AN INTRODUCTION TO CHRISTIAN THEOLOGY

Far from being solely an academic enterprise, the practice of theology can pique the interest of anyone who wonders about the meaning of life. Inviting readers on a journey of "faith seeking understanding," this introduction to Christian theology – its basic concepts, confessional content, and history – emphasizes the relevance of the key convictions of Christian faith to the challenges of today's world.

In the first part, this book introduces the project of Christian theology and sketches the critical context that confronts Christian thought and practice today. In the second part, it offers a survey of the key doctrinal themes of Christian theology – including revelation, the triune God, and the world as creation – identifying their biblical basis and the highlights of their historical development before giving a systematic evaluation of each theme. The third part provides an overview of Christian theology from the early church to the present.

RICHARD J. PLANTINGA is Professor of Religion at Calvin College. He is the editor of *Christianity and Plurality: Classic and Contemporary Readings* (1999).

THOMAS R. THOMPSON is Professor of Religion at Calvin College. He is the editor of *The One in the Many: Christian Identity in a Multicultural World* (1998).

MATTHEW D. LUNDBERG is Assistant Professor of Religion at Calvin College.

AN INTRODUCTION TO
CHRISTIAN THEOLOGY

RICHARD J. PLANTINGA

THOMAS R. THOMPSON

MATTHEW D. LUNDBERG

CAMBRIDGE UNIVERSITY PRESS
Cambridge, New York, Melbourne, Madrid, Cape Town, Singapore,
São Paulo, Delhi, Dubai, Tokyo

Cambridge University Press
The Edinburgh Building, Cambridge CB2 8RU, UK

Published in the United States of America by Cambridge University Press, New York

www.cambridge.org
Information on this title: www.cambridge.org/9780521690379

First published 2010

Printed in the United Kingdom at the University Press, Cambridge

A catalogue record for this publication is available from the British Library

ISBN 978-0-521-87026-9 Hardback
ISBN 978-0-521-69037-9 Paperback

We dedicate this book to a delightful dozen:
To Sharon, Aubree, Nathan, Lukas; to Kelly, Joshua, Jonathan,
Julianna; to Joan, Carrie, Kristie, Matthew — each of our wives and
children three, who continue to ensconce us in their love and
faithfulness. This book is also a fruit of your lives and of our common
journey of faith.

Contents

Illustrations

Tables and figures

TABLES

FIGURES

Preface

This book is both an introduction and an invitation to Christian theology. For many people today theology is a mysterious enterprise – they don't know quite what it is, or what to make of it, or are daunted by its sublime subject-matter (God, creation, and their relation) and lofty claims. Others regard theology as an arcane, academic exercise – too intellectual, too preoccupied with angels and pinheads, too fixated on doctrines of the past to be of any contemporary value or practical relevance.

Through the course of this text, we hope both to inform the uninitiated and to win over those who may hold theology in contempt, as we invite you on a common journey of "faith seeking understanding" – to invoke a classic definition of theology. As a way of easing into our studies, we offer two initial and informal images of theology.

First, theology can be thought of as an intellectual and practical *wrestling with God*. We have in mind here that famous wrestling match between Jacob and the mysterious angel or man, a figure who turns out to be God in person and who changes Jacob's name to *Israel* – a dramatic and signature moment in the life of God's people (Gen. 32:22–32). Throughout a long, dark night of struggle Jacob persists in his quest of the divine identity and blessing. At daybreak he realizes that he has caught a glimpse of God (face to face) and is humbled and changed in the process, as indicated by his wrenched hip and new name. The name "Israel" indicates "one who wrestles with God and with humanity and who overcomes" (v. 28). In Jacob's case, this was an important moment toward the fulfillment of the covenant promise to Abraham that through his legacy all nations of the earth would be blessed (Gen. 12:3; also see 35:9–11). Those who aspire to be the people of God (Israel) are called to represent God to others and others to God as bearers and mediators of God's reconciling grace in a fractured world. The name Israel captures the very mission of God's people – struggling with God and humanity for the sake of the world's blessing. Theology is an important part of this mission – it is an intellectual wrestling with God and humanity (including ourselves, others, and creation at large) for the practical sake of their right relation. Christian theology aspires to be in the service of representing the triune God in the world by bearing the gospel of Jesus Christ, who is himself the true and renewed Israel (see Matt. 1–7). Theology struggles with God and humanity within the various dimensions of creation as a whole for the sake of Christ's reconciling, liberating, and ennobling gospel. This signature image of theology will recur as an important motif in the theological explorations that follow.

A second informal image of theology: When the upstart and controversial rabbi Jesus of Nazareth was pressed by learned scribes to identify the greatest commandment, what he considered the heart and hub of God's law or *torah*, he gave this answer: "'You shall love the Lord your God with all your heart, and with all your soul, and with all your mind, and with all your strength.' The second is this, 'You shall love your neighbor as yourself.' There is no other commandment greater than these" (Mark 12:30–1). While many persons may excel in loving God with heart or soul or strength, fewer seem to be as interested in loving God also with the mind. (Indeed, many verge on anti-intellectualism when it comes to religious or Christian faith.) Theology can be of help here, since it is first a reflective, cognitive discipline. In fact, theology can be thought of as the "intellectual love of God," as a learning to love God with our minds. But just as the mind in Jesus' commandment cannot be divorced from heart and soul and strength, since love of God is a whole-personed act, theology is in the service of these other dimensions as well. Theology informs, clarifies, and helps us to consciously integrate our appropriate response to God.

Jesus' *torah*-in-a-nutshell also reminds us that love of God cannot be divorced from love of neighbor, for the latter is the proof of the former, as the apostle Paul indicates when he states: "For the whole law is summed up in a single commandment, 'You shall love your neighbor as yourself'" (Gal. 5:14; cf. Rom. 13:8–10). Theology, therefore, is in intellectual service to the practical relations of God and neighbor, which properly speaking also includes the whole neighborhood – the breadth of God's good but frustrated creation.

As a persistent wrestling with God and the intellectual habit that serves love of God and neighbor, theology tackles the question of the meaning of life. We think that the answer to this perennial and ultimate question is actually quite simple to state, but most arduous to accomplish. The meaning of life? Here's one simple way of putting it: *learning to love*. From our basic Christian convictions, we believe that such a meaning can only be grounded in the triune God, who *is* Love (1 John 4:8), and God's love for us;

but this is a love that is meant to spill over into all creation. Theology wrestles intellectually in practical service of this love that we hold is supremely expressed, embodied, and available in the gospel of Jesus Christ.

Given these initial informal perspectives on theology, we hope that you will join us in our ongoing journey of faith, a faith that by its very nature seeks an informed understanding in a theological quest to learn to love.

A few words about the text itself. This is an introduction to Christian *systematic theology*. As such, Part I introduces readers to the basic project of Christian theology – what it is and how it works – and attempts to sketch the critical context in which we must forge, refine, and articulate our theology today.

Part II is a survey of the key themes of Christian theology – Christianity's central teachings or doctrines. Under each of these topics (e.g., God, humanity, Christ) we generally sketch out the *biblical basis* for the teaching and review the *historical development* or highlights of the doctrine before we offer a *systematic consideration* of that theme. In this concluding systematic and constructive exploration we note the various ways that different Christian traditions or thinkers have understood the doctrine in question – how they have configured it, what they have emphasized, how they have nuanced their interpretation – many times by mapping out different models of this particular doctrine. While we attempt to do this fairly and squarely, we do not normally remain neutral in our assessment, but will typically take a position on such options, recommending which one we deem "best" – that is, most theologically responsible given our criteria of biblical and confessional *orthodoxy*, broad *coherence*, and practical *relevance*.

Part III is a historical survey of Christian theology through its five significant theological epochs. As such, it can be read profitably and independently before, during, or after Parts I and II. Depending on particular needs and goals, different readers and teachers may wish to utilize this section in varied ways. The historical overlap and occasional repetition between Part III and the historical review of each doctrinal locus is intended to reinforce or "mother" learning. A concluding glossary provides a ready reference for key theological terms.

Finally, we must call attention to the fact that we are not only offering here an introduction to Christian theology as an established, objective discipline and tradition, but also proposing a contemporary statement of Christian theology. While serving as an introduction *to* systematic theology, this book carries out that task by *being* a systematic theology. This is the point of our advocating certain positions on doctrinal subjects. This is also why we first attempt to contextualize the theological project in our contemporary or "postmodern" world (Chapter 2). Given the issues and pressing problems of our times, we are attempting to rally the rich resources of Christian theology within the parameters of historic orthodoxy in a way that is internally coherent and practically relevant to our trying times. That the reader may well not agree with us on some doctrinal points should only serve as stimulus to further theological thinking and discussion. Indeed, such conversation is a key and critical task of the ongoing nature of Christian theology, of our mutual wrestling with God and the world in the quest for an orthodox, coherent, and relevant faith.

Acknowledgments

We are acutely aware of an "embarrassment of debts" in the making of this book. We are indebted to all of our teachers at various levels of education, and from all walks of life – from professors to pastors to the mouths of babes – for the ways they have shaped us theologically in chorus with the wisdom of the historic Christian tradition in all of its breadth and depth. We are especially grateful to Kate Brett at Cambridge University Press for commissioning the book and offering us helpful guidance along the way, as well as to Aline Guillermet and Jo Bramwell for their assistance and careful editorial eyes. Our colleagues in the Religion Department at Calvin College have also been generous in their encouragement and support of this project. And the many students we have taught in our theology classes over the last several years have given us helpful suggestions as they read various renditions of the book's chapters in draft form.

We have received generous institutional support for our work on this book. In particular, we want to express our gratitude to the Calvin College Board of Trustees for the Calvin Research Fellowships we were granted. We are also grateful for the research grants we received from the Calvin Center for Christian Scholarship and the Calvin Alumni Association Board, as well as for the Interim Research Leave extended to us by Dean Uko Zylstra.

Throughout the actual writing of the book, we were assisted by a variety of people. Miriam Diephouse McMillan served most capably as a research assistant for one summer of our work. Jan Curry and Jim Bratt helped to connect us to institutional sources of funding available at the college.

We are also grateful to Peter Williams of the World Council of Churches for helping us to obtain the photographic image of Guido Rocha's "Tortured Christ"; and to Stan Kain of St. Isaac of Syria Skete for providing images of several Orthodox icons.

For a variety of other forms of help and encouragement, we would like to thank Lauren Ciesa, Glenn Fetzer, Simona Goi, Craig Hanson, Dan Harlow, Henry Luttikhuizen, Ken Pomykala, John Stevenson, and Leanne Van Dyk.

For permission to draw upon material published elsewhere, we are grateful to: *Calvin Theological Journal*, for the use of Thomas R. Thompson, "Trinitarianism Today: Doctrinal Renaissance, Ethical Relevance, Social Redolence," *Calvin Theological Journal* 32, no. 1 (1997), 9–42; to InterVarsity Press, for the use of Thomas R. Thompson, "Deity of Christ," in *The New Dictionary of Christian Apologetics*, ed. W. C. Campbell-Jack, Gavin J. McGrath, and C. Stephan Evans, (Downers Grove, IL: InterVarsity, 2006), 207–11; and to Kregel Publications, for the use of Richard J. Plantinga, "God So Loved the World: Theological Reflections on Religious Plurality in the History of Christianity," in *Biblical Faith and Other Religions: An Evangelical Assessment*, ed. David W. Baker (Grand Rapids, MI: Kregel, 2004), 106–37.

The extract from the script of the film *Nuns on the Run*, directed by Jonathan Lynn, is used by permission of HandMade Films plc.

Abbreviations

GENERAL ABBREVIATIONS

BCE	Before the Common Era (equivalent to BC = "Before Christ")
CE	Common Era (equivalent to AD = "In the Year of the Lord")
Gk.	Greek language
Hebr.	Hebrew language
KJV	King James Version, Authorized Version of the Bible
Lat.	Latin language
NASB	New American Standard Version of the Bible
NIV	New International Version of the Bible
NT	New Testament, Christian scriptures
NRSV	New Revised Standard Version of the Bible
OT	Old Testament, Hebrew scriptures
RSV	Revised Standard Version of the Bible
WWI	World War One
WWII	World War Two

BIBLICAL BOOKS USED IN THE TEXT

1 Cor.	1 Corinthians
1 John	1 John
1 Kings	1 Kings
1 Pet.	1 Peter
1 Sam.	1 Samuel
1 Tim.	1 Timothy
2 Cor.	2 Corinthians
2 Kings	2 Kings
2 Pet.	2 Peter
2 Sam.	2 Samuel
2 Thess.	2 Thessalonians
2 Tim.	2 Timothy

Acts	Acts of the Apostles
Amos	Amos
Col.	Colossians
Dan.	Daniel
Deut.	Deuteronomy
Eccles.	Ecclesiastes
Eph.	Ephesians
Exod.	Exodus
Ezek.	Ezekiel
Gal.	Galatians
Gen.	Genesis
Hab.	Habakkuk
Heb.	Hebrews
Hos.	Hosea
Isa.	Isaiah
Jas.	James
Jer.	Jeremiah
Joel	Joel
John	John
Josh.	Joshua
Jon.	Jonah
Lev.	Leviticus
Luke	Luke
Mal.	Malachi
Mark	Mark
Matt.	Matthew
Mic.	Micah
Neh.	Nehemiah
Num.	Numbers
Phil.	Philippians
Prov.	Proverbs
Ps., Pss.	Psalm, Psalms
Rev.	Revelation, the Apocalypse of John
Rom.	Romans
Titus	Titus
Wis.	Wisdom of Solomon
Zech.	Zechariah

PART I

Introduction to theology

The first part of this book introduces theology in general and the discipline of Christian systematic theology in particular. It then sketches out the dominant contours of our contemporary world as the critical context to which Christian theology must meaningfully speak today.

CHAPTER I

What is theology?

INTRODUCTION: THE QUEST(IONS) OF HUMAN EXISTENCE

If one mentions the word "theology" to the average person on the street, one may well be met by a puzzled expression followed by a series of questions: What exactly is theology and what does it have to do with real life? Isn't it something studied only by professionals who have an obscure interest in ancient texts? Don't theologians make unnecessary complexity out of what could and should be simple? Is theology really relevant in our contemporary world?

These perplexed responses are understandable. But theology need not be arcane, enigmatic, or irrelevant. While there is no denying that scholars who undertake its study tend to reject simplistic answers, often use technical terminology, and engage more than two millennia of historical develop-ment, the practice of theology is actually not confined to a small class of scholars. Indeed, we would suggest that anyone who seriously inquires about the basic questions of life is a theologian of sorts. That is to say,

3

human beings are theologically inclined insofar as they wonder about things such as: Where did the world come from? What is the purpose of human existence? Is there any final justice in life? What is the something "other" or "more" that seems to manifest itself in human existence, whether in peak or in depth experiences? What does the "something" – or "someone" – want with us? In short, what is the meaning of life? These are the kinds of questions that theologians think about. But poets, artists, and philosophers wrestle with these very same questions as well. Similarly, we would argue that anyone who seriously grapples with the questions of human existence in search of a meaning to life beyond its mundane and prosaic surface – that is, a transcendent or metaphysical dimension – can be thought of as a theologian.

This existentially inquisitive – and therefore theological – orientation to life was wonderfully expressed in a work by the American poet Emily Dickinson (1830–86):

> This World is not Conclusion.
> A Species stands beyond –
> Invisible, as Music –
> But positive, as Sound –
> It beckons, and it baffles –
> Philosophy – don't know –
> And through a Riddle, at the last –
> Sagacity, must go –
> To guess it, puzzles scholars –
> To gain it, Men have borne
> Contempt of Generations
> And Crucifixion, shown –
> Faith slips – and laughs, and rallies –
> Blushes, if any see –
> Plucks at a twig of Evidence –
> And asks a Vane, the way –
> Much Gesture, from the Pulpit –
> Strong Hallelujahs roll –
> Narcotics cannot still the Tooth
> That nibbles at the soul –[1]

This poem's first line (which functions as its title) asserts that "This World" – the world of our sense experience – is not all there is; it "is not Conclusion." Rather, "A Species stands beyond." What is this "Species"?

---

[1] Emily Dickinson, *The Complete Poems of Emily Dickinson*, ed. Thomas H. Johnson (Boston: Little, Brown & Co., 1960), 243.

Something? Someone? Perhaps God? Dickinson says that the "Species" is "Invisible ... but positive" – in other words, elusive but real. Such transcendence "beckons" but yet "baffles," to the point where philosophers, those lovers of wisdom normally skilled at tackling conundrums, cannot figure "it" out. Scholars fare no better in their quest to determine what this might be. So persistent is its power of attraction, suggests Dickinson, that human beings in their search for this "Other" have suffered indignities such as contempt and even crucifixion – the latter alluding to the original Christian martyr. But the human quest for this "Species," a quest which Dickinson characterizes as "Faith," is a pursuit that does not rest; rather, it seeks evidence, and looks for guidance from various sources. Without coming to a definitive conclusion about God, Dickinson ends her poem by making a strong statement about the human condition: Life involves a quest for a transcendent Other; no other devices – not even drugs – can ultimately "still the Tooth / That nibbles at the soul."

Dickinson's poem tersely illustrates our basic contention: Humanity ineluctably asks questions about its experience in the world in a quest for something more. Given that this "transcendent other" or "metaphysical more" is most typically thought of as a divine being – as God – the quest is ultimately theological, since theology in its most basic sense is an "account of God." More specifically, the term "theology" derives from the Greek (Gk.) word *theologia*, which itself is composed of two smaller Greek words: *theos* and *logos*. *Theos* is the generic Greek term for "god." *Logos* is a more complicated concept with several shades of meaning. It can signify word, speech, talk about, discourse, account, and even reason (our English term "logic" is derived from it). Putting *theos* and *logos* together etymologically, one gets something like "talk about God" or "a reasoned account of God." While different religious traditions will elaborate their own theologies, Christian theology attempts to give a reasoned account of the God made known in the history of Israel and supremely revealed in the incarnation of Jesus Christ. It is striking, however, that the term *theologia* cannot be found in the New Testament (NT), Christianity's charter document, which was first written in Greek. Where then did the term originate?

THE DEVELOPMENT OF THE CONCEPT OF THEOLOGY

Origin of the term "theology"

The origin of the term "theology" lies in the pre-Christian, ancient world, first appearing in the *Republic* by Plato (*c.* 427–347 BCE). In Book II of this famous philosophical text, Plato's spokesperson Socrates criticizes the writers Homer and Hesiod (those great bards of the ancient myths) for their depictions of the Greek gods as engaged in all-too-humanlike intrigues and scurrilous behavior. Their mythical account of the gods, that is, their *theologia*, is misleading and troubling since it misrepresents the true nature of the divine.[2] Following Plato, other ancient Greek philosophers – including Plato's famous student Aristotle (384–322 BCE) – tended to dismiss "theology" as merely mythical speech about the gods. They considered such dubious accounts as inferior to philosophy – the disciplined quest to penetrate the nature of reality through the use of reason and intelligence, leading to a truer understanding of the divine.[3]

Though the term *theologia* first developed as a disparaging term, it was appropriated by Christianity in a very different sense that is captured well by its linguistic roots – *logos* about *theos*. Theology is generally understood today as "reasoned discourse about God." Before discussing the method and dynamics of the theological enterprise more systematically, however, it will be helpful to see how the Christian tradition took up and refined the notion of theology at strategic points in its history.

Brief history of the concept and practice of theology

Patristic developments

As Christianity entered its first era, the "patristic" period (*c.* 100–*c.* 500 CE) of the church "fathers" (Gk. *pateres*), it found itself a minority community in a complex, multicultural, hostile world. Given Jesus' mandate to "make disciples of all nations" (Matt. 28:19), the early Christians needed spokespersons whose task it was to articulate Christian doctrine (Latin [Lat.] *doctrina* = teaching) and defend the faith in the face of persecutions and heresies. As these apologists (Lat. *apologia* = defense) pled for civil and religious tolerance and sought to make converts to the Christian cause, they were eager to characterize their faith not as something radically new or different but as something similar to what already honorably existed in the Greco-Roman world – namely, philosophy. For example, Justin Martyr

---

[2] See Plato, *The Republic*, in *The Collected Dialogues of Plato*, ed. E. Hamilton and H. Cairns, Bollingen Series 71 (New York: Pantheon, 1961), 575–844. For the term *theologia*, see Book II, section 379a, lines 5–6.

[3] Beyond the general Greek philosophical understanding of theology as mythical speech about the gods, which he criticizes, Aristotle does use the term *theologia* positively insofar as he identifies it with metaphysics – an account of the ultimate nature of reality or its first principles. See Wolfhart Pannenberg, *Theology and the Philosophy of Science*, trans. Francis McDonagh (London: Darton, Longman & Todd, 1976), 12–13.

(*c.* 100–*c.* 165) in his *First Apology* avoids the term "theology" in characterizing Christianity instead as the true or highest philosophy.[4]

Gradually, however, the term theology was adopted and adapted by Christian thinkers. Clement of Alexandria (*c.* 150–*c.* 215) was one of the first to distinguish theology in the Greek sense (mythological discourse about the gods) from theology in a Christian sense (the theology of the word, the *logos*, Jesus Christ).[5] Similarly, Eusebius of Caesarea (*c.* 263–339), an early church historian, criticizes the Greek understanding of the term and conceives of theology in a distinctly Christian manner – as the church's practice of proclaiming the biblical God, the creator made known by Jesus Christ.

As Christianity continued to spread, some thinkers sought to articulate its teachings, not so much apologetically to emperors and opponents of Christianity, but more descriptively for believers themselves. Notable in this development are church fathers such as Origen (*c.* 185–*c.* 254), whose work *De Principiis* is a topical arrangement of key Christian doctrines and therefore one of the first systematic approaches to Christian thought.[6] The term *theologia* at this stage most specifically referred to the doctrine of God, with which Origen begins his work. However, Origen's approach showed that it was impossible to examine this foundational doctrine without also considering other doctrines, such as those of Christ, the Holy Spirit, and creation. One therefore sees in Origen a novel structural approach to the practice of theology that is an important milestone in the maturing of the discipline. But it was not until the fourth century that the term "theology" gained broad usage.

The fifth century brought the patristic period to a close. For western Christianity, it was Augustine (354–430) who gathered up the developments of the preceding centuries and constructively shaped them for the subsequent tradition. In his *Confessions*, this pagan-turned-Christian bishop and scholar sculpted an approach to theology that approximates a definition. At the outset of this classic work he argues that the human quest is a restless seeking of God: "our hearts find no peace until they rest in you."[7] Once human beings have encountered God and come to faith, however, they are

---

[4] See Justin Martyr, *The First Apology*, trans. and ed. Cyril C. Richardson, in *Early Christian Fathers*, ed. Cyril C. Richardson, Library of Christian Classics (Philadelphia: Westminster, 1953), 242–89.

[5] See Clement of Alexandria, *The Stromata*, ed. A. Cleveland Coxe, in *The Ante-Nicene Fathers*, ed. Alexander Roberts and James Donaldson (Grand Rapids, MI: Eerdmans, 1993), II: 313.

[6] See Origen, *De Principiis*, trans. Frederick Crombie, ed. A. Cleveland Coxe, in *The Ante-Nicene Fathers*, ed. Alexander Roberts and James Donaldson (Grand Rapids, MI: Eerdmans, 1993), IV: 239–382.

[7] Augustine, *Confessions*, trans. R. S. Pine-Coffin (Harmondsworth: Penguin, 1961), 21.

destined to continue their quest by seeking to understand what it is they have come to believe.[8] Faith or belief coupled with reflective inquiry toward greater understanding – this anticipates the classical description of theology developed more fully in the Middle Ages.

Medieval and Reformation developments

Of the various developments in the concept of theology in the Middle Ages (*c.* 500–*c.* 1400), one of the most important and enduring was authored by Anselm of Canterbury (1033–1109). Following in the tradition of Augustine, Anselm articulated the genius of this approach in striking fashion:

> I confess, Lord, with thanksgiving, that you have made me in your image, so that I can remember you, think of you, and love you … Lord, I am not trying to make my way to your height, for my understanding is in no way equal to that, but I do desire to understand a little of your truth which my heart already believes and loves. I do not seek to understand so that I may believe, but I believe so that I may understand.[9]

Here Anselm portrays theology as the act of "faith seeking understanding" – *fides quaerens intellectum*. This has become the classic definition of theology, one that we gladly employ in this book.

Another medieval development with far-reaching consequences was Christianity's encounter with the Middle Eastern world, especially with Islam during the period of the Crusades. This centuries-long struggle brought Christians into renewed contact with Greek philosophy, especially certain texts of Aristotle which the West had lost but recovered through contact with the Islamic world. A renewed interest in philosophy sparked new inquiry and aided the foundation of Europe's first universities (e.g., Paris, Cambridge, Oxford). This highlighted the question of theology's relationship to philosophy and led to the establishment of theology as an ordered inquiry – in other words, as a science (*scientia*). The science of theology, practiced by "schoolmen" or scholastics, would attempt to articulate the whole of Christian doctrine in a clear, orderly, comprehensive, and sophisticated fashion. During the height of this endeavor, theology was considered the queen of the sciences, with philosophy regarded as its handmaiden.

---

[8] See Augustine, "On the Profit in Believing," trans. C. L. Cornish, in *The Nicene and Post-Nicene Fathers*, 1st series, ed. Philip Schaff (Grand Rapids, MI: Eerdmans, 1993), III: 347–66. Elsewhere in his corpus, Augustine distinguishes three types of theology: natural, mythical, and civil. See Augustine, *The City of God*, trans. Henry Bettenson (London: Penguin, 1972), 298.

[9] Anselm of Canterbury, *Proslogion*, in *The Prayers and Meditations of Saint Anselm*, trans. Sister B. Ward (Harmondsworth: Penguin, 1973), 243–4.

The high-water mark in the scholastic development of theology as a science is found in Thomas Aquinas (*c.* 1225–74). In his master work *Summa Theologiae* (*Summation of Theology*), Aquinas offers a breathtaking overview of theology in an ordered and rigorous fashion.[10] He explores theology's identity and the question of its necessity in relation to the discipline of philosophy. He concludes that theology is necessary because there are essential truths about God that are beyond the grasp of reason alone and therefore beyond the domain of philosophy. These truths are revealed in scripture, the explication of which is the task of theology. Having established the necessity of theology, Aquinas goes on to examine the Christian faith with the aid of (particularly Aristotelian) philosophy.

It was in the Middle Ages, then, that theology was established as a disciplined science practiced in universities, yet in the service of the church. These dual institutional settings would create considerable tension for theology over the centuries to come, as centered on this question: Is theology predominantly an intellectual activity (as *scientia* or knowledge) or is it more practical in nature (as *sapientia* or wisdom)?[11] In the period of the Protestant Reformation, Martin Luther (1483–1546) and John Calvin (1509–64) came to regard much of medieval theology as too scholastic and rationalistic. They believed that theology should be more practical, pastoral, and carefully tied to Christian scripture ("by scripture alone" – *sola scriptura* – was one of the Reformation's central affirmations). In other words, theology is not so much concerned with God's being in abstraction as it is with God in concrete relation to humanity – a subtle but major shift. For Luther, this conviction is expressed in his critique of the medieval desire to visit the mind of God in order to describe the thoughts of God. Over against this rationalistic "theology of glory," he proposed a "theology of the cross" that seeks God concretely in the witness of scripture to the gospel events.[12] In similar fashion, Calvin shows an impatience for speculation and abstraction, always insisting on the concrete relationship between God and humanity. He emphasizes this theme at the very outset of his major work, *Institutes of the Christian Religion*: "Nearly all the wisdom we possess ... consists of two parts: the knowledge of God and of ourselves."[13] For Calvin, there is no knowledge of self without

---

[10] See Thomas Aquinas, *Summa Theologica*, 5 vols., trans. Fathers of the English Dominican Province (Westminster, MD: Christian Classics, 1948).

[11] See Pannenberg, *Philosophy of Science*, 7–14, 228–35.

[12] See Martin Luther, "The Disputation held at Heidelberg," in *Luther: Early Theological Works*, trans. and ed. J. Atkinson, Library of Christian Classics (Philadelphia: Westminster, 1962), theses 19–24 (pp. 290–3).

[13] John Calvin, *Institutes of the Christian Religion*, trans. Ford Lewis Battles, ed. John T. McNeill, Library of Christian Classics (Philadelphia: Westminster, 1960), 35.

knowledge of God – and vice versa. To know God, Calvin argues, what is required is not conjecture about God in God's own being but piety – that is, a relationship to God and a reverence for God.

Modern and contemporary developments

The modern world brought new challenges to the theological enterprise, as rooted in the scientific revolution and the Enlightenment project. Sounding its keynote, the influential philosopher Immanuel Kant urged human beings not to submit to authority and tradition in their thinking but rather to boldly use their own reason. He argued that things beyond general human experience are not knowable, thereby challenging theology's traditional claim that God can be truly and readily known.[14] Sensing the predicament in which religion in general and Christianity in particular found themselves as a result of this Enlightenment criticism, Friedrich Schleiermacher (1768–1834) sought to blaze a new path by attempting to convince skeptics and critics of religion that they had misunderstood that which they had too easily dismissed. In his work *On Religion: Speeches to its Cultured Despisers*, Schleiermacher argued that religion was neither chiefly a matter of knowledge (i.e., doctrine) or of action (i.e., ethics) but was rather something altogether different – namely, a "feeling" or a kind of sense for the wholeness of reality.[15] This non-cognitive conception of religion led Schleiermacher to reconceive the nature of theology, recasting Christian doctrines as descriptions of the Christian religious consciousness, rather than as descriptions of transcendent realities in themselves.[16] In his efforts, Schleiermacher sought to secure a place for theology in the modern university, giving his theology an unmistakable apologetic cast: The one Christian faith must be relevant in both church and academy. Theology cannot be content with addressing the believer in the pew; it must also address the "cultured despisers of religion," whose numbers continued to grow in the post-Enlightenment era and to whom both *theos* and *theologia* became increasingly questionable.

Schleiermacher's conception of theology inspired many nineteenth-century Protestant theologians who sought to negotiate a broad path between

---

[14] See Immanuel Kant, "What Is Enlightenment?," in *On History*, ed. Lewis White Beck, trans. Lewis White Beck *et al.*, Library of Liberal Arts (Indianapolis, IN: Bobbs-Merrill, 1963), 3; Immanuel Kant, *Critique of Pure Reason*, trans. Norman Kemp Smith (New York: St. Martin's, 1965), *passim*.

[15] See Friedrich Schleiermacher, *On Religion: Speeches to its Cultured Despisers*, trans. John Oman (New York: Harper and Row, 1958). The second of the five speeches is particularly relevant to the discussion above.

[16] See Friedrich Schleiermacher, *The Christian Faith*, ed. H. R. Mackintosh and J. S. Stewart (Edinburgh: T. & T. Clark, 1928), 1–128.

church and world, Christianity and culture, faith and science – the approach that came to be known as theological liberalism. The dominating influence of liberalism lasted until the second decade of the twentieth century, at which time a young Swiss Reformed pastor and theologian named Karl Barth (1886–1968) struck out in a new direction. Barth came to reject the approach of Schleiermacher and liberal theology, arguing that theology should not be preoccupied with human piety, consciousness, or feelings – which virtually reduces theology to anthropology – but should concern itself with God, who is "wholly other." In his instructively titled *Church Dogmatics*, Barth argues that the task of theology is rigorous reflection on and correction of the church's proclamation according to its primary norm: Jesus Christ, the reconciling Word of God, as witnessed in scripture. The shift is unmistakable. Barth's chief audience is the church – those inside its walls and who profess its doctrines. His primary category, therefore, is not *religion*, which was Schleiermacher's key category and point of departure, but *revelation*, the utterance of God to humanity.[17]

Since the time that Karl Barth dominated the theological scene – the so-called "neo-orthodox" era (1930s–1960s) – several developments have particularly influenced the present practice of theology as a discipline. Most notably, postmodernism as an intellectual movement has questioned the legacy of modernity and emphasized human subjectivity, historical situatedness, and relativity of perspective in scholarship. Accordingly, theology has become increasingly aware of its historical and cultural dimensions, spawning a variety of "contextual theologies." For example, feminist theologies in the West have sought to liberate the suppressed voices and experiences of women in a male-dominated Christian history and theology.[18] Similarly, Latin American liberation theologians have brought theology to bear on the situation of the poor and the church's practice in their own indigent societies.[19] And African theologians, given the burgeoning of Christianity on their continent, have attempted to come to terms with the theological significance of African primal religion in creating a truly African theology.[20] This

[17] See Karl Barth, *Church Dogmatics*, ed. Geoffrey W. Bromiley and Thomas F. Torrance, 4 vols., various translators (Edinburgh: T. & T. Clark, 1956–75), I/1: xiii–xv, 3–87, 248–92. See also I/2: 797–884.

[18] See Rebecca S. Chopp, "Feminist and Womanist Theologies," in *The Modern Theologians: An Introduction to Christian Theology in the Twentieth Century*, ed. David Ford, 2nd edn. (Oxford: Blackwell, 1997), 389–404.

[19] See, e.g., Gustavo Gutiérrez, *A Theology of Liberation: History, Politics, and Salvation*, trans. Caridad Inda and John Eagleston, rev. edn. (Maryknoll, NY: Orbis, 1988).

[20] See, e.g., Kwame Bediako, *Jesus in Africa: The Christian Gospel in African History and Experience* (Yaoundé, Cameroon: Éditions Clé, 2000).

localization and contextualization of theology have brought a diversity of contributions and voices to the church's ongoing theological task.

From ancient Greece to contemporary Africa, the enterprise of theology has undergone a distinct development and a number of refinements. As "talk about God," Christian theology reflects on the mysterious presence who has created all reality and who over time has revealed the divine reality, particularly through the life of Israel and the person of Jesus Christ as witnessed by scripture, the God to whom human beings are called to respond in faith. Those who come to faith inevitably move from that foundation to seek to comprehend what it is that they believe. As Anselm put it, faith seeks understanding, as to both its content and its implications. Deepened understanding, in turn, generates a reasoned account of theology's subject-matter, which in the case of Christian faith is the triune God, creation, and their relation. Such an account involves a diversity of related topics: the world in which we live (creation); the nature of humanity (image of God); the possibility of undoing the flaw at the heart of human existence (reconciliation); the one who brings hope and salvation to the world (Jesus Christ); and the like – the very doctrines covered in this book.

As "talk about God," theology is bound up with language. Language, however, is a complex and elusive phenomenon – as postmodernism reminds us. We know from life experience that language often fails us at times when it is most needed. In cases where we are called to comfort someone who is suffering, for example, we often cannot find the words. Or in cases where we have undergone some profound experience – say, of beauty or of love – it can be nearly impossible to express the experience and convey it to another. If language fails us in these kinds of moments, how can it possibly serve to describe God and the experience of the divine? How can human words mediate the reality of a transcendent "Species" that "stands beyond"? Theology is nothing if not fraught with peril and bold in its aims. In order to understand how it might be possible to undertake this precarious endeavor, we must examine the architecture and method of theology, beginning with its sources/norms.

THE ARCHITECTURE AND METHOD OF THEOLOGY

The sources/norms and branches of theology

Every discipline or science has sources of knowledge that inform its reflections. Christian theology works from three main sources that also serve as its primary norms. That theology has sources of knowledge about God, of course, presupposes that God can be known. The Christian claim is that God can be known because of God's revelation, the disclosure of the divine life to humanity, since Christianity contends not only that a divine Being exists who is mysteriously present in human experience, but that this God is eminently personal and has over time communicated with us (see Chapter 3). Most audaciously, Christianity claims that God became human in Jesus of Nazareth, whose life, ministry, death, and resurrection constitute the clearest and fullest revelation of God, the account of which is contained in the Christian Bible.

Scripture, therefore, is the primary source for Christian theology because it relates the basic narrative of the triune God, creation, and their relation. This story begins with the creation of the world, relates humanity's fall away from God into sin, and climaxes with the salvific life and death of Jesus Christ, while also anticipating the fulfillment of human history and the renewal of creation. Within this overarching narrative one finds many kinds of writing: history, law, poetry, prophecy, gospels, and letters, among others. Many of these literary genres include what can be called "first-order" language – language that is immediate to experience and as such is often expressive, circumstantial, doxological, poetic, symbolical, or even myth-ical. Such language cries out for interpretation, as is well expressed in the epithet of the French philosopher Paul Ricoeur: "The symbol gives rise to thought."[21] It is the task of theology to reflect upon the biblical narrative as a whole in the effort to synthesize and summarize its major themes. Theology does this with the use of "second-order" discourse – language that attempts, at a reflective remove, to make clear, orderly, and coherent sense of the entire biblical witness. So how to speak about God? Where can one find out first and foremost who God is and what God is like? Christian theology points to scripture as the primary source of theological claims.

But scripture is not the only source of theology. Over the two millennia since Jesus of Nazareth walked the earth, and since the Christian Bible took on its definitive canonical form, there has been a living Christian *tradition* of worship, spirituality, biblical interpretation, and theological reflection. The historic Christian church has thus left behind a great deposit of wisdom in its liturgies, practices, biblical commentaries, and theological writings. The formative theology of the patristic period, for example, falls under this category of tradition. In the early church, as we have seen, there was a need to clarify Christian beliefs in the face of adversity. In response to persecutions and heresies, statements of Christian belief called creeds

[21] Paul Ricoeur, *The Symbolism of Evil*, trans. E. Buchanan (Boston: Beacon, 1967), 348.

(Lat. *credo* = I believe) were developed. There are three ecumenical (i.e., worldwide, universal) creeds that are accepted in most Protestant and Catholic circles as particularly authoritative: the Apostles' Creed, the Nicene Creed, and the Athanasian Creed.[22] In addition to the creeds, particular Christian traditions have produced formal writings or confessions to guide their doctrine and life. For example, Catholics honor the writings of the Council of Trent, Lutherans adhere to the Augsburg Confession, and Presbyterians hold the Westminster Confession in high esteem. Above and beyond these ecumenical creeds and particular confessions, there are the many reflections of Christian theologians from time past, such as Athanasius, Augustine, Aquinas, Luther, and Barth, to name an influential few.

As a source that theologians draw on in their inquiry and discourse, this entire body of received material – which we are calling tradition – has been understood by Protestantism as secondary in terms of normativity, subordinate to scripture as a judge of theological claims. Catholicism and Eastern Orthodoxy, on the other hand, have historically held tradition, especially the definitive dogmas of the church, to be a co-equal authority with scripture – the so-called "two-source" conception of theological authority. Whereas for Protestants, the biblical text should always trump church tradition, Catholicism and Orthodoxy posit a greater interrelation of scripture and the authoritative declarations of the church. But even Protestants must acknowledge this dynamic interaction of scripture and tradition, since the reading of the biblical text always occurs in communities of interpretation, as is reflected in Protestant traditions that respect their denominational confessions. Therefore the reformational battle cry of *sola scriptura* (scripture alone) might better be understood as *prima scriptura* (scripture first) – the methodological primacy and authority of scripture, but not the neglect of tradition.

There is yet one more basic source for the theologian – the best of human learning, which we will summarize as *philosophy* ("love of wisdom"), taken in its classical and broadest sense as the truths resulting from human inquiry. Not everything we hold true comes from scripture or church tradition. There is a whole body of knowledge that human beings acquire by thinking about, and by experimenting with, the world around us. These truths of reason and experience found in the breadth of the arts and sciences provide a third source of data for theological reflection. Wherever truth is found concerning life in creation – in science, literature, or art – it provides essential information for thinking about the triune God, creation, and

---

[22] The Eastern Orthodox churches recognize the authority of only the Nicene Creed.

their relation. If theology is to make contact with the real world, we must constantly ask whether our conclusions on the basis of scripture and tradition make good sense, whether they cohere with the world of our experience. For example, when Copernicus and Galileo argued in the sixteenth and seventeenth centuries on the basis of empirical observation that the Earth moved around the Sun, and not vice versa, they came to know an important truth about the world. This appeared to contradict – but eventually corrected – what Christians traditionally believed and what scripture, in the worldview of its day, assumed about the nature of the cosmos. In their commitment to getting things right, theologians draw on reason and experience via a variety of sciences and studies. As the light of new knowledge improves our understanding and interpretation of scripture, we may have to modify and sometimes even break with traditional beliefs. In such cases philosophy will trump church tradition. But generally speaking, philosophy is a tertiary source and norm of theology. Scripture and the time-tested wisdom of tradition should govern the theological enterprise first and foremost.

To each of these sources of theology there is a corresponding branch of theology. The branch associated with scripture is *biblical theology*. Biblical theology is the study and interpretation of the Bible, with an eye to ascertaining what the text says theologically. Because the Christian Bible is a large and complex text, the biblical theologian will often specialize and restrict her gaze to a particular part of that text – such as the Pauline epistles in the NT in pursuit of a Pauline theology or the prophets in the Old Testament (OT) in articulating a theology of the prophets. Among other features, biblical theology involves the study of the original languages, the historical world, the literary genres, and the formation of the text as a whole. Because it aims to illuminate the primary source and norm of theology, this branch of theology is critical to the functioning of theology as a whole.

Corresponding to the second source and norm of theology, tradition, is the branch known as *historical theology*. Historical theology examines in historical context the content and development of theological ideas throughout the course of the Christian tradition. Given this vast history, the areas of focus and questions of inquiry are legion. For example, what was the predominant patristic conception of God? What are the particular emphases of the ecumenical creeds, and how were they generated? How was the biblical text understood and interpreted in the Middle Ages? How was Luther's doctrine of justification different from earlier views? How did the cultural and political worlds of these theologians inform their theological conclusions? In terms of normativity, after the biblical text, Christian theologians are obligated to listen to and learn from Christianity's past – the sphere of historical theology.[23]

As we have seen, talk about God is funded not just by scripture and tradition, but also by the truths of reason and experience – what we have termed "philosophy" to denote the fruits of human learning in general. The branch of theology that is primarily concerned with this source/norm is called *philosophical theology*, also broadly conceived.[24] This field makes an essential contribution to the work of theology by bringing theology into dialogue with the broad range of human inquiry, whether the arts or the sciences. Working at the intersection of theology and human reason and experience, philosophical theology addresses matters such as the nature and relationship of reason and faith, the possibility of rational arguments for God's existence, and the clarification of Christian doctrines in relation to the contributions of the other sciences. Examples of the latter include such questions as: what brain physiology implies for the notion of the "soul," what consequences evolutionary thought has for the concept of creation, and whether God's foreknowledge is logically compatible with human freedom. In its attempt to mediate between convictions of faith and sound human wisdom, philosophical theology keeps theology rigorous, honest, and true to life by connecting it to other claims regarding the good, true, and beautiful.

This text is a work in *systematic theology*. Systematic theology endeavors to orchestrate these three basic branches of theology and their respective sources, in order to articulate in the most comprehensive, ordered, and coherent way what may be known about the triune God, creation, and their relation – and, importantly, how we are to live in light of this knowledge. Systematic theology draws upon the best of biblical theology, historical theology, and philosophical theology in order to render an account of the big picture of Christian faith – what Christians believe and how they should live – by examining the content and interaction of component Christian doctrines and their practical implications. This means that systematic theology concerns both dogmatics (i.e., basic Christian beliefs or doctrines)

---

[23] Church history – the study of the development of the church as a social institution – is subtly different from historical theology, which is more specifically concerned with the development of Christian doctrines and ideas.

[24] The more traditional and particular sense of philosophical theology concerns the project of discerning what may be known about God through sheer human reason, and was largely restricted to rationally demonstrating God's existence and attributes in the fashion of Thomas Aquinas. We are expanding the sense of philosophical theology to cover the engagement of theology with all disciplines of human inquiry, as in fact is being practiced by philosophical theologians today – the interaction of the current state of human wisdom with Christian theology.

Table 1.1 *The sources and branches of theology*

Source/norm	Corresponding branch	Synthesis
Scripture	Biblical theology	
Tradition	Historical theology	Systematic theology (dogmatics and ethics)
Philosophy	Philosophical theology	

and ethics (i.e., principles of Christian practice) – that is to say, right Christian theory (orthodoxy) and right Christian practice (orthopraxy). Systematic theology is the ongoing work of the Christian church's faith seeking understanding in order to clarify its belief and action in the world. Table 1.1 depicts the sources/norms and branches of theology and their synthesis in systematic theology.

While this book is principally concerned with basic Christian doctrines (dogmatics), these cannot be separated from practical concerns (ethics). Indeed, ethical considerations, primarily the pressing problems of today's world, form the contemporary context in which our theological reflections are situated (see Chapter 2), and which will inform our theological preferences. It is our contention that systematic theology must always be practical – deeply concerned with life's problems and dilemmas, and passionately engaged with the world and time in which we live. All systematic theology, therefore, should be practical theology. Yet we must note that there is a theological sub-discipline more specifically called *practical theology*. In this more technical sense, practical theology deals with the ways in which theology is applied in the institutional life of the church, including the fields of homiletics (preaching), liturgy (worship), pastoral care, Christian education, and church government. Practical theology keeps theology closely connected to the being and life of the church. We must remember, however, that in a broader sense all Christian theology should be practical in nature – concerned with how doctrines intersect with the real world.

With this understanding of the sources and branches of theology in mind, we continue on to other crucial matters. What are the tasks of systematic theology – how does one proceed? And what are the audiences of systematic theology – for whom is such talk about God intended?

The tasks and audiences of systematic theology

In drawing on scripture, in listening to the wisdom of tradition, and in employing the best resources of human learning, the primary purpose of systematic theology is relatively straightforward: it seeks to give an account of the triune God, creation, and their relation for the community of faith in its particular time and location. This large, overarching purpose can be broken down into three basic, interrelated tasks.

First, the systematic theologian seeks to describe the contents (what we believe) and implications (how we should live) of the Christian faith for the Christian church. The systematic theologian assembles the data of scripture, tradition, and human inquiry in order to construct a body of knowledge or statement of Christian belief concerning God, creation, and their relation, most broadly, or any possible theological topic or ethical issue that resides therein – for example, a theology of work or vocation, or a theology of human sexuality. This *descriptive task* of theology thus has the goal of clarifying the believing content and practical implications of the Christian faith.

A second related task of systematic theology involves criticism (Gk. *krino* = to judge). Such criticism will be directed both internally and externally. Since "judgment begins with the household of faith" (1 Pet. 4:17), when a stance of correction is required within the Christian community regarding a position held or a troubling practice, criticism will be aimed at the church itself. For example, theologians in the early church criticized the views of those who held a unipersonal view of God as incompatible with the trinitarian witness of the NT. In the last century, to take a more recent example, theologians such as Karl Barth were compelled to criticize the views of "German Christians" who believed that Christian belief was compatible with the Nazi agenda, resulting in the Barmen Declaration (1934) of the resisting Confessing Church. When, on the other hand, Christians feel strongly about a disturbing occurrence or trend in contemporary society, theologians should offer a word of criticism. For example, if the policies of a government or state are unjust, as with twentieth-century Jim Crow laws in the United States, theologians ought to register their disagreement publicly along with its theological rationale, as many clergy did, such as Martin Luther King Jr., in the civil rights movement. Whether inwardly or outwardly directed, then, theology has a *critical task*. Without this critical edge, theology can easily become ideology – the justification and rationalization of deficient Christian beliefs and dubious practices. To adapt a maxim of Luther in this vein, this is why the word of God must in some sense always come to us as an adversary, given the perennial human penchant for self-justification.

The third task of systematic theology aims to make a case for Christianity in its given context. This is the *apologetic task* of theology, as enjoined by 1 Peter 3:15–16: "Always be ready to give an answer to anyone who demands from you an accounting for the hope that is in you; yet do it with gentleness and reverence." What are the pressing issues of the day? What are the questions being asked? What vocabulary is in vogue? Christian theology must take up those issues and questions and address them in the language of the day. This often involves answering objections to Christian doctrines and positions. While these objections can be generated by those outside the church, even within the church believers struggle with understanding their faith. Such objections or misunderstandings require an apologetic response from the systematic theologian. But such a task also involves showing the beauty and attractiveness of Christian faith, suggesting it as a compelling way to see and live life. The apologetic task thus keeps systematic theology from an unhealthy preoccupation with the church (a ghetto or fortress mentality) at the expense of the church's mission in the world. By engaging society and the domain of culture beyond the walls of the church, the apologetic task makes the case for Christian faith in the world at large.

All good theology implicitly carries out these three tasks. Take the gospels, for example. They are theology in action, as is all of scripture. Each of the four gospels, written decades after Christ's death, takes the received tradition concerning Jesus' life, teachings, and stories, whether oral or written, and describes the theological significance of that life, death, resurrection, and instruction. But each one does so within a particular context and to a particular audience, highlighting certain materials in critique of specific beliefs and practices while making an apologetic case for the significance of the gospel. Or take the Apostles' Creed, for another example. While it might strike the confessor as simply a descriptive statement of Christian faith, it actually contains a pointed polemic against gnosticism, the earliest major heretical challenge to the Christian church (see pp. 153–5, 428–9), and by so doing makes an apologetic appeal for Christian belief within its context. And so on and so on throughout the history of the church – good theology is simultaneously descriptive, critical, and apologetic.

These tasks of systematic theology help to clarify the basic audiences of theology. To whom does systematic theology speak, and for whom does it carry out these tasks? There are three particular target audiences for the theological enterprise: the *church*; the *academy*; and *society or culture*.[25] If theology is a matter of "faith seeking understanding," and the key domain of Christian faith is the church, then theology's first responsibility is to the church – its primary audience. Above all, theology must serve the church and

---

[25] These parallel David Tracy's three "publics" for theology: society, academy, and church. See David Tracy, *The Analogical Imagination: Christian Theology and the Culture of Pluralism* (New York: Crossroad, 1981), 3–46.

its mission – making Christ known, and actively bearing witness to the coming kingdom of God. But since the church must be deeply concerned with the world, theology cannot adopt a fortress mentality and concern itself only with an ecclesiastical audience. It must also engage the truth claims of other disciplines of learning in the academy, a second audience of theology: How do Christian claims relate to truth as known in the other sciences? How can theology speak intelligibly to practitioners of other academic disciplines? Thirdly and relatedly, systematic theology must also be concerned with the relationship between Christian teachings and the broader society and culture. What are the basic human and ethical implications of Christian belief? What does the church have to say both affirmingly and critically to the world at large? Society and culture thus constitute a third audience of theology.

Given these sources/norms, branches, tasks, and audiences, how does systematic theology know when it has been successful in its work? What criteria indicate when theology is responsibly and well done?

The criteria of systematic theology

The question of systematic theology's criteria can be thought of in terms of quality control. In order for a certain doctrinal proposal to be acceptable and convincing, at least three criteria must be met. The first criterion is closely connected with the first two sources and norms of theology, namely, scripture and tradition. For a doctrine to pass theological muster, it must faithfully reflect the teachings found in the Bible and the broad consensus of the Christian tradition – particularly the creeds and confessions. This criterion can be termed *orthodoxy* (right or true teaching), understood as a matter of biblical and confessional soundness. If, for example, someone were to conclude that Jesus Christ was divine but not a real, flesh-and-blood human being, such a position would be out of step with the NT and the ecumenical creeds, and would therefore fail the test of orthodoxy. It is important to recognize, however, that as "right belief," orthodoxy cannot be reduced to parroting the beliefs of the ecumenical or one's confessional tradition, but also includes the need to subject the tradition to critical scrutiny via the norm of scripture. Orthodoxy involves fidelity to both scripture *and* tradition, in terms of their respective normativity.

Fidelity to scripture and tradition, however, is not the only criterion that must be met in order for a theological position to be credible. Fidelity must also be kept with theology's third source and norm, namely philosophy, which actually yields two distinct criteria when philosophy is defined broadly as the human attempt to come to grips with the world through reason and experience. In connection with reason, it should be emphasized that good theology must pass the test of logical *coherence*. What a theologian proposes is not above the logical canons of ordinary discourse. Theology does not have privileged status as a special discipline with its own private rules for communicating clearly and meaningfully. It must be clear about what is a contradiction, what is a paradox, what is a mystery, and where the limits of human inquiry and knowledge lie. If, for example, a theologian concludes that God is both one person and three persons simultaneously – in the same exact sense of "person," as many think the doctrine of the Trinity implies – such a position seemingly smacks of logical contradiction. He or she may wish to pass off such a view as a paradox or a mystery, understandable only through the eyes of faith, but few non-theologians would find this position persuasive (see pp. 141–2).

As regards our second basic component of philosophy – experience – a theological proposition in question must also be fitting in terms of its practical *relevance*. That is, it must ring true in the world of our everyday lives and experience in the world. It must also help Christians better live out their faith. For example, if a person were to conclude that earth-keeping is not a pressing Christian responsibility (because of, say, a low view of the material world and/or a belief in the imminent return of Christ), such a claim would not only be biblically and theologically suspect, but would also fail the criterion of relevance by flying in the face of the experienced and common-sense need to live within limits so as to maintain a sustainable society for future generations.

In sum, from our perspective, systematic theology's criteria are three, as shown in Table 1.2.

The dynamics of systematic theology

As we have just seen, theology does not content itself with fidelity to the past alone (scripture and tradition) or fidelity to the present alone (reason and experience). Privileging the past at the expense of the present – that is,

Table 1.2 *The criteria of systematic theology*

Source	Corresponding criterion		
Scripture	Biblical (fidelity to scripture)	}	= Orthodoxy
Tradition	Confessional (fidelity to tradition)		
Philosophy	Logical (fidelity to reason in particular)		= Coherence
	Practical (fidelity to experience in particular)		= Relevance

concern with maintaining traditional understandings to the neglect of clarity and relevance – can be thought of as conservatism. Privileging the present at the expense of the past – that is, concern with contemporary relevance in lieu of faithfully reflecting the teachings of scripture and tradition – can be thought of as liberalism. It is our contention that good theology rejects both extremes. Theology rightly done involves an ongoing quest, a restless running to and fro between past and present, embracing both fully, seeking to be orthodox (faithful to scripture and tradition – the past) *and* coherent and relevant (faithful to reason and experience – the present) in Christian belief and practice.

This theological restlessness is nicely captured in two maxims. The first of these, already introduced as a classic definition of theology, is the Augustinian-Anselmian notion of *fides quaerens intellectum* – "faith seeking understanding." If one were to draw a slash momentarily between the words "faith" and "seeking understanding," one would see the theological restlessness just described. On the one hand, there is faith – the rock, the foundation on which the Christian life is built. Augustine, in point of fact, spent years wrestling with his own faith before it was firmly established. Once secure, however, he spent the rest of his life seeking to understand what he had come to believe, in terms of both faith's content and its implications: How can a God who is spirit create a material world? How can God be both one and three? Augustine was intellectually restless and perpetually inquisitive, constantly returning to scripture and tradition in dialogue with the present in which he rationally engaged the world of his experience.[26] Faith / seeking understanding: this venerable approach is still a helpful way to conceive the theological quest.

Centuries after the time of Augustine and Anselm, during the Protestant Reformation, another theological maxim came into currency in the circles of Reformed Christianity (i.e., Protestants with roots in the Swiss Calvinist Reformation). As an expression of their identity, Reformed Christians adopted the motto *ecclesia reformata semper reformanda* – the sense of which is "a reformed church will always be reforming." As with "faith seeking understanding," it is helpful to break this phrase into two parts in order to see the theological tension it expresses. "A reformed church" describes a body in which something has been settled – it is reformed (past). "Will always be reforming," however, suggests restlessness and an ongoing task – it is reforming (present progressive), never resting on its laurels, but always wrestling with what it means to be the church in the world.

---

[26] Especially see Augustine's *Confessions*.

Reformed church / always reforming: this Reformation approach is also a helpful way to describe the spirit of systematic theology. The task of theology is ongoing, since theology's work is never done. Every Christian generation must investigate anew the riches of scripture and tradition (past) with the assistance of contemporary human learning (present), so as to seek to understand how it should faithfully live in its time and place.

To understand the architecture of theology – its sources, branches, purpose, tasks, audiences, and criteria – is to grasp its method (Gk. *hodos* = way, road, path). Theology's way or method is an ongoing, committed, persistent way of seeking to understand and then speak about the Christian God in the time and place in which we live. Reflective Christians are always on a journey, always reforming and refining; their theology is a theology "on the way" (*theologia viatorum*), as the German theologian Jürgen Moltmann aptly characterizes this venture.[27] Theology's method thus involves the attempt to grasp the biblical basis of a given Christian teaching, see how that teaching has developed in the history of the church, and ask how it might best be understood and expressed in the present. Method in systematic theology therefore involves constant interplay of theology's sources/norms and tasks, and careful synthesis of the work undertaken by the various branches of theology. Take, for example, the doctrine of creation. A theologian would first turn to key biblical texts concerning creation, such as Genesis 1–2, Psalm 104, Job 38–41, John 1, and Revelation 4. After careful study of these texts, she would engage the wisdom of tradition – the history of the interpretation of these texts and key theological developments (or lack thereof) in creation doctrine. She would at the same time consider contemporary perspectives on and challenges to the Christian conception of creation – such as perspectives offered by modern science (e.g., Darwinism), and the challenge of the environmental crisis. Weaving all of these results together, and bearing in mind the criteria to which systematic theology is subject, the practitioner of "talk about God" attempts to articulate in the most clear, comprehensive, and compelling way what the Christian doctrine of creation entails, which in recognition of changing circumstances and contemporary knowledge may need to be tweaked in different ways and stated with differing emphases than those of previous generations. Moreover, in light of theology's ethical dimension, this reconsideration of creation doctrine must lead to practical guidance for Christian action in the world. Succeeding generations in turn might consult the creation theology produced in our time as they undertake the

---

[27] See Jürgen Moltmann, *Experiences in Theology: Ways and Forms of Christian Theology*, trans. Margaret Kohl (Minneapolis, MN: Fortress, 2000), xvii.

theological task for themselves – for the work is perpetual, ongoing, restless, as Dickinson and Augustine remind us.

Having described the theological enterprise objectively, there is one piece left that we must address before concluding this chapter – that being the subjective location of the theologian.

THE SOCIAL LOCATION AND IDENTITY OF THE THEOLOGIAN

In his work *The Analogical Imagination*, Catholic theologian David Tracy points out a matter that is by now quite obvious and taken for granted in our postmodern world. Tracy argues that when it comes to the practice of theology, it is crucial to identify precisely *who* the theologian is.[28] What theological tradition does she represent and with what agenda and priorities? How do his beliefs and subjectivity enter into the practice of theology? And where is the theologian located? In a university? In the church? Or even in the marketplace, given our claim that everyone is a theologian of sorts? All of these matters affect the process and the product of theology.

If a professional theologian, for example, is employed in a large, public university, he is likely to concentrate on the academy and contemporary society/culture as theology's chief audiences. He is also likely to place a premium on the contemporary relevance of theology and its ability to satisfy the logical rigors of science as practiced in the university. If, on the other hand, a theologian works in a denominational seminary, she is apt to concentrate on the church/denomination as the main audience for theology. She is perhaps more likely to be interested in remaining biblically and confessionally sound, in accordance with the standards embraced by the church in question. Does the university-based theologian also place a premium on biblical-confessional soundness? Is the seminary-based theologian also keen to be rigorously scientific and broadly coherent? The answers certainly depend on the case in point.

Cutting across these social realities is a series of personal coefficients: What is the gender, race, or ethnicity of the theologian? What is her social class? Do his judgments tend to be more conservative or progressive? Do political factors significantly affect their theological judgments? Theologians typically do not tell you about these things outright; you often have to read between the lines to ferret out their point of view, commitments, and the like.

---

[28] See Tracy, *Analogical Imagination*, 3–98.

In light of these considerations, the authors of this book owe you some account of their identity and social location (actually, given three authors, *identities* would be more appropriate, but we will very much speak with one voice in this volume). We have already told you a great deal about ourselves in this chapter by specifying our conception of theology and the theological approach we will take throughout this book. Beyond this, we think it is important to point out that we are professors at a church-related, Protestant college in the Midwest region of the United States. We are white, male, married with children, and middle class. While our theological commitments are broadly ecumenical, we locate ourselves ecclesiastically in the tradition of Reformed Christianity. To employ an image that C. S. Lewis utilizes in *Mere Christianity*, we might observe that while we live in a particular room in the Christian house, we have access to that room only by way of a common (i.e., ecumenical) corridor.[29] We believe that historic, orthodox Christian theology possesses powerful and enduring resources for addressing the problems of today's world. We are furthermore committed to the ongoing task of theology, firm in our belief that the Christian faith is something which one must always wrestle with and refine, not only because it is presumptuous to think that one generation or another can get it right for all time, but because fine-tuning is integral to the task that all Christians take upon themselves as their faith quests for understanding in a diverse and changing world.

The approach employed in this book, therefore, will reflect the method we have just elaborated. In each case where it is possible, a Christian doctrine's biblical basis will be explored, after which some attention will be given to the development of that doctrine in the history of theology. Then the basic systematic question will be asked: How can one best articulate and make sense of this doctrine in our contemporary context, especially given the challenges faced by Christian theology in our world today? We will map out the major issues and positions on each doctrinal question, and we will review what we take to be the strengths and weaknesses in each case. Having considered these positions, we will then respectfully argue for the position that we take to be best – that is, one that we consider responsibly orthodox, broadly coherent, and genuinely relevant to the world in which we live. In this process, we hope that the reader will come to appreciate that Christian beliefs and doctrines resemble fine cloth: tugging at one thread will ineluctably affect other threads and the shape of theology as a whole. Accordingly, the reader will see that our preference for a

---

[29] See C. S. Lewis, *Mere Christianity* (New York: Simon & Schuster, 1996), 11–12.

certain position will generally take into account interrelatedness and overall fit – a key goal of *systematic* theology. For example, our particular recommendation for the doctrine of the Trinity will have important consequences for understanding the person of Christ, as well as for shaping the contours of a doctrine of humanity as created in the image of God. A robust doctrine of creation's goodness will generate a holistic conception of salvation that will challenge an overly spiritual conception of the life to come. In what follows, we will attempt to think about Christian beliefs in a disciplined fashion. But first, given our conviction that theology must be relevant to the world and context of today, we will undertake an examination of the problems and challenges of the contemporary world. For it is in this world that theology must take root as we make the journey of faith.

FOR FURTHER READING

Allen, Diogenes, and Eric O. Springsted, *Philosophy for Understanding Theology*, 2nd edn. (Louisville, KY: Westminster John Knox, 2007).

Anselm of Canterbury, *Proslogion,* in *The Prayers and Meditations of Saint Anselm,* trans. Sister B. Ward (Harmondsworth: Penguin, 1973).

Brown, David, *Invitation to Theology* (Oxford: Blackwell, 1989).

Grenz, Stanley J., and Roger E. Olson, *Who Needs Theology? An Invitation to the Study of God* (Downers Grove, IL: InterVarsity, 1996).

McGill, Arthur C., *Suffering: A Test of Theological Method* (Philadelphia: Westminster, 1982).

Thielicke, Helmut, *A Little Exercise for Young Theologians,* trans. Charles L. Taylor (Grand Rapids, MI: Eerdmans, 1962).

CHAPTER 2

The critical context of theology today

THE CONTEXTUAL DIMENSION OF THEOLOGY

Early in her travels in Wonderland, Alice asks the Cheshire Cat for some direction in the midst of her bizarre adventures:

> "Would you tell me, please, which way I ought to go from here?"
> "That depends a good deal on where you want to get to," said the Cat.
> "I don't much care where –" said Alice.
> "Then it doesn't matter which way you go," said the Cat.
> " – so long as I get *somewhere*," Alice added as an explanation.
> "Oh, you're sure to do that," said the Cat, "if you only walk long enough."[1]

Alice is bewildered by her context. She doesn't quite know what to make of the place she has fallen into (through the rabbit-hole); consequently, she

---

[1] Lewis Carroll, *Alice's Adventures in Wonderland and Through the Looking-Glass* (New York: New American Library, 1960), 62.

really doesn't know where she is going. In negotiating life, context is crucial. In order to get somewhere, we must first know where we are. This is also the case for the venture of theology.

For many people, theology has the reputation of being an abstract and arid intellectual discipline, divorced from *terra firma* and all too often speculating in matters far removed from everyday concerns. This reputation, well earned at certain junctures in Christian history, is unfortunate, for at its best theological reflection is deeply connected to the questions and problems, hopes and fears, of real people in the real world. In fact, it is arguably the case that the most significant theological contributions in the Christian tradition have come from theologians who were deeply engaged with the burning issues of their day. For example, Augustine's *City of God* was written in response to the crisis provoked by the sack of Rome in the early fifth century (see pp. 447–9 below). Thomas Aquinas' two great summaries of theology were in part occasioned by the intellectual challenge of a newly discovered Aristotle and the church's renewed encounter with Islam (see pp. 468–71). Martin Luther's theological protest was forged amid the rapid changes of the early modern world in which disease and war ravaged Europe while new technologies (e.g., the printing press) and new political realities (e.g., the nation-state) were transforming society (see pp. 481–2). In the twentieth century, Karl Barth launched a new theological emphasis, a "theology of crisis," while wrestling with the significance of two world wars, the challenge of Nazism, and the bankruptcy of theological liberalism (see pp. 527–33). More recently, Latin American liberation theology has taken up the themes of Christian faith in response to the scandal of mass poverty in the third world (see pp. 560–4). These examples, among a host of others, illustrate the point that Christian theology is at its best when it engages the problems and challenges of the real world. Indeed, theology ignores its context at its own peril. As with Alice, we can only hope to get somewhere theologically if we have a good sense of where we are.

Over the past few decades theologians have become increasingly aware of this need to connect the theological truths of Christian faith to the real world. This process of bringing theology into engagement with the dynamics of culture is known as *contextualization*. Contextualization stresses the fact that theological work cannot be done in abstraction from the concrete contexts that impinge upon the theologian. The historical epoch, the particular culture, the economic and social needs, the political forms and institutions that structure one's world, as well as the tensions and conflicts that churn in these contexts – these are all deeply relevant to the theological enterprise. As Stephen Bevans writes: "The time is past when we can speak of one, right, unchanging theology, a *theologia perennis*. We can only speak about a theology that makes sense at a certain place and in a certain time."[2] While possibly overstating the point, Bevans is largely on the mark: theology must be made to "sing" in the world of today.

Contextualization is not just a one-way street, however, merely concerned with a conscious application of theology to one's times. Theologians must also become attuned to the ways in which their contexts shape them, since our God-talk cannot avoid being influenced by the dynamics of the culture(s) in which we are situated. One way or another contextualization happens, since theology never occurs in a vacuum.[3] Without such an awareness contextualization undoubtedly takes place *unconsciously*. One evident and often cited example of this is Anselm's eleventh-century explanation of the saving work of Christ, where he employs the categories of lord and vassal drawn from the feudal system of his day (see pp. 271–3 below). Anselm simply took it for granted that these socio-political categories also applied to a theological understanding of the relationship between God and humanity. A less evident example of unconscious contextualization is the way in which certain conceptions of God or Christ over the centuries – whether literary or iconic – have unconsciously privileged certain groups of people. A predominant image of God as Father, for instance, has historically favored the sons of Adam as the true image-bearers of God in slight of the daughters of Eve. Or alternatively, a preference for a portrait of Christ as confident, powerful, and white, as opposed to diffident, weak, and dark-skinned, can be tacitly influenced by, as well as bolster, racist attitudes. Compare, for example, the traditional Byzantine *Christ Pantocrator* (Christ Almighty) to the critical power of Rocha's Brazilian *Tortured Christ*, which strikingly challenges our conventional assumptions about Jesus (see Illustrations 2.1 and 2.2).

In general, the danger of unconscious contextualization is that one's context can easily overdetermine or inappropriately influence one's theological thinking, such that the biblical materials and central affirmations of the Christian tradition, two crucial norms of theology, become overshadowed. While tacit cultural influences can never be wholly avoided, this danger of accommodation – a compromising adaptation of Christian truth to culture – constitutes one reason why many theologians today are convinced that we should *consciously* contextualize our theology. If we take up this task intentionally, we may become more aware of its risks and possible

---

[2] Stephen B. Bevans, *Models of Contextual Theology*, Faith and Cultures (Maryknoll, NY: Orbis, 2003), 5.
[3] Ibid., 7–9.

Illustration 2.1   *Christ Pantocrator*, traditional Byzantine icon (sixth or seventh century).

Illustration 2.2   The Brazilian sculptor Guido Rocha's sculpture *Tortured Christ*, which bears the marks of Rocha's own experiences as a victim of torture.

perils. Moreover, if contextualization is inevitable, one way or the other, it is simply more responsible to take up the task consciously.

If contextualization should be consciously and intentionally embraced by the theological practitioner, what then should it look like? Canadian theologian Douglas John Hall suggests that an appropriate theological engagement with one's context in both an open and a discerning way is best envisioned as a *dialogue*, with theology taking its social context seriously but never losing its own voice in the conversation.[4] Karl Barth is famously reported as saying that theology must be done with the Bible in one hand and the newspaper in the other. In other words, theology that intends to be faithful to the triune God who engages world history through Christ and the Spirit must similarly be engaged in that same historical world. In this book, we hope to foster such a faithful conversation between today's context and the traditional doctrines of Christian faith.

Thus we devote this brief chapter to an exploration of the dynamics of the contemporary world that are particularly germane to Christian theology in order to plot where we are so that we might know whither we theologically venture. We will survey a number of the cultural and intellectual currents, political problems, and social issues that both animate and agitate today's world. We will introduce these problems and challenges here, identifying what issues they pose for contemporary Christian faith and theology in general. Then we will take up many of these concerns elsewhere in the book as they intersect with particular theological themes, sketching the contours of what a faithful Christian response to these challenges might look like.

MODERNITY

Our generation has witnessed tremendous change, change so dramatic and at such an accelerated pace that our times have been dubbed a new epoch – postmodernity. While it remains to be seen what exactly this emerging postmodern ethos will turn out to be, by definition it is touted as an age "after modernity." In our estimation, postmodernity represents both a conscious reaction to and a less conscious radicalization of modernity, which is why, given the latter, some prefer instead to classify our times as "late modernity."[5] Regardless of the label, discerning the spirit of these

---

[4] Douglas John Hall, *Thinking the Faith: Christian Theology in a North American Context* (Minneapolis, MN: Augsburg, 1989), 113–15.

[5] E.g., social theorist Anthony Giddens, *The Consequences of Modernity* (Stanford, CA: Stanford University Press, 1990).

shifting times as the pressing context for the theological enterprise today first requires some acquaintance with the modernity that is currently under siege.

The Enlightenment project

Modernity is an epoch in western civilization that represents a distinctive cultural and intellectual shift from the era that preceded it – premodernity. While such generalized historical periods are notoriously hard to date with any precision, the foundation of the modern mindset is rooted in the Age of Reason (seventeenth to eighteenth centuries), particularly as it comes to expression in the European Enlightenment (eighteenth century) or what has been termed the Enlightenment project. The roots of modernity, however, can be located in the Renaissance, a recovery of classical culture and learning (fourteenth to sixteenth centuries). This "rebirth" instigated a new humanism, a heightened estimate of human capabilities, against the backdrop of medieval times, in which humanity was largely dwarfed by a daunting sense of divine transcendence and its representative temporal authorities of church and state, pope and emperor. Many other factors contributed to the rise of modern times, including religious factors, such as the sixteenth-century Reformation which divided a largely united Christendom, and eventually led to disturbing wars of religion between Christian factions, such as the devastating Thirty Years War (1618–48). These conflicts seemed to many to discredit religious (Christian) belief as a salutary catalyst of civil society. Meanwhile the Renaissance spawned the scientific revolution in which a heliocentric cosmos was being discovered in all its natural order and regularity – the Newtonian world machine. This revolutionary development of modern science and technology became the principal engine of modernity, and seemed to many luminaries to offer a more reliable basis than religion for binding European society together and guiding its future along civilized and prosperous paths.

The Enlightenment project thus made the *appeal to the natural* (order, laws, logic) the basis of truth and certainty in the world as discernible by the *authority of reason*, whether understood in rationalist or in empiricist terms. These commitments entailed a *rejection of tradition*, replacing the authority of divine revelation and church dogma as embraced by faith with the primacy of reason. The new-found faith in reason produced a *belief in progress*, of what human potential could make of the world given scientific, rational, and technological means.

Challenge to Christian orthodoxy

These Enlightenment emphases conspired to present a rationalist challenge to Christian orthodoxy. Generally speaking, Enlightenment thinkers disregarded traditional authorities, whether scripture, creeds, or pope, in the name of autonomous (literally, self-legislating = independent) reason; they ruled out any supernatural causality in the name of autonomous nature – including the foundational miracles of the incarnation and the resurrection; they denied the doctrine of original sin and the consequent need for Christ's atonement in the name of human goodness and potential; and/or they dismissed such doctrines as the Trinity and the divine-human nature of Christ as too paradoxical to pass muster by Enlightenment standards of reasonability and practicality. Much of Christian theology today remains in a defensive posture given the rationalist challenge of modernity, even though the Enlightenment criteria of rationality have subsequently been tried and found wanting – guilty of being too narrow, constricting, and untenable a foundation for the edifice of human knowledge (a postmodern critique). While agreeing with this critique, we nevertheless endeavor in this book to articulate a theology that is broadly orthodox, coherent, and relevant. The last two criteria explicitly take up the Enlightenment challenge of reasonability and practicality, especially in respect to such doctrines as the Trinity (Chapter 5) and the incarnation of Christ (Chapter 9), doctrines that, as traditionally formulated, have often been considered too paradoxical (or illogical) to be of much clear benefit. The requirements of broad coherence and practical relevance are rightly asked of any theology that aims to speak to a world that still has one foot in modernity, since Christian truth (orthodoxy) cannot be exempt from the canons of logic (coherence) upon which the clarity of its application depends (relevance).

Secularization and the rise of modern atheism

Beyond these particular challenges to traditional Christian orthodoxy, Enlightenment emphases had a broader effect on belief in God in general, helping to usher into western society an atheism of unprecedented proportions. This swell of mass atheism was largely the result of the process of *secularization*, the trend toward understanding the world and its activities (science, politics, economics, etc.) in merely natural terms without recourse to supernatural explanation or divine intervention (as in the day, for example, when thunder was attributed to divine disturbance or displeasure). The more the world was discovered in its own structural integrity, the less – and less – God was needed as an explanatory cause or principle of the world's operations. Much of this process, we must be clear, was a natural and inevitable development of natural science and not in the least incompatible with Christian belief (which actually facilitated the rise of modern science – see pp. 159–60 below). But the course of secularization in the West took an atheistic turn, as many came to consider belief in God to be inimical to modern life and human flourishing. Much of the reason for this, we argue, was a particular conception of God long ensconced in Christian theology, a "classical theism" bolstered by questionable philosophical assumptions that tended to exclude more biblical – creational and christological (and therefore more world-affirming and humane) – elements in its conception of God. We therefore will advocate a biblical and christological reformulation of the doctrine of God that addresses this atheistic legacy of modernity, as much of the western world still labors with a sense of the "death of God" – the felt absence or obsolescence of God in the affairs of life (see Chapter 4). Even in the United States, our immediate context, where polls reflect that an overwhelming number of people still believe in God, the influence of the Enlightenment has significantly relegated religious belief to the private, subjective sphere. The corrective to this modern chasing of God from the public to the private realm is a doctrine of God (and especially a doctrine of divine immanence – God's presence within the world) that respects the world in all its created integrity, resulting in a legitimately *Christian* form of secularization and *Christian* humanism (see Chapters 4, 6, 7).

Individualism and dehumanization

Given this cultural de-emphasis of the divine, the human individual has assumed a heightened importance in modern times, one that found its noblest expression in the burgeoning of liberal democracy on the basis of universal human rights. That these democratic rights could be grounded in theistic thought is seen in the American Declaration of Independence, which declares "that all men are created equal, that they are endowed by their Creator with certain unalienable Rights" – an implication of the Christian doctrine that humanity is created in the image of God (see Chapter 7). But the democratic rights of the individual could also be asserted on less religious grounds, as in the French Revolution's declaration of freedom, equality, and fraternity in defiance of an authoritarianism legitimated by "divine right." When not theistically undergirded, this revolutionary flourishing of the individual was bolstered by an Enlightenment anthropology of the rational self, whose autonomous reason could rationally chart and manage the course of life. This modern turn to the human subject, a radicalizing of human subjectivity, has fostered an individualism run amok in the western world, leading to what has been termed a "culture of narcissism."[6] To this extreme individualism, which is paradoxically both challenged and radicalized in postmodernity, a Christian anthropology (Chapter 7) and ecclesiology (Chapter 13) of more social and relational dimensions must serve as a corrective.

On its positive side, the recognition of the individual as one democratically clothed in dignity and rights has highlighted the problems of racism, sexism, and classism that have perennially plagued humanity, since these modern democratic ideals put forward a universal standard of humanization. Reflection on modern (western) history involves the painful recognition of how democratic cultures have often fallen short of their humanitarian ideals. In the United States, for example, many of the founding fathers were slaveholders. Even as late as the 1960s Martin Luther King, Jr. made his non-violent civil rights appeal by holding the American public accountable to the principles of its constitution and the God-given rights it guarantees.[7] This struggle for racial equality continues today in both overt and covert corridors of consciousness and power. Women also continue to labor today for equal recognition and opportunity, having achieved voting rights in the United States only via a relatively late amendment to its constitution (1920). And it has not gone unnoticed that the problems of racism and sexism are typically reinforced and exacerbated by unequal economic structures or classism.

Modernity has historically favored the European male, especially the one who had political and economic means, who though espousing the ideals of democracy often appeared quite oblivious to or simply disingenuous concerning the highly questionable socio-economic forces that motivated and empowered his course of action in the world. One of the greatest contradictions of modernity was the European conquest and colonization of the world at large in the name of Christian civilization, first in a mercantile phase of colonization on the heels of exploration and the commercial revolution (which underwrote the African slave trade), followed by a capitalist phase of imperialism on the heels of the industrial revolution. These endeavors of "manifest destiny" and taking up the "white man's burden" (Kipling) helped to perpetuate a global racism,

---

[6] See Christopher Lasch, *The Culture of Narcissism* (New York: Norton, 1978).
[7] See, e.g., King's famous "I have a dream" speech, August 28, 1963: "I have a dream that one day this nation will rise up and live out the true meaning of its creed: 'We hold these truths to be self-evident: that all men are created equal.'"

sexism, and classism, a legacy that continues to fuel a growing north–south division today in lieu of the East–West conflict of the Cold War era. While heralding a civilized humanism, modernity in its own various ways under-wrote a rampant dehumanization. And while many western nations, and western-influenced nations, have made significant strides toward equality, we have become more globally conscious of the inequities that continue to exist. It is here that Christian theology must continue to be prophetic, insisting that "salvation" is a holistic (cf. whole/holy) matter of both body and soul, including conditions of human dignity and flourishing (Chapter 12) that are part and parcel of a humanity created in the image of God (Chapter 7) – and this against a continuing Christian reductionism of viewing salvation in sheer spiritual terms.

The problem of evil

Given the new emphasis on human freedom and mobility in the world, coupled with the belief in progress, the modern person was no longer resigned to things as they were, as if everything had its ordained, God-given place, whether this concerned social roles or events, especially bad events such as the Lisbon earthquake (1755). Whereas in the premodern "age of faith" all human affairs, even misfortunes, were seen to be under the special guidance of a benevolent divine providence, the Enlightenment rationalist questioned whether such evils really reflected the "best of all possible worlds" and could be squared with an all-good and all-powerful divine Sovereign.[8] Thus the problem of evil was accentuated in modernity, ultimately becoming the capstone in the modern atheistic rejection of God (Chapter 4).

Ironically, considering its loud complaint against the divine – how can there be a God, given a world of egregious suffering? – modernity actually helped to mass-produce the very evidence in its own case against God. On the one hand, one certainly cannot question the countless benefits of modern science, the major engine of modernity, and its technological improvement of life. Advances in all areas – transportation, communication, food production, medicine, and the like – have ameliorated life for

---

[8] Voltaire's *Candide* parodied Leibniz's theodicy conclusion that this was the "best of all possible worlds," especially in view of such events as the Lisbon earthquake. David Hume, reviving Epicurus' formulation, framed the formal problem of evil for modern times (also see pp. 207–8 below): "Is [God] willing to prevent evil, but not able? then is he impotent. Is he able, but not willing? then is he malevolent. Is he both able and willing? whence then is evil?" David Hume, *Dialogues Concerning Natural Religion* (Indianapolis, IN: Hackett, 1990), pt. 10.

millions, though such improvements and accumulation of wealth have not entirely trickled down throughout the globe: while afflicting the northern first world with "affluenza," they have largely left the southern third world low and dry. But on the other hand, the very engine of this (selective) flourishing of life has also driven the technology of death. Promising to tame the future terrors of history, modernity eventually created the world's most ghastly horrors. The twentieth century became the bloodiest on record, inaugurated by the highly technologized and ideologically optimistic "war to end all wars." The second act of this Great War, namely World War II (WWII), witnessed the unspeakable crime of the Holocaust, wherein the most modern and putatively advanced culture of the time attempted the genocide of a chosen people in the name of "living space" – while the rest of the world stood idly by (a scenario that has repeated itself to the present). Only the condition of modernity with its rational planning, bureaucratic execution, and modern factories of death can account for such a diabolical scheme in the name of progress – the possibility of an extermination of a whole race of people.[9]

But this scientific and technological machine grinds on, and many fear it has become a runaway train. What constraints or ethics will harness unbridled investigation – for example, inquiries in genetic engineering, whether of foods or of people? And what is going to stop the continued proliferation and stockpiling of atomic-biological-chemical weapons, whose increasing potency threatens all life on our planet? This is not to mention the modern forces of deterioration already in effect that contribute to the gathering ecological crisis – such as global warming, acid rain, air and water pollution, and the like. In the face of these principalities and powers of ecological degradation, Christian theology must emphasize a doctrine of a good creation and a conception of humanity that highlights human responsibility for and stewardship of a finite but sustainable earth (Chapters 6–7).

Ominously, modernity, while enriching the lives of many, has also created the conditions of the Apocalypse for all. Modernity has ushered in apocalyptic times – the possibility of the end of life as we (like to) know it. Perhaps even more frightful is the prospect that many people around the world seem to be acclimated or resigned to this fate, as if it were an inevitability (a social death-wish?) – including, unfortunately, many Christians who are fixated on

---

[9] See Zygmunt Bauman, *Modernity and the Holocaust* (Ithaca, NY: Cornell University Press, 1989). According to Bauman, the Holocaust was no simple failure of modernity, but one of its "rationalized" products. Only the advanced conditions of modernity make such racism and genocide possible in its quest to design the perfect society by means of social engineering.

a particular scenario of the end times (see Chapter 15). Like the unsinkable ocean liner *Titanic*, a modern marvel, modernity has run aground upon its own hubris. It has become mortally wounded on the sword of its own fashioning. It is this moral bankruptcy, in large part, that accounts for the recent call for a new cultural paradigm – the postmodern.

POSTMODERNITY

Those who herald the postmodern condition have a hard time pinpointing its origin – the thought of Friedrich Nietzsche (ideological), quantum physics and Einstein's relativity theories (scientific), post-WWII consumer culture (economic), the radical 1960s (social)? – as well as identifying its fund of sources. But if modernity idolized the absolute universal truth of nature, autonomous human reason, the role of the individual subject *contra* tradition, and the inexorable march of progress, the contemporary post-modern period has begun to scorn these Enlightenment canons as defective myths of the modern imagination. By contrast, the postmodern intellectual mood is pessimistic about the western path to progress which seems to lead consistently to gross economic imbalance and ecological disaster (and probably war); it is unconvinced that individuals ground their own subjective lives as though they can be abstracted from their historical communities and traditions; it is skeptical that reason is autonomous or impartial, since all thinking is influenced by the interests of the thinker relative to her embeddedness in language, community, and tradition; and it is suspicious that truth can be known as universal and absolute, since we have no "God's-eye view" of the whole, given our radical historical contingency. Indeed, the postmodern mood harbors an "incredulity toward metanarratives,"[10] especially since such "master stories" or "totalizing accounts" have generally functioned to benefit insiders (as powerbrokers of the truth) to the exclusion of others. A primary example: modernity's exclusive – and therefore excluding – stranglehold on the cultural discourse of the West. Instead, postmodernism is a more globally conscious perspective that celebrates the particular, the contingent, the local, the different, the other, the historical, the transient, and the open-ended – championing diversity, pluralism, and relativism. Like its favorite form of art and discourse, postmodernism is a veritable *collage* of ideas and cultural forms, an eclectic taste for this and for that, which means that it resists neat

---

[10] Jean-François Lyotard, *The Postmodern Condition: A Report on Knowledge*, trans. Geoff Bennington and Brian Massumi (Minneapolis, MN: University of Minnesota Press, 1984), iv.

or tidy description. The philosophers and cultural critics who trumpet these changes as much needed advocate *postmodernism* so as to move "beyond modernity" and overcome its hegemony.

The term *postmodernity*, however, refers more neutrally and descriptively to the apparent fact that modern culture has shifted extensively enough that we are entering a new time period – that which comes "after modernity"; as such, it is a controversial term because many claim that modernity has most certainly not yet been left behind. Those who resist the proclamation of a new historical era cite various reasons. For one, the contemporary period is witnessing at an astonishing rate the continuing proliferation of technology that typified the modern world, including the proliferation of weaponry as the modern machinery of war grinds on even in the putatively postmodern world. Moreover, the postmodern respect for the integrity of nature as more than raw material for human consumption has not slowed the march toward ecological catastrophe. For another reason, so-called postmodernity only seems to extend modernity's infatuation with the individual thinking subject, at times affirming the individual even more radically by suggesting that each person possesses his or her own truth. If much of modernity, therefore, remains in play in the West (hence, "late modernity"), then postmodern philosophers cannot be seen as heralds of a new day that is already upon us. They can nevertheless be understood as prophets predicting modernity's doom in order to hasten its demise. In either case, the features now typically associated with the postmodern condition raise challenges for Christian theology that are no less important than those brought by modernity.

The crisis of meaning

Modernity's infatuation with absolute truth – a truth known by right use of reason, rather than through traditions, authorities, or faith – produced numerous challenges to Christian theology. Postmodernity complicates the notion of truth, suggesting that it is a plural category rather than a singular, universal something, with "truths" that emerge from differing historical contexts. The epistemological pluralism that results from radical historical contingency leads to a crisis of meaning in general.

Historical contingency

The modern period itself witnessed an increased appreciation for the historically contingent nature of the world, especially given the ascendancy of the empirical sciences. This intensification of historical consciousness and concomitant rise of historical criticism created problems for traditional religious claims with historical origins. Modernity here held the Christian tradition hostage. The postmodern mood, however, is more open to traditioned perspectives and to forms of truth other than the strictly rational or empirical – such as affective, intuitive, artistic, and historical forms of truth. In this sense, postmodernity is more congenial to religious questions and quests, and would seem therefore to be more open to Christianity as a whole than was modernity. And on the one hand it is. But in the postmodern milieu, the extent to which religious claims "make sense" is largely dependent upon whether one is playing within the "language game" – living within and embracing a particular tradition and its assumptions, rules, and mores. Indeed, the truth of any system is quite compelling within that system, given its presuppositions and logic. But deepened historical consciousness brings with it the realization that things like customs and beliefs have a history, that they evolve, and that they are molded by a myriad of contingent factors – linguistic, personal, historical, social, economic, and political, among others. Why then should we believe the tenets of our tradition? For example, is the doctrine of the Trinity – a central Christian belief foundational for other Christian teachings – simply the result of a confluence of historical factors: Jewish faith plus Jesus Christ plus Greek philosophical thinking? Or is there something more to it (see Chapter 5)? While postmodernity is more open to Christianity than modernity was, it also seems to be equally open to all traditions and perspectives. This raises the specter of relativism.

Epistemological pluralism

If all claims to truth flow from historical contingencies, molded by particular communities and other contingent factors, it is only a short step to say that "truth" is relative. In embracing a relativist approach to truth, postmodernism is suspicious that claims to *the* truth usually involve posturings and ploys for power. While this may often be the case, it also raises some troubling questions. If the search for truth is not a quest for reality as it really is (realism), but involves only the assertion of the interests and culturally constructed traditions of its pilgrims (anti-realism), how can there be any real "meaning" in the world? If truth is wholly relative, how can any claims have enduring significance? This epistemological relativism poses a pointed challenge to orthodox Christian theology, which claims that Jesus Christ *is* in fact the "truth" (John 14:6). Whereas radical modernists simply claimed that Christianity was untrue, postmodern culture often appears to suggest that there are no normative truths; thus the Christian narrative is no more "true" than any other narrative.[11] Some postmodernists would prefer to say that all narratives are indeed true – true, that is, for those who believe them, since there is no other sense of truth (such as universal or absolute truth). The epistemological pluralism of the postmodern world thus challenges what Christians claim is true knowledge with universal significance: that the triune God became present in an utterly unique way in Jesus Christ, who alone brings salvation to a world that is pervasively touched by sin. Here, in the final analysis, postmodernism appears no more congenial to Christianity than was modernism.

But the postmodern condition is both a many-headed Hydra as well as a double-edged sword, an emerging intellectual and cultural ethos that Christian theology will have to negotiate (see pp. 566–70). Whether postmodernity turns out to be a boon or a bane to Christian theology remains to be seen. To the degree that postmodernity overcomes those aspects of modernity that held Christian theology hostage in the past, many applaud and celebrate it as an opening for Christianity to present its case (as one legitimate voice in the conversation). To the degree that postmodern canons impose new and restrictive conditions on the theological enterprise, especially as insisted on by its more radically relativist, even nihilistic expression (itself, arguably, a radicalization of certain features of modernity), the prospects for orthodox Christianity are not so sanguine. But the general postmodern mood is the context in which Christian theology finds itself today, a context whose borders have expanded from the western cultural universe to the diverse cultures of a global community.

Global consciousness

Whereas modernity, a western phenomenon, attempted to winnow all diversity into a singular sameness, postmodernity, by contrast, is more globally conscious and issues a call to recognize and respect the "other." The existence of "otherness" has become more and more undeniable in today's world. All the technological advances in transportation and communication (i.e., the information revolution) have made our world smaller. Whereas it once took weeks to cross the Atlantic Ocean by ship, today we cover the same distance in a matter of hours by air, while our communications zip across the globe in a matter of seconds. But our smaller world has

---

[11] It is ironic, however, that most postmodern thinkers maintain one normative standard – that of justice. While this is a laudable standard, it is hard to explain how they could affirm any normativity given their assumptions and framework that there is no absolute truth.

also unveiled a larger complexity, as we are more aware than in times past of other cultures, religions, and ways of life. There was once a time in which economic, political, and religious realities in one region of the planet did not make much of a difference to other regions. This is no longer the case: what happens in one part of the world inevitably has consequences for other parts of it. In short, today we possess a heightened global consciousness, whereby we pay greater attention to realities beyond our own immediate localities. Greater recognition of the "other" also means that the other has increased effect and affect upon "us," and vice versa. *Globalization* is thus a two-pronged phenomenon – increased awareness of the other, and heightened mutual influence. In the march of globalization today there are three key issues that demand sustained attention by Christian theology.

First, over the course of the last half-century we have become newly conscious of a *north–south disparity*. The world of the north (the so-called first world of Europe and North America), many parts of which possess staggering wealth and prosperity, is much more economically viable and politically stable than the world of the south (the so-called third world of Africa, South America, and parts of Asia), many regions of which experience crushing poverty. The rich north has only just begun to listen to the cries and concerns of the south. Consciousness of the plight of the third-world poor has had an impact on social policy and ethical discussions in the north, given the recognition that life, including politics and theology, cannot be carried on as usual – in light of the local situation alone. Ignorance of others' conditions and concerns in the current global situation is unacceptable, whether in the public or the private sectors of society. Such problems cannot be dismissed by a remote change of channel. Thus the doctrines of salvation and church today must remind the worldwide Christian community of its responsibilities to promote justice and advance the cause of the kingdom of God in wake of the growing north–south divide (see Chapters 12 and 13).

Second, over the course of the last century we have become increasingly conscious of *religious plurality*. Of the nearly 7 billion people who currently inhabit this planet, the major religious traditions claim approximately the number of adherents set out in Table 2.1.[12]

How does one make sense of Christian faith in a religiously plural world such as ours, one in which Christianity is but one of many religious options?

---

[12] The main source for these estimates is the "Religion" entry of the *Britannica Book of the Year, 2008*, retrieved October 28, 2008, from Encyclopædia Britannica Online: http://search.eb.com/eb/article-9439181.

Table 2.1 *Global demographics of religious adherence*

Christianity	2.2 billion
Islam	1.4 billion
Non-religious/atheistic/agnostic	925 million
Hinduism	875 million
Chinese traditional religions (e.g., Confucianism, Taoism, folk religion)	395 million
Buddhism	385 million
Primal and traditional religions	280 million
Sikhism	23 million
Judaism	15 million

If, as most Christians believe, there is "no other name" by which we can be saved (Acts 4:12), how can one make sense of a world in which the name of Jesus Christ is not confessed by the majority of people and sometimes not even known? Christian theology in our time can ill afford to neglect this complex situation and the soteriological questions it raises (see Chapter 14). Even beyond such theological questions, the Christian church must empathetically engage other religious traditions in order to foster dialogue toward mutual understanding, peaceful coexistence, and cooperation in the world at large. This is especially the case with Islam, which has become a major factor in the broader geo-political situation and in international relations. People of good will among these two Abrahamic faiths need to dialogue and come to an appreciable understanding of each another, while honestly acknowledging and respecting their theological differences. Such Christian and Muslim "peacemakers" must then work together for justice and peace in today's world, in the hope of breaking the vicious cycle of these religions' historical antagonism, which continues to fester in fundamentalist attitudes and responses on both sides, often to destructive ends.

Third, today's global world is witnessing the *shifting of Christianity's center*. A century ago, the majority of Christian believers lived in Europe and North America. Today, the majority are found in Africa, South America, and Asia. These demographic changes are nothing short of revolutionary.[13] As the Christian center moves, the fortunes of Christian theology shift with it. In our time, therefore, an account of Christianity's changing nature must be offered. Such an account must pay greater attention to the theologies emerging from different parts of the globe, something we

[13] Philip Jenkins, *The Next Christendom: The Coming of Global Christianity* (Oxford: Oxford University Press, 2002).

attempt to do throughout this book, but especially in Chapter 14. Given their diverse contexts, these Christianities and theologies may look markedly different than those in the western tradition. Moreover, theology in Christianity's recently vacated center – the West – must also rethink its nature and purpose given the dynamics of a changing world. In this globally fluid situation, how does one ensure a unity of Christian theology of the one, holy, catholic, and apostolic church (see Chapter 13)?

CONCLUSION

These are the significant contours of our context and the major challenges and problems that confront theology today. This is the contemporary situation in which theology must venture forth if it seeks to be a relevant rendition of orthodox Christianity, an earnest wrestling with our times. While we have indicated a number of chapters where we more specifically take up these particular problems and issues, the greater postmodern (or late modern) ethos shapes our systematic statement in other diverse ways. We strive to be conscious of this contemporary context so as to intentionally situate our theology, even as we also attempt to be honest and aware of our own personal coefficients – our own perceptual filters of theological tradition, race, gender, class, and the like. Many of the problems we face today are more appropriately (and thoroughly) addressed by the special domain of Christian ethics and related disciplines, and are therefore beyond the scope of an introductory systematic theology. We nevertheless believe that this introductory proposal clarifies much of the essential theological grammar – the basic suppositions and structure of theology – needed to serve as a helpful resource for these problems or issues, since Christian ethics cannot be divorced from theology (nor can theology from ethics).

Back to Alice. She was not satisfied with the Cheshire Cat's directive to simply walk anywhere, so she asked another question in order to locate her whereabouts: "What sort of people live about here?" The Cat proceeded to tell her that a Hatter lived in that direction and a March Hare in that direction, but that they were both mad – in fact, everyone in Wonderland was mad, including even Alice herself just for coming there.[14] With Lewis Carroll, it is not too difficult to make the case that our world is mad, or has gone mad – disordered, uncontrolled, senseless, frenzied, fanatical, panic-stricken, insane in many respects. According to the Christian gospel, it was into such a world that God the Father sent his Son, who in the power of the

---

[14] Carroll, *Alice's Adventures in Wonderland*, 63.

Spirit walked this earth full of truth and grace, preaching and embodying a message of faith and hope and love. But for all his earnest efforts, Christ was nailed to a cross. We crucified God. That is indeed madness – by any standard a murder, an injustice, a tragedy, an absurdity. Headline: Creature Kills Creator. What is even more absurd is that Christ came back to us and issued an "all forgiven." Theology negotiates this madness of divine love in a world still mad, yet searching. That basic condition remains the most crucial context of theology today.

FOR FURTHER READING

Bevans, Stephen B., *Models of Contextual Theology*, Faith and Cultures (Maryknoll, NY: Orbis, 2003).

Jenkins, Philip, *The Next Christendom: The Coming of Global Christianity* (Oxford: Oxford University Press, 2002).

Schreiter, Robert J., *Constructing Local Theologies* (Maryknoll, NY: Orbis, 1985).

Thornhill, John, *Modernity: Christianity's Estranged Child Reconstructed* (Grand Rapids, MI: Eerdmans, 2000).

Vanhoozer, Kevin J., ed., *The Cambridge Companion to Postmodern Theology* (Cambridge: Cambridge University Press, 2003).

PART II

Key themes of Christian theology

The second part of this book surveys the central teachings of the Christian faith, giving special attention to their biblical basis and the highlights of their historical development, before engaging in a systematic consideration of how these themes are variously interpreted in theology today. Throughout this exploration we indicate our perspectives and preferences on particular doctrines as we also seek to propose in the course of this section a contemporary statement of Christian theology – one that strives to be biblically and confessionally orthodox, broadly coherent, and practically relevant.

CHAPTER 3

Revelation and knowledge of God

THE IDEA OF REVELATION

Talk about God and the necessity of revelation

As we have seen in the first two chapters, Christian theology seeks to understand and give a reasoned account of God. But it must do so in a particular time and place, bearing in mind the challenges and concerns of the theologian's specific context. Giving a faithful account of the Christian

God in our day entails recognizing both the legacy of modernity, in which, for example, the matter of secularization and atheism is a key challenge for theology, and the condition of postmodernity, in which the matter of pluralism is increasingly significant. So how do we proceed to speak about God in a world where some deny the divine reality and others view God in terms strikingly different from the Christian tradition? Christian theology proceeds on the assumption that God has already communicated something of the divine life to humanity, that God can be known because of divine revelation. But what sources mediate that revelation? What does knowing God involve? And what are the challenges and liabilities involved in claiming a true knowledge of God? These important questions fall under the canopy of the doctrine of revelation.

Before continuing with our discussion, however, we need to make two important preliminary observations. First, we should note that human knowing is a complex phenomenon, admitting of many gradations that range from sense experience to intuition to demonstrated evidence, and involving many a heady issue in philosophical epistemology (the science of knowing). Such issues have at times, and especially in these postmodern times, mired the theological enterprise in questions of methodology: How do we even *begin* to speak about God? While recognizing the seriousness of these issues, Christian theology can do no other than presuppose revelation, that God has graciously spoken. Theology's reflections and deliberations assume as fact that God has taken the initiative in communicating the divine life to humanity, which it also considers an utter necessity since an adequate knowledge of God is beyond sheer human capacity. In view of this foundational presupposition, considerations of epistemology cannot be granted the exalted role of first determining whether or not God can be known. But they can and should nuance our theological understanding given the working assumption of divine revelation. In other words, philosophy (epistemology) cannot sit in judgment on the viability of the theological enterprise or establish the conditions for its proceeding; yet theology as it proceeds should not neglect the clarifying aid of philosophy and its legitimate epistemological tools. This approach of presupposing the revelation of the triune God as the central grammar of Christian faith is more in line with the community and tradition-affirming sensitivities of postmodernity, over against modernity's obsession with epistemological foundations.

Second, concerning this knowledge of God, it is important to keep in mind a crucial distinction between two different kinds of knowing. The epistemic claim that "I know I have an unread email message from Stacy," for example, is different from the claim "I know Stacy; we go back a long way." In the former, the knowledge in question is factual and concerns an object (an "it"). In the latter, the knowledge referred to is personal and concerns a subject (a "you"). Many languages use distinct words to recognize and differentiate these two sorts of knowing. Spanish, for example, distinguishes between *saber* and *conocer*, French between *savoir* and *connaître*, and German between *wissen* and *kennen* for the factual and personal, respectively. Strangely, the English language does not follow suit. The one English verb "to know" (and the noun "knowledge") must therefore be scrutinized in context in order to discern the difference between factual and personal knowing. So, for example, when the old English Bible states that "Adam knew Eve his wife; and she conceived" (Gen. 4:1, KJV), we understand this to be a most intimate kind of "knowledge" – a personal not a factual knowing. Such a distinction is important in Christian theology, since knowledge of God is first and foremost something personal, relational, and intimate, in addition to involving factual and propositional claims.

As we shall see, Christian thought maintains that human beings cannot come to an adequate or full knowledge of God on their own, by their own will or effort. To know God and know about God truly, revelation is necessary. Only because God discloses the divine identity to humanity in a personal way and invites a faithful, loving response can God be known. But because of the personal nature of divine revelation and the requested human response, this activity on God's part involves risk, for human beings could turn out to be – and in fact do turn out to be – unfaithful, unloving responders, as many a painful episode in the Bible makes clear (see, e.g., Gen. 6:5–6). Whether human or divine, self-revelation entails vulnerability, the risk of rejection and suffering, a freedom which is in fact the condition of love (see pp. 217–18). In this vein, it is instructive to note that Christian theology also maintains that the fullest revelation of the triune God – who is love (1 John 4:8) – takes place at the cross of Christ.

The meaning of revelation

The nucleus of the idea of revelation is this: something unknown must be unveiled or disclosed by an agent. The English term "revelation" comes from the Latin *revelare*, a translation of the Greek *apokalyptein*, which means "to uncover or unveil." Imagine a ceremony in a city square in which a new statue is going to be displayed and dedicated. The statue, hidden behind a covering, is unknown to the bystanders who have gathered for the ceremony, although they may already have some sense of the object of dedication. When the covering is finally removed for the bystanders, they can then see what they had not known before. What was veiled has been disclosed; what was unclear has become clear. The Dutch word for revelation, *openbaring* (cf. the German *Offenbarung*), captures this dynamic well: something comes into view, into the "open," because some agent laid it "bare." As concerns Christian theology, the agent in question is none other than the triune God; revelation is a *divine* act. The intended human correlate and response to revelation is *faith*.

The Bible broadly assumes both the necessity and the reality of revelation but says little about the concept *per se*. The term does of course appear in the biblical text, most notably in the name of the last book of the NT (the book of Revelation, the so-called Apocalypse, from its first Gk. word, *apokalypsis*). Since the notion of revelation remains undeveloped in scripture, it is the task of Christian theology to elaborate this scriptural assumption into an explicit doctrine of revelation.

As Christian theology understands the notion of revelation, then, an agent – the triune God – communicates itself to humanity. But what is the means by which this communication occurs? What form does the communiqué take? And what is the result of the divine revelatory activity? Historically, the Christian tradition has distinguished two kinds or forms of revelation: general and special. These kinds can be differentiated from each other by the type of knowledge they communicate, the primary means or media used, the way they are apprehended, and their resultant theology (see Table 3.1).

Most simply, *general revelation* (sometimes called natural revelation) is a natural knowledge of God via creation and providence, apprehended by human reason, intuition, or conscience, and resulting in what is called natural theology. This kind of revelation is thought to be perceptible in creation, whether in the splendor and beauty of nature (as cosmos) or the inner workings of the human person (as microcosm). Such revelation is considered generally accessible and universally available to all humanity.

Table 3.1 *Kinds of revelation*

Kind of revelation	Type of knowledge	Means/media	Apprehended by	Resultant theology
Special revelation	Revealed knowledge	Redemptive acts/words	Faith (via Holy Spirit)	Sacred theology
General revelation	Natural knowledge	Creation/ providence	Reason/intuition/ conscience	Natural theology

Special revelation, on the other hand, is a revealed knowledge of God via God's particular historical and redemptive acts and words, apprehended by faith (through the work of the Holy Spirit), and resulting in what is called sacred theology. Special revelation is the making known of God to humanity in a supranormal and particular way that is not generally accessible through the structures of creation. This particular "word" that God addresses to humanity includes supremely the Word who became flesh in Jesus Christ, as well as the word contained in the text of scripture. The Christian tradition regards special revelation as available only to those who grasp it with the eyes of faith.

While these basic definitions are rather simple and straightforward, the matters of general revelation and special revelation are in reality much more involved. We will therefore examine both these forms of revelation more closely before addressing the question of how they relate to one another, a discussion that involves the much-debated question of the place of general revelation in Christian theology.

GENERAL REVELATION

Biblical themes

As we have seen, general revelation refers to a knowledge of God that can be gleaned from evidence in the created order. This "knowledge" of God – or "awareness" or "sense" of God's existence and character – is, according to certain key biblical texts, available for all to see. As the Psalmist declares: "The heavens are telling the glory of God; and the firmament proclaims his handiwork. Day to day pours forth speech, and night to night declares knowledge" (Ps. 19:1–2). The apostle Paul affirms something similar:

For the wrath of God is revealed from heaven against all ungodliness and wickedness of those who by their wickedness suppress the truth. For what can be known about God is plain to them, because God has shown it to them. Ever since the creation of the world his eternal power and divine nature, invisible though they are, have been understood and seen through the things he has made. (Rom. 1:18–20)

In both these texts we see the idea that God is made known through the created structures of the world – and therefore all people have some "knowledge" of God. The evidence in the created world serves as the external means of general revelation.

But there is also an internal apprehension of general revelation. Paul indicates as much in the passage just cited: people "know" (sense or intuit) in the depth of their being that there is a God, but they suppress this truth, refusing to recognize it and act upon it. It is as if human beings are created with an inclination to seek God, so as to ultimately know God – but they resist this divine prompting. Even after the fall into sin, general revelation guarantees that the quest(ion) of God cannot be avoided, since human beings "know" deep down that there is a God. Paul makes this point again on his visit to ancient Athens, where he remarks upon how religious – and idolatrous – the Athenians were. Having found an altar "to an unknown God," he first affirms what the Athenians sensed and knew minimally as an inchoate knowledge of God. He then proceeds to proclaim who this God really is: "The God who made the world and everything in it ... is Lord of heaven and earth" (Acts 17:24). Paul concludes that it is humanity's destiny to seek God (see Acts 17:26–31).

It is this general sense of God that Beethoven reflects in his mighty Ninth Symphony, where in the vocal part of the fourth movement, the well-known "Ode to Joy," Schiller's text makes the following claim:

> Above the starry heaven must a loving father dwell ...
> Do you sense the creator, world?
> Seek him above in the starry heaven!
> Above the stars must he dwell.[1]

Or think again of Emily Dickinson's poem "This World is not Conclusion," where she speaks of a "Species" who "stands beyond" the world of our experience and concludes by claiming: "Narcotics cannot still the Tooth / That nibbles at the soul."[2] Something inside needles us to seek something greater beyond ourselves, lending truth to Augustine's famous confession: "Our hearts find no peace until they rest in you."[3]

Natural theology

The theological tradition has overwhelmingly affirmed the existence of general revelation, even if not specifically calling it that. It is little surprise that the great scholastic theologian Thomas Aquinas reflected significantly on this issue. Aquinas assumed that general revelation was clear enough to enable us to elaborate a rather robust *natural theology* on its basis. Natural theology refers to claims about God made on the basis of human reason and

---

[1] Translation ours. The German text of *An die Freude* reads: "über'm Sternenzelt / Muß ein lieber Vater wohnen /... Ahnest du den Schöpfer, Welt? / Such ihn über'm Sternenzelt! / Über Sternen muß er wohnen."

[2] See Dickinson, *Complete Poems*, 243.　　[3] Augustine, *Confessions*, 21.

its reflection on the natural world – that is, theology done on the basis of general revelation alone, apart from special revelation.

To understand Aquinas' account of general revelation and the natural theology it delivers, it is important to grasp that in his view, humanity's natural gifts, including reason, remained basically uncorrupted and largely functional even after the fall into sin. Aquinas thus argues at the beginning of his *Summa Theologiae* that human reason can demonstrate that God exists. Assuming an analogy of being (*analogia entis*) between God and world, Creator and creation, divine cause and creaturely effect, Aquinas argues that there are "five ways" by which reason, via general revelation, can demonstrate God's existence.[4]

Aquinas' first four ways can be taken together since they constitute an argument for the existence of God based on reflection on the origin and grounding of things in the world (*kosmos*) – what is known as the *cosmological argument*. Aquinas points out that we observe various things in the world that in fact exist, but do not exist necessarily – that is, by their own causality. Where did these things come from? What is their cause? What set them in motion? Aquinas argues that since every effect has its cause, and things move only when acted upon by an agent, if one thinks through the nature of things in the world, one must come to the conclusion that there is a First Cause or Prime Mover of the world's effects, who is none other than God.

Aquinas' fifth way constitutes an argument for the existence of God based on reflection on the purpose (*telos*) of things in the world – what is known as the *teleological argument*. Aquinas proposes that we observe purposeful order in the world, even in non-sentient beings that do not consciously will their own ends. There must therefore be an intelligent agent of such design who governs the world and destines created things for certain ends. This agent is none other than God.

Another theologian with a rather developed view of general revelation is John Calvin, as found in his *Institutes of the Christian Religion*.[5] Knowledge of God, asserts Calvin, is naturally implanted in human beings. Each person carries within a sense of divinity (*sensus divinitatis*) or a seed of religion (*semen religionis*), which accounts for the universal phenomenon of religion. All human beings recognize something greater than themselves, since, echoing Paul in Romans 1, God's existence and majesty are seen in the theater of creation. According to Calvin, one cannot open one's eyes in the universe and fail to behold God in the creation and providence of the world. God has designed the created order in such a way that human beings intuit the divine.

---

[4] See Thomas Aquinas, *Summa Theologica*, 1a.2.3.   [5] See Calvin, *Institutes*, 1.3–5.

But Calvin also emphasizes general revelation's decided inadequacy in light of human sin. Despite this general manifestation of God, which is available to all, human beings do not know and revere God truly and rightly because they sinfully distort this natural knowledge. At best, they end up in idolatry, confusing the Creator with the creature. At the least, general revelation keeps humanity accountable to God and prevents it from pleading ignorance for its sinful failure to worship God faithfully (Rom. 1:18–23). Therefore, for a truly reliable and saving knowledge of God there is need for another revelatory measure.

SPECIAL REVELATION

As we described above, special revelation refers to God's disclosure of the divine identity and character by means of particular acts and words through Israel's history and culminating in the coming of Jesus Christ, means that are not generally accessible to all through the structures of creation. But what, more precisely, is special revelation and how is it communicated to humanity? In the Christian tradition there have arisen a variety of emphases as to what particularly constitutes special revelation. Three conceptions or models have been dominant.[6]

A first conception of revelation can be characterized as *historical*. This view contends that human beings come to know the divine by means of God's actions in history – in God's covenantal interactions with Israel, in the incarnation, and in relationship with the church. Special revelation here is predominantly God's historical activity. A second conception can be characterized as *doctrinal*. It views revelation as a communication given to humanity in rather objective form. On this view, revelation is a series of eternal truths or timeless propositions found either in the teachings of scripture (a more Protestant construal) or in the teachings of the church (a more Catholic construal). Special revelation here is predominantly a doctrinal deposit of truth. A third conception is more *experiential*. It conceives of revelation as a communication given to humanity that results in a new subjective reality. Special revelation on this view has to do with religious experience, with an existential sense of divine presence, resulting in a new understanding of God, self, and the world.

As is the case with many conceptual mappings, an important truth is captured in all three conceptions or models. We can assuredly know about

---

[6] Our reflections here are indebted to Avery Dulles, *Models of Revelation* (Garden City, NY: Image Books, 1985), esp. 36–97. While Dulles elaborates five models, we are highlighting what we take to be the three most important ones.

God in the first place because God has acted in the world (i.e., the historical conception), the basis of special revelation. The recording of these divine actions in the world results in a series of truths confessed in faith (i.e., the doctrinal conception), the objective expression of revelation. And God's historical action coupled with the resulting doctrinal beliefs is intended to produce a changed state of being for humanity (i.e., the experiential conception), the subjective appropriation of revelation. All three of these basic models contribute to a full-orbed understanding of special revelation.

The word of God

The most common Christian term for special revelation is the "word of God." For most Christians this refers primarily to the Bible, but this is to overly restrict the locus of special revelation. Here Karl Barth is most helpful in distinguishing a threefold form of the word of God.[7] For Barth, at the heart of the concept "word of God" is a person, a divine person, the Word, sent to live among us to show us the way, the truth, and the life. The Gospel of John declares this foundational Christian truth: "In the beginning was the Word, and the Word was with God, and the Word was God … And the Word became flesh and lived among us" (1:1,14). In its most basic sense, then, the special Word that God addresses to humanity is Jesus Christ, the incarnate Son of God, who is the culmination of God's redemptive acts and words in history. In his person and work, Jesus communicates in the most reliable way *who* God is, *what* God is like, and *how* we are to live in this light. The person of Jesus is what Barth called the Word of God *revealed*.

How do we come to know – and know about – Jesus Christ? Barth answered: through the word of God *written*. Scripture is the faithful witness to God's historical redemptive acts that culminate in the Christ event. The written word has its origin and inspiration in God, but it came to the covenant people through history, culture, language, and human mediation. It can be referred to as the word of God because it faithfully mediates the story of the incarnate Word, the gospel – Christianity's fundamental hope and declaration.

Barth also distinguished a third sense of the word of God, namely, the word of God *proclaimed* by the church. While for Barth such proclamation primarily meant the sermon and the sacraments, we can easily expand this notion of proclamation to the whole ministry of the church. When the church makes Christ known on the basis of scripture, whether it be the

[7] See Barth, *Church Dogmatics*, I/1: 88–124.

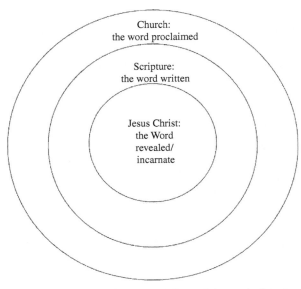

Figure 3.1 Karl Barth's threefold form of the word of God

sermon, the sacraments, speaking an encouraging word, feeding the hungry, clothing the naked, or just being there for someone in need, such acts of proclamation also become the word of God.

What ties these three forms of the word of God together is the theme of faithful witness. Just as Christ is the "faithful witness" to who God is (Rev. 1:5), so also the Bible is a faithful witness to the Christ event. Similarly, the church is called to be a faithful witness through the testimony of scripture to the reality of the God who in Christ is reconciling the world (see Figure 3.1). In this connection, Barth was especially fond of the crucifixion altarpiece of Matthias Grünewald as an image of scripture and church proclamation witnessing to Christ, the true Word (see Illustration 3.1). Just as John the Baptist's elongated finger points away from himself and toward Christ ("He must increase, I must decrease" [John 3:30], the verse highlighting John's witnessing finger), so also the scripture he holds and the church proclamation he embodies are witnesses to Christ. They are the word of God as the Holy Spirit uses them to testify to the revealed Word, Jesus Christ.

This brief discussion indicates that the notion "word of God" is a richly textured matter in Christian theology, the heart of which is the reality of the gospel of Christ. Any Christian doctrine of special revelation must keep this

Illustration 3.1 Matthias Grünewald, Isenheim altarpiece (1512–16).

in mind. Typical discussions of this doctrine, however, have focused special attention on the written word of God. This is because, as the primary source/ norm of theology and the tangible "constitution" of Christian faith, the nature and authority of scripture have been a matter of no little debate.

The doctrine of scripture

Christian scripture (Lat. *scriptura* = writing), usually referred to as the Bible (Gk. *biblion* = book), is in many respects like other ancient writings. As a collection of diverse texts written over time, it contains many common literary genres: story, history, law, prophecy, poetry, letter, and apocalypse. Taking the Bible as a whole, however, the most dominant and overarching literary genre is that of narrative. For Christian theology it is the very nature of this narrative, the very telling of its basic story, that makes the Bible unique. In this it stands apart, or is "holy," as many front covers of the Bible proclaim: it is God's story. In an act of divine condescension, God tells humanity the story of the world in relation to its origin and end, and in so doing, God reveals the divine identity and character to humanity. Like any story, the biblical story is driven by principal characters and moves in a narrative frame from conflict toward resolution. It starts with *creation*, the setting of a good heaven and earth, whose human denizens have the vocation of representing God in the world. Then it moves to the *fall*, the narration of the story of human rebellion and the flaw that was introduced into the good creation. The next major "act" in the story's drama is the divine promise of *salvation* through Jesus Christ, the fulfillment of which is God's solution to the cosmic conflict produced by human disobedience. The conclusion of the story depicts a new creation, a new heaven and a new earth – the anticipated *re-creation* or consummation of creation.

In telling the story of the cosmos, scripture relates the identity of the triune God. The biblical narrative therefore possesses a theocentric character. Given this overarching framework, the principal protagonist is the God who is revealed and whose redemptive plan is recounted in the telling of the story. It is this theocentricity that gives the Bible its special status and authority, since the protagonist is also recognized as its ultimate author, the one who inspired its human authors.

The special authority of the Bible is understood in the Christian tradition in different ways, depending on the ecclesial or theological tradition in question. But all Christian traditions recognize the chief claims made in the biblical text itself. We read in 2 Peter 1:21 that "no prophecy ever came by human will, but men and women moved by the Holy Spirit spoke from God." In 2 Timothy 3:16, Paul states: "All scripture is inspired by God and is useful for teaching, for reproof, for correction, and for training in righteousness." Though the scripture that Paul has in mind in this text is the Hebrew Bible or OT, Christians have extended this claim to include the NT – and therefore the Bible as a whole. The word employed by Paul that is commonly translated "inspired" is *theopneustos*, which literally means "God-breathed." Christians hold that scripture has the very breath of God in it, that the very Spirit of God is at work in and through it.

In Protestant theology in particular, given the primacy it accords to scripture, there is a sometimes sharp debate concerning the scope or extent of scripture's authority. This debate can become considerably complex, but put most simply it revolves around the concepts of *infallibility* and *inerrancy*. Those who hold that scripture is "inerrant" believe that the Bible is wholly without error in everything it addresses, whether this concerns theology and ethics, or scientific and historical truth. Those who consider scripture to be "infallible" make a more modest claim – namely, that scripture will not fail us in what it intends to teach us, which is about the triune God, creation, and their relation (theological truth) and how we are to live in this light (ethical truth). In other words, the infallibilist position contends that scripture is completely dependable and trustworthy for doctrine and life, but not necessarily for other matters. Those who hold to infallibility but reject inerrancy, for example, do not see the Bible as a repository of scientific truth or press it in all its details for precise historical truth, since historical discrepancies do appear in the text (cf. the different ordering in the Gospels of events in the ministry of Jesus – e.g., the orderings of the temptations in Matt. 4 and Luke 4). Indeed, infallibilists hold that inerrantists have adopted an overly modernist and constricting criterion of historical truth (largely in the attempt to meet the Enlightenment challenge on its own ground) that is foreign to the world of the Bible itself.

At the root of this disagreement are different conceptions of biblical inspiration. Let us briefly consider three basic views of inspiration that range on a spectrum from the human to the divine authorship of the word of God (see Figure 3.2). First, a *poetic* or dynamic theory of inspiration presents a picture of the biblical writers as inspired in much the same way as Virgil or Shakespeare were "inspired" to pen their great works. While this theory gives ample play to the human authorship of the biblical writings, it is rather vague and understated with regard to the divine authorship of the word of God. Here it is difficult to distinguish the inspiration of the biblical authors from the inspiration of poets who give nods to the muses. In stark contrast, a *dictation* or mechanical theory of inspiration conjures up a picture of God dictating a message to a scribe, who records it verbatim. This theory obviously reckons with the divine dimension of the word of God but denigrates the human dimension, for on this view the human writer is not really an author but simply a secretary. In between these two extremes, what is known as an *organic* or synergistic theory of inspiration suggests that the biblical writers were indeed directed and empowered by the triune God to write about what they experienced and witnessed, especially regarding

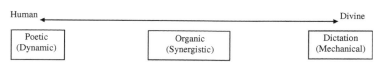

Figure 3.2 Spectrum of biblical inspiration and authorship

God's mighty acts in history, but not at the expense of their own humanity. On this view, scripture reflects its various writers' cultures, experiences, abilities, styles, and the like, while yet truly conveying God's identity, character, and will. The organic view thus seeks to recognize both the human and the divine dimensions of the word of God in a more balanced and synergistic fashion. It views scripture as God's word in human words.

Given these basic views of inspiration, it is easy to see how a dictation or mechanical conception of inspiration would support an inerrantist view of biblical authority. Many inerrantists, for example, would read the first two chapters of Genesis as normative science, reinforcing a young-earth creationism (see pp. 161–2 below). In contrast, a more organic conception would reinforce an infallibilist position. On the infallibilist view, one accepts the creation narratives as divine revelation, which communicate theological and ethical truths without holding that the specifics of ancient near-eastern cosmology, assumed by the Genesis text, are normative science for today. The infallibilist view, assuming an organic conception of inspiration, treasures the Bible as God's word in and through the humble medium of human words, just as Paul suggested when he affirmed that we have the treasure of the gospel in jars of clay (2 Cor. 4:7).

A helpful analogy for understanding this relation is the incarnation itself, where the preexistent Logos, God's personal divine Word, becomes flesh in the human Jesus of Nazareth, speaking the divine word in human words. Just as Jesus Christ is, according to Christian confession, both divine and human, so also does Christian scripture possess both a divinity and a humanity. And just as confessional and conservative Christians more readily affirm the deity of Christ, but often have a much harder time finding a place for the real humanity of Jesus, so also does this seem to be the case with scripture. Yet even as the real humanity of Christ must be emphasized (see pp. 249–56), so also the real humanity of the Bible must be acknowledged, an acknowledgment moreover that may save much effort in defending the Bible's authority on grounds not envisioned by the Bible or the early church itself.

This real historical humanity of scripture can also be seen in the lengthy process of canonization, the process of determining the definitive collection of authoritative OT and NT writings (also see pp. 435–7). The word *kanon* originally referred to a measuring stick that served as an ideal standard, and came to denote the normative fixed series of scriptural writings. Many of the texts of the Hebrew Bible originally existed in an oral form. These texts were eventually written down and preserved in the Jewish tradition. Later, due to the spread of the Jews into the Greek-speaking world, there was a need to translate the Hebrew text. The resulting Greek translation is called the Septuagint. The early Christian tradition accepted the writings of the Septuagint as authoritative, eventually calling it the "Old Testament" when it came to regard other writings – such as the gospels and various letters to early churches – as also authoritative: the New Testament. In early Christianity, the canonization process took centuries as the church doggedly determined which writings about Christ were truly authoritative. Not until the late fourth century was the NT as we know it today recognized by the church at large. The first extant reference to the twenty-seven-book NT canon was Athanasius' Festal Letter in 367. Over the course of the next century, the Christian Bible was translated into the language of the Roman Empire – Latin. This text, known as the Vulgate, was western Christianity's Bible for more than a millennium. Translations of the Bible into vernacular languages, such as German and English, began around the middle of Christianity's second millennium, especially in the wake of the Reformation (e.g., Luther's German Bible and the English King James Version). Clearly, the Christian Bible as written, transmitted, translated, and accepted today was subject to a historical, human process, in contrast to the claims of some other religious traditions, which attribute their sacred books to direct heavenly descent.

Since the Christian canon is composed of diverse texts from many historical periods, it is not surprising that the interpretation of scripture is no simple matter. The science of interpretation is called *hermeneutics*. In theology much attention has been devoted to this complex topic, including the elaboration of hermeneutical "principles" that should guide interpretation of the biblical text, such as sensitivity to issues of original audience, literary genre, and intra-canonicity (interpreting scripture with scripture, given the assumption that the canon as a whole conveys a unified message), among other principles.[8] Given the historical breadth and diversity of the biblical writings, one broader hermeneutical principle that bears importantly on the concept of revelation is the fact that the scriptural drama unfolds gradually and progressively through a lengthy course of salvation history. Rather than appearing at a single sacred place or moment (revelation as epiphany), special revelation's disclosure of the divine identity, character, and will develops over time, gaining further clarity throughout the course of the biblical story. Thus special revelation – as witnessed by

---

[8] An accessible guide to biblical hermeneutics is Gordon D. Fee and Douglas Stewart, *How to Read the Bible For All its Worth*, 3rd edn. (Grand Rapids, MI: Zondervan, 2003). A more sophisticated treatment can be found in Anthony C. Thiselton, *The Two Horizons: New Testament Hermeneutics and Philosophical Description with Special Reference to Heidegger, Bultmann, Gadamer, and Wittgenstein* (Grand Rapids, MI: Eerdmans, 1980).

scripture – must be regarded as a *progressive revelation* that finds its *telos* in the Christ event. Any broader theological hermeneutic, therefore, must be christologically centered and weighted within the ebb and flow of the biblical narrative as a whole. This means in practice that the NT will provide greater revelatory clarity on matters that are perhaps only anticipated or adumbrated in the OT.

As an unavoidable feature of human experience in general – we are always interpretively navigating the landscape of life, whether people, situations, or texts – hermeneutics is a complex and delicate phenomenon. This is even more the case in theology as it approaches a historically situated yet enduringly authoritative text such as the Bible.

THE RELATIONSHIP OF GENERAL AND SPECIAL REVELATION

As we have seen, scripture is special revelation because it authoritatively makes known the true Word of God – Jesus Christ as the fulfillment of the covenant hope of Israel. A remaining question is how this special revelation relates to the general knowledge of God made known through creation. Are both necessary? Does one have priority over the other? There are basically three ways that general and special revelation have been related to each other in the history of Christian thought.

General revelation alone

One position is the idea that general revelation by itself provides an adequate knowledge of God. A prime example of this posture is the Deism (Lat. *Deus* = God) of the Enlightenment period in Europe, which sought rationally to overcome the religious sectarianism that flowed in part from warring interpretations of scripture, as well as scripture's ostensible unscientific supernaturalism. Adherents to this movement believed in a Supreme Being who fashioned the cosmos well and let it run its course, much as a skilled watchmaker crafts a reliable watch. This creator's nature and will for humanity could be deciphered by rational observation of the natural laws of the created order. The founder of Deism in England, Herbert of Cherbury, argued that "Common Notions" – truths that are universally self-evident and rationally decipherable – function as the shared foundation of all particular religions.[9] For Herbert, general revelation suffices to tell us all we need to know about

---

[9] See Herbert of Cherbury, "Common Notions Concerning Religion," in *Christianity and Plurality: Classic and Contemporary Readings*, ed. Richard J. Plantinga (Oxford: Blackwell, 1999), 171–81.

God and the divine will. Special revelation is therefore superfluous, contributing nothing essentially new to our understanding of the divine. This view was also held by other deists, such as John Locke in *The Reasonableness of Christianity* (1695), John Toland in *Christianity Not Mysterious* (1696), and Matthew Tindal in *Christianity as Old as Creation* (1730) – all titles that are quite telling.

But the deistic portrait of God does not allow for the possibility of special divine action within the created order. The watchmaker God sits transcendentally aloof and does not graciously enter into relationship with creatures. This view has no need for special revelation and therefore no room for an inspired scripture, let alone for a divine Jesus Christ, who is reduced to the role of a moral teacher. At best, Christ and scripture merely republish the revelation in creation to which all have rational access. Moreover, other Christian doctrines – such as God being a trinity of persons – must be rejected, since they are not discernible through general revelation. But this is to do away with the central truth of Christianity. For good reason, then, most theologians have held to the necessity of special revelation.

Special revelation alone

As we have seen, the notion of special revelation is fundamental in the theology of Karl Barth. Barth in fact exemplifies a position diametrically opposed to Deism: he suggests that the theologian should focus on special revelation alone and leaves no room for natural theology. For Barth, the true birthright of the theologian is special revelation (God talking) and not religion (human chattering).[10] Barth's rich and complex conception of revelation focuses on the "Word event" of Jesus Christ, and is therefore highly christocentric. In his famous debate with another Swiss theologian, Emil Brunner, Barth issued a terse *Nein!* (No!) to the project of natural theology (see pp. 534–5). He argued that the task of theology involves explication of the scriptural message of revelation, the essence of which is the grace made known in Christ. Theology's task in no way involves interpreting would-be revelation apart from Christ, which humans easily manipulate for sinful ends, a dangerous trend that Barth observed in the theological ideology of Nazi Germany.[11] Instructively, a clear statement of

[10] See Barth, *Church Dogmatics*, I/2: 280–97.
[11] See Emil Brunner and Karl Barth, *Natural Theology: Comprising "Nature and Grace" by Professor Dr. Emil Brunner and the Reply "No!" by Dr. Karl Barth*, trans. Peter Fraenkel (London: Centenary, 1946).

Barth's denial of general revelation is found in the Barmen Declaration of 1934, largely authored by Barth:

Jesus Christ, as he is attested for us in Holy Scripture, is the *one Word of God* which we have to hear and which we have to trust and obey in life and death. We reject the false doctrine, as though the Church could and would have to acknowledge as a source of its proclamation, apart from and besides this one Word of God, still other events and powers, figures and truths, as God's revelation.[12]

It was the Barmen Declaration that launched the Confessing Church's resistance to the "German Christian" capitulation to Nazism, events that formed the crucial context for Barth's contra-traditional position on the efficacy of general revelation.

This complete rejection of any place for general revelation in theology, however, is a difficult position to defend in view of scripture and the Christian tradition. While Barth's position is somewhat understandable in light of his crisis context, it seems to miss the larger biblical claim that something about God *can* be known through creation, although that knowledge is vague and susceptible to sinful distortion, as Brunner argued. Aside from rejection of either special revelation (Deism) or general revelation (Barth), most Christian theologians have attempted to maintain both kinds of revelation.

The integration of general and special revelation

In affirming the propriety of both general and special revelation, the mainstream Christian tradition has argued for both the necessity and the primacy of special revelation. But within this majority opinion, theologians have had differing estimates of the efficacy of general revelation.

Thomas Aquinas stands on one side of this spectrum, though far from the Deist position (see Figure 3.3). As we saw earlier, he had a rather sanguine view of what humanity could know about God through rational reflection on nature. Nevertheless, Aquinas did recognize the limits of what we could know of God through the exercise of natural theology. He actually held that even those things generally knowable by reason need to be specially revealed, and this for a number of reasons: not all people are able to reason effectively; the route of reason to such truth can be a lengthy and arduous process; and reason can in fact yield faulty conclusions.

---

[12] "Barmen Declaration" (1934), in *Creeds and Confessions of Faith in the Christian Tradition*, ed. Jaroslav Pelikan and Valerie Hotchkiss, 3 vols. (New Haven, CT: Yale University Press, 2003), III: 507.

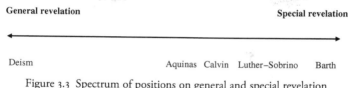

Figure 3.3 Spectrum of positions on general and special revelation

Special revelation guarantees the truths of general revelation for all. Most importantly, however, there are essential truths that reason cannot decipher. For example, while reason may be able to determine that God exists, it is unable to establish that God is triune. Knowledge of God as Trinity requires special revelation as witnessed in scripture. Aquinas thus recognizes the legitimacy of general revelation and the resulting project of natural theology, but thinks this project must be augmented by special revelation.[13]

Not far from Aquinas' view, John Calvin also affirmed the objective availability of general revelation. However, Calvin insisted that the sense of divinity or seed of religion implanted in all human beings as mediated through created things is not enough for *sinful* humanity to elaborate an adequate natural theology, let alone to truly know God. To know God as creator and redeemer in a trustworthy and salvific way, scripture is necessary (i.e., special revelation). The evidence in creation and human nature attracts human beings to a knowledge of God and holds them accountable; scripture delivers the knowledge sought and needed. In fact, Calvin says, scripture can function as a pair of spectacles that allows us to see general revelation in proper focus.[14]

Martin Luther was less sanguine about the efficacy of general revelation. Luther was suspicious of theological approaches that attempted to speak about God based on observation of creation and the exercise of reason, and referred to such a tactic as a "theology of glory." Although humanity may have some natural knowledge of God, to really know God requires seeing the suffering God-man who was crucified at Golgotha, which Luther termed a "theology of the cross."[15] The cross is the supreme revelation of who God is as "God for us" – unveiling paradoxically the power of God through weakness (see 1 Cor. 1:18–25). For Luther, then, there is something which we might term general revelation, but no possibility of natural theology. Because of human sin, general revelation is not efficacious;

---

[13] See Thomas Aquinas, *Summa Theologica*, 1a.1.1; 2a2ae.2.4.   [14] See Calvin, *Institutes*, 1.6–8.
[15] See Luther, "The Disputation held at Heidelberg," 290–3.

theology must therefore focus its attention on God's special revelation in Christ.

Similar to Luther, Latin American Catholic theologian Jon Sobrino has more recently suggested that stressing general revelation in theology (especially the metaphysical view of God historically built on it – see pp. 83–91 below) will inevitably misrepresent the biblical God. Because natural theology focuses on the goodness of creation and ignores evil, sin, and suffering in the world, it produces a theological understanding of God and the world that is oblivious to conditions of poverty and suffering in the world – the reality experienced by people in Latin America on a daily basis.[16] To understand God rightly, Sobrino argues, our theological attention must be focused on the cross of Christ, which is the most reliable revelation of God given the brokenness of the world. With Luther, Sobrino affirms that the core of special revelation is the event of Jesus' crucifixion, an event that has clear theological priority over general revelation.

Luther and Sobrino thus have only a very reserved place for general revelation, placing their positions close to that of Barth. Aquinas and Calvin give more play to the notion of general revelation but contend that it has limits and insist on the necessity of special revelation for knowing and speaking about God. While Aquinas' and Calvin's construals of the relationship of general revelation and special revelation represent the more balanced mainstream Catholic and Protestant views, Luther and Sobrino sound the imperative to keep the theology of the cross at the forefront of the theological enterprise lest Christian theology become overly rationalistic and triumphalistic.

Given the presupposition of general and special revelation, that God speaks and has spoken, how do *we* proceed to speak of God?

SPEAKING OF GOD

Speaking of God has always been a delicate matter. "To whom then will you liken God, or what likeness compare with him?" queries Isaiah the prophet (40:18). Like salvation itself, theologies must be worked out with "fear and trembling" (Phil. 2:12), since in addition to much good done in the name of God, much abuse has also taken place in that same sacred

---

[16] Jon Sobrino, *Christology at the Crossroads: A Latin American Approach*, trans. John Drury (Maryknoll, NY: Orbis, 1978), 195–201. Sobrino draws significantly from the earlier work of Jürgen Moltmann, *The Crucified God: The Cross of Christ as the Foundation and Criticism of Christian Theology*, trans. R. A. Wilson and John Bowden (New York: Harper & Row, 1974), which is itself heavily indebted to Luther.

name. This is because no greater source of justification for one's cause can be evoked than that of "God," as is sarcastically captured in a brief line from Robert Frost, who once wondered whether the war-god was a "dunce, for always fighting on both sides at once."[17] This question therefore must be squarely faced: Is talk about God simply self-serving?

Anthropomorphism

The human tendency to create God in our own likeness and likes was observed early on by the Greek philosopher Xenophanes (*c.* 570–*c.* 480 BCE), who records: "Mortals imagine that the gods are begotten, and that the gods wear clothes like their own, and have voice (or language) and form like the voice and form of mortals." As a consequence, "Ethiopians make their gods snub-nosed and black; Thracians make theirs blue-eyed and red-haired."[18] Attributing human form or characteristics to the divine is called *anthropomorphism* (a closely related term is *anthropopathism* which attributes "pathos" – human feelings, passions, and/or sufferings – to God/gods). Xenophanes rejected any such attribution, since he considered God to be beyond all human form and ascription; any human-looking or human-acting god he considered a projection of human imagination.

The problem, however, is that we can only talk or think about God in human terms, since the only available speech and thought forms we have are those that have been crafted in the matrix of human experience and language. What guarantees do we have that our talk about God is not sheer human projection or fancy?

Accommodation

As we have seen, Christian theology assumes that God takes the initiative in providing knowledge of things divine, by means of revelation. It has traditionally been held that in this process God "adjusts" or "adapts" revelation so that it is "suitable" or "fitting" to human understanding, given the conditions of human finitude and sinfulness. This tempering of the divine communication is known as *accommodation*. Largely assumed throughout the Christian tradition, the notion of accommodation was especially

---

[17] Robert Frost, "To a Young Wretch," in *Robert Frost's Poems*, New Enlarged Pocket Anthology (New York: Washington Square, 1971), 124.

[18] In Kathleen Freeman, ed., *Ancilla to the Pre-Socratic Philosophers: A Complete Translation of the Fragments in Diels*, Fragmente der Vorsokratiker (Cambridge, MA: Harvard University Press, 1948), 22.

emphasized by Calvin as a key principle of biblical interpretation. Calvin writes:

For who even of slight intelligence does not understand that, as nurses commonly do with infants, God is wont in a measure to "lisp" in speaking to us? Thus such forms of speaking do not so much express clearly what God is like as accommodate the knowledge of him to our slight capacity. To do this he must descend far beneath his loftiness.[19]

The idea of accommodation in the Christian tradition served to answer the pedagogical question of how the infinite, eternal creator could communicate with a finite, temporal world, so as to arrest the attention of an errant humanity. At the same time, accommodation could also stand broadly for any concession or self-limitation on God's part, for which the incarnation of the eternal Son – God's self-communication to us in the most human way – was the supreme instance.

But the notion of accommodation also produced tensions in biblical interpretation. Many scripture passages, particularly in the OT, that spoke of God repenting, changing mind, showing emotion, or experiencing suffering, were taken by many to be *mere* accommodation – that is, a sheer rhetorical device on God's part that did not have any real reference in God's own self, since for much early Christian theology it was considered axiomatic that God did not change, feel emotion, or suffer in God's true, essential self. A passage such as Genesis 6:6, for example – "And the LORD was sorry that he had made humankind on the earth, and it grieved him to his heart" – was widely understood as conveying a moral to its readers concerning the gravity of human wickedness, but was not literally applicable to God. Consider, for example, the representative reflections of Augustine on this text:

God's "anger" implies no perturbation of the divine mind. It is simply the divine judgment passing sentence on sin. And when God "thinks and then has second thoughts," this merely means that changeable realities come into relation with his immutable reason. For God cannot "repent," as human beings repent, of what he has done, since in regard to everything his judgment is as fixed as his foreknowledge is clear. But it is only by the use of such human expressions that Scripture can make its many kinds of readers whom it wants to help to feel, as it were, at home.[20]

The tendency to interpret such biblical statements as mere accommodation or sheer anthropomorphism led at times to a two-tiered view of God – the God within the biblical narrative and the God above it; God as related to us

---

[19] Calvin, *Institutes*, 1.13.
[20] Augustine, *City of God*, 15.25. Quoted in Andrew Louth, ed., *Genesis 1–11*, Ancient Christian Commentary on Scripture (Downers Grove, IL: InterVarsity, 2001), 127–28.

(who, for example, grieves) in contrast to God's essential self (which is immune to grief) – with the two conceptions in tension, if not in contradiction, with each other. This interpretive strategy raises the question of whether certain fixed conceptions or preconceptions of God actually do justice to the biblical narrative (see pp. 99–108).

Analogy

Presupposing revelation by way of accommodation, the theological tradition has held that our speaking and thinking about God, in turn, proceeds largely by way of *analogy*. All of our positive affirmations about who God is – for example, that God is (all)-loving, good, powerful, knowing, and the like – are analogical. Originally a mathematical term (*analogia* = ratio, proportion), analogy involves a partial resemblance or similarity among things – in this theological case, between God and creation. As he did for so many theological topics, Thomas Aquinas set the agenda for ensuing discussions of analogy. Of his various statements on analogy, most central and helpful are those concerning the "analogy of attribution," which predicates a similar quality among two subjects. Its theo-logic goes like this: As creator, God is the supreme cause of the effects of creation. Created effects therefore bear some likeness or resemblance to their creator, just as art reflects the artist. Although God is infinite and eternal, while creatures are finite and temporal, we can think our way from creatures to the Creator by means of partial resemblance or analogy. Take the notion of "good" as a simple example. Since God-the-all-Good created a world in which goodness is found in a variety of ways, we may lift our minds from the finite good in creation to think about the perfect cause or author of that goodness, and say, "God is good."

Analogy in Aquinas' thinking is a "middle way" of speaking between univocity and equivocity, positing both likeness and unlikeness between subjects.[21] To speak *univocally* ("with one voice") is to speak of God and creatures in exactly the same sense of a term and risks sheer anthropomorphism by reducing God to the human (e.g., God is Father in exactly the same sense as a human father). To speak *equivocally* ("with different voice") is to speak of God and creatures in a completely different sense of a term and risks sheer agnosticism by communicating nothing about God (e.g., God is Father in a sense totally unlike a human father – what then do we mean when we call God "Father"?). The analogy of attribution presupposes a hinge of likeness or similarity of some quality that mediates a true

---

[21] See Thomas Aquinas, *Summa Theologica*, 1a.13.5.

knowledge of God without fully comprehending or appreciating that quality as God possesses it, which, of course, is in perfect and maximal measure (e.g., God is both like, but also unlike, a human father, since God is the perfect Father).

The analogy of attribution presupposes an "analogy of being" (*analogia entis*) between Creator and creation, attributing a similar sense of being – for example, goodness, truth, and beauty – to both God and creatures. Karl Barth objected strongly to the analogy of being, since he viewed it as a way to "reason to" God apart from the special revelation and grace of Jesus Christ. He preferred instead to think in terms of the "analogy of faith" (*analogia fidei*), which in his view basically equates to special revelation as manifest in Christ, witnessed in scripture, and faithfully transmitted in church doctrine and proclamation (i.e., his threefold form of the word of God). Barth's rejection of the analogy of being is part and parcel of his rejection of general revelation and natural theology in which he feared the captivity of theology by philosophy, the domination and manipulation of revelation by fallible human reason and errant human will.

These two analogical approaches, however, need not work against each other, but can complement each other. An analogy of being (written into creation) without the analogy of faith (based on historical redemption) is susceptible to the danger of neutralizing the grace and clarifying light of special revelation (leading to a rationalist "theology of glory"). But an analogy of faith without the analogy of being depreciates the doctrine of creation and makes special revelation into an esoteric knowledge without any real reflection in, or illumination of, the context of creation. Calvin's contention that the spectacles of scripture (special revelation via analogy of faith) enable us to read creation correctly (general revelation via analogy of being) helps to properly order these two vital senses of analogy, a posture that is also largely followed today in the Catholic understanding of the relationship between nature and grace.

Metaphor

Given the "turn to the rhetorical" of postmodern times and the emphasis on narrative across the disciplines, among other reasons, *metaphor* has taken center stage in recent theological discussions of language for God. In its narrow etymological sense, a metaphor "carries across" or "transfers" a meaning from one thing to another – for example, "God is my rock." A metaphor is an *implied comparison* that talks about one thing (God) in terms of another (rock). It is unlike a simile, which more weakly and formally uses "as" or "like" in speaking comparatively of two objects. The difference between a metaphor and an analogy, on the other hand, is harder to define. In theological description, analogies tend to focus more abstractly on one quality that appears quite appropriate to God, such as goodness, love, or power. With metaphor, however, the comparative point is less usual, more creative, even shocking (e.g., the crucified God), and its sense may be multiple and/or allusive. The effect of metaphor therefore is more felt, intuited, or imagined than cognitively discerned ("unless you eat the flesh of the Son of Man and drink his blood, you have no life in you" [John 6:53]). Metaphors, in other words, resist abstract dissection.

In a broader sense, the "metaphorical" has become an umbrella term for all language, given current sensitivities about the figurative, pliable, and playful nature of human language. The original meanings of almost all words are transferred, and they are continually transferring their sense based on context and use. Given that our understanding and appropriation of our world, culture, or context is a linguistically imaginative affair in which we extend our knowledge by comparing the unknown to the known, there is much truth to the assertion that all language is metaphorical. Theologians accordingly have devoted significant attention to metaphor in describing God. Sallie McFague has especially popularized this trend in her *Metaphorical Theology* and subsequent *Models of God* (defining a "model" as a "metaphor with staying power"). However, given her supposition that all language about God is a human construct, McFague takes significant imaginative license in proposing a new trinity of models of God for our ecological and nuclear times: God as Mother, Lover, and Friend.[22]

The explosion of metaphor in theological discussion today has sharpened this issue: What are the controls for our language about God? For historic Christianity, these controls reside primarily in the biblical text. Yet that text itself employs an abundance of metaphors to describe God, including those of mother, lover, and friend, as McFague points out. Clearly, then, our talk about God will have to be multiple and varied. It will be *metaphorical* in a broad sense, employing a variety of figurative language, including many metaphors in the more narrow sense. It will also be *analogical*, especially if we affirm a strong doctrine of creation. But this also means that our language will be *literal* to some degree, since even the most provocative metaphor implies some literal predication in order to work. For example,

---

[22] Sallie McFague, *Metaphorical Theology: Models of God in Religious Language* (Minneapolis, MN: Augsburg Fortress, 1997); McFague, *Models of God: Theology for an Ecological, Nuclear Age* (Philadelphia: Fortress, 1987).

"God is my Rock" implies at the least that God literally exists and possesses some character of stability, among other possible implications. It is a question finally of what metaphors, analogies, or literal predications are primary and controlling, which is also the question of primary models or paradigms for God. Here the historic Christian tradition becomes an important resource, since it has favored some metaphors and models over others, such as the Trinity of Father, Son, and Spirit, rather than mother, lover, and friend. But many of these traditional models and privileged descriptions of God have been challenged in recent years.

Recent challenges to God-talk

As we have seen, modernity challenged Christian theology to be more rigorously rational in its talk about God (see pp. 33 and 513–6). René Descartes, the father of modern philosophy, sought certainty by subjecting all his beliefs to doubt, with the hope that he would rationally arrive at indubitable truth on which he could build the edifice of human knowledge. Descartes thus bequeathed a certain posture and attitude of doubt to the era he helped shape. Doubt everything; do not accept traditional authority: these are deeply modern instincts.[23] In this modernist ethos, the Christian idea of revelation has not fared well. Modernity has a prejudice against trusting sources, especially ancient ones that claim to reveal things about realities beyond the confines of the world of sense and experience.

More recently, however, postmodernism as a reaction to modernity is more open to traditional Christianity, since in the decline of modernity's restrictive and domineering criteria of truth it boasts a tolerance of various perspectives in which all have a voice in the global conversation. The challenge to Christian theism here is to speak meaningfully of God given the conditions of pluralism, multiculturalism, and relativism. In its more radical wing, however, postmodernism challenges theology's ability even to speak of God *at all*. All God-talk here is considered erring anthropomorphic projection (cf. Xenophanes), since we have no sure way to move beyond our own subjectivities and socio-linguistically constructed worlds.[24] All claims to absolute truth are suspect from the start – if not naive wanderings, then veiled justifications of privilege and power. This postmodern legacy of

---

[23] See Descartes, *Meditations on First Philosophy*, in *Discourse on Method and Meditations on First Philosophy*, trans. Donald A. Cress, 4th edn. (Indianapolis, IN: Hackett, 1998), esp. meditations 1, 2, and 4.

[24] See Mark C. Taylor, *Erring: A Postmodern A/Theology* (Chicago: University of Chicago Press, 1984).

suspicion is rooted in the thought of Marx, Nietzsche, and Freud, who warned against accepting things the way they appear, since ulterior motivations also shape our truth claims – including economic, political, social, and psychological factors.[25] These "masters of suspicion" admonish us to look beneath the surface to see what is really going on, to distrust appearances. Such postmodern sensitivities have caused theology to become preoccupied with issues of method: How do we even begin to speak meaningfully of God?

Along with the challenge of postmodernism, liberation theology in its various forms constitutes an in-house challenge to classical Christian models and language for God. Latin American liberation theology challenges theology to reflect on how its God-talk functions in view of unjust, oppressive conditions and what conceptions of God better facilitate justice and mobilize change in the world. Similarly, black theology, with its striking declaration that "God is black," challenges theological conceptions that glibly reflect the status quo and underwrite prejudice and racism in society.[26] And feminist theology contends that historically dominant conceptions of God as male – God as the Father, or the Trinity of Father, Son, and (He-)Spirit – have reinforced patriarchy in church and society in which women have not been accorded full dignity, rights, and participation. Mary Daly has put the matter most bluntly: "Since 'God' is male, the male is God."[27] Feminist theology joins forces with other liberation theologies in the quest for speech about God that facilitates justice, equality, and human flourishing.

We could go on to talk of other forms and combinations of liberation theology, of Minjung theology in Korea, of black-feminist "womanist" theology in North America, and of the various emerging indigenous theologies in Africa and other areas where Christianity is presently burgeoning. What this current proliferation of liberation and indigenous theologies indicates in general is that theology is a highly contextual affair that is engaged with the crucial, practical issues of our times. What these emerging theologies teach us about God-talk in particular is that it is currently in ferment. But if liberation theology as a whole is critical of traditional Christian theology for not painting the most appropriate portrait of God, what then are the controls for ensuring that various contextual theologies do not wind up

---

[25] See Merold Westphal, *Suspicion and Faith: The Religious Uses of Modern Atheism* (Grand Rapids, MI: Eerdmans, 1993), for a helpful discussion of what Christians might learn from the critiques of Freud, Marx, and Nietzsche.

[26] E.g., James H. Cone, *A Black Theology of Liberation*, rev. edn. (Maryknoll, NY: Orbis, 1990).

[27] Mary Daly, "The Qualitative Leap Beyond Patriarchal Religion," *Quest* 1, no. 4 (1975), 20.

creating God in their own likeness and likes, providing more evidence for Xenophanes' basic suspicion?

CONCLUSION

Clearly, the last several centuries have provided Christian theology with a series of challenges to its basic beliefs and its way of knowing God. It is important for thoughtful believers to take account of these challenges. It is our judgment, however, that we need not become so preoccupied by such issues to the point where theology becomes paralyzed. Challenges notwithstanding, Christian theology presupposes that there is a God who can be known precisely because God has revealed the divine life to humanity through creation (general revelation), but especially through God's redemptive acts in history that culminate in the Christ event as witnessed in scripture (special revelation). Christian scripture – the authoritative, inspired word of God – is trustworthy, because the triune God has providentially acted in such a way that the Christian church has been given a faithful and reliable account of who God is, what God is like, and how we are to live before God (*coram Deo*). The primary check and balance for Christian theology, therefore, is the biblical narrative, the publicly accessible constitution of Christian faith, the special revelation that witnesses to the triune God, especially the incarnate divine Word – Jesus Christ. The biblical materials are the primary source and norm for knowing the identity and character of the triune God. To that most fundamental theological subject, the doctrine of God, we now turn.

FOR FURTHER READING

Abraham, William J., *The Divine Inspiration of Holy Scripture* (Oxford: Oxford University Press, 1981).

Barth, Karl, *Church Dogmatics*, I/1, ed. Geoffrey F. Bromiley and Thomas F. Torrance (Edinburgh: T. & T. Clark, 1975), §4.

Brunner, Emil, and Karl Barth, *Natural Theology: Comprising "Nature and Grace" by Professor Dr. Emil Brunner and the Reply "No!" by Dr. Karl Barth*, trans. Peter Fraenkel (London: Centenary, 1946).

Calvin, John, *Institutes of the Christian Religion*, trans. Ford Lewis Battles, ed. John T. McNeill, Library of Christian Classics (Philadelphia: Westminster, 1960), I.1–6.

Dulles, Avery, *Models of Revelation* (Garden City, NY: Image Books, 1985).

Fee, Gordon D., and Douglas Stewart, *How to Read the Bible For All its Worth*, 3rd edn. (Grand Rapids, MI: Zondervan, 2003).

McFague, Sallie, *Metaphorical Theology: Models of God in Religious Language* (Minneapolis, MN: Augsburg Fortress, 1997).

CHAPTER 4

A tale of two theisms

INTRODUCTION

The question of God is the most basic theological question. Does God exist? If so, who is God? And what is God like? How we answer these interrelated questions will temper everything else we say theologically about life in relation to God (or in the atheist's case *a*theologically – about life without God). The question of God's existence is most fundamental, since in the history of ideas the notion of God has always been thought of in conjunction with the world (*kosmos*) as the world's ground, goal, logic, or meaning. That is to say, theology always implies cosmology or worldview, given that all the basic questions of life intersect in the question of God. If God is regarded as non-existent, the world appears without ground or goal, and the meaning of life is in crisis, since the one standard large enough to measure life in the world – traditionally the role of "God" – has been taken out of the equation.

As indicated in the previous chapter, Christian theology proceeds on the basis that God has already sought us out and revealed the divine identity and purpose. In the quest(ion) of God, therefore, Christian theology presupposes God's existence; but, as faith in quest of understanding, it will be keen to elucidate reasons for affirming that existence. Systematic theology is more deeply concerned, however, to clarify *who God is*, both generally (as *Theos*) and in particular (as Trinity), and to articulate *what God is like*, largely by means of divine attributes. How we flesh out this divine identity and likeness will condition everything else we say about our relationship with God – most importantly, what God's will is for us and what God's designs are for creation at large. Moreover, how we nuance our doctrine of God will have basic implications for all other doctrines (christology, anthropology, etc.). This is why in Christian theology there is no more vital topic than the doctrine of God.

In this chapter we take up the doctrine of God in general while in the next chapter we examine the formal doctrine of the Trinity, the unique Christian understanding of God. While it may initially seem strange to devote two chapters in this fashion to the doctrine of God, there has been in the Christian tradition a pronounced tension between a generalized concept of God and the distinctive trinitarian understanding of God – conflictive accounts of God that virtually constitute a tale of two theisms. We will argue that resolving this tension in favor of a decidedly trinitarian orientation has a number of important consequences for our understanding of the God–world relationship, and, more specific to this chapter, for addressing the problems of basic belief in God raised by many atheists in the modern period.

BIBLICAL FOUNDATIONS

In taking its lead from the biblical narrative, a specifically Christian conception of God – whether Catholic, Protestant, or Orthodox – receives its fullest form from the NT materials. But this form must first be grounded in and bear continuity with the OT presentation of who God is and what God is like.

Old Testament

An appropriate place to begin looking at the OT conception of God is with the names of God. Names were of great significance in the biblical writings, denoting, for example, special circumstances, events, roles, hopes, predictions, personal transformations, or character traits. In order to enter into relationship with someone, it was necessary to know his or her name, since the name represented the person. In the OT there are two sorts of names attributed to God – those of a general sort and those of a particular sort.

We first note that the people of Israel shared with their surrounding polytheistic cultures the general Semitic name for "god" *El* (e.g., Gen. 33:20). Etymologically, *El* most likely connotes power or preeminence and was the name of the supreme god of the Canaanite pantheon. *El* is often qualified in the OT in the superlative sense as *El Shaddai*, "God Almighty" (e.g., Gen. 17:1), *El Elyon*, "God Most High" (e.g., Gen. 14:18–21), and *El Olam*, "Everlasting God" (e.g., Gen. 21:33). The most common general name for "God" in the Hebrew scriptures, however, is *Elohim*. Possibly of a different root than *El*, and of plural form (likely due to its polytheistic background), *Elohim* can indeed refer in the plural to other gods (e.g., Exod. 20:3) or even to angelic beings (e.g., Ps. 82:1).[1] In reference to Israel's God, however, *Elohim* is meant singularly – "God" – since it always takes a singular verb. *Elohim* connotes strength and authority and is accompanied in the OT by many descriptive terms – for example, "God of gods" (Deut. 10:17) or "God Everlasting" (Isa. 40:28).

But these more general names of God that Israel shared with other ancient near-eastern cultures are qualified in the OT by the more specific, personal, and covenantal name of God: YHWH. Called the Tetragrammaton or "four consonants," since ancient Hebrew did not possess letters for vowels, YHWH remains unspoken by pious Jews (referred to simply as "The Name") but is otherwise written and pronounced as *Yahweh* and rendered in most English Bibles by LORD. First announced to Moses by God in the burning bush as "I AM WHO I AM" or simply "I AM" (Exod. 3:14), the distinct covenantal name of YHWH derived from this context is best understood to be a third-person form ("he is") of the verb "to be." Given the Mosaic context of Exodus 3, however, the name is better understood in a future and existential sense, something along the lines of: "I shall be there as who I am shall I be there," and therefore best interpreted as a promise of God's

---

[1] See "Ēl," in *Theological Dictionary of the Old Testament*, ed. G. Johannes Botterweck and Helmer Ringgren, various translators, 15 vols. (Grand Rapids, MI: Eerdmans, 1974–2006), I: 242–61, esp. 244.

faithful presence to sojourning Israel.[2] In this way the name remains somewhat cryptic and enigmatic – "I will be who/what I will be" – and has a certain open-endedness about it. The name YHWH is preeminently a promise of God's presence, to be proven by future faithfulness, which makes it God's name forever, from generation to generation (Exod. 3:15).

It is the covenantal name of Yahweh that identifies God as the particular God of Israel and that qualifies the titles of El and Elohim (e.g., Gen. 17:1). In fact, one of the most common ways in which the OT refers to God is as "Yahweh Elohim," the LORD God, which joins together the particular and general names – perhaps implying that the God making covenant with Israel is in fact the God of all peoples.

It is this covenantal relationship between God and the people of Israel, rooted in Yahweh's promises to Abraham – of many descendants who will flourish in a promised land so as to be a light and blessing to the nations (Gen. 12:2–3) – that informs the characteristics predicated of God in the OT, chief among which are Yahweh's personal-moral attributes. In this checkered love affair between Yahweh and Israel (see, e.g., the book of Hosea), God is revealed as eminently personal, whose gracious election of Israel and continuing provision for her reveal the divine love and faithfulness (*hesed*), but also disappointment and even anger with Israel for not mirroring God's righteousness and justice in life and society:

> The LORD, the LORD,
> a God merciful and gracious,
> slow to anger,
> and abounding in steadfast love and faithfulness,
> keeping steadfast love for the
> thousandth generation,
> forgiving iniquity and transgression and sin,
> yet by no means clearing the guilty.   (Exod. 34:6–7)

That this particular characterization of God echoes over and over again in the OT shows its covenantal and hermeneutical centrality (see, e.g., Ps. 103:7–14; Jer. 32:18; Jon. 4:2). Since Yahweh is holy – set apart in righteousness – Israel is also called to be holy, as she is the nation whose task it is to "sanctify God's name" as a light to the Gentiles (cf. the book of Jonah). This mission requires Israel to be a servant, even a suffering servant, a suffering in which God also participates (cf. Isa. 53; 63:9). Even when Israel becomes delinquent in her mission, God continues to show mercy and forgiveness, and

---

[2] John Courtney Murray, *The Problem of God: Yesterday and Today* (New Haven, CT: Yale University Press, 1964), 10.

promises a special agent of the divine bidding, a royal son of David, the Messiah.

What is most revolutionary in the Hebrew conception of God, given Israel's polytheistic context, is the development of *monotheism* – the claim that there is only one, true God. The influence of this conception of God on Christianity and Islam, and therefore civilization at large, is inestimable. This monotheistic claim is seen in the premier OT confession found in Deuteronomy 6:4. Called the *Shema*, from its first Hebrew word, "Hear," and typically translated "Hear, O Israel, the LORD (*YHWH*) our God (*Elohim*) is One," the *Shema* is the basic Jewish creed, prayed by the devout both morning and evening. In its original setting, however, it was an injunction to *monolatry* – the worship of one god, YHWH, the God of the Israelites as opposed to other gods – and better translated along the lines of "Hear, O Israel, Yahweh is our God, Yahweh alone," as is also conveyed by the first commandment: "You shall have no other gods before me" (Exod. 20:3).[3] In the course of redemptive history, however, the *Shema* gets a fuller monotheistic connotation, as seen especially in exilic Isaiah (chs. 40ff. – e.g., "I am the first and I am the last; besides me there is no god" [44:6b]) or in Jeremiah (e.g., 10:1–16). This monotheistic connotation has everything to do with the Creator/creature distinction: Yahweh, it turns out, is more than just Israel's national god; Yahweh is actually the one true God because Yahweh is the creator of heaven and earth. All other claims to deity are idolatrous assertions, misplaced personifications and worship of creaturely powers (e.g., sun, moon, sky, rain). OT monotheism is the claim that there is one true God by virtue of the uniqueness of this God: YHWH alone is the creator and therefore Lord of creation.

The OT confession that Yahweh is the creator God not only underscores God's transcendence over creation (implying that God is everlasting, all-powerful, all-seeing, and everywhere present), but it also suggests the universality of Yahweh's moral attributes and intentions beyond national Israel. God's love and faithfulness are not just for Israel, but extend to all creation – so also God's demand for human righteousness, justice, and holiness, since, as creator, Yahweh is also the judge of all people and nations. This universality reinforces the fact that Israel's *raison d'être* was missiological – a chosen people and promised land for the purpose of being a blessing to all peoples and lands, the redemptive firstfruits of all God created, since the eschatological goal is a new heavens and earth (Isa. 65:17–25), the renewal of all things.

---

[3] See Patrick D. Miller, *Deuteronomy*, Interpretation (Louisville, KY: John Knox, 1990), 97–104.

New Testament

The NT presupposes the OT conception of God, but adds its own revolutionary twist: the trinitarian understanding of God. With the coming of Christ, understood as the incarnation of a preexistent figure, Yahweh is no longer regarded as a single personal agent, but is personally differentiated – most evidently as Father and Son, but also as Holy Spirit. The trinitarian conception does not cancel out OT monotheism, but does qualify it significantly: there is one, true Creator God, but this Creator God is the Father, Son, and Spirit together. The NT claim concerning the deity of Christ is what first necessitated this trinitarian conception, which was completed by the recognition of the deity of the Spirit. Since a detailed case for these deity claims is made elsewhere in this book (pp. 232–5 and 290–2), we restrict our treatment here to the NT names of God and to the way the incarnate Christ concretizes the OT attributes of God.

Theos is the Greek NT word for God, which is typically the translation of both *El* and *Elohim* from the OT, and which is overwhelmingly (but not exclusively) associated in the NT with God the Father. *Kyrios* is the NT word for Lord, which typically translates YHWH from the OT, and which is overwhelmingly (but not exclusively) associated with Christ the Son in the NT. In fact, the most basic NT confession is "Jesus Christ is Lord" (e.g., Phil. 2:11), as Christ is the one who was given "the name that is above every name" on account of his sacrificial descent into human servitude and death on a cross (Phil. 2:9b; see 2:6–11). Strikingly, the two chief divine names from the OT, God and Lord, come to be shared by Father and Son in the NT, as seen in the following Pauline quotation that reflects expressly on the *Shema*: "We know that … 'there is no God but one' … yet for us there is one God, the Father … and one Lord, Jesus Christ" (1 Cor. 8:4–6). The NT thus presents two personal foci – Father and Son – for the accolade of "Lord our God." Given the development of triadic formulae in the NT that also include the Spirit in the same breath as Father and Son (e.g., 2 Cor. 13:14; Rev. 1:8), it is the singular trinitarian name of Father, Son, and Spirit that is the most proper NT name of God. From a Christian point of view, this name represents the fulfillment of the promise of God's presence – "I will be who/what I will be" – in a most radical way: God's trinitarian presence by means of the incarnation of the Son and abiding presence in the Spirit (see Matt. 28:18–20).

The incarnation of Christ as the definitive form of God's revelation both concretizes and extends the OT personal-moral divine attributes. The oft-quoted John 3:16 implies God's universal love, grace, mercy, and forgiveness: "For God so loved the world [*kosmos*], that he gave his only Son, so that everyone who believes in him may not perish but may have eternal life." Indeed, love (*agape*) becomes the very definition of God: "God is love" (1 John 4:8). As the express image of God ("Whoever has seen me has seen the Father" [John 14:9]), Jesus' life reveals in human form and dimension the righteousness and holiness of God, fulfilling in his life the demands of God's kingdom, which sanctifies God as king of creation. Christ's sonship also clarifies God's fatherhood, and makes this relationship available to all through adoption. As the anticipated Messiah, the anointed of David's line, Christ is also the suffering servant *par excellence*, whose sacrificial death on the cross renews the Abrahamic covenant and reveals the passion of God for all creation.

In his resurrection and ascension to the Father's right hand, Christ is revealed as the transcendent mediator of creation, like the Father the Alpha and Omega of creation (Rev. 22:13), who as "the Son of Man" will come back as the judge of all people and nations and who will remain as Immanuel, "God with us," in the new heavens and earth (Rev. 21).

Until then, the Spirit makes Christ present along with the Father. By implication, the Holy Spirit personally possesses the same divine attributes, but self-effacingly heralds that God is in Christ reconciling the world. While these trinitarian vectors of the NT are treated more thoroughly in the next chapter, it must be said in summary that the NT conception of God maintains continuity with the OT covenantal conception of Yahweh, but as revolutionized in the person of Christ. A christological perspective is the primary lens that focuses the NT trinitarian conception of God.

THE HISTORICAL DEVELOPMENT OF CLASSICAL THEISM

As it reflected on the apostolic witness of the diverse NT documents, the early church quite naturally systematized this biblical picture of God. As the fledgling church developed its theology, it did so in a particular context and with an eye to particular challenges, challenges both *from within* the church in the quest for Christian identity and *from outside* the church in the quest for relevance to the broader culture. Concerning its particular covenantal name for God – Father, Son, and Spirit – it would take the church a few centuries to hammer out the final shape of its trinitarian confession of *God as Three*. That story along with its specific challenges is told in the next chapter. Here we relate the development of what has come to be called "classical theism" – a particular understanding of *God as One* that, together with the trinitarian conception, emerged in the early church in contact with

Greco-Roman culture and has remained influential throughout Christian history, creating certain tensions with basic trinitarian affirmations.[4]

Christianity and Hellenistic culture

Just as Israel had a specific name and conception of God as Yahweh, but also shared the generic divine name *El* or *Elohim* with surrounding cultures, so also Christianity championed a unique name for God as Father, Son, and Spirit, but also shared the general divine name *Theos* with its Greco-Roman environment or Hellenistic culture. Hellenism was the dominant intellectual culture of the Roman Empire, a cultural ethos rooted in Greek civilization (*Hellas* = Greece) that broadly proliferated in the Mediterranean world through the conquests of Alexander the Great and was largely adopted by the Romans (see pp. 420–2). Accordingly, Greek was the common language of the empire, as well as the language of the OT Septuagint and the NT writings. In this formative cultural context the early church was confronted with a variety of challenges in making the case for its gospel and its God. Within this complex interaction with the pervasive Hellenistic culture, Christianity was *Hellenized* in various ways, and Hellenic culture was eventually *Christianized* in other ways, a mix that would perdure in the matrix of western, Judeo-Christian civilization.[5]

Concerning the doctrine of God in particular, it was the pervasive polytheism of the Roman Empire that offered a special challenge to Christian apologists. Acknowledgment of the various gods associated with local traditions, socio-economic guilds, and the empire itself (including emperor worship) was considered a sign of good citizenship and loyalty to the state. Given their denial of these gods, the early Christians were actually accused of atheism, to which the apologist Justin Martyr replied: "We certainly confess that we are godless with reference to beings like these who are commonly thought of as gods, but not with reference to the most true God."[6]

---

[4] A brief word on divine "isms": *Theism* denotes quite simply "belief in God," but connotes more particularly a monotheistic belief in one God who is uniquely distinguished by being the transcendent Creator of all. This makes *theism* characteristic of the three great monotheistic religions of Judaism, Christianity, and Islam – all of which at various times and with varied intensities endorsed the "classical theism" that concerns us here. *Monotheism* is typically contrasted with *polytheism*, belief in *many* gods, *pantheism*, belief that in some sense *all things* are God, and *atheism*, belief that there is *no* God. Elsewhere in the book we will distinguish other divine "isms," such as Deism, naturalism, and panentheism.

[5] On this complex interaction and cross-fertilization of Christianity and Hellenism, see Werner Jaeger's classic, *Early Christianity and Greek Paideia* (Cambridge, MA: Belknap, 1961).

[6] Justin Martyr, *First Apology*, ch. 6 (p. 245).

In making their public case for Christianity and articulating the nature of "the most true God" (only fully manifest as Father, Son, and Spirit), early Christian thinkers drew upon the exalted concept of the One God that had developed over time in Greek philosophy in critical reaction to the anthropomorphic and ethically suspect pantheon of gods of popular Greco-Roman mythology. This *philosophical* monotheism, the largely Platonic conception of God as transcendent Supreme Being then dominant in *Middle Platonism* (a combination of Platonic, Aristotelian, and Stoic thought from the first century BCE to the second century CE), seemed to afford a compatible point of contact with Christian monotheism, a theistic bridge with high culture that would aid in gaining respectability for the Christian message.[7]

For this apologetic move, Christian thinkers had a precedent in the apostle Paul, who, though contending that the message of the gospel was incommensurate with the suppositions of Greek philosophy ("foolishness to the Greeks" [1 Cor. 1:23; cf. vv. 18–25]), nonetheless made some appeal to Greek philosophical sources (Acts 17:22–8). More strongly, however, many early Christian thinkers held that Platonic theism was actually a divine preparation for the Christian gospel – sometimes inspired by the example of Philo of Alexandria (*c.* 25 BCE–45 CE), who had already effected a synthesis of Jewish and Hellenistic thought. Clement of Alexandria, for example, wrote that "philosophy … was given to the Greeks, as a covenant peculiar to them – being, as it is, a stepping-stone to the philosophy which is according to Christ."[8] Along with Justin Martyr and many others, Clement even held that Plato himself had been instructed by Moses and the prophets. Indeed, it was widely held by Christian thinkers that Greek philosophy had originally "plagiarized" its truth from the Hebrew scriptures. What had been borrowed therefore could easily be reclaimed.

Middle Platonism tended to view God as an impersonal principle of supreme being – "God" as the immaterial and transcendent ground, unity, and structure of being, the veritable fullness of life. This theistic concept evolved mainly out of the early philosophical question of "the One and the many." Its basic theo-logic runs as follows: given that our experience in the material world is of the manifold, of the "many" – things, aspects, moments, and so on – there must be a "One" that transcends, grounds, and unifies the many-ness of life and gives it coherence and meaning. For the early Greek

---

[7] For a general treatment of the conceptions of God in Platonic, Aristotelian, and Stoic philosophy, see Christopher Stead, *Philosophy in Christian Antiquity* (Cambridge: Cambridge University Press, 1994). For their congealing in Middle Platonism, see esp. pp. 54–62.

[8] Clement of Alexandria, *Stromata*, Book 6, ch. 8 (p. 495).

philosophers, material multiplicity was a problem in itself, since everything with parts eventually over time changes for the worse; everything with parts wears down, deteriorates, dies, and, by all appearances, dissolves into oblivion – witness, for example, the human body. Only an immaterial, transcendent One, without parts, would be immune to this physics of decay and death. This One Supreme Being, or God, would be characterized by the highest perfection, and so would be the supreme instance of all the positive or good things in life: the all-true, good, beautiful, happy, self-sufficient One. Conversely, God would be the opposite of all the bad things. Therefore many of the divine attributes must be expressed as negations. Since material parts or divisibility lead to decay and death, God would have to be *im*material and *in*divisible – One simple, single spiritual thing. As the transcendent One without parts, God would be free from change and therefore *im*mutable, since change involves being affected by another (moreover, if God could change, this would entail that God is not perfect – since change is assumed to be either for the worse *or the better*, and God must by definition already be the best). As immutable, God must also be *im*passible or *a*pathetic – neither affected by another, not even emotionally, nor prone to suffering. All of this entails that the One could not be temporal or "ternal" – that is, in time, the realm of transience and death – but rather *e*ternal, dwelling in timeless transcendence.

The patristic legacy

Early Christian thinkers were certainly aware that this Greek natural theology or philosophical monotheism was not wholly compatible with Christian theism, particularly with its trinitarian confession. But even as a doctrine of God as One, there was a major difference: Greek theism had no doctrine of creation *ex nihilo* ("out of nothing"), since it considered physical matter to be eternal. For Middle Platonism, God was more like the "world principle," the comprehensive ground of the world's working, which set the ethical agenda and goal of life. To the degree that God was conceived of as mind (a more personal concept), this simply served to guarantee the immanent rationality of the world. In short, in Greek monotheism, even as in Greek polytheism, God or the gods cannot be conceived of apart from the world, unlike in Christian thought, where God can: as the Creator *ex nihilo*, the triune God existed everlastingly before the world came into being (see pp. 153–5).

Nevertheless, most early Christian theologians embraced a significant compatibility between Greek and Christian monotheism when thinking of

God as One – especially in terms of divine attributes. This point of contact with Hellenistic culture aided the universal claim of the Christian gospel and its Creator God, and the highly ethical, even religiously mystical project bound up with Greek philosophical monotheism appeared congenial to a Christian morality and spirituality. With the apostle Paul (see again Acts 17:22–8), Christian thinkers thought they could present Christian theism as the revealed fulfillment of the natural inclinations of Greek monotheism. But this gift of the Greeks, which significantly facilitated the acceptability and spread of early Christianity, became, at least for the doctrine of God, something of a Trojan horse.

One finds in the church fathers, therefore, a fairly standard treatment of divine attributes. On the one hand, there are trinitarian affirmations as required by the biblical text – for instance, that God in Christ, the eternal Son of the Father, became incarnate, suffered, died, was bodily resurrected, and will return again in judgment, all of which on the face of it seems to imply a divisibility, mutability, passibility, pathos, and temporality in God. But on the other hand, one also finds an array of Greek metaphysical attributes that assert the opposite – for example, that God is indivisibly simple, absolutely immutable (and therefore impassible or apathetic), and timelessly eternal, a metaphysic that the church fathers largely regarded as consistent with the biblical terminology that God is One (Deut. 6:4), unchanging (e.g., Mal. 3:6), and eternal or everlasting (e.g., Ps. 90:2). Such negative attributes comple-mented the positive, maximal attributes, that array of "omni"-attributes such as omnipotence, omnipresence, and omniscience, all of which were intensi-fied in Christian thought given the more transcendent notion of God implied by its creation doctrine. Even Tertullian, who is renowned for his suspicion of philosophy and who affirms more than most of the fathers the biblical affirmations of divine relationality, change, and suffering, is dogged by this philosophical monotheism.[9] In part, this was simply the intellectual air that the patristic theologians breathed, reinforced by a "scientific" Aristotelian-Ptolemaic cosmology that demeaned the material, variable earth in view of the spiritual, empyrean heaven, bolstering a philosophical conception of God as a fixed transcendent Being (see pp. 155–7).

This patristic legacy endured in both eastern and western Christianity. John of Damascus (*c.* 675–*c.* 749), for example, both sums up and perpet-uates this mixture of attributes for the East in his influential *Exposition of the*

[9] See Tertullian, *The Prescription Against the Heretics*, in *Early Latin Theology*, ed. and trans. S. L. Greenslade, Library of Christian Classics (Philadelphia: Westminster, 1953), ch. 7; Tertullian, *Treatise Against Praxeas*, ed. and trans. Ernest Evans (London: SPCK, 1948), pt. 29.

Orthodox Faith, which from the start intones the attributes of the One God before addressing the trinitarian conception:

> We, therefore, both know and confess that God is without beginning, without end, eternal and everlasting, uncreate, unchangeable, invariable, simple, uncompound, incorporeal, invisible, impalpable, uncircumscribed, infinite, incognisable, indefinable, incomprehensible, good, just, maker of all things created, almighty, all-ruling, all-surveying, of all overseer, sovereign, judge; and that God is One, that is to say, one essence; and that He is known, and has His being in three subsistences, in Father, I say, and Son and Holy Spirit.[10]

Similarly, Augustine both sums up and perpetuates this admixture for the Catholic and Protestant West across the breadth of his influential writings. For example, his provocative *On The Trinity*, while reflecting on the biblical, trinitarian materials from beginning to end, also affirms from the start the array of classical theistic attributes: "So then it is difficult to contemplate and have full knowledge of God's substance, which without any change in itself makes things that change, and without any passage of time in itself creates things that exist in time."[11] Augustine's ponderous reflections on the Trinity are rife with his assumption of divine simplicity, due especially to the influence of Neoplatonism on his theology. Indivisibility (simplicity), immutability (implying impassibility or apathy), and eternality (timelessness) are logically cut from the same metaphysical cloth, and have long been considered orthodox divine attributes.

Scholasticism and Thomas Aquinas

The influence of this Greek theism became formalized in medieval scholasticism, as fathered by Anselm. In his *Proslogion*, where he elaborates a "perfect being theology," a rationalist conception of God as "that thing than which nothing greater can be thought," Anselm deduces the range of classical theistic attributes – both positive and negative – as great-making properties of divine being. In a striking passage on the question of God's mercy, the tension that this philosophical conception of God makes for a more biblical, trinitarian affirmation can clearly be seen:

---

[10] John of Damascus, *Exposition of the Orthodox Faith*, trans. S. D. F. Salmond, *Nicene and Post-Nicene Fathers*, second series, ed. Philip Schaff and Henry Wace (Grand Rapids, MI: Eerdmans, 1993), IX: Book I, ch. 2 (pp. 1–2).

[11] Augustine, *The Trinity*, trans. Edmund Hill, The Works of Saint Augustine 1/5 (New York: New City, 1991), 1.3 (p. 66).

But how can you be at the same time both compassionate and beyond passion? If you are beyond passion, you cannot suffer with anyone; if you cannot share suffering, your heart is not made wretched by entering into the sufferings of the wretched, which is what being compassionate is. But if you are not compassionate, where does so much consolation for those who are wretched come from?

How then, Lord, can you be compassionate and yet not compassionate, unless you are compassionate from our point of view and not from yours? According to our meaning, not according to yours? When you look upon our wretchedness, we experience the effect of your compassion, but you do not experience the emotion. So you are compassionate, when you save wretches, and pardon those who sin against you; but you are not compassionate because you do not experience the feeling of compassion for wretchedness.[12]

It is Thomas Aquinas, however, who is widely considered the eminent representative of classical theism in the Christian tradition. More clearly than any before him, he sums up both the content *and method* of this core philosophical theism and formalizes its place for the trajectory of Catholic and Protestant theology. Thomas's theological achievement, epitomized in his *Summa Theologiae*, must first be appreciated as an apologetic response to the growing attitude of many of his contemporaries that philosophical reason jeopardizes the essential truths of Christianity, a rationalist challenge to Christianity in the wake of the rediscovery of Aristotle (see p. 469). For this reason, Thomas takes up the doctrine of God at the outset of the *Summa*, but formally divides this foundational doctrine into two treatises: the doctrine of the One God, known through reason; and the doctrine of the triune God, known only through revelation. Thomas's noble intent was to show the limitations of human reason (nature) and the necessity for revelation (grace) to come to a full understanding of Christian truth. He holds that while human reason can achieve some significant knowledge of God as One, including God's existence and divine attributes, it requires faith in revelation to come to a full knowledge of God as Three.

Aquinas begins his discussion of the One God with the question of God's existence. Here we have Thomas's famous "Five Ways" (see Table 4.1), the first four of which as *cosmological* arguments all argue in different ways from the cosmos as effect to the world's causal ground (e.g., God as First Cause, Prime Mover, etc.). Thomas's Fifth Way, the *teleological* argument, cites the order and purpose (*telos*) in the world as pointing to an Intelligent Being. Thomas's point is that human reason

---

[12] Anselm, *Proslogion*, ch. 8 (p. 249).

Table 4.1 *The "Five Ways" of Thomas Aquinas*

First Way	Argues from *motion* in the world to God as the foundational *Prime Mover*.
Second Way	Argues from *effects* in the world to God as *First Cause*.
Third Way	Argues from the world's *contingent being* to God as *Necessary Being*.
Fourth Way	Argues from the *graded perfections* of creaturely beings to God as *Maximally Perfect Being*.
Fifth Way	Argues from the *design* or purpose manifest in the world to God as *Intelligent Designer*.

and philosophy, when properly applied, seem to be able to reason to something we typically call "God."

Similarly, human reason can say something about what that God is like, and it can do this in one of two ways. These have become known as the *via negativa* and the *via positiva*, the negative and positive ways of deriving God's attributes.[13] It is telling that at the very beginning of his discussion of the divine attributes, right after his discussion of God's existence, Aquinas devotes a whole section to divine simplicity, which he strongly supports in his theology as a whole. Recall that simplicity is characteristic of the One in negation of the material many (*in*divisibility), and is actually the linchpin of other significant negative attributes, which Thomas also endorses: immutability (impassibility) and eternality. These negative attributes are complemented by the *via positiva* attributes. Since God must be the eminent ground and cause of all the positive things in the world, Aquinas reasons, following Anselm, that God is maximally perfect. Hence God is omnibenevolent, omnipotent, omnipresent, and so forth. The best of human reason therefore appears to be able to establish both the existence of God and a significant number of divine attributes, just as Greek theism had held.

Again, Thomas's intention was actually to show the limitations of sheer human reason, that it did not get you to the full – and salvific – knowledge of God in Christ, a trinitarian theism found only through special revelation. Accordingly, Thomas's treatment of the Trinity soon follows in the *Summa*. But Thomas's methodological strategy of dividing the doctrine of God into two treatises had certain consequences – one more innocent, one less so. On the one hand, it simply clarified the two theisms that had been tenuously mixed together throughout the Christian tradition: the unique trinitarian theism of the biblical narrative (revealed, sacred theology) and the classical theism of Greek philosophy (reasoned, natural theology) that had long been

---

[13] The *via positiva* is also known as the way of eminence (*via eminentiae*).

Christianized and exerted pressure on the former. Thomas's work nicely demarcated their boundaries. But on the other hand, his strategy of placing the doctrine of the One God before that of the triune God tended to isolate the Trinity and make it secondary in importance, particularly as Thomas's method was historically appropriated, since it set the theological pattern for the Catholic and Protestant West.[14] Its effect was to subordinate affirmations one would be inclined to make about the triune God from the biblical narrative (trinitarian theism) to the affirmations about the One God derived from a philosophical theology (classical theism). We will argue that a number of these affirmations – by way of both presupposition and content – are in conflict with a trinitarian theism and ought to be revised in light of the biblical narrative. This is also to say that methodologically, in terms of our approach to the doctrine of God, a trinitarian form of theism ought to have primacy: the triune God as revealed in the biblical narrative ought to control and interpret the concept of the One God, not vice versa. There is much at stake here – namely, a faithful representation and witness to the distinctive Christian concept of God. To get a flavor of these high stakes, we take up the issue of modern atheism, the major crisis of belief in the modern world. Along with other notable theologians, we contend that much of modern atheism is a reaction to a concept of God that is more influenced by classical theism than a trinitarian theism, and that a robust trinitarianism, in addition to being a more biblical kind of theism, can serve as an important apologetic response to this lingering crisis of faith in the late-modern western world.[15]

THE SPECTER OF MODERN ATHEISM

Atheism as we know it today, what we call philosophical atheism – the complete denial of God or the notion of God – is predominantly a modern phenomenon, not so prevalent in the ancient world. The Bible, for instance, knows of no philosophical atheist. The "fools" who "say in their hearts, 'There is no God'" (Ps. 14:1) are denying not the existence of God, but the relevance of God for their lives. Theirs is a *practical* atheism marked by

---

[14] See Karl Rahner, *The Trinity*, trans. Joseph Donceel (New York: Crossroad, 1997), 10–21.

[15] This basic thesis was embraced by many theologians during the last century, most notably Karl Barth and Jürgen Moltmann. For an excellent treatment of their trinitarian apologetic to the crisis of modern atheism, see W. Waite Willis Jr., *Theism, Atheism, and the Doctrine of the Trinity: The Trinitarian Theologies of Karl Barth and Jürgen Moltmann in Response to Protest Atheism* (Atlanta: Scholars Press, 1987). Willis covers much of the same ground that we traverse in the remainder of this chapter.

Illustration 4.1 The April 8, 1966, cover of *Time* magazine.

foolish character and behavior. By the twentieth century, however, it was commonplace to hear about the "obsolescence," "eclipse," or "death" of God in western civilization, even on the front cover of *Time* magazine (see Illustration 4.1).[16]

What contributes to this reversal of theistic fortune is, on the one hand, the rise of the modern world (see pp. 507–10). But this inevitable and understandable process of modernization and secularization is not enough to account for the modern mass rejection of God. A certain conception of God was also rejected, one that was considered inimical to a world "coming of age" (predominantly, classical theism). While there are different ways to categorize modern atheism, we will look at four major types, two of which

---

[16] For a helpful treatment of the rise of modern atheism in general, which our presentation will echo in places, see Walter Kasper, *The God of Jesus Christ*, trans. Matthew J. O'Connell (New York: Crossroad, 1984), 7–46.

follow closely from key Enlightenment themes, and two of which represent different temperaments of atheism.

Scientific atheism

As modern science developed and the world was being discovered in its natural integrity as a well-oiled machine run by natural laws (the Newtonian world), less and less was God needed as an explanatory principle of the world's workings. Life phenomena that were mysterious to the ancients and medievals – take thunderstorms or earthquakes – were generally attributed to the spiritual forces of the gods/God. As the operations of the world were discerned as natural laws, the cosmos was significantly demystified and God was increasingly pushed to the periphery of human knowledge. But this is to make God the "God of the gaps" of human knowledge, invoked only when natural explanations fail. What happens to God when the gaps of scientific knowledge are eventually filled in?[17] This trend of "scientific atheism" is captured well in the story of Napoleon and Pierre Laplace. Upon reading Laplace's *The System of the World*, Napoleon is purported to have asked him where God fit into his scientific scheme, to which Laplace replied: "Sire, I no longer have the need of that hypothesis."[18]

Historically, developments in science facilitated modern atheism as scientific explanation replaced divine explanation. But it must be recognized that while the rise of modern science was quite a natural course of history, the rejection of God that attended it was not. Something else was at work to foment the modern rejection of God, a factor we see more clearly in other types of modern atheism.

Humanistic atheism

If "scientific atheism" (naturalism) develops historically from the Enlightenment emphasis on the appeal to nature and its newly discovered autonomy, "humanistic atheism" arises from the Enlightenment's emphasis on the authority of reason and human autonomy (see p. 511).[19]

The eminent representative of humanistic atheism is Ludwig Feuerbach (1804–72). Feuerbach's thought builds on the major developments in

---

[17] See, e.g., Diogenes Allen, "Has Science Replaced God?," ch. 2 of *Christian Belief in a Postmodern World* (Louisville, KY: Westminster John Knox, 1989), 35–49.

[18] Cited in Kasper, *God of Jesus Christ*, 24.

[19] Kasper characterizes these two atheisms as emphasizing the autonomy – self-governance or independence – of nature and the human subject (ibid., 18–19).

modern philosophy beginning with Descartes and extending to Hegel (see pp. 511–20). Put most simply, Feuerbach thought that the notion of God was a projection of human imagination; "God" was a human fancy, a person blown up to infinite, eternal size (recall Xenophanes' suspicion – see p. 69). Moreover, Feuerbach considered theism a pathology: humanity projects an image of itself as "God" and lavishes on it all our best features and attributes in God-sized measure, but then so objectifies this image transcendentally that in view of God humans become but poor, wretched sinners, unable to do any good. In this "God pro-ject" we have judged and alienated ourselves from our good, rational nature and human potential. This mental illness of theism has stymied the more positive effect human beings might have in the world. So Feuerbach, originally trained in theology, set out to unveil the true origin and order of theological matters: whereas in Christian theism God is the Creator and we the creatures, the truth of the matter is that we are the Creator and God the creature (of our imagination); whereas in Christian theism, human beings are the image of God, the truth is that God is the image of human beings; whereas in Christian theism, idolatry is worship of the creature, the truth of the matter is that idolatry is worship of the Creator, since this alienates us from our true selves. For Feuerbach, all theology was really anthropology, and to face up to this truth is the first step in liberating humanity for positive social and political action in the world. Given his elaboration of the projectionist theory of theistic belief, Feuerbach is considered the father of modern, humanistic atheism.

Feuerbach's projectionist thought was taken up in different ways in the atheism of Karl Marx (1818–83) and Sigmund Freud (1856–1939). Marx thought not only of God as a human projection, but of religion in general as an ideology that all too easily justified – economically and politically – the status quo of haves over have-nots. Although religion was the "sigh of the oppressed," it was also the "opium of the people" in that it narcotized them to their present plight, promising only compensation in the life beyond. It therefore served no liberating function for present inequities. Freud, on the other hand, proposed a psychological explanation for the "illusion" of God: it is the infantile desire or "wish-fulfillment" for a father-figure beyond the limitations of our earthly fathers.[20]

---

[20] Marx's basic criticism of religion can be found in "Towards a Critique of Hegel's *Philosophy of Right*: Introduction," in Marx, *Selected Writings*, ed. David McLellan, 2nd edn. (Oxford: Oxford University Press, 2000), 71–82. Freud's major criticism of religion is found in *The Future of an Illusion*, ed. James Strachey (New York: Norton, 1989).

Humanistic atheism comes to a climax in the fascinating and controversial figure of Friedrich Nietzsche (1844–1900). Nietzsche is rightly dubbed the modern "prophet of the death of God" for two reasons. *Prescriptively*, Nietzsche boldly preached atheism, advocating it largely for the same reasons as Feuerbach, but most particularly because what he observed in Christianity was a deleterious depreciation of life in this world, what he called a "Platonism for the 'people'."[21] But more importantly, *descriptively*, Nietzsche predicted that the secularization of modern life that de-centered the divine, even making God obsolete, would bring about a crisis of meaning or nihilism, given the centering, ethical role played by Judeo-Christian monotheism in western civilization. This vision is captured most vividly in Nietzsche's parable of the madman, who with ironic lantern in hand one bright morning roams the marketplace in search of an honest answer to his question "I seek God! I seek God! ... Whither is God?" Receiving no forthright answer, the madman sheds his own light on God's absence: "Whither is God?... I will tell you. *We have killed him* – you and I. All of us are his murderers ... God is dead. God remains dead .... What was holiest and mightiest of all that the world has yet owned has bled to death under our knives." The madman then prophetically proclaims the revolutionary consequences of the death of God, consequences that teeter toward nihilism:

What were we doing when we unchained this earth from its sun? Whither is it moving now? Whither are we moving? Away from all suns? Are we not plunging continually? Backward, sideward, forward, in all directions? Is there still any up or down? Are we not straying as through an infinite nothing? Do we not feel the breath of empty space? Has it not become colder? Is not night continually closing in on us?[22]

Nietzsche saw clearly that, given their traditional connection, the death of God would lead to the death of humanity unless something else filled the divine vacuum. For that role Nietzsche recommended a new breed of humanity, the *Übermensch* or "Overman" – those who could face up to this new atheistic condition and by force of will overcome themselves and live lives of great and noble achievement. In Nietzsche the prophet we find both a proclamation of a divinized humanity – that "man is the measure of all things" (Democritus) – and a foretelling of the nihilistic tendencies of the twentieth century.

---

[21] Friedrich Nietzsche, *Beyond Good and Evil: Prelude to a Philosophy of the Future*, trans. Walter Kaufmann (New York: Vintage, 1989), preface.

[22] Friedrich Nietzsche, *The Gay Science: With a Prelude in Rhymes and an Appendix of Songs*, trans. Walter Kaufmann (New York: Vintage, 1974), 181.

Apathetic atheism

In addition to these two interrelated atheisms that most generally characterize the modern period – scientific atheism and humanistic atheism – we also note two different temperaments of atheism. Nietzsche's premonition concerning the death of humanity leads to another type of atheism: the atheism of indifference, or "apathetic atheism." While Nietzsche prescribed the Overman in view of the trends of secularization and atheism, he also described the "last man." The last man is the atheist of indifference, that herd of humanity who, given the glut of modern culture, are dead to the great questions and quest of life:

Behold, I show you the *last man*.

"What is love? What is creation? What is longing? What is a star?" thus asks the last man, and he blinks.

The earth has become small, and on it hops the last man, who makes everything small. His race is as ineradicable as the flea-beetle.[23]

The last men are so satisfied with their lives of immediate gratification that they are no longer concerned with the great issues of life, including the question of God (see Illustration 4.2). They represent the death of humanity. One cannot help but think here of the general malaise of modern (and now postmodern) consumer culture and of the consequences of the clamoring for this culture worldwide. Has Nietzsche's prophecy come true?

Protest atheism

But there is yet another, more noble atheism: "protest atheism." This is a nobler atheism since it is a passionate remonstrance against God in view of the fractured human condition. That is, it takes up the plight of humanity in the face of seeming divine indifference. Take the father of modern atheism, Feuerbach, for example. His atheism is also a form of protest atheism, which we can describe as *a general humanistic protest*:

Certainly my work is negative, destructive; but, be it observed, only in relation to the *un*human, not to the human elements of religion.[24]

What is truly negative is theism, the belief in God; it negates nature, the world and mankind: *in the face of God, the world and man are nothing* ... For the true theist the power and beauty of nature, the virtue of man, do not exist; a believer

[23] Friedrich Nietzsche, *Thus Spoke Zarathustra*, in *The Portable Nietzsche*, ed. and trans. Walter Kaufmann (New York: Penguin, 1982), 129.

[24] Ludwig Feuerbach, *The Essence of Christianity*, trans. George Eliot, Great Books in Philosophy (New York: Prometheus, 1989), xvi.

Illustration 4.2 "Who's God?" Cartoon by Werner Wejp-Olsen. Used by permission (www.cartoonstock.com).

in God takes everything away from man and from nature in order to adorn and glorify God.[25]

As we see in these quotations, Feuerbach was not against religion *per se*, but only that type that seemed to negate human dignity and responsible action in the world. He apparently considered Christian theism to be of this latter sort. But is his assessment fair? In order to answer this question, we must ask two other important questions, as we must of any atheist: (1) What is the concept of God that Feuerbach is protesting? and (2) Is that particular concept the most appropriate Christian understanding of God? Again, we will argue that much of modern atheism, as seen especially in its protest variety, is a reaction more to classical theism than to a trinitarian theism, a reaction to a doctrine of God informed more by Greek metaphysics than by the biblical narrative, and that the latter, a trinitarian theism, can actually

---

[25] Ludwig Feuerbach, *Lectures on the Essence of Religion*, trans. Ralph Mannheim (New York: Harper & Row, 1967), 282–3.

serve to apologetically address the major protests of modern atheism. But let us first elaborate two other poignant expressions of protest.

Albert Camus (1913–60) articulates a *protest of life's absurdity*. Camus's writings have been associated with atheistic existentialism – generally, the view that in the absence of metaphysical absolutes or any pattern of life's meaning, as traditionally grounded in God, the individual must resolutely define and "authenticate" his or her own life. His short essay *The Myth of Sisyphus* creatively encapsulates this protest. Sisyphus was the tragic hero in Greek mythology whose audacious human exploits so offended the gods that they condemned him in the underworld to roll a rock unsuccessfully, and therefore eternally, to the top of a mountain. Sisyphus' condition represents the seeming absurdity of life and divine indifference. Nonetheless, Sisyphus resolves to roll his rock, to create his own meaning and destiny, an attitude, writes Camus, that

drives out of this world a god who had come into it with dissatisfaction and a preference for futile sufferings. It makes of fate a human matter, which must be settled among men … [Sisyphus'] fate belongs to him. His rock is his thing. Likewise, the absurd man, when he contemplates his torment, silences all the idols [i.e., gods].[26]

For Camus, the absurdity of life appears incompatible with any notion of providential governance of the world; rather, the world seems to be inhabited by "a god who had come into it with dissatisfaction and a preference for futile sufferings." Sisyphus' resolve to live in some dignified way "silences all the idols," rejecting belief in any god of this sort. Like others, Camus cannot reconcile traditional theism with the absurd conditions of human existence.

Camus's protest anticipates the most piercing reason for protest atheism: the *protest of human suffering*. One of the most poignant and oft-quoted texts that elaborate this protest is a small chapter in Fyodor Dostoevsky's magnum opus, *The Brothers Karamazov*, entitled "Rebellion." In it Ivan, the elder, intellectually inclined Karamazov brother, takes the most innocent case, that of children, and relates a litany of heart-wrenching stories concerning their gratuitous suffering at the hands of adults, asking where God is in all of this. Ivan's main point is that human freedom does not appear worth the price we pay for its misuse given the history of human suffering. Given the persistent cry of the innocent, he cannot accept a world so

---

[26] Albert Camus, *The Myth of Sisyphus and Other Essays*, trans. Justin O'Brien (New York: Vintage, 1991), 122–3.

arranged, even if it purports to serve some higher divine purpose or promises ultimate justice:

And if the sufferings of children go to swell the sum of sufferings which was necessary to pay for truth, then I protest that the truth is not worth such a price ... I don't want harmony. From love for humanity I don't want it ... Besides, too high a price is asked for harmony; it's beyond our means to pay so much. And so I give back my entrance ticket, and if I am an honest man I give it back as soon as possible. And that I am doing. It's not God that I don't accept, Alyosha, only I most respectfully return the ticket to Him.[27]

Thus Ivan rejects any God who would will suffering as part of the good creation.

But here is where protest atheism slurs into a *protest theism*, for Dostoevsky writes in the Christian tradition, and Ivan, a serious voice of Dostoevsky, is not an atheist *per se*, but simply thinks that the problem of human suffering renders any notion of divine providence questionable, if not blasphemous. And it is here that the Christian theist ought to have the deepest empathy for the concerns of the protest atheist; indeed, it is here that the Christian theist ought to join in protest if in fact, as Feuerbach imagines, God negates life in creation; if, as Camus holds, God is indifferent to the absurdities of life; if, as Ivan Karamazov complains, God necessitates or has a positive place for human suffering. But again, the important question to ask here is what conception of God is the object of protest, and whether this represents the best Christian understanding of God. Whence comes the negative view of God of much of modern atheism? Here, finally, we must tell the tale of two theisms.

A TALE OF TWO THEISMS

Classical theism

Our claim is that much of modern atheism is a reaction to a conception of God that more closely resembles classical theism than a trinitarian theism. We observed the development of classical theism, as rooted in Greek metaphysics, as embraced by the majority of church fathers, as reinforced by the Aristotelian-Ptolemaic cosmology of the day, and as formalized by Aquinas in the doctrine of the One God. To simplify, we may characterize classical theism thus: in terms of *method*, it is a reasoned understanding of

---

[27] Fyodor Dostoevsky, *The Brothers Karamazov*, trans. Constance Garnett (New York: New American Library, 1980), 226.

God via general revelation (i.e., natural theology), whose *content* is a philosophical conception of the One God as Supreme Being, with the *result* that God is conceived of in absolutist terms as omnipotent, immutable, impassible, and the like, related to the world as distant Creator or external Cause.[28] Just as Aquinas apologetically put this philosophical monotheism front and center in view of the rationalist challenge of medieval Aristotelianism, so also did the Catholic and Protestant West emphasize it as Christian belief in God was challenged in the rise of modernity and Enlightenment rationalism. Ironically, however, it appears that it was precisely this reasoned or philosophical conception of God that excited much of modern atheism. How so?

The recipe is quite simple, and the ingredients are as follows: if one conceives of God primarily in the category of causality (the world as an effect of the First Cause); and if one places that transcendent Cause outside of the world in eternal timelessness; and if one considers God's will and plan toward the world to be absolutely immutable (because everything in the divine being is unchanging, since there is no movement in God, given that God is one, simple, single thing); if one puts these ingredients together as the controlling features of the doctrine of God, what kind of relationship do we get between God and the world? The answer is: one characterized by *determinism*. So conceived, whatever God timelessly wills toward creation will, as an inexorable cause, work its way out in the world. God's providential relationship with creation becomes deterministic, a theological consequence that is not just the case for Calvin, who is typically associated with a predestinarian theology, but is also true of Augustine, Aquinas, and Luther, among many others. In fact, throughout the breadth of historic Christian theology, one finds doctrines of providence – of the God–world relationship – that look highly deterministic, with all things being eternally fixed by God's will. The doctrine of predestination then becomes a mere subset of an otherwise providentially determined world.

This classical theistic determinism was largely what provoked the most general protest of modern atheism, whose overarching complaint was that there was no room in Christian theism for the true freedom and dignity (i.e., relative autonomy) of the human person. With the rise of modernity and all the various, even religious, influences that contributed to secularization, there was a new emphasis on human responsibility in a less cosmologically and more historically conceived world. Could the Christian conception of God accommodate this important shift? Unfortunately,

---

[28] The simplified characterization and contrast of these two theisms by way of method, content, and result is indebted to Willis, *Theism*, 9–15.

most atheists thought that it could not, and the reason, we would argue, was the dominance of classical theism. It is this basic freedom–dignity concern that largely motivates the atheism of Feuerbach, who rejects a religion that is not socially or politically responsible. In fact, if we recall the second quotation from Feuerbach –

What is truly negative is theism, the belief in God; it negates nature, the world and mankind: *in the face of God, the world and man are nothing* … For the true theist the power and beauty of nature, the virtue of man, do not exist; a believer in God takes everything away from man and nature in order to adorn and glorify God[29]

– one can see quite clearly that his objection to Christian theism is based on a conception of God derived principally *via negativa* and *via positiva* – the methodology of classical theism.

Likewise with protest atheist Camus, who objects to a God who appears existentially indifferent to (and therefore metaphysically aloof from) the absurdities, injustices, or suffering in the world, a conception of God reinforced by the classical attributes of immutability and impassibility. For Camus such indifference renders the notion of God unbelievable. Similarly with protest *theist* Ivan Karamazov (i.e., Dostoevsky), who cannot accept the suffering in the world as though it contributes to some ultimate divine plan. In a world so arranged, Ivan wishes to return his ticket of admission. But the question remains, however, whether these objections and protests are as crushing when given a trinitarian theism.

Trinitarian theism

By a trinitarian theism, we mean a Christian conception of God that is derived first and foremost from the biblical narrative, especially as focused by a christological lens. By way of contrast with classical theism, we may characterize trinitarian theism thus: in terms of *method*, it is a revealed understanding of God via special revelation (i.e., sacred theology), whose *content* is a theological conception of the triune God as Supreme Communion, with the *result* that God is conceived of in personalist terms as Father, Son, and Spirit, related to the world as historically involved creator, redeemer, and glorifier.

In the biblical narrative, God is revealed not as a metaphysical principle, but as personal – ultimately tripersonal. As the Supreme Communion of

[29] Feuerbach, *Essence of Religion*, 282–3.

Father, Son, and Spirit, God-as-Love (1 John 4:8) is a relational God, composed of divine persons in right relation who accord one another the dignity of equality and responsible freedom. God shares this communion with humanity, which is expressly created male *and* female as God's image in the world with the responsibility to cultivate God's earthly garden and to direct its history along just paths. In this project of creation, the triune God is intimately involved, establishing and reestablishing covenant (relationship) with a people, whose renewed humanity and mission invitingly reach out to all creation. Ultimately, the eternal Son himself becomes incarnate, lives, suffers, and dies on a cross, indicating that God can change in striking ways, can be deeply affected by creation, and suffers because of and for creation in the hope of the resurrection and renewal of all things.

This trinitarian theism speaks to Feuerbach's complaint that Christian theism negates the goodness of creation and the freedom and dignity of humanity in its ethical responsibilities; it takes up Camus's complaint that God is indifferent to the injustices and absurdities of the world, since the Son of God experienced the highest injustice and absurdity imaginable – as the divine Son suffering the ignominy of the cross, whereby the creature crucifies the Creator (which also renders dubious the accusation of anthropomorphic projection); it therefore goes some distance in addressing Ivan Karamazov's poignant concerns, since the passion of Christ takes into the trinitarian life the sufferings of the world (albeit sufferings that are still, in Jürgen Moltmann's words, the "open wound of life").[30] Since many of the concerns of modern atheism, especially of the protest variety, appear to be a reaction to classical theism, we put forward and accentuate a trinitarian theism in apologetic response, for a robust trinitarianism addresses many of these concerns, in addition to being a more faithful reading of the biblical narrative.

Classical theism is a natural theology. While we think that natural theology has its place in Christian theology, its role is limited insofar as reason is unable to secure the truths of faith and is inevitably distorted by human sinfulness. Therefore, when a proposal in natural theology conflicts with trinitarian theism, with central affirmations about God from the biblical text, then trinitarian theism methodologically trumps that natural theology. What this means concretely is that a number of classical divine attributes may need to be revisited in light of the biblical text.

---

[30] Jürgen Moltmann, *Trinity and the Kingdom: The Doctrine of God*, trans. Margaret Kohl (Minneapolis, MN: Fortress, 1993), 49.

Reconsidering divine attributes

Ever since history came fully into its own as an important category of truth (in the nineteenth century) and Christian theology began to think of the God–world relationship in more dynamic and historical terms, theologians (especially in the twentieth century) have begun to rethink many of the classical divine attributes from a more biblical perspective. While this reconsideration includes attributes derived both *via positiva* and *via negativa*, the traditional *via positiva* attributes, on the whole, are less problematic for a trinitarian theism. We are concerned here with three major *via negativa* attributes, already highlighted, that have created the most dissonance between classical and trinitarian theism – namely, indivisibility (simplicity), immutability (including impassibility or apathy), and eternality. Historically, the particular content of these classical attributes has been informed more by Greek metaphysical suppositions than by the biblical narrative. We have already seen the basic logic of these attributes, which all hang together given their origin in the Greek philosophical problem of the One and the many: unlike the world of the many, where *parts* break down, undergo *change* and deterioration, and over *time* dissolve into oblivion, God must be conceived as One simple, single thing, unchangeable, unaffected and unafflicted by anything, secure in a transcendental timelessness. The result of these *via negativa* attributes, so conceived, is that God has no real relation – that is to say, personal give-and-take – with the world. This was the major complaint against classical theism by process theologians, who led the way in the twentieth century in revision of these attributes (see pp. 546–8). But one need not endorse all the suppositions of process theology, especially given its deficient creation doctrine, to appreciate its critique, or to join the chorus of revision, which theologians of more orthodox stripes have done, such as Barth, Bonhoeffer, and Moltmann, among a gathering host of others.

The major problem with this complex of *via negativa* attributes is the supposition that parts, change, and time are necessarily bad. In the Greek understanding of the world, such things could not dignify God (the One), since they were associated with corruption and death – to which God, the fullness of being, must be contrasted. But we must regard this as a gnostic supposition, which holds that the material world is intrinsically evil (see pp. 153–5). We need only turn to the first chapter of Genesis, however, to see quite an opposite affirmation: that God creates many different sorts of things and *parts*, including a differentiated humanity whom God blesses, instructing them to be fruitful, to multiply, and to care for the earth, all of which requires *change* and *time*. Now if this created realm of composition, movement, and temporality is called "very good" by God, and indeed is actually a divine blessing (Gen. 1:28–31), is there any reason why parts and change and time cannot also be appropriately applicable to God? There is therefore eminent biblical warrant for rethinking the following three *via negativa* attributes that have especially worked against important trinitarian (biblical) affirmations.

Simplicity

Most Christians have not even heard of the doctrine of divine simplicity, that God is one simple, single thing. At first glance, it seems to militate against the notion of the Trinity. Indeed, the affirmation of divine simplicity has been the biggest reason why the Trinity has been presented as an impenetrable mystery of faith, a logical paradox of three persons who are also one person or thing, and why most Christians finally tend to have a unipersonal view of God – typically associated with the Father. We believe that this attribute has no real biblical basis and has in fact worked to defeat the resources of a full-fledged trinitarianism. While the Bible certainly does speak of the oneness or unity of God, its content is not the metaphysical simplicity of Greek theism. Since we treat the doctrine of the Trinity formally in the next chapter, however, we will leave our discussion of the biblical content of divine oneness or unity until then. But if the traditional notion of divine simplicity can be trumped by a more biblical notion of divine oneness or unity, then the way is open for also rethinking our other two *via negativa* attributes that depend on simplicity as their linchpin.

Immutability

If God has no parts, in the fashion of Greek theism, then there is no change in God, since change is a movement of one thing in reference to another, or an effect of one thing upon another. Moreover, it was thought that if God is perfect, any change in God would be either a diminishment of divine perfection or an admission of its lack.

Strict immutability, however, seems to fly in the face of basic biblical affirmations. Take creation, for example: since in Christian confession the world is not eternal, but was created *ex nihilo*, God once was not, but then *becomes*, the creator of the world. Or, more tellingly, take the incarnation: there was a time when the eternal Son of God was not incarnate (as the preexistent Logos), but then takes on human flesh – another change of personal status. Or, more generally, take the entire sweep of the biblical narrative: does not God interact with human beings in give-and-take relationships in which there is change, a developing history of relationship?

To be sure, the Bible does say that God is unchanging (e.g., Mal. 3:6; Jas. 1:17), but the clear consensus of biblical scholarship today is that, taken in context, such texts refer not to a metaphysical principle of being, but to the constancy of God's character and promises – God is unchanging in reference to God's nature (e.g., as the good, true, and beautiful) and is faithful to God's promises.[31] It is important to note here that God changes not out of a deficiency of being (the Greek concern) but as a function of being in genuine relationships – change that flows from loving interaction. What trinitarian theism teaches us is that God should be conceived first and foremost in the category of personhood, not in the category of impersonal being or nature. And persons – divine or human – change in the course of relationship.

Persons are also affected by one another, and so it seems that the classical attribute of *impassibility* or *apathy*, a corollary of immutability, also works against the biblical narrative. Perhaps God really was grieved at an errant creation and really did regret the risk with the human creature (Gen. 6:6); perhaps God really is a jealous God, eager for our loyalties and therefore not immune to emotions (Exod. 20:3–5). Again, if the incarnation of Christ is the NT key for understanding the divine identity, what more evidence do we need that God is deeply affected by creation, since God, as Dietrich Bonhoeffer strikingly put it, "lets himself be pushed out of the world on to the cross"?[32] If God can be affected by creation in this way, then it seems that God can also suffer. For centuries it was axiomatic in Christian theology, apart from notable exceptions like Luther, that the divine nature did not suffer. But taking this tack again is to conceive of God principally in the category of divine Being (*vis-à-vis* the world of the many) and not in the category of Personhood. Moreover, it contravenes the principal affirmation of the Christian gospel – that God in Christ suffered and died for our sakes, the event known tellingly as the *passion* of Christ. We will later see how the affirmation of immutability and impassibility was often assumed in christology, creating a logical paradox for understanding the unity of Christ's person given both his deity and humanity. For now it must be noted that in contemporary theology, the new axiom is virtually that of the divine

[31] See, e.g., Abraham Joshua Heschel, *The Prophets* (Peabody, MA: Prince, 2003); Terence Fretheim, *The Suffering of God: An Old Testament Perspective*, Overtures to Biblical Theology (Minneapolis, MN: Fortress, 1984).

[32] Dietrich Bonhoeffer, *Letters and Papers from Prison*, ed. Eberhard Bethge, trans. R. H. Fuller *et al.*, enlarged edn. (New York: Macmillan, 1972), 360.

pathos – that God can and does suffer, not out of deficiency of being, but personally, voluntarily, out of the abundance and power of divine love. This claim makes better sense of the biblical witness to the Father's grief and compassion, the Son's passion, and the Spirit's present groaning and travail with an enslaved creation (Rom. 8:18–27).

Eternality

Of the three *via negativa* attributes highlighted here, revisions of divine eternality have been most controversial. Certainly the Bible declares that God, in contrast to creation, is eternal or – as alternatively translated into English – everlasting (e.g., Ps. 90:2). But what is meant by God's eternality? Within a Greek metaphysic, it signified that God transcended time, was outside of time, and therefore was timeless, since time was ultimately seen as a vicious cycle and an enemy of life. In short, God must not be subject to the ravages of time. As appropriated by Christian theology, this meant that time was a created entity that governed creation, and that all points of historical time come to God as a simultaneous whole (*simul totem*). While God could act in time, in God's transcendent self all times were the same, one "eternal present": Adam's creation was simultaneous with Moses' call, was simultaneous with Christ's birth, was simultaneous with Christ's second coming. The question therefore of what God was doing prior to creation was considered inappropriate. (To this question Augustine jokingly said that God was preparing hell for those who pry into such matters!)[33]

But is this really such an impudent question? If God is conceived of principally as a trinity of persons, is it not possible to conceive of Father, Son, and Spirit as relating to one another in an everlasting divine life; and if relating, is there not a dynamism and movement in the divine life; and if there is personal movement in the divine life, is there not something like temporal sequence – certain things happening before and after others? And is this not analogous to time as a measurement of movement, of certain things past, present, and future?

The problem with the timeless view of divine eternality is that it is very hard to make sense of God's real relationship to creation as it unfolds in the biblical narrative. How can there be real covenantal interaction between God and the world if all temporal events are finally experienced by God "at the same time"? Here again we would have to posit a two-tiered understanding of God – God as God relates to us in time, and God in God's own essential being experiencing everything at once. The latter seems to nullify

---

[33] Augustine, *Confessions*, Book 11, ch. 12.

and defeat the former. Not only is it difficult to make any sense of God's real relation with creation, but it also seems to logically make creation (and everything in it) eternal, a very unorthodox and incoherent position given the confession of *creatio ex nihilo*.

For these reasons some contemporary theologians have proposed an alternative understanding of God's eternality. Oscar Cullmann, a NT scholar, argued that only a more linear understanding of time *and eternity* was compatible with the biblical history of creation and redemption, in opposition to the Greek cyclical understanding that cast salvation as a spatial transcendence in a timeless heaven. Since the OT Hebrew (*olam*) and NT Greek (*aion*) words that are translated "eternal" and "everlasting" are rooted in the time-fraught word "age," the biblical notion of eternality can best be understood as an unending duration of time – as the endless succession of ages.[34] Similarly, philosophical theologians such as Nicholas Wolterstorff have proposed that we think of God's eternality more in terms of "everlastingness," that the divine life, even apart from creation, has a temporal sequence to it – a past, present, and future.[35]

The proposal of understanding divine eternality as everlastingness – the unending temporal sequentiality of divine life – instead of eternity as atemporal timelessness is really quite modest. It holds that God is from everlasting to everlasting (Ps. 90:2) – God has always been, God presently is, and God will always be (see Rev. 1:4). At some temporal point in the divine life God created a world with its own history, and at a different point in the divine life the Son became incarnate. On this view, since the time sequence in creation and the divine life are basically analogous, it is easier to see how there could be a real history of relationship between God and creation: what is past for one is past for the other (e.g., the crucifixion of Christ); what is future for one is future for the other (e.g., the second coming of Christ). In this way there is a real history of relationship between God and creatures that is not relativized by eternal timelessness. Time on this proposal is no metaphysical entity in itself, but is simply a measurement of movement or sequentiality.[36]

---

[34] Oscar Cullmann, *Christ and Time: The Primitive Christian Conception of Time and History*, trans. Floyd V. Filson, rev. edn. (Philadelphia: Westminster, 1964), esp. 37–68.

[35] See Nicholas Wolterstorff, "God Everlasting," in *God and the Good: Essays in Honor of Henry Stob*, eds. Clifton Orlebeke and Lewis B. Smedes (Grand Rapids, MI: Eerdmans, 1975), 181–203.

[36] The debate surrounding divine eternality can quickly become dense and complex. This revisionary approach to classical eternality is particularly controversial because of its possible implications for divine omniscience. One of the considered advantages of the traditional view of eternity as time-lessness is the way it seemingly accounts for God knowing all things, since all temporal things – past, present, and future – are present to God in one simultaneous whole. But if God is "in time," how can

We think that a reconsideration of these three *via negativa* attributes is warranted given the problematic gnostic suppositions that undergird their classical expression (a natural theism gone astray), and especially given the priority of the biblical narrative and a trinitarian theism. Moreover, we hold that a revisionist view of these three attributes is especially key in liberating the full resources of trinitarian theism, and for appreciating the dynamic historical relation between the trinitarian God and a creation that bears a trinitarian likeness. It is to the formal doctrine of the Trinity that we now turn.

FOR FURTHER READING

Dostoevsky, Fyodor, *The Brothers Karamazov*, trans. Constance Garnett (New York: New American Library, 1980), Book 5, chs. 4–5.

Gunton, Colin E., *Act and Being: Towards a Theology of the Divine Attributes* (Grand Rapids, MI: Eerdmans, 2003).

Jaeger, Werner, *Early Christianity and Greek Paideia* (Cambridge, MA: Belknap, 1961).

Kasper, Walter, *The God of Jesus Christ*, trans. Matthew J. O'Connell (New York: Crossroad, 1984), ch. 1.

Migliore, Daniel L., *The Power of God and the gods of Power* (Louisville, KY: Westminster John Knox, 2008).

Morris, Thomas V., *Our Idea of God: An Introduction to Philosophical Theology* (Downers Grove, IL: InterVarsity, 1991).

Westphal, Merold, *Suspicion and Faith: The Religious Uses of Modern Atheism* (Grand Rapids, MI: Eerdmans, 1993).

God know future events, as seems to be required by biblical prophecy and the classical concept of God? On these issues in general, see Gregory E. Ganssle, ed., *God and Time: Four Views* (Downers Grove, IL: InterVarsity, 2001).

CHAPTER 5

The triune God

INTRODUCTION

The previous chapter stressed the importance of a trinitarian *method* in crafting a Christian conception of God. Rather than taking our first or strongest cue from a general, abstract monotheism based on natural theology, it is the dynamic interaction of Father, Son, and Spirit as portrayed in the biblical narrative that should inform and control our understanding of God's attributes (being) and interaction (act) with creation. When the biblical materials are given their due, the trinitarian conception emerges as the distinctive Christian understanding of God, just as the early church confessed and taught: three divine persons in one God. This chapter explores the venerable *doctrine* of the Trinity.

This trademark Christian teaching, however, has not always been the easiest to appreciate, let alone understand. Historically, the Trinity has been a difficult and perplexing doctrine, one often considered of little relevance or practical value. Such an impression lingers today. Consider, for example, the following dialogue from a 1990 film in which actor Eric Idle (of *Monty Python* fame) seeks clarification on the matter of the Trinity from his fellow "nun on the run":

> Explain the Trinity!
> Mmm, well, it's a bit of a bugger.
> Well it can't be that difficult. You've been a Catholic all your life.
> Yeah. Well, here's the pitch [lights up a cigarette]: You got the Father, the Son, and the Holy Ghost. The three are one, like a shamrock, my old priest used to say – three leafs, but one leaf. Now the Father sent down the Son, who was love. And then when he went away, he sent down the Holy Spirit, who came down in the form of a ...
> You told me already, a ghost.
> No, a dove.
> The dove was a ghost?
> No, the ghost was a dove. And ...
> Let me try and summarize this: God is his Son, and his Son is God. But his Son moonlights as a Holy Ghost, a Holy Spirit, and a dove. And they all send each other even though they're all one and the same thing?
> Got it.
> What?
> You really could be a nun.
> Thanks ... Wait a minute. What I said, does that make any sense to you?
> Well no, no. But it makes no sense to anybody. That's why you have to believe it. That's why you have to have faith. I mean if it made sense, it wouldn't have to be a religion, would it?[1]

Unfortunately, this sketch captures all too well a common impression of the Trinity. For many people today, the teaching that God is both three and one remains at best paradoxical or mysterious, at worst contradictory, but in any event not very graspable. And if the Trinity "makes no sense," it is hard to see the practical value of the doctrine. For this reason, many Christians largely ignore this central confession.

---

[1] *Nuns on the Run*, directed by Jonathan Lynn, 1990. By permission of Hand Made Films plc

It was this lack of appreciation for the doctrine of the Trinity, especially in the West, that led Karl Rahner (1904–84), the eminent Catholic theologian, to lament that "despite their orthodox confession of the Trinity, Christians are, in their practical life, almost mere 'monotheists'."[2] Rahner surmised that if the Trinity were dropped from Christian confession, it would hardly alter the vast majority of Christian literature and spirituality. The Trinity, he observed, simply has little play in most Christians' thinking and practice.

But Rahner's lament concerning this sorry state of Trinity doctrine seems to have been a rallying cry of the sentinel, as the decades since have seen a resurgence of interest in the Trinity and its relevance for the life and mission of the church.[3] What occasions this groundswell of trinitarian thought is not simply a commitment to the indispensability of the Trinity as the distinctive Christian doctrine of God – that is, the unavoidable grammar of the NT and the historical confession of the church. This renaissance also springs from the growing conviction that the Trinity has rich practical consequences for Christian life. The reasons for this renaissance will become clear in our historical treatment of Trinity doctrine, and its practical consequences will be elaborated in our systematic treatment. To begin, however, we turn to the biblical basis of this central doctrine.

THE BIBLICAL BASIS OF THE DOCTRINE OF THE TRINITY

Scholars agree that the Bible does not contain the formal *doctrine* of the Trinity in any explicit fashion. One certainly cannot point to a single biblical text that declares as clearly as the Athanasian Creed, for example, that

> the Father is God, the Son is God, and the Holy Spirit God;
> and yet there are not three gods, but there is one God.[4]

But the Bible in its unfolding narrative, and therefore progressive revelation, does imply the trinitarian conception of God, the vectors of which, upon reflection on the Bible as a whole, are systematized by the church's ecumenical confessions. For this biblical development the OT is foundational.

---

[2] Rahner, *The Trinity*, 10.

[3] See Thomas R. Thompson, "Trinitarianism Today: Doctrinal Renaissance, Ethical Relevance, Social Redolence," *Calvin Theological Journal* 32, no. 1 (1997), 9–42.

[4] Verses 15 and 16 of the so-called "Athanasian Creed," a classic summary statement of western trinitarianism. See Pelikan and Hotchkiss, *Creeds and Confessions*, 1: 676.

Old Testament

We noted in the previous chapter the revolutionary development of mono-theism in Israel within its polytheistic context. More than just Israel's God, Yahweh is ultimately acknowledged as the one true God by virtue of being the Creator of all things. That is the basic monotheistic claim and the baseline of Jewish faith. But does this monotheistic oneness admit of *any* plurality in God? While Yahweh in the OT does seem to be a single personal agent, "the name" itself (YHWH) does not rule out personal plurality, since, as we have contended, it is rather cryptic and open-ended: "I will be who/what I will be." Moreover, the "oneness" of God referred to in the famed *Shema* of Deuteronomy 6:4, a oneness of which the OT as a whole says rather little, has ultimately to do with the "uniqueness" of God. OT monotheism appears to be the claim that there is one true God by virtue of Yahweh's unique status as Creator and therefore Lord of history. All other claims to deity are idolatrous assertions of creatures.

But the OT itself, Christian theologians have long contended, is open to and even intimates a plurality in God. They have cited, for example, the plural form of *Elohim* as referent for Israel's singular God. They have also noted how God sometimes speaks in the plural (Gen. 3:22; 11:7), especially in striking vacillation with the singular (Gen. 1:26; Isa. 6:8). They have addi-tionally observed how God seems to appear in differentiated, bodily form (called "theophanies" – e.g., Gen. 32:22–32; Josh. 5:13–15), many times as "the angel of the Lord" (e.g., Gen. 16:7–13; 21:17–18). Most striking to the early church fathers was the convergence of such elements in Genesis 18:1–15, where Abraham entertains three strangers who turn out to be a visitation of the Lord (YHWH). The church fathers interpreted this episode as an adumbration of the Trinity, and the scene became a genre of iconography in Eastern Orthodoxy for its intimation of the Trinity, of which Andrei Rublev's icon is the most famous example (see Illustration 5.2). While scholars today generally find these texts questionable as proofs of the Trinity, theolo-gians are on surer grounds by focusing on the important OT notions of the Spirit, Wisdom, and Word as suggestive of some kind of differentiation in God's personal being, since these notions are expressly taken up by the NT to identify the Holy Spirit and Christ.[5]

In the OT, the more it became clear that Yahweh was the sole Creator God, the more Yahweh's *transcendence* was emphasized, that God is high

---

[5] See Arthur W. Wainwright, *The Trinity in the New Testament* (London: SPCK, 1962), esp. 29ff. for what follows.

above and quite other than creation (e.g., Isa. 57:15). But if Yahweh is not like the other gods, incomparable to mere creatures, how does one affirm the divine *immanence*, that God is still within and involved with the world? The OT affirms this through the dynamic media of Spirit, Wisdom, and Word.

- The Spirit of God (*ruach* – literally "breath" or "wind") is the power by which God variously animates creation, empowers special agents such as the prophets (and the coming Messiah), and renews the earth in righteousness. While mostly portrayed as an impersonal force in the OT, the Spirit is also talked about in personal terms, as one who guides (Ps. 143:10), teaches (Neh. 9:12), and even grieves (Isa. 63:10).

- The Wisdom of God (*chokmah*) is even more clearly *personified* in the OT – as witnessed, for example, in Proverbs 8–9, among other wisdom texts. Closely related to God's law, and as one who helps Yahweh create and structure creation (8:22–36), "Lady Wisdom" is immanent within the nature of things, through which she makes a personal appeal, as if in the public square, for people to heed her counsel.

- The word of God (*dabar*) is a third important way the transcendent God communicates in creation and effects the divine purpose, whether it be productive of creation itself (Gen. 1: "And God said"), for example, or the means of prophetic utterance ("The word of the LORD came to …"). While not personified in the OT itself, the notion of God's word was personified by Philo, the important first-century Jewish apologist. Philo found a great compatibility between the word and a Platonic understanding of *Logos* (Word), and virtually spoke of the Logos as a conscious person in distinction from God. The concept of divine wisdom also continued to be personified during this intertestamental period, as can be seen dramatically in Sirach (Ecclesiasticus) (ch. 24) and Wisdom of Solomon (esp. chs. 7–9). These developments during the intertestamental period as reflected in its literature as a whole must be considered an influential context for the NT writings.

In the OT, then, Spirit, Wisdom, and Word are the central ways through which the transcendent God interacts with creation. They make Yahweh immanent or personally present within the world in word and deed. As such, they are an extension of the divine personality. However, even though such media are closely associated and even identified with Yahweh, they also seem at times to take on a life of their own as an independent personal existence. Even if this OT trend toward personification is mere literary device, such notions would provide the NT writers with a segue for thinking about the real, historical person of Jesus the Christ (as Word and

Wisdom) in relation to the one God of Israel, and later, by analogy to Christ, the person of the Holy Spirit (as Spirit).

That the OT tradition as a whole is flexible enough to be open to a plurality in God is seen even in the history of Jewish thought, particularly in the rabbinic doctrine of the *Shekinah* ("dwelling"), the suffering divine presence that follows God's people into exile, and which sympathetically remains with them awaiting deliverance. In Jewish cabalistic mysticism, the Shekinah is considerably personified, suggesting a self-differentiation between the transcendent God and God the immanent, exiled sojourner.[6] Such developments indicate that Jewish monotheism is a less rigid form than that found, for example, in Islam. They also show a striking formal parallel with NT developments.

New Testament

In Christian thought, personal distinction within the being of God does not become clear apart from the claims of Jesus Christ and the NT interpretation of his person. That Jesus of Nazareth was a truly *human* person is the clear assumption of the NT, the keynote of the synoptic gospels. From this perspective, what the NT also asserts, astonishingly, is his *deity*. The Gospel of John, while still presupposing Jesus' humanity, is especially explicit about his deity and represents the height of NT reflection on the trinitarian issue. This NT witness to Christ's deity is the linchpin of Trinity doctrine. Once Christ's status was clarified as a second divine person, the way became open for recognition of a third person in God, the Spirit, and thus the distinctive Christian trinitarian conception of God.

The NT case for Christ's deity is both comprehensive and compelling. Since this case is presented more thoroughly in Chapter 9 on the person of Christ, we only briefly summarize it here. There are three major NT lines of argument for Christ's deity: (1) the titles he is given; (2) the divine functions he assumes; and (3) the worship he receives.

Christ is given the title *God* (*Theos*) in three sure instances (John 1:1; 20:28; Heb. 1:8–9) and in another probable five instances (John 1:18; Rom. 9:5; Titus 2:13; 2 Pet. 1:1; 1 John 5:20). Jesus' own favorite self-designation as the *Son of Man* also likely implies divinity when understood as the coming apocalyptic judge (cf. Mark 14:61–4). But a more evident association with deity is found in the title *Son of God* as an exclusive claim for Christ, as in

---

[6] See Franz Rosenzweig, *The Star of Redemption*, trans. Barbara E. Galli (Madison, WI: University of Wisconsin Press, 2005).

John's assertion that he is the unique or "only [begotten] Son" (e.g., John 3:16). Similarly, *Lord* (*kyrios*), as in the basic confession "Jesus is Lord," also connotes deity since it is the Greek word used to translate the Hebrew divine name, YHWH.

The highest sense of these titles is reinforced by the divine functions associated with Christ. Various NT assertions affirm Christ's key role in the *creation* of the world (Col. 1:16; Heb. 1:3; John 1:3) – including its sustenance (Col. 1:17), fulfillment (Eph. 1:9), and re-creation (2 Cor. 5:17); the *judgment* of the world (Matt. 25:31–46; Mark 8:38); and the *salvation* of the world, including the power to forgive sins (Luke 7:48; Mark 2:1–12) and to effect the future resurrection of the dead, an event associated with his second coming (John 5:25–9). These functions of creating, judging, and saving place Christ in the closest association with God the Father, since they are considered in the Hebrew scriptures to be uniquely divine acts, performed by the power and prerogative of God alone.

Most telling for Christ's deity, however, is the fact that he was worshipped together with the Father. All the titles of *God* ascribed to him, noted above, are likely of liturgical origin, indicating that Christ was worshipped in NT times. This conclusion is bolstered by the ascription of doxologies to Christ (Rom. 9:5; 2 Tim. 4:18; 2 Pet. 3:18), as well as prayers offered to Christ in his own right (Acts 7:59–60; 1 Cor. 16:22; 2 Cor. 12:8). If worshipped, Christ had to be considered on the divine side of the Creator/creature divide, since to worship him as a creature would constitute both idolatry and polytheism.

Beyond these "proof texts," the Gospel of John integrates this variety of evidence for Christ's deity in a sustained fashion. John develops the relationship between the Father and Son more fully than any other NT book, affirming both their personal distinction and divine equality, as seen already in 1:1 (Christ the Word both is "with God" and is "God"). Whereas the Son as the humanly incarnate "sent one" is subordinate to God, he is at the same time so united or "one" with the Father (10:30) that to see him is to see the Father (14:9). In John, Jesus' calling God his own Father and therefore claiming to be the Son of God provokes the accusation of blasphemy, since he, by all appearances a man, makes himself equal to God (5:18; 10:33; 19:7). It is in John's development of the Father–Son relation that the trinitarian conception emerges most distinctly in the NT. But we have also seen in Chapter 4 that the apostle Paul is aware of the trinitarian issue when he refers the *Shema* to both Father and Son (1 Cor. 8:4–6).

The Spirit's status both as person and as divine is not as textually obvious. Since this material is treated more fully in Chapter 11 on the Holy Spirit, we again only summarize here. Although the distinct *personhood* of the Spirit is not as self-evident as in the case of Christ, the NT does deepen the personalization of the Spirit begun in the OT. To be sure, the Spirit still appears as a dynamic force or divine power that, variously, is poured out, fills, and empowers, all of which could be understood in a merely impersonal sense as the power of the Father or the Son. But one need only look to the book of Acts, which records the church's Spirit-empowered mission to the world, to see an accumulation of personal traits and actions associated with the Spirit. There, for example, the Spirit speaks (1:16), is lied to (5:3), is tempted (5:9), and so forth – all subjective or personal acts that the NT generally attributes to the invisible, elusive Spirit.[7]

The *deity* of the Spirit is also not as pronounced as that of Christ. Of the NT texts that possibly identify the Spirit as God in an explicit way, only one has exegetical plausibility (2 Cor. 3:17–18), and even that interpretation is questionable (see p. 291 below). Unlike Christ, the Spirit is not given an array of *titles* that intimate deity. Nor is there any NT evidence that the Spirit was *worshipped*, doxologized, or prayed to directly. The Spirit is, however, associated with an array of divine *functions*, playing an integral role in creation (Gen. 1:2), in judgment (John 16:8–11), and in re-creation (John 3:5–8). Since the latter – new creation – is such a strong soteriological motif in the NT, this directly associates the Spirit with salvation, an act that can only be performed by God, even though the Spirit is never expressly called Savior.

It is again the Gospel of John that casts this trinitarian person in starkest relief. John does this by analogy to the person of Christ, when Christ himself states that in his absence the Father will send "another Advocate" ("Paraclete") – implying the Son is the first advocate. An eminently personal term, traditionally pronominalized as a "he" (John 14:16–17), the Spirit as Paraclete is sent by Christ (16:7) to glorify him (16:14), instructing the disciples (14:26), and convicting and judging the world (16:8–11). All of these functions distinguish the Spirit's person and work from that of the Father and the Son, indicating that the Spirit is not merely their dynamic, impersonal power or force. In sum, though John's Gospel does not expressly say the Spirit is a third divine person, it strongly suggests as much by its analogy between Christ and the Spirit.

The Spirit's deity is implied even more by the raft of triadic formulae peppered throughout the NT witness.[8] Over and over again, both explicitly and implicitly, the breadth of NT writers place Father, Son, and Holy Spirit

---

[7] See Wainwright, *Trinity*, 199ff., esp. 201, n. 1   [8] Ibid., 237–47.

together in the same breath. The most famous of these texts is the baptism formula of Matthew 28:19: "Go therefore and make disciples of all nations, baptizing them in the name of the Father and of the Son and of the Holy Spirit." What is the name of the God with whom Christian believers identify and to whom they profess their allegiance? The name (singular) of Father, Son, and Holy Spirit. We consider this name to be the most proper name for God disclosed to humanity this side of the eschaton, the penultimate fulfillment of Yahweh's enigmatic promise that "I will be who/ what I will be" (see pp. 79–80). (The ultimate fulfillment will be the eschaton itself, where the Trinity will dwell with us in person in the new heaven and earth – see pp. 410–4.)

The apostle Paul makes frequent use of this triadic pattern. Consider, for example, 1 Corinthians 12:4–6:

Now there are varieties of gifts, but the same Spirit; and there are varieties of services, but the same Lord; and there are varieties of activities, but it is the same God who activates all of them in everyone.

In this text it is the diversity-in-unity of God (Father), Lord (Son), and Spirit (Holy Spirit) that unifies the diversity of spiritual gifts. Or consider the triadic nature of this well-known Pauline benediction: "The grace of the Lord Jesus Christ, the love of God, and the communion of the Holy Spirit be with all of you" (2 Cor. 13:14). Even the book of Revelation highlights this triadic pattern in its opening greeting, albeit in typically figurative fashion:

Grace to you and peace from him who is and who was and who is to come, and from the seven spirits who are before his throne, and from Jesus Christ, the faithful witness, the firstborn of the dead, and the ruler of the kings of the earth. (Rev. 1:4–5)

In short, from Matthew to Revelation, triadic references abound. What they suggest is that the Christian experience of God bears a distinct trinitarian imprint, an irreducible triadic pattern. The Son cannot be reduced to God the Father: he is Christ the Lord. Nor can the Spirit be reduced to the mere power of the Son or the Father: the Spirit is "another Advocate." As the tradition would later put it, God's movement toward humanity both in creation and redemption is "from the Father, through the Son, in the power of the Spirit," while our response to God is, conversely, in the power of the Spirit, through the Son, to the Father. To put it simply, the Christian experience of God is trinitarian; it concerns a relationship with a God whose name is Father, Son, and Holy Spirit.

It was these basic NT materials, including their vectors and implications, that the early church would sift through and reflect on for centuries before formulating the official church dogma of the Trinity, a process fostered by certain proposals that were finally deemed out of bounds as heterodoxy ("other opinion"), or more pejoratively, heresy. Through this historical development, detailed in the next section, the trinitarian confession emerged as the characteristic Christian conception of God, since it was considered the necessary grammar for interpreting the biblical witness.

THE HISTORICAL DEVELOPMENT OF TRINITY DOCTRINE

Church fathers and heresies

The so-called apostolic fathers in the first half of the second century do not really advance the trinitarian issue beyond the NT level of discussion. It was rather the apologists later in that century who first probed the trinitarian issue beyond its NT foundations. In their scholarly endeavors to gain respectability for the Christian faith within a Hellenistic milieu, the apologists eagerly employed the Logos concept, which in the reigning Middle Platonism of the day referred to the (divine) rational structure of the cosmos, which the human rational soul, as microcosm, could discern. This concept seemed to offer a perfect bridge for the Christian gospel, especially since the Gospel of John had identified Christ as the Logos, the Word (1:1), the one who brings light to everyone in the world (1:9). Locating the unity or oneness of God in the "monarchy" (*mone* = one; *arche* = rule) or single rule of the Father, the apologists employed the Stoic distinction between the *immanent Logos* and the *expressed Logos* to account for both the unity and the diversity of the Christian God. As the immanent Logos, Christ is the inner mind or thought of God the Father. As the expressed Logos, Christ is the creative Word that goes forth when the Father decides to create. In this way, Christ is begotten of the Father as the firstborn of creation (Col. 1:15), the wisdom that mediates and inheres in creation (Prov. 8), who ultimately becomes incarnate in Jesus of Nazareth. Since the Logos in Greek philosophy was considered the universal reason of the cosmos, the apologists' "Logos doctrine" was thought to give universal grounds and appeal to Christianity. But the weaknesses of this particular construal would soon appear, not least of which was its total neglect of the place of the Spirit.[9]

---

[9] For a helpful introductory treatment of these early trinitarian developments, see Thomas Marsh, *The Triune God: A Biblical, Historical, and Theological Study* (Mystic, CT: Twenty-Third Publications, 1994), 50–94.

Inheriting this legacy of the apologists, Irenaeus of Lyons (*c.* 130–*c.* 200) devotes greater attention to the roles of both the Son and the Spirit as the "two hands of the Father."[10] Equating the Son with the OT "word" and the Spirit with OT "wisdom" (as did other church fathers), Irenaeus elaborates their roles in the divine "economy" (*oikonomia*) – the first theologian to use this important term. "Economy" (the law [*nomos*] of the household [*oikos*]) has to do with the administration or ordering of affairs – theologically speaking, with the way God administers creation and salvation through the Son and the Spirit. Eventually, the term "economic Trinity" would come to refer to the Trinity as revealed in history – the Father, Son, and Spirit in their dynamic movement in creation and redemption – in distinction from the "immanent Trinity," the Trinity as it is eternally in itself, even apart from creation. But overall, Irenaeus does not provide a substantial or consistent statement on the doctrine of the Trinity.

Of the early church fathers, it was Tertullian (*c.* 160–*c.* 220) who considerably advanced Trinity doctrine, clarifying key trinitarian concepts. Situated in the West, Tertullian writes mostly in Latin and coins many new theological terms. "Trinity" (*trinitas*) is his most famous. "Person" (Lat. *persona* = Gk. *prosopon*, most literally "face") is his most controversial. Tertullian uses "person" as the threeness or differentiating term for Father, Son, and Spirit, by which he means a distinct individual existence. In order to fully appreciate his employment of this term, however, it is necessary to identify a trinitarian proposal that Tertullian was attempting to rule out – namely, that of *modalism.*

As Christ was recognized as truly divine, yet, as the Logos, was distinguished from God the Father, some Christians became anxious that the monotheistic principle or oneness of God was being compromised. At this time the divine unity was understood to reside in the monarchy, the single rule or authority of God the Father. Zealous for both the deity of Christ and the strict oneness of God, as strongly reinforced by a commitment to divine simplicity, some regarded Christ as a *mere manifestation* of God the Father. Later termed "modalism," this position took a variety of forms, but its common denominator was the denial of any real and enduring personal distinction between Father, Son, and Spirit. Such distinctions were regarded as only apparent in revelation, differing manifestations of the one monarch, the one person of God. The most famous statement of this

---

[10] Irenaeus, *Against Heresies*, ed. A. Cleveland Coxe, in *Ante-Nicene Fathers*, ed. Alexander Roberts and James Donaldson (Grand Rapids, MI: Eerdmans, 1993), 1: 4.20.1; 5.1.3; 5.5.1; 5.6.1.

position is the one associated with Sabellius, to the extent that "Sabellianism" has become a synonym for modalism.

Sabellius (early third century) apparently believed that in the divine economy the one God (a singular divine monad) engages in three different operations or "modes" of self-expression – hence the term "modalism." As Creator, the one God is the Father; as redeemer the Son; as sanctifier, the bestower of grace and eternal life, the Holy Spirit. One might imagine here one real-life actor playing three different roles in three successive scenes: creation, redemption, sanctification. Father, Son, and Spirit therefore are merely names for the one divine actor, the one monarch and person that God is. One implication of this teaching is that the Christ suffering on the cross is also actually the Father – thus the term *Patripassianism* ("the Father suffers") became a code word for modalism, considered problematic in doctrinal history not only because of its association with modalism, but also because it violated the assumed axiom of divine apathy or impassibility.

It was his argument with the modalist Praxeas, who collapsed the trinitarian members into "the very selfsame Person,"[11] that occasioned Tertullian's clarification of "person" as the basic threeness term. Citing the Father–Son relation in John's Gospel (e.g., John 10:30: "I and the Father are one" – "are" as a *plural* verb), Tertullian argued that the trinitarian members were distinct agents, persons that can be counted – distinct but not divided, discrete but not separated. Moreover, he suggested that just as a single human monarchy could be administered by several persons – for example, by a father and son together – so too could the divine monarchy. This led Tertullian to introduce a new term for the divine unity, that of the divine *substance* (*substantia*) – what Father and Son possess in common, by nature – in place of the reigning concept of divine unity, that of the single monarchy of the Father. This development is significant because the subsequent western tradition would gravitate to "substance" as its principal concept of divine oneness, while the eastern tradition would continue to incline to the person of the Father. But for all his gains in trinitarian thought, Tertullian himself was still plagued by the apologists' Logos model in which the Son and the Spirit do not appear to be distinct persons until their expression in and with creation (i.e., their begottenness and procession by the will of the Father for the purpose of creation and redemption). In short, Tertullian's is still a mere economic trinitarianism.

---

[11] Tertullian, *Against Praxeas*, trans. Peter Holmes, ed. A. Cleveland Coxe, in *Ante-Nicene Fathers*, ed. Alexander Roberts and James Donaldson (Grand Rapids, MI: Eerdmans, 1993), ch. 2 (III: 598).

It would be the eminent eastern theologian Origen (185–254) who would clarify personal distinction in the eternal Trinity itself. In his systematic work *On First Principles*, Origen describes each trinitarian member as a *hypostasis*, considering each a distinct individual existence in the Godhead.[12] *Hypostasis* would eventually come to function together with Tertullian's *persona* and its Greek equivalent *prosopon* as personal, differentiating terms for the threeness of God (see Table 5.1). With respect to the Father and Son relation, Origen asserts that the Son is eternally begotten from the Father, a generation "as eternal and everlasting as the brilliancy which is produced from the sun."[13] This means that the Son was "never at any time non-existent."[14] Similarly, the Spirit's existence and procession are eternal, which Origen treats more fully than his predecessors. For Origen, the Father communicates his deity to the Son and to the Spirit eternally. It is in this affirmation that he goes beyond the economic trinitarianism of Tertullian and other early church fathers, for whom the Son and the Spirit become distinct persons only in creative or redemptive expression. By placing such personal distinctions eternally in God, Origen secures the immanent Trinity – God as triune in God's own being even apart from creation. As the later tradition will affirm, God is Father, Son, and Spirit by nature, not by will or decision.

While Origen anticipates the main lines of what would become trinitarian orthodoxy in the "Cappadocian settlement" around the Council of Constantinople (381), it took the fourth-century Arian controversy to push the early church to the clarification of this doctrine. Instigated by Arius (*c.* 250–*c.* 336), a priest in the Alexandrian church, this particular debate served to clarify the subordinationist tendency in much emergent trinitarian thinking (including even some inconsistent threads in Origen's thought) that regarded Christ the Son as substantially inferior to the Father. In tandem with modalism, Arianism represents a second major foil in the development of trinitarian doctrine. While modalism recognizes the Son's full deity, but absorbs his distinct personhood into that of the single monarchical person that God finally is, Arianism, conversely, recognizes the Son's full and distinct personhood, but subordinates him in deity to God the Father.

[12] Origen, *De Principiis*, trans. Frederick Crombie, ed. A. Cleveland Coxe, in *Ante-Nicene Fathers*, ed. Alexander Roberts and James Donaldson (Grand Rapids, MI: Eerdmans, 1950–1), 1.2.2 (IV: p. 246); 1.1.3 (IV: p. 243).
[13] Ibid., 1.2.9 (p. 247).   [14] Ibid., 1.2.9 (p. 249).

Endorsing a strict monotheistic concept of God as indivisible, immutable, and incommunicable – one divine Monad properly referred to as God the Father – Arius held that Christ the Son as a discrete person could not share this same divine nature. Rather, Arius considered Christ the preeminent creature, "the firstborn of creation" (Col. 1:15), created by the Father's will for the purpose of mediating between the eternal, immutable, unknowable God and the temporal, suffering, searching world – a metaphysical bridge between God and humanity. Though the Arians worshipped Christ together with the Father, he was not accorded the same divine status, since, taking Christ's begottenness from the Father in stricter analogy to human begottenness, they affirmed – in pointed contradiction to Origen – that "there was [a time] when he was not."[15]

The Arian position was censured at the first ecumenical council at Nicea in 325. Convened by the first Christian emperor, Constantine, to quell this potentially destabilizing controversy that was upsetting the empire, the bishops at Nicea declared that Christ the Son was *homoousios* – "of the same essence" – with God the Father. In pointed condemnation of Arius' position, they declared that Christ possessed a divine status and dignity equal to that of the Father.

But Nicea did not end the Arian controversy. In addition to many political factors and machinations, much of the controversy concerned the sense and propriety of the Nicene Creed's key term. *Homoousios* was a highly freighted philosophical term that admitted a range of meanings. Its employment at Nicea actually hardened the resolve of many Arians, since this philosophical term did not reflect the "common sense" language of the Bible, as well as its images of Christ as "begotten" (John 1:14, NASB), as "firstborn of creation" (Col. 1:15), or as the "wisdom brought forth by God" (Prov. 8:25ff.). To the Arians such biblical imagery proved that Christ was of creaturely status, and therefore only "similar to" (*homoios*) or "unlike" (*anomoios*) the Father. The vast majority of the eastern church, however, was also suspicious of the Nicene *homoousios* because it was eagerly embraced by the modalists to identify Father and Son as the same identical person or being. Their suspicion was reinforced by the fact that the original creed drafted at Nicea (not yet the version of the Nicene Creed confessed today) used the term *hypostasis*, which, in the East since Origen, had been

---

[15] Cited by Alexander of Alexandria in his attack on Arianism. In William G. Rusch, ed. and trans., *The Trinitarian Controversy*, Sources of Early Christian Thought (Philadelphia: Fortress, 1980), 35. Alexander's reference reflects Arius' own statement, as expressed in his letter to Eusebius of Nicomedia (ibid., 30).

used for differentiating the three divine persons, as a synonym or equivalent for *ousia*, the accepted oneness term, encouraging the perception that Nicea posited only one person of the divine being. Due to this modalist interpretation of Nicea, many in the East preferred the term *homoiousios* – "of similar substance" – to secure both Christ's deity with the Father and their personal distinction.

It was in this theologically fluid and politically unstable situation that Athanasius (*c.* 295–373) arose as the champion of Nicene orthodoxy. Athanasius attacked the Arian interpretation of scripture, arguing that it focused too selectively and too literally on certain biblical texts (cited above) without taking into account the larger drift and scope of scripture that secures Christ's deity. Athanasius emphasized that specific, individual texts must be read in light of the whole Bible, whose overall sense might be rendered more precisely and faithfully in extrabiblical words and terms, such as the term *homoousios*. In his theological hermeneutic Athanasius passionately held that Christ had to be God, not simply on account of the biblical materials as a whole, but because otherwise we could not through Christ become "partakers of the divine nature" (2 Pet. 1:4) – a key soteriological motif in eastern Christian thought (i.e., deification – see pp. 268–70 below). He also argued that God could not be "Father" by nature unless he eternally had a "Son," which implies the Son's deity. In his theological labors Athanasius helped to clarify key trinitarian issues, arguing strongly for the deity of the Holy Spirit (*Letters to Serapion*), as well as, finally, the distinction between *hypostasis* and *ousia* that Nicea appeared to conflate. In these endeavors Athanasius was able to convince many *homoiousios* proponents of their conceptual kinship with Nicea, which led to the broader eastern acceptance of the *homoousios*, resulting in united stands against both modalism and Arianism. This winning of the East was significantly aided by the work of three theologians from the province of Cappadocia in Asia Minor, who in taking up Athanasius' cause would further clarify the orthodox logic and terminology of the doctrine of the Trinity.

The Cappadocians and the East

Basil of Caesarea (d. 379), his younger brother Gregory of Nyssa (d. *c.* 395), and their friend Gregory of Nazianzus (d. 389) are known as the Cappadocian Fathers. Their various writings and influence upon the second ecumenical council at Constantinople (381) settled the trinitarian question confessionally for the church. They accomplished this settlement in two major ways.

First, they clarified the status of the Holy Spirit. Against those who in an Arian vein subordinated the Spirit to the Father, called *pneumatomachians* ("fighters against the Spirit") among other names, Basil (*On the Holy Spirit*) and Gregory of Nazianzus (*Theological Orations*) argued strongly for the deity of the Spirit as a third divine person. Gregory even used the Nicene *homoousios* to describe the Spirit's relationship to Father and Son.[16] The deity of the Spirit was affirmed as official orthodoxy by the Council of Constantinople (381), called by Emperor Theodosius I to unite the eastern church in the Nicene faith. What we today call the Nicene Creed is the product of this council's expansion and modification of the creed issued at Nicea (325). In this Niceno-Constantinopolitan Creed, as it is sometimes named, the Spirit's deity is secured by calling the Spirit "the Lord" (the divine title based on 2 Cor. 3:17), "and Giver of life" (the divine function of creating and re-creating), "who together with the Father and the Son is worshipped and glorified" (a clear statement of divine worship). With the recognition of the Spirit's deity, the trinitarian issue was finally fully trinitarian.

Second, the Cappadocians clarified the essential logic and terminology for Trinity doctrine. What Nicea had confusingly used as synonyms for the divine essence, *ousia* and *hypostasis*, the Cappadocians clearly distinguished. They used *ousia* for the one divine essence or nature that Father, Son, and Spirit share, and, following Origen's lead, used *hypostasis* for each of the three persons. The technical trinitarian formula became "three *hypostaseis* (persons) and one *ousia* (essence)." The way that Basil explained this basic terminological distinction is as follows:

> The distinction between *ousia* and *hypostasis* is the same as that between the general and the particular; as, for instance, between the animal [i.e., genus] and the particular man. Wherefore, in the case of the Godhead, we confess one essence or substance so as not to give a variant definition of existence, but we confess a particular hypostasis in order that our conception of Father, Son and Holy Spirit may be without confusion and clear.[17]

Following Basil's lead, Gregory of Nyssa utilizes this distinction in his "three men" analogy for the Trinity. Peter, James, and John – the inner

---

[16] Gregory of Nazianzus, *The Theological Orations*, trans. Charles Gordon Browne and James Edward Swallow, in *Christology of the Later Fathers*, ed. Edward Rochie Hardy and Cyril C. Richardson, Library of Christian Classics (Philadelphia: Westminster, 1954), 199.

[17] Basil of Caesarea, "Letter 236," trans. Blomfield Jackson, in *Nicene and Post-Nicene Fathers*, 2nd series, ed. Philip Schaff and Henry Wace (Grand Rapids, MI: Eerdmans, 1993), VIII: 278.

Table 5.1 *Trinitarian terminology*

Threeness (differentiating) terms		
Greek	*Latin*	*English*
Prosopon	Persona	Person
Hypostasis	Subsistentia	Hypostasis/subsistence/person
Oneness (unifying) terms		
Greek	*Latin*	*English*
Ousia	Substantia	Essence/substance
Physis	Natura	Nature
Theos	Deus	God
Theotes	Deitas	Deity/divinity/Godhead/Godhood

circle of disciples – though three particular men, are nonetheless participants in one humanity since they all possess the same general human
essence or nature. Gregory propounds this analogy in his *On Not Three
Gods* in defense of the charge that positing three distinct persons in God
entails tritheism. Gregory of Nazianzus also employed this distinction and
experimented with a social analogy for the Trinity, reflecting on the primal
family of Adam, Eve, and Seth as an example of how different persons are
unified in nature.[18] While the clarity and consistency of the social model in
the Cappadocians is compromised by their commitment to a Platonic
conception of universals, as well as by the encroachment of divine simplicity, they are generally credited with maintaining a crisper distinction of the
trinitarian persons than their western counterpart Augustine. Since Father,
Son, and Spirit are quite evidently individuated by distinguishing characteristics (e.g., fatherhood, sonship, spiration), they constitute three personal
existents or *hypostaseis* (*contra* modalism) who share the same divine nature
or *ousia* (*contra* Arianism) – three persons in one God. Table 5.1 clarifies the
basic trinitarian terminology, including parallel terms, Greek and Latin
equivalents, and English translations.

   Beyond settling the basic trinitarian definition for the church at large, the
Cappadocians' explorations put a particular imprint on the eastern approach,
which generally maintains a greater emphasis on the threeness of the trinitarian
persons than the western approach. For this reason, the important trinitarian
notion of *perichoresis* took its rise in the East, as first found in John of
Damascus' *The Orthodox Faith* (eighth century). Based on the sublime oneness
or "in-ness" of Father and Son in John's Gospel (e.g., 10:30), *perichoresis*

---

[18] See Gregory of Nyssa, "Answer to Ablabius," and Gregory of Nazianzus, *Theological Orations*, in
   Hardy and Richardson, *Christology of the Later Fathers*, 256–67, 128–214.

connotes "mutual indwelling," "interpenetration," "fellowship," and functioned to shore up the unity of the Trinity in light of the distinction of persons. The strong trinitarianism of the eastern church is manifest by its centrality in the Orthodox liturgy as well as in its iconography, as seen in Andrei Rublev's famous Trinity icon (*c.* 1425 – see Illustration 5.2). Here the Trinity is adumbrated as three distinct, angelic persons who are lovingly, perichoretically inclined to one another – an image which both mirrors and invites participation in the trinitarian life. Given these perduring liturgical and artistic representations of trinitarian faith, this doctrine did not historically experience the same decline in the East as it did in the modern West.[19]

Augustine and the West

Augustine of Hippo is the patriarch of the western doctrine of the Trinity. His *On The Trinity*, written over the course of some twenty years, represents his seasoned trinitarian thought that would long influence the western church. In his extensive reflections, Augustine gives primacy to the one divine substance as the trinitarian point of departure, after which, secondarily, the three divine persons are considered and accommodated. In this way Augustine takes up Tertullian's introduction of the term "substance" for the divine unity and makes it his primary reference for "God," in contrast to the Cappadocian penchant for beginning with the persons and giving primacy to the Father as the principle of divine unity. Augustine specifically rejects Nyssa's three-men analogy,[20] and is quite uncomfortable with the notion of "person" in trinitarian description: "Yet when you ask 'Three what?' human speech labors under a great dearth of words. So we say three persons, not in order to say that precisely, but in order not to be reduced to silence."[21] In point of fact, given Augustine's strong commitment to divine simplicity (reinforced by his Neoplatonic background), which allows only one substantial thing in God, the trinitarian "persons" or hypostases are not ultimately discrete entities, but they reduce to sheer "relations" within the one divine substance: the Father *just is* the individuating characteristic of fatherhood (*paternitas*), the Son *is* the relation of sonship (*filiatio*), and the Spirit *is* merely the characteristic of being breathed out (*spiratio*).[22]

---

[19] The strong mystical and apophatic orientation of Orthodox theology, however, did at times impair the distinction of trinitarian persons, as in the later Palamite tradition (fourteenth century) that made such a strong distinction between the divine essence and divine energies, the former of which was considered unknowable and with which the divine persons were associated (see pp. 452–3 below).

[20] Augustine, *The Trinity*, 7.11 (pp. 229–30).   [21] Ibid., 5.10 (p. 196).   [22] E.g., ibid., 5.6 (p. 191–2).

Augustine also proposed a series of analogies in his quest to better understand the Trinity. Taking a cue from Genesis 1:26, he reasoned that if God is truly a Trinity who creates humanity in the divine image and likeness, then we ought to find in human beings a trinitarian imprint or vestige that could illumine our trinitarian confession. That likeness which Augustine identified as the comparative point of the *imago Dei* was, in characteristic Greek fashion, the rational soul. Human beings are like God by virtue of their rationality. With a little help from Plato's illumination doctrine, Augustine discerned a threefold division of the rational soul into mind, knowledge, and love,[23] or memory, understanding, and will,[24] among other tripartite variations,[25] corresponding to Father, Son, and Spirit, respectively. Augustine's preference for a psychological analogy – faculties of one *psyche* or mind – would significantly influence the course of western trinitarianism.

Augustine also experimented with a love analogy, proposing that three essential components of love – the Lover, the Beloved, and the bond of Love the two share – mirror the Father, Son, and Spirit.[26] While Augustine himself does not push this analogy, his emphasis in other writings on the Spirit as the gift and bond of Love between Father and Son, along with this analogy's parallelism with a psychological analogy, accounts for the western emphasis on the double procession of the Spirit from the Father *and the Son* – the *filioque* clause added later by the West to the Nicene Creed that would contribute to the formal split with the eastern church in 1054. The filioque controversy (see pp. 295–6, 301–3, 456–8) underscores the difference of trinitarian approach between East and West.

Later in the course of western trinitarianism, Richard of St. Victor (d. 1173) proposed a more robust love analogy, arguing that the claim "God is love" (1 John 4:8) logically requires a plurality of divine persons since love is supremely a predicate of persons-in-right-relation. If God were not personally differentiated in God's self, God could not be "love" before creation, apart from someone else to love. In fact, Richard contended that this necessitated at least *three* divine persons, since love in its noblest expression is always a "shared love" of two for a third (see pp. 465–6).

But Richard's was a minority voice. The majority of western theologians followed the lead of Augustine and his psychological analogies, especially as scholastically endorsed and embellished by Thomas Aquinas. We noted in the previous chapter the formal shift made by Thomas in the doctrine of God, treating first the doctrine of the One God – the existence, nature, and attributes of God *simpliciter*, largely through human reason – before

---

[23] Ibid., Book 9.   [24] Ibid., Books 10 and 14.   [25] Ibid., Books 11–13.   [26] Ibid., 8.14 (p. 255).

addressing the revealed conception of the Trinity. This methodological approach in itself reinforces the Augustinian penchant for prioritizing the one divine substance over the persons of the Trinity. In Thomas's formal treatment of the trinitarian processions, persons, and relations, the analogy of the divine intellect (i.e., rational soul) is controlling, and it is even clearer here than in Augustine that the persons reduce to "subsistent relations."[27] Thomas's account of the Trinity would become standard textbook fare in the western theological tradition in both Catholic and Protestant orthodox circles.

The modern demise of Trinity doctrine

The Enlightenment posed a rigorous intellectual challenge to traditional Christianity. Its heady confidence in the ability of human reason to map the world and chart the course of life without recourse to traditional authority or supernatural ideas conspired against Christian teaching, the doctrine of the Trinity notwithstanding. Where these Enlightenment currents did not lead to atheism, they reinforced forms of unitarianism, as in Deism, which boasted a strict monotheism that reduced Christ to a mere human teacher and moral example. The received doctrine of the Trinity as fathered by Augustine and developed by Aquinas was found wanting, owing in no small measure to its perceived irrationality and impracticality. It was especially the claim that God is a simple, indivisible spiritual entity but also three distinct, discrete persons that aroused jeers about "the incomprehensible jargon of the Trinitarian arithmetic, that three are one, and one is three."[28] Immanuel Kant, the Enlightenment champion of a rational and ethical religion, made this famous pronouncement: "The doctrine of the Trinity, taken literally, has *no practical relevance at all*, even if we think we understand it; and it is even more clearly irrelevant if we realize that it transcends all our concepts."[29]

Taking up modern advances and challenges in his theological program, Friedrich Schleiermacher, the "father of modern theology," made little use of the doctrine of the Trinity. Due to its ostensible logical problems and lack of immediacy to Christian piety, Schleiermacher treated it only summarily at the conclusion of his magisterial *The Christian Faith*. Thus it is typically said of

---

[27] Thomas Aquinas, *Summa Theologica*, 1.27–43, esp. 39–41.

[28] Thomas Jefferson's ridicule of the doctrine in a letter to Timothy Pickering, cited in Thomas Cuming Hall, *The Religious Background of American Culture* (Boston: Little, Brown, & Co., 1930), 172.

[29] Immanuel Kant, *The Conflict of the Faculties*, trans. Mary J. Gregor (New York: Abaris, 1979), 65, italics original.

Schleiermacher, whose own sympathies toward the Trinity were distinctly Sabellian, that he relegated the Trinity to the status of a mere appendix to theology. Schleiermacher's legacy to Albrecht Ritschl (1822–89), the "father of liberal theology," was effectively unitarian, a tendency that is vividly seen in the last great Ritschlian, Adolf von Harnack (1851–1930). Harnack considered such dogmatic formulations as the Trinity to be the weedy intrusion of Greek philosophy on the soil of the simple gospel that Jesus preached, which was more meagerly concerned with the fatherhood of God, the brotherhood of man, and the commandment to love (see p. 528).[30]

A trinitarian renaissance

As the twentieth century dawned, the doctrine of the Trinity was being either pronounced dead by the rationalists, liberally effaced by the unitarians, or tediously transmitted in rather embalmed scholastic form by the Catholic and Protestant orthodox – that is, until Karl Barth entered the scene.[31] It was Barth who instigated the reconsideration and renewal of Trinity doctrine that is flourishing today. Bucking the Thomistic trend of subordinating the Trinity to the doctrine of the One God, Barth nestled the Trinity at the very beginning of his magisterial *Church Dogmatics*, making this doctrine part and parcel of his emphasis upon God's self-revelation as the theological point of departure.[32] For Barth the very analysis of Christian revelation cannot but evoke discussion of the Trinity. In restoring revelation to its prominence, Barth therefore elevated the Trinity as the leitmotif and interpretive key for the whole breadth of Christian theology, a theological corrective of its eclipse since Schleiermacher.

Yet, Barth's trinitarian initiatives did not really catch on in the "neo-orthodox" movement launched by his program. Surprisingly, the movement's strong christological concentration did not so much blossom into a vibrant trinitarianism. Hence Karl Rahner's lament in the late 1960s that Christians were still practically "mere monotheists." To ameliorate this situation Rahner proposed his own constructive statement of the Trinity governed by the rule: the economic Trinity is the immanent Trinity and vice versa.[33] That is to say, the God who is revealed to us in the history of salvation as Father, Son, and Spirit (the economic Trinity) is truly who God

---

[30] See Adolf von Harnack, *What is Christianity?*, trans. Thomas Bailey Saunders (New York: Harper & Row, 1957), lecture 4, pp. 57–74.
[31] On this renaissance, see Thompson, "Trinitarianism Today," 10–19.
[32] Barth, *Church Dogmatics*, I/1: 295–489.   [33] Rahner, *Trinity*, 23.

is eternally, apart from creation, in God's self (the immanent Trinity). Similar to Barth, Rahner's primary intent with this rule was to overcome the dichotomy in the doctrine of God between treating God first simply as One (God *simpliciter*) and only then to consider God as Trinity, revealed in God's economy or actions toward us. The myopic emphasis on the doctrine of the One God tended to subordinate, if not defeat, trinitarian distinctions and resources. Happily, Rahner's lament and rule instigated a new level of inquiry in Catholic and Protestant circles that has led to a veritable renaissance in trinitarian thought.

The key to this western trinitarian renaissance has been a shift to a more personalist, dynamic, and relational approach to the doctrine of God. As the modern world became more historically oriented, history came more fully into its own as an important category of truth, and the God–world relation was understood in more dynamic terms. This development encouraged theology to emphasize the God revealed in history – as a Trinity of persons – and to prioritize the data of the biblical narrative over traditional philosophical perspectives on God – as absolute being or supreme substance, rooted in a cosmological approach (i.e., the One and the many; see pp. 84–6, 99–101). Moreover, the postmodern penchant to view things contextually and holistically, in reaction to the individualizing and objectivizing strains of modern thought, has led to more relational accents in theology, emphasizing the interpersonal or social dynamic of humanity in its environment. These developing theological sensitivities to the personal, historical, and relational inevitably highlighted the trinitarian God – as three persons in dynamic, interpersonal relation. We regard these as welcome developments in theology since they accentuate the Trinity as a ready foundation and resource for the gamut of Christian doctrines. While this book will highlight the trinitarian resources for various doctrines at their appropriate junctures, such applications still turn on the particular model of the Trinity that one finally embraces.

A SYSTEMATIC CONSIDERATION OF THE TRINITY

A typology of models

In order to evaluate the doctrine of the Trinity systematically in quest of a vital trinitarian confession and practice, it will be helpful to work with a typology of trinitarian models. This is a typical systematic strategy: map out a variety of options or possibilities on a given theological issue (many times by means of models), assess their respective strengths and weaknesses, and be honest about which option one deems "best," that is, most responsible in view of one's theological criteria – in our case, the threefold criteria of orthodoxy, coherence, and relevance.

Every useful typology is governed by a clearly defined issue or set of issues. The fundamental issue that shapes the following trinitarian typology is the question of *divine personhood*. This has historically been the most difficult of trinitarian issues: just what is meant by "person" in the confession "three persons in one God"? That God is personal has hardly been disputed in the history of Christian thought. But just how this personal dimension is to be understood in a trinitarian framework has been much debated and has led to different approaches to the Trinity.

Let us suppose that a person constitutes a center of thought, will, act, love, and therefore consciousness. This low-level description of personhood is quite uncontroversial; most of us would easily attribute it to any human person. But we could also quite easily attribute it to God in general – would it not fit, for example, Yahweh in the OT? Such a description, however, has been controversial when applied to the trinitarian members severally. Given this working definition of "person," we can map out three basic positions on the Trinity that have arisen in doctrinal history and remain in debate today.[34] These positions would suggest, differently, that God-as-Trinity is

One Person existent as Father, Son, and Spirit (1)

Three Persons – Father, Son, and Spirit – who are also One (Person?) (3 = 1)

Three Persons – Father, Son, and Spirit – who together comprise the one true God (3)

The crucial difference between these three options is this: given our working definition of person, the first option holds that God-as-Trinity is supremely one divine person (1); the third position opts for three divine persons (3); and the middle option seems to want it both ways: three persons on the one hand, yet finally one divine person on the other hand (3 = 1).

Before we begin our analysis of these three positions, it is important to keep in mind the creedal parameters for an orthodox doctrine of the Trinity. These are tersely summarized in the Athanasian Creed, verse 4, which indicates that if one wants to confess the Trinity rightly, one must neither "confuse the persons," which has the modalist heresy in view, nor "divide the essence," which has the Arian heresy in view. These are the foul lines for trinitarian orthodoxy. Any position that follows these creedal rules is a fair trinitarian proposal.

---

[34] The following typology is based on that proposed by Cornelius Plantinga Jr., "The Threeness/ Oneness Problem of the Trinity," *Calvin Theological Journal* 23 (1988), 37–53.

The western paradoxical Trinity

We begin our analysis with the middle option (3 = 1), since this is the model that best represents the classic western trinitarianism of the Augustinian-Thomistic tradition. This is the position rather crassly reflected in the opening dialogue from the film *Nuns on the Run*. In this model, the Trinity appears to be a mathematical conundrum of three equaling one, the kind of view that roused the scorn of Thomas Jefferson and other Enlightenment deists. Because it possesses this paradoxical character, we will call it the western paradoxical model. Theologians who hold this view do not formulate the position in quite these contradictory terms, but we will see why it often leaves this impression. While we attempt to explain this model fairly, it will become clear that we ultimately consider it lacking.

This model of the Trinity presupposes divine *simplicity*, the idea that God is a single, simple being. Assumed by most early Christian thinkers, simplicity was especially prominent in Augustine's construal of the Trinity (particularly in *On the Trinity*, Books 5–7) and has continued in his legacy. If the teaching of divine simplicity is sound, then there can only be one "thing" in God. Therefore, if one wants to affirm, on the one hand, that Father, Son, and Spirit are "persons" in any discrete, distinct way (as in Tertullian's use of *persona* or Origen's and the Cappadocians' understanding of *hypostasis*), then to also affirm, on the other hand, that God is one simple, single thing requires quite a juggling act. The assumption of simplicity leaves a rather indeterminate place for the three persons. Each person in fact becomes identical with the one simple thing that God is (as in our opening dialogue: "they're all one and the same thing"). The three persons as concrete existent entities must be identical with the numerically singular thing that God is, since God's simplicity admits of no divisions, distinctions, or parts. Most Christians have never even heard of simplicity as a divine attribute, but it is the theological underpinning of the western "paradoxical" view of the Trinity.

Echoing Augustine's reservations about the notion of "person," proponents of this model tend to identify the trinitarian persons as "relations" within the one divine essence. The notion of a "subsistent relation" – a conceptual half-breed between Aristotle's categories of substance and accident – was introduced by Augustine and developed by Aquinas in order to account for the distinctions of Father, Son, and Spirit in the Godhead. Since, on the assumption of simplicity, there can be only one substantial thing in the divine essence, the divine persons cannot be discrete "things" in their own right. They therefore reduce to the *sheer* relations of fatherhood (*paternitas*), sonship (*filiation*) and spiration (*spiratio*) that are somehow subsistent in the one God. The Father, for example, just is fatherhood, and the Son is sonship. But what is a "sheer relation"? We really don't know, because we have no experience of one. In human experience, relations exist between concrete, distinctive things, most notably persons. A daughter's relationship with her mother, for example, is based on both being concrete individual persons. A sheer relation is when you take away both mother and daughter as distinct personal entities and simply have the abstracted "relation" of "daughterhood" or "motherhood." In our experience, this is unimaginable, yet this is what the western paradoxical view affirms about God: the divine persons are really relations. Such is the complexity created by divine simplicity.

This analysis suggests that this view nominally affirms the three persons, but only through the concept of "subsistent relations." Due to the pressure of divine simplicity any common-sense notion of "person," as in our working definition, can only be attributed to the oneness of God – the one substantial "thing" that God is. If the three persons are identical to the one divine substance, and therefore identical with one another, then they appear to be one. One what? One person – one singular consciousness (3 = 1).

Given that this model suggests a logical contradiction, why has it been so prevalent and popular in the western tradition? A first reason is the commonly held intuition that belief in one God entails that God is one single thing or person. We can call this the "monotheistic intuition." This common impression is reinforced by a number of factors, particularly (a) philosophical monotheism (think of Thomas's Five Ways) in which human reason can discern only one first divine principle, be it one Mover, Cause, or Mind; (b) the OT portrayal of Yahweh as ostensibly one personal agent (though we should keep in mind the roles of Spirit, Wisdom, and Word noted above); and (c) the NT, which continues the OT portrayal by principally identifying "God" with the person of the Father. But the latter, we have seen, is not exclusively true, since the Son is also considered divine, as is the Spirit. The bottom line: the monotheistic intuition does not pan out or prove true. If this were the biblical sense of monotheism, it is hard to see how the doctrine of the Trinity could even begin to take shape in the first place, since it requires a plurality of persons in God – most starkly suggested by the relationship between the Father and the incarnate Son. Yet many people tacitly or unconsciously hold this "intuition," which is a significant reason why the Trinity seems for them to be a mathematical conundrum of three persons equaling one person. It is therefore important in evaluating these different models of the Trinity to bracket this problematic intuition or tacit assumption, and to remember that biblical monotheism has everything to do with the Creator/creature divide, rather than with God simply being a singular person.

A second basic reason why in this model three persons appear to collapse into one person has to do with Augustine's influence. Augustine's psychological analogy for the Trinity became standard fare in western trinitarianism for centuries and continues to have considerable influence today. His basic method is sound: if God is a Trinity and has created humanity in the divine image (*imago Dei*), then a trinitarian imprint or vestige ought to be found in the human image. But Augustine's choice of a psychological approach is questionable. While one could ask whether the rational soul so easily admits of three distinct faculties, a more important question is whether the "rational soul" is the best candidate for the point of divine likeness in humanity in the first place. We will argue that a more biblical understanding of the divine image in humanity points to *persons* in relation (cf. Gen. 1:27; see pp. 189–94 below), a likeness that better reflects the portrayal of Father, Son, and Spirit as distinct but interrelated players in the divine drama. But here is the major point: if one's primary analogy for the Trinity is a *one-person* analogy – three faculties of one rational soul, one individual psyche – it is easy to see how the confession of three persons keeps reducing to one person.

A third major reason for the collapse of three persons into one is one we've already seen – the assumption of divine simplicity. If divine simplicity is axiomatic, then there can be only one singular "thing" in God. The three persons must be identical with this one "thing," which is generally depicted as a single person. But we have seen in the previous chapter the metaphysical logic of divine simplicity and the biblical grounds for questioning it. It appears to be a proposition of natural theology that has no warrant in the Bible itself and therefore is open to revision. But it more than any other factor produces the popular impression that in confessing the Trinity the Christian is affirming that three persons are also at the same time one person – that three equals one.

It is clear from our analysis that we consider this model to have its share of shortcomings. But what are the strengths of the western paradoxical model to which its proponents commonly point? For one, it is strongly traditional, rooted in an august theological patriarch, Augustine, and endorsed by a gallery of eminent western theologians. For another, it has a strong unity claim, emphatically securing the oneness of God. For yet another, it seems to preserve a strong sense of the mystery of the Trinity, which is especially attractive to those inclined to think that God in principle is "beyond our understanding."

But strengths, when pushed too far, can also be weaknesses. For one, the theological enterprise is all about clarifying our understanding of God (and the world, and their relation). Mystery notwithstanding, we need to ask questions, to probe, to see if we can gain a better understanding of our faith, including the Trinity, since faith by its very nature seeks understanding (*fides quaerens intellectum*). Second, one can have too strong a divine unity claim if it does not maintain the distinction of persons, which the western paradoxical model arguably does not, laying it open to the charge that it actually "confuses the persons" – one of the foul lines in the Athanasian Creed (i.e., modalism).[35] Third, while tradition is an important and eminent dialogue partner, it does not have the last word in systematic – and therefore constructive – theology. The biblical narrative must be consulted again and again in the continuing theological quest for a right understanding of God.

The neo-modal Trinity

Let us now consider the first option, which we will call the neo-modal model of the Trinity.[36] Given our working definition of personhood, this view posits that God-as-Trinity is supremely one person. If we were to understand this proposal in the sense that God is one person *manifest* as Father, Son, and Spirit, then we would be back to classic modalism along the lines of Sabellius, where the divine "persons" are simply names or roles for various manifestations of the one divine actor. The early church, we have seen, censured this position since it "confuses the persons" – a heresy ruled out of bounds by the Athanasian Creed.

But the stated sense of this option, one person *existent* as Father, Son, and Spirit, captures well both Karl Barth's and Karl Rahner's similar trinitarian proposals, so instrumental in the recent trinitarian resurgence. In their highly sophisticated theologies, Barth and Rahner are united in maintaining a singular subjectivity of God's self-revelation or self-communication of grace. They are not convinced that the early church understood the notion of trinitarian "person" in any common-sense way (as in our working definition), especially if *self-consciousness* is regarded as an essential constituent of personhood. They prefer instead to think of the trinitarian "persons" as God's eternal "modes of being" (Barth) or "manners of subsisting"

---

[35] Such an assessment is reflected in Adolf von Harnack's oft-quoted remark concerning Augustine's Trinity doctrine that he "only gets beyond Modalism by the mere assertion that he does not wish to be a Modalist, and by the aid of ingenious distinctions between different ideas." *History of Dogma*, trans. E. B. Speirs and James Millar (London: Williams & Norgate, 1898), IV: 130–1, n. 1.

[36] To describe this trinitarian model we borrow the label "neo-modal" from William J. Hill, *The Three-Personed God: The Trinity as a Mystery of Salvation* (Washington DC: Catholic University Press, 1982).

(Rahner), with our definition of personhood applying only to the one God singularly.[37] By positing that these modes or manners are eternal, they lay claim to an immanent Trinity, which distinguishes their position from Sabellius' sheer economic trinitarianism.

One strength of the neo-modal model is its coherence, since it is more thinkable than the western paradoxical view. It is easier to imagine one person playing three different roles, or being in three different modes or manners *at the same time*, than it is to envision one person also being three persons. For example, one can easily think of Bill Gates simultaneously being the president of Microsoft, the father of his children, and a waxing humanitarian.

A second strength of the neo-modal view, like the western paradoxical position, is its unity claim. In this model, however, the oneness of God is secured primarily in the supreme person that God is (which Barth and Rahner largely identify with the Father), not in the divine essence. But like the western view, herein lies a weakness of the neo-modal view, namely, its apparent depreciation of the distinction of the trinitarian persons. Barth and Rahner have been routinely criticized for their "modalistic" tendency, since critics have found the terms "modes" or "manners" deficient in their ability to dignify and distinguish Father, Son, and Spirit as personal objects of worship. Given the foul lines of the Athanasian Creed, Barth's and Rahner's very similar constructs also tend to "confuse the persons," even if they are a significant improvement over classic modalism.

Sometimes advocates of this model defend their position by arguing that the very use of *prosopon* and *persona* by the early church suggested a weak, even a modalistic, sense of the trinitarian "person," since these terms actually originate from the theatre in denoting the masks worn by actors (cf. *dramatis personae*; *per-sona* = to sound through; *prosopon* = face). But if it were the case that "person" had the much weaker sense of "mask," then ancient modalists would have eagerly embraced the idea of three *personae/prosopa* in the one God, when in fact they were routinely criticized in the early church for positing only one. Thus even for modalists "person" had a deeper sense, one that they restricted to the one God. It is interesting to note in this connection that slaves in ancient Greece were called *aprosopa* (literally, those without faces; metaphorically, non-persons) – indicating that the notion of personhood had at least something to do with individual rights and dignity.

Given the origin of the word "person" as mask or face, it is best to see this as a case of synecdoche – part for the whole – the face representing the whole

---

[37] Barth, *Church Dogmatics*, 1/1: §9; Rahner, *Trinity*, 103–15.

person, as we principally imagine people in their absence (i.e., by their face rather than in terms of, say, their big toes). This makes *prosopon* or *persona* an eminent term for the person and therefore fitting for trinitarian description – a point recognized even by Thomas Aquinas:

Although this name *person* may not belong to God as regards the origin of the term, nevertheless it excellently belongs to God in its objective meaning. For as famous men were represented in comedies and tragedies, the name *person* was given to signify those who held high dignity ... Now the dignity of the divine nature excels every other dignity; and thus the name *person* pre-eminently belongs to God.[38]

This understanding of face as synecdoche for person also coheres with the biblical terminology, which, lacking a word for *person*, uses "name" and "face" as the closest conceptual equivalents. The depth of the term "person" as a discrete individual entity is actually guaranteed by the synonym *hypostasis* (a concrete individual existent), as is also manifest in Boethius' classic definition of person: "an individual substance of a rational nature," which became standard terminological fare in western trinitarian discussion.[39] With the Christian tradition, therefore, we regard *person* as the best possible *denotation* (term) for the trinitarian members – they cannot be paid any higher distinguishing compliment. But it is the ongoing task of systematic theology to clarify the most appropriate *connotation* (sense) of trinitarian personhood – just as theology does, for example, in clarifying the appropriate sense or content of the divine attributes (see pp. 103–8). If the Father and the Son were the same person, per the modalistic hypothesis, it would make a mockery of the Father–Son relationship as presented in the gospels. This is the Achilles heel of classic modalism and the neo-modal Trinity: if God is unipersonally in Christ, then who, for example, is the Son talking to in the garden of Gethsemane; or who during the incarnation is minding the celestial store? From all gospel appearances, our low-level working definition of personhood (center of thought, will, consciousness, etc.) seems to apply to both the Father and the Son and rules out any form of modalism.

The social Trinity

With little apology for a strong sense of the trinitarian person, the third option, which we will call the social Trinity, holds that God is three such persons – three discrete centers of thought, will, and consciousness. This

---

[38] Thomas, *Summa Theologica*, 1a.29.3 ad 2. The problem in Aquinas is that the discrete persons of Father, Son, and Spirit fade – they are "effaced" by the one divine substance.

[39] Boethius, *A Treatise Against Eutyches and Nestorius*, in *The Theological Tractates*, trans. H. F. Stewart and E. K. Rand, Loeb Classical Library 74 (Cambridge, MA: Harvard University Press, 1936), Part 3.

position is a social model of the Trinity, since the analogies that best convey it are personally pluralist: God is like a family, a community, or a society of persons. Hearkening back to the Cappadocians' suggestions and the rumi-nations of Richard of St. Victor, but not as well represented in the lengthy history of trinitarian thought, the social model of the Trinity has become an attractive option for many contemporary theologians because of its ability to meet key theological criteria.

But if the Trinity substantially comprises three distinct persons, how is it that they still constitute but one God? The first and major concern with this model is the question of divine unity. To secure this important oneness claim, social trinitarians would cite the following three forms of unity.

Forms of unity

The first is *essential divine unity*. The classic trinitarian formula is three persons in one divine essence. The divine essence (or substance, nature, Godhead) is that which the three persons possess in common and which makes them divine, and is typically described in terms of attributes, as in the Athanasian Creed, where various attributes (e.g., eternal, almighty) are each ascribed to Father, Son, and Spirit. While the neo-modal view does not concern itself so much with the category of essence (or substance) as it does the category of person (wherein the divine oneness is principally located), the western paradoxical position understands the divine unity principally *as* the divine essence. Given its strong simplicity claim, however, it so subordinates the trinitarian persons in any individuated or substantial sense that they are dissolved into sheer relations. The social model, however, does the opposite: While still employing the category of essence, it subordinates it to the category of personhood. The notion of the divine essence as the divine unity or oneness must therefore be understood in a different sense. The key to this sense is the question of the meaning of the Nicene *homoousios*, the ecumenical ruling that the Son was "of the same essence" as the Father. Here Aristotle's classic distinction between primary and secondary essence is help-ful: a primary essence is the *thing itself*, the single, particular thing something is; a secondary essence is the *sort of thing* something is – that is, its kind or class.[40] Take the human person for example: each of us has both a primary and secondary essence – the single, individual thing we are (a person) and the sort of thing we are (human). Utilizing Aristotle's distinction, how should the Nicene *homoousios* be understood – as a primary or secondary essence? To

---

[40] Aristotle, *Categories*, in *The Basic Works of Aristotle*, ed. Richard McKeon (New York: Random House, 1941), ch. 5. Cf. Basil of Caesarea, Letter 236, p. 278.

understand Christ's "same essence" with the Father in a primary sense would make them the same individual thing or person, which would head in the modalistic direction of "confusing the persons." So it seems better to understand the Nicene *homoousios* in a secondary sense: Father and Son (and Spirit) are of the same essence in the sense that they are the same sort, same class, same kind – persons who are all divine, who share a generic essence, each one manifesting the requisite divine attributes (eternal, almighty, etc.).[41] Applied to the Trinity, on this view there are three persons as three primary essences united in one divine secondary essence, satisfying the classic trinitarian formula. Given its assumption of divine simplicity, however, the western paradoxical model can understand the Nicene *homoousios* only in a primary sense, since God can only be strictly one numerical entity.

The second form of unity, *quasi-genetic unity*, captures the deeper sense of the Nicene *homoousios* – that of a relationship of derivation.[42] Here the trinitarian members share a sort of genetic unity or family bond. Two of the divine names indicate this quite clearly, that of Father and Son. According to John, the Son is the only-begotten (1:18; 3:16). Against Arius, the Council of Nicea understood such begottenness or generation to be eternal, since there was never a time when the Son was not. As much as this assertion may transcend our understanding, it underscores a unity of Father and Son that goes beyond their simply being members of the same divine class, for they also possess a familial relationship of derivation. According to the orthodox tradition, the Son is eternally *generated* and the Spirit eternally "breathed out" or *spirated* from the Father as the fount of divinity (*fons divinitatis*). While this characterization of the Spirit's "relation of origin" is not explicitly familial, it nonetheless underscores an intimacy of relationship that together with the Father–Son relationship is best likened to a genetic bond or family tie. This relational unity means that the divine persons cannot exist without one another. The Father, for example, is always the Father of the Son. The trinitarian persons, so to speak, are always a "package deal" in the context of this familial unity.

A third form of unity is the *perichoretic unity* of persons in community. Recall that *perichoresis* was a term that originated in the East to emphasize the divine unity in light of the distinction of persons. As employed today by many trinitarians it underscores the volitional ties of life and love shared by

---

[41] See Christopher Stead, *Divine Substance* (Oxford: Clarendon, 1977), 245–50, for a discussion of the nuances of the notion of substance in connection with the Nicene *homoousios*.

[42] The term "quasi-genetic" is taken from Cornelius Plantinga Jr., "Social Trinity and Tritheism," in *Trinity, Incarnation and Atonement: Philosophical and Theological Essays*, ed. Ronald J. Feenstra and Cornelius Plantinga Jr. (Notre Dame, IN: University of Notre Dame Press, 1989), 21–47.

the persons, their unity of purpose, fellowship, and love (1 John 4:8). In the divine communion, the three persons mutually and intimately indwell one another. Therefore beyond being members of the same class of divine person (essential divine unity), and beyond being members of the same family (quasi-genetic unity), Father, Son, and Spirit are also united in purpose, fellowship, and love (perichoretic unity).

The question of tritheism

Do these forms of unity suffice in securing the oneness claim, that there is only one true God? That is to say, does the social Trinity maintain sufficient continuity with Jewish monotheism such that it does not constitute tritheism (a species of polytheism), as some fear the social analogy entails? It depends on what exactly monotheism and tritheism are. As noted earlier, biblical monotheism appears to be the claim that the one true God is distinguished as such by being the Creator of all; all other so-called gods are the idolatrous assertions of creatures. The social model maintains this monotheistic claim, since it holds that Father, Son, and Spirit are all on the divine side of the Creator/creature divide. In light of the NT, the Creator God is not simply the Father, but the Holy Trinity: the Father creates through the mediation of the Son in the power and energies of the Spirit. Creation, in other words, is a trinitarian act. Only by some other definition does the social Trinity violate monotheism, as in, say, the dubious "monotheistic intuition" that holds that God can only be one exact thing or person (as reinforced by simplicity doctrine). Tritheism, conversely, was identified early on in church history in quite particular and concrete terms – it is Arianism.[43] By grading the divinity of the trinitarian members – whereby the Father alone is truly God, and the Son and Spirit are of a lesser, created divine status – Arianism divided the divine essence and mixed its worship of God between Creator and creature, which constitutes polytheism. The social view, however, does no such thing: Father, Son, and Spirit are all equally co-eternal divine persons who together constitute the one Creator God. The social analogy neither "confuses the persons," like modalism, nor "divides the essence" among Creator and creature, like Arianism. It therefore falls within orthodox confessional parameters in indicating how three divine persons are nonetheless One God.

Social trinitarians are fond of pointing to Jesus' "high-priestly prayer" in John 17 as express biblical warrant for their model. There, amid the perichoretic language of "oneness" and "in-ness," Jesus prays to the Father that believers (the church) "may be one, as we are one." For "one" John uses the generic Greek

[43] Ibid., 34.

word *hen*, which admits of a plurality, not *heis*, which refers to a strict numerical oneness (17:22; cf. 17:20–3). In John's simple, but subtle, syntax he presents the trinitarian unity here as the model or paradigm for the church's unity. The church therefore in turn becomes an analogy for the Trinity: a diversity of persons united by human genus, spiritual birth, and Christian purpose, one body of witness in the world (cf. Paul in 1 Cor. 12:4–12). And if the church is an analogy for the Trinity *in redemption* by virtue of being the renewed image of God, then one can also find this analogy *in creation*. That paradigmatic precedent is the one humanity that comes packaged in a diversity of persons, created in the image of God as "male and female" (Gen. 1:27), whose loving procreation perpetuates that image in other persons (Gen. 5:3). The family image in creation and the church image in redemption reflect the divine Trinity and, by extension, human community or persons-in-right-relationship in general.

Trinitarian mystery

Another common concern about the social model is whether it robs the Trinity of mystery. The answer depends, of course, on what one means by mystery – by its very definition neither a clear nor a distinct idea. It is possible to identify a variety of senses of mystery, not every one of which is helpful theologically. A key NT sense of mystery, especially in the Pauline letters, is that of something that was hidden, but is now revealed for our salvation (e.g., Eph. 3:4–5). This "mystery of salvation" (*mysterium salutis*) is certainly true of the Trinity – hidden in the OT but revealed in the NT. Another sense of mystery endorsed in the theological tradition is a "mystery strictly speaking" (*mysterium stricte dictum*), referring to that which is undiscoverable by human reason alone and therefore requires revelation. This sense also is well applicable to the Trinity, since the Trinity is a datum of special revelation. But the social trinitarian is skeptical about a third sense of mystery that is usually invoked when it comes to the Trinity's threeness-oneness relation – the so-called "logical mystery" (*mysterium logicum*). As we will argue more fully in Chapter 6, we do not believe that one must embrace the contradictory in theology. As a "logy," a broadly logical account, theology must press on toward coherence where paradox *appears* and where illogic is asserted. We do not think that the Trinity's threeness-oneness relation must be embraced as contradictory, as has largely been the case when the Trinity has been declared a "mystery" – of logic.

Yet there is a fourth sense of mystery which is profoundly applicable to the Trinity. This may be called the "mystery of communion" (*mysterium communionis*), in which our relationships with other persons, whether human or divine, constitute an inviting horizon of mystery. A moving statement of this type of mystery is found in one of Dietrich Bonhoeffer's sermons, delivered one Trinity Sunday. In it, Bonhoeffer contends that mystery is not simply a matter of not knowing something. For example, it is not the most distant star that presents the greatest mystery; on the contrary, a more profound mystery resides in the persons who are closest to us: "It is the deepest of all mysteries when two people come so near that they *love* one another." In similar fashion, the divine mystery does not so much concern God's transcendence and unknowability as it concerns God's love and nearness to us, a loving reach that correlates with our experience of the Trinity:

> The mystery of God means to be loved by God and to love God – but to be loved by God signifies Christ; and to love God signifies the Holy Spirit. God's mystery therefore means Christ and the Holy Spirit; God's mystery signifies the Holy Trinity ... The meaning of the doctrine of the Trinity is enormously simple, so that any child can understand it: there is truly only one God, but this God is consummate Love.[44]

Bonhoeffer's reflections suggest that mystery need not be reduced to an epistemological problem. Indeed, his inviting concept of mystery as a mystery of communion is eminently compatible with a robust and coherent doctrine of the Trinity.

Given our typology and governing theological criteria, we endorse the social view as the most orthodox and coherent model of the Trinity. It is orthodox in satisfying the classic trinitarian definition of three unconfused persons and one undivided essence. But its orthodoxy is more aptly found in this model's greater ability to account for the contours of the NT narrative. The social Trinity is also a more coherent account of the trinitarian confession than what has been taken for orthodoxy in the western tradition, namely, the paradoxical model (but so also is the neo-modal Trinity). Since the social model is more thinkable or graspable, the way is clearer to see how the doctrine of the Trinity may function more practically, thus also meeting the criterion of relevance. We conclude our trinitarian proposal with three of these important practical applications.

Practical advantages of the social model

A first practical advantage of the social model is that it affords us a better definition of human personhood. It is a safe judgment that the western democratic notion of the person, as one clothed in rights and dignity, is in

---

[44] Sermon entitled "Geheimnis," delivered May 27, 1934, in *Gesammelte Schriften*, ed. Eberhard Bethge (Munich: Chr. Kaiser Verlag, 1972), v: 515–20, italics original (translation ours).

no small measure a Christian contribution, arising principally out of the early christological and trinitarian debates.[45] It is also a fair judgment that particular conceptions of God reinforce certain perceptions and patterns of human personhood, especially when given that human beings are created in God's likeness (*imago Dei*). It is at this anthropological juncture that the sort of trinitarian model one advocates becomes crucial. A number of theologians have argued that the dominant one-person view of God in the West, the legacy of the Augustinian model, has contributed significantly to the rampant individualism in western society.[46] To this malady (and resulting malaise), a more relational notion of the person grounded in the social conception of the Trinity can serve as an important antidote, for while the trinitarian members are distinct and irreducible persons, they are not autonomous "individuals." The Father is never Father, for example, without the presence of the Son and Spirit. As we will elaborate in Chapter 7, a more relational view of the human person as *imago Dei* has been loudly trumpeted in recent theology as a more wholesome interpretation of scripture. If it is true that we read our concept of person off God, a social Trinity would better account for this relational accent.

Second, on the basis of this conception of personhood, the Trinity readily becomes an exemplary model for human community – including the church, the family, and society at large. The perichoretic cooperation, mutuality, and deference of the trinitarian persons provides the ultimate model for persons-in-right-relations, whatever the social configuration. Here the venerable Christian ethic of the "imitation of Christ," sometimes harnessed to an individualistic spirituality, finds its larger social context in the "imitation of the Trinity," a more socially conscious and communal spirituality.[47]

A final practical advantage of the social Trinity may well be the most important: the social model better clarifies the fundamental Christian *vision* of God. One of the more intriguing developments in recent theology has been the comeback of the religious imagination against its modern, scientific demise.[48] That humans are fundamentally imagistic beings, of necessity nourished by myth and ritual, symbol and story, is a fact with which theology is reckoning. If it is the case that at base in human consciousness

[45] See Thomas F. Torrance, "The Goodness and Dignity of Man in the Christian Tradition," *Modern Theology* 4, no. 4 (1988), 309–22.

[46] See, e.g., Colin E. Gunton, *The Promise of Trinitarian Theology* (Edinburgh: T. & T. Clark, 1991), esp. ch. 6: "The Human Creation: Towards a Renewal of the Doctrine of the *Imago Dei*."

[47] See Thomas R. Thompson, "*Imitatio Trinitatis*: The Trinity as Social Model in the Theologies of Jürgen Moltmann and Leonardo Boff" (PhD dissertation: Princeton Theological Seminary, 1996), ch. 6.

[48] See, e.g., Garrett Green, *Imagining God: Theology and the Religious Imagination* (Grand Rapids, MI: Eerdmans, 1989).

Illustration 5.1 Michelangelo, *The Creation of Adam*, Sistine Chapel.

stands an imaginative backdrop of pictures, stories, and myths of the way things sit in the world, then this must also be considered a religious consciousness, including some image of what is ultimate. Here the question of one's vision of God becomes acute.

Christianity has its own authoritative story, a guiding myth which is also fact. But how are we to *envision* the principal protagonist of this story – the trinitarian God? Is this God rightly viewed in the fashion of, say, Michelangelo's Creator, whose solitary finger touches that of a solitary human figure strikingly bearing his personal likeness? Or is this God better imagined in the form of, say, Andrei Rublev's Trinity, as three angelic-like persons lovingly inclined toward one another (see Illustrations 5.1 and 5.2)? To imagine God as both one and three persons at the same time appears impossible. The difficulty in envisioning a contradictory portrait of God may go some distance in explaining why western Christians have predominantly been "mere monotheists" (Rahner): what we have been taught about the Trinity is unimaginable (i.e., 3 = 1); and when given an accentuated oneness, Michelangelo wins.

But the NT story tells of three agents, Father, Son, and Spirit, whom the early church subsequently all recognized as divine and denoted as "persons." Here the Rublev icon better captures the theological imagination, and the social analogy is a better way to conceptually unpack this Christian vision of God – and, conversely, to clarify and warrant that vision theoretically, which is to say, to articulate it as a doctrine.

The person of the Father has probably been the dominant image of God in the western religious imagination, as in Michelangelo's famous depiction. What effect this has had on western thinking and practice might be hard to

Illustration 5.2 Andrei Rublev, *The Holy Trinity*, fifteenth-century icon.

say and document; but it could very well reinforce cultural trends toward individualism. Feminists contend that it has also reinforced other harmful human behaviors. The social trinitarian considers the Michelangelo vision incomplete, and would want to add a couple of persons to the imaginative equation – on both the divine and the human side. And if a more pluralistic conception of the *imago Dei* has been a recent, welcomed and little-disputed theological insight, why not also regarding the divine archetype?

CONCLUSION: THE QUESTION OF "GOD"

So what do we finally mean when we say "God"? For the Christian there seem to be three viable referents.[49] First, the NT referent for God is

---

[49] Also see Plantinga, "Threeness/Oneness," 52.

overwhelmingly that of God *the Father*. This is understandable given that the primary vantage point of the NT is that of the incarnation, and therefore a view from the perspective of the humanity of the Son. But since the Son and Spirit were also discerned to be divine, a second sense of "God" is that of the *deity*, the divine essence or nature that each person fully possesses. Here "God" typically functions as a predicate adjective, as in the Athanasian Creed: So the Father is God (i.e., divine), the Son is God, and the Spirit is God. But, finally, "God" in Christian perspective ought to refer first and foremost to the *Holy Trinity* – the whole community of Father, Son, and Spirit – even as Gregory of Nazianzus observed: "But when I say God, I mean Father, Son and Holy Ghost."[50]

Given the current options in trinitarian discussion, we think that the social Trinity best accounts for the trinitarian confession and is the most coherent and consistent model that gathers up the personal, dynamic, and relational gains in the doctrine of God and facilitates their application to other doctrines and issues. With social trinitarianism as our working presupposition, we will chart the riches of these trinitarian resources across the terrain of Christian theology.

FOR FURTHER READING

Augustine, *The Trinity*, trans. Edmund Hill, The Works of Saint Augustine I/5 (New York: New City, 1991).

Barth, Karl, *Church Dogmatics*, ed. Geoffrey W. Bromiley and Thomas F. Torrance (Edinburgh: T. & T. Clark, 1975), I/1: §§8–9.

Gregory of Nyssa, "An Answer to Ablabius: That We Should Not Think of Saying There Are Three Gods," trans. Cyril C. Richardson, in *Christology of the Later Fathers*, ed. Edward R. Hardy, Library of Christian Classics (Louisville, KY: Westminster John Knox, 1954), 256–67.

Gunton, Colin E., *The Promise of Trinitarian Theology* (Edinburgh: T. & T. Clark, 1991).

O'Collins, Gerald, *The Tripersonal God: Understanding and Interpreting the Trinity* (New York: Paulist, 1999).

Plantinga Jr., Cornelius, "The Threeness/Oneness Problem of the Trinity," *Calvin Theological Journal* 23 (1988), 37–53.

Rusch, William G., ed., *The Trinitarian Controversy*, Sources of Early Christian Thought (Philadelphia: Fortress, 1980).

Wainwright, Arthur W., *The Trinity in the New Testament* (London: SPCK, 1962).

---

[50] Gregory of Nazianzus, "Oration 38," trans. Charles Gordon Browne and James Edward Swallow, in *Nicene and Post-Nicene Fathers*, 2nd series, ed. Philip Schaff and Henry Wace (Grand Rapids, MI: Eerdmans, 1993), ch. 8 (VII: p. 347).

CHAPTER 6

The world as creation

INTRODUCTION

The triune God is the principal protagonist of the Christian story. The second main character is creation. The opening verse of the Hebrew Bible casts the relationship of these respective parties as follows: "In the beginning God created the heavens and earth" (Gen. 1:1). In Judeo-Christian thought there is no more fundamental distinction than that between Creator and creature, a distinction on which much rides theologically. The basic problem is that the creature has become an antagonist. More particularly, humanity, the key representative of God within creation and commissioned caretaker of the earth, has not always considered itself part of a dependent creation, but has sinfully declared its own independence from God. Neither has our species always had a sufficient appreciation for creation beyond its own anthropocentric concerns. In this chapter, we will contend that a robust doctrine of creation is essential for the health of all Christian theology, and especially for understanding humanity's God-given vocation as the image of God. This creational emphasis is particularly important today given that our very survival as a species hangs in the balance, dependent as it is with the rest of created life on human responsibility for a unique blue-green planet.

THE BIBLICAL AFFIRMATION OF CREATION

Old Testament

We have argued that a limited knowledge of God as Creator is possible via general revelation (see pp. 52–6). In terms of the progressive unfolding of special revelation in the history of Israel, however, Israel's knowledge of God as Redeemer comes first (as the God of Abraham, Isaac, and Jacob, and the God of the exodus). A deeper understanding of Yahweh as the unique Creator God comes only later, a point already made in our discussion of the *Shema* (see p. 81). It was largely the Babylonian exile that accelerated this clarification of monotheism. Given this conquest and exile from the land of Judah, the Jews questioned whether the Babylonian gods were stronger than Yahweh. The prophetic answer, particularly in Isaiah and Jeremiah, is negative. Israel has indeed incurred divine judgment for its sins, but its exile will come to an end (e.g., Isa. 40:1ff.; Jer. 30–3). The guarantee of this promise is that Yahweh is not just the God of the Jews, but in fact the Creator of all – heaven and earth and all its peoples (e.g., Isa. 44:6–24; Jer. 10:1–16). Since Yahweh is the Creator, Yahweh alone is God.

Most biblical scholars hold that the prologue to the Hebrew (and Christian) canon, Genesis 1:1–2:3, comes from this exilic period. This classic text on creation, which sets the tone for the Bible as a whole, is a finely structured theological declaration that God is King of a good creation. Sharing many of the features of ancient near-eastern cosmology (primeval watery chaos, waters above a solid heavenly dome, waters under the earth, etc.), God is portrayed as the heavenly King who uniquely creates, not by giving birth to the world or through cosmic conflict as in so many other ancient "creation" stories (e.g., the *Enuma Elish*), but by sheer word of command (divine fiat). In this highly stylized text, God first separates and forms in successive steps the three basic spheres of the Israelite cosmos (days 1, 2, 3) and then fills them with their respective inhabitants (days 4, 5, 6).[1] In this process all other so-called gods are dethroned – most pointedly, the sun and moon, considered gods in the ancient Near East, are not even mentioned by name, but are called the "greater and lesser" lights to show that they are sheer creatures. While the climax of the sixth day is the creation of humanity in God's very image to represent God in creation (see Chapter 7), the completion of creation is the Sabbath, the seventh day, in which God rests from all creative labors. The Sabbath sanctifies or sets apart the creation as very good and hallows God as its benevolent Creator.[2] Genesis 2:4 then introduces the history of the God–world relation by offering a differing but complementary perspective on creation (2:4a–25), one that highlights the origin of humanity and its God-given vocation to tend the earthly garden.

The biblical canon therefore introduces God as Creator King. It is this strong affirmation of God's sovereignty over a good creation that resonates throughout the OT – as in the creation psalms (e.g., Pss. 8; 33; 104; 139), the wisdom literature (e.g., Job 38–41), and especially in the exilic and post-exilic prophets such as Isaiah and Jeremiah, who declare the confusion of creature with Creator to be sheer folly (e.g., Isa. 40:18ff.; 44:9–20; Jer. 10:1–16). Since creation is established in God's wisdom (Prov. 8), it is inherently meaningful, a domain that makes wisdom available to those who fear Yahweh and who respectfully observe creation:

> But ask the animals, and they will teach you;
>   the birds of the air, and they will tell you;
> ask the plants of the earth, and they will teach you;
>   and the fish of the sea will declare to you.
> Who among all these does not know
>   that the hand of the LORD has done this?   (Job 12:7–9)

The doctrine of an inherently good and meaningful creation encouraged in Israel's wisdom school a proto-scientific inquiry of the world, an observance of order and regularities and a cataloguing of natural phenomena: "But you have arranged all things by measure and number and weight" (Wis. 1:20).[3]

---

[1] See Daniel C. Harlow, "Creation According to Genesis: Literary Genre, Cultural Context, Theological Truth," *Christian Scholars Review* 37, no. 2 (2008), 163–98.

[2] See Abraham Joshua Heschel, *The Sabbath: Its Meaning for Modern Man*, rev. edn. (New York: Farrah, Straus & Co., 1951).

[3] See Gerhard von Rad, *Wisdom in Israel*, trans. James D. Marton (Nashville, TN: Abingdon, 1972), esp. ch. 7.

But it is not only the good *space* of creation that is the domain of God's created kingdom; it is also the good *time* of creation. God continues to create in time, in history. The very same word used in the OT for the unique creative activity of Yahweh in the beginning, *bara*, as in Genesis 1:1ff., is also used of God's present and future actions – for example, a future generation is "a people not yet created" (Ps. 102:18, NIV), each individual is created by God (Eccles. 12:1), as well as the continuing generations of animals (Ps. 104:30), all of which, we should note, normally takes place through "natural causes" – a hint toward the fact that God's continuing creative activity makes use of natural processes. It is not surprising, then, that God's redemptive actions are also considered creative acts: "Create in me a clean heart, O God" (Ps. 51:10). Both the nation of Israel (Isa. 43:1, 7, 15) and her redemption (Isa. 41:20; 45:8) are considered unique creative acts of God (employing *bara*).[4]

In the OT it is this creation, both its good space and good time, that is the proper *and final* locus of the God–world relation – not an ethereal heaven as in Greek antiquity. In this God–world relation humanity plays a key role as the image-bearer or representative of God's presence in the world. According to the OT, human default on its God-given responsibility has serious consequences for creation – indeed, it leads to the undoing of the earth. This is seen early on in Genesis, where the proliferation of human wickedness results in the implosion of a good earth, as the flood of judgment (Gen. 6–9) is depicted as a reversal of creation, taking it back to its watery, chaotic beginnings. Yet God begins anew with Noah and a colorful promise of a renewed earth. And God begins again with Abraham after the confusion of Babel (Gen. 11). In Abraham, the faithful patriarch of Israel, we continue to see the close connection between human responsibility and the earth, since the divine promise to Abraham includes not only the fruitfulness of persons, but also the fruitfulness of the land (Gen. 12:1–3), both of which hark back to God's original blessing in Genesis 1:28. The land of Canaan, so central to God's covenant with Israel, was to be a land flowing with milk and honey (Exod. 3:8), in which righteous Israel would be a light and a blessing to the nations (as particularly symbolized by Jerusalem, the antici-pated "city of peace"). But similar to the Noahic flood, Israel's disobedience caused the land to "vomit" them out in exile (Lev. 18:28; cf. Deut. 4:25ff.). Yet a remnant returned to begin anew. In Isaiah's vision of this restoration of Israel, the future New Jerusalem symbolizes the righteous society and

---

[4] See Karl-Heinz Bernhardt, "*bara*," in Botterweck and Ringgren, eds., *Theological Dictionary of the Old Testament*, II: 246–8.

fortunes of the land. But in Isaiah's visions and proclamations, Jerusalem's and therefore Israel's restoration morphs into a vision of a new heavens and earth (chs. 54ff.). The city of God is then envisioned as the entire world, God's renovation of the earth (Isa. 65:17–25; 66:22–3). Just as the garden of Eden represents the whole earth, so also the land of Canaan was to be an anticipation and firstfruits of God's broader cosmic redemption. Israel's expectation of salvation was earthy, for it understood God's kingdom as having to do with creation at large.

New Testament

The NT presupposes the strong affirmation of creation found in the OT (e.g., Heb. 11:3; Rom. 4:17; 11:36a). Building on this inheritance, but given the central NT focus on Christ, not only as the expected Messiah but also as the Son of God, one preoccupation of the NT is to affirm Christ's role as mediator not simply of salvation but of creation as well (e.g., 1 Cor. 8:6; Col. 1:16). Creation is seen to have its basis (Rev. 3:14) and goal in him (Heb. 1:11f.). The God who is in Christ reconciling the world, therefore, is none other than the one Creator God. The deity of Christ necessitates such an identification, an affirmation most resounding in John's vision in Revelation of the heavenly liturgy surrounding God's throne where Christ the Lamb-Lion is also centered. Here God is worshipped first as Creator God (Rev. 4) and then as the Redeemer God and Lord of history (Rev. 5).

It is striking that in the NT the land of Canaan is no longer in focus as an essential inheritance of Abraham's promise. Apparently, just as the promise of many descendants has been universalized – the "Israel of God" (Gal. 6:16) in Christ is no longer an ethnic issue about Jew or Gentile, but includes a kingdom of priests purchased "from every tribe and language and people and nation" (Rev. 5:9) – so also the promise of the land has been universalized to include the whole earth, even as Isaiah anticipated. The kingdom of God, the dynamic rule and realm of God, is no longer localized in a particular land but has broken into all the world historically in the person and work of Jesus Christ. In the NT it is the "body of Christ," the worldwide and multicultural church, that has become the temple of God's presence, whose members are the redemptive "firstfruits of all God created" (Jas. 1:18). Given the advent of Christ whose resurrection from the dead makes him the firstborn of creation (Col. 1:15–20), creation theology in the NT has been taken up into new-creation or re-creation theology. The new creation therefore becomes the central soteriological hope for which the whole frustrated creation yearns, waiting for this redemptive drama to play itself out in anticipation of its own liberation (Rom. 8:19–21). What the NT envisions is the redemption of the whole cosmos, a new heaven and earth (Rev. 21), in which God will be "all in all" (1 Cor. 15:28). The closing chapters of the Christian canon depict this renewed creation in terms of the descent of the New Jerusalem, the righteous city or civilization of God's original intention (Rev. 21:1–5). In short, in the NT, creation cannot be seen apart from redemption (new creation), nor redemption apart from creation. A renewed creation in which God rests in manifest presence is the fulfillment of God's original "heavens and earth."

Given this emphasis on new creation and de-emphasis of "the land," the NT sometimes appears less concerned with explicit creation theology than the much larger OT. This impression has been unfortunate for the course of Christian history and theology, for the church, at times neglecting the very earthy OT, as well as neglecting the inseparability of creation and redemption, has been quite susceptible to influences that depreciate the material creation, influences that crystallized later on as the movement of gnosticism. But in fact, the NT itself presupposes the OT, and it explicitly combats an incipient or proto-gnosticism in its first-century setting. There is a warning of "the profane chatter and contradictions of what is falsely called knowledge [= *gnosis*]" (1 Tim. 6:20), of teachers that "forbid marriage and demand abstinence from foods, which God created to be received with thanksgiving" (adding the rebuttal: "For everything created by God is good" – 1 Tim. 4:3–4). 1 John combats a "spirit of the antichrist" that does not acknowledge that Christ came in the flesh (1 John 4:1–3). And Paul contests an array of gnostic tendencies in the Corinthian church (1 Cor. 8:1), not least of which is a neglect, even denial, of the bodily resurrection of the dead (1 Cor. 15). In all these respects, the NT presupposes the strong OT emphasis on a good material creation, an emphasis further presupposed in the central Christian affirmations of the incarnation, resurrection, sacraments, and new heaven and earth that embrace the fleshly, bodily, physical elements of the material world.

THE DOCTRINE OF CREATION IN HISTORICAL PERSPECTIVE

While the goodness of creation as affirmed by both the OT and NT was a theme of early Christian theology, it did not take long for gnosticism to make significant inroads into the church.

Gnosticism and creatio ex nihilo

We have already spoken of gnosticism in a variety of settings, since its tendencies have historically harassed an array of Christian doctrines. The term itself was coined by modern scholarship for the general characteristics of a diversity of systems and movements that claimed a special *gnosis* or knowledge of cosmic origins, the plight of humankind, and the way of salvation – namely, escape from the material cosmos.[5] In its origins and development, which largely parallel Christian origins and development, gnosticism is both syncretistic and eclectic, combining elements from a variety of sources – most notably, Greek philosophy, near-eastern astral religion, and Jewish and Christian elements. While it is likely that gnosticism had already made significant inroads into Hellenistic Judaism, and from early on had garbed itself in Christian imagery, it was not until the second and third centuries that "Gnosticism" became a more clearly defined aberration of Christian doctrine. In this crucial post-apostolic contest of orthodoxy, the importance of creation doctrine became more transparent, and would play a strategic role in the clarification of other central Christian teachings.

At the heart of gnosticism is a radical dualism of spirit and matter, soul and body. The one true God dwells in utter spiritual transcendence above the material world, since the latter is a mis-creation of a lesser divine being, typically called the Demiurge and generally identified with the God of the OT. Human beings have their preexistent origin in this fullness (*pleroma*) of the divine, but as "sparks of deity" they have fallen into the material soup of the cosmos and as imprisoned souls they have forgotten whence they come. But a divine revealer descends, like unto Jesus Christ, to disclose to the elect the secret, esoteric knowledge of their origins, of who they really are. Once enlightened, those "in the know" may begin the process of their ascent out of the material world, since that world is intrinsically the realm of darkness, suffering, and evil.[6] This process of ascent involves the education and cultivation of the soul in disdain of the body, which usually takes the form of an extreme asceticism, a rigorous denial of bodily pleasures, and which is completed at death when the soul leaves the body behind.

---

[5] For a classic treatment of gnosticism see Kurt Rudolph's *Gnosis: The Nature and History of Gnosticism*, trans. Robert McLachlan Wilson (New York: HarperCollins, 1984).

[6] As the gnostic *Gospel of Truth* puts it: "If anyone has gnosis he is a being who comes from above ... He who in this manner shall have gnosis knows whence he is come and whither he goes." Quoted in Rudolph, *Gnosis*, 56.

Given its formal similarities with Christianity, the lines between gnostic and Christian believers were not always easy to draw, particularly since many gnostic groups also considered themselves Christian. Concerning belief in the person of Christ and the chief entailments of the gospel, however, the differences began to sort themselves out. Gnostics typically held that Christ was a divine revealer, but not a fully human redeemer, since any emissary from the pure spiritual realm would never deign to take on real flesh and blood in order to redeem an intrinsically defective material world. Accordingly, for the gnostic, the resurrection of the body was an absurdity, at most a mere metaphor for the ascent of the soul to its true home in heaven. By the second century it became clear that the crux of the doctrinal differences between Christians and gnostics lay in the doctrine of creation.

It was Irenaeus of Lyons, as seen in his *Against Heresies*, who took the lead in elaborating a strong doctrine of creation against the gnostic threat, directed mainly against the teaching of Valentinus. Central to his rebuttal is the contention that God created *ex nihilo* or "out of nothing," which became the foundational tenet of Christian creation doctrine: "While men, indeed, cannot make anything out of nothing, but only out of matter already existing, yet God is in this point preeminently superior to men, that He Himself called into being the substance of His creation when previously it had no existence."[7] For Irenaeus this view implies not only that creation is a *free* act of an omnipotent God, but also that its materiality is a *good* product of an omnibenevolent God. As Colin Gunton notes, Irenaeus' reasoning is christologically and soteriologically motivated: "If God in his Son takes to himself the reality of human flesh, then nothing created, and certainly nothing material, can be downgraded to unreality, semi-reality or treated as fundamentally evil."[8] Moreover, in contrast to the gnostics, creation as a whole is the object of God's redemption – its destiny, like that of human beings, is maturation and perfection, a process that is related to Irenaeus' understanding of Christ's work as a fulfillment of creation (see pp. 267–8). While other church fathers, such as Tertullian (*Against Hermogenes*), strongly echoed Irenaeus' emphasis on *ex nihilo*, others, more attracted and influenced by Platonism, did so less. For example, before Irenaeus, Justin Martyr denied *ex nihilo* outright, holding that God created out of preexistent formless matter.[9] And later, Origen held a

---

[7] Irenaeus, *Against Heresies*, 2.10.4 (p. 370).
[8] Colin E. Gunton, *The Triune Creator: A Historical and Systematic Study*, Edinburgh Studies in Constructive Theology (Grand Rapids, MI: Eerdmans, 1998), 52.
[9] Justin Martyr, *First Apology*, ch. 10.

sort of half-way view: God created *ex nihilo*, but only upon the occasion of the fall of preexistent spirits from their pure spiritual unity with God.[10] While Justin is a rare exception to the patristic affirmation of *ex nihilo*, and while Origen was considered highly unorthodox in his affirmation of the preexistence of the human soul, they do illustrate the ambiguity of a strong affirmation of creation in the early Christian tradition.

It is our view that this ambiguity, seen in the historical recurrence of gnostic tendencies – in short, a depreciation of the material creation – has badgered the Christian tradition throughout its lengthy history and continues to do so today on a number of doctrinal fronts, including the doctrines of God, Christ, humanity, salvation, and last things. To this tenacious gnostic spirit, a strong doctrine of creation is the proper antidote. While the reasons for this lingering influence are historically varied, one contributing factor is that the general view of the cosmos that dominated classical through medieval times, the very period through which Christian doctrine was first forged and tempered, reinforced a gnostic orientation to life. That cosmology can generally be termed Aristotelian-Ptolemaic geocentrism, and is the topic of the next section.

Geocentric cosmology

While the biblical understanding of the origins of the world (encapsulated by *creatio ex nihilo* doctrine) was at odds with the Greek assumption that matter was eternal, Christian theologians of the patristic and medieval eras adopted by default the regnant classical understanding of the physical structure of the cosmos. Based on his dualism between appearance and reality, correlating to matter and mind, Plato had proposed that the Earth was a material sphere at the center of the cosmos surrounded by the ideal sphere of the heavens, wherein the motions of the planets and stars were perfectly uniform and circular as governed by the intelligence of a divine soul (see his *Timaeus* dialogue). Aristotle modified and elaborated this Platonic legacy in greater physical detail. He held that the realm under the moon was the realm of transience – of birth, change, decay, and death. Within Aristotle's physics, motion was accounted for in three basic ways. First, to the degree that something consisted of the four primal elements, it sought its proper place of rest based on its elemental weight or nobility, from heaviest to lightest: earth, water, air, and fire. Hence, a ripe apple fell to the ground not because of gravity, but because it, consisting mostly of earth, was seeking its proper place

---

[10] Origen, *De Principiis*, 2.9.

of rest. Water spread out over the earth; air hovered above both, and fire leapt up. Second, according to Aristotle's hylomorphism, things moved on the basis of potency and act – correlating with matter (*hyle*) and form (*morphe*) – as things materially seek to realize their structured purpose or form. Third, things also move by virtue of local motion, if by continuous direct contact they are pushed or pulled. Such physics reinforced Aristotle's view of the realm of the heavens, from the moon on up, as the realm of unchanging perfection, where the planets and stars moved in uniform circles around the Earth in indestructible crystalline spheres of "ether" (the fifth basic element). The material earth, by contrast, constituted the dregs of the cosmos.

Aristotelian geocentrism was the basic "scientific" air that Christianity breathed in the patristic and early Middle Ages, a cosmology that debased the earth in view of the divine heavens above. In the Middle Ages, Aristotle's writings were rediscovered in the West along with those of the influential astronomer Ptolemy (second century CE), whose mathematical calculations underwrote and consolidated this geocentrism. When these were "reconciled" with Christian doctrine in the synthesis of Thomas Aquinas, they codified a scientific-sacred worldview that oriented people to the heavens above, especially in quest of the empyrean heavens where God dwells. And when given that Greek – especially Platonic – thought encouraged the separation of the soul from the body, the proper place of rest for the latter was considered the earth, the dregs of the universe, whereas the proper place of the ethereal soul was the heavenly realm of light. This is to say that the very "scientific" logic of the cosmos as embraced by Christianity until roughly the sixteenth century reinforced a gnostic orientation to life: the human being is essentially soul, only accidentally body, and our real home is not the material creation, but the spiritual heaven.

This geocentric universe and its upward-looking soul culture, rooted in ancient Greek philosophy, is strikingly portrayed in Cicero's *Dream of Scipio* (first century BCE),[11] a perspective that is astoundingly still dominant a millennium later in Dante's classic Christian work, *The Divine Comedy* (early fourteenth century), particularly volume III, *Paradise*, where the last leg of the pilgrim's journey to God ascends through the nine crystalline spheres (the moon, planets, Sun, and stars) to the fiery empyrean heaven, the realm of pure light and rest where God dwells and where elect souls are transfixed by the beatific vision – the intellectual contemplation of the divine essence (see Illustration 6.1).

---

[11] This text is extant in the work of the fourth-century Neoplatonist Macrobius: *Commentary on the Dream of Scipio by Macrobius*, trans. William Harris Stahl (New York: Columbia University Press, 1952), 67–77.

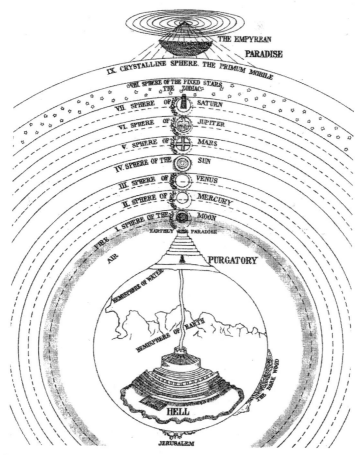

Illustration 6.1 A modified version of a nineteenth-century diagram of Dante's picture of the cosmos.

It would be the overcoming of this geocentrism and its Aristotelian physics that would herald a revolutionary age, the rise of modern science.

Heliocentrism and the rise of modern science

Aristarchus of Samos had actually proposed a heliocentric model of the solar system as early as 250 BCE, but his perspective lost out to Aristotle, especially when endorsed by the most learned and reputable astronomer of ancient times, Ptolemy. It would not be until the sixteenth century that helio-centrism would come back for serious discussion in western civilization when Nicolas Copernicus (*On the Revolution of the Celestial Spheres*, 1543) proposed that placing the Sun in the center of the solar system, besides producing a simpler mathematical model, made better sense of the growing body of observed phenomena than did Ptolemaic astronomy. Copernicus' inclination was followed by Kepler and, more famously, by Galileo.

Acquiring a state-of-the-art telescope, Galileo observed such features as pockmarks on the moon (imperfection), sunspots (violence and decay), and moons circling Jupiter (counter-motion) – all evidence that contradicted Aristotelian-Ptolemaic assumptions that the astral heavens were a place of perfection, tranquility, and uniform motion around the Earth. But it was Galileo's and others' work on motion that especially undermined Aristotelian physics and metaphysics. The motion of bodies depends, it appeared, not on their material density, purposive form, or continuous local contact, but on their material relations as governed by natural laws such as gravity and inertia. It was Sir Isaac Newton's *Principia Mathematica* (1687) that would finally provide the mathematical proof of heliocentrism, and so stamp the enterprise of modern science as "Newtonian" – the investigation of a physical world well ordered by virtue of regular and uniform natural laws, much like a machine.

The hallmark of modern science is the observation of quantitative fact – the empirical investigation of the physical properties, behavior, relations, and causation of material things. This is qualitatively different from Greek science, which was a quest to discern the inherent form of something – its formal, essential, or purposive structure, which correlated with the function or end that it served.[12] Modern science could never arise on the basis of Aristotle's matter–form physics, since the *material* element itself played no appreciable role in understanding the what and why of worldly phenomena. Though Aristotle thought the world was intelligible and fraught with purpose, its intelligibility and purposeful motion (teleology) was not found within its material qualities or relations. Only by overcoming Aristotle's physics and its larger metaphysical assumptions (geocentrism, divinity of the heavens, etc.) did modern science break out of the mold of its Greek inheritance.

There are, to be sure, many factors that contributed to the rise of modern science, including nominalism and Renaissance humanism (see pp. 475–6), not to mention the rediscovered contributions of the Greeks themselves. But

---

[12] See, e.g., Langdon Gilkey, *Maker of Heaven and Earth: The Christian Doctrine of Creation in the Light of Modern Knowledge* (Garden City, NY: Doubleday, 1959), 123–9.

ever since Michael Foster's seminal articles in the 1930s, there has been a growing contention that Christianity – primarily its creation doctrine – played an important if not essential role in the rise of modern science.[13] Since empirical science can only proceed on the working assumption that nature is uniform and subject to universal and necessary laws, and since this presupposition cannot be established by the inductive method of science itself, the question arises: Whence come these larger suppositions? Many scholars today believe that Christianity's creation doctrine slowly encouraged the requisite philosophy of science needed to supplant Aristotelian cosmology, citing in particular the following implications of this doctrine:[14]

1. *Nature (i.e., the physical world) is contingent, a product of the divine will.* That the world is created and contingent on God's good will denies that the world or any part of it is divine (e.g., the heavens), or that God is part of the world (e.g., the world's animating soul or structure). Since nature has a beginning in time, and is not eternal or divine, it can rightly be studied and analyzed by human beings.

2. *Nature is good, created by a good God.* Since matter is good and not intrinsically evil or irrational, and since history is good and meaningful, and not an enemy from which to escape, material entities in their cause and effect relationships in time and space should be appreciated and studied in their own integrity.

3. *Nature is orderly, created by a wise God.* Since there is one Creator God, creation is a singular entity whose uniformity and order reflect the divine wisdom. As such, we can expect to discern an intelligible order of nature, since nature's goodness, truth, and beauty reflect the will and wisdom of God.

4. *Nature's flourishing is a cooperative endeavor, superintended by humanity as God's representative steward.* Created in God's image, humanity has a special responsibility for its earthly home, given God's blessing to be fruitful and mandate to subdue the earth (Gen. 1:26–8). The scientific enterprise was seen to be an essential aspect of the basic human vocation – to discover nature's potencies and potentialities for the benefits of humanity and creation at large. That human beings were "rational souls" (the dominant traditional interpretation of the image of God in humanity) implied the intelligence to do so; that human beings were commanded to

---

[13] The first of these seminal articles is Michael B. Foster, "The Christian Doctrine of Creation and the Rise of Modern Science," *Mind* 43 (1934), 446–68.

[14] See, e.g., Stanley Jaki, *Science and Creation: From Eternal Cycles to an Oscilla Universe* (Edinburgh: Scottish Academic Press, 1974); and Allen, *Christian Belief in a Postmodern World*, esp. ch. 1.

have "dominion" over the earth (another prevalent interpretation of the *imago Dei*) implied the warrant to do so. As we will see, these two dominant interpretations of what it means to be created in God's image could easily coalesce into more exploitative attitudes toward nature. But in the rise of modern science they also served the good intention of facilitating the noble endeavor of scientific inquiry and application.

If indeed Christianity contributed significantly to the rise of modern science, mainly by way of its creation theology, a contention bolstered by the Christian orientation of most of its pioneering scientists, then why do we have the popular impression today that Christianity and science are at odds with each other, that faith and reason inevitably clash? Here the trial of Galileo (1633) is often cited, in which Galileo was forced to recant his Copernican tendencies, and heliocentrism was condemned by the Roman Catholic Church. However, as Diogenes Allen points out, the case of Galileo was more of a complex affair of personalities, historical accidents, and political intrigues than it was a wholesale rejection by the church of free scientific inquiry (remember: the *proof* of heliocentrism comes only later with Newton). Nonetheless, the Galileo affair became the paradigm case of the clash of forward-looking science and repressive religion, of the incompatibility of scientific reason and Christian faith.[15] This seeming antagonism continued with the rise of evolutionary thought.

Creation and evolution

Among many things, this new empirical emphasis aided the rise of historical science (see pp. 512–13), which brought a greater appreciation of the importance of change and development over the course of time. When combined with geological study, this new historical emphasis also suggested a much older Earth than previously thought. Up to this juncture it was largely assumed, on a *prima facie* reading of scripture, that the Earth was young and that its present geologic features, including its peculiar fossil deposits, resulted from a combination of God's recent creation some 6,000–10,000 years ago and the catastrophes of the fall and worldwide flood. But the pioneers of modern geology (James Hutton and Charles Lyell) proposed a more uniform approach – that geologic processes have always been of the same nature and rate as observed today – a view which eventually won the day, requiring a very lengthy terrestrial history.

[15] See Allen, *Christian Belief in a Postmodern World*, 27–34.

An old Earth was a necessary condition for Charles Darwin's revolutionary theory of evolution. Given the data Darwin amassed on his famous *Beagle* expedition (1831–6), which he continued to add to and analyze for decades after, he became convinced that only an evolutionary model could account for the biological and geological patterns of the world's flora and fauna. But unlike proponents of other evolutionary theories in the air, Darwin offered a more natural, mechanistic explanation. Taking a cue from Thomas Malthus, who argued that a population naturally grows more quickly than food production can supply, Darwin reasoned that in such a competitive struggle where species produce more than an ecological niche can support, those who have variations that give them an advantage to survive will better perpetuate themselves – hence, natural selection. And when given a vast stretch of time – millions of years – species can evolve into other species, even from a common ancestor. Darwin published his theory as *The Origin of Species* (1859).

Unsurprisingly, the initial reaction of the churches was not one of great enthusiasm, since Darwin's theory proposed a much more fortuitous world than was the sense conveyed by certain scripture passages – as one *directly* well designed by its Maker. But it is interesting that by the twentieth century much of mainstream Christianity had reconciled itself to the possibility (if not actual idea) of evolutionary process as the means by which God created organic life – including even the likes of B. B. Warfield (1851–1921), the Princeton theologian who, ironically, is widely considered to be the architect of the twentieth-century doctrine of biblical inerrancy.[16] This is to say that, early on, scientific evolutionary perspectives were not viewed as irreconcilable with theological affirmations of creation, in contrast to the views of many Christians today.

The creation–evolution debate did not really heat up until the rise of fundamentalism, which is typically traced to the publication of *The Fundamentals* (1910–15), twelve mass-produced pamphlets that attempted to stake down the non-negotiable beliefs of evangelical Christianity. The epitome of this clash was the Scopes (monkey) trial of 1925 in which the nationally prominent anti-evolutionist crusader William Jennings Bryan was made sport of by the urbane trial lawyer Clarence Darrow. It was the fundamentalist movement with its commitments to an inerrantist scripture and literal hermeneutic that gave birth to the twentieth-century "creation science" movement.

---

[16] See David N. Livingstone, *Darwin's Forgotten Defenders: The Encounter Between Evangelical Theology and Evolutionary Thought* (Grand Rapids, MI: Eerdmans, 1987). For a history of the reception of Darwin, see Ronald L. Numbers, *The Creationists* (New York: Knopf, 1992).

Though there were precursors, Henry Morris's *The Genesis Flood* (1961), written in collaboration with OT scholar John Whitcomb, is the foundational document of current creation science.[17] In it they argue for a strict, literal read of the early chapters of Genesis as normative for science: God created the world in six twenty-four-hour days no more than 10,000 years ago, yet with an appearance of age. Originally a canopy of water enveloped the earth, producing a tropical terrarium effect that suppressed disease, accounting for the ancients' longevity (e.g., Methuselah's 969 years – Gen. 5:27). Only the fall brought death and carnivoric activity, and the torrents of the Noahic flood removed the terrarium effect and created the fossil record.

There have been many subsequent developments in the creation science movement that have attempted to shore up its scientific credentials. While not necessarily endorsing a young-earth perspective, the latest and most sophisticated version of creationism flies under the banner of *intelligent design*. It claims to argue from scientific evidence alone, apart from any scriptural basis, for the high probability of a Creator God. Regardless, the various manifestations of creation science are united in their opposition to evolutionary thinking, which they largely believe underwrites an irreligious atheism and undermines Judeo-Christian values. That the creation science movement today represents a force to be reckoned with is continually seen in polls which indicate that a near majority of Americans embrace creationist perspectives rather than evolutionary ones.[18]

Presently there is a range of positions on the creation–evolution question due to graded commitments to religion and science. On one end of this spectrum is (1) *evolutionary naturalism* or evolutionism, which considers itself a purely scientific posture with no religious elements; on the other end is (2) *(young-earth) creation science*, which privileges scripture as scientifically normative to the exclusion of any evolutionary science. Each of these extremes in its own way can be considered a "folk science" – the misuse of science to confirm an ideological commitment either unwarranted or unwarrantable by scientific inquiry – evolutionism reaching beyond the bounds of science's competence in ruling out a Creator God, creation science

---

[17] John C. Whitcomb Jr. and Henry M. Morris, *The Genesis Flood: The Biblical Record and its Scientific Implications* (Philadelphia: Presbyterian & Reformed, 1961).

[18] Over the two decades since the late 1980s, numerous Gallup polls have consistently shown that 44–7 percent of Americans agree with the statement: "God created man pretty much in his present form at one time within the last 10,000 years." For the most recent poll (as we write), see Alec M. Gallup and Frank Newport, eds., *The Gallup Poll: Public Opinion 2007* (Lanham, MD: Rowman & Littlefield, 2008).

imposing a questionable paradigm (young earth, flood geology) upon select – and therefore tendentious – empirical evidence.[19] Between these two extremes are a host of mediating positions, most generally (3) *progressive (old-earth) creationism*, which allows for an old earth and some evolutionary processes, but which holds that divine intervention (i.e., a miracle) is occasionally necessary to account for some new life forms, particularly humanity; and (4) *theistic evolutionism*, which holds that God uses evolutionary means and mechanisms to bring about created life forms.

Many Christians today are convinced that the evolution of organic life is a compelling scientific model, and that this model does not compromise the non-negotiables of creation doctrine – that God is the Creator (Designer and Sustainer) of life who providentially superintends an evolutionary process as a means of creation, and that human beings are created in the divine image, even if they are also the product of evolution. What is more difficult to specify theologically, given a theistic evolutionary model, is *how* God's creating hand or divine providence guides the evolutionary process without lapsing into a deistic understanding of this process. An evolutionary perspective also creates some theological tension for the question of the fall into sin – its time and nature – as well as for the dynamic of physical death in this theological mix.

Such issues notwithstanding, an evolutionary perspective, if true (and we have no better scientific model), must be addressed theologically. In so doing, we may find that it actually confers certain advantages theologically, among which is a greater appreciation for humanity's kinship with creation as a whole in contrast to historically dominant anthropocentric perspectives. This may be a timely theological emphasis, especially in view of the gathering ecological crisis and the question of human responsibility for and in this crisis.

Today's ecological crisis

Although degradation of the earth has taken place in many different localities throughout human history, it is only recently, given the expansive run of western industrialization, that we have created an ecological crisis of global proportions. It was especially the post-WWII industrial and economic boom, coupled with the growing threat of nuclear holocaust, that

[19] For a helpful treatment of both of these extremes as "folk science," see Howard J. Van Till, Davis A. Young, and Clarence Menninga, *Science Held Hostage: What's Wrong with Creation Science and Evolutionism* (Downers Grove, IL: InterVarsity, 1988).

awakened an ecological awareness in the socially conscious 1960s and thereafter, as expressed, for example, in Marvin Gaye's song "Mercy, Mercy Me (the Ecology)." The bloating litany of ecological concerns has since become a familiar refrain: air and water pollution; overpopulation; resource, ozone, and species depletion; global warming; acid rain; deforestation; genetic manipulation; threats of nuclear, biological, and chemical warfare; and the ghastly like.

In 1972 a group of young MIT scientists warned of a coming environmental train wreck that would occur in the absence of serious modification of human patterns of growth and consumption. They observed that since population grows exponentially (and along with it such factors as pollution and resource depletion), finite resources – including food production (the Malthus thesis) – will not, under current growth and consumption rates, make for a sustainable global society (in their estimate, in about 100 years). Three decades later, during which time the earth's population almost doubled, the authors updated their research and affirmed their original thesis – albeit this time estimating 70 years and counting.[20] Ecological prophets are not in short supply today – both pessimistic doomsayers and hopeful visionaries. The earth is groaning and threatens to spew us out of the land.

Ever since Lynn White Jr.'s seminal essay, "On the Historical Roots of our Ecologic Crisis" (1967), Christianity has been implicated as a major contributor to the ecological crisis.[21] White's main criticism was that Christianity, in aiding the rise of modern science, gave unbridled blessing to science's technological applications and exploitation of the earth. While White's chief complaint is debatable, subsequent criticisms of Christianity in this vein have generally been the following three:

1. Christianity promotes a dualism of spirit and matter that depreciates the physical earth.
2. Christianity fosters an anthropocentrism that exalts humanity at the expense of the non-human world.
3. Christianity advocates an escapist eschatology that neglects historical responsibility in view of an impending rescue to heaven.

While the causes of today's ecological crisis are many and more complex than can be laid upon any one scapegoat, we think that Christianity *historically and sociologically* has in varying degrees been guilty of these charges and ought to

---

[20] Donella Meadows, Jorgen Randers, and Dennis Meadows, *Limits to Growth: The 30-Year Update* (White River Junction, VT: Chelsea Green Publishing, 2004).
[21] Lynn White Jr., "On the Historical Roots of our Ecologic Crisis," *Science* 155 (March 10, 1967), 1203–7.

own up to any culpability. But we also hold that Christian *theology* at its best points us in a very different direction. We will pick up these three charges at the end of this chapter and indicate how one particular application of creation doctrine addresses these various criticisms apologetically, pointing a way forward for the church in the world.

A SYSTEMATIC CONSIDERATION OF CREATION DOCTRINE

Implications of creatio ex nihilo *doctrine*

In laying out in systematic fashion what the Christian doctrine of creation teaches about the God–world relationship, it is hard to improve upon the pedagogical structure of Langdon Gilkey's classic work, *Maker of Heaven and Earth*,[22] which delineates the basics of creation doctrine under the following three propositions. While employing Gilkey's basic rubrics, we nonetheless develop these ideas in our own way.

"God is the source of all that there is"
The linchpin of the doctrine of creation is the assertion that God creates *ex nihilo* – out of nothing. It is interesting to note, however, that few biblical scholars today think that this essential qualification can be read directly out of the Genesis 1 account, the classic text on creation, given its assumption of ancient near-eastern cosmology (presupposing the primeval watery chaos) and its basic polemical intent. The first clear statement of the *ex nihilo* idea comes only in the second-century BCE apocryphal book 2 Maccabees, which states: "I beg you, my child, to look at the heaven and the earth and see everything that is in them, and recognize that God did not make them out of things that existed" (7:28). In the NT, *creatio ex nihilo* is perhaps implied in Romans 4:17, which speaks about God "who gives life to the dead and calls into existence the things that do not exist," and Hebrews 11:3: "By faith we understand that the worlds were prepared by the word of God, so that what is seen was made from things that are not visible." But while explicit biblical reference to *ex nihilo* is slim, the teaching is a necessary theological implication of the overall biblical witness to the nature of God and the God–world relation. What *ex nihilo* most explicitly rules out is that God creates out of something – namely, preexistent matter. In Christian thought, whatever is eternal must also be divine. Since the triune God alone is God, nothing else, not even inert matter, can be considered eternal,

---

[22] Gilkey, *Maker*, esp. ch. 3.

since it would then in some sense rival or condition God – an affront to monotheism.

In this way, the early Judeo-Christian assertion of the *ex nihilo* claim excluded any form of *dualism*, such as that of the eternal conflict between spirit (God) and matter, as principally found in Greek and gnostic thought. We may take Plato's own "creation" account as a prime example. In his *Timaeus*, Plato sets out an account of the formation of the universe. He introduces a figure called the Demiurge or "craftsman" to mediate between the transcendent realm of being – that truly real realm of the forms – and the illusory material world of becoming. With an eye to the exemplary forms, the Demiurge imposes rational structure onto matter, changing the preexistent chaos into an ordered cosmos. Without this ordering action of the Demiurge based on the fixed and intelligible forms, the world would remain in chaos, since matter *per se* is intrinsically irrational and unstable. Plato's account, as we can see, presupposes a preexistent matter that conditions the shaping of the universe, and is therefore not a creation account in the sense of *ex nihilo*.

For Plato and the Greeks in general the material world was considered eternally existent. But since the physical world was a changeable world, ultimately involving disintegration and death, any sort of salvation had to be sought in a transcendent, non-material realm. Such a logic reinforces the soteriological and ethical dualism of gnosticism, which baldly posits that spirit is good and that matter is bad on account of its intrinsic irrationality. It is against this metaphysical and ethical dualism that Christianity affirms that God creates *ex nihilo* – matter is neither eternally existent nor intrinsically deficient, but is created by God. This leads into a second major affirmation.

"Creatures are dependent, yet real and good"

That creatures are good is the obvious implication of being created by a good God, and rules quite directly against any gnostic dualism. But this second proposition also rules out metaphysical *monism*. If in dualism there are two ultimate principles – such as spirit (the divine) and matter – in monism there is only one ultimate principle, namely, God or the divine, which alone possesses reality. Monism is also known as *pantheism*, which literally means that "all things are God." Classically found in some eastern religions, such as certain forms of Hinduism, a monistic construal of reality can also be found in western versions of philosophical idealism and romantic transcendentalism (e.g., Emerson), as well as in various manifestations of "new age" thought. While pantheists do not naively deny the physicality of the material world (as, for example, when bumping into a chair), when compared to the truly real thing – God – the finite and physical world pales in significance. In metaphysical monism it is as if, by comparison to God, the world were mere illusion. For the pantheist there is finally only one metaphysical reality – the eternal, infinite divine, the "All" – and anything that has any real substance participates in this divine All. The basic problem for the pantheist therefore is the delusion that we are finite and individuated beings. If we were really enlightened to the true nature of reality, we would realize that we are all a part of God – we are all divine. Consequently, the goal in the pantheist system is to achieve unification with God, which is the same thing as realizing one's own essential divinity. Though we are inclined to think that we are as individual droplets of water, we need to find ourselves dissolved in the ocean of the All. We might also note here that certain versions of Christian mysticism, especially those influenced by Neoplatonism, have also appeared to pursue this salvific goal – to be so absorbed into the reality of God that one's discrete personal existence disappears.

It is against this pantheistic orientation to life that the Christian doctrine of creation declares that creatures are dependent on God: we are not God or an essential part of God, but *creatures* of God. There is indeed one ultimate principle, God, but God is not the only *real* thing. On the contrary, our creatureliness is both real and good – it is not illusory and therefore something to be overcome. The fact that creatures are finite and individuated celebrates the diversity and beauty of God's creation. Each and every creature possesses an intrinsic goodness and worth, a discrete existence that glorifies the Creator.

How then do we characterize the Christian metaphysic? That is to ask, what is its basic ontology, conception of being, or view of ultimate principles? In a metaphysical dualism there are two eternal principles – spirit (the divine) and matter. In metaphysical monism or pantheism there is only the first of these principles, the divine, which possesses true reality. *Naturalism*, on the other hand, is a monism of the second principle, asserting the eternality and reality of matter alone. The Christian metaphysic is neither dualistic, monistic, nor naturalistic. Rather, it is best characterized as a *duality* that embraces two sorts of things: Creator and creature. The first of these, God, is primary and necessary; the second, creation, is derivative and contingent, since there was a time when creation was not, a time when only the triune God existed – a significant implication of *creatio ex nihilo*. Given the act of creation, however, the Christian metaphysic is a duality of Creator and creature, two distinct entities that must never be confused, as they are in the three other metaphysical systems. In gnostic dualism, human souls are deified and the rest of the material world is denigrated; in monism, all that truly exists is deified; and in naturalism, the material world takes the place of God as the ultimate principle. Each of these systems of thought in its own way confuses God and the world (or some particular aspect of the world, such as the human soul), a confusion that in biblical thought constitutes idolatry – elevating the creature to the status of God. According to Christianity, creatures are not God, but are radically dependent upon God as entities both real and good, each in its own integrity reflecting the goodness, truth, and beauty of the Creator.

"God creates in freedom and with purpose"

The first half of Gilkey's third proposition affirms that God creates freely, ruling out the position that God *had to* create for some reason or other. This conclusion is a further implication of *creatio ex nihilo*, since the fact that creation had a beginning in time and is not eternal indicates that it is not a necessary constituent for an everlasting God. Creation, accordingly, is a grace-ful affair – freely chosen and freely bestowed by God, which makes every created existence and moment a gift of God's grace.

One popular violation of this affirmation is the answer parents sometimes give their children when asked why God created the world: because God was lonely; God needed to create in order to have someone to love. A much more sophisticated version of this answer was given by the modern idealist philosopher Hegel, who in his complex philosophy made the world a necessary constituent or moment of God's being (see pp. 519–20). To simplify his thought: conceiving God principally as Love, but as only one divine person (the Father), Hegel necessitated creation as "the other" (symbolized by the Son) to which God must enter into relationship – even painfully so – in order to become Love in the process of world history (symbolized by the Spirit). In other words, God needs the world in order to love and become the love that God by definition is. While Hegel thought that he was rescuing the doctrine of the Trinity from Enlightenment criticisms that heralded its obsolescence, his apologetic for the Trinity falls short of orthodox standards, for Hegel proposes only an economic Trinity: God *becomes* a Trinity only in view of the world, only in the process of the God–world relation (reducing Christ and the Spirit to the creaturely level as symbols of this relation). Hegel's construct shows the importance of the doctrine of the immanent Trinity. That God is *eternally* a Trinity of persons, and not just one person, ensures that God eternally is Love. God does not have to create another to overcome loneliness or to enter into love. There is no deficiency in God's eternal personal being to which creation is a remedy. God creates freely, and creation is a product of God's gracious and beneficent will. This preserves God's sovereign freedom and transcendence over creation.

But this does not mean that the act of creation is willy-nilly, a capricious action or hastily made product on God's part. While affirming God's freedom on the one hand, Christian theology also affirms that God creates with purpose. This is to say both that God has good reason to create (in motive) and that the result of God's creation (in content) is inherently meaningful. First on *motive*: what could possibly motivate the triune God to create? We have ruled out loneliness or the need to love an other, on the basis of an eternal, immanent Trinity. One traditional answer is that God created for God's own glory or self-glorification. But this is sometimes presented in such a way that it makes God seem to be ego-deficient, as though God were in need of a chorus of creatures to sing God's praises. But let us return for a moment to the motive of love, not in the Hegelian sense, but in the sense of Richard of St. Victor, who observed that love by its very nature desires to share itself with others (see pp. 127, 466). Might God have created in order to share the trinitarian love and life, much like married couples who desire children, whether natural or adopted, or like families who gladly extend hospitality to others, a vocation the church itself is called to practice? And what about the motive of creativity itself? If it is human to be creative (productive), and if this is a virtue, perhaps even an aspect of the divine image in humanity, could not creativity also be a motivating factor for God? We must be careful here, however, not to necessitate creation and impugn the divine freedom. But what we can say is that given the fact of creation (that is, speaking *ex post facto*), it seems eminently appropriate – right and fitting – that the triune God would be a creative God. Whatever the case, given God's character, creation could not be ill motivated.

In addition to purposeful motive, the resulting product or *content* of creation must also be seen to be fraught with purpose. This is to say that creation itself is inherently meaningful; it is not thrown together in some *ad hoc* fashion, like many a warehouse piece of ersatz art. Since God is by nature the Good, the True, and the Beautiful, whatever God creates cannot but reflect God's character. Therefore creation is steeped in goodness, truth, and beauty. This means that we side with the realists over the nominalists in the medieval debate over what is supreme or "controlling" in God (see pp. 474–6). This debate centers on the extent of divine freedom and has important consequences for the theological enterprise itself. On one side, the nominalists held that what was supreme in God was God's free, sovereign will or power. God, they maintained, was free to will and to do whatever God wanted, because God by definition possesses *potentia absoluta*, absolute power. By the nominalist assumption, God could have created a very different world than the one we know – for example, one in which sins, as we classify them, would have been virtues, and virtues, as we know them, sins. For a nominalist, *something is good because God wills it*. But on the other side, the realists held that something like goodness or love is supreme in God, that God has an eternal nature that is good, true, beautiful, loving, and the like, and that God cannot do anything that would contradict this character. Therefore the realist actually contends that there are many things that God cannot do – for example, God cannot make a square circle, pronounce murder a virtue, commit deicide, and the like. For a realist, *God wills something because it is good* by the standard of God's eternal nature. The nominalist position, in our estimation, though nobly attempting to preserve the sovereignty of God, allows for too much caprice in God. Given the nominalist assumption, what is to say that God could not change God's mind at any time – say, about God's promise of future salvation? Actually, no nominalist can faithfully live like a nominalist, and so nominalism itself makes a distinction between *potentia absoluta* and *potentia ordinata,* ordained power. In God's primal self God has absolute power, but after God determines the ground rules for creation – what is good and true and beautiful – God restricts the divine power and remains faithful to the rules ordained for creation. But this still creates something of a crisis for our knowledge of and language for God, for on the nominalist score there is no real connection between our understanding of what is good, true, and beautiful and God's essential being. On the realist account, however, there is, for whatever in creation manifests goodness, truth, and beauty is a pointer to and reflection of what its Creator God essentially and eternally is. It is in this realist sense that we affirm an "analogy of being" – that creation in its very being and structure bears some likeness, some analogy to who God essentially is (see pp. 71–2). Without this basic analogy of being, the doctrine of general revelation is in jeopardy, which then means that special revelation comes in a vacuum – without any resonance or reflection in the created nature of things. A strong doctrine of creation as proposed here facilitates the theological enterprise by helping to secure a true knowledge of God.

Divine transcendence

While the doctrine of *creatio ex nihilo* implies these three particular affirmations about the God–world relationship, what this doctrine underscores most generally is God's radical *transcendence* over creation – that God surpasses and cannot be reduced to creation. Divine transcendence has important implications both ontologically – in respect to the issue of God's being *vis-à-vis* the world – and epistemologically – in respect to the route of human knowledge of the triune God.

Ontological implications

First, concerning God's being, it must be established that God (as Creator) is not a being among (created) beings, but has a different ontological status than creatures; God is of a different order of being. Simply stated, the triune God plus creation is not greater than the triune God alone. In our creational experience, being plus being occasions an increase: one apple plus one apple equals two apples – an increase in being. With God, however, things are different. God's uncreated being is so maximally perfect and sufficient that nothing added to God (e.g., creation) can increase or supplement God's being, even though God's dynamic interaction with creation can occasion an increase of divine glory, involve a new set of relationships, and the like. The triune God plus creation is not greater than the triune God alone. Whereas creatures are dependent on God for their being, God is independent of anything outside of God's own self. Another way of saying this is that creatures are *contingent* beings, meaning that our existence is conditional – it may or may not possibly be – whereas God's existence is *necessary*. What does it mean to be a necessary being? It means that God cannot but exist. Such a concept is the basis of Anselm's famous argument for the existence of God.

Anselm was the first to elaborate what has been called an *ontological argument* for God's existence. Unlike the cosmological or teleological arguments that reason *a posteriori* (based on observation or experience) from the effects or design of the world to their divine Cause or Designer, the ontological argument reasons *a priori* (before experience) – simply by thinking about the nature of God's being (see Table 6.1). In his *Proslogion*, Anselm proposes the working definition that God is "that thing than which nothing greater can be thought."[23] Given this sheer idea that can be thought by believer and atheist alike, it must be the case that God exists not only in our minds but also in reality, since if God existed only in our minds we could yet think of a greater possible being – namely, one that existed both in our minds *and in reality*. Anselm here treats "existence" as a divine perfection. Just as it is impossible that God be God apart from being just or wise, so also, he

---

[23] Anselm, *Proslogion*, 244.

Table 6.1 *Major types of theistic argument*

Type	Argument	Representatives
Cosmological argument	Argues variously from the effects in the world (*kosmos*) to God as their First Cause, Prime Mover, etc.	Aquinas' first four "Ways"
Teleological argument	Argues from the design, order, and purpose (*telos*) of the world to God as Designer.	Aquinas' fifth "Way"; Deists
Ontological argument	Argues from the sheer concept of God as greatest possible being (*on*) to God's necessary existence.	Anselm, René Descartes
Moral argument	Argues from the objectivity or necessity of human morality to God as Lawgiver and Guarantor of the moral project.	Immanuel Kant, C. S. Lewis

reasons, it is impossible that God be God apart from the fact of existing. God by definition exists, necessarily; therefore God is a necessary being.

While the philosophical debate has raged as to the plausibility and merits of Anselm's argument, it is best to understand it as a case of "faith seeking understanding," for which Anselm is also famous. This can be seen at the very outset of his argument, which begins with a prayer:

Now, Lord, since it is you *who gives understanding to faith*, grant me to understand as well as you think fit, *that you exist as we believe, and that you are what we believe you to be*. We believe that you are that thing than which nothing greater can be thought.[24]

Anselm already presupposes (believes) the divine reality he sets out to "prove" (understand). His argument is therefore circular. But that is the very nature and dynamic of theological thought – thinking through that which one already believes by faith – hence, faith seeking understanding. The crucial presupposition of Anselm's argument here is the Creator–creature distinction stemming from the *ex nihilo* claim. Since God is not a being among (created) beings whose existence is contingent, as the Creator, God's existence is necessary. God is a necessary being.[25]

This qualitative difference between God and creatures distinguishes monotheistic belief from all other metaphysical systems that conceive of God within a general category of being. In Greek mythology, for example, the Homeric gods cannot be conceived of apart from the world – they are

---

[24] Ibid., italics added.
[25] For the role of the Creator/creature distinction in Anselm's argument, see Robert Sokolowski, *The God of Faith and Reason: Foundations of Christian Theology* (Notre Dame, IN: University of Notre Dame Press, 1982), 1–11.

"principalities and powers" of the world (e.g., Poseidon is the power of the sea). If you take away the world, you take away the gods. In monotheistic thought, however, given creation out of nothing, when you take away the world, you still have God. God's being is independent and necessary. In this way God radically transcends the world.

Epistemological implications

From this ontological distinction of Creator and creature there follows an important epistemological implication. Put most simply, in the theological enterprise *faith transcends reason*. As the advances of modern science and technology demonstrate, human reason, when not impaired by ill will, works reasonably well on a functional level within the world. We are basically able to investigate our world rationally and apply such knowledge in constructive ways. Now if God were a being among beings, God would also be rationally discernible and subject to the laws of our reasoning within a general category of being. But since God radically transcends the world, revelation and faith are warranted – indeed necessary – avenues for knowing God. What the critiques of reason from Kant to the postmodern present teach us is that human reason has its distinct limitations – it is functionally limited to our finite, empirical world (and even then, as postmodernism reminds us, is significantly influenced by many other factors). Christianity can readily agree with the postmodern consensus that human reason *qua* reason cannot discern final or absolute truth. What is required for the fuller picture of life is a word or perspective from beyond our creaturely capabilities – that is, a revelation from God. The very doctrine of creation warrants this need for revelation as an implication of the Creator–creature distinction. In this sense, faith (accepting something as authoritatively true based on God's revelation) conveys a knowledge that transcends what human reason is able to establish on its own. Once a truth is revealed and accepted by faith, however, reason can go to work to make that faith more understandable (faith seeking understanding) and to articulate its (reasonable) connections to our creaturely world of experience. Here is where an analogy of being becomes so important. Since the triune God as the Good, True, and Beautiful created a world that is fundamentally good, true, and beautiful, God's revelation from beyond the creaturely realm has reflection and resonance within creation itself. This means therefore that the truths of revelation are not finally irrational within created existence, but are quite reasonable – indeed, they light up the landscape of creaturely existence.

Take the confessional truth of the Trinity, for example. Even Thomas Aquinas, who had a high estimate of human reason, argued that though reason could perhaps discern a First Cause, Prime Mover, and the like, it could not establish that God was a Trinity of Father, Son, and Spirit. The truth of the Trinity is a datum of special revelation. Once revealed, however, human reason can go to work to make sense of the doctrine and to show its reasonable connections with created experience. We would contend, for example, that a trinitarian conception of God better accounts for the unity and diversity of our world, for a social conception of humanity created in God's image, and for the basic human quest of meaningful relationships – that is, love – grounded in the relational Love that the Trinity eternally is. In other words, the trinitarian conception of God illuminates the landscape of experience in creation.

Or take the confessional truth of creation itself. Again, Aquinas rightly held that sheer human reason could not establish whether the physical world was created or existed eternally. Like the Trinity, the doctrine of *creatio ex nihilo* is a datum of special revelation. Once accepted by faith, however, the theistic assumption of a good, intelligible, and ordered creation makes better sense of life within our world. As we have contended, it was such positive assumptions about creation that facilitated the rise of modern science, which continues to be a reasonable endeavor today when ethically normed. Herein lies the moment of truth of "intelligent design": though it cannot be proven by scientific means (and even makes for a "folk science"), once accepted by faith that creation has a wise Maker, such an affirmation lights up the landscape of an intelligible world. It simply makes more sense of our experience to suppose that our world was designed than that it was not. This has always been the *faith*-driven truth of the teleological argument, even if this argument does not finally work as an independent *rational* demonstration of God's existence.

In sum, if we think through the epistemological implications of the Creator–creature distinction, we can generally conclude the following. Faith that embraces the deliverances of special revelation (the theological criterion of orthodoxy) transcends human reason. Once accepted by faith, however, reason can be rigorously employed to show the coherence of such doctrines (coherence criterion) and their reasonable connections with life in creation (relevance criterion).[26] This is especially the case if we assume an analogy of being between Creator and creature, for then special revelation does not come in a vacuum but illuminates general revelation within creation. Given the logic of *creatio ex nihilo*, implying the finitude of human reason, faith in response to divine revelation not only appears

---

[26] See pp. 20–1 for our theological criteria.

warranted, but is in fact necessary to truly know God and better grasp the larger picture of life – that is, to see the world in its necessary divine context. Indeed, when seen in this light, faith actually appears to be the most reasonable option. Otherwise we must capitulate to skepticism. While circular in form, this is theology as faith seeking understanding – thinking through the implications of the doctrine of creation.

Divine immanence

If we were to leave the discussion here, stressing only divine transcendence, we would be telling only half the story; we could also be in danger of promoting a more deistic conception of God as distant, aloof, and indifferent to the everyday affairs of the world. In addition to emphasizing God's transcendence over creation, therefore, we must also equally affirm God's *immanence* – the idea that God is also radically involved *within* creation. Such divine immanence takes a variety of forms.

Informally considered, we might say that God is radically in creation *as an artist's touch*.[27] Just as a work of art "contains" the artist, reflecting her imprint on every detail, so also creation reflects its divine artist in every good, true, and beautiful aspect. One can see, hear, smell, taste, touch, reason, and intuit the artifacts of creation and experience the touch of creation's Artificer, who is not just over creation, but who also delights within creation. In this sense all of created life is sacramental – mediating, participating, and pointing beyond itself to the divine presence.

A more traditional way of articulating God's immanence in creation is *via providence*. The doctrine of divine providence was typically conjoined to creation as its *alter ego*. Whereas creation was principally conceived of as "creation in the beginning," as an act completed in the past, providence was considered the means by which God continued "to provide" for creation. Some theologians break the doctrine of providence down into parts, such as preservation and governance. Preservation concerns the way that God continues to sustain creation in its natural integrity; governance concerns the way that God intervenes in the affairs of the world so as to direct history to God's desired goal. The affirmation of God's providence was seen to be the principal bulwark against a deistic conception of God. As we saw in the biblical section, however, the Bible does not draw a sharp distinction between creation and

---

[27] Cf. Daniel L. Migliore, *Faith Seeking Understanding: An Introduction to Christian Theology*, 2nd edn. (Grand Rapids, MI: Eerdmans, 2004), 110–13, for a helpful discussion of various models of creation, in which he proposes "artistic play" as the best approximate model of *creatio ex nihilo*.

providence. Rather, the Bible conveys something more along the lines of continuing creation (*creatio continua*), a more fluid concept that would also better account for the lengthy formative history of the cosmos, including the evolutionary development of organic life.

A third form of immanence concerns the particular trinitarian way in which God is radically within creation, namely, *in the Spirit*. A classic way of understanding the general pattern of God's actions toward the world is "from the Father, through the Son, in the Spirit" (whereas creation's response, conversely, is "in the Spirit, through the Son, to the Father"). As with all of God's workings, creation is a trinitarian act, a cooperative effort of all divine persons. The Father creates through the mediation of the Son in the power and energies of the Spirit. Therefore, apart from the period of Christ's earthly life, there is a distinct sense in which the person of the Spirit is the nearest or most immanent divine person, the one who presently mediates the trinitarian presence in creation. Given the Spirit's vivifying role in creation, sanctifying role in redemption, glorifying role in the anticipated new creation, and ubiquitous empathetic presence, we might say that the triune God is radically immanent in creation through the presence and work of the Spirit (see Chapter 11).

Retrieving immanence in view of the ecological crisis

Building on this pneumatological perspective, Jürgen Moltmann in *God in Creation* proposes that God's immanence in creation also implies that creation exists "in the Spirit" – the personal divine energies, presence, even "womb" in which "we live and move and have our being" (Acts 17:28). Moltmann proposes this more reciprocal understanding of the God–world relation as a needed perspective in today's ecological crisis. With many others, he fears that modern industrial and technological society has forfeited any sense of divine immanence. This "practical atheism" has reinforced an objectification of nature as a sheer object for our knowledge (science) and manipulation (technology), justifying its exploitation and contributing to the ecological crisis. Recapturing a sense of divine immanence, in addition to viewing the world as flourishing in God, could aid in re-envisioning the world as God's creation and reinvigorating the human responsibility this implies.[28]

The retrieval of God's immanence in creation helps to address the eco-criticism that Christianity promotes a dualism of spirit and matter that

---

[28] Jürgen Moltmann, *God in Creation: A New Theology of Creation and The Spirit of God*, trans. Margaret Kohl (San Francisco: Harper & Row, 1985), esp. 72–103.

depreciates the physical earth. But this is only one piece of the apologetic retrieval of immanence. We have emphasized that Christian theology concerns (1) the triune God, (2) creation, and (3) their relation. As practiced in much of Christian history, however, especially when given a weak creation doctrine, Christian theology has appeared to be more concerned, reductively so, with (1) the one God, (2) humanity, and (3) their historical relation. Accordingly, each of these component parts – God, humanity, and history – has been regarded as so transcendent over the non-human creation that they have depreciated creation as a whole. Since we have already suggested ways in which God the Trinity can be perceived more immanently in creation, it remains to be seen how both humanity and the history of the God–human relation need to be viewed more immanently in the space-time dynamic of creation as a whole.

That humanity is created in God's image is actually a very important form of divine immanence. But the dominant historical interpretation of the image – as the rational soul (see pp. 166–8) – has so privileged the human over every other creature as to disparage the rest of creation. This interpretation has promoted an unhealthy anthropocentrism: created in God's image, humans have considered themselves the transcendent lords and masters of creation – and in this sense the only creatures that really matter. The rest of creation – animate or inanimate – has largely been relegated to the status of "raw material" for the building of human culture. While not disputing the uniqueness of humanity, we think that such uniqueness is better viewed along the lines of possessing a special task of stewardly responsibility – of tending the earth and directing history along just paths. This means that we need to emphasize that humanity is immanent in creation, just as any other creature. In this connection, Moltmann helpfully suggests that human beings are not only created *imago Dei*, but also *imago mundi* – in the image of the earth. Created from dust, we also return to the dust (Gen. 3:19). We are not spirits who fell from heaven, but are rooted in the earth, a perspective that can also accommodate an evolutionary understanding of human development.[29] As the crowning complexity of organic creation, endowed most articulately with the gift of language, we are the priests of creation who specially mediate the God–world relation: we represent God to creation and creation to God. We embody in a unique way the divine presence and in turn give voice to all of creation's praise.[30]

[29] See ibid., 185ff.
[30] See Douglas John Hall, *Imaging God: Dominion as Stewardship* (Grand Rapids, MI: Eerdmans, 1986), 183–205, esp. 204–5.

A strong doctrine of creation, while placing human beings in the exalted role of being God's vice-regents (*imago Dei*), also places us knee deep in creation's mud, sweat, and tears (*imago mundi*). In view of the ecological crisis, we must envision ourselves as not only transcendent over creation, but also immanent within it. This change of mentality, along with a consistent enacting of it in practice – the more important piece – would address the ecological criticism that Christianity fosters an anthropocentrism that exalts humanity at the expense of the non-human world.

The third component that needs to be viewed more immanently is the history of the relation between God and creation. In premodern times, as we have seen, the category of history was not taken seriously enough, and the God–human relation was understood in more spatially transcendent terms – as the journey of the soul to the heaven of God's dwelling. Only in the nineteenth century did history come fully into its own as an important category of truth, an intellectual development that we consider a theological gain, since it better reflects the Judeo-Christian embrace of time. But in modernity history itself became overemphasized, leading to a type of historicism, whereby the truth of anything was reduced to "what actually happened," especially in its meaning and significance for the history-maker, humanity. This shift in emphasis from the cosmological to the historical thus also accentuated the priority of the God–human relation, wherein what really matters is the history of God and "man" (exclusion intended). Here again, history overly dominates the broader compass of creation, making creation the mere "stage" for the divine–*human* drama. What is needed as a corrective is to see history more immanently in creation at large, and to remember that the whole of creation is taken up in relation to God. If the beginning of this relationship with God involves a whole creation that is "very good" – including both its good space and time (Gen. 1) – the end of this relationship envisions the whole of a glorified creation, a new heaven and earth (Rev. 21–2). Here history does not hover over creation, concerned only with the God–human relation, but takes up the whole of creation into the trinitarian history of God with the world. To see the history of the God–human relation in these more immanent terms is a helpful step in counter-ing the eco-criticism that Christianity advocates an escapist eschatology in neglect of historical responsibility (see p. 401).

While there are other necessary and complementary perspectives, to think theologically about the gathering ecological crisis requires a more immanent perspective on God, humanity, and the history of their relation within the context of the earth and creation as a whole. These are all implications of a strong doctrine of creation. Once again, however, the main rebuttal to such ecological criticisms of Christianity can come only through a seriously altered Christian witness in living sensibly in creation. Such responsible living in creation is part of humanity's vocation as the image of God (*imago Dei*), the topic of our next chapter.

FOR FURTHER READING

Gilkey, Langdon, *Maker of Heaven and Earth: The Christian Doctrine of Creation in the Light of Modern Knowledge* (Garden City, NY: Doubleday, 1959).

Gunton, Colin E., *The Triune Creator: A Historical and Systematic Study*, Edinburgh Studies in Constructive Theology (Grand Rapids, MI: Eerdmans, 1998).

Harlow, Daniel C., "Creation According to Genesis: Literary Genre, Cultural Context, Theological Truth," *Christian Scholars Review* 37, no. 2 (2008), 163–98.

Moltmann, Jürgen, *God in Creation: A New Theology of Creation and the Spirit of God*, trans. Margaret Kohl (San Francisco: Harper & Row, 1985).

Roukema, Riemer, *Gnosis and Faith in Early Christianity: An Introduction to Gnosticism*, trans. John Bowden (Harrisburg, PA: Trinity Press, 1999).

Van Till, Howard J., *et al.*, *Portraits of Creation: Biblical and Scientific Perspectives on the World's Formation* (Grand Rapids, MI: Eerdmans, 1990).

CHAPTER 7

Humanity in the image of God and the disfigurement of sin

THE QUESTION OF HUMAN IDENTITY

In his classic work *The Nature and Destiny of Man*, American theologian Reinhold Niebuhr observed that humanity is a puzzling paradox.[1] On the one hand, we fancy ourselves spiritual beings who transcend the sheer dictates of nature, yet we are also quite evidently children of the natural world, bearing a likeness and kinship with other animals – the paradox of our earthly stature. On the one hand, we seem to occupy center stage of the cosmic drama, yet we are easily dazzled and dwarfed by the vast spaces and

---

[1] Reinhold Niebuhr, *The Nature and Destiny of Man: A Christian Interpretation* (New York: Charles Scribner's Sons, 1943), 1.

times of the universe – the paradox of our place in the cosmos. On the one hand, we consider ourselves basically good and have proven that we are capable of great virtue, but at the same time we have perpetrated the greatest evils and acts of barbarity – the paradox of our virtue. For example, the same human race that includes Mother Teresa and Gandhi, who gave of their lives selflessly, has also produced Hitler and Stalin, who took countless lives through mass murder; the same humanity that makes astounding medical advances in preservation of life has also manufactured factories of death, perpetrating practices of abortion, euthanasia, and even genocide. Such paradoxes raise the question of human identity: What is humanity? What is it that makes a person human? In short, who are we?

A biologist might say that human beings are soft machines, forms of life in which a series of chemical reactions and other natural processes take place. A sociologist might observe that human beings are communal creatures, needing interaction with others in order to exist and flourish. A psychologist might suggest that humanity's uniqueness consists in its consciousness, in its capacity to be cognizant of self and of others. A linguist might point to humanity's refined facility for complex and meaningful communication. A philosopher might argue that what makes human beings unique is their intellect, their rationality, or their capacity for abstract thought. A scholar of religion might say that human beings are set apart by their possession of a spiritual dimension. So what is a human being? As we can see, a variety of answers can be offered to this basic anthropological question from a host of disciplinary perspectives.

While appreciating all such "definitions" of humanity, Christian theology insists that the question of human identity can be resolved only in relationship to God. As Emil Brunner argues, humanity "must first of all be defined theologically; only then may the philosopher, the psychologist and the biologist make their statements."[2] This insistence flows from the conviction that, in the final analysis, human beings cannot be understood in terms of themselves. Rather, our identity must be anchored in something greater or transcendent – ultimately God our Creator. Interestingly, the word "identity" comes from the Latin word *idem*, which means "same." In identity formation, we always associate ourselves with things with which we claim some sameness or similarity, whether this be our age, gender, relationships, profession, possessions, political preference, or other category *ad infinitum*. Such associations can change considerably throughout the course

---

[2] Emil Brunner, *Man in Revolt: A Christian Anthropology*, trans. Olive Wyon (London: Lutterworth, 1939), 102.

of a lifetime, creating many an identity crisis. In modern western culture, people (especially men) tend to articulate their identity in terms of their profession and possessions. In this way, we principally identify ourselves as doctors, lawyers, merchants, plumbers, nurses, and the like, or we prize ourselves as members of a certain social or economic class – proclaiming our "sameness" with these groups. Christian theology, however, would not want to reduce human identity to these dimensions, but would rather express that identity in terms of that which is most fundamental *outside* the sphere of the human. Theologically speaking, a human being is first and foremost a being created for relationship with God. Only this divine reality beyond ourselves secures our true, stable, and enduring identity. Dietrich Bonhoeffer once expressed this truth in a poem he wrote while imprisoned by the Nazis during WWII, which movingly asks the question "Who Am I?" For most of the poem, Bonhoeffer vacillates in his reflections between how others perceive him – as strong, calm, courageous, and full of faith in the face of his trying prison circumstances – and how he perceives himself – as weak, restless, frightened, and beset by doubt. He then ponders which person he truly is. Without coming to any conclusion, he nonetheless takes solace that whoever he is, he belongs to God.[3] Bonhoeffer's poem suggests that the fundamental identity of human beings can be grasped only in relation to God our Creator. In Christian thought, this dynamic of human identity is captured succinctly in the doctrine that humanity is created in the image and likeness of God (Gen. 1:26). The ultimate likeness or sameness (*idem*) that identifies humanity beyond its own fleeting and insecure confines and classifications is its association – even, astonishingly, its similarity – with God. The affirmation that humanity is created in the "image of God" (*imago Dei*) is the most fundamental anthropological datum in the biblical text.

THE IMAGE OF GOD IN THE BIBLICAL TEXT

Old Testament

The OT references to the image of God are restricted to the book of Genesis.[4] In fact, they are all found in a rather limited part of it – the literary unit often known as the primeval history (chapters 1–11). The first of

---

[3] See Bonhoeffer, *Letters and Papers*, 347–8.
[4] The following account of the biblical materials draws upon G. C. Berkouwer, *Man: The Image of God*, trans. Dirk W. Jellema (Grand Rapids, MI: Eerdmans, 1962), 67–118; Anthony A. Hoekema, *Created in God's Image* (Grand Rapids, MI: Eerdmans, 1986), 11–32; J. Richard Middleton, *The Liberating Image: The* Imago Dei *in Genesis 1* (Grand Rapids, MI: Brazos, 2005), 43–90.

these references sounds the keynote. After Genesis 1 relates the ordering of creation and the bringing forth of creatures "according to their various kinds" (1:11, NIV), the text then depicts God's culminating act as the summoning forth of a creature made according to the *divine* likeness:

Then God said, "Let us make humankind in our image [*tselem*], according to our likeness [*demut*]; and let them have dominion over the fish of the sea, and over the birds of the air, and over the cattle, and over all the wild animals of the earth, and over every creeping thing that creeps upon the earth." So God created humankind in his image,

> in the image of God he created them;
> male and female he created them.

God blessed them, and God said to them, "Be fruitful and multiply, and fill the earth and subdue it; and have dominion over the fish of the sea and over the birds of the air and over every living thing that moves upon the earth." (Gen. 1:26–8)

As God addresses the heavenly court ("Let us"), the role of gendered humanity ("male and female") in the new created order is specified in terms of rule ("have dominion") and (pro)creativity ("be fruitful and multiply"). But the biblical text is terse and compact in its expression here, not immediately elaborating the precise meaning and implications of humanity's being created in the image of God.

The other few references to the "image of God" in Genesis help to complement our understanding in the following ways. Genesis 5:1–3 reiterates the claim made in Genesis 1:26–8 that humanity is created in the image of God. This reiteration is significant because the intervening narrative includes the fall into sin (Gen. 3), thus indicating that in some real way the image of God survives the scars of human sin. In similar fashion, Genesis 9:6 concludes that since humanity is created in the image of God, human blood may not be shed. In other words, human beings possess a dignity and should be accorded respect by virtue of their special status. This exalted status is signaled elsewhere in the biblical text, nowhere more notably than Psalm 8, which begins with a declaration of Yahweh's majesty – beside which human beings pale in comparison. Then comes a key disjunction – "yet": "Yet you have made them a little lower than *God*, and crowned them with glory and honor. You have given them dominion over the works of your hands; you have put all things under their feet" (8:5–6, italics added).[5]

---

[5] The Hebrew term for God in verse 5 is "Elohim," which can also be rendered as "angels," as followed by some English translations, to the effect that God has created human beings a little lower than the angels. However, we agree with the NRSV's translation (used above) that compares human beings with God rather than angels, since the God–humanity relation is the point of comparison in the *imago Dei*, which Psalm 8 appears to explicate, even without using the phrase.

The high view of humanity as *imago Dei* that is implied by Psalm 8 and the Genesis "image of God" references can be further explicated by looking closely at the key terms involved in the keynote text, Genesis 1:26–7. What, more precisely, are the meanings of "image" and "likeness"? "Likeness" (*demut*) functions quite simply as a synonym for "image." It is not a separate concept but an instance of the Hebrew penchant for poetic parallelism.[6] The Hebrew term for "image" (*tselem*) is the more crucial term. A *tselem* in the OT typically refers to a statue or idol. Most instructively, a *tselem* could refer to a monument crafted in the likeness of an ancient near-eastern king that would be set up in and at the borders of his domain in order to identify his claim of dominion – *this* is the ruler of this kingdom (e.g., Dan. 3). By analogy, as OT theologian Gerhard von Rad points out, the King of heaven and earth places a divine image or *tselem* in creation – humanity: "Just as powerful earthly kings, to indicate their claims to dominion, erect an image of themselves in the provinces of their empire where they do not personally appear, so man is placed upon earth in God's image as God's sovereign emblem."[7] Humanity, fashioned in God's likeness, thus reflects and represents God in creation in some special royal way – declaring the earth to be God's kingdom. This is in all likelihood why there is a proscription against physical representation or likenesses of God in Israelite law (see Deut. 5:8). God already has an image, a divine likeness in creation: humanity. Human beings are God's living statues on the earth, bearing God's likeness, declaring that the "earth is the LORD's and all that is in it" (Ps. 24:1).

With the idea of humanity standing as the *tselem* or representative of God in creation as a key for understanding the notion of the image of God in the OT, a number of crucial implications follow: First, the image cannot be limited to a single point of likeness between God and humanity (as the tradition has often proposed, usually by focusing on human reason), but includes the whole array of ways in which humanity resembles God, both in character and in activity. Second, the general human vocation has a sacramental quality about it, pointing beyond itself to the reality of God. Third, the visible and physical body cannot be depreciated or excluded from the image of God, as it often has in the history of theology (see pp. 186–8), since the function of an "image" resides in its visibility. Fourth, as God's royal representative, humanity bears a significant responsibility for the earth

---

[6] As we will shortly see, some interpreters in the Christian tradition have considered the two terms to have distinct meanings.

[7] Gerhard von Rad, *Genesis: A Commentary*, trans. John H. Marks *et al.*, rev. edn. (Philadelphia: Westminster, 1972), 60. Also see von Rad, *Old Testament Theology*, I: *The Theology of Israel's Historical Traditions*, trans. D. M. G. Stalker (New York: Harper & Row, 1962), 146–7.

and its history. And fifth, human beings possess great dignity, unlike the estimate held by other ancient near-eastern cosmologies, as in the *Enuma Elish*, where human beings are viewed as slaves to the gods, destined for mere drudge labor.[8] We will draw upon and develop these important implications when elaborating our systematic statement of the image of God.

New Testament

Whereas the OT introduces the theme of humanity's image-bearing, the NT develops and refines this important idea. While some texts simply reiterate the general OT teaching of the fact of humanity's special status as the created image of God (see, e.g., Jas. 3:9), other texts, more importantly, equate the image (Gk. *eikon*) with Jesus Christ. We read in 2 Corinthians 4:4, for example, that "the god of this world has blinded the minds of the unbelievers, to keep them from seeing the light of the gospel of the glory of Christ, who is the image of God" (see also Col. 1:15; Heb. 1:3). Therefore, while presupposing and reaffirming the OT account of the image, the NT diverges strikingly in specifying one particular person – Jesus Christ – as the special embodiment of the image. Why is this the case?

An answer to this question might be introduced with an analogy. Suppose that we were to visit the Louvre Museum in Paris in order to behold a famous painting, such as the Mona Lisa. Suppose that after viewing it one day, we returned the next day for further observation and reflection. During the intervening night, however, some vandals broke into the Louvre and sprayed pink paint all over the painting. As we behold the disfigured painting, now barely recognizable, we stammer the question: "Is that the Mona Lisa?" Well, yes – in some sense it still is. But it is awfully hard to recognize. What it now requires, of course, is restoration. Analogously, an act of disfiguration has occurred to the image of God in humanity – an act called the fall into sin. While we will discuss sin more fully in the second half of this chapter, we observe here that human sin and rebellion distorted creation and its goodness, including the image of God. This distortion meant that the image of God needed to be restored in creation – like a vandalized painting. As Anselm once wrote: "But that image is so worn and blotted out by faults, so darkened by the smoke of sin, that it cannot do that for which it was made, unless you renew and refashion it."[9] This restoration was made possible by the incarnation and ministry of the second person of the Trinity, Jesus Christ, the proper image of God. Important NT texts thus

---

[8] Middleton, *Liberating Image*, develops this thesis at length.   [9] Anselm, *Proslogion*, 244.

point to the need for a remaking, renewing, or restoration of the image. In Romans 8:29, for example, we read that God's chosen are called "to be conformed to the image of his Son." Other NT texts call for putting off the "old self" and putting on the "new self," which is another way of referring to the renewal of the image of God (see 2 Cor. 3:18; Col. 3:9–10; Eph. 4:22–4). Thus it makes sense that the NT would describe Jesus Christ as the proper image of God, the one through whom our defaced image is restored.

Clearly, the idea that humanity is created in the image of God is an important teaching in the biblical narrative. That teaching, however, is not elaborated in great detail or explicitly systematized in the text. The Christian tradition has therefore made varied use of the theme. After reviewing some key interpretations offered in the history of theology – one from each of the tradition's first four main periods – we will offer a systematic interpretation of the theme.

THE IMAGE OF GOD IN THE HISTORY OF THEOLOGY

Irenaeus

As noted in the last chapter, in his famous work *Against Heresies* Irenaeus develops his major theological positions in dispute with the heresies of his day, especially gnosticism.[10] However, in spite of Irenaeus' polemic against gnosticism and his disdain for influences foreign to Christianity, he remains rather indebted to the assumptions of Greek philosophy in his anthropology. For Irenaeus, a human being consists of an immortal soul united with a mortal body. As he interpreted the biblical teaching about humanity's special created status, Irenaeus strongly distinguished between "image" and "likeness" (rather than seeing the two terms as roughly synonymous as the biblical writers likely intended). In his view, the *image* of God concerns humanity's natural capacities and primarily involves the immortal soul's rationality and freedom. This image remained in humanity after the fall into sin. *Likeness* to God, on the other hand, concerns humanity's original righteousness and special relationship with God. This supernatural endowment was lost as a result of the fall into sin and stands in need of restoration, which takes place through the incarnation of the Logos (Christ thus truly reveals both the image and the likeness of God).[11] Only believers possess the restored likeness, which Irenaeus calls the spirit – a third dimension of his anthropology, in addition to the body and the rational soul, a dimension which is a gracious endowment of the Holy Spirit bestowed only upon redeemed human beings.

[10] See Irenaeus, *Against Heresies*, esp. 3.23; 4. preface; 4.4, 37–9; and 5.6, 16.
[11] See Brunner, *Man in Revolt*, 93, 503–5.

For Irenaeus, then, following the blueprint of Greek philosophy, the image of God is something largely equated with the soul's rationality and freedom – capacities of the soul not lost in the fall into sin. This Greek-influenced interpretation of the image as the rational soul set the tone for the subsequent Christian tradition. For Irenaeus, however, humanity's original righteousness and special relationship with God were lost through the fall into sin. Irenaeus thus senses that something about humanity's special created status remains in human beings despite sin, but something else is indeed lost.

Thomas Aquinas

In his discussion of creation in the *Summa Theologiae*, Thomas Aquinas claims that the image of God is found chiefly in intellectual creatures, who most image God when they reflect the divine self-understanding and love.[12] In focusing on the rational soul as the locus of the image of God, Thomas's theology is clearly informed not only by the assumptions of Greek philosophy (as was Irenaeus'), but also by Augustine's psychological analogy for the Trinity – the rational mind (Father) that both knows itself (Son) and loves itself (Spirit).[13] The primacy of the intellect for Thomas's view of the image can be seen in the fact that he argues that the image is found more perfectly in angels than in human beings, since angels have a superior intellectual nature. With respect to humanity, the image of God is present in three different but related ways.[14] First, by nature all human beings have a capacity – found in the mind – for understanding and loving God. This aspect of the image is unaffected by sin and reflects Thomas's strong view of the enduring integrity of created human nature. Second, by grace some human beings ("the just") do in fact know and love God to some degree, the degree to which they are being restored in the image through Christ. Third, those human beings who have gone to glory ("the blessed") know and love God perfectly by virtue of their participation in the beatific vision – the contemplation of the divine essence or nature of God. All persons thus bear the image of God to some degree, even after the fall into sin, although believers, and especially those in heaven, image God more purely. Aquinas thus recognizes that the residual image in sinful humanity stands in need of restoration.

John Calvin

At the outset of his *Institutes of the Christian Religion*, John Calvin argues that only in the light of knowledge of God can we human beings know ourselves.

---

[12] Thomas Aquinas, *Summa Theologica*, 1a.93.2–6.   [13] See, e.g., ibid., 1a.93.8.   [14] Ibid., 1a.93.4.

Accordingly, after examining the nature of God, Calvin proceeds to a discussion of theological anthropology.[15] In his view, human beings consist of a mortal body and an immortal soul. The soul inhabits and animates the body, which Calvin describes in rather Platonic fashion, even calling the body the "prison house" of the soul.[16] In his understanding of the image of God in its pre-fall, integral state, Calvin focuses on Adam's original clarity of intellect, rational governance of the passions, and proper regulation of the senses. Like Irenaeus and Aquinas, therefore, Calvin conceives of the image in predominantly spiritual terms, since its primary locus is the rational soul, although he states that the divine image also shines forth in some degree through the body. After the fall into sin, which resulted in alienation from God, humanity's special status as the image of God was not completely destroyed, but it was horribly disfigured. The image of God therefore stands in need of restoration. Thus Calvin thinks that a clearer understanding of the divine image can be found only by looking at the Second Adam, Jesus Christ, who is the proper image of God. When the divine image is seen in Christ, it is clear that true knowledge of God, as well as "pure righteousness and holiness," are integral to that image. But then Calvin reverts in his discussion of the image to an examination of the faculties of the soul.

Our consideration of a representative theologian from each of the patristic, medieval, and Reformation periods has shown the dominance of the rational soul as the central feature of the divine image in humanity. This interpretation, or some variation on its theme – the image as intellect, conscience, spirituality, immortality, freedom – has tended to accentuate an individualistic conception of the image of God. In the twentieth century, however, we can detect a shift of emphasis to a more relational conception of the *imago Dei*. Highlighting the fact that humanity is created "male and female" (Gen. 1:27), theologians such as Barth, Brunner, and Bonhoeffer took this gendered qualification of humankind as a key interpretive principle in order to emphasize a more social and relational theological anthropology.

Emil Brunner

Swiss theologian Emil Brunner has been especially influential in elaborating a relational perspective.[17] Highlighting the distinction between the ideal state in which humanity was created (i.e., good) and the actual state in which human beings exist (i.e., sinful), Brunner argues that with respect to

---

[15] Calvin, *Institutes*, 1.15.   [16] Ibid., 1.15.2.

[17] See especially Emil Brunner, *Dogmatics*, II: *The Christian Doctrine of Creation and Redemption*, trans. Olive Wyon (Philadelphia: Westminster, 1952), 55–61, 75–8. See also Brunner, *Man in Revolt*.

the *imago Dei*, attention must be paid to the centrality of divine love and the desire on God's part to have fellowship and relationship with humanity. The loving God endowed human beings with freedom and the capacity to respond to God, a capacity which Brunner calls the "formal image" – a teaching that he largely associates with the OT texts reviewed above. The formal image is something we never lose; not even the vitiating effects of sin undo it. However, our actual response to God has been compromised by sin. We do not respond to God properly – that is, lovingly, willingly, gratefully. This proper response is what Brunner calls the "material image" – a view he associates with the teachings of the NT on the subject: "The loss of the *Imago*, in the material sense, presupposes the *Imago* in the formal sense."[18] In order to enable a proper response to God, the image must be restored, and this occurs through faith in the incarnate Jesus Christ, who is the true image of God. In focusing on responsibility as a formal constituent of humanity, albeit materially impaired by sin, Brunner underscores *relationality* as central to the image of God. In sum, we are called to live in right and responsible relationship with God and with one another, a vocation that is the essence of the image of God, and which is paradigmatically expressed in the fact that humanity is created "male and female," fashioned for relationship as social beings.

THE IMAGE OF GOD: A REPRESENTATIONAL-RELATIONAL CONCEPTION

In crafting a view of the image of God that gathers together the key elements of the Bible's teaching in dialogue with the best insights of the tradition, our model emphasizes the representational function of the image – humanity as the royal stewards of the divine King of creation – and its relational dynamic. Accordingly, the following proposal traces this image through the matrix of its various relationships – with God, with other human beings, and with nature – giving special attention to God's designs for the *original* image before the fall into sin and the *restored* image that is revealed in the incarnation of Christ.

Relationship between God and humanity

As we contended in the previous chapter, the triune God creates the world not out of need but out of love. In so doing, God desires fellowship with

---

[18] Brunner, *Creation and Redemption*, 60.

creation, and particularly with humanity, on whom special status is bestowed. God makes space for humanity so as to enable a relationship of a free and loving kind, and reveals the divine identity and will to this special creature who, bearing the divine image, is endowed with the capacity for free response or "response-ability." Clad with freedom and responsibility, humanity is called to reflect God's likeness and character in the range of its relationships – not only to be the visible *image of God* (noun) in creation, but also *to image God* (verb) concretely in all of its tasks and activities. What is central to this pivotal divine–human relationship, therefore, is God's gracious act of bringing humanity into being, revealing the divine life, and then calling human beings to respond in right relationship to the God who first seeks them. Since God creates humanity out of sheer grace and unconditional love, each person possesses an ineradicable dignity and worth.

If we bear in mind the ancient near-eastern conception of *tselem*, humanity can be understood as the living representation of God, called to mark out and take care of God's created domain. A proper relationship with God, therefore, is the prerequisite for humanity to live out its vocation as the representative of God's concerns in the world. This relationship ought to be characterized by *faithfulness*. As the earthly steward of the heavenly King, humanity is the royal servant, whose vocation requires faithful obedience. Rather than living egocentrically for the concerns of the self, humanity is called to live exocentrically (other-centered) for the divine interests in the larger world. Mired in sin, however, the human race rejects its center in God, striving instead in egocentric directions, creating idols to and of the self, and living in disobedience rather than in faithfulness. In such a condition, humanity evidences little of the faithfulness that befits its role as the divine representative in creation. We must look therefore to the *restored* image of God for a healthier glimpse of this image. In the incarnation, cross, and resurrection, Jesus Christ is the true image of God, the eminent representative of the triune King in creation, who as the true human being models for us a faithful and obedient likeness of God in the world.

The first representative of humanity, the "first Adam," did not accept the limitations of earthly life as the servant of God, but wanted to be "like God" (Gen. 3:5), a disobedience that led to death. But the second representative of humanity, the "last Adam" (1 Cor. 15:45), who ironically was already like God, did not hoard his equality with God but humbly accepted the limitations of earthly life – an obedience that leads to life and salvation (see Phil. 2:5–11). Instructively, the German word for "obedient" is *gehorsam*, a word whose core is the verb "to hear" (*hören*). An obedient person is one who hears the word and listens to the will of God – and then acts accordingly. In the incarnation, Jesus subordinated his will to that of the Father, followed the bitter path to the cross, and was obedient even unto death. Seen through Christ, to be in God's image means to hear God's word and to respond obediently to the will of God, living one's life *coram Deo*, before the face of God, faithfully reflecting God's character and concerns in the world.

Relationship between human beings

Being created in the image of God, however, involves more than living faithfully in the divine–human relationship. It is also intimately linked to our relationship with our fellow human beings. Genesis 1:27 uses poetic parallelism to make this point:

> in the image of God he created him [*Adam*];
> *male and female* he created them.   (RSV, italics added)

Since the one God is ultimately revealed to be a social being (a Trinity of loving persons), it is not surprising to find that the humanity created in the divine image bears a distinct social impress, underscored paradigmatically by sexual distinction. The one *Adam* ("man" = humanity) is both "male and female." Since God *is* the Trinity, it makes sense that human beings exist as social beings. The image of God (*imago Dei*), therefore, is none other than the image of the Trinity (*imago Trinitatis*).

Sexually differentiated humanity is blessed with the charge to be fruitful and to fill the earth (Gen. 1:28), reflecting how God filled the emptiness of space with a material order. Humanity fulfills this blessing quite literally by procreating, producing daughters and sons in God's image (Gen. 5:1–3). Yet we may take sexual distinction and procreation as a paradigm case for the many ways in which a diversity of persons – by way of gender, race, ethnicity, gifts, talents, and callings – come together and complement one another in creative and productive ways. Living as the image of God means being fruitful and resourceful in a variety of relationships – living fruitfully with the "other" as a primary concern in our decisions and way of life. Our relationships to our fellow human beings are an inextricable dimension of the image of God. Indeed, love of neighbor seems to be a crucial measure of one's love of God (Gal. 5:14).

However, just as with the divine–human relation, sin disrupts this second form of relationship. We put ourselves first, subordinating others to our own egocentric interests, defacing God's image in the process. So once again, we need to look at the restored image, Jesus Christ, to see more clearly what imaging God to our neighbor looks like. In the incarnation, Jesus revealed the true nature of exocentricity. He did not live for himself but focused his concern on others: he fed the crowds; he healed the sick; he served his disciples by washing their feet; and ultimately he gave up his life for sinners. Christ's behavior reveals what it means to be the restored image of God in our relationships with others.

What undergirds a posture of proper exocentricity is self-giving love – what the NT calls *agape*, that which supremely characterizes, even defines, the triune God (see 1 John 4:8). Such love is not motivated by what the self can derive from a relationship – say, from the beauty or worth of another object or person (*eros*). Neither is this love mere natural affection for one's family members (*storge*). Nor is this love mere concern for one's fellow humanity, especially one's friends (*philia*).[19] Self-giving *agape* is the kind of love that God has for creation, as especially manifest in the self-sacrifice of Christ, which is a model for the kind of love and faithfulness that the imagers of God are called to embody – with spouses, parents, children, co-workers, roommates, and so on.

In sum, being restored to the image of God means *learning to love*, which is one terse way of describing the meaning of life. The church is to manifest this life of the renewed image of the Trinity. Here a diversity of persons – male and female, Jew and Gentile, slave and free (Gal. 3:28), with manifold gifts, talents, and abilities – become one body (of Christ), one new humanity (Eph. 2), in order to be a creative, transforming, and life-giving force in history through love of God *and* love of neighbor. Only in right and loving – that is, self-giving – relationships with others do we truly image God, though as God's image-bearers every person possesses inherent equality, dignity, and respect, and is therefore precious and worthy of esteem as a distinct individual.

To put this another way: to be a person in the image of God is to be a person-in-relation. Again, we are suggesting that Christians ought to derive their conception of personhood not from western culture, which is strongly and dangerously individualistic, but from the Trinity, in which persons dwell in communion and in perichoretic love with one another. Such persons are lovingly inclined to one another (see the Rublev icon, Illustration 5.2); they defer to one another and subordinate their wills to one another in selfless devotion. The Trinity is the exemplar of persons in right relation, of persons in love, and it is in this divine reality that the fractured image is renewed.

[19] See C. S. Lewis, *The Four Loves* (New York: Harcourt & Brace, 1960).

Relationship between humanity and nature

Proper obedience to God and self-giving relationships with others do not exhaust what it means for human beings to bear the *imago Dei*. As Genesis 1 puts it, humanity is to "have dominion" over creation. As God's representatives in a world deemed "very good," human beings are called to responsibly tend the earthly garden (Gen. 2:15ff.). Just as God is a benevolent and wise ruler of the cosmos, human beings are called to image God by wisely and benevolently supervising the earthly microcosm.

But the biblical text indicates that human sin also introduced a strained relationship with the rest of nature. In the course of history, human beings have considered themselves autocrats who have free license to do with created reality whatever they wish. Indeed, in the western tradition, the notion of "having dominion," when coupled with an interpretation of the image as primarily the rational soul, has conspired to reinforce an attitude toward nature of rational domination and technical manipulation (also see pp. 163–5).

While confessing Christian culpability in ecological matters, we again look to Christ for a proper understanding of image-bearing. Since Jesus Christ is the restored image of God, his lordship sets the example for human lordship of the earth, a conception of power that Christ embodied in self-sacrifice and explicitly defined as the power of servanthood (Matt. 20:20–8). Among other things, then, we would argue that being created in God's image ethically entails wise and provident stewardship of creation's resources. All material things, the theological tradition has held (via an analogy of being), bear some trace resemblance to God – reflecting God's goodness, truth, and beauty. All of life is sacramental in this sense, pointing beyond itself to its source in God. Humanity as the fullest resemblance of God must therefore respect all of life – from the less sentient to the inanimate – which possesses its own worth as a medium of God's presence and as an object of God's cosmic redemption. While material things are subject to our discerning use and responsible enjoyment, there is no biblical or theological license to exploit nature. What we are thus pleading for, especially given the tenuous ecological times in which we live, is an ethic of creation care – a crucial implication of Christianity's teaching about humanity's being created in the image of God.

This and the previous chapter of this book have stressed that creation is good and that humanity has special status in creation owing to its bearing of God's image. But as seen repeatedly above, reference to sin is inescapable in any discussion of the image of God. That is to say, a concrete examination of humanity as the bearer of the divine image also requires attention to the many ways in which the image is disfigured by sin. For this reason, our examination of theological anthropology takes us next into the topic of sin.

SIN AND THE IMAGE OF GOD

Defining sin

The Bible never really defines sin in a neat and tidy way, but implies from the beginning (Gen. 3) that sin at its core is a rebellion against God. Adam and Eve reject the divine will for their lives and find themselves estranged from their Creator and from each other. The same point is visible in the famous David and Bathsheba episode (2 Sam. 11–12), which also punctuates the deleterious effects of sin on other human beings: sin is rooted in disregard for God's will, manifests itself as an unbalanced concern for the desires of the self, and results in pain and destruction for others. The Bible also makes it clear that sin is a reality that enslaves humanity, skewing the will and robbing us of our true freedom (e.g., Rev. 1:5). In short, while sin harms the sinner, as well as other human beings, it is at its core an offense against God (Ps. 51:4) for which forgiveness is necessary in order for the relationship between God and humanity to be renewed (1 John 1:9).

These biblical themes are variously systematized and formalized in the confessional writings of different Christian traditions. For example, the Catholic catechism defines sin as "an offense against reason, truth, and right conscience; it is failure in genuine love for God and neighbor caused by a perverse attachment to certain goods. It wounds the nature of man and injures human goods ... Sin is an offense against God ... which sets itself against God's love for us and turns our hearts away from it."[20] Here sin is portrayed as a reality rooted in rebellion against God that defaces the natural orders of creation and resists God's gracious love. In Lutheranism, the Augsburg Confession conceives of all sin as the result of Adam's fall from obedience to God, a fall that results in a failure to fear and trust God and produces the tendency to satisfy the desires of the self rather than the precepts of God.[21] Similarly, in the Reformed tradition, the Westminster Confession focuses on sin as a transgression against God's love that results in guilt, divine wrath, and the penalty of death, in addition to suffering and evil.[22]

---

[20] *Catechism of the Catholic Church* (New York: Doubleday, 1994), 1849–50.
[21] See "Augsburg Confession," in Pelikan and Hotchkiss, eds., *Creeds and Confessions*, II: 59 (art. 2).
[22] See "Westminster Confession of Faith," in Pelikan and Hotchkiss, eds., *Creeds and Confessions*, II: 614 (ch. 6).

The biblical materials and these confessional descriptions of sin show that sin is a distortion or corruption of God's will for human beings. Cornelius Plantinga Jr. aptly terms sin a "culpable disturbance of shalom."[23] If *shalom* in the Hebrew Bible refers to the vital flourishing of all things in right relationship with one another, then sin can be described as that which corrupts, distorts, and taints that universal flourishing. Where obedience is called for, disobedience reigns. Where faithfulness to God and other human beings ought to be the norm, faithlessness shatters our lives. Where freedom ought to be used for the benefit of others, the shackles of selfish desires, slothful inaction, and broken relationships tie human beings down. Plantinga's description suggests that sin most fundamentally is a disturbance of *shalom* for which human beings are guilty – a corruption of God's created order caused by responsible moral agents.

Inasmuch as sin is first and foremost a personal reality – a presence in the lives of human persons that results from and affects our wills – it must also be described as a disfigurement of the *imago Dei*. God's will for human beings is that they represent God in creation with integrity, that they have dominion over the world in responsible, stewardly ways, and that their fruitfulness be a blessing to those around them. In short, as persons-in-relation, they are called to live with and for one another in ways that mirror the divine love. But this basic human vocation and *raison d'être* is opposed and undermined by the overly proud bearers of the image itself. To adapt Calvin's phrase, human sin is a "frightful disfigurement" of the image of God.[24]

This whole discussion, however, may appear to raise a most obvious question, a question that has occupied the attention of Christian theologians from the beginning of the Christian era: *How* has sin become part of our experience and a force in our lives? That is to ask, what is the genesis of sin in creation? This has always been a rather vexing question in Christian theology given this tradition's high estimate of creation. How can it be that a good creation, created by a perfect and loving God, could become sinful? Grappling with this question has led to the doctrine of original sin.

Original sin

The early chapters of the OT suggest that in some way all of humanity is united as an organic whole, both by virtue of sharing in the *imago Dei* and by its common sinfulness. Genesis 3 portrays Adam and Eve as rejecting the limits

---

[23] Cornelius Plantinga Jr., *Not the Way It's Supposed to Be: A Breviary of Sin* (Grand Rapids, MI: Eerdmans, 1995), 18, italics removed.
[24] Calvin, *Institutes*, 1.15.4.

placed on them by God, preferring instead to "be like God" on their own terms (3:5). The result is their separation from God, as they are expelled from their original habitat with curses that apparently apply to all other human beings who come after them (3:16–19). Hence the degenerative path of the early Genesis narrative, eventuating in the flood which punished sinful humanity with near-total destruction, and climaxing in the Tower of Babel episode, which describes all of humanity banding together to "make a name" for itself apart from communion with and obedience to God (11:1–9). The primal sin of Adam and Eve, the narrative implies, begets the continuing and worsening sinfulness of all humanity. While this point of the biblical narrative is clear enough, the precise implications to be drawn from it are less clear, for while the word *Adam* functions in the text as a proper name, its meaning and sense also refer to humanity in general. And *Eve* is defined as the "mother of all living" (Gen. 3:20), perhaps due to the closeness of the name Eve to the Hebrew word for "living." So, then, should "Adam and Eve" in the biblical text be understood as two historical human beings, a literal first couple to which all subsequent human beings owe their lineage and their heritage of sin? Or are "Adam and Eve" literary personifications of all humanity that are used narratologically by the authors of Genesis to make a point about the organic unity and universal sinfulness of humanity at large? Which interpretation is best, the historical or symbolic, and what are the theological implications of each view?

The patristic theologians generally (but not unanimously) believed Adam and Eve to be a literal first couple. They were considered the biological progenitors of all humanity. And inasmuch as they had fallen into sin, their generations of descendants – the whole human race – were also stuck in sin apart from the gracious redeeming work of Jesus Christ. This view became known as the doctrine of *original sin* – the idea that all instances of sin in the world can be traced to a common historical origin.

The most famous elaboration of this doctrine, and one whose influence in the theology of the West can hardly be overestimated, comes from Augustine in the early fifth century. Augustine's formulation of his doctrine of original sin was provoked in part by his opposition to the views of a British monk named Pelagius, whose teachings about humanity, sin, and grace became fashionable in the Roman world around the turn of the fifth century.[25] Pelagius thought that the commandment "Be perfect, therefore,

---

[25] For texts representative of Augustine's position in debate with Pelagius, see Augustine, *The Perfection of Human Righteousness*, trans. Roland J. Teske, in *Answer to the Pelagians*, The Works of Saint Augustine I/23 (New York: New City, 1997); and Augustine, *On Nature and Grace*, in *Four Anti-Pelagian Writings*, trans. John A. Mourant and William J. Collinge, The Fathers of the Church 86 (Washington DC: Catholic University of America Press, 1992).

as your heavenly Father is perfect" (Matt. 5:48) ought to be taken as a real human possibility, one that could actually be achieved. God would not have commanded such perfection if it were not attainable. It must therefore be possible in principle for human beings, via their natural faculties, to live perfectly. Pelagius' view denied that Adam's primal sin had any inevitable effect on later human beings, other than by setting a bad example by which subsequent generations were tempted and which they overwhelmingly imitated, falling into sin of their own individual accord. Salvation, accordingly, is possible on the basis of a person's works, with no need of grace other than the natural capacities with which God has endowed humanity in creation – especially rational free will. God graciously offers forgiveness for past sins, as well as provides the example of Jesus' moral perfection, which should serve as a model for our lives. Pelagius' distinct emphasis is on the call to humanity to use its God-given abilities to live perfectly, which remains a possibility given his rejection of the idea of original sin.

Augustine reacted vehemently to Pelagius' proposals because he thought that they nullified the supernatural grace of Christ that is witnessed in scripture. In Augustine's view, salvation cannot be achieved by human works, but requires the special grace of Christ to be infused into the human soul. In other words, our created capacities are not enough to live rightly because the human will is bent toward sin. Humanity is gravely infected by sin and requires the grace of divine healing. But how did humanity come to be so decisively infected by sin? Augustine's answer comes in the form of his doctrine of original sin. Inherent in the created goodness of Adam and Eve was the gift of freedom. In misusing their freedom in primal rebellion against God, they infected human nature itself, acquiring a disease that involves both guilt for sin and an unconquerable inclination toward sin, which is biologically transmitted to all other human beings through the propagation of the race (via sexual intercourse). Augustine followed the implications of this idea of original sin in such a rigorous and consistent way that he thought that infants who died before being baptized would certainly be damned, since their conception in original sin included an inheritance of guilt that needs to be washed away in the waters of baptism.[26] Augustine's position attempts to show the utter necessity of grace for salvation because of the inevitability of sin. He locates this inevitability in sin's reception by all human beings

---

[26] See Augustine, *The Punishment and Forgiveness of Sins and the Baptism of Little Ones*, trans. Roland J. Teske, in *Answer to the Pelagians*, The Works of Saint Augustine I/23 (New York: New City, 1997), chs. 21–36.

by virtue of the common stock into which they are born (i.e., human nature).

But this teaching of Augustine's, which became *de facto* orthodoxy in the Latin West, includes certain implications that many modern theologians find troubling. For one, the idea that infants merit punishment for sin that they inherit appears counter-intuitive and raises questions about the loving character of God. In fact, the general idea that one person, apart from her own actions, could receive condemnation for the actions of another (i.e., Adam) runs counter to human conceptions of justice. Recent discussions of the need for reparations to be made by one generation for the crimes of a previous generation (e.g., against Native Americans) show some possibilities for thinking about a common guilt and a justice not directly tied to individual actions. But it is hard to see the applicability of this analogy to the personal guilt of newborn infants. Many also find the Augustinian idea of a primal first couple hard to maintain in face of contemporary scientific perspectives and historical evidence (e.g., evolutionary perspectives).

But on the other hand, Augustine's claims about the inevitability of sin, given a fallen creation, and the utter necessity of grace appear strongly backed by the biblical materials. Moreover, Pelagian alternatives tend not to take the tragedy of sin seriously enough, overestimating the capacities of human beings, while underestimating the value and necessity of the cross of Christ. So, is there a way to preserve in a reformulated doctrine of original sin the two indispensable Augustinian insights – namely, the necessity of grace and unavoidability of sin (thus avoiding the Pelagian heresy) – without lapsing into the particular problems of the Augustinian approach?

The suggestions of Friedrich Schleiermacher on this topic are worthy of consideration at this point. Schleiermacher is cognizant of the deep paradox of human sin: we sense that sin is something for which we are responsible, yet also perceive it as something that originates prior to us.[27] As a result of this paradox, Schleiermacher is compelled to give some account of "original sin," but wants to avoid the problems of the traditional Augustinian account. Accordingly, Schleiermacher locates the transmission of original sin in the social and historical dynamics of human life. Since the interrelated systems, institutions, and cultures of human society have been permeated by sin (whose ultimate origins are mysterious), all those born into that social history are conditioned by these very same sinful forces. But original sin never remains something that simply occurs in humanity passively, for all human beings, as historical and social creatures, eventually participate

[27] Schleiermacher, *Christian Faith*, 279–81.

willfully in sin. Up to the point of the actualization of original sin, it is best regarded, according to Schleiermacher, as "originat*ed* original sin" because it is a sinfulness that is inevitably acquired by human beings as they develop as members of a sin-infected human society. But when a person actualizes that original sin, that is, actually sins, it becomes "originat*ing* original sin," for his sinful actions beget even more sin and corruption both in the individual self and in others around him.[28] In other words, one's own sinful actions contribute to the ongoing sinfulness of history and society. Guilt, therefore, for Schleiermacher, results from our willful participation in the sinfulness into which we are born; guilt itself is not inherited. It is only when human beings – gradually and at an unspecifiable point in time – actualize sin in their own lives that they become guilty and remain guilty for perpetuating the tragedy of sin in the world.

Schleiermacher's framework allows for a distinction between the *propensity* toward sin that is part of the human condition, given the mysterious entrance of sin into the histories and societies of this world, and the *guilt* for sin that comes from our own acts of sin for which we are responsible – two dimensions that were a package deal for Augustine. Thus an infant can be understood to inherit unconquerable propensities toward sin by virtue of being born into a sinful world, but is actually guilty for sin only in connection with his own eventual willful participation in that society. Moreover, Schleiermacher gives a more compelling account of how sin is passed down from generation to generation than Augustine's proposal of a biological infection of "human nature." Schleiermacher is not willing to specify exactly *how* sin entered into the world in the first place (which remains a mystery), but given that it has, he maintains that it is transmitted historically and socially, not through the reproduction of the species. Nevertheless, his view holds on to the most crucial tenets of the Augustinian position – the inevitability of sin and the utter necessity of grace. There is no way for human beings to conquer the temptation of sin by the sheer force of their own will, for they are situated in and affected by a world whose history and society have become decisively corrupted by sin. Even Jesus, on Schleiermacher's model, required divine grace in order to remain sinless. Other human beings are therefore even more dependent on God's grace in Christ to rescue them from their sinful plight.

Schleiermacher's reconsideration of this doctrine of original sin, placing it in the categories of history and society rather than human biology, alleviates some of the questions about the justice of God that are raised by

---

[28] Ibid., 287, italics added.

Augustine's own approach. It therefore strikes us as a valuable rethinking of this important doctrine that is worth serious consideration – one that is ultimately Augustinian, *not* Pelagian. Whatever the status of Adam as a historical person in Genesis, this approach captures the deeper biblical sense that *Adam* is all humanity organically bound together, and therefore sharing the tragic human plight of sin and concomitant need for redemption. An additional benefit of Schleiermacher's approach is that it tightly connects the question of sin's origins, that is, sin as a *state* of humanity, to the *acts* of sin that we human beings commit. None of us can plead innocence or disclaim responsibility for sin on the basis of "original sin," for each of us as an embodiment of *Adam* is guilty and each contributes to the ongoing catastrophe of the world's sinfulness in our own concrete acts of sin. Thus our discussion of original sin must give way to a consideration of what is usually called "actual sin."

Actual sin

As we have seen, both Augustine and Schleiermacher reject any attempt to see sin as merely an "original" reality. Sin is also something for which we are responsible – something that we willfully and culpably commit. Thus Plantinga's definition of sin as "disturbance of shalom" includes the decisively important qualifying adjective "culpable." This dimension of actual, agential sin raises the question of the character of the acts of sin that we commit on the basis of the tendencies inculcated in us by original sin. Drawing upon Genesis's portrayal of Adam and Eve as rejecting their creatureliness and striving to be like God, the Christian tradition has generally pointed to *pride* as the quintessence of our act of rebellion against God, which is why pride heads the list of the classic "seven deadly sins." Reinhold Niebuhr defines pride as a matter of "overreach[ing] the limits of human creatureliness" by a "will-to-power," making the self a god.[29] Niebuhr also specifies *sensuality* as a contrasting second form of human sin. Sensuality refers to hiding from our human freedom by giving in to certain desires of the self (such as sexual desire) that cause us to make something outside of the self a god.[30] As such, sensuality also has its roots in the self-love of pride and its rejection of the lordship of God. Feminist theologians have objected to Niebuhr's (as well as the broader Christian tradition's) reduction of sin to pride by pointing out the experience of many women who overly suppress an appropriate sense and esteem of self (self-loathing,

[29] Niebuhr, *Nature and Destiny of Man*, 178.   [30] Ibid., 233–40.

self-degradation) in response to the pressures of patriarchal society and sexist oppressors.[31] The main sin for women in those situations is not excessive self-love or pride, but actually the converse – an insufficient estimation, love, and care of the self as one created in God's image.

This feminist observation is well taken: our acts of sin can express attitudes of either excessive self-love or stultifying self-loathing. That is to say, we sin both "above ourselves" and "beneath ourselves." It is probably true, however, that the most overt acts of sin in human history, especially those that have produced the horrors of history, have resulted from excessive self-love and the will-to-power run amuck. But in either case, the result of actual sin, whatever its particular character, is the distorting of relationships. And if living in right relationship with God and others is a key component of the image of God, then actual sin is a decisive corruption of that image. As we have seen, by virtue of being in the image of God, human beings are called to live rightly with God and others, to have stewardly dominion over creation, and to be fruitful in relationally appropriate ways that seek the good of others and creation at large. The acts of sin that we commit corrupt that basic human vocation and disrupt the matrix of life's relationships.

The first and most fundamental human relationship – of *persons with God* – is distorted as human beings live according to their own plans and desires, rather than striving to live obediently before a holy God as the divine representatives in creation. We rebel against God, rejecting God's righteous demands and resisting God's saving grace, either considering ourselves to be lords of our own lives, or, conversely, regarding ourselves as unworthy of God's attention. The irony of our sinful distortion of this first relationship is that it destroys our lives. The God we reject is the one who knows what is best for us, whose moral demands embody that "best" that will enable the flourishing of our lives. Therefore Plantinga is right to note that one key feature of sin is its character as "folly."[32] By living against God rather than with God, we foolishly destroy our own lives and our own well-being (see, e.g., Prov. 1:8–19).

The most obvious way in which our prideful or self-loathing rebellion against God's designs brings destruction into our lives is through the perversion of the second basic human relationship – of *persons with one another*. Rather than seeking the good of the other before that of the self, we put our own plans first; rather than seeking the wholeness of the self in

[31] See, e.g., Valerie Saiving Goldstein, "The Human Situation: A Feminine View," *Journal of Religion* 40, no. 2 (1960), 100–12.
[32] Plantinga, *Not the Way*, 121–8.

appropriate relationships in order to contribute to the humanity and the needs of others, we enter into destructive relationships of co-dependency. The command to "be fruitful" is twisted into the tragedy of children imitating the vices of their parents; and the broken lives of abused daughters and sons are in turn reiterated in the histories of their own children. Men abuse women, parents take advantage of their children, bosses mistreat their employees, the rich lord their wealth over the poor. In short, our sin wrenches and perverts the whole spectrum of intra-human relationships from loving, mutual, and beneficial expressions of care into selfish, divisive, and ungrateful expressions of the desire for unbridled primacy.

This effect of sin can also be seen in the third relationship – of *persons with nature*. The command to "have dominion" is twisted into license for domination and exploitation of nature. Rather than acting as careful stewards of the world in which we live, human beings have raped and pillaged the land, water, and air. The synergy intended by God between all creatures is twisted into an unequal and unhealthy use and abuse of the world's natural resources and its non-human creatures rather than seeing them as gifts to be cherished and well tended. This approach, however, involves a massive folly – human sinfulness in this relationship imperils the planet upon which we depend for our very existence.

The distortion of these three basic human relationships helps to illuminate the Pauline contention that the "wages of sin is death" (Rom. 6:23). Certainly the most obvious meaning of the statement has to do with the NT's claim that personal sin reaps a punishment of death that can only be borne by Jesus Christ if we are to have any hope. But we should not ignore the fact that the distortion of our relationships with God, with one another, and with our world can bring death into life. For the child abused by a father, life can seem to be hardly worth living. For the poor who struggle for daily bread, death is lurking at any moment in a tortured existence. For the person who lives estranged from God, hopelessness can make life a living hell. In short, both in the guilt we bear for sin and in the degraded character of the relationships that constitute human life, sin brings death.

This death brought by sin also takes on corporate shape and cumulative force. While each of these three basic human relationships distorted by sin involves actions by individuals – for example, persons ignoring God, men abusing women, people contaminating their water supplies – we must recognize that individual sin only scratches the surface of the complex reality of sin. The various sins of persons bloat into larger realities – such as poverty, sexism, and species extinction. In other words, sin can never be regarded as merely an individual or personal reality, although it never ceases to be such; it is also necessary to talk about *structural* or *systemic* sin. Sin transcends persons and becomes a force or dynamic that permeates the institutions, attitudes, structures, and systems of society. Economic systems, for example, tend to favor the rich (those with capital) and make it more difficult for the poor (lacking capital) to compete in the market. Democratic political structures intended to empower people can become corrupt vehicles for the advancement of politicians, corporations, and the upper crust of society. In short, the interrelationship of personal sin and structural sin produces a vicious and tragic cycle of sin and death in our world.

Seen from a slightly different angle, personal sin and structural sin taken together can be called *evil*. Human history has never lacked examples of evil, especially in recent centuries. The existence of such evils – such as the event of the Holocaust – constitutes a painful thorn in the flesh of Christianity and its theology, given its affirmation of a world created good by the triune God of love. We therefore pause in the next chapter to address the poignant problem of evil as a major challenge to the Christian confession.

FOR FURTHER READING

Augustine, *On Nature and Grace*, in *Four Anti-Pelagian Writings*, trans. John A. Mourant and William J. Collinge, The Fathers of the Church 86 (Washington, DC: Catholic University of America Press, 1992).

Hall, Douglas John, *Imaging God: Dominion as Stewardship* (Grand Rapids, MI: Eerdmans, 1986).

Middleton J. Richard, *The Liberating Image: The* Imago Dei *in Genesis 1* (Grand Rapids, MI: Brazos, 2005).

Niebuhr, Reinhold, *The Nature and Destiny of Man: A Christian Interpretation* (New York: Charles Scribner's Sons, 1943).

Plantinga, Cornelius, Jr., *Not the Way It's Supposed to Be: A Breviary of Sin* (Grand Rapids, MI: Eerdmans, 1995).

Schleiermacher, Friedrich, *The Christian Faith*, ed. H. R. Mackintosh and J. S. Stewart (Edinburgh: T. & T. Clark, 1928), 270–304.

CHAPTER 8

The problem of evil and the question of theodicy

THE NATURE AND REALITY OF EVIL

Our examination of sin in the previous chapter emphasized that sin is rebellion against the divine will with deleterious consequences, including the estrangement of human beings from God, from one another, and from nature. Sin is a potent reality in human life, which unleashes dark forces in creation that cause incalculable misery. This is perhaps why the NT reminds us that humanity's real battle in life is with fallen "principalities and powers" (see Eph. 6:12), which can be understood as forces of *evil*, both spiritual and structural, that harass persons, from both within and without.[1] In addition to sin, therefore, we must consider the sinister presence of evil – a power that causes suffering and destruction – in God's good but fallen creation.

Evil takes a variety of forms. It is customary in theology to distinguish between two main types of evil. On the one hand, there is *natural evil*, which occurs when seemingly senseless but potent natural forces oppress and devour innocent victims, such as when tornadoes, tsunamis, and earthquakes suddenly wreak havoc on entire communities, or when diseases stalk and attack countless people. On the other hand, closely related to sin, there is *moral evil*, which occurs when acts perpetrated by accountable moral agents result in suffering. Human beings, it seems, have a pronounced penchant for inflicting cruelty on their fellow creatures: assault, rape, and murder are frighteningly common in our disordered world, to say nothing of attempts to exterminate entire races of people, among other unspeakable atrocities and acts of terror. Such moral evil, moreover, is not only perpetrated by individuals, but can also be inscribed into the very way we organize our societies and formulate our policies (i.e., systemic forms of moral evil, such as racism, sexism, and classism).

How can this be? Why do the innocent so often suffer? Why do the wicked prosper? How can such powers run seemingly rampant in a good creation ruled by the triune God – the loving and powerful Creator? These questions raise the theological problem of evil.

THE PROBLEM OF EVIL

Thus far in this book we have addressed several of Christian theology's central *doctrines*. In this chapter, however, we address not a doctrine but a vexing *problem*. That evil exists and is a problem goes without saying – it is something we all sense to be true. Christian theology must squarely face this brute fact of evil because of the tension it creates for many central Christian doctrines – such as the doctrines of God, creation, and humanity. So how shall we articulate the nature of this problem? Generally speaking, evil does not seem to fit in a *good* creation governed by a *sovereign* God, who is *love*. Before tackling this problem more formally, however, it is helpful to

---

[1] For a helpful study of the NT's conception of "the powers," see Walter Wink, *The Powers*, 1: *Naming the Powers: The Language of Power in the New Testament* (Philadelphia: Fortress, 1984).

highlight two distinct but ever-related dimensions to the problem of evil – one experiential and the other intellectual.

Dimensions of the problem

The experiential force of evil

The experiential dimension of the problem of evil is undeniably real and lamentably tragic. In the course of human life, many people experience profound pain and all people encounter difficulties of various kinds. Natural evil claims many victims, who experience loss due to the unfeeling and unremitting forces of nature – whether untamed forces in the environment or dysfunction in the body. Moral evil also intrudes frequently and terribly in human life and creaturely experience, when people brutalize one another and other creatures. In short, creatures *suffer* in various ways in the course of their lives: this is the experiential dimension of the problem of evil, which is deeply and ineluctably *felt* in the form of suffering.

This experiential dimension of the problem of evil was given profound literary expression by Fyodor Dostoevsky in his novel *The Brothers Karamazov*. In a little chapter entitled "Rebellion," Ivan, the eldest Karamazov, relates to his younger brother Alyosha a litany of heart-wrenching stories about the gratuitous suffering of children at the hands of adults.[2] Given this history of violence, Ivan can only conclude that the freedom human beings possess is not worth the price we pay for its misuse. He cannot accept a world so arranged and has deep reservations about the wisdom and justice of the God who is its director. To such a theater of the absurd, Ivan seeks to "return his ticket" of admission.[3]

The intellectual conundrum of evil

But this poignant chapter of literature, with its true-to-life tragedies, shows that there is an inevitable intellectual dimension to consider when confronting evil, as it is the overwhelming experience of suffering that gives rise to Ivan's intellectual wrestling with this vexing problem. In short, human beings are inclined to ask "Why?" in response to suffering. While moral evil is perhaps easier to understand than natural evil in this regard, since it involves a clear and accountable agent, even moral evil prompts the larger question "Why?" – Why do people seem to perpetuate disruptive acts? What possesses us to do such things? Why does evil seem to run so rampant in our world? Historically, human cultures and civilizations have felt the

---

[2] Dostoevsky, *Brothers Karamazov*, Book 5, ch. 4.　　[3] Ibid., 226.

need to come to terms with chaos, disorder, malfunction, suffering, and death. In seeking some semblance of an answer, the strategy most generally employed is to situate the experience of chaos and suffering in a larger context of order and meaning. Let us take two examples from history.

First, consider Jerusalem in the year 586 BCE. Judah's capital city lies in ruins, and its temple has been destroyed. In this pivotal OT crisis, Yahweh's chosen people, who long ago were promised a secure land and assured of God's enduring presence with them, are being led away into exile, seemingly abandoned by their covenant God. How do the people of Judah endure this crisis of faith as they trudge toward faraway Babylon? Perhaps they speculate that Yahweh has been defeated by the gods of the Babylonians. Perhaps they regard this catastrophe as punishment for living waywardly, for being unfaithful to the covenant, and for ignoring the prophets who brought them the admonishing word of the Lord. Or perhaps they find reason to hope that although the present moment is filled with chaos and darkness, order and light will one day return when they – or at least their descendants – return from exile, rebuild their lives and temple and city, and rededicate themselves to covenant relationship with Yahweh.

For our second example, consider the evening of June 5, 1944, in southern England. Allied soldiers have just learned that D-Day is imminent. Within hours, they will cross the English Channel in order to storm the beaches of Normandy and begin the liberation of Nazi-occupied Europe. These soldiers will face great dangers and experience horrible suffering. It is entirely possible and even likely that one day from now, they will no longer be alive, or, if they do remain alive, may be scarred or dismembered for life. How do they move forward with courage and hope? Perhaps they think to themselves that although they may die (subjective mortality), the cause for which the Allies are fighting will live on (objective immortality). As in the first example, the present moment of chaos and suffering is placed into a larger context of order and meaning.

The issue of suffering is most perplexing when God enters into the equation. In its most formal and abstract form, the intellectual dimension of the problem of evil was tersely stated by Epicurus (*c.* fourth century BCE), the ancient Greek philosopher, who held that it was impossible to hold these three propositions together:

1. God is all-powerful.
2. God is all-good.
3. Evil exists.

Epicurus' argument was revived in the eighteenth century by the skeptical Scottish philosopher David Hume. In Hume's own words: "Is [God] willing to prevent evil, but not able? then is he impotent. Is he able, but not willing? then is he malevolent. Is he both able and willing? whence then is evil?"[4] Given the indisputable existence of evil, Hume's argument, if sound, prompts one of two conclusions: either (1) God is a rather different being from the one portrayed in the Christian tradition; that is, if God exists, God may be *either* all-good *or* all-powerful, but cannot be both. Or (2) God does not exist.

Combined with general Enlightenment critiques of Christianity, Hume's challenge put Christianity on the defensive. While the existence of evil is a challenge for all religions, it is a greater challenge for monotheistic religions – distinguished as they are by a strong creation doctrine, which in accentuating the transcendence of God and the goodness of creation emphasizes divine omnipotence and omnibenevolence. The existence of evil calls into question the nature and therefore the existence of the *Theos* of monotheistic confession. In the enlightened eighteenth century, the need to respond to the problem of evil gave rise to the conscious project of *theodicy*, a term coined by the German philosopher Leibniz.[5] From the Greek words *Theos* (= God) and *dike* (= justice), theodicy most literally is the attempt to "justify God," as being both good and powerful, in the face of evil. More particularly, theodicy refers to an argument that attempts to specify why God and evil are compatible realities. This endeavor has produced a variety of explanations or theodicies, as we will shortly see.[6] But before we discuss the project of theodicy in greater detail, we first explore how the problem of evil became more acute in human experience during the course of the twentieth century, making the question of theodicy even more pressing today.

Twentieth-century intensification of the problem of evil

The nineteenth century was a time of tremendous optimism. In this period, human beings generally believed that they had in their own hands the ability to solve all problems and correct all injustices. This spirit of optimism carried over into the twentieth century, which was predicted by many to be the "Christian century," the age when war would be abolished, injustices removed, and the world Christianized. As a symbol of this cultural

---

[4] Hume, *Dialogues Concerning Natural Religion*, ch. 10.

[5] See Gottfried Wilhelm von Leibniz, *Theodicy: Essays on the Goodness of God, the Freedom of Man, and the Origin of Evil*, ed. Austin Farrer, trans. E. M. Huggard (La Salle, IL: Open Court, 1985).

[6] In its broadest sense, the term theodicy is also used simply as a synonym for the general problem of and response to evil.

optimism, think of the *Titanic*, which was christened in 1912. This new ship was considered to be a technological marvel that could not be sunk. *Titanic*, of course, sank on her maiden voyage across the Atlantic, with hundreds of lives lost in the tragedy. Like the *Titanic*, nineteenth-century optimism proved to be naively idealistic, dashed as it was by the hard, cold brutalities of the twentieth century. Two years after *Titanic* sunk, war broke out in Europe. The democratic nations thought that this conflict would be over quickly and decisively, even trumpeting it as the "war to end all wars." Instead, an appalling and hideous trench war dragged on for four long years (1914–18) and introduced tremendous instability into the period that followed.

This "Great War" sowed the seeds for the bloody conflict that followed from 1939 until 1945 – WWII. By the time this second act ended, upwards of 50 million people lay dead. A new term was even coined – genocide – the systematic attempt to eradicate an entire race of people. The Nazis had set up in the German Reich a series of camps dedicated to the methodical murder of the Jewish people. The most famous of these death camps was Auschwitz, which has become a chilling symbol for the evil that human beings can inflict upon one another. In his book *Night*, Elie Wiesel (b. 1928) powerfully depicts the horror of Auschwitz as well as its insidious capacity for hollowing out the human soul. Wiesel writes:

Never shall I forget that night, the first night in camp, which has turned my life into one long night, seven times cursed and seven times sealed. Never shall I forget that smoke. Never shall I forget the little faces of the children, whose bodies I saw turned into wreaths of smoke beneath a silent blue sky ... Never shall I forget these things, even if I am condemned to live as long as God Himself. Never.[7]

Tragically, the Holocaust was but one attempt at genocide. Despite humanity's promise afterwards that such slaughter would happen "never again," several more attempts have ensued during the strife-ridden decades that have followed: Cambodia, Bosnia-Herzegovina, Rwanda, and Sudan, to name a few. These atrocities in contemporary history pose the problem of evil with undeniable force to Christianity. To put it most starkly, can there be a God in a world in which genocide has become a common occurrence and household term? If so, where is God? Or, to heighten the stakes, is belief in God possible when humanity has harnessed for itself the power to threaten and destroy all life on the planet (i.e., the specter of nuclear or

---

[7] Elie Wiesel, *Night* (New York: Bantam, 1960), 32.

Illustration 8.1 Picasso's *Guernica*, which depicts the bombing of the Spanish city of Guernica in the 1930s, captures the pain and anguish of twentieth-century mechanistic terrors.

ecological extinction)? Does Christian faith make sense in such a fractured world (see Illustration 8.1)?

THEODICIES IN THE WESTERN TRADITION

Given a world in which horrendous suffering has become all too common and ominously threatening, the specter of evil is a pressing challenge for Christian theology today. Though the term "theodicy" was not coined until the eighteenth century, explanations of evil (which are the essence of theodicy) are as old as religion itself, since evil is a problem that all cultures and religions inevitably address. The following is a survey of some of the major types of theodicy in the western tradition.

Evil as inherent in the material world

The ancient world into which Christianity was born and flourished was populated by many rival religious movements. One of these was gnosticism, which, as we have seen (see pp. 153–5 and 428–9), taught a dualism of spirit and matter: the realm of spirit is good (e.g., soul), and the domain of matter is evil (e.g., body). The true God dwells far above the material world in the realm of spirit; the material world, which was seen as the source of evil and suffering, was fashioned by an inferior god known as the Demiurge, who was often associated with the Creator God of the OT.

The gnostic analysis of reality thus suggests a theodicy. The true God of the transcendent realm is not responsible for evil; only the inferior Demiurge, who fashioned the world from matter, bears the blame. But the true God makes salvation possible by means of escape from the evil material world through a special "knowledge" (= *gnosis*). This salvific knowledge is provided by the emissary of the true God – the Christ, who, masquerading as a human being (Jesus), sneaked behind enemy lines to reveal to the chosen few the path to redemption. In short, in this dualistic metaphysic, evil is regarded as intrinsic to a material world, for which the true spiritual God bears no blame.

Evil as non-being

In addition to various religious movements in the ancient world, there were also philosophies in antiquity with which Christianity had to contend, and by which it was also influenced. One of these was a school of thought deeply impressed by the teachings of Plato. Founded by Plotinus in the third century CE, Neoplatonism was a monistic system that saw one utterly transcendent God (about whom little can be said) as the foundation of reality.[8] The material world emanates from this Supreme Being, who is all good. The world is thus not evil *per se* – but neither is it truly good. Being at the far reaches of the divine emanation, the sensible world of the many is of a lesser degree of being than God the One. In its ontological distance from God, the highest Good, evil can exist only as a kind of *non-being*. For example, just as darkness is the absence of light, the material world is the absence of the fullness of divine being – virtually nothing in and of itself in comparison to God.

Plotinus' understanding of evil thus suggests a theodicy. On his view, evil is not real, *ontologically* speaking, but is simply an absence or "privation" of the good. The perception of evil results from the material realm's metaphysical distance from God the Supreme Good. Evil is, however, certainly real, *experientially* speaking. One clear danger with this view is that it tends to spiritualize evil, making it a mere illusion, and thus does not take evil seriously enough. In Christian theology, Augustine, who was significantly influenced by Neoplatonism, inclined to this conception of evil's metaphysical status as one of his many theodical proposals.

---

[8] See Plotinus, *The Enneads*, trans. Stephen Mackenna (New York: Larson Publications, 1992), I.8. See also Frederick Copleston, *A History of Philosophy*, I: *Greece and Rome* (New York: Image Books, 1993), 463–75.

Evil as condition for human becoming

These first two theodicies developed outside the domain of Christian theology, but nonetheless influenced Christianity in various degrees. The following three theodicies, however, are more typical of the monotheistic metaphysic, which in highlighting the Creator–creature distinction does not compromise the power or goodness of God. The first of these theodicies was articulated by Irenaeus and has more recently been popularized by John Hick, who called it a "soul-building" theodicy.[9] For Irenaeus, humanity was created with the capacity to know and freely choose between good and evil. Having been created good but not perfect, that is, still immature, human beings must make good and right decisions in order to *become* the persons of God's created intention, that is, mature. In other words, the presence of finitude and evil in created reality is a necessary condition for humanity to be able to choose rightly and thereby mature into the stately creature of God's purpose and design. It is by encountering evil – by being tempted by its very possibility – that we can know and choose the good. Evil, therefore, is not inconsistent with either God's existence or nature, but fits into God's plan for human beings to grow into the stature of their full humanity.

Evil and cosmic beauty

Augustine was another patristic theologian who gave serious consideration to evil and offered a variety of responses to it. In addition to his Neoplatonic view that evil does not exist in any full metaphysical sense, that it is merely a privation of goodness, Augustine also offered an "aesthetic" theodicy. As the good Creator of the cosmos, God would not have fashioned a world in which evil existed but did not serve the broader purpose of the divine plan. In God's sovereignty and wisdom, evil stands in an aesthetic relation to the good, thereby contributing to the overall harmony and beauty of God's world. It is as though in the greater tapestry of life, darker, drabber colors (various experiences of evil) highlight or accentuate the brighter, cheerier colors (experiences of goodness). With eschatological hindsight we will be able to appreciate the beauty of the whole of life's portrait to which even evil makes its contrasting contribution. Augustine's conception emphasizes that God foresaw the possibility of bad human choice which could result in evil, but created a world in which a greater good was also foreseen – in other

---

[9] John Hick, *Evil and the God of Love*, rev. edn. (New York: HarperSanFrancisco, 1977). See Irenaeus, *Against Heresies*, esp. 4.37–9; Irenaeus, *Proof of the Apostolic Preaching*, trans. Joseph P. Smith (Westminster, MD: Newman Press, 1952), 47–57.

words, a world in which good would triumph over evil, and the resulting whole would be all the more glorious.[10] Augustine's aesthetic theodicy thus underscores that the world has a certain order and design, the beauty of which includes (even requires?) the experienced fact of evil.

Evil and submission to the divine will

Augustine's position implies that the will of God is opaque to human beings, who therefore have no right to charge God with injustice for allowing evil. This view, along with its implications, has been championed by others in the Christian tradition, including John Calvin. In good Augustinian fashion, Calvin emphasized humanity's fall into sin as the source of evil in the world. But Calvin also understood God's sovereignty in a rather deterministic way, wherein God specifically ordained every event that takes place in the world, even acts of sin and evil (see pp. 493–5 below). Since God is good and just by definition, and every event has its divine determination – its actively being willed by God – all events must somehow fit in with the divine goodness and plan. Human beings therefore have no right to complain about evil or to question God's justice.[11] But there seems to be little room for human freedom in Calvin's account of things, and scholars have pondered whether events and acts foreordained by God are actually compatible with human freedom – with these acts also being freely chosen by human agents. Those who answer in the affirmative are known as *compatibilists*, and those who answer in the negative are called *incompatibilists*. According to compatibilists (such as Calvin), whose position presupposes divine determinism, it follows that in the face of evil, human beings can only trust the sovereign God, who governs the cosmos in its every detail. Before the mystery of evil and the opaque all-determining divine will, human beings must simply submit to God's higher ways and standard of justice.

A THEOLOGICAL RESPONSE TO THE PROBLEM OF EVIL

While there are many other explanations of or approaches to evil that fly under the banner of theodicy, the foregoing represent some of the central theodicies of the western and Christian tradition.[12] Each of the monotheistic

---

[10] See Augustine, *City of God*, Book 11, ch. 18 (p. 449).   [11] See Calvin, *Institutes*, 1.16–17.
[12] For a helpful survey of theodicies both eastern and western, see James C. Livingston, *Anatomy of the Sacred*, 5th edn. (New York: Prentice Hall, 2004), ch. 11.

theodicies appears to capture a moment of truth in the encounter with evil. For example, many people will testify that they have learned from difficult times or past mistakes and have become better persons for it (soul-building theodicy); that they have had experiences of evil or suffering that make them more appreciative of the goodness and beauty of life (aesthetic theodicy); and that even when baffled or bewildered as to why certain events befall them, they seem to be left with no other response than to trust that God is ultimately in control (submission theodicy).

Moreover, one can find biblical texts that will support a variety of theodical positions. Take the OT book of Job, for example, a *locus classicus* in scripture regarding evil, human suffering, and justice. In this fascinating text, Job becomes a seeming plaything in a cosmic drama as God allows an adversary (Satan – literally, the "accuser") to wreak havoc on the life and well-being of this good man. Left unprotected by God and set upon by Satan, Job loses his children and many of his possessions, as well as his own health. His wife and friends offer him counsel, and it is in these exchanges that the roots of many theodicies are found (such as the possibility that Job's plight is the consequence of his own sin). Through all of his seemingly senseless suffering, righteous Job shows patience and keeps faith; he refuses to curse God – although he does lament his plight, which is not of his own making. At the end of the ordeal, Job's patience and faith are rewarded with the restoration of his material possessions. The book of Job as a whole suggests that relatively innocent human beings may have suffering visited upon them in order to test their faith (soul-building); Job's climactic chapters (38–42) appear to suggest, more particularly, that human beings have little right to question the justice of the God who is Lord and Creator of all (submission).

Yet other biblical texts press the question of divine justice. The OT book of Habakkuk is instructive in this regard. Habakkuk questions why it is that the righteous perish while the wicked flourish, and how it is that God can use the wicked (the Babylonians) to chastise God's own chosen people (Hab. 1:1–2:1). To his audacious complaints, Habakkuk receives this cryptic answer: the righteous will live by faith (2:4) – implying that any true answer to the problem of evil and divine justice is still pending, as though the issue is still an open question.

The problem of theodicy

It is this latter biblical attitude that fuels a certain suspicion about any theodicy which attempts a definitive answer to the problem of evil. Among Christian philosophers and theologians today there is a growing unease about the basic project of theodicy, a hesitation that can be stated as follows. While theodicy attempts to justify God (God's goodness, power, and therefore existence) in view of the presence and persistence of evil, such arguments many times have the opposite effect: they justify evil in view of the presence (goodness and power) of God. That is to say, theodicies can argue too strongly for a positive role for evil in God's good creation. Take the soul-building theodicy, for example. It is one thing to say that God allows evil, and that our unpleasant encounters with it can result in lessons learned and human maturation, an observation that many people make after the concrete fact (*a posteriori*) or particular experience of evil; it is another thing, however, to specify generally and abstractly beforehand (*a priori*) that the reason God allows evil is *for the purpose* of human maturation, for the latter suggests that God has good reasons for evil and that it actually plays a positive role in God's good creation. Here, instead of justifying God in view of evil, evil is justified in view of God, for the argument implies that humanity could not mature without the presence of evil, virtually necessitating evil for a positive outcome. Or take the aesthetic theodicy as a second example. It is one thing to say that the experience of evil which God allows can result in a greater appreciation for the good things and beauty of life; but it is another thing to specify *a priori* that the presence of evil is *for the purpose* of accentuating the goodness and beauty of life, as if these could not be appreciated without their contrasting evils. Any such argument which stipulates that God allows evil for a good purpose has virtually made evil into a positive force in the world for which God has good reasons – and therefore actively wills. Such arguments ultimately trivialize the tragic and heinous nature of evil as well as the experience of those who suffer it.

This boomerang effect of theodicy was keenly recognized by Elie Wiesel, who expressed the point in an arresting literary way. From his experience in Auschwitz, Wiesel recalled three rabbis who once put God on trial for allowing the horrendous extermination of the Jews. In his play *The Trial of God*, set in the Ukraine in 1649 after yet another pogrom, Wiesel stages a mock trial (a *Purimspiel* in celebration of the festival of Purim) in which God is tried for indifference and complicity – silence and inaction – in the face of Jewish suffering and murder.[13] Berish, a Job-like figure, eagerly assumes the role of prosecutor, but no one volunteers to play the defense attorney, until, that is, a stranger named Sam suddenly shows up to advocate for God. Sam is intelligent and witty and appears to be a pious

---

[13] Elie Wiesel, *The Trial of God* (New York: Schocken, 1995).

Jew. In the course of his defense of the "Master of the Universe," Sam argues for a range of traditional theodicies, with a heavy emphasis on submission. Sam's summation: "It's simple. Faith in God must be as boundless as God Himself. If it exists at the expense of man, too bad. God is eternal, man is not."[14] The conclusion of the trial, however, is interrupted by yet another pogrom, so no verdict is reached. But as a last ceremonial gesture, the actors put on their Purim masks. Sam's is the mask of Satan. Wiesel's striking verdict: theodicies can be diabolical; instead of justifying God, they often only justify evil at the expense of suffering humanity. The breadth of Wiesel's writings on the problem of evil breathe the spirit of Habakkuk. For him, any definitive "answer" to the "why?" of the Holocaust is still an open question, one he awaits in faith, albeit a wounded one. Wiesel protests any glib or easy answers that justify or trivialize unjust suffering.

The free-will defense

Does this mean, then, that we have no recourse to an intellectual address of the problem of evil? Not exactly. The liability, certainly, of any intellectual discussion of evil is that it can trivialize the pain of present suffering, as it is indeed an experiential or existential answer to this problem for which we yearn and that alone could satisfy – the Christian hope which we have yet to sketch out. But we cannot avoid an intellectual discussion of the issue, especially since the question arises so naturally and inevitably in the course of honest theological reflection on God and creation. But instead of a theodicy, perhaps the best we can offer is a weaker argument, what Christian philosopher Alvin Plantinga calls a "defense." Plantinga defines the difference this way: whereas a theodicy attempts to state what God's reason *is* in permitting evil, a defense only attempts to state what God's reason *might possibly be*.[15] A defense is not as ambitious an argument, and therefore it is less susceptible to the adverse consequence of unintentionally justifying evil. We might think of a defense as an argument "from below," in contrast to a theodicy as an argument "from above" – the latter assuming a "God's-eye" view of the reason or purpose for evil. In a defense, one more modestly specifies a possible condition by virtue of which the existence and amount of evil in the world do not disprove the existence of God as all-good and all-powerful.

---

[14] Ibid., 157.
[15] See Alvin Plantinga, *God, Freedom, and Evil* (Grand Rapids, MI: Eerdmans, 1974), 28.

The best available defense is the "free-will defense." In simple terms it can be stated as follows: the existence and amount of evil in the world do not necessarily nullify the existence of an all-good and all-powerful God, because it is perfectly possible that God deemed it a greater good to create creatures that were morally free, *even at the risk of their misuse of freedom* (i.e., sin), than to create creatures that were not free.[16] The free-will defense does not directly specify a good reason for God permitting evil, but only a condition for the possibility of sin/evil, a condition that is compatible with God's existence and nature. Most importantly, it does not accord evil a positive role. Though the difference between a theodicy and a defense can be subtle, it is nonetheless an important difference.

We might reflect further upon the possible reason why God thought it a greater good to create creatures that were morally free than creatures who were not. The simple answer here is that God desired that moral creatures freely respond to God – that is, in love, of which freedom is a necessary condition. A love that is not free is not love in its noblest sense or expression. This is actually an answer that Dostoevsky offers in his provocative chapter "The Grand Inquisitor," which follows on the heels of "Rebellion" in *The Brothers Karamazov*.[17] Recall that in "Rebellion" Ivan argued that the freedom humans possess is not worth the price we pay for its misuse, given the world's history of gratuitous violence and innocent suffering. While asserting this on the one hand, Ivan in "The Grand Inquisitor" relates his own story about the return of Christ to sixteenth-century Spain during the fires of the Inquisition. The "grand inquisitor" is not happy to see Jesus and accuses him, summarily, of making the "way of Christ" too hard for the mass of common folk. More particularly and strikingly, the inquisitor chastises Christ for resisting the three temptations in the wilderness, since in doing so he rejected the "miracle, mystery, and authority" which most human beings substitute for their dependence upon God and for which they gladly relinquish their freedom. He berates Christ for demanding too much of humanity, all in the name of and desire for a pure faith and love that are free. In all of this upbraiding, Christ is silent and does nothing but listen to the inquisitor respectfully and compassionately. In the end, Christ kisses the wizened inquisitor on his bloodless lips. The implication: he respects the inquisitor's freedom to reject him, since he desires a loving

---

[16] For a sophisticated and analytical treatment of the free-will defense, see Plantinga, *God, Freedom, and Evil*. Augustine also argues along these lines, although in stronger theodical fashion, as a key variant of his Neoplatonic "privation" theory of evil. See *City of God*, 12.7.

[17] Dostoevsky, *Brothers Karamazov*, Book 5, ch. 5.

response that is free. These two poignant chapters in Dostoevsky, which have become classic texts in the discussion of God and evil, imply a free-will defense: while human freedom does not seem to be worth the risk of its egregious abuse, it nevertheless remains the necessary condition of love, for a free response to God in Christ.

The origin of evil

Another reason for skepticism regarding the project of theodicy is that it tends to specify the origin of evil in rather glib fashion. Think of the *dualist* theodicy of gnosticism, for example. It easily identifies the origin of evil in one word: matter. Or think of the *monist* theodicy of Neoplatonism (or other monistic systems), which identifies the origin of evil in non-being, making evil a mere chimera or illusion. Or consider even the *naturalist* account of evil in much current atheistic materialism (the view that the material cosmos is all there is), which must locate the origin of evil in something like the blind workings of nature. In all of these major metaphysical systems, the origin of evil is readily identified. These proposals obviously conflict with a Christian (monotheistic) metaphysic, which considers created matter to be good, evil real, and the workings of the world under the governance of more than a "blind watchmaker."[18]

Given the Christian Creator/creature metaphysic, we think it best *not* to specify the origin of evil, but rather to leave this question open as a mystery – to be more precise (and harking back to the free-will defense), a mystery of the misuse of creaturely freedom. To say anything more than this, to specify any further why free human creatures have rebelled against God (blaming it on some external stimulus, such as the serpent or a built-in weakness for apples) is to introduce a causality of sin into the world beyond the mysterious and responsible realm of human choice. To explain the cause of the misuse of creaturely freedom would not only rob humanity of this freedom (since the efficient cause would be other than the actual exercise of this freedom), but would also imply that the origin of sin in God's creation results from some created deficiency. This would not only exculpate humanity of its responsibility for sin, but would ultimately reflect poorly on God as somehow the author of sin – both of which violate essential theological principles. As G. C. Berkouwer has rightly noted, we

---

[18] See Richard Dawkins, *The Blind Watchmaker: Why the Evidence of Evolution Reveals a Universe Without Design* (New York: Norton, 1987).

must leave the origin of evil as a mystery, a mystery of the misuse of human freedom.[19] By so doing, we make sin our common human confession: We – each and every one of us – have sinned against God. Collectively, we are culpable for sin and responsible for the moral evil that pervades our world and history. Moral evil is a human problem that cannot be blamed on anything else – whether it be a deficiency in creation, the devil, or God's own self. Original sin is a collective human confession: *Mea culpa, mea maxima culpa.*

The present and future status of evil

The question of origin inquires into the source of evil. Where did it come from? How did it make its appearance in a world created good and ruled by a loving, triune God? As we have seen, it is finally difficult to say much about that topic, given that evil presents us with a true theological mystery. The more pertinent questions have to do with the *status* of evil – namely, what we are to make of evil in our present experience, given its lurking and ineluctable presence, and what we are to make of God's seeming silence in the face of continuing evil. In Christian perspective, this means pondering the connection between evil and God's history of the salvation of the world, especially the central christological events of the NT narrative.[20] What are we to make of evil now? And what of evil's future? Will it have the last word?

Good Friday: Trinity and cross

The God in whom Christians confess their faith is the triune God – the God who desires the flourishing of all beings in creation. The linchpin of God's saving action with respect to sin, evil, and suffering is the incarnation, where the eternal Logos entered into the human condition in order to share the human plight and redeem it from within. The one who dies on the cross, bearing the pain of the world's evil in solidarity with sufferers, is truly divine, "of the same essence" as the Father and the Spirit. This event therefore constitutes God's *com-passion* or "suffering with" the world. When we suffer, we can be assured that God is present with us in compassionate love. From one angle, it is hard to see how it could have been otherwise. How could a God who *is* love (see 1 John 4:8) and who loves the

---

[19] See G. C. Berkouwer, *Sin*, trans. Philip C. Holtrop (Grand Rapids, MI: Eerdmans, 1971), chs. 1 and 5.
[20] The following section echoes the approach taken in Matthew D. Lundberg, "The Problem of Suffering and the Theology of the Cross," *Covenant Quarterly* 66, no. 1 (2008), 11–20.

world (see John 3:16) stand idly by in the face of the suffering of creatures? As Psalm 145:9 indicates: "The Lᴏʀᴅ is good to all, and his compassion is over all that he has made." The triune God through the poignancy of the incarnation thus understands what it is to undergo trials: physical pain, uncertainty, loneliness, anticipation of death, psychological anguish, God-forsakenness, and death itself. As Hebrews 4:15 notes concerning Christ the Son: "we do not have a high priest who is unable to sympathize with our weaknesses, but we have one who in every respect has been tested as we are, yet without sin." The cross of Good Friday is the high point of the divine compassion. The Son experiences the height of human trials, as epitomized by his cry of dereliction ("My God, my God, why have you forsaken me?" – Mark 15:34), which expresses his experience of divine abandonment or hell. Given the perichoretic love of the Trinity, however, it would also make sense that as the Son suffers horribly on the cross, the Father and Spirit, far from remaining unmoved, suffer with the Son, as well as suffer the loss of the Son. The cross therefore is the triune God's decisive act of sharing in human suffering. It is in God's co-suffering presence, instructively, that many of the poor and oppressed of the world find deep comfort.[21] And it is largely for this reason that Good Friday is the preeminent holiday of Catholic Latin America.

Like the crucified Christ, human sufferers cry out not just for God's comforting presence, but for vindication and restoration – for their suffering to be removed. In many ways, however, the cross by itself, while providing some solace by manifesting the compassion of God in Christ, also heightens the problem of evil. Writing through the grief of the death of his own son, Nicholas Wolterstorff stresses this point in relation to the cross: "Instead of hearing an answer [to the problem of evil] we catch sight of God himself scraped and torn. Through our tears we see the tears of God. A new and more disturbing question now arises: Why do you permit yourself to suffer, O God? If the death of the devout costs you dear (Psalm 116:15), why do you permit it? Why do you not grasp joy?"[22]

Easter Sunday: resurrection and new creation

Finally, but only after walking through Good Friday's valley of the shadow of death, we must also look to the light of the empty tomb, just as Christ's immediate followers did. The "good news" of the NT hinges on the claim

[21] See, e.g., Jon Sobrino, *Christ the Liberator: A View From the Victims*, trans. Paul Burns (Maryknoll, NY: Orbis, 2001), 268–74.

[22] Nicholas Wolterstorff, *Lament For a Son* (Grand Rapids, MI: Eerdmans, 1987), 80.

that Good Friday and the cross do not have the last word with respect to evil. The injustice of Jesus' death was redressed when he was vindicated through the resurrection. His suffering was removed when his death was transformed into incorruptible life. Easter Sunday and the empty tomb radically modify the status of evil, most notably its future. "He is risen!" goes the old Christian refrain on Easter Sunday. The resurrection signifies that evil has been defeated, because the resurrection stands as the promise of new creation for all creatures in the kingdom of God. Despite appearances to the contrary, therefore, evil has been defeated. The same divine power that called Jesus back from the dead will be manifested eschatologically at the final triumph over evil in the resurrection of body and the final judgment. God has sent a promise (*pro-missio*) into the present from the past. As Paul writes in 1 Corinthians 15, Christ's resurrection is the basis for Christian hope regarding the general resurrection and the renewal of all things.[23]

A helpful analogy for thinking about this victory can be drawn from WWII.[24] On June 6, 1944 – D-Day – the allies landed at Normandy, an initiative that proved successful as the turning point of the conflict. The war in Europe, however, dragged on for almost another year; hostilities did not cease until May 8, 1945 – VE-Day. In the meantime, battles were lost and many soldiers and civilians were killed. But D-Day sealed the fate of the Nazi regime and assured the outcome of the war, despite further setbacks and suffering. Analogously, Easter Sunday is D-Day. Evil has been dealt a definitive blow, and the ultimate outcome of the war is assured in the form of promise. But until VE-Day – the final eschatological victory over evil through the return of Christ (see pp. 397–415) – battles will be lost and evil will often seem to continue to have its way.

Christian belief in the significance and profundity of the resurrection, the symbol of the final defeat of evil, has been given beautiful and profound expression by artists over the centuries. In order to illustrate our theological point here, we enlist the theological and musical insight of Johann Sebastian Bach (1685–1750), arguably the greatest composer in the western tradition. Bach composed a great deal of church music – much of it offering rich theological commentary – including works for Sunday worship called cantatas, works for Good Friday observance called passions, and even a Catholic mass – the majestic "Mass in B Minor."[25] The mass begins with a

---

[23] See Jürgen Moltmann, *Theology of Hope: On the Ground and the Implications of a Christian Eschatology*, trans. James W. Leitch (New York: Harper & Row, 1967), 139–48.
[24] This analogy is suggested by Cullmann, *Christ and Time*, 84.
[25] On the Mass in B Minor, see George B. Stauffer, *Bach: The Mass in B Minor: The Great Catholic Mass* (New Haven, CT: Yale University Press, 2003).

Kyrie (invoking divine mercy), moves to a *Gloria* (expressing glory to God in the highest), proceeds to a *Credo* (a setting of the words of the Nicene Creed), continues with a *Sanctus* (addressing divine holiness), and ends with an *Agnus Dei* (a plea directed to the "Lamb of God"). We wish to focus on some key movements in Bach's framing of the *Credo* in this profound work.

In setting the Latin words of the Nicene Creed regarding Christ's taking on flesh and becoming human ("*Et incarnatus est*"), Bach depicts this mystery with consummate skill. Just as Christ came down to dwell with us, the musical phrases in "*Et incarnatus est*" are falling phrases, ones in which the sequence of notes generally proceeds downward. Bach next sets the words of the creed that deal with the death of Christ ("*Crucifixus etiam pro nobis sub Pontio Pilato, passus et sepultus est*" – "He was crucified for us under Pontius Pilate, died and was buried"). Instructively, Bach places the *Crucifixus* at the very center of the *Credo*, indicating its importance symbolically and musico-theologically. Bach's setting of these words is very soft (*piano*). The piece is also in a relatively dark key, a minor key (E minor, whose key signature has only one sharp [#], which resembles a cross – instructively, the German word for "sharp" is *Kreuz*, which is also the German word for "cross"). The *Crucifixus* ends very softly – the words *passus et sepultus est* are almost inaudible. Then after a short pause, Bach bursts forth with the theme of the resurrection ("*Et resurrexit tertia die secundum scripturas*" – "And he rose on the third day according to the scriptures"). Bach's account of the *Et resurrexit* is comparatively loud (*forte*). The setting is in a bright-sounding major key, and it includes celebratory instruments such as trumpets and tympani. Befitting the theme of Christ's rising from death, the musical phrases are rising, ones in which the sequence of notes is generally upward. The musical symbolism and theological point are unmistakable. Further in the *Credo*, Bach seeks to emphasize that there is a crucial connection to be made between the death and resurrection of Christ and that of the believer. Near the end of the *Credo*, when he sets the words describing the general resurrection of the dead ("*Et expecto resurrectionem*" – "And I await the resurrection"), there are some notable musical similarities between the *Et expecto* and the *Et resurrexit*, including similarities of melody, key, and instrumentation.

Christ has come in the flesh – a mystery. Christ was crucified – a tragedy. But Christ rose again from death and conquered evil – a glorious transformation. Bach reminds us that the resurrection is the key source of hope for the believer. But we are permitted to celebrate only *after* taking up our crosses and walking through the valley of the shadow of death – a point also convincingly made in Gustav Mahler's searching Symphony No. 2, "Resurrection."[26]

In sum, the events of Passion Week reveal the lengths to which the triune God is willing to go to address evil. While the silence of God was a major theme in twentieth-century theology, philosophy, and the arts, we would argue, with Bach, that God has in fact spoken powerfully and loudly to evil – but ironically beginning with the agony of the cross and its divine silence. It is then through the resurrection (and its eschatological vectors) that God's powerful response to evil and suffering resounds. But the question that now remains is this: How do we live in between the "already" of Christ's resurrection and the "not yet" of the new creation?

Holy Saturday: lament, protest, and hope

From a theological perspective, the first point to be emphasized about evil is its continuing reality in our world. In this sense, we are still living in the shadow of Good Friday with the realities of sin and evil even as we strain in hope for the new creation promised in Easter Sunday. Thus it is possible to regard present existence metaphorically as the in-between time of Holy Saturday. Evil continues to exert a real and tragic force in human experience, and Christians should forthrightly acknowledge this fact. We should not seek to explain it away in some fashion – whether by denying its reality (consigning it to the domain of passing illusion) or by justifying it through some theodical strategy (declaring it necessary to God's plan). Christians are called to recognize evil as evil and to name it as such. Life here and now is lived in the shadow of the cross, with the promise of new creation only partially fulfilled. We should therefore *lament* evil's presence in creation. Such lament is found in many OT texts, particularly the Psalms, which cry out to Yahweh that the world seems disordered and upside down, insistently asking Yahweh to step down from lofty inactivity and create justice in the world (e.g., Pss. 22; 44; 88). We can learn much from the Jewish tradition in this respect, which has been less hesitant than the Christian tradition to cry out to God in lament – and even in *protest*. As the writings of Elie Wiesel show us, it can be a facet of the life of faith to lament and to cry out in protest, for to protest is to decry the injustice in our world. Such protest is first directed against the clear perpetrators of injustice who must be thwarted and held accountable for their crimes; protest is also directed to those who remain silent and indifferent – apathetic – in the face of injustice

---

[26] See Constantin Floros, *Gustav Mahler: The Symphonies*, trans. Vernon Wicker and Jutta Wicker, ed. Reinhard G. Pauly (Portland, OR: Amadeus Press, 1993), 51–82.

in the world; and sometimes, in the passion of the moment, such protest even questions God's mysterious silence and inaction in the midst of a particular crisis: "My God, my God, why have you forsaken me?" (Mark 15:34). This order is significant, for what it indicates is that even before we may ask the question of theodicy – How is God justified in view of evil? – we must first ask the question of *anthropodicy*: How is humanity justified in view of the evil we ourselves perpetrate and about which we so often remain apathetic? Moral evil is first a problem about humanity and its justification (righteousness) before it is a problem about God and divine righteousness. This, in important point of fact, is the presupposition of the free-will defense.

In this sense, perhaps Dostoevsky's Ivan Karamazov should speak for us all: there is something deeply disturbing, even absurd, about a world in which innocent children suffer. We protest – and we should. As a body of people who are ostensibly concerned with righteousness (= justice), Christians are called to shake their fists at evil, not look past it or explain it glibly away, and to advocate for justice in the world. Only when we recognize the force of evil – that is, only when such evil overwhelms us – can our questioning of God become, understandably, a passionate prayer, a demand, even a protest to the God who allows it to happen: "How long, O Lord, before you come and judge the inhabitants of the earth?" (Rev. 6:10). Such an attitude ought to be part and parcel of a Christian spirituality that wrestles with God for the sake of God's world – a spirituality of passionate involvement, a spirituality of *chutzpah*. As Wiesel puts it for his own faith tradition: "Only the Jew knows that he may oppose God as long as he does so in defense of His creation."[27]

Parenthetically, we pause to note that evil can play a pedagogical role in the development of the Christian life; through the crucible of human suffering it is possible for the virtues of patience, humility, compassion, and even faith to be refined. That is to say, when we suffer, the experience changes us – and sometimes makes us better people. Many attest to this happening in their own experience.[28] This can happen, perhaps, because God can turn evil to good – even though it is often not clear to us how and when this happens, and we should be ever so careful not to let this claim slur over into the related but perverse claim that God *willed* evil for the sake of good (bearing in mind, once again, the point of the distinction between a theodicy and a defense). Any good that God brings out of evil is purely *in*

---

[27] Elie Wiesel, *A Jew Today* (New York: Vintage, 1978), 7.
[28] See, e.g., Simone Weil, *Waiting for God*, trans. Emma Gruafund (New York: Putnam, 1951).

spite of evil. Moreover, it is only in retrospect that we can see how some good resulted from senseless suffering. This is the moment of truth in the soul-building theodicy – namely, that evil *can* contribute to human becoming as we mature in a finite, imperfect world. That suffering can play a pedagogical role in some people's lives may describe what sometimes happens, but this should never become an axiomatic explanation for all suffering in general.

But just as present lament shades over into present protest, so both shade over into *hope* for the future, for the Christian has reason to hope that evil does not have the last word. The present in-between of Holy Saturday, with the shadow of the cross and Good Friday looming, peeks in hope at the glimmer of new creation at the horizon of the eschatological Easter Sunday, for evil does not belong in the world created by the triune God. Evil and suffering are destined to be eradicated. Christians can have this radical hope because evil is not intrinsic to the world as creation (as it is in dualism or naturalism). Evil is *accidental* to creation, not an *essential* part of it. As such it is a perversion of and a parasite on a good creation. This is to say that in Christian thought evil is not necessary to the good, it is not essential to its definition, since given the doctrine of creation *ex nihilo*, good can exist independently of evil (either in God or in a good creation). To the contrary, it is evil that is dependent and parasitic on the good for its very definition and existence. To illustrate: you can explain healthy cell division without reference to cancer; but you cannot explain cancer without reference to healthy cell division. Analogously, the doctrine of creation establishes the primacy of the good and defines the nature of the good upon which evil is an inessential and accidental parasite. And parasites, as we well know, can be excised. So while the doctrine of *creatio ex nihilo* initially exacerbates the problem of evil for monotheism, by accentuating the transcendent power and goodness of God, it is that doctrine alone that provides the metaphysical condition for hope in the radical removal of evil. The resurrection of Jesus Christ promises this radical surgery in a renewed heaven and earth, the re-creation of all things.

CONCLUSION

The question about God's seeming unconcern and silence in the face of human suffering has concerned many a person, both Christian and non-Christian, over the course of the years and has intensified during the last violent and bloody century. But is God really silent about the problem of evil? The God of Christian confession is none other than the triune God, who, far from being unconcerned about a suffering creation, sends one of its own, the only begotten Son, into the world out of love for that world. The Christian claim is that God has spoken powerfully to this problem in the Word who became flesh. The Christ event shows the dramatic and self-giving lengths to which God was willing to go in order to address evil and injustice. The Word spoken to creation in the incarnation defeated the powers (including evil) on Easter Sunday and will consummate his cosmic rule in the last days. The personal identity of the one sent to accomplish this task – Jesus Christ – is the subject of our reflection in the next chapter.

FOR FURTHER READING

Dostoevsky, Fyodor, *The Brothers Karamazov*, trans. Constance Garnett (New York: New American Library, 1980), Book 5, chs. 4–5.

Hall, Douglas John, *God and Human Suffering: An Exercise in the Theology of the Cross* (Minneapolis, MN: Augsburg, 1986).

Hick, John, *Evil and the God of Love*, rev. edn. (New York: HarperSanFrancisco, 1977).

Wiesel, Elie, *The Trial of God* (New York: Schocken, 1995).

Wink, Walter, *The Powers, 1: Naming the Powers: The Language of Power in the New Testament* (Philadelphia: Fortress, 1984).

Wolterstorff, Nicholas, *Lament for a Son* (Grand Rapids, MI: Eerdmans, 1987).

CHAPTER 9

The identity and person of Jesus Christ

INTRODUCTION: THE QUEST(ION) OF GOD

In an episode recorded in all three synoptic gospels, Jesus once asked his disciples: "Who do people say that the Son of Man is?" (Matt. 16:13). The Matthean version continues as follows: "And they said, 'Some say John the Baptist, but others Elijah, and still others Jeremiah or one of the prophets.' He said to them, 'But who do you say that I am?' Simon Peter answered, 'You are the Messiah, the Son of the living God'" (16:14–16). Jesus went on to tell Peter that this was revealed to him by his Father in heaven, and that the disciples must keep quiet about Jesus' identity, since he must first go to Jerusalem to suffer, die, and then be raised from the dead.

Christian faith hinges on the identity of Jesus Christ. While people across the centuries have acknowledged Jesus as a significant historical figure, a good teacher, or a moral example, the Christian creedal tradition has followed in the wake of Peter's confession: Jesus of Nazareth is the long-expected messiah who fulfills OT hopes, yet who does so in a most unexpected way: as the Son of God, veritable God in the flesh, he suffers the powers of death in order to inaugurate a new creation.

For the Christian, the quest(ion) of God cannot be pursued apart from the drama surrounding Jesus Christ. This "Christ event" – Christ's incarnation, life, ministry, crucifixion, and resurrection – represents a surprising culmination of the OT portrayal of God. In that ancient polytheistic context, the question of God was largely an ordeal of power, as conflicts among nations were also seen to be conflicts among competing gods. One nation's political fortunes in conflict or combat with another became a referendum on that nation's god(s). In short, the true God is the one who "wins" history. So, for example, in Moses' showdown with Pharaoh, Yahweh proved to be stronger than the Egyptian gods; or in the confrontation with Jericho, Yahweh proved mightier than Jericho's gods. This is why the Babylonian exile created such a crisis of faith for Judah, since it posed the question whether the Babylonian gods were stronger than Yahweh. This crisis, as we have seen, occasioned the deepening of creation theology and the fuller recognition that Yahweh was the sole Creator of heaven and earth (see pp. 81 and 148). Even after their restoration to the land, however, the Jewish remnant lived largely under foreign rule. During this intertestamental period the rise of apocalyptic literature intensified the question of God, especially under the pressure of persecution. How long would it be before Yahweh would come in apocalyptic splendor to manifest the divine righteousness, bringing justice to the earth and thereby proving in world history to be the one true God?

Enter Jesus of Nazareth, born of humble Mary in a lowly stable, raised in relative obscurity, but who raised quite a ruckus in the final years of his life. In his teaching, Jesus announced the coming kingdom of God, and claimed to be the apocalyptic figure who would implement Yahweh's universal reign of righteousness and peace. Entering Jerusalem as a triumphant king, albeit riding on a donkey, Jesus' proclamation led to his execution as a religious blasphemer and political criminal. All these events would have amounted to little more than an interesting chapter in the history of first-century Palestine were it not for one persistent claim: that Jesus of Nazareth rose from the dead – an event which appeared to vindicate Jesus' claims and ministry, and which set in motion for his followers a new movement of spiritual and missional verve. For the Christian, therefore, the question of God inextricably revolves around the question of Jesus Christ: Who do you say that I am?

This chapter takes up this basic question of Jesus' identity – who is this *person* of Jesus Christ? – while the subsequent chapter takes up the issue of Christ's *work* – what is it that Christ does to accomplish salvation? While these christological aspects can never be separated, since they fit hand in glove, they are traditionally distinguished in order to clarify who exactly Christ is that qualifies him to perform the work of salvation. Importantly, how one answers the question of Christ's person will be telling for how one understands the salvific work he undertakes.

Ever since the apostle Paul, "Jesus Christ" has for all practical purposes become a proper name, as though Jesus' last name were Christ. But Christ is really a title, since *Christos* is the Greek equivalent for the Hebrew "Messiah" – the anointed one. "Jesus Christ" – or better, Jesus the Christ – is really the confession that Jesus of Nazareth is the Messiah. The primary biblical identity of Jesus Christ therefore is that of a special agent anointed to do God's salvific bidding. We therefore begin our biblical survey with the messianic expectations of the OT, followed by the NT claims that Jesus of Nazareth is that long-anticipated Messiah.

BIBLICAL MATERIALS

Old Testament messianic expectations

In light of the discovery of the Dead Sea Scrolls in the late 1940s, as well as the accumulating research on intertestamental literature, scholars today are confident that at the time of Jesus' appearance there was no singular conception of or common Jewish hope for the messiah. Rather, there were a variety of messianic conceptions and expectations that, according to the NT, are fulfilled singularly in Jesus – but in quite unexpected ways.[1]

The most popular and dominant of these various messianic strains was that of an ideal Davidic *king*, one who would subdue Israel's enemies and rule in righteousness. Such an expectation is rooted in Nathan's oracle to David:

Moreover the LORD declares to you that the LORD will make you a house. When your days are fulfilled and you lie down with your ancestors, I will raise up your offspring after you, who shall come forth from your body, and I will establish his kingdom. He shall build a house for my name, and I will establish the throne of

---

[1] See, e.g., John J. Collins, *The Scepter and the Star: The Messiahs of the Dead Sea Scrolls and Other Ancient Literature* (New York: Doubleday, 1995), whose treatment informs the following.

his kingdom forever. I will be a father to him and he shall be a son to me ... Your house and your kingdom shall be made sure for ever before me. (2 Sam. 7:11–14, 16)

In ascending to the throne, this messianic king is considered the son of God by adoption and is, therefore, God's representative and righteous agent on earth (as is reflected, e.g., in Pss. 2; 45:1–9; and Isa. 9:6–7).[2] When Israel experienced exile and the loss of the Davidic kingship, the prophets continued to rouse hope in a coming king, as a shoot from the stump of Jesse who would be endowed with God's Spirit to rule in righteousness (Isa. 11:1–9), as a branch of David who would execute justice (Jer. 23:5–6). While this messianic expectation waned thereafter in the early Second Temple period (c. sixth century BCE to first century CE), it revived later on in the literature of the Hasmonean era – named for those non-Davidic kings who ruled Judea up into the Roman period which ended shortly after Herod the Great's reign (c. 37–4 BCE). Here the messianic hope for the Davidic king took on sharp warrior qualities, in anticipating one who would restore Israel to her former grandeur by overthrowing all of Israel's enemies in a final, eschatological war. According to John Collins, "the concept of the Davidic messiah as the warrior king who would destroy the enemies of Israel and institute an era of unending peace constitutes the common core of Jewish messianism around the turn of the [Christian] era."[3]

But other messianic strains were present as well. In connection with another "anointed" office, there was an expectation for a *priestly* messiah, one who would mediate between Yahweh and Israel in an unprecedented way (see Lev. 4; Dan. 9). This expectation was sometimes held in tandem with the kingly messiah, reflecting Zechariah's "two sons of oil" (4:12), which referred to the last Davidic king, Zerubbabel, and the high priest, Joshua, who shared leadership of the post-exilic Jewish community (late sixth century BCE). Additionally, there was a hope for a *prophetic* messiah, based on Deuteronomy 18:18, where Yahweh promises one like Moses: "I will raise up for them a prophet like you from among their own people; I will put my words in the mouth of the prophet, who shall speak to them everything that I command." Interestingly, in this vein, the literature of the Dead Sea Scrolls talks about a "teacher of righteousness" who would come at the "end of days" to inaugurate a messianic age of holiness and justice.[4]

A fourth prominent messianic strain arose in intertestamental apocalyptic literature – the messiah as the *Son of Man*. This expectation is based on

---

[2] Ibid., 22–3.   [3] Ibid., 68.   [4] Ibid., 74–135.

the book of Daniel, the best representative of apocalyptic literature in the Hebrew Bible, where one vision records:

> I saw one like a [Son of Man]
>   coming with the clouds of heaven.
> And he came to the Ancient One
>   and was presented before him.
> To him was given dominion
>   and glory and kingship,
> that all peoples, nations, and languages
>   should serve him.
> His dominion is an everlasting dominion
>   that shall not pass away,
> and his kingship is one
>   that shall never be destroyed.   (Dan. 7:13–14)

The prospect of an apocalyptic Son of Man entailed the hope that a transcendent figure of heavenly origin would come to bring salvation to the righteous and judgment to the nations, a messianic motif that sometimes melded with that of the Davidic kingly messiah.[5]

New Testament fulfillment

The NT declares that Jesus of Nazareth fulfills these various messianic expectations, but that he does so in surprising ways. Though Jesus himself never expressly claims to be the messiah, neither does he deny the identification (e.g., Matt. 16:13–16; Mark 14:61–4). His wariness over the title and the reason why he implores his disciples to keep quiet about this identity (the so-called "messianic secret") likely stem from the popular conception of the Davidic king as one who will militarily overthrow the Gentiles (Romans) and reinstate Israel's political independence. Instead, Jesus' triumphal entry into Jerusalem as *king* is nonviolent and lowly – riding on a donkey – and instead of ascending a throne, he is enthroned upon a cross. There he is hailed the "King of the Jews" only with bitter irony – while suffering humiliation, execution, and defeat. (His conquering ascension takes place only through his resurrection.)

Jesus' ministry is also interpreted by the NT to be that of a *priest*, but his priesthood is of a different order – not that of Aaron or Levi, but, mysteriously, that of Melchizedek (Heb. 6:19ff.; cf. Ps. 110) – whereby he not only mediates the relationship between God and humanity, but is, strikingly, the

---

[5] Ibid., 173–94.

sacrifice of reconciliation itself (Heb. 7:27; 9:11–15, 26). Moreover, Jesus is also assumed to be the expected *prophet* (Luke 24:19; John 6:14), one who teaches a righteousness that is not for the sectarian or pious, but that he offers graciously and promiscuously to sinners, with whom he freely and scandalously associates.

Jesus' most explicit identification with messianic expectations, however, is as the *Son of Man*, his favorite self-designation, which associates him with the Danielic figure that comes on the clouds as the agent of God's final judgment. That this appears to be the chief way that Jesus interpreted his messianic vocation can be seen in the episode recorded in Mark 14:61–4, where Jesus claims, to the high priest's chagrin, that he is indeed the apocalyptic Son of Man.[6] But Jesus did not usher in the climax of history, at least not in the expected sense (though there is another sense in which he did indeed inaugurate the "last days" – see pp. 392–5 below). This is in fact the primary obstacle for Jewish belief in Jesus as the Messiah: the world as we know it did not end. In Christian thought this apocalyptic climax is deferred to his second coming.

In summary, the primary identification of Jesus Christ in the NT, in continuity with the OT, is as the Messiah, a confession now etched in his very name. Jesus' fulfillment of this variegated office, however, happens in quite unexpected ways, especially the way he fulfills the kingly role through suffering and humiliation, which comports with the "suffering servant" imagery from Isaiah 52–3 (e.g., Mark 8:31). But the biggest surprise in Jesus' messianic identification comes with the deity claim, for in NT and Christian thought Jesus the Christ turns out to be no mere human being, but the very Son of God in the flesh. While such a claim went far beyond typical messianic expectations, it is the compelling testimony of the NT at large.

The deity of Christ

The humanity of Christ is not at issue in the NT. That Jesus of Nazareth was truly human – that he was born of a woman, that he matured, hungered, thirsted, was tempted, got angry, died a painful death, in the same fashion as other human beings – is the clear keynote of the synoptic gospels and is assumed by the NT at large. But what intrudes into the NT witness is the claim that Jesus is also divine, that he ultimately belongs to the divine side of the Creator/creature distinction. There are three indisputable

---

[6] See also Raymond E. Brown, *An Introduction to New Testament Christology* (Mahwah, NJ: Paulist, 1994), 89–100.

texts where Christ is expressly identified as "God": John 1:1; 20:28; and Hebrews 1:8–9, along with five other probable instances: John 1:18; Romans 9:5; Titus 2:13; 2 Peter 1:1; and 1 John 5:20. But the NT case for the deity of Christ is much more extensive than mere proof texts and includes a consideration of (1) other *titles* Jesus is given; (2) the *divine functions* he assumes; and (3) the *worship* he receives.[7]

(1) Jesus' principal title as the *Messiah* does not imply divinity, which is the most striking anomaly of Christ's fulfillment of OT messianic expectations. But Jesus' favorite self-designation as the *Son of Man* may imply divine status. Though this Hebrew phrase can simply refer to a human being, as in Ezekiel's use of it, given the intertestamental development of Daniel's heavenly savior figure, Jesus' claim to be the Son of Man goes beyond sheer human status, as seen by the fact that it provoked accusations of blasphemy (Mark 14:61–4).

Christ's association with deity is more readily secured in the title *Son of God*. While "divine sonship" manifests a range of senses in the OT (e.g., angels, the Davidic king, even the Hebrew nation), a unique and exclusive sense is attributed to Christ in the NT, one that Jesus himself accepts (Mark 12:6–7; 13:32; Luke 10:22), and which culminates in the claim that he is God's "only Son" (John 3:16). This affirmation both distinguishes Christ personally from God the Father and yet situates them in the closest possible relationship of deity. In fact, John 1:18, traditionally translated "only begotten Son," is better translated "only begotten God" according to the best manuscript evidence (cf. NRSV and NASB).

The title *Lord* can also be variously interpreted (e.g., sir, master, household lord). In the basic NT confession "Jesus is Lord," however, it likely implies deity, since "Lord" (Gk. *kyrios*) is the word used to translate the divine name (YHWH) in the Septuagint, the Greek version of the OT utilized by the majority of NT authors. To call Jesus "Lord," therefore, especially in the context of worship, would be tantamount to calling him "God."

(2) Christ's divine functions further justify this high interpretation of his titles, as activities considered the domain of God alone in the OT are in the NT also ascribed to Christ. Yahweh's status as *Creator*, for example, distinguished the God of Israel from all the other putative deities – showing them to be mere creaturely powers and therefore idols. Various NT texts assert Christ's role in the creation (Col. 1:16; Heb. 1:3; John 1:3), sustenance

---

[7] What follows draws significantly from Thomas R. Thompson, "Deity of Christ," in *The New Dictionary of Christian Apologetics*, ed. W. C. Campbell-Jack, Gavin J. McGrath, and C. Stephen Evans (Downers Grove, IL: InterVarsity, 2006), 207–11.

(Col. 1:17), fulfillment (Eph. 1:9–10), and re-creation (2 Cor. 5:17) of the world, thus strongly implying his deity.

Even more significant is Jesus' claim that he will be history's *Judge* at the end of the world – the dreaded Day of the Lord (Matt. 25:31–46; Mark 8:38) – an assertion intimately bound up with Jesus' self-designation as the "Son of Man." The NT at large associates Christ's return with the final divine judgment of human actions and attitudes, and Paul even speaks of this day as "the day of the Lord Jesus" (2 Cor. 1:14).

In close connection with judgment, the NT also indicates that Jesus has the power to forgive sins (Mark 2:1–12; Luke 7:48), a prerogative unique to God as *Savior*. Similarly, Christ is also seen as the figure who will effect the general resurrection of the dead, which is an event tied to his second coming in judgment (John 5:25–9). These two acts associated with salvation – forgiveness and resurrection – link Christ in the closest possible way to the God of the OT.

(3) But the most compelling evidence for the deity of Christ is the NT witness that he was worshipped along with God the Father. This is evidenced by the ascription of doxologies to Christ (Rom. 9:5; 2 Tim. 4:18; 2 Pet. 3:18), as well as prayers *to* Christ (Acts 7:59–60; 1 Cor. 16:22; 2 Cor. 12:8). Moreover, it is likely that all the direct predications indicating that Christ is "God," as noted above, are of liturgical origin. If Christ was worshipped during NT times, it was because he was considered divine, otherwise the early Christians would have been committing acts of idolatry by worshipping a creature.

The Gospel of John especially integrates this variety of evidence, affording a compelling case for Christ's deity beyond general proof-texting. As noted above, John contains two of the three clear references to Christ as "God": at the very outset – "In the beginning was the Word, and the Word was with God, and the Word was God" (1:1) – and near the very end – doubting Thomas's reverent recognition of the risen Christ: "My Lord and my God!" (20:28), which ascribes to Jesus both of the divine designations of the *Shema* (Deut. 6:4). During the course of this gospel, John seeks to persuade his readers that Jesus is both Messiah and Son of God, so that they may have salvation in his name (20:31). In the NT, the relationship between the Son and the Father is most fully developed in this gospel, portraying them as both distinct from and equal to one another (cf. 1:1, where Christ as Word both is "with God" and is "God"). Although the Son is subordinate to God the Father in the incarnation, he is simultaneously so united with the Father (10:30) that seeing him is equivalent to seeing the Father (14:9). In fact, when Jesus calls God his own Father, his utterance is judged to be blasphemous (see 5:18; 10:33; 19:7). This association with Israel's God is strikingly emphasized in John by a series of "I am" sayings that identify Jesus with the divine name (YHWH) revealed to Moses at the burning bush: "I AM WHO I AM" (Exod. 3:14). John employs the "I am" designation on multiple occasions in both an absolute sense (e.g., 8:58: "before Abraham was, *I am*") and with predicates (e.g., 11:25: "*I am* the resurrection and the life"). In addition to these divine *titles*, Jesus in John is also associated with the spectrum of divine *functions*: as the preexisting agent of creation (1:1–3), the coming judge (5:22–30), and the savior of the world (4:42, 11:25). As in Thomas's climactic confession of *worship*, John's Gospel boldly portrays Jesus as both Lord and God.

The cumulative case for the deity of Christ in the NT is compelling. In addition to his true humanity, the NT witness – both directly and indirectly – asserts his deity. Yet in reflecting on this apostolic witness, it would take the patristic church some years to formulate an ecumenical consensus concerning the person of Christ. That historical development is our next topic.

HISTORICAL DEVELOPMENT

The long road to Chalcedon

The culminating statement of the early church's assessment of the personal identity of Jesus Christ was formulated at the fourth ecumenical council, held at Chalcedon in 451. The so-called "Chalcedonian definition" of the person of Christ has since been regarded as the benchmark of christological orthodoxy. In the long and winding road to Chalcedon, a number of christological proposals were ruled as unacceptable (i.e., as unorthodox or heretical) by various conciliar decisions. Given Christ's dual identity, some of these proposals stressed his humanity at the expense of his deity, while others stressed his deity to the neglect of his humanity; still others grappled with the question of how two such natures could reside in one person. The following is a simplified account of the lengthy and complex theological process that led to the Chalcedonian definition of Christ. Though this doctrinal history was often fraught with political intrigues and the clash of personalities, here we can address only the basic theological issues involved (see also pp. 437–42 below).[8]

---

[8] For a fuller treatment of this doctrinal history, see J. N. D. Kelly, *Early Christian Doctrines*, 2nd edn. (New York: Harper & Row, 1960); and Jaroslav Pelikan, *The Christian Tradition: A History of the Development of Doctrine*, 5 vols. (Chicago: University of Chicago Press, 1971–89), 1: 226–77.

The Ebionitic strain and the Council of Nicea (325)

The Ebionites were a second-century group of Jewish Christians who retained much of their Judaism in belief and practice, including an adherence to strict monotheism that recognized only God the Father as divine (as Yahweh). Consequently, many Ebionites held that Jesus, although he was a great prophet – indeed, the promised Messiah – was not fully or eternally divine. Denying his preexistence, they held that Christ was born of Mary *and Joseph*, but at his baptism was specially endowed with God's Spirit and elevated as the Messiah into a special relationship with God. The Ebionites have subsequently lent their name to the basic type of christological tendency that emphasizes Christ's humanity to the depreciation of his deity.

This tendency was continued by Paul of Samosata, a third-century bishop of Antioch. Like the Ebionites, Paul held to a rigid monotheism and therefore denied the preexistence of Christ, contending that the person of Jesus is "from below" – human in every ordinary way. What is novel about Jesus is that at his baptism the Logos or Word of God, which Paul considered the supreme divine attribute, comes to indwell him, launching and empowering his messianic mission. It is at his baptism that Jesus the man is adopted into divine sonship and given superstar status. Paul of Samosata has become the classic representative of *adoptionism*, which holds that Jesus Christ acquires his "divinity" or God-likeness by means of adoption; he does not essentially possess full deity by means of an eternal begottenness. Adoptionism is typically characterized as a "low" christology.

The Ebionitic strain of thought came to a head at the Council of Nicea (325). This council, we recall, was precipitated by the Arian crisis (see pp. 121–3). Although Arius was not an adoptionist *per se*, given that he affirmed a preexistence of Christ, he did not think that that preexistence was an eternal one. For Arius, once again given a rigid monotheism that brooks no personal distinctions in God, Christ the Son was a creature, created by the Father's will for the purpose of mediating between the eternal, infinite God and the temporal, finite world. We nevertheless include Arianism in the Ebionitic strain since it fails to recognize the full deity of Christ and precipitated the council that secured that deity claim (in actuality, Arianism also has little if any place for the humanity of Christ). In terms of Christian orthodoxy, Nicea sounded the death knell of the Ebionitic strain by declaring Christ the Son *homoousios* with God the Father, co-equal in deity. Christ is eternally and fully divine, which rules out any adoptionism of ontological proportions.

The docetic strain and the Council of Constantinople (381)

Concurrent with the Ebionitic impulse, there developed an opposite strain of christological thought known as docetism, which stressed the deity of Christ to the neglect of his humanity. Gnosticism is an early representative of this tendency, which flourished in the second century (see pp. 153–5 above). Shunning the material world as intrinsically evil, gnostics generally understood Christ to be the eternally existent and fully divine *revealer* of the way to salvation. Christ, however, did not really become flesh in Jesus of Nazareth, for such embodiment was considered beneath the dignity of divine spirit. Rather, Christ's humanity and the suffering weakness it displayed only "seemed" or "appeared" to be real, since the divine, by definition for the gnostics, cannot suffer – hence the docetic label (Gk. *dokeo* = to seem or appear). Though there were many different gnostic systems and speculations, their common christological denominator was a depreciation of Christ's humanity, which was considered irrelevant in the gnostic understanding of salvation.

Another example of the docetic strain is Apollinarius in the fourth century. Though he was a firm adherent of the Nicene *homoousios* – the claim that Christ as a person distinct from the Father was fully divine – Apollinarius also held that in the incarnation the preexistent Logos (i.e., the divine person of Christ) took the place of the human rational soul of Jesus of Nazareth. Therefore, though Christ had human flesh (i.e., a body), he was not a full human person, since he lacked a decisive component of what it means to be human – namely, a rational soul, the seat and animating principle of human personhood. Apollinarius' views were a significant factor in the convening of the second ecumenical council, held at Constantinople (381), which declared that Christ was fully human, both in body and soul, officially sounding the death knell of the docetic strain.

The Alexandrian and Antiochene schools and the councils of Ephesus (431) and Chalcedon (451)

Apollinarius' christological speculation represents the tendency of the *Alexandrian* school of theology (in Egypt) in contrast to the *Antiochene* school of thought (in Syria), which could claim Paul of Samosata as a sympathizer. These two dominant scholastic centers in the patristic era had particular theological tendencies that fueled a rivalry which, among other things, produced the fourth- and fifth-century christological debates. One artistic way of envisioning their basic difference is to consider Raphael's famous painting *The School of Athens*, which highlights at its center the two

Illustration 9.1 Raphael, *The School of Athens.*

eminent philosophers of antiquity, Plato and Aristotle (see Illustration 9.1).
Raphael portrays Plato as holding his speculative *Timaeus* in one hand,
while raising his other hand high with one finger pointing up to the
heavens. This represents Plato's philosophical quest for the one ideal truth
that transcends the world of the many. By contrast, Aristotle, with his more
practical *Ethics* in hand, points out toward the world with all fingers
extended. This represents his philosophical emphasis on the observation
of the manyness or particulars of the world of human experience.

The Alexandrian school was decidedly oriented to Plato as an aid to its
theological elaborations, while the Antiochene school was much more
indebted to Aristotle. These orientations can be seen in their respective
approaches to biblical exegesis, with Alexandria promoting a more allegorical style that attempted to discern the higher, even mystical truth beyond
scripture's literal meaning, while Antioch was more content with the literal,
historical meaning of the scriptural text. As these tendencies applied to
christology, Alexandria was more concerned with the transcendent deity
of Christ and the unity of his person as the divine Logos, while Antioch
was preoccupied with securing the flesh-and-blood humanity of Christ.
Accordingly, Alexandria promotes what has been called a *Logos-sarx* or
"Word-flesh" model of the incarnation, wherein the eternal Logos assumes
human flesh. The persistent question with this model, however, is whether
it makes sufficient room for a human soul and therefore the full humanity

of Christ (the major problem in Apollinarius and the docetic strain). Antioch, on the other hand, promotes what has been called a *Logos-anthropos* or "Word-man" model of the incarnation, wherein the eternal person of the Logos conjoins himself to a whole human person (Jesus of Nazareth), both body and soul. While this model secures Christ's full humanity, it leaves in doubt the question of Christ's personal unity, of how the divine Logos and the human rational soul are still one person.

Nestorius, a fifth-century patriarch of Constantinople, is an extreme representative of Antiochene christology that brings our narrative to the third ecumenical council. To simplify a complex episode: while accepting the preceding ecumenical tradition that Christ has both a divine and a human nature, Nestorius could not conceive of a "nature" without a corresponding "person" (*prosopon* or *hypostasis*), and therefore gave the impression in his christological reflections that he advocated not one but two persons in Christ – one divine and one human, united only by a moral union of wills – the divine person of the Logos indwelling and morally influencing the human person of Jesus. Though Nestorius' position is actually more nuanced than this, the part of his christology that really provoked Alexandrian ire was his glib dismissal of the *Theotokos*, the popular liturgical custom of referring to the Virgin Mary as the "bearer of God." For the Alexandrians, the confession of the *Theotokos* was a necessary theological truth because it affirmed the personal unity of Christ's deity and humanity by implying that the eternal Logos is identical with the Jesus born of Mary.

Cyril, the patriarch of Alexandria, took the lead in opposing Nestorius, whose christology he thought smacked of adoptionism. With Cyril's Alexandrian cohorts dominating what became known as the third ecumenical council at Ephesus in 431, Nestorius' position was ruled out of bounds in the council's affirmation of one *hypostasis* or person of the Word made flesh (including a human rational soul) as well as a strong affirmation of the *Theotokos*.

Subsequent to Ephesus, however, a figure named Eutyches, in opposition to the Antiochenes, pushed the Alexandrian tendency even further. Seizing on an ambiguity in Cyril's formulations and sympathetic to Nestorius' strict correlation between nature and person, Eutyches taught that the one person of Christ has but one nature, a third sort of thing (*tertium quid*) that emerges through the incarnation, a divine–human hybrid or fusion in which the deity of Christ overwhelms his humanity. Eutyches is often considered the founder of *monophysitism*, the belief that Christ has but one nature. The Antiochenes regarded this view as unacceptably docetic in its failure to preserve the integrity of Jesus' humanity.

In light of the Eutychian controversy, appeal was made to Pope Leo (the Great) of Rome, who issued a long dogmatic letter, now known as Leo's *Tome*. Leo's response ruled against Eutyches and tried to strike a compromise between Alexandrian and Antiochene concerns. In the spirit of Leo's *Tome*, and borrowing much of its wording, the fourth ecumenical council at Chalcedon (451) made its famous ruling on the person of Christ:

> So, following the saintly fathers, we all with one voice teach the confession of one and the same Son, our Lord Jesus Christ: the same perfect in divinity and perfect in humanity, the same truly God and truly man, of a rational soul and a body; consubstantial [*homoousios*] with the Father as regards his divinity, and the same consubstantial [*homoousios*] with us as regards his humanity; like us in all respects except for sin; begotten before the ages from the Father as regards his divinity, and in the last days the same for us and our salvation from Mary, the Virgin God-bearer [*Theotokos*] as regards his humanity; one and the same Christ, Son, Lord, Only-begotten, acknowledged in two natures [*physis*] which undergo no confusion, no change, no division, no separation; at no point was the difference between the natures taken away through the union, but rather the property of both natures is preserved and comes together into a single person [*prosopon*] and a single subsistent being [*hypostasis*].[9]

This Chalcedonian definition represents the high-water mark of patristic christology. Most centrally, this statement affirms that Christ is one person (*contra* Nestorius) in two natures (*contra* Eutyches), one nature being divine (*contra* the Ebionitic strain) and one nature being human (*contra* the docetic strain), and that these natures are without confusion or change (*contra* Eutyches) and without division or separation (*contra* Nestorius). In this way Chalcedon sums up the ecumenical tradition and strikes a rather balanced compromise between Alexandrian and Antiochene concerns (see Figure 9.1).

The Chalcedonian definition of the person of Christ provides the touchstone for the subsequent orthodox tradition, which is carried on in Eastern Orthodoxy, Roman Catholicism (especially as refined scholastically by Aquinas), and in Protestant traditions. Both Luther and Calvin, for example, accepted the early church's ruling, though some have made the case that Luther's christology tends in a Eutychian direction, while Calvin's leans toward the Nestorian. Subsequent Protestant orthodoxy and more recent conservative evangelicalism also endorse Chalcedon. Although these various traditions may emphasize different features of Christ's *work* (see next

---

[9] "The Council of Chalcedon, the Definition of Faith," in Pelikan and Hotchkiss, eds., *Creeds and Confessions*, 1: 181.

The Council of Chalcedon
(451)

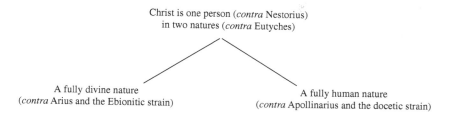

Christ is one person (*contra* Nestorius)
in two natures (*contra* Eutyches)

A fully divine nature
(*contra* Arius and the Ebionitic strain)

A fully human nature
(*contra* Apollinarius and the docetic strain)

Natures that are:

without confusion or change (*contra* Eutyches)
without separation or division (*contra* Nestorius)

Figure 9.1 The Council of Chalcedon

chapter), they are all united in their agreement with the "two-natures" teaching of Chalcedon concerning Christ's *person*.

Modern developments and reaction

The modern period, however, gave rise to new theologies that challenged the Chalcedonian legacy. Already in the time of the Reformation, fringe groups such as the Socinians, promoting a unitarian conception of God in rejection of the Trinity, denied Christ's personal preexistence and therefore his full deity. They esteemed Jesus only as the perfected human being who mediates our relation to God. As unitarian theologies became standard modernist fare, christologies gravitated lower. Supposing only a human origin of the person of Christ, these usually promoted either an *adoptionism*, whereby the human Jesus eventually achieves a degree of divinity or special closeness to God, a *functionalism*, which locates Jesus' "divinity" in the particular work or activity that God performs through him, or an *exemplarism*, which simply sees in the human Jesus the exemplary teacher or moral leader.

The last of these was the tendency of the natural theologies rooted in the Enlightenment. The Enlightenment's rejection of traditional authority and its attempt to base truth on reason alone bolstered Deism, which saw in Jesus the exemplary moral teacher. Immanuel Kant, for instance, whose religious thought is broadly deistic, asserted that human reason alone, particularly "practical reason," is sufficient to discern the "idea of a person morally well-pleasing to God."[10] He conceded, however, that for those who required additional inspiration, there was one historical example of such moral rectitude, Jesus of Nazareth. Jesus' life and death, however, could not substitute for one's own responsibility to become morally pleasing to God. Kant shows, incidentally, that the tendency to reduce Christ to a moral example accompanies a diminished estimate of his death as an atonement for sin.

Friedrich Schleiermacher, regarded as the father of modern theology, attempted a wholesale reformulation of Christian belief in view of modern scientific and philosophical developments. In *The Christian Faith*, he offers a stinging critique of Chalcedon's "two-natures" conceptuality, charging it among other things with incoherence, since in his view *one* person cannot possess *two* natures.[11] Rather, based on his theological method of elaborating the historical contents of the Christian religious consciousness (i.e., piety or affections), Schleiermacher develops a functional christology. Jesus Christ is not a preexistent divine person but a fully human person who possessed an "absolutely potent God-consciousness" manifest in a life of absolute dependence upon God. His perfect God-consciousness reflected God's redemptive activity through him, which itself constitutes his divinity: "The Redeemer, then, is like all men in virtue of the identity of human nature, but distinguished from them all by the constant potency of His God-consciousness, which was a veritable existence of God in Him."[12] Schleiermacher's relative neglect of the classical doctrine of the Trinity in preference for a Sabellian approach also reinforces a functional christology: Jesus' divinity is, quite simply, God's working in him. Schleiermacher has been considered the progenitor of modern "low" christologies.

Albrecht Ritschl, whose name is synonymous with classical liberal Protestantism, follows Schleiermacher's lead. Ritschl similarly eschews all metaphysical or ontological categories in theology as outside the bounds of religious knowledge, which he asserts is concerned only with ethical or practical value. His program of the "moralizing of dogma" leads him to emphasize the historical *effects* of Jesus' life as the perfect embodiment of the kingdom of God – Ritschl's central theological category and concern – which he understands as the human task of fashioning a moral society by means of love-inspired action. Consequently, Ritschl dismisses Chalcedon's categories as illegitimately speculative. At best, Christ preexisted only in the

---

[10] Immanuel Kant, *Religion Within the Limits of Reason Alone*, trans. Theodore M. Greene and Hoyt H. Hudson (New York: Harper & Row, 1960), 56; see esp. 54–72.
[11] Schleiermacher, *Christian Faith*, 391–8.   [12] Ibid., 385.

mind and will of God the Father. Christ's "divinity" is, therefore, found in his vocation as the exemplary model and the human embodiment of the kingdom of God.[13]

Concurrent with and informing these modernist christologies was the movement known as "the quest of the historical Jesus." As the modern science of historiography sought to discern "what actually happened," and when this technical study was combined with Enlightenment suppositions that challenged traditional authorities such as Bible and creed, it produced a severely critical approach to both the biblical and orthodox portrayal of Christ, one that excluded any supernatural causation or explanation in the name of natural truth. This modern quest for the historical Jesus is considered to have begun with the posthumous publication of Hermann Samuel Reimarus's *Wolfenbüttel Fragments* in 1778, which, disallowing the resurrection, asserted that Jesus' crucified body was stolen by his disciples, who then made up the story of the resurrection and the Christian gospel.[14] For Reimarus, the Jesus of history was simply an aspiring messiah who taught the natural truths of religion (i.e., Deism), but who now was dead.

Many attempts to uncover the authentic Jesus from the dress of church dogma were launched, as documented by Albert Schweitzer's *The Quest of the Historical Jesus*.[15] Some of these proposals were nobly motivated by the attempt to appreciate the historical humanity of Jesus over against a docetic portrait of Christ, which they considered to be the legacy of Chalcedon. The effect of this broad movement, however, was to drive a wedge between the "Jesus of history" and the "Christ of faith." Generally speaking, while Jesus of Nazareth was largely appreciated for being a significant personality, a moral example, or a teacher of important religious truths, the Christ of Chalcedonian faith was rejected. Such quests resulted only in an Ebionitic Christ.

Karl Barth reacted strongly against this modernist trend in christology, as did other so-called neo-orthodox theologians: Brunner, Bonhoeffer, and Bultmann. Stressing the transcendent otherness of God, Barth emphasized the deity of Christ as God's free and sovereign Word of revelation, while also seeking to account for the humanity of Jesus in paradoxical

---

[13] See especially Albrecht Ritschl, *The Christian Doctrine of Justification and Reconciliation*, III: *The Positive Development of the Doctrine*, ed. and trans. H. R. Mackintosh and A. B. Macaulay (Edinburgh: T. & T. Clark, 1900), 385–484. This tendency toward a functionalist or exemplarist christology is also clearly seen in the last great Ritschlian, Adolf von Harnack (see p. 528 below).

[14] Hermann Samuel Reimarus, *Fragments*, ed. Charles H. Talbert, trans. Ralph S. Fraser (Philadelphia: Fortress, 1970).

[15] Albert Schweitzer, *The Quest of the Historical Jesus: A Critical Study of its Progress from Reimarus to Wrede*, trans. William Montgomery (New York: Macmillan, 1961).

juxtaposition to his strong emphasis on Christ's deity. He therefore embraced the ecumenical decisions that culminated in Chalcedon, yet recast Chalcedon's abstract language of "natures" into more dynamic, "actualistic" categories, wherein Christ's being is construed in terms of his work.[16]

Reacting to what he considered a docetic preoccupation with the divine "Christ of faith" in neo-orthodox theologies (such as Barth's) to the neglect of the real history and humanity of Jesus, Wolfhart Pannenberg proposed a christology "from below."[17] Pannenberg's point of departure is not the perspective of the incarnation and Christ's deity – the traditional tack "from above" – but the man Jesus, and his human history, which culminates in his death and resurrection. Making a strong case for the historicity of the resurrection, Pannenberg views it as key to Christ's divine identity. Yet Pannenberg's point here is more than methodological. It is not simply that the resurrection *vindicates* Christ's claims, ministry, and special relationship with God, which is certainly the historical order through which the apostles and early church came to recognize Christ's deity. Rather, for Pannenberg, Christ's resurrection also *constitutes* – that is, ontologically establishes – his eternal deity. But Pannenberg's proposal is compelling only if one can accept his complicated notion of "retroactive ontology," whereby the future has reverse causality for the past. Many critics who find this notion problematic consider Pannenberg's approach "from below" to entail adoptionism.

To conclude our brief historical survey, we can only note that at present, reflecting the pluralism of our postmodern condition, one can find a veritable smorgasbord of christological positions and proposals. These range from generally orthodox portrayals of the person of Christ to those that merely see in the human Jesus an example or symbol of religious truth.

A SYSTEMATIC CONSIDERATION OF THE PERSON OF CHRIST

In examining the person of Christ systematically, we are not left with many models to consider. Since we accept the Chalcedonian standard as an orthodox benchmark, considering it to resonate sufficiently with the biblical materials, we can only endorse an incarnational model of the person of

---

[16] See, e.g., Barth, *Church Dogmatics*, I/2: 132–71.
[17] Wolfhart Pannenberg, *Jesus – God and Man*, trans. Lewis L. Wilkins and Duane A. Priebe (Philadelphia: Westminster, 1968).

Christ that begins "from above" with his preexistence as an eternal member of the Trinity. This rules out any adoptionism of ontological proportions, wherein the merely human Jesus, who originates "from below" – from human parents (plural) – is adopted into special relationship with God the Father (a starting point also presupposed by functionalist and exemplarist christologies). Regardless of how exalted Christ's status *becomes*, an adoptionistic model fails the test of trinitarian orthodoxy that Christ's *being* as the eternally begotten Son is co-equal with that of God the Father. At the same time, we must acknowledge and be able to account for the distinct adoptionist strain in the NT (e.g., Rom. 1:3–4; Heb. 1:3ff.; Phil. 2:9–11), which will enable us to take the humanity of Jesus seriously as we read the biblical narratives in their progressive historical revelation of Christ's divine identity, which is the methodological truth of a christology from below.

Given that an incarnational approach is the only theological tack that preserves the high christology of the biblical witness and the Chalcedonian standard, we are really left with only two particular models to consider – the two-natures model and the kenotic model of the incarnation.

The two-natures model

As we have seen, a two-natures model of the incarnation has been the regnant orthodox understanding of the person of Christ since the decision of Chalcedon. It has the endorsement of a litany of prominent theologians in the Orthodox, Catholic, and Protestant traditions. Taking the Chalcedonian standard directly as a conceptual model, the two-natures option posits that Jesus of Nazareth is identical with the person of the preexistent Logos, that he is one person who possesses both a fully divine nature and a fully human nature, natures that are without confusion or change, division or separation. These natures and the respective attributes they manifest are united in the one person of Christ by means of the "hypostatic union" and the resulting "communication of attributes" (*communicatio idiomatum*), which allow characteristics of both humanity and deity to be attributed to the one person (or *hypostasis*) of Christ. Thus the range of attributes that manifest the divine nature, such as omnipotence, omniscience, and omnipresence, are communicated to Christ's person and available to him in the incarnation, as are the attributes that manifest his human nature, such as weakness, limited knowledge, and being localized in a body. In this way the Christ of the incarnation is both fully divine and fully human, which seemingly accounts for his dual identity in the scriptures and for the various characteristics that manifest his divine and human capacities, ranging from powerful miracles to all too human weaknesses.

This two-natures model, however, has come under sharp criticism in modern times, by both friend and foe of Christian orthodoxy. In addition to challenging the adequacy of its abstract categories of substance (essence, natures), since people today tend to think more concretely in terms of persons and their historical relations, the main criticisms of the two-natures model fall under four headings. These involve questions concerning (1) its coherence, (2) its possible docetic tendency, (3) its ability to maintain the unity of Christ's person, and, taken all together, (4) its fidelity to the biblical portrayal of Jesus the Messiah.

First, critics have charged that the model is incoherent on a number of scores. For one, it is hard to conceive of a single individual possessing two actualized natures of distinctive quality – as, for example, in a pet that is both fully canine and fully feline at the same time, simultaneously manifesting both dog and cat characteristics and behaviors. This is simply beyond our intelligible experience. For another, it is difficult to conceive in any positive or unified sense how such natures could be simultaneously "without confusion or change, without division or separation," as Chalcedon requires. How exactly should we specify their relationship? Most problematic, however, is the question of how attributes of two different natures that are polar opposites could coexist within one person – how, for example, Jesus of Nazareth could be both omnipotent and weak at the same time, or how he could simultaneously be both omnipresent and localized in a human body. This question is most acute when it comes to the issue of Christ's knowledge. If, possessing a fully divine nature, Jesus was omniscient, how could he also in his one person and frame of mind be humanly limited in his understanding, as the scriptures portray (e.g., Luke 2:52; Matt. 24:36)? Technically speaking, to be both consciously omniscient and non-omniscient is a contradiction – one cannot both know something and not know it at the same time. Yet many see this essential paradox as a strength of the two-natures model, given the utter uniqueness of the incarnation, especially when coupled with the conviction that God's ways are simply beyond our understanding.

This leads directly into a second criticism of Chalcedon, namely, that the two-natures model is susceptible to docetism. This model posits that Christ the Logos retains his fully divine nature in the incarnation, primarily because of the doctrine of divine immutability – God does not change, so neither does the divine Son, even in the incarnation. What the

Son does is "assume" a human nature while remaining essentially the same in his deity. But then the question arises whether Jesus' humanity can be taken seriously. Once again, if Christ is omnipotent (for which his miracles have been cited as evidence), can his human weakness be taken seriously? Or if Christ is omniscient, can his manifest ignorance be taken as anything other than feigning? Or if he is omnipresent, can the incarnation be anything other than partial, since Christ continues to exist beyond the bounds of his humanity? This assertion was already articulated as early as Athanasius:

He was not, as might be imagined, circumscribed in the body, nor, while present in the body, was he absent elsewhere; nor, while he moved the body, was the universe left void of his working and providence; but, thing most marvelous, Word as he was, so far from being contained by anything, he rather contained all things himself; and just as while present in the whole of creation, he is at once distinct in being from the universe, and present in all things by his own power ... thus, even while present in a human body and himself quickening it, he was, without inconsistency, quickening the universe as well.[18]

In postulating the fully actualized deity of Christ in the incarnation, the two-natures model has been less than successful in demonstrating the place of Christ's full and true humanity – apart from merely *asserting* that this just is, paradoxically, the case. It is this legacy of docetism that has especially beleaguered the two-natures model.

One of the most impressive defenses in recent times of a two-natures model is found in Thomas V. Morris's *The Logic of God Incarnate*.[19] Presupposing a classical form of theism in the tradition of Anselm, which entails that Christ in his incarnation possesses all the attributes of deity in their maximal strength, Morris proposes a "two-minds" view of the incarnation. In this construct, the preexistent Son takes on a human body and mind and thus experiences in a human consciousness the full range of the human condition and nature – its limitations, growth, and dependencies – out of which, asserts Morris, Jesus normally lives. Yet, states Morris, Jesus still possesses a divine mind, which enables his continuing divine consciousness and which can access his divine nature and

[18] Athanasius, *On the Incarnation of the Word*, in *Christology of the Later Fathers*, ed. Edward Rochie Hardy and Cyril C. Richardson, Library of Christian Classics (Louisville, KY: Westminster John Knox, 1954), 70–1.
[19] Thomas V. Morris, *The Logic of God Incarnate* (Ithaca, NY: Cornell University Press, 1986). Morris reiterates his basic strategy in shorter form in "The Metaphysics of God Incarnate," in *Trinity, Incarnation, and Atonement*, ed. Ronald J. Feenstra and Cornelius Plantinga Jr. (Notre Dame, IN: University of Notre Dame Press, 1989), 110–27.

powers when need arises. These two minds of Christ bear an "asymmetric accessing relation" to each other – the human mind is a subset of the divine mind, which means that the divine mind completely experiences the human mind but not vice versa. Such a duality of consciousness, according to Morris, allows for the full humanity of Jesus and the range of human experiences attested by scripture, while not diminishing the classical deity claim. Morris experiments with various analogies to illustrate his two-minds model, such as shifting centers of dream consciousness (where the person is both dreamer and actor in the same dream), multiple layers of consciousness (conscious–subconscious), and the phenomenon of multiple or split personalities.

But the very name of Morris's proposal, "two minds," betrays for some critics a third lingering weakness of the two-natures model – the question whether it maintains the unity of Christ's person as also required by Chalcedon. If the incarnate Christ has a dual consciousness – a fully divine awareness and a fully human awareness – this would seem to split the unity of his person, given that mind and consciousness are better seen as constituents of personhood rather than of nature. But this very tendency has been endemic to the two-natures model ever since the sixth ecumenical council (Constantinople III – see pp. 454–5) declared that as a consequence of Christ having two natures (*diophysitism*) he also had two wills (*diothelitism*) – regarding will as a function of nature. Along with many contemporaries, however, we contend that the category of personhood ought to have priority over that of abstract "natures," and that it makes better sense to see the will, along with mind and consciousness, as constitutive of personhood. Again, the issue of Christ's knowledge best clarifies the problem. If Christ is both omniscient (as divine) and non-omniscient (as human), this seems to divide his person as a subjective center of consciousness, mind, and will. In this way, the two-natures model itself appears to harbor Nestorian tendencies, as Morris's "two-minds" defense tellingly suggests.

Finally, the preceding considerations raise a fourth issue. This is the critical question whether a two-natures model does justice to the biblical – and especially synoptic gospels' – portrayal of Jesus' genuinely human life and messianic mission, which biblical scholars today would strongly contend excludes docetic perspectives and presents a more unified portrayal of the historical person of Christ.

In sum, while the two-natures model is a viable interpretation of Chalcedon and has been endorsed as orthodoxy across the centuries by the preponderance of theologians, it raises a number of questions as to its coherence, its liability to docetism, its tendency to divide Christ's person, and its overall fidelity to scripture.

The kenotic model

Concerned with the liabilities of the two-natures model, but wishing to remain faithful to the confessional tradition of Chalcedon, a number of nineteenth-century theologians proposed a different model of the incarnation. Here they took a cue from Philippians 2:6–7, which states concerning Christ that "though he was in the form of God, did not regard equality with God as something to be exploited, but emptied himself, taking the form of a slave, being born in human likeness." Keying on the term "emptied" (from the Gk. verb *kenoo*; noun: *kenosis*), such theologians proposed that upon the event of the incarnation and through the period of his humiliation the preexistent Son of God voluntarily relinquished or "emptied" himself of all maximal divine attributes, powers, prerogatives, and/or glory that were incompatible with his becoming truly and fully human. (Such attributes were to be taken up again after the period of his humiliation in his exaltation.) Beginning with Gottfried Thomasius (1802–75) and running up to H. R. Mackintosh (1870–1936), a flurry of kenotic statements were proposed with various strategies as to which divine attributes were relinquished (or emptied) and of how a kenotic Christ would still qualify as truly divine.[20] Appreciating and endorsing the new historical emphasis on Jesus' humanity, the kenoticists explored this model as a way of better capturing the incarnational christology of Chalcedon and its non-negotiable affirmations: preexistence, true deity, true humanity, and the unity of Christ's person.

This kenotic movement waned around the time of WWI, rejected by the liberal left as still too mythological, working as it does with a christology "from above," and judged by the conservative right as insufficiently securing the deity claim of the incarnate Christ. Neo-orthodox theologians such as Barth also found the kenotic model wanting, desiring instead to emphasize the incomprehensibility of the incarnation. More recently, however, kenotic christology has come back for reconsideration by a number of theologians. We are among those who find this model quite promising as

---

[20] The most important texts of Thomasius' kenoticism have been translated and edited by Claude Welch in *God and Incarnation in Mid-Nineteenth Century German Theology* (New York: Oxford University Press, 1965). See also H. R. Mackintosh, *The Doctrine of the Person of Jesus Christ* (Edinburgh: T. & T. Clark, 1913).

a way of capturing the biblical portrayal of Christ, the essential affirmations of Chalcedon, and important practical implications of the incarnation. In what remains of this chapter, we outline the case for a kenotic model of the incarnation.[21]

It is important first of all to make a distinction between Chalcedon's two-natures *doctrine* – its essential teachings concerning the person of Christ – and a two-natures *model* – taking Chalcedon strictly or straightforwardly as a prescriptive paradigm. The kenotic model purports to be an interpretation of the former, the doctrine, while being an alternative to the latter, the model. We take Chalcedon as principally prescribing parameters or boundary lines concerning Christ's person, and not as a model *per se* – that is, one that constructively proposes a unified conceptual account of the person of Christ. This is to say that what the Chalcedonian definition primarily does (in the original sense of *de-finire*) is to *set limits* on what can be said by ruling out specific positions – namely, the Ebionitic, docetic, Arian, Apollinarian, Eutychian, and Nestorian proposals. To press Chalcedon's statements into a positive model leads to the irresolvable paradoxes or contradictions that plague its coherence. It is understandable, however, why Chalcedon was taken as a prescriptive model throughout the centuries. This was due to the tradition's strong commitment to the classical attribute of divine immutability. As long as God, or the divine nature, was considered strictly immutable, absolutely without change (which the Chalcedonian context presupposes), then the divine nature of Christ also had to be unchanged and fully actualized in the incarnation. Strict immutability necessitates taking Chalcedon as model. Along with the nineteenth-century kenoticists, however, we have objected to this classical attribute (which derives more from Greek philosophy than from the biblical text) and offered a reinterpretation of immutability or God's unchanging nature as faithfulness to God's character and promises (see pp. 104–6 above). If strict immutability is considered a non-negotiable axiom of orthodoxy, then a kenotic understanding is clearly ruled out; but if it is deemed foreign to the biblical text, the way is open to explore kenoticism. Even Thomas Morris, who adheres to a strong version of immutability, acknowledges that besides a two-natures model, kenoticism is the only other viable incarnational option in the spirit of the high christology of Chalcedon.[22]

---

[21] For a brief history of the kenotic project, see Thomas R. Thompson, "Nineteenth-Century Kenotic Christology: The Waxing, Waning, and Weighing of a Quest for a Coherent Orthodoxy," in *Exploring Kenotic Christology: The Self-Emptying of God*, ed. C. Stephen Evans (Oxford: Oxford University Press, 2006), 74–111.

[22] Morris, "Metaphysics of God Incarnate," 126–7.

So let us suppose that in the incarnation the eternal Son of God voluntarily relinquishes, gives up, or empties himself of all maximal divine attributes, privileges, powers, and/or glory in order to become *truly* human, and to live within the confines of a human condition and life with all its trials, tribulations, limitations, and even death. Supposing all this, that Christ became truly human, how is it that he would still qualify as being truly divine? It is the deity claim that has been considered the Achilles' heel of kenotic christology.

We can offer three reinforcing strategies for securing the deity of a kenotically incarnate Christ. These strategies actually parallel the three forms of unity we elaborated in Chapter 5 to bolster a social trinitarianism (i.e., how three distinct, discrete divine persons nevertheless constitute one God). We should note in this connection, if it is not already evident, that in clearly distinguishing the incarnate Son from the Father and Spirit, a kenotic christology presupposes and is consistent with some form of social trinitarianism.[23]

Recall the first form of unity, essential divine unity, which posited that all trinitarian members share a common nature, each possessing the range of attributes that qualifies them as divine. On a kenotic model of the incarnation, however, the Son freely relinquishes these attributes in their divine form and strength so as to become truly and fully human – exchanging omnipotence for weakness, omniscience for limited knowledge, and the like. But even on a kenotic model there is one divine attribute that the Son cannot relinquish, one which he could still possess without impairing his true humanity, but which nonetheless would still qualify him as divine – namely, his *eternality*, albeit understood along the revisionist lines of everlastingness (see pp. 106–8). Even on a kenotic model, Jesus Christ is still an eternal person; he is one who has always existed. This is the truth of his preexistence. According to John's Gospel, this was a claim that Jesus himself made in striking conjunction with the divine name: "Before Abraham was, I am" (John 8:58) – a claim that registered accusations of blasphemy. In Christian thought, whatever is eternal is divine, which is why Christianity rejects metaphysical dualism – not even inert matter can be considered eternal, since it would condition or rival God (hence Christian theology's embrace of *creatio ex nihilo*). The attribute of eternality alone is sufficient to qualify Christ as divine. But such eternality-as-everlastingness need not

---

[23] For an elaboration of this point, see Thomas R. Thompson and Cornelius Plantinga Jr., "Trinity and Kenosis," in *Exploring Kenotic Christology: The Self-Emptying of God*, ed. C. Stephen Evans (Oxford: Oxford University Press, 2006), 165–89.

impair the experience of Christ's true and full humanity. What it does underscore, however, is that though truly and fully human, Jesus Christ is not *merely* human – he is, even in a kenotic incarnation, an eternal divine person. This fact alone can secure the deity claim.

Our second form of trinitarian unity, the quasi-genetic unity, concerned the familial bond that unified Father, Son, and Spirit. In a kenotic model this form of unity is never broken. In addition to being the Messiah, Jesus' principal identity throughout his life is as the Son of the living God, the unique Son, the only begotten of the Father. This is a claim for his personal divine identity, not for an abstract nature. Even if kenotically emptied of all maximal divine attributes, Jesus of Nazareth is still a divine person, one whose familial bond in the Holy Trinity was never severed. This also reinforces the deity claim.

The third form of trinitarian unity, the perichoretic unity of divine persons, underscored the volitional ties of life and love shared by Father, Son, and Spirit. These also were never severed in the incarnation, given a kenotic model. Though Christ was truly tempted, given his experience of the full human condition, he never sinned or severed fellowship with the Father and Spirit, though this was no simple feat (think of the episode in the garden of Gethsemane). Even at the point of his greatest separation from the Father, his cry of dereliction from the cross – "My God, my God, why have you forsaken me?" (Mark 15:34) – his will was nonetheless united with the Father and Spirit for the greater purpose of the salvation of the world. Christ's abiding perichoretic unity within the Trinity further secures the deity claim, even given a kenotic model of the incarnation.

As a rough analogy for the kenotic model, think of a maximally great athlete, say Pelé or Michael Jordan. Suppose he showed up for a game one day but volunteered to play in a heavy suit of medieval armor. This would sorely limit his usual superstar, even god-like performance: his speed would be diminished, his power and agility impaired, his stealth compromised. Yet, even with these diminished capacities, it is still his identity as Pelé or Michael Jordan – and the usual glories of his stardom – that define his person, which he can easily prove in the very next game by sloughing off his armor and resurrecting his full abilities.

So let us suppose that in the incarnation the eternal Son of God voluntarily relinquished his divine powers, prerogatives, and glory so as to live strictly within the confines of our human condition. What would be the advantages of such a model? For one, it would capture the confession of Christ's true and full humanity in an incarnational christology from above, but in a way that is less prone to the charge of docetism than the traditional two-natures model. It also better preserves the confessional truth of Christ's single personhood. On a kenotic model there are not two minds or wills or ranges of consciousness – features which appear to be clear constituents of personhood – but one human mind, will, and consciousness. Here there is no divine *alter ego* that would overshadow Christ's true and full humanity: no omnipotence that would trump his human strength, no omniscience that would trivialize his human range of knowing, no omnipresence that would dwarf his localization in the body of Jesus of Nazareth. This would also mean that the kenotic model offers a more coherent understanding of the person of Christ, who prior to the incarnation was the divine Logos with a divine nature, but who in the incarnation becomes a human person with a human nature while retaining his depth of personal identity as the eternally (pre)existent Son of God. This model, in short, is more thinkable and graspable, since it does not require accepting contradictory assertions concerning his person.

Apart from the classical assumption of immutability, which we think can be legitimately revised, a kenotic model satisfies the confessional parameters laid down by Chalcedon, which is to say that it is neither Ebionitic nor docetic, neither Arian nor Apollinarian, neither Eutychian nor Nestorian. While some have regarded kenoticism as Eutychian, given a certain formal similarity, in actuality the kenotic model is materially and therefore qualitatively different, since it does not fuse the divine and human natures into a third metaphysical sort between God and humanity. Rather, kenoticism takes seriously the Johannine claim that the Logos "became" flesh (John 1:14) and Hebrews' claim that Jesus "had to become" like his brothers and sisters in every respect (Heb. 2:17).

Most importantly, we think that a kenotic christology, in comparison to the two-natures model, better accounts for the biblical portrait of Christ. While securing the necessary deity claim of the overall NT witness, a kenotic christology can also account for Christ's full humanity in all of its growth, development, trials, and limitations. One key christological feature that is easily downplayed by a two-natures model is the role of Jesus as Messiah. This is, after all, his principal role and title – Jesus the Christ, Jesus the Messiah, which means that he is the special one anointed and empowered by God's Spirit. Our reading of the historical Jesus, the Jesus of the gospels, is that he lived his life as a man in utter dependence upon God the Father in the power and energies of the Spirit. For example, Jesus performed his miracles, it seems, not by virtue of his own divine power, but by his dependence upon the Spirit, like other miracle-working biblical persons. (Note in this connection the fact that Jesus performed no miracle prior to his baptism by the Spirit.) The same would hold true for his knowledge, his prophetic prescience and insight, since Jesus also manifested a limited knowledge, even an ignorance of certain things. These also were endowments of the Spirit, similar to the other prophets, not due to his own divine powers of omniscience.

What a kenotic model allows for is the real human growth and development of Jesus of Nazareth (Luke 2:52) as well as a real faith development without docetic depreciation. In the epistle to the Hebrews, which begins with a high christology (i.e., a clear affirmation of Christ's deity [1:3ff.]), Jesus' humanity is portrayed in striking ways: as one who "had to become like his brothers and sisters in every respect, so that he might be a merciful and faithful high priest in the service of God" (2:17); as the pioneer of our salvation who was made perfect through suffering (2:10); as "one who in every respect has been tested as we are, yet without sin" (4:15). Note especially the text from 5:7–10:

In the days of his flesh, Jesus offered up prayers and supplications, with loud cries and tears, to the one who was able to save him from death, and he was heard because of his reverent submission. Although he was a Son, he learned obedience through what he suffered; and having been made perfect, he became the source of eternal salvation for all who obey him, having been designated by God a high priest according to the order of Melchizedek.

Only a true and full humanity of Christ can account for these notes, true to the gospel accounts, of Jesus' "faith development" – of struggling with temptation, of learning obedience through what he suffered, and of becoming perfect so as to be the source of salvation (see Illustration 9.2). Such a portrayal also comports well with the recent discussion of the Pauline locution "faith of Christ" (*pistis tou Christou*, Rom. 3:22; Gal. 2:16; 3:12), which has traditionally been interpreted to mean "faith in Christ," but which is better understood exegetically and theologically as "Christ's faith or faithfulness" – the human life of faith that Christ lived in his role as the Messiah.[24]

By better accounting for the humanity of Christ, the kenotic model also facilitates the imitation of Christ (*imitatio Christi*). Since Christ's life is a human life of faith – a fulfillment of true Israel (cf. Matt. 1–5) and true humanity (cf. Paul's "last Adam" motif, e.g., in 1 Cor. 15 and Rom. 5) – we may also emulate Jesus' life as re-presented and made available in the life of the Spirit. Here Christ's life does not hover docetically and inimitably over the horizon of history, due to his own inherent divine nature and advantage;

---

[24] See pp. 324–5 below on this discussion.

Illustration 9.2 Andrei Rublev's *Christ of Zvenigorod*, as marred over time, captures both the divine personhood of Christ and the blemishes of his historical humanity.

rather, Christ's life exhibits a life lived profoundly in the human condition, showing us what it is to live in utter dependence upon God the Father in the power and energies of the Spirit. As a truly human being, Christ leads us into our true humanity, into what God intended us to be. A kenotic christology delivers this exemplary humanism, a Christian humanism, capturing as well the truth of scripture's adoptionist strands without sacrificing the necessary deity claim and christology from above, which signify that Christ's work mediates the saving presence of the triune God.

While there are other issues to be considered in determining a preference for the two-natures or kenotic model, these two models appear to be the only viable possibilities for those committed to the high incarnational christology of Chalcedon. We find the kenotic model especially promising as an orthodox, coherent, and relevant portrayal of the person of Christ.

It affords a way of securing the necessary deity claim while allowing for the full play of Jesus' humanity, a humanity that is essential to understanding Christ's work, the topic of the next chapter.

FOR FURTHER READING

Brown, Raymond E., *An Introduction to New Testament Christology* (Mahwah, NJ: Paulist, 1994).

Collins, John J., *The Scepter and the Star: The Messiahs of the Dead Sea Scrolls and Other Ancient Literature* (New York: Doubleday, 1995).

Evans, C. Stephen, ed., *Exploring Kenotic Christology: The Self-Emptying of God* (Oxford: Oxford University Press, 2006).

Morris, Thomas V., *The Logic of God Incarnate* (Ithaca, NY: Cornell University Press, 1986).

Norris, Richard A., Jr., ed., *The Christological Controversy*, Sources of Early Christian Thought (Philadelphia: Fortress, 1980).

Schwarz, Hans, *Christology* (Grand Rapids, MI: Eerdmans, 1998).

Schweitzer, Albert, *The Quest of the Historical Jesus: A Critical Study of its Progress from Reimarus to Wrede*, trans. William Montgomery (New York: Macmillan, 1961).

CHAPTER 10

The reconciling work of Jesus Christ

INTRODUCTION

The Christian scriptures loudly proclaim that "salvation" is accomplished by Jesus of Nazareth, the Christ or Messiah. It is through the work of this person – Christ's incarnation, life, ministry, death, and resurrection – that wholeness, righteousness, and reconciliation with God are made available.

Understanding the "work" of Christ, as well as articulating this doctrine today in a theologically responsible way, requires a clear understanding of its placement in the broader web of Christian beliefs. We spent the previous chapter examining the person of Christ, emphasizing the need to affirm both his divine identity and the fullness of his humanity within the singularity of his person. There we contended that these basic creedal affirmations are best captured by means of a kenotic model of the incarnation, wherein the second person of the Trinity, the divine Logos, freely "empties" himself of maximal divine attributes and prerogatives in order to become *genuinely* human. On this model it is consistent to say that God the Son *became* human (see, e.g., John 1:14). As this chapter on the work of Christ unfolds, we will see that both the deity and humanity of Jesus Christ are necessary to fully account for his salvific work. For reasons that will become clear, we will privilege the language of "reconciliation" as the summary term for the saving life, death, and resurrection of Jesus Christ.

BIBLICAL ROOTS OF THE CHRISTIAN UNDERSTANDING OF RECONCILIATION

In the NT there are a variety of perspectives on the work of Christ – a diversity of metaphors and images that complement one another in describing what Christ does to provide salvation. But these images are not all created equal. To sort out the relative importance of these various motifs we must first take a look at the OT narrative to see how salvation or reconciliation through Christ fulfills OT expectations and maintains continuity with Christianity's Jewish heritage.

Old Testament

The life of the nation of Israel was established by the gracious covenant initiated by Yahweh. Yahweh pledged to be the God of Israel, to faithfully protect, guide, and bless the nation; the people of Israel, in turn, promised to be faithful and obedient to their God and Lord. The theme of Israel as the covenant nation dominates the attention of the OT. But this central theme takes its ultimate meaning from the context of creation as a whole, since the particular election of Israel as the chosen nation serves a more universal end. This connection is visible by the fact that the "all nations" introduction to the book of Genesis (chs. 1–11) is immediately followed by God's announcement of the covenant to Abram: "In you all the families of the earth shall be blessed" (12:3). Accordingly, Israel is to play a special role in God's cosmic redemption; she is to be a "light" to the nations (Isa. 49:6). The creational *shalom* described in Genesis 1–2, whose corruption is portrayed in Genesis 3, remains the essential backdrop of the covenant. Seen in this context, Israel represents all of humanity as the redemptive firstfruits of all creation.

When Israel broke her covenantal requirements as expressed in the Mosaic law, the nation became estranged from Yahweh, requiring that the relationship be restored. This reconciliation was ordinarily achieved in the OT by means of the sacrificial system, as prescribed particularly in the book of Leviticus. Sacrifices had to be performed by a priestly representative *of* the people who also served as Yahweh's representative *to* the people. Chapter 16 of Leviticus is of special importance, as it describes what is called the "Day of Atonement." This chapter elaborates how the high priest was to present various animals as "sin offerings" that would "make atonement" for the people of Israel (16:5–6), reconciling them to Yahweh.

From these brief considerations we see that central to the OT understanding of atonement or reconciliation is the *covenantal framework*, the need for *priestly representation* of the sinful person or nation, and the centrality of the *sacrifice* as the means by which God's disfavor is assuaged and guilt is forgiven. The NT will apply all these elements to the person and work of Jesus Christ. But Christ's particularity must also be seen in view of the universality of God's reign over creation. Just as Israel's covenantal election and reconciliation with the covenanting God are oriented toward the blessing of all the nations, so also Christ's particularity as the one who brings reconciliation envisages the redemption of all creation.

New Testament

The NT takes great pains to stress that Jesus of Nazareth, believed by Christians to be the Messiah, is the Savior. Following the OT understanding of reconciliation, Christ is identified as the priestly *representative* who, strikingly, also serves as the *sacrifice* for the sin of humanity. One of the early annunciations by John the Baptist bluntly makes this point: "Here is the Lamb of God who takes away the sin of the world" (John 1:29). As the representative of the world, Jesus is the sacrificial "lamb," and the result of his death is the removal of the world's sin. This interpretation of Jesus as the sacrificial lamb must be understood in the light of the Day of Atonement in Leviticus 16. The result of his representative priesthood and sacrificial work is the establishment of a "new covenant," which renews, fulfills, and subsumes the previous covenants of God with Israel. This new covenant, announced in Jeremiah 31:31–7 and actualized in Christ, was understood by the earliest Christians to be open to all of humanity beyond the confines of ethnic Israel and the law of Moses (see Acts 15; Gal. 2–3; Eph. 2).[1]

The NT book of Hebrews is instructive in this regard. One of the main themes of Hebrews is the supremacy of Jesus, that is, his superiority as the Son of God to both the angels and Moses, particularly in his role as the high priest: "Since, then, we have a great high priest who has passed through the heavens, Jesus the Son of God, let us hold fast to our confession" (4:14). Jesus' task as high priest is to represent the people to God and to offer sacrifice for their sins (5:1). However, Jesus is not only the high priest, but also the sacrifice itself. Moreover, his sacrificial death is unique: it is not a sacrifice that must be repeated, but one that is sufficient "once for all" for the sins of the people (7:27; cf. 10:1–18). Seen in the context of the gospels, this sacrifice at the cross is the culmination of Jesus' ministry of proclaiming and embodying the kingdom of God. He is accused by the Jewish authorities of being a blasphemer (e.g., John 19:7), and he is condemned and executed by the Romans as a political criminal. Thus he dies a judicial death, which other NT writings interpret as a vicarious (substitutionary) death in place of the death owed by humanity for its blasphemy and treason against God's righteousness and sovereignty. As a substitutionary death, the cross must be understood in terms of the OT sacrificial tradition. The cross is a sacrifice that brings salvation – that is, forgiveness and reconciliation. According to Hebrews, the sacrificial and priestly work of Jesus, especially on the cross, constitutes the institution of the new covenant that Jeremiah announced long before (Heb. 8:8–13).

This discussion shows why it makes sense that the cross has ordinarily been seen as the quintessence of the saving work of Christ. This line of thinking, however, has unfortunately suggested that the *life* of Jesus has little to do with his saving work, or that it is only an incidental prologue to his accomplishment of reconciliation on the cross. This underplaying of the significance of the life of Christ for his salvific work has been a lamentable tendency of the Christian tradition. When the NT portrays the cross as *the* event that secures salvation, however, this is best regarded as a synecdoche: the cross as the culminating *part* of Christ's work that epitomizes and

---

[1] It is significant that John 1:29 uses the term "world" (*kosmos*) and does not restrict the sin that will be taken away by the Lamb of God to the sin of Israel.

represents the *whole* of his reconciling activity, inclusive of his incarnation, life and ministry, and resurrection.

This intimate connection between Jesus' life and death can be seen in the book of Hebrews, which while stressing the centrality of the death of Jesus, certainly does not ignore his life. Hebrews in fact stresses the sinlessness of the life of Jesus as a necessary condition of his sacrificial death, a sinlessness wrought in the face of recurrent temptation: "For we do not have a high priest who is unable to sympathize with our weaknesses, but we have one who has been tempted in every way, just as we are – yet was without sin" (4:15). As was also noted in the previous chapter, this is Hebrews' understated way of affirming the significance of the fully human, yet sinless *life* of Jesus. Without that life, it is clearly implied, Jesus' death would not have sacrificial and reconciling merit:

During the days of Jesus' life on earth, he offered up prayers and petitions with loud cries and tears to the one who could save him from death, and he was heard *because of his reverent submission.* Although he was a son, *he learned obedience* from what he suffered and, *once made perfect, he became the source of eternal salvation* for all who obey him and was designated by God to be high priest in the order of Melchizedek. (5:7–10, NIV, italics added)

From this it is clear that the dimensions of Christ's *person* discussed in the previous chapter, not only his divine identity as the Son of God but also, poignantly, the genuine fullness of his humanity – including suffering, temptation, deepening faith, and growth toward perfection, albeit without the taint of sin – are intrinsic to his redemptive work. Paul makes the same point about the humanity of Christ when he casts Jesus as the "last Adam" (1 Cor. 15:45; cf. Rom. 5), the one who comes in the very same likeness of the "first Adam" to show us the way to true humanity.

If we are to understand the NT seeds of the Christian doctrine of the work of Christ, therefore, it is necessary to think further about the life and ministry of Jesus, and to connect his life and ministry to the pivotal events of the crucifixion and resurrection. This approach will also provide the resources by which to evaluate the Christian tradition's teaching on the atonement so as to strengthen its fidelity to the primary norm of theology – the biblical text. In this regard, it is imperative to remember something that NT scholars have long noted – namely, the centrality of the kingdom of God in the ministry and preaching of Jesus.[2] For example, early in the Gospel of Mark, Jesus inaugurates his ministry with the following words: "The time is fulfilled, and

[2] See, e.g., Joachim Jeremias, *New Testament Theology: The Proclamation of Jesus*, trans. John Bowden (New York: Charles Scribner's Sons, 1971), 96–7; see also 31–5 and 103ff.

the kingdom of God has come near; repent and believe the good news" (1:15). Jesus rarely preaches about himself, but rather calls his listeners' attention to the "kingdom of God" (and the "God of the kingdom," to borrow a parallelism used by Jon Sobrino).[3] The point of Jesus' parables is to convey the "secret of the kingdom of God" (Mark 4:11). Typical of Jesus' rhetoric is his response to the wise teacher of the law: "You are not far from the kingdom of God" (Mark 12:34). In line with these statements, Jesus implies that he himself constitutes the *personal* presence of the kingdom of God (e.g., Luke 17:21).

But what *is* the kingdom of God that is given such prominence in the gospels? In short, the kingdom of God is the dynamic rule of God whose realm includes the entire breadth of creation. In light of sin's corruption of that reign, however, the term "kingdom of God" in the gospels refers primarily to the comprehensive *renewal* of all reality, the transformation of creation and its history so that the world once again reflects the character, sovereignty, and will of God. Interestingly, the *Magnificat*, Mary's song of jubilation after she was told that her unborn child would be the Messiah, is one of the most direct descriptions of the kingdom. It tells of the proud being humbled, the rulers of the world being dethroned, the poor and hungry of the world being filled (Luke 1:46–55). It is in this same spirit that Jesus announces the kingdom as one of "good news to the poor," of "release to the captives and recovery of sight to the blind," and of liberation of the oppressed (Luke 4:18). This expansive scope of the kingdom of God is a perspective that coheres with the eschatological compass of other biblical writings, particularly the "new heavens and the new earth" of Isaiah 65–6 and Revelation 21, a redemptive scope that is also famously claimed by John 3:16: "God so loved the world (*kosmos*) that he gave his only Son."

Therefore, Christ's work will be misunderstood if its all-embracing nature is neglected. Jesus' work not only represents and reconciles humanity to the triune God, but includes the "reconciliation" of all creation as well – the renewal of the cosmos so that *shalom* is restored. The NT relates that this broad work of Christ is achieved in an astonishing way: by the crucifixion of Jesus – his sacrificial death – and his surprising resurrection, which enables that sacrifice to suffice for all and to give hope to all. We see this in the fact that the gospel writers juxtapose Jesus' broad concern for the kingdom of God (e.g., Mark 10:14–15) with his seemingly unavoidable journey to Jerusalem – the path of suffering and death (e.g., Mark 10:33–4). The apostle Paul styles Jesus' life, death, and resurrection as the "firstfruits" (Rom. 8:23)

---

[3] Jon Sobrino, *Jesus the Liberator: A Historical-Theological Reading of Jesus of Nazareth*, trans. Paul Burns and Francis McDonagh (Maryknoll, NY: Orbis, 1993), 135–6.

of the perfected version of the kingdom of God.[4] The universal scope of Jesus' particular life, death, and resurrection corresponds to the universal purpose of the original covenant, when God announced to Abram that his descendants (Israel) would bless the entire world. Such an understanding also comports with the apostolic church's affirmation that through Christ the "new covenant" of Jeremiah is extended to the Gentiles beyond the confines of the Jews (e.g., 2 Cor. 3:6).

Root metaphors and images

The full swath of the biblical narrative is foundational for an adequate understanding of the work of Christ. Within that narrative, however, a wide variety of metaphors and images are used to characterize Christ's saving work. Within this variety, we can point to several families of images or root metaphors as being of special importance, especially given their lasting influence on the doctrinal tradition.

In connection with the suffering servant text of Isaiah 53:5 that "by his bruises we are healed," a central component of Jesus' ministry was the bringing of health and wholeness, paradigmatically expressed through his healing of diseases (Mark 1:40–4). In the vicinity of this *medical* metaphor, Jesus is portrayed as the one who provides for and makes possible the well-being of his people – he is the "Good Shepherd" who protects those under his care, even if that protection requires the loss of his own life (John 10:11–18; cf. Matt. 18:10–14); or he is the "bread of life" (John 6), whose work provides sustenance for the hungry, an idea reinforced by Jesus' feedings of the thousands (e.g., Matt. 15:29ff.) and institution of the Lord's Supper. Prominent as well are *military* metaphors. For example, the Gospel of Matthew portrays Jesus as the new "Moses" who will liberate God's people from the slavery of their own sin. His salvific work is also depicted as the defeat of demonic powers that enslave (e.g., Mark 1:21–8), the calming of the frightening powers of nature (Mark 4:35–41), and the defeat of death (John 11:43–4). As 1 John 3:8 puts it: "The Son of God was revealed for this purpose, to destroy the works of the devil." *Financial* metaphors are also frequently employed, as especially embodied in those familiar terms of "redemption" and "ransom" (Mark 10:45; 1 Tim. 2:6), which portray humanity as being "purchased" from the powers that imprison it.

---

[4] Paul does not use the term "kingdom of God" in this passage, but the broader context of his discussion is the salvation of all creation, which in both the OT and the NT is synonymous with the kingdom of God.

Two other sets of images stand out in importance. The *legal* metaphor involves the largely synonymous concepts of "reconciliation" and "atonement." These terms highlight the fact that the Hebrew law or *torah* (in the OT), and the death and resurrection of Jesus Christ (in the NT), make possible a renewed relationship between the holy God and sinful humanity through the forgiveness of the offense of sin. That is to say, we are reconciled to God through Christ's atonement for sin (Eph. 2:14–16). But of all the root metaphors in the NT, the one that stands in the most crucial continuity with the OT is the *sacrificial* metaphor. As we have seen from the book of Hebrews, Christ is both the priestly representative of God and of humanity, and the sacrifice itself. His death, accordingly, is a "vicarious" or "substitutionary" sacrifice that reconciles God and humanity. He is the lamb of God who takes away the sin of the world; his sacrifice is a "fragrant offering" to God (Eph. 5:2, echoing the book of Leviticus). We will see the importance of these metaphors in our historical discussion of atonement theories.

Broader biblical perspectives

While such metaphors and images are central to describing the work of Christ, they can never be isolated from the broader biblical perspectives on salvation that frame Christ's coming into the world. Three of these perspectives are especially important to keep in mind.

The first of these is a trinitarian perspective, one that especially dovetails with our argument for a social doctrine of the Trinity (pp. 137–45) – namely, that Christ is the one who opens up the triune life of God to humanity. As the natural "Son" of God, he is the one who provides access to the life of God through "adoption" in the power of the Holy Spirit (see Gal. 4:5 and Eph. 1:5, as well as pp. 321–3 below). Through Christ, God's eternally begotten Son, human beings can become adopted sons and daughters of God. By virtue of his divine sonship, in fellowship with Christ we become children of God (e.g., John 1:12–13), members of the family of God (1 Pet. 4:17), participants in the trinitarian life.

A second perspective focuses on the role of Christ in restoring *shalom*, the "peace" or wholeness and well-being of creation, which has become chaotic and violent through the power of sin. In his post-resurrection appearances, Jesus blesses his disciples: "Peace be with you" (e.g., John 20:21), and the Pauline epistles declare that Christ is our peace (Eph. 2:14) and the Lord of peace (2 Thess. 3:16), whose peace should rule in our lives (Col. 3:15). Altogether, this particular idea suggests that Christ's work is a matter of reestablishing the *shalom* of creation that has been disrupted by sin, and of enabling the harmonious quality of that *shalom* to characterize the lives of those who work for Christ's kingdom in anticipation of its full eschatological realization.

A third important broad perspective focuses on Jesus' identity as the long-expected Messiah. Elaborating the image of messiah (Hebr. *mashiach* = anointed one), there is a venerable Christian tradition of interpreting Christ's work as the fulfillment of three OT offices that required anointing – namely, the roles of prophet, priest, and king (which, we have seen, became distinctive messianic expectations). Christ as prophet is the one who discerns God's will, calls God's people to repentance, teaches the way of righteousness, and instills hope in God's future salvation. Christ as priest is the one who represents God to the people and the people to God, intercedes for sinners, and provides sacrifice for reconciliation. Christ as king is the one who rules and protects the people in representation and restoration of God's kingdom and creational rule. While the OT looked forward to the coming of the messiah predominantly in kingly terms as one who would restore the fortunes of Israel in a form reminiscent of the Davidic kingship, the NT perspective on Jesus' messianic mission arguably focuses more on his priestly and sacrificial work, by integrating the suffering-servant motifs of Isaiah 53 with the OT title of "Son of Man," Jesus' favorite self-designation.[5]

It is important to note that all three of these broad biblical perspectives are eschatological in character. Messianic hope anticipates the coming of the anointed one who will set history right, ushering in a kingdom of *shalom* that will involve nothing less than the renovation of creation, wherein human beings will find a full flowering of fellowship with the triune God.

All of these various metaphors, images, and broader perspectives are firmly rooted in the biblical text, and each one of them brings valuable insight to the complex task of making sense of the work of Christ. But it is probably the messianic and priestly perspective that dominates the pages of the NT, which has led historically to the privileging of the notion of "reconciliation" as the central category through which to understand Christ's salvific work. As a synonym of reconciliation, the term "atonement" has come to be particularly central in the English language, such that the wide variety of explanations of *how* Christ brings salvation or

---

[5] Oscar Cullmann, *The Christology of the New Testament*, trans. Shirley C. Guthrie and Charles A. M. Hall, rev. edn. (Philadelphia: Westminster, 1963), 51–82.

reconciliation have come to be known as "atonement theories." Most literally, the concept of atonement focuses on the fact that Christ's work brings a new situation of unity between estranged parties – God and humanity – such that they are once again right or "at one" with one another, hence *at-one-ment*.[6] This reconciliation has traditionally been understood to have been transacted by Christ's sacrificial atonement on the cross. But as we have already seen, the cross alone is too narrow a focus to account for the saving work of Christ, which encompasses the entirety of his incarnate life, ministry, death, and resurrection. Used as a general rubric today, however, atonement theories are conceptual elaborations that draw out the logic and implications of central biblical metaphors concerning Christ's saving work. After surveying the most significant attempts to understand *how* Christ's work brings salvation – all of which fly loosely under the banner of "atonement theories" – we will offer our own proposal to make broad coherent sense of the variety and breadth of the biblical threads discussed above, some of which have received insufficient attention in traditional discussions of Christ's work.

TRADITIONAL CHRISTIAN ATONEMENT THEORIES

Unlike the doctrines of the Trinity and the person of Christ, there has never been *one* orthodox formulation of the work of Christ. This is likely due to the diversity of the biblical materials that by virtue of their quantity recommend a variety of perspectives on the work of Christ. But based largely on the key biblical metaphors just reviewed, a number of atonement proposals have risen to prominence in the course of the Christian theological tradition. In reviewing these major atonement theories, we will examine their basic theo-logic, observe how they vary depending on the cultural and historical context of the theologian or movement in question, and offer some evaluation of them in preparation for our own synthetic-constructive proposal.

Patristic theology

The theology of the early centuries of the church reflects the intersection of the Jewish heritage, the Greco-Roman culture of the ancient Mediterranean world,

---

[6] The English term dates to the early sixteenth century. See W. S. Reid and Geoffrey W. Bromiley, "Atone, Atonement," in *The International Standard Bible Encyclopedia*, rev. edn., 4 vols., ed. Geoffrey W. Bromiley (Grand Rapids, MI: Eerdmans, 1979), 1: 352. It was the term chosen by the translators of the King James Version of the Bible (1611) to render the Hebrew verb *kaphar* and the noun *kiphur*, and the Greek word *katallage*. These terms were translated into Latin as *reconciliatio*, which underscores the synonymous nature of reconciliation and atonement.

and the Christian claim regarding the ultimacy of Jesus Christ (see pp. 420–2). By the time of the second century, however, patristic theologians were often willing to trade on continuity with Judaism in order to make their claims more convincing in the Greco-Roman milieu. Thus many of their "atonement" ideas bear the stamp of the cultural and philosophical concerns of the Hellenistic world. This is not to say, however, that these early theories ignored the NT text. Indeed, most were guided by one or more of the relevant biblical motifs that we have already surveyed.

Recapitulation

One of the first major post-NT theologians, Irenaeus of Lyons, drew upon Paul's First Adam / Last Adam parallelism (see Rom. 5:15–21 and 1 Cor. 15:22) to elaborate his theory of "recapitulation" (*anakephalaiosis*). Irenaeus claims that Christ, as the second Adam, relives the life of the first Adam, retracing his steps and experiencing all of the stages of human life, but with one major difference: unlike the first Adam, who faltered in obedience to God, Christ does not succumb to temptation, but remains faithful and obedient to God. In this work of summing up or "recapitulating" the trial and temptations of human life, Jesus Christ sanctifies humanity:

He therefore passed through every age, becoming an infant for infants, thus sanctifying infants; a child for children, thus sanctifying those who are of this age, being at the same time made to them an example of piety, righteousness, and submission; a youth for youths, becoming an example to youths, and thus sanctifying them for the Lord.[7]

Christ sanctifies each stage of human existence by living it faithfully – without sin – serving as a model of how we should live as true human beings.

What, then, is the significance of the death of Christ? Here Irenaeus does not focus on sacrificial imagery, but rather says that Jesus died so that he would defeat the powers of death, illustrating what Swedish theologian Gustaf Aulén famously called the *Christus victor* (Christ the victor) atonement motif.[8] For Irenaeus, Christ destroys the powers of sin, death, and the devil through his obedient reiteration of the phases of human life. But precisely *how* his obedient life-unto-death provides salvation is not something that Irenaeus answers with great clarity. He appears to think that

---

[7] Irenaeus, *Against Heresies*, 2.22.4. Interestingly, Irenaeus speculates that Jesus (despite gospel evidence to the contrary) must have been at least fifty years of age before he died, so as to sanctify the "old age" stage of human life.

[8] Gustaf Aulén, *Christus Victor: An Historical Study of the Three Main Types of the Idea of Atonement*, trans. A. G. Hebert (New York: Macmillan, 1951).

Jesus' righteous recapitulation of human existence somehow brings humanity from death to life, from corruptibility to incorruptibility, by enabling it to participate in the divine life.[9] This idea of the transfer of the life of God to humanity became known as "deification" (*theopoiesis* or *theosis*), an idea that we will examine further in conjunction with Athanasius. Irenaeus simply claims that Christ's life and death bring humanity the "life of God."[10] This participation in the divine life is actually the culmination of human development, since according to Irenaeus human beings were not created "perfect" in the beginning, but rather were created by God to grow into maturity (cf. the "soul-building" theodicy on p. 212 above). Since the first Adam defaulted in this process of maturation, this human *telos* is only now accomplished by the life of Christ, who is none other than the eternal Word of God.[11]

In developing the Pauline Adam motif, Irenaeus' proposal powerfully shows the importance of the full humanity of Jesus and the significance of his whole life. However, Irenaeus' lack of sacrificial imagery prevents him from offering greater precision on *how* Jesus' life of obedience-unto-death makes salvation a reality.

Deification

The most succinct statement of the deification theme is found in the great theologian Athanasius: "For [Christ] was made man that we might be made God."[12] By this remark, Athanasius did not intend to suggest that the incarnation of the Logos allows human beings to transcend the ontological divide between Creator and creature; nor did he ostensibly mean that redeemed human beings somehow leave their humanity behind. Similar to Irenaeus, he meant that the event of the incarnation breathes a new and incorruptible kind of divine life back into the very *being* of humanity, a humanity that finds itself collapsing into non-being and death because of its finitude compounded by sin. It is on account of the incarnation that we "may become participants of the divine nature" (2 Pet. 1:4).

Understanding why Athanasius thinks of salvation in these terms requires a look at his view of creation and fall. According to Athanasius, because humanity is created *through* Christ, we are created through the divine rationality (the Logos), which enables us to rightly contemplate God.

---

[9] Irenaeus, *Against Heresies*, 3.19.3.   [10] Ibid., 4.22.1.   [11] Ibid., 4.38.1.

[12] Athanasius, *On the Incarnation*, 107. For a detailed historical study of this motif, see Norman Russell, *The Doctrine of Deification in the Greek Patristic Tradition*, Oxford Early Christian Studies (Oxford: Oxford University Press, 2004).

Contemplating God by participating in the rationality of the Logos is what constitutes our very being and gives us life. As a result of sin, however, our contemplation of God is impaired, leaving our lives "disintegrated" and "bereft even of being."[13] Just as God had warned Adam and Eve that sin would be punished by death, humanity began to lapse into physical and metaphysical death.[14]

The only one who can rescue humanity from its plight is the Logos, the very same one through whom God made humanity in the first place. Since death is necessary as the punishment for sin, Christ the Logos has to assume a human body to bear that punishment. But since he is in fact fully divine – the second person of the Trinity – he brings to humanity once again the possibility of incorruptibility through restored contemplation of God. While this possibility is achieved by the incarnation, everlasting life is actualized only by means of the resurrection. The resurrection completes the incarnation's healing of human nature from the disease of sin that leads it toward death.[15] This is the sense in which Athanasius understands deification.

Athanasius' account of deification, however, raises a few critical questions. First, while it is apparent that his view of the work of Christ certainly requires the deity of Christ, the necessity of Christ's humanity is much less clear. Apart from the need for a body to die the death of punishment, Athanasius seems to have little theological role for the humanity of Christ. Second, it is questionable whether his deification theory sufficiently recognizes the centrality of sacrifice in the biblical narrative. As such, this view may concentrate on the incarnation to the relative neglect of the cross. Third, the language of "deification" can easily be misunderstood as implying that salvation somehow entails transcending one's humanity *en route* to divinization, as in the gnostic ascent to salvation. While subsequent accounts of deification guard against these tendencies, a helpful qualification, we will suggest, is to view salvation more along the lines of "humanization" – the reclamation of true humanity – as anticipated by Irenaeus' Adam typology. Nonetheless, deification is a venerable perspective on Christ's work in the Christian tradition, one that is particularly significant in light of the NT's use of "adoption" into the trinitarian life as a key perspective that frames Christ's work (see p. 264). Deification continues to be the central soteriological motif in Eastern Orthodoxy, is operative in the

---

[13] Athanasius, *On the Incarnation*, 59. The fact that sin affects our very *being*, such that we are headed toward death rather than life, is why theologians sometimes describe Athanasius' theory of reconciliation as an "ontological" theory.

[14] Ibid., 60–3.

[15] The "healing" metaphor becomes central in paragraphs 22–6 of *On the Incarnation*.

Roman Catholic understanding of the "beatific vision," and has even enjoyed renewed appreciation in Protestant circles today.

Ransom

Gregory of Nyssa is another early theologian who employed the deification motif. But Gregory also famously elaborated another prominent patristic perspective that has become known as the "ransom" theory of atonement, harking back to the financial metaphor of the Son of Man becoming a "ransom for many" (Mark 10:45; cf. 1 Tim. 2:6). Interestingly, the most significant formulation of Gregory's ransom theory in his *Great Catechism* is nestled in the middle of an extended discussion of the "deifying" operations of the work of Christ, demonstrating the patristic penchant for sampling a variety of reconciliation motifs.[16]

In elaborating the ransom theme, Gregory first affirms that the manner of God's redemptive work must not be at odds with divine justice – that is, God must respect the legitimate rights that the devil has over sinful human beings.[17] Gregory then likens sinners to those who have "bartered away their freedom for money" and therefore are "the slaves of those who have purchased them." Thus any rescue of self-enslaved humanity must not be an arbitrary wrenching of human beings away from the grasp of the devil, but rather one that is "consonant with justice," which is to say, a legitimate ransom.[18] Accordingly, the only ransom the devil would accept would be something greater than the sinful humanity he holds captive. Only the miracle-worker of the gospels, whose perfect humanity is undeniable, appears to the devil as a ransom that would be worth more than the loss of sinful humanity. But in this transaction God engages in a bit of deception, since Christ is really true deity cloaked in human flesh.[19] What the devil does not realize is that in accepting this ransom he is gaining not an ordinary human being whom he could possess, but the divine one whom he *cannot* enslave. So the devil loses both his original possession (sinful human beings) *and* the ransom for which he unwittingly overreached (Jesus Christ), when by means of the resurrection Christ's deity is unveiled.

The shortcomings of the ransom theory are rather obvious. It takes one isolated biblical motif and spins it into a full-blown theory that is quite speculative. It also gives a more prominent role to the devil than is

---

[16] Gregory of Nyssa, *The Great Catechism*, trans. William Moore and Henry Austin Wilson, in *Nicene and Post-Nicene Fathers*, 2nd series, ed. Philip Schaff and Henry Wace (Grand Rapids, MI: Eerdmans, 1993), V: 487–95.

[17] Ibid., 492–5.   [18] Ibid., 492–3.

[19] Gregory claims that the deception is justified because its purpose is salvation (ibid., 495).

warranted by the biblical witness as a whole, taking the emphasis away from a focus on *human* sin and culpability, and therefore human responsibility. Lastly, the ransom theory underemphasizes the centrality of the humanity of Christ in his redeeming work, making it a mere cloak for the Son's powerful deity.

Medieval and Reformation theology

Satisfaction

Unease with the "ransom" idea of atonement was one of the major factors that prompted the development of the major medieval theories of atonement. The most significant medieval view of Christ's work is the "satisfaction" theory of Anselm of Canterbury, which has played an influential role in the subsequent western tradition. Like his patristic forebears, Anselm tightly connects questions about the work of Christ to the reality of the incarnation, as is seen in the title of his famous treatise *Cur Deus homo*, "Why God Became Human."[20] As a scholastic theologian, Anselm aims to rationally demonstrate how it is only through the incarnation that salvation could be achieved.

As theologians and historians have long recognized, Anselm draws heavily on his medieval feudal context for the categories he uses in his atonement theory, applying the logic of the relationship between a landowning lord and his vassals or serfs to the relationship between God and humanity. In feudal society, if an offense was committed against a lord, the offending vassal or serf could only rectify the relationship by making "satisfaction" for the offense, since it would not be honorable or just for the lord simply to forgive. For example, satisfaction in the case of a robbery would require the repayment of the stolen amount, as well as an additional amount that restored the honor of the offended party. Should the offender not be able to repay or provide the honor-restoring "extra," the only way by which the lord could preserve his honor was through punishment. Anselm compares this state of affairs to the situation of sinful humanity before God. Human beings, as vassals of God, owe a perfect, infinite God perfect, infinite loyalty – that is, true obedience every moment of their lives: "Every inclination of the rational creature ought to be subject to the will of God."[21] To sin is to withhold loyalty that is due to God. Humanity cannot repay what it has stolen from God, because even one moment of disobedience falls short of perfect loyalty. In other words, once surrendered, the perfect loyalty owed to God is forever lost and can never be

---

[20] Anselm of Canterbury, *Why God Became Man*, in *A Scholastic Miscellany: Anselm to Ockham*, ed. Eugene R. Fairweather, Library of Christian Classics (Philadelphia: Westminster, 1956).
[21] Ibid., 119.

repaid. It is therefore also impossible for human beings to provide any extra that would constitute "satisfaction" for an infinite God's offended honor.

Since sinful human beings cannot make satisfaction, it would seem that punishment must necessarily occur in order for the honor of God and the social order of the cosmos to be preserved. Were God to punish humanity for its sin, God's honor would certainly be upheld. But in so doing, God's original purpose for human beings (blessedness) would be undermined, and this, Anselm reasons, would be unfitting for God. Satisfaction, therefore, is the only adequate option. But again the dilemma: since the offense belongs to humanity, it is humanity which must make satisfaction; but humanity lacks the necessary resources. Anselm's resolution: only God can manage such an achievement. The only way out of this dilemma is through the satisfying work of a "God-man" – hence the incarnation.[22] Here we see Anselm's connection between the work of Christ and the person of Christ.

Christ's life of obedience to God is owed simply by virtue of his being a human person. To make satisfaction for humanity, he has to give something more, which can only be his death, since he does not owe that to God by virtue of his sinlessness. According to Anselm, because of the divine identity of the one who dies, his freely given human death becomes so valuable that it outweighs the offense committed by sinful humanity. The value of this superabundant gift merits for Christ a reward, a reward that he (being divine and therefore perfect) does not personally need. So he transfers the reward to humanity as its satisfaction, which preserves God's honor and rescues humanity from the punishment of death.

Anselm's theological achievement was considerable, for his framework provided the atonement logic for most of the Latin West after him. The indebtedness of his theory to the categories of his culture is evident and not unproblematic, but the affinity of those categories to some of the major motifs in the biblical materials has enabled it to weather the test of time. However, the strict logic of Anselm's approach – claiming the utter "necessity" of God redeeming us in *this* particular way – does seem to denigrate the gracious and merciful love of God's provision of reconciliation. Theologians have also recognized another problem in Anselm's approach, namely, that his focus on satisfaction *instead of* punishment seems to betray the biblical logic of the crucifixion as a vicarious sacrifice on behalf of humanity. So a major subsequent revision of the Anselmian construal was the rejection of his feudal framework of either satisfaction or punishment. Thomas Aquinas, for example, proposed that satisfaction took place *through* punishment, with Christ paying the "debt

[22] Ibid., 152.

of punishment," an idea that became central to the reformers' understanding of Christ's reconciling work.[23]

Penal substitution

Among the reformers who embraced this revision of the satisfaction theory, John Calvin's statement is one of the most systematic. Calvin structures his broader explanation of Christ's "work" under the famous rubric of Christ's threefold "office" as prophet, priest, and king, as introduced above.[24] His expanded discussion of Christ's priestly office focuses on the work of Christ on the cross, though Calvin certainly realizes that the cross cannot be separated from the resurrection, since the latter makes possible the new righteousness of sinful humanity forgiven through the cross.[25] For Calvin, a central feature of the fallout of sin is that it occasions the wrath of God. While the pre-fall attitude of God toward humanity was one of favor, the holy God's countenance becomes wrathful in the face of sin for which God demands punishment. Since the penalty for sin is eternal death – estrangement from its Creator – humanity is doomed before the wrath of God. But according to Calvin, God still loves the world and therefore finds a way to rescue sinners from their plight while still requiring the penalty for sin.[26]

This rescue is found, of course, through Jesus Christ, who through a life of perfect obedience dies a substitutionary death on behalf of humanity, bearing the punishment that is the penalty that makes satisfaction for sin, thus appeasing God's wrath. This form of satisfaction theory is usually called a "penal substitution" theory. In freely giving himself up for a sacrificial death, Jesus Christ bears God's wrath and pays the penalty for sin in humanity's stead.[27] "This is our acquittal," states Calvin: "the guilt that held us liable for punishment has been transferred to the head of the Son of God."[28] Humanity, in turn, is given the favor earned by Christ, completing the substitution.[29]

---

[23] Thomas Aquinas, *Summa Theologica*, 3.48.4.   [24] Calvin, *Institutes*, 2.15.

[25] Ibid., 2.16.13. Calvin explicitly calls the cross a synecdoche, identifying the cross as shorthand for the whole ministry and fate of Christ.

[26] Ibid., 2.16.1–4.

[27] Because it is the *penalty* for sin, Calvin considers it important to see that Christ died the death of a criminal, albeit one who was clearly himself innocent (ibid., 2.16.5).

[28] Ibid., 2.16.5.

[29] Calvin's emphasis on life-long obedience in fact constitutes a recapitulation element in his penal substitution theory. The Bible's focus on Christ's death – which becomes Calvin's own focus – should not, in his view, displace the redemptive importance of Christ's *life*. Calvin also stresses that death and the devil are destroyed by Christ's atoning work, thus showing that the *Christus victor* motif is also present in Calvin (ibid., 2.16.7 [p. 512]). While also employing imagery of Christ's victory over the powers of death and the devil, Martin Luther similarly focused his attention on the substitutionary satisfaction in which Christ, in the place of sinners, bears the righteous God's wrath against sin. On Luther's view of the work of Christ, see Bernhard Lohse, *Martin Luther's Theology: Its Historical and Systematic Development*, trans. Roy A. Harrisville (Minneapolis, MN: Fortress, 1999), 223–8.

This revised form of Anselm's theory was prevalent until the rise of modern theology. A major strength of this view is that it employs the priestly and sacrificial imagery that is central to the biblical materials. By way of weakness, an emphasis on God's wrath raises some difficult questions about the divine love, since it seems to necessitate the Father's punishment of the Son, which has been criticized as a form of child abuse.[30] The substitutionary theory also gives the impression that Christ's work of atonement is narrowly concerned with human beings, rather than with the broader scope of creation, a weakness that generally applies to most of the theories we have surveyed.

Modern theology

Exemplarism

The dominant theory of the work of Christ in nineteenth-century Protestant liberal theology resembles certain statements made by one of the major medieval theologians, Peter Abelard. In one of his writings, Abelard suggests that Christ's death is not a sacrifice or a means of satisfaction, but an *example* of God's love. Christ's exemplary devotion to God, even unto death, which pierces the hardness of the sinful human heart, leads humanity to love God, which in turn leads to forgiveness.[31]

Following this thread of Abelard's reflections, Albrecht Ritschl, the theologian who is typically called the "father" of Protestant liberalism, dismissed Anselm's emphasis on the removal of human beings' objective guilt and the fulfillment of God's justice, and focused instead on the removal of human beings' *subjective* guilt or "consciousness of guilt."[32] Ritschl does not conceive of sin as an objective offense against God that requires punishment and expiation. Rather, Christ's exemplary life of true love captivates the lives of the members of the Christian community so that they lose *their* enmity toward God.[33] Following Christ's example enables them to fulfill their moral responsibility. Reconciliation is simply the matter of the person being liberated from self-imposed guilt and set free for moral community. Ritschl's focus is the subjective transformation of the human being, not any kind of objective change in the legal contours of the God–sinner relationship. Christ's death is

---

[30] See, e.g., Rita Nakashima Brock, "And a Little Child Will Lead Us: Christology and Child Abuse," in *Christianity, Patriarchy, and Abuse: A Feminist Critique*, ed. Joanne Carlson Brown and Carole R. Bohn (New York: Pilgrim, 1989), 51–4.

[31] Peter Abelard, "Exposition of the Epistle to the Romans," in Fairweather, *Scholastic Miscellany*, 283.

[32] Ritschl, *Justification and Reconciliation*, III: 54.　　[33] See esp. ibid., III: 72–9.

not a literal sacrifice, but an inspiring example of love lived self-sacrificially with no reserve.

Historically speaking, the exemplarism that nineteenth-century liberalism espoused lost its relative dominance due to the influence of Karl Barth's theology in the twentieth century. As is well known, liberal theology's optimism regarding humanity's ability to turn to morality through Christ's example was shredded by the horrors of WWI. Liberalism also ignored the weight of the biblical evidence that requires the cross to be seen as some kind of representational sacrifice that addresses sin as an objective offense. Barth himself held to a substitutionary account in the vein of Calvin.[34]

The kingdom of God

Beginning in the late 1960s and early 1970s, Latin American liberation theology developed a more historical orientation to the work of Christ by highlighting the NT notion of the kingdom of God as the historical act by which God brings liberation to the oppressed. Jon Sobrino, one of the leading liberation theologians, criticizes the substitutionary Anselmian tradition as "unhistorical" on two accounts: first, by virtue of its abstracting the cross of Christ from Jesus' radical life of love and the historical forces of sin that caused his death; and second, by focusing on sin simply as a personal offense against God rather than as a complex, systemic reality that leads to poverty and oppression in the real, historical world.[35] Sobrino observes that focusing only on the removal of the *offense* of sin fails to address the question of the *sin itself*, especially the destructive effects it has wrought in the world.[36] For him, sin is not only personal, but is primarily social, structural, and historical. Accordingly, Sobrino largely rejects the judicial terms of substitutionary theologies of atonement and points instead to the kingdom of God as the saving work of Jesus. The kingdom of God, embodied and represented by Jesus, is the salvation that God brings into *history*. It includes the transformation of history itself into a realm of life rather than death, into a world of liberation rather than oppression.

Interestingly, Sobrino's principal reflections on atonement also include significant elements of exemplarism. Jesus' liberative life in service of the "God of life" rather than the "idols of death" provides an example of authentic love which ought to awaken human beings to follow Jesus by working for the poor and downtrodden. In this way, Sobrino identifies the work of those who imitate

---

[34] On this see Bruce L. McCormack, *For Us and Our Salvation: Incarnation and Atonement in the Reformed Tradition*, Studies in Reformed Theology and History (Princeton, NJ: Princeton Theological Seminary, 1993), 28–34.

[35] Sobrino, *Christology at the Crossroads*, 191–3.   [36] Ibid., 190.

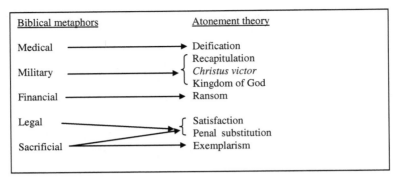

Figure 10.1 Biblical metaphors and atonement theories

Christ's liberative example with the kingdom's amelioration of structural sin, implying that human beings are the primary means by which Christ's kingdom is ushered into history. Sobrino's exemplarism is even more apparent when he speaks of salvation through the cross as an "exemplary cause" and not as, in the substitutionary sense, an "efficient cause."[37] In this approach, the connection between the cross and the forgiveness of personal sin is rather ambiguous.

Sobrino and other liberation theologians clearly indicate a lacuna in traditional Anselmian and substitutionary understandings of atonement. The limitation they highlight is the failure of these traditional understandings to address the relationship between Christ's reconciling work and the *social* and *structural* sin that is as real in the world as personal sin. In other words, if Jesus is "the Lamb of God who takes away the sin of the world" (John 1:29), how is it the case that his life, death, and resurrection "take away" both the personal *and* structural sin of the world? But this strength of Sobrino's approach also becomes its weakness: in his preoccupation with structural sin, he fails to sufficiently address the theme of personal sin, and ultimately lapses into a rather conventional form of exemplarism.

Thus far in this chapter we have surveyed the important narrative themes and biblical motifs related to Christ's work, and we have discussed the most important atonement theories in the Christian tradition that are conceptual elaborations of one or more of the central biblical metaphors (see Figure 10.1). We have also seen that each atonement theory contributes important insights into the work of Christ, but that taken alone they each contain shortcomings. In our view, the best way to remedy these deficiencies is not by choosing *one* theory

---

[37] Sobrino, *Jesus the Liberator*, 230.

over the others, but by integrating the insights of the various theories with one another in the context of the broad sweep of the biblical narrative. The remainder of this chapter constitutes our attempt to synthesize these atonement motifs into a coherent whole that remains biblically faithful and yet compelling in today's world.[38]

A NARRATIVE PROPOSAL FOR RECONCILIATION THEOLOGY

In elaborating a theology of reconciliation that does justice to the central biblical themes surveyed above, we must pay close attention to the structure and flow of the biblical narrative of salvation history, particularly its NT moments. Since sacrificial and substitutionary ideas are central to the biblical text, they must play a pivotal role in any systematic account of the work of Christ. But recent theological developments, such as liberation theology, have reminded us that any adequate doctrine of reconciliation must extend beyond merely personal and individualistic concerns into the sphere of social, systemic, and structural considerations. Thus the kingdom of God must be the broadest context of any contemporary proposal. But we also deem Irenaeus' recapitulation motif of great importance because it underscores the creational and representational significance of Jesus' humanity in the context of his *whole* life, not merely his death on the cross. To anticipate, the central elements of our constructive proposal are as follows:

- The kingdom of God as the horizon of the ministry of Jesus, in connection to the triune God's broader lordship over all creation.
- The significance of the incarnation and whole life history of Jesus, who as the last Adam recapitulates the life history of all human beings (the first Adam), whom he represents before God.
- The cross of Christ as the culmination of his representative work of recapitulation, serving as a substitution for the punishment deserved by those whom he represents.
- The liberating importance of Christ's resurrection as the cosmic transformation that makes it possible for sinners to participate in the project of God's coming kingdom, thereby actualizing their true humanity and promising the new creation.

---

[38] Another contemporary proposal that is rather synthetic in nature is Robert Sherman's *King, Priest, and Prophet: A Trinitarian Theology of Atonement*, Theology for the Twenty-first Century (New York: T. & T. Clark, 2004), which integrates various biblical motifs and atonement theories under the rubric of Christ's threefold office.

Creation as kingdom of God

Following the lead of contemporary biblical theology, the liberation theologians are right to emphasize the centrality of the kingdom of God in Jesus' teaching and ministry. Jesus proclaims not primarily himself, but the great reign of God that promises to transform all of history. This focus on the kingdom of God as the all-embracing, eschatological renewal of reality coheres with the OT's portrait of Yahweh as the Lord or King of all creation, since creation in the beginning is portrayed as the kingdom of God (see pp. 148–51 above). As seen above, the OT situates Israel's election and covenant in Yahweh's broader international and cosmic purposes. In the same way, the NT interprets Christ's coming both as the fulfillment of the covenant (in a way that embraces all the nations) and as the embodiment of the kingdom of God (which transforms all reality). Thus the triumph of the kingdom in history is something that happens, first and foremost, *through him*. The kingdom is something objective, something happening even apart from human participation in it – God's reign as a force that eschatologically transforms history. Seen in this light, Jesus is the personal representative of God's kingdom. Cast in more trinitarian terms, Jesus as God the Son is the representative of the triune God's kingdom, whose person and work constitute the decisive moment in the divine project of reclaiming all of creation from the tyranny and violence of sin and evil. With this broad framework, it is impossible to reduce the significance of Christ's work to that of "forgiveness" for the human "soul" (also see pp. 314–5 below). Christ's work, ultimately, promises the renovation of all creation into the kingdom of God.

Incarnation as recapitulation

If Jesus' person and work constitute the crucial moment in reestablishing the kingdom, then reconciliation takes place through the whole course of the incarnation. On the one hand, Jesus (as the second person of the Trinity) is the divine representative of God's kingdom. But, on the other hand, through his self-emptying incarnation as a historical human being, he also serves as the representative of all humanity. Human beings, as the primary progenitors of sin in creation, are the special focus of Christ's work of inaugurating the kingdom that extends to all creation, particularly given the special human vocation that includes responsibility for creation. While the kingdom is first and foremost God's work, and not directly dependent on human participation, the reconciliation of sinful human beings is nevertheless a strategic moment in the witness, embodiment, and life of that kingdom. Paul's "last Adam" motif, so central in

Irenaeus' theology, is indispensable at this point. Christ is the eschatological Adam, the one who represents sinful humanity, embodies true humanity, and eschatologically renews the human race. This motif picks up essential points made by the Genesis narrative, which underscores the fundamental unity of all humanity. All human beings are God's creatures, made in the divine image to represent God to creation and creation to God; and all human beings share in sin. That is why it is fitting that God redeems through *one* who is the representative of *all* humanity.

Moreover, since sin, at its heart resident in the human person, becomes a reality that affects the structures of society and under which all creation groans, it is important that Christ's reconciling work connect to every dimension of human existence. If sin in the personal sense is essentially disobedience and rebellion against God, it is fitting that the representative of humanity who neutralizes the effects of that rebellion live all of the stages of human existence rightly, obediently, faithfully, and sinlessly. As highlighted in the book of Hebrews, Jesus as the representative of all humanity even needed to prove his righteousness and representational status by faithfully living an authentic human life. Thus his person and work serve not only as a redemptive counterpoint to humanity's disobedience, but also as the revelation of true humanity – what it is to be the *imago Dei* before the face of God.

Crucifixion as substitutionary death

The recapitulating life of Jesus Christ, however, culminated in his execution on the cross. Hence the substitutionary tradition of atonement, which need not be at odds with the recapitulation motif: while the first Adam's disobedient life led to the punishment of death, through the last Adam's obedient life-unto-death, a death on a cross, life is once again restored to humanity. Indeed, the substitutionary motif brings greater precision to the recapitulation theme, showing *how* the obedience of the incarnate Logos made reconciliation possible as the inauguration of the kingdom of God. It does this by specifying the meaning of that death, interpreting the crucifixion against the background of the OT sacrificial system, which sees sin as an offense that alienates the sinner from God and which therefore must be removed if God and humanity are to be reconciled. The substitutionary character of Christ's death means that the punishment for sin – something never downplayed by the biblical materials – is assumed by Jesus: the ones who deserve to pay the punishment are acquitted of their guilt. The one whose death takes the place of those who deserve to die is in fact the representative of all humanity; thus his substitutionary death is sufficient for all.

Illustration 10.1 Marc Chagall's provocative *Yellow Crucifixion* paints the death of Jesus the Jew in the apocalyptic colors of the chaos, displacement, and fires of the Holocaust.

Christ's death, however, need not be interpreted as *directly* caused or *prescriptively* willed by the Father, as though it were the whole point of the incarnation – a scenario that gives rise to the criticism of divine child abuse. Here we must let the gospel story first play itself out. Historically speaking, we – humanity – crucified the Son of God. Jesus died as a religious blasphemer and political criminal at the hands of the human powers that be (see Illustration 10.1). Given his innocence of these charges (the truth of which fully comes to light only in the resurrection), Jesus' death on the cross is nothing less than a travesty of justice, a gruesome murder, and ultimately a cosmic absurdity given Jesus' full identity, wherein humanity crucifies the eternal Son of God. Jesus' own parable of the tenants makes this perspective clear: how outrageous it would be for the tenants of the vineyard to kill its owner's son (Luke 20:9–19). But this is exactly what humanity did, not God the Father. Yet through the resurrection God creates good out of bad, salvation out of evil, by accepting the sacrificial life of Christ that culminates in his death as the ultimate and final sacrifice (indeed, the end of sacrifice – Heb. 7:27) that pardons and atones for sin. It is only in the light of the resurrection, retrospectively, that one may interpret Christ's death as an atoning sacrifice for sin, not prospectively.

However, it must be remembered that Jesus is not only the representative of humanity; he is also the representative of the kingdom of God, which is proven by his resurrection from the dead, wherein the incarnate second person of the Trinity is unveiled and confessed as Lord. Therefore his substitutionary death becomes a decisive moment in the eschatological coming of the kingdom – but only in connection to his resurrection.

Resurrection for liberation, humanization, and cosmic shalom

The release of sinners from their personal guilt stands as the promise of the eventual demise of the sinfulness of the structures of the world. In other words, the death of death through the punishment of the cross also marks the promise of the liberation of all creation and history itself. Through the hope of Christ's resurrection and the promise of their own resurrection, forgiven sinners are liberated to participate in the fashioning of the kingdom of God that was embodied by Jesus and inaugurated into history through the incarnation and cross. Thus the kingdom of God, established at creation, bursts in a new and redemptive way into history through the scandal of the cross and the power of the resurrection, and is open to the participation of those who are liberated by the forgiveness of the cross and resurrection. This is the truth of the exemplarist motif as emphasized in liberation theology.

In having their sin forgiven on the basis of the substitutionary death of Christ, people are liberated to become fully human. More than providing "divinization" in the ontological language of the early church, the cross and resurrection make humanization possible.[39] Through Christ's substitutionary death and the liberation of the resurrection, it becomes possible for people to actualize their true humanity by following the Last Adam, the

---

[39] The concept of "humanization" is central in Paul L. Lehmann, *Ethics in a Christian Context* (New York: Harper & Row, 1963), and Sobrino, *Christ the Liberator*, 232–6.

truly human one. As such, they participate through Christ in the gracious coming of God's kingdom by living righteously, thankfully, and justly in recapturing their true humanity as the image-bearers and adopted children of God.

The newness and restoration inaugurated by the resurrection are not restricted to human beings, but include the renewal of the whole breadth of the triune God's creational kingdom. While the kingdom of God is only present in provisional form through Christ's life, death, and resurrection, these point forward eschatologically, promising the general resurrection of the dead and the new heaven and the new earth in which creational *shalom* will be finally and fully realized. Thus the liberative participation of humanity in the fashioning of the kingdom of God, which humanizes humanity, must always be a hope-filled and forward-looking effort that anticipates God's definitive work at the return of Christ.

CONCLUSION

This chapter has surveyed the biblical roots of the important Christian doctrine of Christ's work. It has examined the church's historical attempts to come to grips with this doctrine. Finally, it has proposed a way of integrating these central biblical themes and historical theories in a narratival way. In so doing, we have attempted to show the congruence between the doctrine of Christ's *person* and the doctrine of his *work*, how both Christ's divine identity and the fullness of his humanity are indispensable in appreciating his salvific work. The important recapitulation element of our narrative proposal presupposes the previous chapter's kenotic construal of the incarnation. By emptying himself of his divine prerogatives, the second person of the Trinity became genuinely and fully human so as to re-create a true and faithful humanity. As the authentic representative of humanity, who is also, as God's Son, the authentic representative of the triune God, Jesus Christ secures the kingdom of God in history through his obedient life, his self-giving sacrificial death, and the great power of his resurrection, which liberates sinners to participate in God's renovation of creation.

Since reconciliation is not only a christological event, but most broadly a trinitarian event, much remains to be said about the role of the Holy Spirit's person and work. While focusing on Christ's person and work for the last two chapters, we now bring the Spirit's person and work to the foreground.

FOR FURTHER READING

Anselm of Canterbury, *Why God Became Man*, in *A Scholastic Miscellany: Anselm to Ockham*, ed. Eugene R. Fairweather, Library of Christian Classics (Philadelphia: Westminster, 1956), 100–83.

Athanasius, *On the Incarnation of the Word*, in *Christology of the Later Fathers*, ed. Edward Rochie Hardy and Cyril C. Richardson, Library of Christian Classics (Louisville, KY: Westminster John Knox, 1954).

Aulén, Gustaf, *Christus Victor: An Historical Study of the Three Main Types of the Idea of Atonement*, trans. A. G. Hebert (New York: Macmillan, 1951).

Boersma, Hans, *Violence, Hospitality, and the Cross: Reappropriating the Atonement Tradition* (Grand Rapids, MI: Baker Academic, 2004).

Sherman, Robert, *King, Priest, and Prophet: A Trinitarian Theology of Atonement*, Theology for the Twenty-first Century (New York: T. & T. Clark, 2004).

Sobrino, Jon, *Christology at the Crossroads: A Latin American Approach*, trans. John Drury (Maryknoll, NY: Orbis, 1978).

CHAPTER 11

The person and work of the Holy Spirit

INTRODUCTION: THE CINDERELLA OF THE TRINITY?

In the history of Christian theology, the doctrine of the Holy Spirit, or
pneumatology (Gk. *pneuma* = spirit), has not always received its own
distinct chapter. This is due to a number of factors. For one, the fact that
God by nature is spirit (John 4:24) and that all of God's works are therefore
"pneumatic" in effect has meant that the particular personhood of the
Spirit, by virtue of both name and prominent manifestation as a power or
force, is not as transparent as that of the Father or the Son. For another, the

work of the Spirit has typically been subsumed under the doctrine of salvation (soteriology), since the Spirit's principal role has been seen to be the *application* of Christ's saving work to believers (in short, sanctification) in the life and mission of the church and in the eschatological consummation of salvation (glorification). Because of "its" elusive personhood and seemingly subordinate work, the Spirit has not always been appreciated as a full divine person alongside the Father and Son. Therefore, in evaluating doctrinal history, it has become fashionable to say that the Spirit is the forgotten or neglected member of the Trinity, even the Cinderella of the Trinity (or, in view of the feminist critique, the Cinderfella of the Trinity). Given twentieth-century theological developments, however, this relative neglect of the Spirit has been considerably remedied, bringing with it quite a pneumatological windfall. For reasons that will become clear, the person and work of the Spirit rightly warrant a distinct chapter before we take up the doctrines of salvation and the church, which, as the topics of the so-called "third article" of the creed, are principally ascribed to the pneumatic work of the third person of the Trinity.

BIBLICAL MATERIALS

Spirit in the Old Testament

The foundational image for "spirit" in the OT is that of a blowing "wind" or "breath," as the Hebrew word *ruach* can be variously translated.[1] Ezekiel 37:1–14, for example, plays on all three of these senses.[2] As applied to humanity, *ruach* is the principle of life that animates the individual; the human spirit therefore is virtually identical with the "person" or "self" (e.g., Ps. 31:5; cf. Gen. 2:7). As applied to God, the divine *ruach* depicts God's presence, power, or activity in creation. That is to say, the Spirit of God is the agency of divine action in the world; the Spirit is "God in action."

While most of the activities attributed to the Spirit of God in the OT have to do with the life, mission, and hope of the people of Israel, we also see many references in the Hebrew Bible to the role of God's Spirit in creation.

---

[1] See "Pneuma," in *Theological Dictionary of the New Testament*, ed. Gerhard Kittel and Gerhard Friedrich, trans. Geoffrey W. Bromiley, 10 vols. (Grand Rapids, MI: Eerdmans, 1969–76), VI: 332–455. For a very good article on Spirit in the biblical materials, see D. A. Tappeiner, "Holy Spirit," in *International Standard Bible Encyclopedia*, II: 730–42. Alasdair I. C. Heron, *The Holy Spirit* (Philadelphia: Westminster, 1983), esp. 3–60, also informs the following.

[2] In Ezekiel 37:1–14, *ruach* is best translated as "spirit" in vv. 1 and 14 and as "breath" in vv. 5, 6, 8, and 10; in v. 9 the implied sense is "wind."

In Genesis 1:2, the Spirit of God is poised for creation, brooding over the primeval waters.[3] Similar to the parallelism of Psalm 33:6 — "By the word of the LORD the heavens were made, and all their host by the breath (*ruach*) of his mouth" — so also creation in Genesis 1 can be seen to be a product of God's creative word in tandem with God's mighty Spirit. This life-giving function of God's Spirit is reiterated in Genesis 2:7, where God breathes life into the "man" (*adam*) formed of the dusty ground (*adamah*). And it is the Spirit of God that preserves created life, as affirmed in Psalm 104:27–30: "These [creatures] all look to you to give them their food in due season ... When you hide your face, they are dismayed; when you take away their breath (*ruach*), they die and return to their dust. When you send forth your spirit (*ruach*), they are created; and you renew the face of the ground." In addition to its agency in creation and preservation, the Spirit of God manifests the universal divine presence in creation: "Where can I go from your spirit? Or where can I flee from your presence? If I ascend to heaven, you are there; if I make my bed in Sheol, you are there" (Ps. 139:7–8).

The preponderance of OT references to God's Spirit, however, are concerned with divine activities within the life of the nation of Israel. One particular area of manifestation is when various persons are specially endowed or equipped with the Spirit for the purpose of leadership. This is seen vividly in the book of Judges, where the Spirit of Yahweh empowers various leaders to deliver besieged Israel, such as Gideon (6:34) and, most famously, Samson, upon whom the Spirit comes at various times to enable him to tear apart a lion (14:6) or to slay a thousand men with the jawbone of an ass (15:15). Similar empowerments for leadership are attributed to Saul (1 Sam. 10:1–13), David (1 Sam. 16:13ff.) and even the post-exilic Zerubbabel, the last of the Davidic kings (Zech. 4:6).

Prophecy is another area particularly attributed to the Spirit of God. Early attestations depict the Spirit coming ecstatically upon a person, such as Balaam (Num. 24:2) or Saul (1 Sam. 10:10). While the classical pre-exilic prophets place more emphasis on the Word of God coming to the prophet, Hosea nonetheless identifies "prophet" with "man of the Spirit" (Hos. 9:7), and Micah claims that his vocation is impelled by the Spirit: "But as for me, I am filled with power, with the spirit of the LORD, and with justice and might, to declare to Jacob his transgression and to Israel his sin" (Mic. 3:8).[4] Later exilic prophets such as Ezekiel and Isaiah explicitly associate their

---

[3] This is a highly debated text. Some biblical scholars translate *ruach* in Genesis 1:2 simply as a "mighty wind."

[4] Tappeiner, "Holy Spirit," 730.

prophetic acts with the Spirit of God: "The spirit of the Lord GOD is upon me, because the LORD has anointed me; he has sent me to bring good news to the oppressed ... to proclaim the year of the LORD's favor" (Isa. 61:1–2; see also Ezek. 2:1–2; 3:12ff.). In the prophetic literature overall we again see a parallelism between the working of God's Spirit and God's Word.

A final important area of reference to the Spirit in the OT concerns Israel's hope for an unprecedented age of the Spirit, a time when God's Spirit would be poured out without measure. This hope centers most explicitly on the OT's messianic expectations of one who would come in Yahweh's name specially endowed with the Spirit, as Isaiah highlights in 11:1–2: "A shoot shall come out from the stump of Jesse, and a branch shall grow out of his roots. The spirit of the LORD shall rest on him, the spirit of wisdom and understanding, the spirit of counsel and might, the spirit of knowledge and the fear of the LORD" (see also 11:3–9; 42:1; 62:1). In addition to these messianic hopes, the prophets spoke of a time in which God's Spirit would come upon all God's people in an unprecedented way, as especially promised in Joel: "Then afterward I will pour out my spirit on all flesh; your sons and your daughters shall prophesy, your old men shall dream dreams, and your young men shall see visions. Even on the male and female slaves, in those days, I will pour out my spirit" (Joel 2:28–9; cf. also Isa. 32:14–18; 63:7–19; Ezek. 39:29). This promised infusion of the Spirit appears to parallel the promise of a new covenant, as is implied by Ezekiel: "A new heart I will give you, and a new spirit I will put within you; and I will remove from your body the heart of stone and give you a heart of flesh. I will put my spirit within you, and make you follow my statutes and be careful to observe my ordinances" (Ezek. 36:26–7; see also Isa. 59:21ff. and Jer. 31:31–4; 32:37–40). Such an era would be a time of spiritual renewal, a renewal not only of the people of Israel, but also of the land of Israel, and ultimately of the whole earth, since embedded in these promissory contexts is the anticipated renewal of all creation (see in particular Isa. 11: 6–9; 32:14–18; 44:3–5; 65:17ff.; 66:22ff.; Joel 2:18–29). This brings the Spirit's role in the OT full circle, as the Spirit's vivifying power in new creation is seen in continuity with its originating role in creation.

During the intertestamental period, amid the ebb and flow of messianic expectations, there grew a nostalgia for the prophetic Spirit of Israel's former days, an activity which now appeared quiescent. Along with the rise of apocalypticism there emerged a more detailed angelology and demonology of good and evil spirits. In Hellenistic (diaspora) Judaism in particular there developed a virtual identification of God's Spirit with the divine wisdom immanent in creation, as reflected in the Wisdom of Solomon (*c.* 50 BCE): "For wisdom [the fashioner of all things] is more mobile than any motion; because of her pureness she pervades and penetrates all things. For she is a breath of the power of God, and a pure emanation of the glory of the Almighty" (7:24; see also 7:21–30). In this way the Spirit is personified as Yahweh's partner, who as the wisdom resident in creation gives universal testimony to God's presence and truth (see also Prov. 8:22–31).

The Holy Spirit in the New Testament

The NT proclaims that the OT's anticipated "age of the Spirit" has arrived in the coming of Jesus the Messiah. The advent of Christ, accordingly, sharpens the focus on the person and work of the Spirit in the NT. In contrast to only two passages in the OT (Ps. 51:11; Isa. 63:10–11), the Spirit is overwhelmingly called the *Holy* Spirit in the NT.

Among the synoptic gospels, Luke is particularly keen to depict the workings of the Holy Spirit. His early references to Elizabeth (1:41), Zechariah (1:67), and Simeon (2:25–7) as prophesying filled by the Spirit not only signal a continuity with the OT emphasis on the Spirit of prophecy after its intertestamental quiescence, but also heralds something new, anticipating that time foretold by Joel when even sons and daughters would prophesy (cf. also Mary, 1:46–55, and Anna, 2:36–8). All of these prophecies, of course, center on Jesus Christ, who is the unique bearer of the Spirit – the Messiah. As the one anointed by God, Jesus is uniquely conceived by the Holy Spirit (1:35), is specially endowed by the Spirit at his baptism for his subsequent ministry (3:21–2), is immediately "led by the Spirit" into the wilderness to be tempted (4:1ff.), and then, "filled with the power of the Spirit," returns to Galilee (4:14). At Nazareth he claims to fulfill Isaiah's prophecy: "The Spirit of the Lord is upon me, because he has anointed me to bring good news to the poor" (4:18ff.; cf. Isa. 61:1ff.). With this announcement, Luke implies that Jesus' entire ministry is empowered by the Spirit, as indicated, for example, when "the power of the Lord was with him to heal" (5:17). Luke's gospel ends with Jesus' ascension, telling his disciples to wait in Jerusalem for the Spirit, the "power from on high" which the Father promised (24:49).

Luke's second volume, the Acts of the Apostles, picks right up on this scene: "But you will receive power when the Holy Spirit has come upon you; and you will be my witnesses in Jerusalem, in all Judea and Samaria, and to the ends of the earth" (1:8), anticipating the plot of Acts. The Spirit then comes in dramatic fashion at Pentecost (2:1ff.; also see Illustration 11.1), which Peter interprets as a fulfillment of Joel's prophecy concerning the

Illustration 11.1 An iconographic depiction of the giving of the Holy Spirit to the apostles at Pentecost, by Theophanes the Cretan (sixteenth century).

coming age of the Spirit: "In the last days it will be, God declares, that I will pour out my Spirit upon all flesh" (2:17ff.; cf. Joel 2:28ff.).

This pneumatic event at Pentecost, according to Peter's sermon, vindicates Christ as both Lord and Messiah, since upon his ascension and exaltation to God's heavenly throne he was given the promised Holy Spirit, whom he poured out in inauguration of the messianic age (Acts

2:32–6). The Spirit now becomes available to all who confess that Jesus is Lord (2:38–9). The rest of the book of Acts is studded with references to the Spirit filling, empowering, and directing the early church's life and mission.

While Luke records the historical march of the Spirit, the Pauline epistles develop a rich theology of the Spirit. For Paul, life in the Spirit is the all-encompassing mode of Christian existence. Therefore to be "in Christ" – a favorite Pauline locution signaling new creation (see 2 Cor. 5:17) – is synonymous with being "in the Spirit" (e.g., Rom. 8:9–11), since union with Christ can be experienced only in the Spirit, in the "Spirit of life in Christ Jesus" (Rom. 8:2). Indeed, Paul even states that "the Lord is the Spirit" (2 Cor. 3:17), placing the Holy Spirit and Christ in the most intimate relationship, since Christ is the Lord of the new age of the Spirit, the new creation. The Holy Spirit mediates the presence, power, and life of Christ in the world in inauguration of that new creation and anticipation of its full realization. It is in this eschatological vein that Paul calls the Spirit the "firstfruits" of the glorious redemption that is to come, for which the whole creation pines (Rom. 8:18–25), as well as a "seal" and "deposit" guaranteeing this inheritance to come (Eph. 1:13–14).

The Spirit therefore qualifies every aspect of Christian existence, since life "in the Spirit" contrasts with life "in the flesh" – that is, life outside of God and Christ, life lived by human strength alone, which leads to sin and death (e.g., Rom. 8:1–13).[5] It is the Spirit who indwells the believer, whose body is the temple of the Holy Spirit (1 Cor. 6:19), and who is the source of the "fruit of the Spirit" (Gal. 5:22ff.). Life in the Spirit is life in the "body of Christ," Paul's favorite image of the church, since the Spirit vivifies and unifies the community of Christ (e.g., Rom. 12:4–8; 1 Cor. 12:17–31). It is the Spirit who empowers the church with special gifts (*charismata*) for ministry (Rom. 12:3–8; 1 Cor. 12:4–30) and impels the church to worldwide mission. In sum, the Holy Spirit is the all-encompassing power who animates new life in Christ, who personally represents Christ, and as such is the agent and medium of the new creation.

The personhood and deity of the Holy Spirit

As we noted already in our discussion of the Trinity, the Holy Spirit's status as both personal and divine is much more elusive than in the case of Christ. In the OT, the Spirit is susceptible to a mere *dynamistic* or impersonal

---

[5] See Rudolf Bultmann, *Theology of the New Testament*, trans. Kendrick Grobel, 2 vols., (New York: Scribner, 1951–5), 1: 232ff.

interpretation, as simply representing Yahweh's divine presence or power. Yet there are exceptions to this rule, as when the OT suggests, for example, that the Spirit instructs (Neh. 9:20), guides (Ps. 143:10), or even grieves (Isa. 63:10), which constitute more *animistic* or personal descriptions. We also note in this connection the tendency of intertestamental wisdom literature to personify the Spirit, primarily as a "she." Whether this is sheer poetics or a movement toward the hypostatization (personalization) of the Spirit is debatable, though in the case of the rabbinic doctrine of the Shekinah, it seems to veer toward the latter (see p. 114 above). While the Spirit in the NT still often appears in dynamistic mode, as the power of the Father or Son, the NT also significantly deepens the personalization of the Spirit. Luke's record of the work of the Spirit in Acts, for example, predicates a variety of personal traits of the Spirit. There the Spirit speaks (1:16), is lied to (5:3), is tempted (5:9), bears witness (5:32), is resisted (7:51), snatches (8:39), sends (13:4), thinks good (15:28), forbids (16:6), prevents (16:7), and appoints (20:28) – all personal acts, examples of which can be multiplied from the breadth of the NT writings.[6] Especially noteworthy is the fact that the Spirit can be blasphemed (Mark 3:28–9; 12:32), which seems to require for the Spirit both a personal and a divine identity. In short, in the NT, the animistic or personal presentation of the Spirit is prevalent and persistent.

The evidence for the deity of the Spirit is also not as cumulative as in the case of Christ. There are no biblical texts that explicitly identify the Spirit as God. The one passage that has been rallied to this cause, "Now the Lord is the Spirit" (2 Cor. 3:17), is best understood in context as a statement of the mode of Christian experience of Jesus the Lord – that is, in the Spirit of the new covenant as opposed to the letter of the old. Moreover, the Spirit is not given any *titles* that intimate deity. Nor is there any direct NT evidence that the Spirit was *worshipped* along with Christ, whether through doxology or prayer.

But the Spirit does participate in the range of divine *functions*. We saw in the OT that the Spirit plays an integral role in creation (Gen. 1:2), especially if we allow for the Spirit's identification with God's Wisdom (Prov. 8). The Holy Spirit also plays a vital role in judgment (see John 16:8–11), and in re-creation (e.g., John 3:5–8). Since new creation is a pervasive soteriological theme in the NT, this includes the Spirit in the work of salvation, which, as with the other divine functions, can be performed only by God, even though the Spirit is never explicitly called Savior.

---

[6] See Wainwright, *Trinity in the New Testament*, 199ff.

As with the case of Christ, it is the Gospel of John that portrays the trinitarian person of the Holy Spirit with greatest distinction. John secures this distinction by analogy to the person of Christ when he depicts Jesus stating that after his departure the Father will send (literally) "another paraclete" (Gk. *parakletos* = advocate, counselor), implying that the Son is the first paraclete (14:15ff.; cf. 1 John 2:1). This is an eminently personal term, pronominalized as a "he" (14:16–17). The Spirit is the Paraclete (NRSV "Advocate") who proceeds from the Father (15:26) and is sent by Christ (16:7) to glorify the Son (16:14) by way of hearing and speaking what Christ directs (16:13–14), teaching and reminding the disciples (14:26), and convicting and judging the world (16:8–11). These sections of Jesus' farewell discourse (14:15–16:16) differentiate the Spirit's person and work from that of the Father and the Son, signifying that the Spirit is not merely their dynamic and impersonal power, force, or presence. In short, while John does not expressly say that the Spirit is God, the Spirit's divine personhood is strongly suggested by analogy to Christ.

Such an identity is implied even more by the wealth of triadic formulae and patterns spread throughout the NT witness.[7] As we argued in Chapter 5, over and over again, both explicitly and implicitly, the NT writings place Father, Son, and Holy Spirit together in the same breath. The most famous of these is the baptism formula of Matthew 28:19: "Go therefore and make disciples of all nations, baptizing them in the name of the Father and of the Son and of the Holy Spirit" (see also 1 Cor. 12:4–6; 2 Cor. 13:13; Rev. 1:4–5).[8] The name of the God with whom Christian believers identify and profess their allegiance is that of Father, Son, and Holy Spirit – the most proper name for God revealed in the NT.

In short, the NT is studded with triadic patterns, indicating that the Christian experience of God bears a distinct trinitarian impress. In this experience of God the Spirit cannot be reduced to the mere power of the Son or the Father, for the Spirit is "another Advocate." It may in fact be the inclusion of the Spirit in the triadic formulae and trinitarian name that accounts for the lack of more specific deity claims for the Spirit, since, unlike the case for the Son, who was quite evidently human, the Spirit would be considered divine by mere trinitarian association. These then are the basic biblical materials that would eventually lead to the creedal claim that the Spirit is a personal divine member of the Holy Trinity.

---

[7] Ibid., 237–47.

[8] The concentration of trinitarian persons in the book of Luke at the annunciation (1:35), the baptism (3:21–2), and, arguably, the transfiguration (9:28–35) of Jesus is also noteworthy.

HISTORICAL DEVELOPMENTS IN PNEUMATOLOGY

Given the diversity and complexity of issues surrounding the person and work of the Holy Spirit, we can only highlight some of the important historical developments in Christian pneumatology.

The patristic era to the Council of Constantinople

Writing in the third century, the early church father Novatian noted that the Spirit

> gives similar gifts, like jewels, to the Bride of Christ, the Church. He causes prophets to appear in the Church, instructs the Church's teachers, encourages tongues, obtains power and health, works wonders in the Church, brings about the discernment of spirits, helps those who govern the Church, inspires the Church's councils and dispenses the other gifts of grace. In this way, he perfects and completes the Church of Christ everywhere and in all things.[9]

While Novatian gives evidence of a vital spiritual dynamic in the life of the patristic church, Montanism was an early movement that pushed the limits of pneumatic experience. Beginning in the mid-second century, Montanus and his followers Priscilla and Maximilla laid claim to a special indwelling of the Paraclete and to new revelations, including prophecies that the end of the world would occur with the descent of the New Jerusalem in Phrygia, Asia Minor, in 177. Montanist enthusiasm for immediate experience of the Spirit spread throughout the Mediterranean basin, disrupting many area churches. Montanism was eventually deemed heretical, with the result that almost all historical assessments of it are negative. A notable exception to this judgment, however, is found in Tertullian, who was attracted to this movement especially for its moral discipline and ascetic rigor, if not also for its charismatic claims and sense of eschatological urgency. The Montanist movement prompted further theological reflection on the question of spiritual authority both in relationship to the institution of the catholic church (i.e., the emerging episcopate or hierarchy of bishops) and the biblical writings (i.e., the developing canon).

Irenaeus' notable reflections on the Holy Spirit were forged in combat with gnosticism toward the end of the second century. In his argument against the gnostic bifurcation of the God of the OT (the inferior

---

[9] Novatian, *De Trinitate Liber*, ch. 29, quoted in Yves M. J. Congar, *I Believe in the Holy Spirit*, trans. David Smith, 3 vols. (New York: Seabury, 1983), 1: 68. Congar's work, together with Heron, *Holy Spirit*, serves as an important source for this historical section.

Demiurge) and the God of the NT (the loving God of Jesus Christ), he made special appeal to the Spirit. Inclined to the tradition that associated the Spirit with Wisdom, Irenaeus considers the Spirit/Wisdom one of the "two hands" of the Father, along with the Son/Word, through which God created all things.[10] As he did with Christ, Irenaeus accords to the Spirit a role in both creation and redemption, as the Spirit who is given to all whether "by way of creation, the gift of being" or "by way of adoption, the gift of rebirth as sons of God."[11]

It was the Arian crisis, however, that particularly sharpened the debate concerning the Spirit's divine status and place in the Trinity. Once Jesus the Son was recognized to be of divine status, the question turned to the relationship between the Spirit and the Father and Son. As he did for the deity of Christ, Athanasius also contended for the Spirit's deity. Against a group known as the Tropici, who in the vein of the Arians held that the Spirit was an angel-like creature, Athanasius argues in his *Letters to Serapion* for the triadic tradition of the church as rooted in the NT and as particularly expressed in the baptismal formula (Matt. 28:19). In Athanasius' view, since it is the Spirit who sanctifies or deifies us, uniting us to God and making us partakers of the divine nature, the Spirit must also share by nature in the being of Father and Son. Against a similar group called the Pneumatomachians (literally, "fighters against the Spirit"), the Cappadocian fathers took up and expanded Athanasius' arguments for the deity of the Spirit, with Gregory of Nazianzus even directly calling the Spirit "God" and extending the Nicene *homoousios* also to the Spirit.[12]

The Cappadocians considerably influenced the pneumatological deliberations at the ecumenical Council of Constantinople (381). Whereas the creed that issued from Nicea in 325 only tersely affirmed: "And [we believe] in the Holy Spirit," the second ecumenical council, convened to unite the eastern church in the Nicene faith, expanded the confession of the Spirit. The Niceno-Constantinopolitan Creed reads: "And [we believe] in the Holy Spirit, the Lord, the giver of life, who proceeds from the Father, who together with Father and Son is worshipped and glorified, who spoke through the prophets."[13] In this fashion, the Nicene Creed recited today affirms the deity of the Spirit by attributing to the Spirit a divine title ("the Lord" – based on 2 Cor. 3:17), the divine function of creating and re-creating ("the giver of life"),

---

[10] Irenaeus, *Against Heresies*, 4.20.1.
[11] Ibid., 5.18.2. Quoted in Heron, *Holy Spirit*, 65; see more broadly 64–7.
[12] Gregory of Nazianzus, *Theological Orations*, chs. 10–11 (pp. 199–200).
[13] "The Niceno-Constantinopolitan Creed," in Henry Denzinger, ed., *The Sources of Catholic Dogma*, trans. Roy J. Deferrari (St. Louis: Herder, 1957), 35.

and the honor of divine worship ("who together with Father and Son is worshipped and glorified"). The Cappadocians' technical formula for the Trinity, three *hypostaseis* (or *prosopa*) and one *ousia*, also clearly assumes the distinct personhood of the Spirit. From the time of Constantinople on, the Spirit's full personhood and divine nature have been confessed in formal analogy to that of Christ the Son.

The emphasis in the Cappadocians and other eastern fathers on deification – as a deliverance from corruption and mortality through the renewal of the image of God – would place the Spirit front and center in Eastern Orthodox spirituality as the agent of participation in the divine life.

Augustine, the West, and the filioque clause

Early in his theological career, Augustine noted that "many books have been written by scholarly and spiritual men on the Father and the Son ... The Holy Spirit has, on the other hand, not yet been studied with as much care."[14] Augustine set out to rectify this lacuna. Among his various reflections, which range over the course of many works, Augustine's most important and concentrated pneumatological contribution is found in his *On the Trinity*. There, one of his favorite psychological analogies for the Trinity was that of the *mind*, its *knowledge* of itself, and its *love* for itself (Books IX and X), which also correlated with his analogy of *lover, beloved,* and the *love* they share (Book VIII). These analogies reinforced for Augustine a view of the Spirit primarily as the "bond of love" (*vinculum caritatis*) shared by Father and Son. Augustine thus emphasized the unifying character of the Spirit, not only for the Father and Son relation, but also for the relationships between the church and Christ, the soul and God. Given his dominant psychological model, Augustine concludes that the Spirit proceeds not only from the Father, but also from the Son, as the love they share.[15] Augustine makes this claim not only with reference to the *economic* Trinity – the Trinity of revelation and redemption, for which he adduces a number of biblical passages that indicate that the Son is also the giver of the Spirit (e.g., John 20:22; Acts 2:37–8) – but also with reference to the *immanent* Trinity – that is, concerning the eternal trinitarian relations in God. Just as the Son is eternally begotten from the Father, so also the Spirit eternally proceeds from the Father *and* from the Son.

[14] Augustine, *De fide et symbolo*, 9.18–19, quoted in Congar, *Holy Spirit*, I: 77.
[15] Augustine, *Trinity*, 15.29.

It was thus Augustine's influence that accounts for the western addition of the *filioque* – "and the Son" – to the Nicene Creed, which originally stated that the Spirit "proceeds from the Father" alone. As a clear implication of Augustine's trinitarianism, with considerable biblical evidence (that is, post-resurrection), the *filioque* clause first appeared in local church liturgies in Spain as a way of combating a residual Arianism, since the assertion that the Holy Spirit proceeds *a patre filioque* – "from the Father and the Son" – reinforces the deity claim for the Son. The *filioque* was eventually adopted by local councils, such as the Council of Toledo (589), and was formally added to the creed in the West in 1014 by Pope Benedict VIII. This creedal addendum became the focus of the theological debate that led to the formal split between the western Roman Catholic Church and the eastern Byzantine Orthodox Church in 1054, churches that for years had been developing their own distinctive theological ethos, due in no small measure to linguistic, ethnic, and cultural differences (see pp. 456–8).

The eastern church objected to the *filioque* clause for a number of reasons. Besides the ecclesiastical objection that it involved a unilateral act of the West and therefore constituted an unecumenical tampering with an established, authoritative council, the East regarded the *filioque* as theologically suspect for (1) endangering the monarchy of the Father as the fount of divinity and personal unity of the Godhead, (2) blurring the distinction between Father and Son, and (3) unduly subordinating the Spirit to the Son. The subsequent argument over the *filioque* has been intense, complex, and sometimes even pedantic. Since much of this debate concerns two differing models of the Trinity – roughly, the Augustinian and the Cappadocian – we shall briefly take it up again in our systematic considerations in the context of renewed dialogue between East and West.

The Middle Ages and the Reformation

Augustinian trinitarianism and its *filioque* pneumatology became the mainstay of the Roman Catholic tradition. In the Middle Ages, Anselm and Aquinas added little to this framework by way of novelty, but did strengthen this basic position by way of their scholastic prowess. Beyond this mainstream Catholic theology, however, one might note some interesting reflections on the Spirit by some of the medieval mystics. Hildegard of Bingen (1098–1179), for example, was fond of conceiving of the Spirit as the "greening" power of God (for which she coined the Latin term *viriditas*) in highlighting the Spirit's fructifying presence in creation and in the life of the believer.[16] And Joachim of Fiore (*c.* 1135–1202) prophesied a coming new age of the Spirit based on a trinitarian scheme of history: the age of the Father (OT), characterized by slavish obedience to the law, is succeeded by the age of the Son (NT), characterized by the more intimate relationship of sonship, which will yet be followed by the age of the Spirit, in which the letter of the NT will be radically transcended by a time of freedom and universal love – the true maturity of humanity. Joachim's teachings greatly influenced the spiritual Franciscans, who considered this third millennial age to have dawned with St. Francis. Joachim's vision of a new historical epoch has also served as inspiration for a variety of reform and progressivist movements, influencing thinkers of the Renaissance, the Enlightenment, and beyond, and may even have inspired the terminology of "the Third Reich."[17]

Both Luther and Calvin agreed with established Catholic doctrine concerning the Trinity and *filioque*, but developed their own pneumatological accents based on their common reformational battlefronts – in contrast to the authority claimed by the Roman Catholic hierarchy, on the one side, and the new spiritual freedom claimed by various Anabaptist groups, on the other side. Based on his conviction of the sole authority of scripture, Luther argued for the liberation of the Spirit from the Catholic sacramental system, where he believed the Spirit's work was held captive to the institutional church as the dispenser of grace. At the same time, he argued against the *Schwärmer*, those fanatical enthusiasts who were claiming a libertine spirituality based on their own experience and interpretation of the Spirit. Luther thus argued for the complementarity of word and Spirit, asserting that

God only gives his Spirit of grace through or with the previously existing external word. This is our safeguard against the enthusiasts, in other words, those spirits who flatter themselves that they have the Spirit independently of the word or before it and who consequently judge, interpret and extend Scripture or the word of the mouth according to their will ... Everything that is said of the Spirit independently of this word and sacraments is the devil.[18]

Similarly, Calvin also emphasized the correlation of word (including sacraments) and Spirit, which work together hand in glove, since scripture's primacy and authority are authenticated by the "inner testimony of the Holy Spirit."[19] Calvin went on in his *Institutes* to elaborate in a rather

---

[16] See Veli-Matti Kärkkäinen, *Pneumatology: The Holy Spirit in Ecumenical, International, and Contextual Perspective* (Grand Rapids, MI: Baker Academic, 2002), 49–55, where he summarizes the pneumatological reflections of four medieval mystics: Hildegard of Bingen, Bernard of Clairvaux, Bonaventure, and Catherine of Siena.

[17] See Congar, *Holy Spirit*, I: 126–37.   [18] Quoted in ibid., I: 139; see also 138–41.

[19] See Calvin, *Institutes*, 1.7.4.

unprecedented way the work of the Spirit through the various moments of salvation – faith, regeneration, repentance, and the like (the so-called "order of salvation") – as fruits of our union with Christ (Book III) before addressing the "external means" by which the Spirit of God brings us and holds us in fellowship with Christ through the ministry and sacraments of the institutional church (Book IV). In this way Calvin accentuated both the word's (scripture's) authority over the church and the Spirit's unity with the word.

The Anabaptists, on the other hand, while associated early on with a number of extremist elements that helped to win them the title of "Radical Reformation," eventually gave rise to a variety of free-church traditions. To generalize, the Anabaptists intensified the reformational stress on the "priesthood of all believers" in structuring the church and interpreting the Bible, arguing for the primacy of the work of the Spirit through believers in the church and in relation to the word. While they held to the authority of scripture, they maintained that the word, originally inspired by the Spirit, would remain a dead letter unless illumined and appropriated in the believer's life by the work of the Holy Spirit.

Other Anabaptists allowed for a word of the Spirit not bound by the objective letter – especially a word of prophecy. George Fox (1624–91), founder of the Quakers, is an extreme example of this tendency. He rejected any established ministry or sacraments as structured means of the Spirit's work, and instead prescribed for Christian worship a silent listening to God via one's inner, divine light – a word which when received may be shared.[20] As a whole, however, Anabaptism gave birth to a number of free-church traditions that are variously structured – some more so, some less.

Modern developments

The rise of modernity brought shifting fortunes for pneumatology. Reacting to a perceived spiritual *rigor mortis* in the reformational churches due to their preoccupation with doctrinal orthodoxy (viz., the period of Protestant orthodoxy, or, more pejoratively, scholasticism), pietism became a movement of significant spiritual verve in the seventeenth and eighteenth centuries across the spectrum of Lutheran, Reformed, and Anabaptist churches, emphasizing the experiential dimension of Christian life. Meanwhile, the Enlightenment's rationalist challenge to Christianity and its doctrines, especially the Trinity, engendered a waxing unitarianism that

---

[20] See Congar, *Holy Spirit*, 1: 141–3.

demoted the Spirit from person to power – whether conceived of as the power of God the Father, the spirit of Jesus' life and teaching, or even the spiritual principle of a human life of virtue – an example of the latter being Immanuel Kant's low view of the Spirit within the framework of his reduction of Christianity to ethics.[21] Two particular reactions to this Enlightenment challenge are especially noteworthy in the saga of the Spirit.

The first is the reaction by Friedrich Schleiermacher, the "father" of modern theology, who early in his life was deeply impressed by pietism and later in his life by romanticism. In his attempt to root Christian theology in religious experience, especially the "feeling of absolute dependence" (see pp. 520–3), and as shaped by his Sabellian-tending approach to the Trinity, Schleiermacher conceived of the Spirit as the power of (the one person of) God that effected the unique and absolute "God-consciousness" of Jesus and that mediates this saving consciousness to us by means of the historical community of believers. In Schleiermacher's own words, "the Holy Spirit is the union of the divine essence with human nature in the form of the common Spirit animating the life in common of believers."[22] In other words, the Spirit is really the enlivening power of the church.

Second, Georg W. F. Hegel tried to take the Enlightenment rationalist challenge head on. Since for Hegel only the rational and historical are the truly real, he conceived of God as *Geist* – "Spirit" or rational "Mind" – which was dynamically unfolding in the process of history. Hegel believed that his integrative philosophy clarified the truth of Christianity as symbolized by the Trinity: abstract, ideal Being or Spirit ("thesis" or Father) must encounter the existence of the concrete, material world ("antithesis" or Son) in order to arrive at self-consciousness as Absolute Spirit in the process of world history ("synthesis" or Holy Spirit). This dialectical process of God's "trinitarian" self-realization takes place through the various expressions of human consciousness or spirit – such as culture, art, and religion. Thus Hegel conceived of the whole of history as a march of the Spirit. His pantheistic-tending philosophy, which virtually identifies the divine and the human spirit, would exert considerable influence in modern theology.

The philosophical-theological programs of Kant, Schleiermacher, and Hegel all influenced in various ways the nineteenth-century theological movement known as classic liberalism, as exemplified in the theologies of Albrecht Ritschl and Adolf von Harnack (see pp. 527–8). Since both Ritschl and Harnack considered the traditional doctrine of the Trinity to be overly fraught with metaphysical speculation, their pneumatological reflections

[21] See Kant, *Religion Within the Limits*, 65, 131n., 136 and n.   [22] Schleiermacher, *Christian Faith*, 569.

concern only the work (in negation of the person) of the Spirit, which they both nearly identified with the workings of the human spirit in the ethical project of the kingdom of God. The Holy Spirit *is*, in a sense, what human beings achieve in the "Christianizing" of society.

In line with his general assessment of liberal theology (as more preoccupied with anthropology than with theology), Karl Barth considered its anthropocentric pneumatology to be a domestication of the Holy Spirit within the confines of the human spirit – human consciousness, faith, and works – to the point that it jeopardized a true knowledge of God. In reaction Barth emphasizes God as "Wholly Other" and God's revelation in Christ as absolutely necessary for true and saving knowledge of God. Accordingly, in his revelational model of the Trinity (i.e., Revealer, Revelation, Revealedness), Barth set the Holy Spirit as God's third "mode of being" in complete disjunction to the human spirit. As the "subjective" reality of revelation (with Christ as the "objective" reality), the Spirit creates faith and sustains belief, but this is never a personal possession of the believer or a historically locatable experience. God always remains sovereign over revelation, the gracious act which manifests the single and indissoluble subjectivity of God as revealer (Father), revelation (Son), and revealedness (Holy Spirit).[23]

In addition to these developments in more academic theology, we must also note the phenomenal rise of Pentecostalism and present-day charismatic movements. Already anticipated in modern times by the "Irvingites," a London-based "pentecostal" church that followed the lead of Edward Irving (1792–1834) in claiming the powers of signs and wonders, tongues and healing, twentieth-century Pentecostalism traces its beginnings to revivals early in the century, such as Charles Parham's Topeka, Kansas, revival in 1901, and William Seymour's Azusa Street revivals in Los Angeles several years later.[24] Significantly informed by nineteenth-century Wesleyan-Holiness movements that laid stress on a "second work of grace" – a supernatural experience of instant and complete sanctification of the individual subsequent to justification – Pentecostal churches emphasized the "baptism of the Spirit" as a special experience subsequent to conversion, constituting a special empowerment of the Spirit and typically signaled by the ability to speak in other tongues. Pentecostalism spilled beyond the bounds of its own various

---

[23] See Barth, *Church Dogmatics*, I/1. While Barth does examine the Spirit more expansively in IV/1, §62; IV/2, §67; and IV/3.1, §72, he does so in a way that implies that Christ is the personal *agent* of the Spirit's work, leaving in doubt the Spirit's own personhood.

[24] See Kärkkäinen, *Pneumatology*, 87–98, whose treatment informs the following.

churches around the 1960s in what became known as the "charismatic movement." Given its trans-denominational character, charismatic theology is generally not as doctrinaire as the more established Pentecostal denominations – for example, in insisting on "baptism of the Spirit" as a distinctive experience subsequent to conversion and water baptism, or in insisting that tongues are a necessary sign of Spirit baptism. At the heart of their spirituality, Pentecostals/charismatics tout a supernatural encounter with God in both worship and daily life that includes manifestations of extraordinary *charismata* – the gifts of the Spirit, such as prophecy, healings, and speaking in other tongues. Due to their zealous commitment to evangelism, the Pentecostal and charismatic movements became in the twentieth century alone the largest single Protestant group (half a billion strong), the majority of whose members reside in the impoverished third world.

The Pentecostal/charismatic movement is certainly one of the reasons why the Holy Spirit has come into greater theological prominence in contemporary theology. A second major reason is the renaissance in trinitarian theology of the last four decades that we noted in Chapter 5. Since this renewal in Trinity doctrine was largely driven by a more differentiated understanding of the divine persons (as opposed to a "mere monotheism"), it naturally produced a renewed consideration of the distinct person and work of the Spirit. This in turn opened up a greater dialogue between East and West over the central theological topic of their centuries-old schism – the *filioque* clause. The Catholic, Lutheran, and Reformed churches have all formally engaged Eastern Orthodoxy in conversation over the *filioque* in the effort to speak a common Christian confession; and many individual theologians from a variety of church traditions have ventured their own mediating statements in this discussion, including Thomas Weinandy (Catholic), Wolfhart Pannenberg (Lutheran), Jürgen Moltmann (Reformed), and Dimitri Staniloae (Orthodox).[25] Discussion about the Spirit today has helped to unify the one, holy, catholic, and apostolic church – characteristics, interestingly, that make up a central feature of the "third article" of the Creed devoted primarily to the work of the Spirit. Such dialogue has also helped to clarify a more robust doctrine of the Spirit, so much so that in the following systematic section we will largely confine ourselves to a consideration of the key gains that have come out of this recent revitalization of pneumatology.

---

[25] For an examination of this ecumenical discussion, see Lukas Vischer, ed., *Spirit of God, Spirit of Christ: Ecumenical Reflections on the* Filioque *Controversy* (London: SPCK, 1981).

SYSTEMATIC CONSIDERATIONS

The filioque *clause*

We begin our systematic reflections with a consideration of the *filioque* clause, which has famously divided eastern and western Christianity for nearly a millennium. While the issues surrounding the *filioque* debate can quickly become complex, they involve at base a difference of trinitarian approaches and emphases (see pp. 123–8 above). The *filioque* addition is a logical implication of Augustinian trinitarianism, given its preference for the psychological-love analogy and strong emphasis on divine simplicity. By contrast, the *filioque* does not fit well with the contours of Cappadocian trinitarianism, given its greater differentiation of divine persons and its emphasis on the person of the Father as the fount of trinitarian life.

Given our preference for a social analogy of the Trinity, our kinship resides more with the Cappadocian than with the Augustinian orientation to the Trinity. This means that we are sympathetic to a revisionary approach to the *filioque* clause. While we do not agree with every feature of Cappadocian trinitarianism or every aspect of the Orthodox critique of the *filioque*, we do think that its addition has unduly subordinated both the person and the work of the Spirit to that of the Son.

Concerning the *person*, a social Trinity assumes and highlights the distinct and discrete personhood of the Spirit beyond that of being simply the "bond of love" between Father and Son. The latter image tends to conceive of the Spirit in a sheer dynamistic and therefore impersonal sense – as the power that unifies Father and Son. Concerning the *work*, a social model allows us to view the Spirit's contribution in a more discrete way. The tendency of *filioque* doctrine in the West has been to reduce the Spirit's work to that of *applying* Christ's accomplished work to the life of the believer and church, a work that has been summed up by the term *sanctification* (and its culmination in *glorification*). Though we wholeheartedly agree that this is an important component of the work of the Spirit, one that will be elaborated in the next chapter, this cannot be considered the only work of the Spirit. While there are NT texts (many cited by Augustine) which suggest that, in addition to the Father, the resurrected Son also gives the Spirit, to focus on those texts alone is to neglect the redemptive work of the Spirit *prior to* the incarnation – for which there is plenty of OT evidence – in addition to the essential work of the Spirit *in* the very life of Jesus the Christ or Messiah, by very title the one especially anointed with the Spirit. Our reflections on and preference for a kenotic christology are especially germane here, since that christological model attempts to capture the role of the Spirit in every facet of Jesus' life, from birth to resurrection. So while Jesus, the resurrected and ascended Lord, does indeed send the Spirit (John 16:7; Acts 2; cf. 1 Cor. 15:45), the Spirit's work does not originate here, but has from the beginning been involved in God's redemptive initiatives.

But the Spirit's work cannot be limited to that of redemption, even broadly conceived, for the Spirit also plays a vital role in creation. While this role has been variously acknowledged in doctrinal history, it has not always been fully appreciated, especially in the course of western theology. This is certainly due to a number of reasons – the high frequency of biblical references to the Spirit in the context of redemption, and the lingering gnostic tendency in the church that depreciates creation in general, in addition to the legacy of the *filioque* clause. But another contributing factor may be that creation has been largely seen as the domain of the Father, as the Father's work alone. To understand why this is the case, it is necessary to delve into the doctrine of appropriations.

Trinitarian appropriations

Concerning the Trinity, the doctrine of appropriations is the teaching that certain works of the Trinity toward the world – such as creation, redemption, and sanctification-glorification – are "appropriated" in theological discourse to one or another of the trinitarian persons because they seem "most appropriate" to that person. For example, since according to scripture the Son alone became incarnate and suffered bodily for our salvation, it seems most appropriate to attribute to him the trinitarian act of redemption. In similar fashion, creation was appropriated to the Father, and both sanctification and glorification were appropriated to the Spirit. The theory of appropriations was necessitated by the teaching that the operations of the Trinity toward the world (that is, outside of the inner trinitarian relations) are "indivisible" (*opera trinitatis ad extra sunt indivisa*). Given the assumption of divine simplicity, it was held that all things in God, that is, in the divine nature, are radically simple or singular, *except for* the distinguishing relations that internally differentiate the divine persons – that is, "relations of opposition" such as *paternitas, filiatio,* and *spiratio* that Father (paternity), Son (sonship), and Spirit (spiration or "breathing out") each uniquely possesses. Since they all share in the one singular nature (indeed, are each identical with it), Father, Son, and Spirit are all identically present as the One God works in the world, whether that be in creation, in redemption, or in sanctification. But since from the biblical record it appears to be the case, for example, that it was the Son alone who became incarnate, it is *appropriate* to attribute redemption primarily to him, even though the whole Trinity works indivisibly in redemption.

The doctrine of appropriations underscores the truth that the Bible presents a differentiated portrait of the works of the trinitarian persons. But this theory may not be necessary if one contests the doctrine of divine simplicity as an unwarranted philosophical intrusion into the Christian understanding of God, as we have already done (see pp. 104 and 132–5, especially the discussion of the western paradoxical Trinity). On the assumption of divine simplicity, one cannot *really* distinguish the persons in their operations in the world, since those works are performed indivisibly by the one divine nature. Hence appropriation becomes a necessary strategy in order to maintain the formal doctrine of the economic Trinity's resemblance to the biblical record. But if we are not constrained by the doctrine of divine simplicity, we need not make this tortuous move, whose logic, for example, led Augustine to the conclusion that the Son must have been actively involved in his own virgin birth![26] Rather, we may take the biblical record straight on as presenting three distinct but unified persons working cooperatively in the world, but in which operations one person may take the lead – as the Son does in redemption, the Father in creation, and the Spirit in sanctification and glorification. Even on a social model of the Trinity there is still the affirmation that the works of the Trinity are "indivisible," if this is understood as an indivisibility (i.e., unity) of *the persons* working cooperatively, and not the *divine nature* working indiscriminately as one. Creation, for example, is a trinitarian act in which all divine persons are involved, but which can be more discretely understood as orchestrated by God the Father, through the mediation of the Son, and performed in the power and energies of the Spirit. Similarly redemption has a "principal player" in the incarnation of the Son, and sanctification and glorification appear particularly spearheaded by the Spirit – even though these are all *trinitarian* acts, a cooperation of all trinitarian members, as are all of God's operations toward the world.

The traditional doctrine of appropriations, however, helped to reinforce the impression that the Spirit's work was both subordinate and subsequent to that of Father and Son, concerned "only" with sanctification-glorification. As a result, recognition of the Spirit's important role in creation suffered. One of the most important rediscoveries in the recent renaissance in trinitarianism and pneumatology is the role of the Creator Spirit.

---

[26] Augustine, *Trinity*, 2.9 (pp. 102–3).

Recovery of the "Creator Spirit"

Even though the vast majority of biblical references to the Spirit come in the context of redemption, we have seen that the OT locates the work of the Spirit first in creation. The Spirit's link with creation is reinforced in the OT if we associate the Spirit with the Wisdom of God resident in creation (e.g., Prov. 8), as we are inclined to do, but it is certainly strengthened by the Spirit's role in the new creation as anticipated in the OT and inaugurated in the NT. Analogous to the Spirit's function in creation, the Spirit plays a principal role in the new creation, which implies the unity and continuity of creation and redemption, rather than their separation as in gnostic thought, a point that Irenaeus emphasized early on. That the Spirit is not only the Redeemer Spirit but also the Creator Spirit has a number of important implications that will carry us through to the end of this chapter.

Jürgen Moltmann is one contemporary theologian who has emphasized the Creator Spirit in a strong trinitarian theology. His book *God in Creation* focuses on the Spirit in pursuit of a pneumatological doctrine of creation that recognizes the Spirit in all created things, and all of creation in God-the-Spirit. Such a program is continued in his most explicit pneumatology, *The Spirit of Life: A Universal Affirmation*, whose German subtitle (*Eine Ganzheitliche Pneumatologie*) is better translated as "A Holistic Pneumatology."[27] Here Moltmann argues that "the operations of God's life-giving and life-affirming Spirit are universal and can be recognized in everything which ministers to life and resists its destruction. This efficacy of the Spirit does not replace Christ's efficacy, but makes it universally relevant."[28] Moltmann forges a path between the antithetical approaches of Schleiermacher and Barth, between their exclusive-tending emphases on immanent human experience (human spirit) and transcendent divine revelation (God's Spirit), respectively – alternatives that have dominated twentieth-century discussions of pneumatology. By virtue of the Creator Spirit, however, Moltmann's path is to affirm God's *immanence* in human experience, and human *transcendence* in God: "Because God's Spirit is present in human beings, the human spirit is self-transcendently aligned towards God. Anyone who stylizes revelation and experience into alternatives, ends up with revelations that cannot be experienced and experiences without revelation."[29] With due recognition of the Creator Spirit, the wellspring of life and animating principle of all

---

[27] Jürgen Moltmann, *The Spirit of Life: A Universal Affirmation*, trans. Margaret Kohl (Minneapolis, MN: Fortress, 1992).
[28] Ibid., xi.   [29] Ibid., 7.

things, it becomes possible "to experience God *in, with, and beneath* each everyday experience of the world."[30] Only an appreciation for the cosmic breadth of the Spirit can overcome the gnostic reductionism of salvation, since the sanctifying Spirit cannot be divorced from the vivifying Spirit. Indeed, when dealing with "sanctification" – traditionally a category of Christian growth in faith, and largely conceived individualistically – Moltmann expands this notion creationally: "'Sanctification today' means first of all rediscovering the sanctity of life and the divine mystery of creation, and defending them from life's manipulation, the secularization of nature, and the destruction of the world through human violence. Life comes from God and belongs to God, so it has to be sanctified through the people who believe God."[31]

Eugene F. Rogers also intones a creational emphasis in his provocative *After the Spirit*.[32] Arguing as well for a more fluid understanding of the Spirit's relationship with Christ than the *filioque* has allowed – preferring John of Damascus's formulation, "the Spirit rests on the Son" – Rogers states: "To think about the Spirit, you have to think materially, because, in Christian terms, the Spirit has befriended matter. She has befriended matter for Christ's sake on account of the incarnation."[33] In reflecting on the distinctly trinitarian scenes of the annunciation, baptism, transfiguration, and resurrection, all of which narrate actions of the Spirit upon Christ's bodily existence, Rogers concludes: "Because this Spirit is the Creator God, the Giver of Life, it announces and sanctifies, transfigures and gives life to other human beings too and the whole world."[34] Examples of contemporary pneumatologies that emphasize the Creator Spirit could be multiplied. This recognition of the Creator Spirit is also deeply rooted in ancient forms of Christian piety, as shown by the tenth-century Latin prayer, "Come, O Creator Spirit, come":

> Come, O Creator Spirit, come,
> and make within our heart thy home;
> to us thy grace celestial give,
> who of thy breathing move and live.
>
> O Comforter, that name is thine,
> of God most high the gift divine;
> the well of life, the fire of love,
> our souls' anointing from above.

---

[30] Ibid., 34.　　[31] Ibid., 171.
[32] Eugene F. Rogers Jr., *After the Spirit: A Constructive Pneumatology from Resources Outside the Modern West* (Grand Rapids, MI: Eerdmans, 2005).
[33] Ibid., 58.　　[34] Ibid., 210.

Thou dost appear in sevenfold dower
the sign of God's almighty power;
the Father's promise, making rich
with saving truth our earthly speech.

Our senses with thy light inflame,
our hearts to heavenly love reclaim;
our bodies' poor infirmity
with strength perpetual fortify.

Our mortal foes afar repel,
grant us henceforth in peace to dwell;
and so to us, with thee for guide,
no ill shall come, no harm betide.

May we by thee the Father learn,
and know the Son, and thee discern,
who art of both; and thus adore
in perfect faith for evermore.[35]

Spirit and flesh

Part of Christian theology's problem in not recognizing the Spirit's and therefore God's presence in all created things has been the way that "spirit and flesh" (*pneuma* and *sarx*) in the NT have often been played off against each other, especially in interpretation of the Pauline epistles. Paul frequently denigrates "the flesh" – for example: "For I know that nothing good dwells within me, that is, in my flesh" (Rom. 7:18) – and presents "flesh" in antithesis to "the spirit" – for example: "For what the flesh desires is opposed to the Spirit, and what the Spirit desires is opposed to the flesh" (Gal. 5:17). While it is true that the term *sarx* can refer variously to the human body (e.g., Rom. 2:28; 1 Cor. 5:5), humanity in general (Rom. 3:20; Gal. 2:16), and therefore human life in all its "earthly" weakness and transitoriness (1 Cor. 15:42ff.), when contrasted with *pneuma*, Paul has a specific eschatological sense in mind. Since to be "in the Spirit" is to be in the new situation brought about by Christ's resurrection – that is, the new creation (Rom. 8:1ff.) – to be "in the flesh" refers to life in the old order of things, the old aeon characterized by human sin and rebellion. Such a contrast corresponds precisely to Paul's typology of the two Adams (Rom. 5:15–21; 1 Cor. 15:22). "Flesh" in contrast to "Spirit" therefore should not be confused with the material creation *per se*, as represented by the body; its

---

[35] This translation is from Robert Seymour Bridges and H. Ellis Wooldridge, eds., *Hymns: The Yattendon Hymnal* (Oxford: Oxford University Press, 1899).

theological sense is that of *sinful* human nature, as is conveyed in newer Bible translations such as the NIV. Without this eschatological qualification, the contrast with Spirit easily becomes susceptible to a gnostic interpretation.[36]

Holistic spirituality

What these trends in pneumatology, as represented by Moltmann, Rogers, and a host of others, rightly emphasize is a holistic spirituality and a sacramental view of life. If Christian spirituality (including belief, character, piety, behavior, and vocation) concerns life in the Spirit, and if the Spirit is not only the *Spiritus Redemptor* but also the *Spiritus Creator*, then the salvation accomplished by Jesus Christ that the Spirit applies to our lives (especially in sanctification) cannot be defined over and against the material creation, but should actually lead us more deeply and transformatively into that creation. The way of Jesus Christ is a way *in* this world, a "worldly spirituality" that concerns not only inner states of prayer and contemplation, but also noisy intersections of commerce and vocation. Wherever the Spirit is, and whatever concerns the Spirit, become in fact a matter of Christian spirituality. The breadth of one's total life context and the depth of the particulars that make up that context, from lofty experiences to the most mundane – these all become matters of life before the triune God: "Where can I go from your Spirit?" (Ps. 139:7).

The corollary to this holistic spirituality is a sacramental view of life. If the world's truth, goodness, and beauty reflect that of its Maker, who also resides within that creation principally in the person of the Spirit, then the whole world can be seen as a sacrament of God's gracious presence. Similar to formal church sacraments such as baptism and eucharist, where the common material elements of water, bread, and wine become means of grace, so too can the creational elements of the world at large in various sacramental densities point to, mediate, and participate in the life of the Creator, Redeemer, and Sanctifier of life. Such a sacramental spirituality is difficult to cultivate without a strong doctrine of creation, and difficult to sustain without a recognition of the personal presence of the Spirit at work in creation at large. With this holistic and sacramental spirituality in mind, there are two other implications of the Creator Spirit that we wish to briefly note – the theological resources this offers for (1) the ecological crisis, and (2) Christian dialogue with other religions of the world.

---

[36] See Herman Ridderbos, *Paul: An Outline of His Theology*, trans. John Richard De Witt (Grand Rapids, MI: Eerdmans, 1975), 64–8.

The Creator Spirit and the ecological crisis

We have already indicated in Chapter 6 how, by viewing creation as a trinitarian act, an appreciation of the immanence of the Spirit aids in re-envisioning the earth as God's world in view of the ecological crisis. These creational resources of pneumatology have been significantly taken up by many theologians today who are addressing our world's pressing environmental issues. One of the more daring proposals is that of Mark Wallace's *Finding God in the Singing River*, which, keying on the Creator Spirit, portrays the earth as "the green face of God." Taking a cue from the inaugural image of the Spirit in Genesis 1:2 as the "Mother Bird God" brooding over the world, Wallace reflects on the various incarnations of the Spirit in the primal elements of earth (as dove, Matt. 3:13–17), water (John 7:37–8), wind (John 3:6), and fire (Acts 2:1–4) to suggest that the Spirit is the "Earth God": "God as Earth Spirit, the compassionate, all-encompassing divine force within the biosphere who inhabits earth community and continually works to maintain the integrity of all life forms."[37] Wallace's work is but one of a host of projects that represent "the greening of theology" in which the person and work of the Spirit is key, echoing Hildegard of Bingen's verdant intuitions. And while a number of these proposals, including Wallace's, play quite loose with more orthodox trinitarian perspectives on the Spirit – endorsing a process panentheism or even pantheism – their insights can usually be accommodated within a more orthodox framework. Notably, many of these proposals have also found it helpful to conceive of the Spirit in more maternal or feminine terms, for which there is both biblical and historical precedent, especially in the Syrian Christian tradition, which identifies the Spirit with God's Wisdom and often calls the Spirit "Mother."

The Spirit and the world's religions

The recovery of the Creator Spirit has also become a prominent feature in the discussion of Christianity's relationship with other religions. While we take up this issue more fully in Chapter 14, the Spirit's complementary role in creation and redemption has become a powerful theological resource for engaging other religions – another pressing global development. Within the recent trinitarian renaissance, Catholic theologian Gavin D'Costa, following the lead of Vatican II, has been one of the first to develop an explicit trinitarian approach to Christianity's encounter with other religions. In his

---

[37] Mark I. Wallace, *Finding God in the Singing River* (Minneapolis, MN: Fortress, 2005), 6.

various writings, he appeals to a strong pneumatology in order to discern the ways that the triune God may be at work in other religions (whose approximate truths must be respected) as a basis for dialogue, mutual enrichment, and Christian witness.[38] On the Protestant side, evangelical theologian Clark Pinnock has also tackled this issue. In his *Flame of Love*, Pinnock takes up Karl Barth's end-of-life desire to see a dogmatics written from the perspective of the third article of the creed, as Pinnock develops a theology of the Holy Spirit through the variety of theological loci.[39] In so doing, he devotes entire chapters to "Spirit in creation" and "Spirit and universality." According to Pinnock, as the life-giver and universal divine presence, the Spirit sustains life, gives it meaning, and moves history toward the goal of participation in the trinitarian love of God: "By acknowledging the work of the Spirit in creation, we are actually allowed a more universal perspective where Spirit can be seen as seeking what the Logos intends and where one can believe and hope that no one is beyond the reach of grace. A foundation is laid for universality if indeed the Spirit pervades the world and if no region is closed to his influences."[40] Pinnock reasons that if it is the case that the Spirit is universally at work in the world doing the Trinity's bidding, then it should also be possible to see glimmers of this, of all places, in the area of religion. Such a conviction warrants an openness to how the Spirit may be working in other religions, creating points of contact and conditions for dialogue. Both Pinnock's and D'Costa's trinitarian pneumatologies as the basis of inter-religious dialogue constitute an "inclusivist" approach to other religions (see pp. 370–1).

We applaud all of these current emphases in the theological retrieval of the Creator Spirit. Given that many of these issues are still in a state of ferment and ongoing formulation, we have sought to present them as positive trends more than to adjudicate them as "dogmatic theses," many of which, due to their complexity, would require a more strenuous discussion. While the next chapter will concentrate on the Spirit's work of applying the redemption accomplished by Christ – what has traditionally been summed up by the term "sanctification" – we will conclude this chapter by discussing the other traditional appropriation of the Holy Spirit: the role of the Spirit in glorification, which is also an important implication of the Creator Spirit.

---

[38] See Veli-Matti Kärkkäinen, *Trinity and Religious Pluralism: The Doctrine of the Trinity in Christian Theology of Religions* (Burlington, VT: Ashgate, 2004), 67–80.

[39] Clark H. Pinnock, *Flame of Love: A Theology of the Holy Spirit* (Downers Grove, IL: InterVarsity, 1996).

[40] Ibid., 63.

The Spirit in glorification

Glory in its original Hebraic sense has to do with "weightiness" or importance, and can variously refer in the Bible to divine honor, splendor, power, or radiance. In the NT, "glory" becomes a way of talking about salvation as a matter of the creature's participation in the divine life. In systematic theology, glorification refers to the eschatological completion of salvation – the complete transformation and transfiguration of our bodies and the world whereby we are saved from the presence of sin, pain, and death in the new heaven and earth (see Rev. 21). Just as sanctification is rightly appropriated to the Spirit – as the lead agent – so also is the completion of that process, since the Spirit is portrayed biblically as the principal agent of creation's glorification. Such a role for the Spirit can be quickly glimpsed in Romans 8, a chapter that speaks much about the Spirit and much about glory. In a dense trinitarian statement, Paul asserts: "If the Spirit of him who raised Jesus from the dead dwells in you, he who raised Christ from the dead will give life to your mortal bodies also through his Spirit that dwells in you" (v. 11). As the agent of the resurrection (cf. 1 Cor. 6:14), the Holy Spirit is the dynamic source of the new creation. While that new creation has begun for believers, this is a process of salvation that is complete only in glorification: "And those whom he predestined he also called; and those whom he called he also justified; and those whom he justified he also glorified" (v. 30). So while believers have "the first fruits of the Spirit," the fullness of salvation takes place only with the "redemption of our bodies" (v. 23) – that is, in the resurrection. But this is not only a hope for believers; it is a hope for the entire creation. Speaking of this future glory, Paul states:

I consider that the sufferings of this present time are not worth comparing with the glory about to be revealed to us. For the creation waits with eager longing for the revealing of the children of God; for the creation was subjected to futility, not of its own will but by the will of the one who subjected it, in hope that the creation itself will be set free from its bondage to decay and will obtain the freedom of the glory of the children of God. (vv. 18–21)

It is for this liberation from sin into glory that both believer and creation at large groan (vv. 22–3). We should especially note in this Pauline chapter, a chapter that also speaks about the antithesis of "Spirit and flesh" (vv. 3–9), that it is the resurrection of the body that is the path to glorification, which, rooted in Christ's resurrection, provides the analogue for the transfiguration of creation itself. This emphasis on the material world once again underscores the continuity between the Spirit's creative and redemptive work as the Sanctifier and Glorifier of creation. Indeed, it is the original and abiding presence of the Spirit in a frustrated creation that especially gives poignant voice to creation's travail – be they the groans of a sentient believer or the less sentient creation.

In the following chapter we will highlight the Spirit's role in applying the accomplished work of Christ – the important moment of truth of the *filioque* and the trinitarian appropriation of sanctification to the "third" person of the Trinity, whose historical neglect and doctrinal under-appreciation are currently being remedied in contemporary theology.

FOR FURTHER READING

Congar, Yves M. J., *I Believe in the Holy Spirit*, trans. David Smith, 3 vols. (New York: Seabury, 1983).

Heron, Alasdair I. C., *The Holy Spirit* (Philadelphia: Westminster, 1983).

Moltmann, Jürgen, *The Source of Life: The Holy Spirit and the Theology of Life*, trans. Margaret Kohl (Minneapolis, MN: Fortress, 1997).

Rogers, Eugene F., Jr., *After the Spirit: A Constructive Pneumatology from Resources Outside the Modern West* (Grand Rapids, MI: Eerdmans, 2005).

CHAPTER 12

Dimensions of salvation

INTRODUCTION

The red thread that runs the length of the Jewish and Christian scriptures is the theme of salvation. The God of the Bible, revealed in the OT as Yahweh and in the NT as Father, Son, and Holy Spirit, is the saving God who brings *salus* – health and wholeness – to a world of sin, violence, and despair, the God who forgives sinners, brings justice to the poor, and encourages the downtrodden and weary. The biblical text as a whole can justly be regarded as a narrative of salvation – the story of the triune God's salvific initiatives, which begin with the covenantal election of Israel. The climax of this story is the provision of salvation for all people and all nations through the person and work of Jesus Christ, who is the fulfillment of the covenant. The dénouement of this story is the final eschatological restoration of God's saving kingdom, which we now anticipate in hope.

Given this central theme of the Bible, "salvation," quite understandably, has been a preoccupation of Christian theology and the church's mission. But the Christian church has at times conceived of salvation in rather narrow or reductionistic terms as, for example, a reality that concerns only the escape of the soul to heaven, or as a mere acquittal of human guilt for sin, or as a singular event of conversion – a rather glib transaction enacted by a formulaic prayer by which one "gets saved." As we will see, such conceptions are problematic because they reduce to a simple reality what is a rather complex, variegated, and multidimensional phenomenon. In the biblical witness, "salvation" and related terms are used in a wide variety of ways to refer to a full-orbed experience of forgiveness, righteousness, and wholeness.

For this reason, the basic strategy in this chapter is similar to our consideration of the work of Christ in Chapter 10. Just as we argued there that only a multidimensional understanding of the reconciling work of Christ does justice to the biblical complexity of the theme and the varied insights of the Christian tradition, so also here with the topic of salvation. Only by taking many complementary perspectives into consideration can one do justice to the biblical and theological profundity of salvation. Moreover, because it is Christ who accomplishes salvation, our historical and systematic examination of the "dimensions" of salvation in this chapter will be tightly connected to our narrative proposal in Chapter 10 regarding the work of Christ. We have already seen in that chapter how direct discussion of Christ's work slurs into considerations of soteriology (Gk. *soteria* = salvation). Conversely, we shall observe in this chapter that direct discussion of the key dimensions of salvation requires us to recall their corresponding moments in Christ's reconciling work.

A traditional way of relating the work of Christ to soteriology is to employ the distinction between redemption "accomplished" and "applied." This distinction serves well to connect the work of Christ to the work of the Spirit, for Christ "accomplishes" reconciliation and the Holy Spirit "applies" that salvation to people's lives. As the Redeemer Spirit, the Spirit's work is to make Christ known and to bind human beings to him. For this reason the Christian tradition has often understood soteriology to be about the Holy Spirit's work of actualizing the reconciling work of Christ in human life. Given this redemptive focus on the Holy Spirit, this chapter continues what was begun in the previous chapter, but now with a particular eye to what salvation itself looks like.

The distinction between redemption "accomplished" and "applied" becomes problematic only when it is construed in too wooden a fashion – for example, in overestimating the neatness of the distinction or in restricting the Spirit's work to the sphere of redemption. Close attention to the discussions in Chapter 10 (Christ's reconciling work), Chapter 11 (the person and work of the Spirit), and this present chapter (the Spirit's work of actualizing reconciliation), will show that the *accomplishment* and *application* of salvation are thoroughly interwoven. These interrelationships once again demonstrate the "webbed" nature of the various themes of systematic theology.

THE BIBLICAL BREADTH OF SALVATION

The traditional tendency in soteriology has been to regard salvation in rather individualistic and otherworldly terms. According to this view, salvation is predominantly a matter of a personal relationship with God that ensures one's happy existence after death. As a result, "getting to heaven" and "saving the soul" are often presumed to be the best short definitions for the theological term "salvation." This inclination, which reflects the lingering influence of gnostic tendencies in Christian theology (see pp. 153–5), obscures the fact that, while salvation is certainly portrayed in the biblical materials as having an eschatological component, it is first and foremost a reality pertaining to *this* world, one that certainly includes, but is never restricted to, individual human persons.

Salvation in biblical perspective

Old Testament

While in prison before his martyrdom at the hands of the Nazis, the German theologian Dietrich Bonhoeffer noted in his famous prison letters that the OT understanding of salvation was much more "earthy" in character than has been commonly recognized:

Does the question about saving one's soul appear in the OT at all? Aren't righteousness and the Kingdom of God on earth the focus of everything …? It is not with the beyond that we are concerned, but with this world as created and preserved, subjected to laws, reconciled and restored. What is above this world is, in the gospel, intended to exist *for* this world.[1]

Bonhoeffer's intuition is right on the mark, since the paradigm event of salvation in the OT is the exodus of the enslaved Israelites from Egypt, an event that obviously cannot be reduced to an otherworldly form of

---

[1] Bonhoeffer, *Letters and Papers*, 286.

salvation or interpreted as something pertaining solely to the "soul." As a matter of fact, the OT at large shows little if any concern for human existence beyond that of an earthly, embodied existence. More than anything else, the OT has a very this-worldly kind of rescue in mind when it speaks of "salvation." For example, when Moses and the people of Israel sing that "the LORD is my strength and my might, and he has become my salvation" (Exod. 15:2), they are celebrating Yahweh's works of liberation in the exodus, particularly the parting of the Sea of Reeds (vv. 4–10). When King David speaks of Yahweh as the "horn of my salvation" and as a "tower of salvation for his king" (2 Sam. 22:3, 51), he has in mind God's work of delivering him from his enemies. While such examples could be multiplied, the point should be clear: the OT generally sees salvation in quite mundane terms, a perspective that culminates in Isaiah's eschatological vision of a new heaven and *earth* (see Isa. 11:1–9; 65:17–25).

This does not mean, of course, that the OT never speaks of salvation in more personal and individual terms, for it is also concerned with the status of the relationship between sinful persons and the holy God. For example, in Psalm 51, David asks for forgiveness for his affair with Bathsheba and his successful plotting of her husband's death: "Wash me thoroughly from my iniquity, and cleanse me from my sin" (51:2). Here David calls God the "God of my salvation" (v. 14) and asks Yahweh to "restore to me the joy of your salvation" (v. 12). While "salvation" in these latter verses is still a this-worldly deliverance, it is closely linked to God's merciful forgiveness of sinful David from his personal guilt.

It is easy to see the OT connection between salvation as forgiveness or the restoration of holiness, and salvation as historical deliverance when we remember that creation is the realm of God's kingdom. When the Israelites cried out for Yahweh to release them from slavery or death at the hands of their enemies, they were calling for him to manifest the justice and *shalom* of his creational kingdom, which Israel as the particular chosen representative was called to herald. But David's plea for forgiveness clearly manifests the idea that his participation in God's broader divine purposes, especially as king of the covenant people, required his own holiness. Thus the "earthy" sense of salvation as the deliverance of the oppressed and the more personal sense of salvation as forgiveness of guilt converge in the broader notion of the kingdom of God. Salvation, therefore, is inseparable from Yahweh's "justice" and "righteousness" – both translations of the Hebrew *tsedaqah* – a righteousness and justice that not only forgives sinners but also insists on conditions of justice for the poor and oppressed (Pss. 146:7; 103:6; Deut. 10:18; Isa. 1:17). It is telling, for example, that Psalm 103's praise of Yahweh connects Yahweh's "vindication and justice for all who are oppressed" (v. 6) with the need for forgiveness of sins (vv. 8–13), and points to all of this as the establishment of Yahweh's kingdom (v. 19). In short, the OT ties together a broad sense of salvation as God's renewed reign over all creation with a more narrow sense of salvation as deliverance from oppressive captivity and the forgiveness of one's sin. Salvation has to do with health, well-being, rescue, forgiveness, holiness, justice, and ultimately with dwelling rightly within God's reign in creation.

New Testament

These OT themes are continued in the NT portrait of salvation, with some important christological developments and changed emphases. The earthy emphasis of the OT sense of salvation is best seen in the centrality of the resurrection of the body – rather than an emphasis on a disembodied immortal soul. This glorified existence of the person finds its proper home in a new creation, a new heaven and new earth (2 Pet. 3:13; Rev. 21). Jesus' own proclamatory focus on the kingdom of God is rife with the sense of salvation as the renewed creational reign of God in which right relations flourish between God, humanity, and the world at large.

Concerning this cosmic breadth of salvation, it is instructive to note the NT word for salvation, *soteria*. Literally denoting "safety" or "preservation," *soteria* in its broader connotation refers to a person's secure existence, protected from assailing powers (including death), enabling one to prosper. In certain contexts *soteria* appears to have the sense of "health" (e.g., Acts 27:34). As such, it can be understood as referring to the right ordering of the body, that is, to the harmonious integration of all organs such that the body functions properly. By broadening this analogy, it is possible to say that salvation in the cosmic sense of the "kingdom of God" refers to the harmonious interrelation of all reality, the balanced coexistence and flourishing of all creatures with their triune Creator. For example, Revelation 11:15 presents voices in heaven proclaiming: "The kingdom of the world has become the kingdom of the LORD and of his Messiah." Whatever salvation is, it cannot be divorced from the breadth of the kingdom of God, the most comprehensive context of salvation.

At the same time, the NT also speaks of salvation in a more personal and individual sense – that of the forgiveness of the person and her transformation into one who lives as a child of God. The NT use of "salvation" in this more personal sense is implied by the growing NT conviction that "salvation" is not only for the Jewish nation, but is also intended for the Gentiles – that is, for all humanity. The apostle Paul declares at the beginning of the letter to the Romans that salvation is for "everyone who has faith, to the Jew first and also to the Greek [i.e., Gentile]" (1:16). On the one hand, this extension of salvation to those outside of Israel presupposes a strongly personal sense of salvation – salvation is for persons, so it can be offered through Christ not only to the ethnic children of Abraham, but also to non-Jews. But, on the other hand, the more corporate and cosmic sense also applies here. If God's kingdom is not restricted to Israel, but through Christ extends to all the nations, to the ends of the earth, then salvation cannot be reduced to the individual rescue of persons, but must be seen as the transformation of all reality – persons, nations, structures, systems, nature, and the like.[2]

These suprapersonal dimensions of salvation in the biblical witness warrant emphasis, given the individualistic focus of much modern western Christianity. But at the same time, this should not obscure the personal sense of salvation in the NT. Romans 10:10, for instance, speaks of a person believing in Jesus Christ, resulting in righteousness, with the outcome being "salvation" (*soteria*). This shows that one's personal stance toward Christ – one's faith or lack thereof – is decisive in determining whether one is "saved" in the personal sense. But what exactly does this being "saved" involve?

The NT asserts throughout that salvation is something that is the result of the grace of God (see, e.g., Titus 2:11), which involves, among other things, faith (2 Thess. 2:13), repentance (2 Cor. 7:10), forgiveness of sins or justification (Matt. 26:28; Gal. 2:15–17), and the obedience and effort (Phil. 2:12) that are part of sanctification (2 Thess. 2:13). The NT also connects this present reality of salvation to its eschatological fulfillment in a new creation (see Rom. 13:11; 1 Pet. 1:5). Hebrews 9:28, for example, shows this eschatological tension in respect of the forgiveness of sins: "So Christ, having been offered once to bear the sins of many, will appear a second time, not to deal with sin, but to save those who are eagerly waiting for him." As an eschatological reality, "salvation" involves both transformation in the here and now *and* future deliverance from the powers of death. We are given "a new birth into a living hope" (1 Pet. 1:3), a hope for the rebirth of all creation (Jas. 1:18). As such, salvation is a reality with eternal consequences (Heb. 5:9). The Gospel of John in particular tends to use "eternal life" to denote salvation (e.g., famously, 3:16). That this cannot be taken reductionistically as sheer immortality or as an insurance policy for the soul is seen in John's qualitative description of

---

[2] This universal vision is implied by the opening chapters of Genesis (chs. 1–11), the so-called "all-nations narrative," which situates the story of Israel in the broader context of creation, implying that what happens to Israel through the covenant bears significance for the whole earth.

eternal life as relational knowledge of God through Christ (John 17:3). Such a characterization, of course, does not exclude everlasting life in the more literal sense of life after death, given the hope of the healing power of the resurrection (cf. 1 Cor. 15). But it also reminds us that the saving character of that eternal life resides in its communion with the triune God.

It is a clear teaching of the NT, therefore, that salvation is a personal reality. 1 Peter 1:9 for example, even uses the language, which became common in Christianity, of salvation of "souls." We must keep in mind, however, that "soul" (*psyche*) in the NT cannot ultimately be abstracted from the whole person, given the central NT hope of the resurrection of the dead. By remembering the broad biblical affirmation that the human being is inextricably linked to creation, we will guard against a gnostic or reductionistic construal of personal salvation. In other words, everlasting life for the person requires a renewed creation as its final context.

Personal and cosmic salvation

To summarize the foregoing biblical discussion: in Christian terms, salvation must be understood as a reality that is both *personal* – transforming human beings in their relations with one another and with God – and *cosmic* – extending to the heights and depths of all creation. The tendency of the theological tradition has been to focus on salvation of persons, a focus that will indeed occupy much of our attention in the historical and systematic section below. But just as human persons are creatures who flourish only in the context of creation as a whole, so also personal salvation makes sense only when seen against the backdrop of the salvation of all creation – the restoration of creation so that it fully becomes the kingdom of God.

These are the two key foci that encapsulate the particular and universal dimensions of Christian salvation. But a sub-category of the latter must also be recognized, one that has been more recently highlighted by political and liberation theologies in the global south – namely, the category of structural salvation (see pp. 560–5). This category refers to the fact that sin manifests itself in systemic and structural ways – such as in poverty, political oppression, sexism, racism, environmental exploitation, and the like. If salvation, ultimately speaking, concerns God's reign over all dimensions of creation, such that creational *shalom* is restored, then the restoration of political, economic, cultural, and social structures must be included. The new heaven and earth, after all, are symbolized in the book of Revelation as the New Jerusalem – the righteous civilization and city of God's dwelling (ch. 21). As we shall see below, the category of structural salvation has key implications for sanctification, wherein "saved" persons are called to participate, as agents of renewal, in God's broader work of transforming creation into the kingdom of God.

THE QUESTION OF THE *ORDO SALUTIS*

Having surveyed some salient features of the Bible's portrayal of salvation in both its particular and its universal dimensions, it is now possible to address the traditional question of the "order of salvation" (*ordo salutis*) – that is, the logical ordering of the key components of salvation with respect to the individual. The *locus classicus* for this approach is Romans 8:29–30: "For those whom [God] foreknew he also predestined to be conformed to the image of his Son, in order that he might be the firstborn within a large family. And those whom he predestined he also called; and those whom he called he also justified; and those whom he justified he also glorified." The project of looking to this and other such texts for an ordering of the realities involved in salvation has spawned a variety of proposals concerning the process of salvation, whose sequencing can often become rather lengthy and ornate. For example, John Murray specified the *ordo* as: calling→ regeneration→ conversion (including repentance and faith)→ justification→ adoption→ sanctification→ perseverance→ glorification.[3]

While the *ordo salutis* approach can become a problem if it reduces salvation to the individual, given the biblical breadth reviewed above we do see that the NT demonstrates a strong concern with the category of personal salvation. To that degree, and to the degree that the categories used in the *ordo salutis* are clearly attested in the biblical witness, they must be included in an account of the Christian doctrine of salvation. This approach is a significant improvement over the rather crass understanding of salvation as "getting saved" or "going to heaven" that is all too prevalent today, since the *ordo salutis* recognizes, at least on the personal level, that salvation is a multifaceted reality that cannot be reduced to only one thing. In it we see, among other elements, that salvation involves the initiative of God (calling), a particular attitude and stance on the part of the person (faith), a change in the self (regeneration), a new relationship to God (adoption), the forgiveness of sins (justification), and the moral and spiritual transformation of the person (sanctification), all of which will be incomplete until the eschaton (glorification).

---

[3] Cited in Anthony A. Hoekema, *Saved by Grace* (Grand Rapids, MI: Eerdmans, 1989), 12.

But this raises a critical question: are the concepts included in the *ordo salutis* sufficiently distinct from one another in scripture that they should be considered discrete categories? For example, is regeneration different enough from sanctification that it warrants its own category? Some theologians, such as John Calvin, see those terms as synonyms, in addition to being roughly equivalent to a third term – conversion.[4] In other words, the "order of salvation" approach sometimes ossifies rather fluid biblical terms into hardened systematic categories.

With these considerations in mind, in our historical and systematic section below, "Dimensions of salvation in historical and systematic perspective," we will present a pared-down *ordo salutis* with the following caveats. First, since we consider "election" to be a missiological category, we will not discuss "calling" here, but will subsume it under our discussion of election in the next chapter. Second, we will follow Calvin and treat regeneration and conversion largely as synonyms for sanctification. Third, we will not discuss "adoption" as a distinct reality, to be merely set alongside justification and sanctification, but will regard it as a comprehensive image that describes salvation as a whole. In fact, all of the elements of this "bare-bones" *ordo salutis* result from the Holy Spirit's work of uniting us to Christ in adoption as daughters and sons of the triune God. For this reason, we will first explore the notion of adoption as an all-embracing metaphor for the salvation of persons, before broaching the dimensions of salvation typically associated with the *ordo salutis*.

THE SAVING WORK OF THE HOLY SPIRIT: ADOPTION INTO THE TRIUNE LIFE

In a comprehensive sense, all of the dimensions of personal salvation can be tied together in the metaphor of "adoption" into the triune life. On this metaphor, the root meaning of salvation is fellowship with the triune God. But how is the sinner "adopted" into fellowship with the triune God? One key biblical answer, which became an important soteriological theme in the tradition, is that it is *union with Christ*, the eternally begotten Son, that effects our adoption as daughters and sons of the triune God. The apostle Paul in particular frequently speaks of salvation as a matter of being united to the very person of Jesus Christ. For example, in Romans 6, Paul claims that through baptism the Christian has been included in the death and resurrection of Christ, a union that gives hope of salvation: "If we have been united with him like this in his death, we will certainly also be united with him in his

---

[4] Calvin, *Institutes*, 3.11.1.

resurrection ... Now if we died with Christ, we believe that we will also live with him" (6:5, 8, NIV).

Paul links union with Christ to adoption when he speaks of the Holy Spirit as the "spirit of adoption" (Rom. 8:15) that enables people to have God as their Father: "For all who are led by the Spirit of God are children of God ... It is that very Spirit bearing witness with our spirit that we are children of God" (8:14, 16). This passage concludes with Paul's declaration that adoption includes the benefit of being "heirs of God" (8:17). But this inheritance is possible only because those heirs are "joint heirs with Christ" who suffer with him and therefore can expect to share in his glorification (8:17). In short, adoption as a child of God comes through union with Christ through the Spirit. In developing these metaphors Paul is offering a comprehensive description of the whole reality of salvation.

The idea of "union with Christ" became central for later Christian theologians such as John Calvin, who suggested that the work of Christ remains useless to the human person unless she becomes united to Christ: "As long as Christ remains outside of us, and we are separated from him, all that he has suffered and done for the salvation of the human race remains useless and of no value for us."[5] Following Paul and the Augustinian tradition, Calvin states that "the Holy Spirit is the bond by which Christ effectually unites us to himself."[6] For Calvin, salvation as a whole can be summarized as adoption by God through union with Christ.

Summing up the reality of salvation as adoption, we should note, requires speaking of the "saved" as children of *God the Father* through adoption with *Christ the Son* as empowered by the *Holy Spirit*. Thus salvation in Christian terms must be understood in a trinitarian perspective. Simply put, salvation is a matter of being ushered into the fellowship of the Trinity. This understanding of salvation is especially appropriate in view of the social model of the Trinity that we advocated in Chapter 5. If God is a community of three divine persons who are characterized by perfect, self-giving, and other-affirming love, it makes eminent sense that the Bible describes salvation as a matter of being invited into the trinitarian fellowship as "children of God." Such participation in the divine community, of course, does not mean that children of God cease to be creatures, but that their creaturehood is affirmed, renewed, and perfected by being brought into fellowship with their Creator – the triune God.

Since the triune God is undertaking the work of renovating all of creation into the kingdom of God, salvation as fellowship with God includes the

[5] Ibid., 3.1.1.   [6] Ibid.

fellowship of human beings with one another and with nature – *shalom* in a full-orbed sense. If salvation is ultimately the triune God's *creational* kingdom, adoption into fellowship with God also includes the human vocation toward, and fellowship with, all of God's creatures. Thus "adoption" is an apt image that brings together both the personal and the cosmic aspects of salvation. It is this larger context of adoption into the triune life that must be borne in mind for our historical and systematic consideration of the more particular dimensions of salvation that follows.

DIMENSIONS OF SALVATION IN HISTORICAL AND SYSTEMATIC PERSPECTIVE

In approaching the particular dimensions of salvation, our discussion here will take a lead from John Calvin's laudable minimalism with respect to the "order of salvation." As described above, Calvin claims that salvation is at its root the Spirit's work of uniting the believer to Christ. The result of this union with Christ is the double grace of *justification* and *sanctification*.[7] While these two are the key classic categories to describe personal salvation, we must first discuss the sign of "union with Christ," which, according to Calvin, as well as the majority report of the ecumenical Christian tradition, is *faith*.

Faith

Faith has always been considered a central facet of the Christian life – that is, the "saved" life. Thomas Aquinas, for example, described faith as the essential theological virtue that enables one to see and understand God's supernatural revealed truth.[8] The Reformation, however, heightened the emphasis on faith in order to stress that salvation is by God's grace through faith and is not achieved by human "works." Martin Luther, for prime example, was tormented by his inability to feel that he had done enough penance or ascetic practices in his life to merit God's grace. His theological breakthrough that precipitated the emergence of Protestantism was predicated on the insight that forgiveness (justification) cannot be earned, but only received: "Now because this must be *believed* and may not be obtained or grasped otherwise with any work, law, or merit, it is clear and certain that faith alone justifies us."[9] For Luther, "faith" is the opposite of "works." Faith is the great anti-work, a total disavowal of the abilities of the self in

---

[7] Ibid., 3.11.1; cf. 3.3.1. [8] Thomas Aquinas, *Summa Theologica*, 2a.62.3.
[9] Martin Luther, *The Schmalkald Articles*, trans. William R. Russell (Minneapolis, MN: Fortress, 1995), 6.

favor of full reliance on God and God's grace in Christ that comes by hearing the word. Faith is purely a *response* to God's active initiative (made possible by the Spirit), and never something in its own right.[10]

Calvin defines faith as "a firm and certain knowledge of God's benevolence toward us, founded upon the truth of the freely given promise in Christ, both revealed to our minds and sealed upon our hearts through the Holy Spirit."[11] According to Calvin's definition, faith is a trustful knowledge, involving both head and heart, of the fact that God loves humanity – a kind of trust that is possible only because of Christ's reconciling work and the Spirit's illumination. Calvin here defines faith in trinitarian terms, with special emphasis on the work of the Spirit.

The Reformation accent on faith as the fruit of the Spirit's work of uniting the believer with Christ coheres with the biblical understanding of salvation as a matter of God's gracious promise and faithfulness to the covenant – the covenant with Israel and ultimately through Jesus Christ with all creation. Genesis 15 recounts Yahweh's promise to the elderly and childless Abram that his descendants will be as numerous as the stars (v. 5). It is by this means that God will fulfill his earlier promise to Abram that "in you all the families of the earth shall be blessed" (Gen. 12:3). Despite the outlandish and incredible nature of the promise, Abram "believed the LORD; and the LORD reckoned it to him as righteousness" (15:6). The apostle Paul recounts this episode in making the claim that became so important for the Reformation, namely, that faith in Christ's grace, rather than performance of works of the law, is what brings righteousness (Gal. 3). That is to say, the response required of human beings in God's work of salvation, in both the OT and the NT, is faith. It is through faith that humanity can fulfill its commitments to the covenant with God that was begun with Abraham and was renewed and universalized in Jesus Christ. This is why the great twentieth-century theologian Karl Barth structured his mammoth discussion of the person and salvific work of Christ with a particular eye to the covenant, and highlighted faith as central to that covenant.[12]

In broader perspective, the centrality of "faith" as the sign of salvation and work of the Holy Spirit corresponds well to one of the "work of Christ" themes that we discussed in Chapter 10 above – namely, Jesus' life and

---

[10] See Paul Althaus, *The Theology of Martin Luther*, trans. Robert C. Schultz (Philadelphia: Fortress, 1966), 43–53.

[11] Calvin, *Institutes*, 3.2.7.

[12] For his own summary account, see Barth, *Church Dogmatics*, IV/1: 22–78.

ministry as a faithful recapitulation of the history of humanity. Jesus is the "last Adam" who retraced all the stages of human life, but did so obediently and faithfully, relying on God the Father in the power of the Spirit rather than on his own initiative. It is important to note in this vein that many contemporary NT scholars have come to the conclusion that Paul's use of the phrase "faith of Jesus Christ" (*pistis Iesou Christou*, in, e.g., Rom. 3:22; Gal. 2:16; 3:12), traditionally translated "faith in Jesus Christ" (with Christ as the object of faith) is more accurately rendered as "the faithfulness of Jesus Christ" (with Christ as the subject of faith).[13] What brings salvation is the faithfulness of Jesus, as God the Son, to the covenantal plan of God the Father. This is a salvific counterpoint to the First Adam's faithlessness and rejection of God's plan in Genesis 3. Jesus relies in faith on the Father's leading, even subjecting his own will to the Father's purposes (cf., e.g., Matt. 26:39). In light of this facet of the work of Christ, it is fitting that salvation involves human faithfulness in response to God's call of salvation through Christ's pioneering faithfulness to the covenant. With this in mind, we proceed to what Calvin called the "double grace" that resulted from the Spirit's work of awakening faith in the believer who is united to Christ and thereby adopted as a child of God.

Justification

The first component of this double grace is justification. In the minds of many people, justification is the central notion of salvation, since it often functions as a synecdoche for salvation in general. Even the apostle Paul in his lengthy discussion in Galatians 2 and 3 focuses on justification as the quintessence of salvation: "We know that a person is justified not by the works of the law but through faith in Jesus Christ" (2:16). In its most literal sense, "justification" refers to the "becoming just" or "becoming righteous" of the sinful human being. Ordinarily it is associated with God's forgiveness of sin through faith in Christ, because in forgiveness the unjust or unrighteous person is given a clean slate, as God ceases to hold sin against the sinner. But the precise manner in which the sinner is forgiven and thereby "justified" is a question whose answers have varied over the Christian centuries.[14]

---

[13] N. T. Wright, *Paul in Fresh Perspective* (Minneapolis, MN: Fortress, 2005), 112, 119–20. See also Richard B. Hays, *The Faith of Jesus Christ: The Narrative Substructure of Galatians 3:1–4:11* (Grand Rapids, MI: Eerdmans, 2002).

[14] On the history of the doctrine of justification see Alister E. McGrath, *Iustitia Dei: A History of the Christian Doctrine of Justification*, 3rd edn. (Cambridge: Cambridge University Press, 2005). Also see pp. 472–3, 475–6, and 482–4.

Thomas Aquinas, for example, regarded justification as an instantaneous movement from injustice (disorder in the person) to justice (proper ordering of the self in relation to God) that was made possible by an infusion of Christ's grace into the sinner through the church's sacraments. This infusion of grace made it possible for the sinful, disordered human will to turn away from sinful desires and turn back towards God. The result of this process is the forgiveness of sins – God's recognition and reward of the reordering or renewed "justice" of the human being.[15] As such, Thomas's understanding involves "merit," inasmuch as the immediate reason God forgives sin is that God recognizes the transformation that has taken place in the human will, such that it is once again "just." Since this merit is made possible only by the gracious work of the Holy Spirit, Thomas's view clearly avoids Pelagianism.[16]

Some views of justification in the centuries after Thomas, however, tended to accentuate the role of human merit in justification. Certain theologians, such as the late medieval adherents of the *via moderna* (often called the nominalists – see pp. 474–5), even claimed that God required human beings to turn minimally toward God of their own initiative in order to merit sanctifying grace which would enable further good works that would warrant forgiveness.[17] They argued that this was not a "Pelagian" view, because God's decision to accept people's own initiative was an expression of divine grace.[18] It was this sort of view that led the young monk Martin Luther to significant agony over whether he was performing the minimal good works necessary to merit grace.

In the context of his spiritual struggle to measure up to the divine standard, Luther came to a new understanding of justification that sparked the Protestant Reformation. According to Luther, justification cannot be "earned" by any works, but can only be received as a gift. For him, the righteousness of justification is better understood as

the confidence of the heart in God through Christ Jesus. Such confidence is accounted righteousness for Christ's sake. Two things make for Christian righteousness: Faith in Christ, which is a gift of God; and God's acceptance of this imperfect faith of ours for perfect righteousness. Because of my faith in Christ, God overlooks my distrust, the unwillingness of my spirit, my many other sins. Because the shadow of Christ's wing covers me I have no fear that God will cover all my sins and take my imperfections for perfect righteousness.[19]

---

[15] Thomas Aquinas, *Summa Theologica*, 2a.113.1.   [16] Ibid., 2a.114.3.
[17] McGrath, *Iustitia Dei*, 83–91.   [18] Ibid., 170.
[19] Martin Luther, *Commentary on Galatians*, ed. John Prince Fallowes, trans. Erasmus Middleton (Grand Rapids, MI: Kregel, 1979), 198.

In speaking of faith as being "accounted righteousness," Luther thinks of justification as a double "imputation" or "reckoning" (following the language in Genesis 15 and Romans 4). On the negative side, one's own sin is *not* "reckoned" as one's own, but is forgiven. On the positive side, Christ's righteousness *is* graciously "reckoned" to the believer – that is to say, God considers it as the believer's own. Justification therefore is entirely the act of God, who forgives the believer's sin on the basis of Christ's substitutionary death and views the believer as if she possesses the righteousness of Christ. In and of themselves, Christians are sinful; but when Christ's righteousness is imputed to them and they are forgiven of their own sin, they are justified. For this reason, in Luther's view, Christian existence is a paradox – the Christian is *simul iustus et peccator* (simultaneously justified and a sinner), sinful in his own right, but righteous in God's eyes.[20]

Most Protestant theologians followed the basic direction of Luther's view of justification. In this model, human works have no bearing on justification, since reliance on them to earn God's good favor (an impossibility) constitutes unbelief and serves only to earn condemnation. Justification, in short, is wholly the gracious act of God. From this perspective, any growth in human righteousness has to do with the *sanctification* that justification makes possible. While the Christian should strive to perform good works, such good works are no basis for justification – they belong instead to a different category.

More recently, however, a cadre of NT scholars have questioned whether this shunning of the relevance of human works to justification is in fact faithful to the teachings of the Pauline epistles. This so-called "new perspective on Paul" cautions us not to read Luther's particular understanding of justification back into Paul, since the Pauline conception of justification is much more nuanced.[21] E. P. Sanders, a foremost advocate of the "new perspective," argues that in Paul the judicial character of justification refers only to forgiveness (acquittal of guilt), not to a positive imputation of Christ's righteousness to the believer.[22] Therefore when Paul talks about "righteousness by faith," he is simply opposing the idea that obedience to the law is required to merit salvation.[23] Furthermore, according to Sanders,

---

[20] Martin Luther, *Lectures on Romans*, ed. and trans. Wilhelm Pauck, Library of Christian Classics (Philadelphia: Westminster, 1959), 125.

[21] This is especially important with respect to Romans 7, where the struggle described by Paul has been traditionally understood by Protestants (with Luther's own struggle in mind) to refer to the *Christian* struggle with sin, whereas most Pauline scholars today think that Paul is referring here to the *pre-Christian* struggle with sin.

[22] E. P. Sanders, *Paul and Palestinian Judaism* (Philadelphia: Fortress, 1977), 492, esp. n. 57.

[23] Ibid., 492.

Paul proclaims *salvation* by grace through faith, but also *judgment* by works. Good works do not earn salvation, but they are the condition of remaining in the covenant.[24] Christians are Christians by faith, to be sure, but they should still fulfill the covenantal law – a possibility only through faith.[25]

Most recently, N. T. Wright, another scholar who generally fits into the "new perspective," has interpreted Paul's view of justification by faith as an "anticipatory judgment" of the "eventual judgment which will be announced, on the basis of the whole life led, in the future."[26] The "whole life led" can be worthy of salvation because with faith comes the gift of the Holy Spirit, who makes good works possible. One is granted this anticipatory judgment of forgiveness because faith brings one into God's covenant people, which includes the vocation of participating in the mission of that people.[27] The faithfulness of one's participation in God's work through the Spirit is the basis of the final judgment that will come with God's new creation.[28]

Despite these disagreements in Pauline perspective, it remains the case that "justification" in all its orthodox formulations emphasizes *God's* gracious activity in the covenant rather than human activity. Faith is made possible by the Spirit as the person's acceptance of grace.[29] Thus it is appropriate that in his discussion of justification, Karl Barth emphasizes *God's* activity in the covenant. Justification, says Barth, represents God saying, "I will be your God." Justification is the triune God's gracious act of remaining faithful to the covenant and maintaining a relationship with sinful creatures who have spurned friendship with God.[30]

The atoning moment that corresponds to justification is Christ's substitutionary sacrifice on the cross. Because Christ takes the punishment that human beings owe, they are granted a forgiveness that they do not deserve. This sacrifice is acceptable to God because of the perfect life of Jesus that fulfills the covenant, just as forgiveness is appropriately granted to human beings who faithfully trust that Christ alone makes justification possible.

But with the covenant there is always the question of the behavior required of God's covenant partner. To put it simply, God's *justification* of the sinner also entails personal righteousness and works of love and *justice* as a faithful response. While the new perspective on Paul emphasizes that justification never stands independent of the works that God's grace makes

[24] Ibid., 516–17.
[25] E. P. Sanders, *Paul, the Law, and the Jewish People* (Philadelphia: Fortress, 1983), 93–114.
[26] Wright, *Paul in Fresh Perspective*, 57, cf. 148.   [27] Ibid., 147.   [28] Ibid., 121.
[29] Cf. ibid., 176.   [30] Barth, *Church Dogmatics*, IV/2: 499.

possible, traditional Catholic and Protestant theologies at their best have never totally ignored this connection. Traditional Thomistic Catholicism is formally similar to the new perspective's reading of Paul, although it ties forgiveness and becoming righteous more tightly to the sacramental system. Traditional Protestant theology, on the other hand, has simply considered works to belong to a different category, that of *sanctification*, which nonetheless is an inseparable and indispensable moment of salvation.

Sanctification

There is more to the salvation of the human being than forgiveness of sin. There is also the positive reality of being conformed in disposition and behavior to the image of Christ (see Rom. 8:29), which is typically called sanctification. In its most literal sense, "sanctification" refers to the process of becoming holy (Lat. *sanctus* = holy). As we saw above, Thomas Aquinas considered sanctification to be internal to the process of justification. As one's will moves toward God and away from sin, one becomes just. The new perspective on Paul also closely connects growth in holiness to justification – both as its fruit and as the basis of future judgment, which justification anticipates in forgiveness.

Traditional Protestantism, however, has remained wary of connecting any growth in righteousness or works to justification, given its dominant fear of works righteousness. But even so, justification and sanctification are not disconnected realities. For example, Calvin, as we saw above, considered sanctification as part of the "double grace" that flows from union with Christ by the Holy Spirit. Strikingly, he even discusses sanctification *before* justification, even though he clearly thinks of the latter as the logical ground of the former. According to Calvin, the essence of sanctification is *repentance*:

> The meaning is that, departing from ourselves, we turn to God, and having taken off our former mind, we put on a new [mind] ... [Repentance] is the true turning of our life to God, a turning that arises from a pure and earnest fear of him; and it consists in the mortification of our flesh and of the old man, and in the vivification of the Spirit.[31]

Sanctification or repentance is a turning to God that involves a transformation of the person, both outwardly in works and inwardly in the heart.[32] It consists of two basic movements: *mortification* refers to a dying to the self as one turns away from sin toward reliance on God; *vivification*

---

[31] Calvin, *Institutes*, 3.3.5.   [32] Ibid., 3.3.6.

signifies new life in the Spirit, coming alive to obedience as a new creation. Deeper and deeper recognition of how far one falls short of God's will and how greatly one needs Christ is thus a significant part of what constitutes growth in Christian holiness. The result of sanctification for Calvin is the restoration of the image of God – which he defined as true righteousness and holiness.[33] Yet Calvin scorns all forms of perfectionism, as if a Christian could achieve a sinless life this side of the eschaton (i.e., glorification): "But sin ceases only to reign; it does not also cease to dwell in them."[34]

Calvin is clear that justification is the ground of sanctification.[35] He maintains that sanctification is grounded in *grace*, since it is part of the "double grace" given through the Spirit's work of uniting the believer to Christ. Yet human effort and activity remain central to sanctification as fruits and works of the Spirit. Karl Barth put this relationship similarly: justification is the presupposition of sanctification, and sanctification is the goal of justification.[36] Barth's covenant-oriented discussion of salvation is once again helpful at this point. He interprets sanctification in terms of both humanity's privilege and its obligation as God's covenant partner. If justification emphasizes God's act of establishing and preserving the covenant ("I will be your God"), sanctification refers to God's act of enabling the fitting human response to Christ's grace ("You will be my people").[37] Sanctification, therefore, refers to *living as God's people* both ethically and spiritually as those who are grateful for the triune God's gift of reconciliation in Christ.

What does the life of sanctification involve? While the Protestant tradition has usually interpreted sanctification in individual terms as personal growth in piety and purity, liberation theology has instructively challenged the Christian church to remember the concrete, political, and often conflictual dimensions of sanctification. Highlighting its broader biblical sense, liberation theology insists that God's righteousness/justice not only justifies sinners, but also creates conditions of justice for the poor and oppressed. True sanctification, therefore, which is inseparable from justification, requires a "preferential option for the poor," that is, for the church to adopt the same disposition and ethical response that God makes on behalf of the downtrodden of the world.[38] Sanctification – living the Christian life responsibly and growing in holiness – requires an advocacy for the poor,

---

[33] Ibid., 3.3.8–9. For Calvin's discussion of the image of God, see 3.15.3–4.   [34] Ibid., 3.3.10–11.
[35] Ibid., 3.3.19–20.   [36] Barth, *Church Dogmatics*, IV/2: 508.   [37] Ibid., IV/2: 499.
[38] See Gustavo Gutiérrez, "Option for the Poor," trans. Robert R. Barr, in *Mysterium Liberationis: Fundamental Concepts of Liberation Theology*, ed. Ignacio Ellacuría and Jon Sobrino (Maryknoll, NY: Orbis, 1993), 235–50.

broadly conceived. As James reminds us, true religion involves not only personal holiness, but also social justice: "Religion that is pure and undefiled before God, the Father, is this: to care for orphans and widows in their distress and to keep oneself unstained from the world" (1:27). Seen in this light, it can be argued that justification, the assurance of forgiveness for sins, frees and empowers Christians for responsible ethical activity in sanctification beyond the paralysis of guilt. Living a concrete life of sanctification prevents justification from becoming what Dietrich Bonhoeffer called "cheap grace."[39] While liberation theology may at times insufficiently acknowledge the importance of justification/forgiveness of the sinful person, it must be credited with restoring in theology a more appropriate understanding of the particular works required for authentic sanctification in the broader structures of life.

Finally, it must be noted that the relationship between sanctification and justification parallels the relationship between the resurrection and the cross, since to become sanctified is to live in a way that corresponds to the new life made possible in Christ's resurrection (see pp. 281–2). This new life of sanctification can be realized only on the basis of the word of forgiveness in justification, which flows from Christ's substitutionary sacrifice on the cross. Being liberated from sin makes it possible to enter into the difficult task of participating in God's work of renewing justice, love, and life in creation. Such sanctification is a matter of following the example of Jesus Christ, who identifies with the "least of these" – the hungry, thirsty, stranger, naked, sick, and imprisoned (Matt. 25:31–46).

Cosmic salvation and personal vocation

Our discussion of the dimensions of salvation to this point has focused on the human being's appropriation of the benefits of Christ's work through the activity of the Spirit. Along the way we have pointed out the correspondences between these facets of soteriology and the moments of the work of Christ that we discussed in the last part of Chapter 10. Faith as a dimension of salvation, accordingly, was seen to parallel the faithfulness of Christ in his recapitulative life and ministry. Justification was shown to correspond to the substitutionary sacrifice of Christ's cross. And sanctification was described in terms that bear affinity to the resurrection of Christ and the liberative effects of a new creation.

---

[39] Dietrich Bonhoeffer, *Discipleship*, trans. Martin Liske, Ilse Tödt, Barbara Green, and Reinhard Krauss, ed. Geffrey B. Kelly and John D. Godsey, Dietrich Bonhoeffer Works 4 (Minneapolis, MN: Fortress, 2003), 43–4.

Although we took great pains earlier in this chapter to show that salvation is a reality that cannot be reduced to the personal or individual level, it is necessary to make that point once again by highlighting the broadest dimension of salvation. Since the horizon of Christ's work is the all-embracing kingdom of the triune God, the horizon of the dimensions of salvation is the all-embracing restoration of the cosmos. Salvation in its fullest, all-encompassing sense is the triune God's reclamation of all of creation as the kingdom of God. While one important component of that work of reclamation is the forgiveness and sanctification of individual persons, these personal dimensions of salvation fit in the context of God's larger work of renovating all of created reality. Again, liberation theology has emphasized this breadth, pointing out the social, political, and economic dimensions of salvation. As Jesus shows by his work for the kingdom of God, salvation includes the rescue of the poor and disadvantaged from the plight that keeps them from the abundance of life. God's work for the kingdom includes unifying divided societies, rectifying political corruption, and making unjust economic systems righteous, in anticipation of God's final eschatological salvation – the new creation – even if such work is not obviously visible here and now. The broad Christian conviction is that salvation applies to all creation, and that salvation is God's work in Christ through the Spirit.

However, human beings as the image and representative of the triune God are participants in God's renovation of all reality, partners in the building of the kingdom, a kingdom that comes only by grace, but a grace that invites and energizes the work of individuals and corporate humanity. Thus the forgiven sinner, who in faith is becoming more righteous through the process of sanctification, has in this process the *vocation* of participating in God's mission (*missio Dei*) in the world – the transformation of all reality, including the reconciliation of persons and social structures. The kingdom of God is first and foremost the gracious work of God and therefore a *gift*, achieved through the gracious election of Israel and the church through Jesus Christ, who is the personal embodiment of the kingdom and the foretaste of the kingdom's final form. The church, however, as the body of humanity graciously elected by God through Christ, possesses the calling (vocation) of participating in the coming of the kingdom through its work for the transformation of all dimensions of society. For example, in light of the looming ecological crisis, the concrete vocation of the church would certainly include making personal and political decisions that will preserve and restore the natural environment upon which all life depends. In short, the gift of salvation implies the vocational *task* of the church.

To summarize this scaled-down *ordo salutis*, the church is the believing body (faith) of humanity that has been forgiven on the basis of Christ's cross (justification), and is being made holy by the Spirit's power (sanctification), a holiness that is authenticated by works of love and justice within the world (vocation), in participation in the kingdom of God (new creation). Such dimensions, taken together, constitute salvation in a Christian sense.

CONCLUSION

As we noted at the outset of this chapter, Christian faith is a faith in God's salvation, for salvation is the theme that runs through the biblical narratives and binds the various Christian doctrines together. This chapter has described the triune God's project in the world as the renovation of persons and society, the scope of which is as wide as the creation itself. This salvation is made possible by the self-emptying grace and service of Christ, whose work makes forgiveness and liberation present in the world as the coming kingdom of God that is effected by the Holy Spirit. Thus many of the theological loci we have discussed in earlier chapters of this book have intersected with this chapter. This systematic intersection will continue to be visible in the chapters that are to come, for the visible body of the "saved" is the church of Jesus Christ (Chapter 13), whose mission embraces all nations (Chapter 14), in view of the eschatological horizon that promises the salvation of all creation (Chapter 15).

FOR FURTHER READING

Calvin, John, *Institutes of the Christian Religion*, trans. Ford Lewis Battles, ed. John T. McNeill, Library of Christian Classics (Philadelphia: Westminster, 1960), Book 3.

Gutiérrez, Gustavo, *A Theology of Liberation: History, Politics, and Salvation*, trans. Caridad Inda and John Eagleston, rev. edn. (Maryknoll, NY: Orbis, 1988).

McGrath, Alister E., *Iustitia Dei: A History of the Christian Doctrine of Justification*, 3rd edn. (Cambridge: Cambridge University Press, 2005).

Wright, N. T., *Paul in Fresh Perspective* (Minneapolis, MN: Fortress, 2005).

CHAPTER 13

The church and its mission

INTRODUCTION

The previous chapter emphasized that the triune God's gift of salvation extends beyond human persons to the heights and depths of creation itself. With this universal scope of salvation always in view, the primary focus of the biblical narrative is nonetheless on humanity, which specially bears God's image as the divine representative in creation. We have contended that this human image of God is a matter of the human community representing God's dominion in creation in a way that is faithful in its relationships with God, one another, and the natural order (see pp. 189–94). Accordingly, salvation cannot be seen in personal or individualistic terms alone, for God's saving work has always taken place through communities for the benefit of the world at large. In the OT the community of salvation was the nation of Israel, and in the NT it is the multicultural Christian *church*.

The theme of the church has been implicit throughout our exploration of Christian theology, even from the beginning, when we discussed the church as the primary audience of theology (pp. 19–20). In the present chapter we turn our attention more explicitly to the *doctrine* of the church or ecclesiology (Gk. *ekklesia* = church). We shall first explore the most basic question: What *is* the church? That discussion will naturally give rise to a second question: What is the church about, or what is it supposed to be *doing* – that is, what is its mission in the world?

THE NATURE AND IDENTITY OF THE CHURCH

The biblical witness

The very word that the Greek NT uses to refer to the Christian community, *ekklesia*, is instructive as a starting point for our inquiry into the nature and identity of the church. *Ekklesia* is a combination of two words, *ek* (out of) and *kaleo* (to call), suggesting that the church is a group of persons who have been "called out of" a larger group of people for a particular purpose. Long before the writing of the NT, *ekklesia* was the common Greek word used to denote an assembly of people.[1] It was accordingly the natural choice of the translators of the Septuagint (Greek OT) to render the Hebrew word for the assembly of the Israelites, *qahal*. In order to grasp the theological significance of the church as the people "called out of" the broader society to do God's work in the world, we first need to examine the role of the chosen community in the OT.

Old Testament
As we have seen repeatedly, the OT begins with a vision of all creation and all of humanity, the so-called "all nations" narrative of Genesis 1–11. Quickly thereafter, however, it turns its attention to a specific person, Abram, his family, and eventually the many-tribed nation constituted by the descendants of Abraham,

---

[1] See "Ecclesia," in Kittel and Friedrich, *Theological Dictionary of the New Testament*, II: 513–17.

whose new name, notably, means "father of many nations." From this juncture forward in the narrative, the main concern of the OT is this particular corporate body of people and its religious and political fortunes as a nation.

God's purpose in choosing Israel was to employ it as an instrument for reclaiming creation from its bondage and decay.[2] Yahweh's covenant with Abraham and his descendants is the means by which this particular people becomes God's agent for the blessing of all nations. Yahweh promises to be faithful to Israel, favoring and preserving her, and in turn calls the Israelites to be faithful and obedient: "I will indeed bless you, and I will make your offspring as numerous as the stars of heaven and as the sand that is on the seashore. And your offspring shall possess the gate of their enemies, and by your offspring shall all the nations of the earth gain blessing for themselves, because you have obeyed my voice" (Gen. 22: 17–18). The basic notes of the Abrahamic covenant – a fruitful progeny, an abundant and stable land, and blessing to the world at large – hark back to God's original blessing of humanity to be fruitful and cultivate the earth as a habitable home for the flourishing of all life (Gen. 1:26–8). Israel was to be instrumental in the renewal of this original blessing of creation.

Ironically, perhaps, Yahweh's redemption of all nations through Israel requires that Israel be set *apart* from the rest as a holy nation: "You shall be holy, for I the LORD your God am holy" (Lev. 19:2). Vast sections of the OT, most notably the book of Leviticus, describe in meticulous detail the ways in which Israel was called to distinguish itself from the surrounding nations. Israel's correct worship of the one true Creator God, and its moral behavior in which justice prevailed in society – in short, its holiness before God in all dimensions of life, instead of conformity to social norms and prevailing injustice – would be a beacon to the surrounding nations, calling them to such a way of life as well. One of the servant poems in Isaiah tersely combines these themes:

> Thus says God, the LORD,
>   who created the heavens and stretched them out,
>   who spread out the earth and what comes from it,
> who gives breath to the people upon it
>   and spirit to those who walk in it:
> I am the LORD, I have called you in righteousness,
>   I have taken you by the hand and kept you;
> I have given you as a covenant to the people,
>   a light to the nations,
>   to open the eyes that are blind,

---

[2] See Wright, *Paul in Fresh Perspective*, 121, cf. 38.

> to bring out the prisoners from the dungeon,
> from the prison those who sit in darkness.   (42:5–7)

But how exactly will Yahweh redeem creation through his servant Israel? Aside from the above-mentioned features of Israel's worship of the true God, her ethical conduct that includes the just treatment of the least fortunate, and her overall distinctive way of life, the OT does not explicitly spell out how Israel's election by Yahweh would effect the blessing of all creation. The OT focus is predominantly on political and spiritual Israel, in particular Israel's experience in and out of the "promised land," which the Jews regarded as central to their experience of Yahweh's favor.[3]

Bearing in mind the narrative placement of the initial announcement of the covenant to Abraham, however, can help with this matter of determining how Israel's election would bless all creation. Again, the introduction of the covenant comes in Genesis 12, right after the conclusion of the "all nations" narrative in the Tower of Babel episode (11:1–9) – the scene of the scattering of humanity, a judgment that accrues to the human hubris that attempts to unify itself without reference to God. Whatever else the election of Israel may signify, it must be seen above all as Yahweh's answer to the problem of a sinful humanity that has rebelled against God, distorted the goodness of creation, and become disjointed into countless factions – the legacy of Genesis 3–11.

And indeed, as the OT narrative progresses, more light is shed on the relationship between Israel and the nations. Through the course of the prophetic books, especially during and after the destruction of Israel in the north (eighth century BCE) and the exile of Judah in the south (sixth century BCE), the Jews developed an increasing sense that their faithfulness to Yahweh does not depend primarily on ritual sacrifice *in* the temple *in* the promised land, but that faithfulness to God's law is possible anywhere, even in exile. And it becomes clearer and clearer that Yahweh's covenant purposes with the nation of Israel cannot in fact be restricted to Israel, for the ultimate goal of the Abrahamic covenant is God's mission to the nations. This is the lesson of the prophet Jonah, whose reluctance to preach to the Ninevites and chagrin at their repentance functions as a critique of Israel's dereliction in mission. Given this default of covenantal responsibility, a new covenant is envisioned (see Jer. 31), a covenantal renewal that not only has ethnic Israel as its covenant partner, but embraces all nations in creation. How is that new covenant enacted? The NT answers: through the

---

[3] See Walter Brueggemann, *The Land: Place as Gift, Promise, and Challenge in Biblical Faith*, 2nd edn. (Minneapolis, MN: Fortress, 2002).

incarnation, life, death, and resurrection of Jesus Christ. The NT multicultural church then becomes the renewed people of Israel who bear witness to that covenant and its incarnational mission.

New Testament

When Jesus began his public ministry, one of his first acts was to call together a band of close followers, his disciples (see, e.g., Matt. 4:18–22). Through a variety of experiences, these disciples came to regard Jesus not only as an amazing teacher, but eventually as the unique representative of Yahweh – the Messiah or Christ – and ultimately as the veritable Son of God. The disciples' faith in Jesus waxed and waned in their time with him – waning significantly after the crucifixion when the one they had trusted and followed was dead; but waxing joyously in light of the resurrection when the crucified one was restored to life and shown truly to be the Son of God. Despite the ebb and flow of their faith in Jesus, the disciples served throughout his ministry as his close confidants and special agents in extending his work on behalf of the kingdom of God (cf. Mark 6:7–13).

The disciples' role as followers of Jesus came especially into its own after his ascension, when they were designated *apostles* (Gk. *apostoloi* = those who are sent), the representatives of Jesus charged to bring the gospel of Christ to the ends of the earth. Jesus' parting command to them, known as the Great Commission, instructs: "All authority in heaven and on earth has been given to me. Go therefore and make disciples of all nations, baptizing them in the name of the Father and of the Son and of the Holy Spirit, and teaching them to obey everything that I have commanded you. And remember, I am with you always, to the end of the age" (Matt. 28:18–20). Thus the apostles are those who are "sent" to spread the gospel of Jesus Christ throughout the nations. They do so in the physical absence of Christ, yet in his presence through the power of the Holy Spirit (see John 14:15–17). The story of Pentecost recounts how the Spirit fills and empowers the fledgling church in order that it might faithfully carry out its mission (Acts 2:1–4). Through the power of the Spirit the church of Christ, founded on the apostles, is sent into the world to continue the mission of Christ, whom Hebrews calls *the* apostle sent from the Father (3:1).

The book of Acts narrates the history of the primitive church carrying out its mission "to the ends of the earth" (1:8). It begins with a small gathering of Jesus' followers in Jerusalem led by the apostle Peter's mission to the Jews (1:4–14), and ends with the church's presence in Rome, the very center of the civilized world, through the work of the apostle Paul to the Gentiles (28:16–31). In being "sent" by the risen Christ and the Holy Spirit on its worldwide mission, the church understands itself in "missional" terms (Lat. *missio*, from *mitto* = to send = Gk. *apostello*). Like OT Israel, the NT church is the community of persons who serve as Christ's representatives in the world; it is the community that is "elect" not for its own sake but for the sake of the world that God loves and is in the process of redeeming through the covenant in Christ. 1 Peter states: "But you are a chosen race, a royal priesthood, a holy nation, God's own people, in order that you may proclaim the mighty acts of him who called you out of darkness into his marvelous light" (2:9). Similar to Israel, whose social-ethical conduct (such as care for the alien and orphan) was to be a "light" to the nations, the church – as the renewed Israel – is called by 1 Peter to "conduct yourselves honorably among the Gentiles, so that, though they malign you as evil-doers, they may see your honorable deeds and glorify God when he comes to judge" (2:12).

Just as the work of Jesus was to establish and proclaim the kingdom of God – the Trinity's dynamic reign in history – Jesus' mandate for his disciples as contained in the Great Commission is best seen as the call to participate in the advent of this kingdom. Indeed, the things that Jesus commanded his followers to do are concrete ways of witnessing to that kingdom. Take, for example, Matthew's Sermon on the Mount, where the church is enjoined to witness to God's kingdom in various ways, such as by mourning the world's evil and suffering with creation (5:4), yearning for righteousness (5:6), working for peace (5:9), modeling reconciliation in a world of festering hatred (5:23–6; cf. 6:14–15), reflecting God's faithfulness in human relationships (5:31–2), loving enemies and shunning vengeance (5:38–43), and doing God's work humbly (6:1–6). In sum, witnessing to the kingdom means doing the will of God in every dimension of life (see 7:21–3). And like the nation of Israel before her, the church's work in the world as the servant of the triune God requires special concern for the weak and disadvantaged. The striking parable of the sheep and the goats makes this clear, as Jesus reminds his disciples/apostles that "just as you did it to one of the least of these [the hungry, thirsty, strangers, naked, the imprisoned] … you did it to me" (Matt. 25:40). In short, according to the NT, the church is that community of people that continues the apostolic mission of following Jesus by being sent into the world to make God's kingdom known in both word and deed. In carrying out this work as God's renewed covenant people, the church is frequently called by Paul the "church of God" (e.g., 1 Cor. 11:22).[4] While this appellation reminds us that the church is not first

---

[4] See "Ecclesia," 506–7.

and foremost a human enterprise, as God's agent in the world, the work of the church is concretized only through human action.

Key biblical images

Given this glance at the place of the church in the biblical narrative, it is possible to highlight some key scriptural images of the church that have come to have special prominence for conveying the church's identity and role in the world. One central image that accents the continuity of the Christian church with the chosen nation of Israel is that of the "people of God." Throughout the OT, Israel is considered to be Yahweh's special people, elect among the nations in order to bless and restore creation through the covenant.[5] All of the variants of this phrase in the OT stress the communal nature of the covenant and the special significance of the congregation of Israel. This communal emphasis finds its way into the NT portrayal of the church, as reflected in the 1 Peter passage cited above: "But you are a chosen race, a royal priesthood, a holy nation, God's own people ... Once you were not a people, but now you are God's people" (2:9–10). That such OT language is used for the Christian church is all the more remarkable given that this letter appears to be directed toward a Gentile audience (see 1:18). Other NT texts also pick up on this imagery, which connects the church to Israel as God's people through the renewed covenant. Paul, for example, speaks of those who trust in Christ rather than the law as "the Israel of God," referring to both Jew and Gentile (Gal. 6:16; cf. Rom. 9:6). The "people of God" image underscores the church's status and task as God's covenant people in continuity with the Abrahamic covenant.

A second central NT image, the church as the "body of Christ," stresses the church's newness in the Christ event. While this metaphor also captures the communal character of the church – many parts but one body (1 Cor. 12:12ff.) – it especially underscores the fact that the church is not the "people" or "community" of God apart from its particular relationship to Jesus Christ. While Paul obviously uses the term "body of Christ" to refer to Christ's incarnate, human existence (e.g., Rom. 7:4), he also uses it as a metaphor to describe the church as the continuing presence of Christ in the world (1 Cor. 12:27). In some mysterious but concrete way the church is a sacrament of the incarnate Christ by virtue of its corporate identity and mission of continuing the work of its ascended Lord. Importantly, as the *body* of Christ, the church cannot be understood

---

[5] E.g., Deut. 7:6; 2 Sam. 7:23; Isa. 40:1; cf. the covenant formula of Exod. 6:7.

apart from reference to its *head*: "We must grow up in every way into him who is the head, into Christ" (Eph. 4:15). Only in vital connection with the head can the members of Christ's body function fruitfully: "From [Christ] the whole body, joined and knit together by every ligament with which it is equipped, as each part is working properly, promotes the body's growth in building itself up in love" (4:16).

Ephesians links together the themes of continuity and newness that we see in "people of God" and "body of Christ" by means of a third image, the "household of God."[6] The members of the Gentile church are "no longer strangers and aliens, but ... citizens with the saints and also members of the household of God, built upon the foundation of the apostles and prophets, with Christ Jesus himself as the cornerstone" (2:19–20). This declaration also suggests that the human situation of disunity and discord under sin, as symbolized by Babel, has been remedied by Christ, who creates "in himself one new humanity" (2:15). The NT contains a host of other metaphors and images in referring to the church.[7]

Central biblical images of the church have given rise to particular models of the church's self-understanding and practice. Catholic theologian Avery Dulles has helpfully identified and addressed five of these dominant models in the history of the church. The church, he suggests, can be seen as: (1) *institution*, which emphasizes its visible organization and structure; (2) *mystical communion*, which highlights its dynamic community as the body of Christ; (3) *sacrament*, which accents its role as the visible and gracious presence of Christ in the world; (4) *herald*, which concentrates on its work of proclaiming the gospel; and (5) *servant*, which emphasizes the church's mission of service to the world.[8] While different church traditions may incline to one or another model, Dulles irenically contends that all of these models have their legitimate place as complementary facets of the ecumenical church of Christ.

The Nicene notes of the church

Although various theologians and traditions have emphasized different images and models of the church, there is a general consensus in the

---

[6] Cf. Lesslie Newbigin, *The Household of God: Lectures on the Nature of the Church* (London: SCM Press, 1957).

[7] See Paul S. Minear, *Images of the Church in the New Testament*, New Testament Library (Louisville, KY: Westminster John Knox, 2004). In addition to "people of God" and "body of Christ," Minear devotes considerable attention to "new creation" and "fellowship in faith," while identifying a total of ninety-six images of the church.

[8] See Avery Dulles, *Models of the Church*, rev. edn. (New York: Doubleday, 2002), chs. 2–6.

Christian tradition, at least formally, about what the church should be *like*.
When asked what characteristics ought to typify the faithful church of
Christ, the most common answer points to the Nicene Creed, which affirms
belief in "one, holy, catholic, and apostolic church."[9] These attributes of
unity, holiness, catholicity, and apostolicity are commonly called the
Nicene "marks" or "notes" of the church. However, while the Christian
tradition has formally agreed *that* this is what the church ought to look like,
it has not always agreed materially on *how* exactly to understand these notes.

Unity

There are thousands upon thousands of Christian churches in the world.
However, a central theological conviction is that there is but *one* church of
Jesus Christ. The term "church," therefore, is used both for the plurality of
local churches, and also for the single church of Christ that has many
instantiations. Here the problem of the "one and the many" is an ecclesiological problem. How are the diverse "local" churches related to the one
"worldwide" church? How is it the case that the church is *one* when we see
so many churches and confessional traditions throughout the world and
in history? This issue is especially problematic in the schismatic age of
"denominationalism" that has come to pass since the Reformation era.
Prior to the Reformation, at least in the West, the unity of the church
appeared more straightforward, for one pointed to the Roman Catholic
Church as *the* one church of Christ. The Reformation, however, precipitated a turn of events that eventually produced the Lutheran, Reformed,
Anglican, Mennonite, Baptist, and Methodist traditions, among many
others, most of which are further subdivided.

But the picture of a strongly unified church before the Reformation is
itself something of an illusion. Since the eleventh century the Roman
church has existed in division from the Eastern Orthodox church – a schism
that formalized deep cultural, political, and theological differences that had
existed for centuries before their official split in 1054 (see pp. 456–8).
Moreover, from the early history of the church one can point to sects that
diverged from mainstream theology and church practice (such as the
Ebionites and the Monophysites; see pp. 426, 454–5). When branded as
"heretical," these groups were considered by the "orthodox" to be unchris-
tian or extra-ecclesial, thus posing no problem for ecclesiastical unity. Such
heterodox groups, however, considered themselves to be faithful followers
of Christ, and therefore regarded themselves as the one true church over and

---

[9] "Niceno-Constantinopolitan Creed," in Pelikan and Hotchkiss, eds., *Creeds and Confessions*, I: 163.

against the "apostate" mainline church. The point here is this: the divisions that have plagued the church from its very beginnings, and which today are as evident as ever, pose the very concrete question as to where the unity of the church is to be found.

Since the late nineteenth and early twentieth centuries, the ecumenical movement (Gk. *oikoumene* = world) has addressed this question by attempting to repair – piece by piece – the shattered unity of the church. The largest and best-known ecumenical body, the World Council of Churches, describes its mission as follows: "to call one another to visible unity in one faith and in one eucharistic fellowship, expressed in worship and common life in Christ, through witness and service to the world, and to advance towards that unity in order that the world may believe."[10] In partial fulfillment of this goal, the ecumenical movement has fostered the reunion of some previously estranged denominations (e.g., in the United States, several Methodist denominations joined together to form the United Methodist Church). Even when not leading to tangible institutional unity, the ecumenical movement has often facilitated theological dialogue and understanding that has enabled centuries-old disagreements to be relativized in the hope that divergent church bodies would at least be able to work together for Christ in the world. One significant example of such dialogue is the *Joint Declaration on Justification* by the Lutheran World Federation and the Catholic Church, which facilitated closer agreement on a central doctrine that has famously divided these churches for almost half a millennium.[11]

Despite all of the important progress made by ecumenical efforts over the past century or so, the Christian church remains painfully divided and fragmented. Traditions battle with one another over basic Christian doctrines and practices. Currently, many denominations are considering splitting over divisive issues, such as the morality of homosexuality. Denominationalism, it seems, in spite of its obvious affront to the unity of the church, is alive and well. This is not to mention the all too apparent but seldom acknowledged division within the Christian church between the poor and the rich – between those who lack the basic necessities for life and those whose possessions and economic power far surpass the category of "needs." As noted in Chapter 2, one of the challenges facing the church and its theology in our time is the continuing existence of mass poverty. Currently Christianity is experiencing

---

[10] World Council of Churches, *Constitution and Rules of the World Council of Churches*, available at www.oikoumene.org/index.php?id=2297, accessed November 18, 2008.
[11] The Lutheran World Federation and the Roman Catholic Church, *Joint Declaration on the Doctrine of Justification* (Grand Rapids, MI: Eerdmans, 2000).

a boom in places with high levels of poverty, such as Africa (see pp. 373–4). How then is there *one* church of Christ when it includes astoundingly wealthy congregations and astonishingly impoverished churches on both the global and local level? And what about the glaring racial divisions found in the churches of many communities, where Sunday morning worship remains one of the most segregated hours of the week?

The solutions to such problems are never simple; and the theological response to such a complicated socio-political problem is not obviously apparent. For this reason, it is important to remember that the unity of the church should not be located primarily in the churches themselves. Ultimately, the unity of the church can be found only in its head, Jesus Christ. It is *Christ*, the Lord over the church and whose gospel is to be proclaimed in all of the churches, who constitutes the unity of the church. To the degree that the churches proclaim one faith in Christ, they possess a confessional unity: "There is one body and one Spirit, just as you were called to the one hope of your calling, one Lord, one faith, one baptism, one God and Father of all, who is above all and through all and in all" (Eph. 4:4–6). But in fidelity to the one Christ's lordship, it is the church's responsibility to strive for ever more concrete and visible signs of its unity in Christ. In short, the unity of the Christian church is caught up in the eschatological tension of the already and the not yet. In Christ, the head of the church, we have a promissory glimpse of the unity of the church that will be completely realized only in the fulfilled kingdom of God. Until then, the work of growing up into this unity and forging ever more authentic unity is an ongoing task for the church.

Holiness

The second Nicene note of the church is holiness. As we saw in our biblical discussion above, the nation of Israel was called to be holy – set apart in reflection of her covenant God so as to be a beacon to the nations: "You shall be holy, for I the LORD your God am holy" (Lev. 19:2; cf. 11:44 and Isa. 42:5–7). That central OT refrain is echoed in the NT, as the church is also called to be holy in imitation and representation of the Holy Trinity (see, e.g., 1 Pet. 1:16). But descriptively speaking, this characteristic of the church also seems to be lagging, as the church all too often is anything but holy. It is easy to amass evidence of the church's unholiness. One can quickly recall the ways in which the church has even participated in egregious evils, such as its active promotion of the medieval Crusades or its passive silence in the face of the Holocaust (not to mention the recent genocides in Bosnia, Rwanda, and Sudan). How, then, is it possible to speak of the church as holy?

This question not only reverberates in today's church but is as old as the church itself. For example, the Donatist conflict in the fourth century (see pp. 445–6) was concerned with the holiness of the church. In their zeal for the church's purity, the Donatists considered church leaders who had renounced their faith under persecution to be "traitors" to Christ – even if it was only a momentary lapse that they later regretted. The Donatists considered them to be unholy and therefore an affront to the purity of the true church. This became especially important on a practical level when the Donatists argued that sacraments performed by such "traitor" clergy were invalid because of their forfeited holiness. In the Donatist view, priests ordained by apostate clergy should be replaced by priests who had been ordained by unstained bishops.

While this controversy started early in the fourth century, it was still being sharply debated when Augustine became a bishop in North Africa in 395. Augustine took the Donatists to task, claiming that they were locating the identity and holiness of the church in the wrong place – in sinful human beings, rather than in the sinless one, Jesus Christ.[12] Certainly there are hypocrites in the church, Augustine maintained, but ultimately God is the only one who can distinguish between true and false believers. It is incumbent upon Christians to trust that the visible church is a communion of saints which manifests God's work, and especially to trust in Christ as the one who himself constitutes the church's holiness. For that reason, sacraments performed and received with right intentions, even if administered by sinful clergy, were considered by Augustine to be valid.

Augustine points us in the right direction on the question of how the church is holy. From a sheer empirical perspective, there are countless ways in which the church is quite unholy, and has even been complicit in some of history's most shocking evils. But from a theological perspective, as the body of its head, Jesus Christ, and the adopted people of the triune God, the church is in a derivative sense holy because *God* is holy. If the church's identity comes from outside of itself – from the triune God – then the church possesses a kind of alien holiness. It is then an ongoing task for the church to become a holy community in actuality, to grow in sanctification through the renewing energies of the Holy Spirit. In other words, the gift of Christ's holiness becomes a project for the church: learning to live out that holiness in more faithful ways in its interaction with the world, the world to

---

[12] For an example of his basic approach, see Augustine, *On Baptism, Against the Donatists*, trans. J. R. King, in *Nicene and Post-Nicene Fathers*, 1st series, ed. Philip Schaff (Grand Rapids, MI: Eerdmans, 1993), IV: 411–514.

which the church has been sent out with the gospel. As with the note of unity, holiness has an eschatological texture, for the church is always "on the way" to embodying in reality this characteristic that it has in Christ, but which it will not completely possess until the fullness of the kingdom comes.

Catholicity

The third note of the church mentioned in the Nicene Creed is catholicity. The word "catholic" is best understood as "universal," which means that this characteristic overlaps somewhat with unity.[13] The term originally referred to the extension of the church as a whole in both time and space, meaning that various instantiations of the church from different ages and in different locales are still the one church of Jesus Christ. "Catholicity" was later commonly used to refer to orthodox as opposed to heretical forms of Christianity. Combining these two senses, this note emphasizes that the church that is spread out through time and space is nonetheless the *same* church of Christ, largely because of the doctrinal and missional continuity of the universal church. In specifying *how* this is true, Roman Catholic theologian Hans Küng describes catholicity as follows: "The catholicity of the Church ... consists in a notion of entirety, based on identity and resulting in universality."[14] Rather than focusing on the temporal and spatial connections of the universal church, Küng helpfully focuses on the church's identity as the body of *Christ*. The catholic church is the church with a worldwide mission, whose identity in Jesus Christ connects it with the church of all times and places in doing the work of God. Once again, similar to the first two notes of the church, we see that the church's catholic character is grounded in its head – Jesus Christ. And once again, the church sounds these notes only in eschatological relief, as it grows into the likeness of the triune God. The church's catholicity creates space (and makes time) for all Christian churches – Orthodox, Catholic, Protestant, and other Christian traditions – to be members of the body of Christ, the catholic church.

Apostolicity

The final Nicene note of the church is apostolicity. This characteristic has traditionally referred to the link between the present church and the church's foundations, indicating that the authentic church of Christ here

---

[13] For a helpful discussion of this term, see Edmund P. Clowney, *The Church*, Contours of Christian Theology (Downers Grove, IL: InterVarsity, 1995), 90–8.

[14] Hans Küng, *The Church*, trans. Ray Ockenden and Rosaleen Ockenden (London: Burns & Oates, 1967), 296–313, quotation at 303.

and now is connected to the age of the apostles in which the Spirit of Christ was active in a special way in the establishment of the church. However, there are various ways to understand the church's connection to the apostles. In the patristic era it was common for theologians, such as the apostolic fathers, to connect the identity of the church to the apostles by pointing to the leaders of the church – its bishops – as the successors of the apostles. For example, Ignatius of Antioch wrote in the early second century: "For when you obey the bishop as if he were Jesus Christ, you are (as I see it) living not in a merely human fashion but in Jesus Christ's way ... It is essential, therefore, to act in no way without the bishop ... Rather submit even to the presbytery as to the apostles of Jesus Christ."[15] From this starting point, the idea developed that the church was "apostolic" because its leaders, the bishops, could be traced back along a line of succession to the first apostles themselves. This became known as the idea of "apostolic succession."

This idea presents several problems. For one, it is unlikely that the line of succession is pristine or unbroken, despite the claims of some, especially in the Roman Catholic and Orthodox traditions. For another, on this view all other traditions, such as the Protestant churches, must be regarded as "non-apostolic." For these reasons, it is more common today in Protestant churches for "apostolicity" to be understood in terms of the church's foundational message. That church is apostolic which faithfully proclaims the *teaching* of the apostles. That is to say, it is the proclamation of Jesus Christ in word, sacrament, and deed that constitutes the apostolicity of the church.

While this modification is a helpful first step, it is insufficient for a full appreciation of the church's apostolicity. It is also necessary to recapture a second meaning of "apostolicity" that centers on the literal sense of the word itself – "sent." The "apostolic" church is the body that is sent into the world to do God's work; it is the "missional" church.[16] To be apostolic is to be grounded in Christ's gospel (as witnessed and transmitted by the apostles) and to be engaged in the task of taking that gospel – in word and deed – into the world to which the church is sent by the Holy Spirit as Christ's representative. Thus this final Nicene note describing what the church should be like broaches our next topic – namely, what the church is called to be doing in the world.

[15] Ignatius of Antioch, "Letter to the Trallians," in *Early Christian Fathers*, ed. Cyril C. Richardson, Library of Christian Classics (Philadelphia: Westminster, 1953), 98–9.
[16] See Darrell L. Guder and Lois Barrett, eds., *Missional Church: A Vision for the Sending of the Church in North America* (Grand Rapids, MI: Eerdmans, 1998).

THE MISSION OF THE CHURCH

While the preceding has considered the question of what the church *is*, we have already seen that this first question is inseparable from a second question: What should the church be *doing*? At this point, therefore, we turn our attention more fully to the question of the church's mission. As we saw above, the biblical text portrays the central mission of the church as, in a nutshell, witnessing to God's coming kingdom by making Christ known in proclamation. Such proclamation must be understood holistically – in word, deed, and the very life of the church. So how does this proclamatory mission work itself out concretely in ecclesial life?

Tasks of the church

Proclamation through preaching

The most obvious task of the church according to the Great Commission (see p. 338) is that of making disciples of all nations. Disciples, however, can be made only if people hear the message of Christ (see Rom. 10:14–15). The means by which the church makes disciples and teaches people the way of Christ is known as "proclamation." According to Karl Barth, proclamation is the "announcement" of the triune God's promise to be with creation, a love supremely manifest in the death and resurrection of Jesus and in the continuing presence of the Spirit.[17] Such proclamation happens most obviously through preaching in the context of Christian worship. The Protestant tradition has especially highlighted this role, giving the sermon (Lat. *sermo* = word) a central liturgical place. The church is called to announce, explain, and interpret the gospel through the preaching office of its ministry. But Christian proclamation cannot be reduced to the preaching of the gospel, for it is not only the spoken word that announces the good news of God's kingdom.

The sacraments as proclamation

The so-called "sacraments" are a second means by which the church proclaims the triune God's work in the world, a means often under-appreciated in the Protestant world, but liturgically central in the Catholic and Orthodox traditions. While the preached word can be grasped by the mind and heart, as embodied persons, human beings also require a more tangible, physical manifestation of the gospel. The sacraments provide this more concrete,

---

[17] Karl Barth, *Church Dogmatics*, I/1: 59.

even sensual, experience of God's word as the physical sign (e.g., water, bread, wine) symbolizes and makes present the reality that it signifies (i.e., the gospel promise). As such, sacraments are typically regarded as "means of grace" – ways by which the triune God heals and guides the people of God.

The original Greek term for "sacrament" was *mysterion*, although it is never used in the NT to refer to what later became known as "the sacraments," since it more generally means "mystery." It was likely Tertullian who rendered the Greek *mysterion* into Latin as *sacramentum*, which found its way into the western tradition via the Vulgate and eventually came to refer to a fixed set of rites.[18] The classic definition of a sacrament in the western-Augustinian tradition is that of a visible sign of an invisible grace. Later thinkers in this tradition developed this definition by clarifying in their view what *happens* when Christ's invisible grace is made present through a visible sacrament. John Calvin, for example, defined a sacrament as "an outward sign by which the Lord seals on our consciences the promises of his good will toward us in order to sustain the weaknesses of our faith."[19] Calvin takes great care to emphasize that sacramental actions mean nothing apart from the gospel message that they proclaim. But as "seals" they authenticate and actualize those promises in the minds and hearts of those who receive them in faith; this partaking in turn is a visible and outward confession of faith before God and the world.

Baptism, the rite of passage into the Christian church, and the *Eucharist* (or Lord's Supper), the rite of spiritual sustenance, have almost universally been accepted as sacraments in the Christian tradition. In baptism, the initiate is included in the saving promises connected to the death and resurrection of Christ, as symbolized by her rising up out of the waters of death (see Rom. 6:3–4). In the Eucharist, the body and blood of Christ, given as a saving atonement for sinful human beings, are represented and remembered through the consumption of bread and wine, a sacrament that is meant to nourish Christian faith, hope, and love.[20]

These two sacraments, one that is oriented to the beginning of the Christian life and the other that concerns the ongoing nurture of the Christian life, are accepted by most Protestant churches, since they clearly

---

[18] Ann Loades, "Sacrament," in *The Oxford Companion to Christian Thought*, ed. Adrian Hastings, Alistair Mason, Hugh Pyper, Ingrid Lawrie, and Cecily Bennett (Oxford: Oxford University Press, 2000), 635.

[19] Calvin, *Institutes*, 4.14.1.

[20] There is, as is well known, an ongoing debate whether infant baptism is an acceptable practice, a debate that we do not have time to explore. There is also a continuing debate about how Christ is actually present in the supper (see pp. 459–60, 486–7, 491–2, and 496).

refer to the death and resurrection of Christ and were specifically commanded by him to be observed (e.g., Matt. 28:19 and 26:26–8, respectively). In the Roman Catholic tradition, however, there are seven sacraments. In addition to baptism and the Eucharist, this tradition also includes confirmation, penance (which Luther accepted in a qualified way), marriage, ordination, and last rites. In a very nuanced way the *Catechism of the Catholic Church* argues for the appropriateness of these seven by pointing to the fact that they "touch all the stages and all the important moments of Christian life: they give birth and increase, healing and mission to the Christian's life of faith. There is thus a certain resemblance between the stages of natural life and the stages of the spiritual life." The *Catechism* distinguishes between sacraments of initiation (baptism, confirmation, and Eucharist), sacraments of healing (penance, last rites / anointing of the sick), and sacraments that contribute to the salvation of others (ordination and marriage). It also calls the Eucharist the "sacrament of sacraments," to which all the other six point.[21] By identifying the Eucharist as the central sacrament that gives meaning to the others, the Catholic tradition offers a credible response to the Protestant critique that Catholicism includes as sacraments rites that do not clearly signify the death and resurrection of Christ. A further strength of the Catholic view is the manner in which its third category of sacraments connects Christian vocation to the mission of the church, showing the sacredness of proclaiming the gospel through formal ministry, family, and life in society.

The sacraments, especially baptism and the Eucharist, which have explicit NT claim to primacy in the church's grace-laden mission, are the Christian church's rites that accompany the spoken gospel. The message of Christ's salvation and the church's corresponding mission is written into all of them, when they are properly understood. The life and mission of the church therefore includes the administration of the sacraments as one of its central tasks, alongside the preaching of the gospel.

The enacted proclamation of the living church community

In proclaiming the good news of the triune God in its preaching and sacraments, and in bearing witness to the kingdom of God, the church is called to be a distinctive community. It is to be a holy community, "set apart" from the ordinary ways of a world that labors under sin, in order to be a salvific presence in and light to that world. The distinctiveness of the church community and its life-affirming way of being within the world

---

[21] *Catechism of the Catholic Church*, 1210–11.

constitute another means of proclaiming the joy and justice of the gospel of Christ. But the discussion of *how* the church is to be a distinctive community raises the perennial question of the relationship between the church and the world, between Christianity and culture. A helpful approach to this question is the typology provided by H. Richard Niebuhr, who distinguished five different responses to the question of the relation of Christ and culture.[22]

The idea of the church as a distinctive community has at times been understood in a sectarian way. Niebuhr identifies this approach as the "Christ against culture" type. This is a separatist stance that concludes that fidelity to Christ's lordship requires "the rejection of cultural society."[23] This was often the case in the pre-Constantinian church, which experienced Roman persecution, and whose congregations had little choice but to stand at the fringes of their cultural world.[24] However, this sectarian stance, which lingers throughout church history, was many times reinforced by the anti-creational supposition that since the world at large was evil, Christians should have little to do with earthly or cultural matters.

Other Christian traditions have suggested that the church must be deeply involved in the world. Niebuhr's second type, accordingly, which resides at the opposite end of the continuum from the first type, is the "Christ of culture" approach. This stance posits a very congenial relationship between the work of God and the work of humanity, so much so that the two virtually coincide. A prime example of this approach is nineteenth-century Protestant liberalism (see pp. 527–8 below), which viewed the finest products of human culture as noble expressions of the Christian spirit, a movement that Karl Barth criticized as "culture Protestantism."

Between these two extremes, Niebuhr cites three mediating positions. First, there is the "Christ above culture" position, most famously embodied by Thomas Aquinas (see pp. 468–73). While this view sees the natural truth, goodness, and beauty of culture to be valuable in their own right, because they come from God, it regards such cultural products as incomplete without the special truth, goodness, and beauty of Christian grace. A second mediating position is what Niebuhr calls "Christ and culture in paradox." Largely exemplified by Luther's "two kingdom" theory (i.e., church and state), this approach is paradoxical because it judges it impossible either to

---

[22] H. Richard Niebuhr, *Christ and Culture* (New York: Harper & Row, 1951). [23] Ibid., 47.
[24] See, e.g., "The So-Called Letter to Diognetus," ed. and trans. Eugene R. Fairweather, in *Early Christian Fathers*, ed. Cyril C. Richardson, Library of Christian Classics (Philadelphia: Westminster, 1953), ch. 6.

fully reconcile Christ and culture (since society is always corrupt) or to take refuge from culture in a Christian community free from sin (since the church is populated by sinners and always situated in the world). The fifth position is what Niebuhr calls "Christ the transformer of culture." Following Christ's redemptive approach to a sinful world, this view sees the church as possessing a vocation to engage and transform the sinful aspects of culture – an approach that can be witnessed in the Augustinian tradition and in contemporary liberation theology.

Which approach is most promising in thinking about how the church should fulfill its mission in the world as the distinctive community of Christ? While Niebuhr holds that each "Christ and culture" type has its legitimate time and place, he indicates a preference for the last – Christ the transformer of culture, a view with which we generally agree. Given a strong doctrine of the goodness of creation, human culture and its products must generally be held in high regard. But given a realistic view of sin, culture must also be seen as tinged by human fallenness. Since history is the sphere in which the triune God is acting redemptively through Christ and the Spirit, one distinctive feature of the church should be its involvement in the real historical world with a transformational goal in mind. This is to say that the church's mission is to be caught up into the mission of God (*missio Dei*) in the world. The church as the covenant community exists to serve God's kingdom goals for all of creation. However, enthusiasm for the transformationalist motif must avoid the temptation of triumphalism by being careful not to overestimate the extent to which the church can bring about "transformation" in society. And the church of any age must also remember that it is inevitably and in various ways shaped by the culture of its day – the very context of its ministry – from which it can also learn.

The church cannot fulfill its mission of cultural engagement, however, without governing itself and its corporate life in a distinctive way. Recently, theologians such as Stanley Hauerwas have exhorted the church to embrace its identity as a people set apart from the broader society so as to live as an alternative community in witness to the Christ who can change the world: "The church must recognize that her first social task in any society is to be herself." This task, continues Hauerwas, "does not involve a rejection of the world, or a withdrawal from the world; rather it is a reminder that the church must serve the world on her own terms."[25] Thus, the distinctive

---

[25] Stanley Hauerwas, "The Church and Liberal Democracy: The Moral Limits of a Secular Polity," in *A Community of Character: Toward a Constructive Christian Social Ethic* (Notre Dame, IN: University of Notre Dame Press, 1981), 84–5.

features and practices of the church are the necessary infrastructure of the church's renewing presence in the world. Corporate worship of the triune God, forthright proclamation of the gospel, and faithful administration of and participation in the sacraments are all necessary if the church is to own its identity in carrying out the Great Commission and in witnessing tangibly to the kingdom of God. Only by being itself, a distinctive community within the world, by means of its distinctive practices, can the church serve the world without being absorbed by it. But true religion, according to James 1:27, involves not only holiness – keeping oneself from being polluted by the world – but also works of justice – looking after orphans and widows in their distress. Within the world the church must manifest the righteousness of the coming kingdom in concrete works of love and acts of justice, such as by clothing the naked, feeding the hungry, visiting those in prison, and the like (see Matt. 25:31–46). In exemplifying such righteousness within its own ranks, and in advocating for justice within the world at large, the church announces, lives out, and anticipates the *shalom* of God's coming (eschatological) kingdom. This task of being a distinctive community that embodies love of God and neighbor requires the practice of the whole range of the church's missional tasks. Taken all together, preaching, sacraments, and the living witness of the church community in its concrete life and acts of righteousness constitute its broad proclamation of the gospel of Christ's kingdom.

Mission and election

The question of how the church relates to the broader world out of which it has been called to be a distinctive community broaches the issue of election, since God's election is the very basis of the church's existence. The connection between election and church has typically been made through the traditional distinction between the visible church and the invisible church.

Visible and invisible church

In conjunction with the Donatist and Pelagian controversies (see pp. 445–7 below), Augustine reflected at length on the fact that the church includes not only true believers, but also those who masquerade as believers. In other words, the visible church is a mixed body. But Augustine stressed that only God ultimately knows which members of the visible church are true believers and which are hypocrites. It is therefore not the church's job to separate the wheat from the weeds (see Matt. 13:24–30). Only at the last day will God unveil the true church – the invisible church – which was partially cloaked in the visible church. In *The City of God* Augustine writes eloquently of how "many reprobates are mingled in the Church with the good, and both sorts are collected as it were in the dragnet of the gospel; and in this world, as in a sea, both kinds swim without separation, enclosed in nets until the shore is reached. There the evil are to be divided from the good."[26] But what is it, precisely, that constitutes the invisible church? For Augustine the answer is clear: God's predestining will. The true saints of the invisible church are God's elect, and in the visible church they are mixed up with false believers, who, along with the rest of humanity outside of the church, are the reprobate.[27] For Augustine, the visible/invisible distinction in ecclesiology depends on the doctrine of double predestination.

On the basis of his doctrine of original sin, whereby all human beings inherit Adam's sin and guilt (see pp. 195–8 above), as well as his particular reading of Paul (especially Rom. 9–11), Augustine teaches that God predestines both the "saved" and the "damned" to their respective ends: "All pass into condemnation ... unless they are born again in Christ, even as He has appointed them to be regenerated, before they die in the body, whom He predestinated to everlasting life, as the most merciful bestower of grace; whilst to those whom He has predestinated to eternal death, He is also the most righteous awarder of punishment."[28] Many major theologians of the western tradition have followed Augustine in this doctrine. For example, Martin Luther's *The Bondage of the Will* presupposes it.[29] But it is John Calvin who is probably best known for advocating this doctrine of double predestination. Calvin writes: "We call predestination God's eternal decree, by which he compacted with himself what he willed to become of each man. For all are not created in equal condition; rather, eternal life is foreordained for some, eternal damnation for others. Therefore, as any man has been created to one or the other of these ends, we speak of him as predestined to life or to death."[30]

One might be surprised that the issue of predestination has not already been addressed in this book in the places where it is traditionally treated – namely, in the doctrines of God, creation, or salvation. It is our conviction,

---

[26] Augustine, *City of God*, 18.49.
[27] While the "visible/invisible" language comes from later theologians, the basic concept is clearly present in Augustine. See, e.g., *On Rebuke and Grace*, trans. Peter Holmes, Robert Ernest Wallis, and Benjamin B. Warfield, in *Nicene and Post-Nicene Fathers*, 1st series, ed. Philip Schaff (Grand Rapids, MI: Eerdmans, 1993), chs. 20–3 (v: pp. 479–81).
[28] Augustine, *The Nature and Origin of the Soul*, trans. Roland J. Teske, in *Answer to the Pelagians*, The Works of Saint Augustine I/23 (New York: New City, 1997), Book 4, ch. 16.
[29] Martin Luther, *The Bondage of the Will*, trans. J. I. Packer and O. R. Johnston (Old Tappan, NJ: Revell, 1957).
[30] Calvin, *Institutes*, 3.21.5.

however, in line with a growing consensus in contemporary theology, that *election* rather than predestination is the more important biblical category, and that this topic is most appropriately discussed in relationship to the church. The theme of election makes best sense when thinking about the *mission* of God's people *to* the world, rather than when simply thinking about Christians being chosen and saved *from* a condemned world. The biblical basis of our view should be clear from the discussion above, as well as from the biblical sections included in the chapters on the doctrines of God, creation, and salvation. In those discussions we began by talking about the election of Israel as part of the covenant, which is the instrument of God's mission to the world. The election of OT Israel and subsequently of the NT church, we would contend, is ultimately missiological. To make this case in more convincing, systematic terms, however, especially with respect to the question of predestination, requires a more detailed examination.

Rethinking election

It is our view that double predestination, despite being taught by some of the most significant theologians in the Christian tradition, is a mistaken interpretation of scripture's depiction of election. The traditional view relies heavily on Romans 9–11, especially Paul's typological use of Jacob and Esau: "Even before they had been born or had done anything good or bad (so that God's purpose of election might continue, not by works but by his call) [Rebecca] was told, 'The elder shall serve the younger.' As it is written, 'I have loved Jacob, but I have hated Esau'" (9:11–13). In the traditional view of double predestination, this text is taken to mean that God has freely chosen to elect some to salvation (as an expression of grace) and to reject others (as an expression of justice). However, this interpretation ignores the covenantal context that lies behind the passage, especially the fact that God's election of the nation of Israel and individuals within the nation was always *instrumental* in character – that is, done with the intention that those chosen would participate in God's broader rescue of creation from its sin and brokenness.[31] Moreover, the traditional interpretation misses the fact that Romans 11 (the culmination of this difficult Pauline passage) even speaks about the rejection of Israel and the inclusion of the Gentiles in the covenant as being instrumental to the salvation of both: "And even those of Israel, if they do not persist in unbelief, will be grafted in, for God has the power to graft them in again. For if you have been cut from what is by

---

[31] See N. T. Wright, *Simply Christian: Why Christianity Makes Sense* (New York: HarperCollins, 2006), 73–5.

nature a wild olive tree and grafted, contrary to nature, into a cultivated olive tree, how much more will these natural branches be grafted back into their own olive tree" (11:23–4). The climax of the whole passage is the inclusion of the "full number of the Gentiles" (11:25) in the covenant through Christ, as well as the fact that "all Israel will be saved" (11:26). In short, use of this passage to support the notion of the double predestination of individuals is to wrench what Paul says about election from its communal, covenantal, and salvation-historical context in order to support an abstract theology of the absolute decree of God and an individualistic conception of salvation that were foreign to the mind of the apostle.[32]

For these reasons and others, including the fact that most traditional theologies of predestination tend to view election and reprobation as taking place without respect to Christ, this doctrine has been radically rethought from the ground of its biblical roots up in recent theology. The most prominent – and Reformed/Calvinist – attempt at reworking this doctrine comes from Karl Barth.[33] Barth worried that the traditional parallelism between election and reprobation took the *good* news of Christ from the center of the theological stage. The traditional interpretation made it seem as if God's choice to elect some and reject others was merely arbitrary, and therefore lost sight of God's *loving* character. Barth reminds us that God's election has to do first and foremost with the fulfillment of the covenant in Jesus Christ; individuals come into play only as they are included through the corporate people of God. According to Barth, Jesus Christ is both the electing God and the elect human being, which means that any faithful doctrine of election must be thoroughly christological. Through Christ's incarnation, Barth sees election as God's decision to be the God of covenantal faithfulness – to be "for us" – and through Christ's atonement sees election as including God's *own* acceptance of humanity's reprobation through sin. Rather than referring to individual beings who were eternally rejected by God, reprobation has to do with what Jesus Christ suffered on the cross: "Rejection cannot again become the portion or affair of man. The exchange which took place on Golgotha ... took place once and for all in fulfillment of God's eternal will, and it can never be reversed."[34]

As the fulfillment of the covenant, Barth thinks that the election (and reprobation) that took place in Christ (as the fulfillment of the triune God's eternal will) is mediated through God's choice of a people: "According to Scripture, the divine election of grace is an activity of God which has a

---

[32] Cf. Wright, *Paul in Fresh Perspective*, 108–29.
[33] See Barth, *Church Dogmatics*, II/2: §§32–5.   [34] Ibid., II/2: 167.

definite goal and limit. Its direct and proper object is not individuals generally, but one individual [Jesus Christ] – and only in Him the people called and united by Him [the church], and only in that people individuals in general in their private relationships with God."[35] Barth suggests that the purpose of election is mediation – God's choosing of a community in order to make Christ known to the nations. Thus, in line with what we argued above in our biblical portrait of the church, election ought to be seen as a missiological category. The nation chosen in the OT to bear God's promise to the rest of the world was Israel. The history of that nation culminated in the incarnation and saving death of Jesus Christ, the one who bears the rejection for sin and in whom salvation is to be found. The church is elected by God to testify to the fulfillment of God's promises in Jesus Christ and is *sent* into the world to make the good news known. In this OT and NT dynamic of election, the choice of the particular serves the blessing of the universal creation. This point is also emphasized by Reformed theologian and missionary Lesslie Newbigin: "To be chosen, to be elect, therefore does not mean that the elect are the saved and the rest are the lost. To be elect in Christ Jesus, and there is no other election, means to be incorporated into his mission to the world, to be the bearer of God's saving purpose for his whole world, to be the sign and the agent and the firstfruit of his blessed kingdom which is for all."[36] In summary, the traditional doctrine of election is being reconsidered today more in terms of mission than as a strict soteriological category (i.e., the question of the "saved"), more in terms of a corporate covenantal body than in a strict individualist fashion, and, we might additionally note, more in terms of doxology (thanksgiving to God for a prevenient grace received) than as a timeless eternal decree. Indeed, the principal passages that speak expressly of "predestination" are found in texts that are chiefly doxological in character (Rom. 8:28–39; Eph. 1:3–14).

In light of this rethinking of the doctrine of election, there follows a way to reconstrue the visible/invisible distinction regarding the church. Fittingly, this reconstrual draws upon another important ecclesiological distinction – that between the church *militant* and the church *triumphant*. Traditionally, this latter distinction referred to the pilgrim church in the world that still battles against sin and evil (church militant) and the dead saints in heaven who have been relieved of their struggle (church triumphant). While it certainly makes sense to think of the visible church in history as the church militant – the church that is, by the power of the

[35] Ibid., II/2: 43, see also 233–40.
[36] Lesslie Newbigin, *The Gospel in a Pluralist Society* (Grand Rapids, MI: Eerdmans, 1989), 86–7.

Spirit, struggling against sin, evil, and the powers of death for the sake of Christ and the world – we deem it better to think of the invisible church in historical and eschatological terms. Instead of referring to the unknowable number of the elect, the invisible church is the church that will triumph in the coming kingdom of God, when the triune God's covenant purposes are fulfilled and all of creation is healed of its brokenness and sin. The triumphant church is the invisible church that we do not *yet* see, since we are still in history, a history whose meaning will be revealed only in light of its fulfillment. The triumphant church is the church of the future when its particular election culminates in God's universal blessing of all creation.

CONCLUSION: A CHURCH *FOR* THE WORLD

This chapter has suggested that the church, while certainly *in* and populated by citizens *of* the world, is called out as the *ekklesia* to be a distinctive community that lives by the commandments of Christ, the principles of God's kingdom, and the power of the Spirit. By living in such a way – through proclaiming the gospel, administering the sacraments faithfully, and ethically embodying the character of the kingdom – the church is graciously invited to participate in the covenant renewal of the world through Christ. This means that the church, while called to be a distinctive community in the world, is also called to be a church *for* the world in reflection of the triune God, "who so loved the world" (John 3:16) and who has sent the church into the world to serve God and neighbor. Our next chapter will explore what it means for the church today to carry out this mission in a pluralistic and globalized world.

FOR FURTHER READING

Clowney, Edmund P., *The Church*, Contours of Christian Theology (Downers Grove, IL: InterVarsity, 1995).

Dulles, Avery, *Models of the Church*, rev. edn. (New York: Doubleday, 2002).

Guder, Darrell L., and Lois Barrett, eds., *Missional Church: A Vision for the Sending of the Church in North America* (Grand Rapids, MI: Eerdmans, 1998).

Küng, Hans, *The Church*, trans. Ray Ockenden and Rosaleen Ockenden (London: Burns & Oates, 1967).

Macquarrie, John, *A Guide to the Sacraments* (London: SCM, 1997).

Minear, Paul S., *Images of the Church in the New Testament*, New Testament Library (Louisville, KY: Westminster John Knox, 2004).

Newbigin, Lesslie, *The Household of God: Lectures on the Nature of the Church* (London: SCM Press, 1957).

Niebuhr, H. Richard, *Christ and Culture* (New York: Harper & Row, 1951).

CHAPTER 14

Christianity in a global context

INTRODUCTION: TWO THEATERS AND CHALLENGES TO THE MISSION OF THE CHURCH

According to the eminent historian of religion Wilfred Cantwell Smith, people in the modern West are inclined to think of religions as discrete, static, self-enclosed entities. On this view, Christianity and Islam, for example, are rather thought of as parallel lines that do not really change over time or intersect with each other in space. Smith argues that it would be better to regard "religions" as complex, dynamic combinations of both faith (the personal dimension, focused on human beings) and cumulative tradition (the impersonal dimension, focused on things such as texts, history, etc.) that interact with one another in the world and subtly change over the course of history.[1] For Smith, multifaceted historical realities such as Christianity are always developing and morphing into new forms, with the result that being a Christian today is very different than it was, say, in the Middle Ages.

In the last century, Christianity has undergone changes that have been profound and wide-ranging.[2] Reflecting a new global consciousness, Christianity changed significantly in two different theaters. In the *western* world, Christianity began a precipitous *decline* in power, prestige, and influence as the process of secularization intensified and as westerners became increasingly aware of the existence and significance of the other great religions of the world. But during this same period of time in the *non-western* world, Christianity began a mighty *ascent* in terms of numbers of adherents and institutional presence as Africans, Asians, and South Americans embraced a new faith, a burgeoning that continues today. Both of these regional changes present significant challenges to the church's self-identity and pursuit of its mission in the contemporary world. Let us begin by examining the first challenge.

WESTERN CHRISTIANITY

The decline of Christianity in recent centuries

Christianity's demise in the modern, western world – what can thought of as its secularization – has been centuries in the making (see pp. 507–16).[3] While a myriad of causes have been at work in this complex development, a key contributor during the last century has been the dawning awareness of the complexity of the world's religious situation. As westerners became increasingly conscious of the reality, size, and wisdom of religious traditions other than those resident in their own culture, they often concluded that such a situation somehow relativized the claims of their own Judeo-Christian

---

[1] See Wilfred Cantwell Smith, *The Meaning and End of Religion* (New York: Harper & Row, 1978). Given such considerations, Smith even suggests that the term "religion" ought to be abandoned.

[2] The presentation on Christian thinking about other religions in this chapter draws significantly on the following: Richard J. Plantinga, "God So Loved the World: Theological Reflections on Religious Plurality in the History of Christianity," in *Biblical Faith and Other Religions: An Evangelical Assessment*, ed. David W. Baker (Grand Rapids, MI: Kregel, 2004), 106–37; Richard J. Plantinga, ed., *Christianity and Plurality: Classic and Contemporary Readings* (Oxford: Blackwell, 1999).

[3] For a penetrating sociological account of the secularization of religion in general and Christianity in particular, see Peter L. Berger, *The Sacred Canopy: Elements of a Sociological Theory of Religion* (Garden City, NY: Doubleday, 1969). In light of the proliferation of religion across the globe, however, Berger has since rethought and qualified his secularization thesis.

tradition. If, as Christians confess, Jesus Christ is the sole savior of the world, what is one to make of a world in which two-thirds of its people confess faiths in which Christ is marginal or even irrelevant?

Heightened awareness of the complexity of humanity's religious history

A century or two ago, even a basic awareness of religious plurality was not very prevalent in the West. As literate and informed a nineteenth-century figure as Ralph Waldo Emerson, for example, could mistakenly categorize the Hindu classic, the *Bhagavad-Gita*, as a Buddhist text.[4] Such errors of classification by educated westerners are difficult to conceive of today. A variety of factors have brought about this new consciousness of religious plurality. Let us review seven such factors that have contributed to this new appreciation of the world's manifold religiosity – the first four rooted in pre-twentieth-century history and the last three originating in twentieth-century events.

A first factor is the importance of European exploration of the globe, beginning in the fifteenth century. In what might be called the *Columbus factor*, European seafaring nations in particular became aware of impressive civilizations beyond the confines of the West, often to exploitative ends. These civilizations, of course, also contained complexes of religious belief and practice. In time, exploration of the globe would be followed by colonialism and missions, which would further open the eyes of the West to the reality of a larger world filled with cultural and religious diversity.

Second, around the same time, the Protestant Reformation was beginning to make itself felt in parts of Europe. By the time the sixteenth century had ended, the Reformation had changed western Christianity in crucial ways. Most importantly, perhaps, the *Reformation factor* introduced a variety of ecclesiastical ways of being Christian. No longer was there only the Roman Catholic Church in the West; there were now several other churches and fledgling theological traditions, including the Anglican, Lutheran, Calvinist, and Anabaptist branches of Protestant Christianity. The result of the Reformation was thus greater intra-Christian diversity.

Third, due in part to the discord, even warfare, brought about by the religious disagreement of the Reformation and its aftermath, some thinkers in seventeenth- and eighteenth-century Europe began to rethink the nature of religion and its role in society. Seeking to avoid the hot passions that

---

[4] See Eric J. Sharpe, *The Universal Gītā: Western Images of the* Bhagavadgītā (London: Gerald Duckworth & Co, 1985), 22.

religions, rooted in the dictates of gods (via their particular revelations), seemed capable of fanning, these thinkers instead counseled the use of reason in order to arrive at a sober, realistic assessment of human problems and their solutions. Emancipated reason, especially as embodied in modern science, became the new judge of faith; and in the implied trial, Christian faith – and its correlate, special revelation – were found wanting. This *Enlightenment factor* thus provoked something of a crisis of credibility for Christianity as its positions were attacked and not always satisfactorily defended. In this encounter with modernity, Christianity found itself rather besieged – an attack that summoned forth a defensive posture from Christianity, contributing further to the substantial weakening of Christianity as a force in modern, western life. The Enlightenment dissatisfaction with the conflicts and discrepancies among particular religious traditions led to the quest for a universal religion of reason, further facilitating a global perspective on religion in general.

Fourth, drafting off the previous factor, the nineteenth century witnessed a number of changes in the curricula of western universities. Alongside of the sciences of the human mind (psychology), preliterate cultures (anthropology), and society (sociology), other new fields of study came to be formalized in the expanding research university, such as "religious studies" or "comparative religion" – the multidisciplinary, poly-methodic examination of the world's faith and religious traditions.[5] As this new field came to expression in university courses, translations of sacred texts, and scholarly monographs, a new generation of influential learners came to a sustained awareness of the complexity of humanity's religious history – the *scholarship factor.*

Fifth, as the twentieth century dawned, it became increasingly clear that Europe was on the brink of a major conflict – in fact, a series of conflicts. As WWI ended in 1918, a time of intense and unsettling questioning set in. This period saw the rise of communism in Russia and fascism in Germany and Italy. Such economic and political uncertainties eventually flowed into another global conflagration, WWII. In this sustained period of crisis for western civilization, existential questions gave way to religious questions that were asked of mainline religious traditions, especially Christianity. Particularly after the end of WWII, in which neologisms were coined to name new horrors – for example, "genocide" (Auschwitz) and "A-bomb" (Hiroshima) – westerners entertained further doubts about the existence and nature of a God who allowed such unspeakable atrocities. Was this God both loving and powerful? Was Christianity still capable of addressing

---

[5] See Eric J. Sharpe, *Comparative Religion: A History*, 2nd edn. (LaSalle, IL: Open Court, 1986).

the concerns of humanity in a technological, nuclear age? Or was the West headed toward a religionless, secular era? This *western crisis factor* thus served as a further challenge to Christian truth claims. It also forced new thinking about religion and its role in public and private life.

Sixth, while the West was undergoing this period of self-questioning and even self-doubt, there were signs of new life stirring across the globe. Of special significance were the developments in Asia, where there was increasing dissatisfaction with western colonial presence in various countries such as Indonesia, Vietnam, and India. As the citizens of these countries declared themselves non-Dutch, or non-French, or non-British in recovery of their indigenous religio-cultural identities, they also implicitly and often explicitly declared themselves non-Christian in the process. Mahatma Gandhi, for example, in distancing himself from things western and British, became a Hindu in the process of leading his country to independence. This *Asian renewal factor* thus symbolizes a kind of rebirth of the non-West, the effects of which would impress themselves on western consciousness over the decades that followed. Particularly noteworthy in this connection is the renewed vitality of Islam, as both a religion and a political force.

A seventh factor that fostered a heightened western awareness of religious plurality is the *globalization factor* – an umbrella term subsuming a diversity of phenomena. It has become common to assume and assert that during the course of the twentieth century the world became smaller, as it became increasingly clear that events and decisions in one part of the world affected other areas as well. Whereas in prior centuries the activities of a person seeking increased power might have seemed irrelevant thousands or even hundreds of miles away, in 1990, for example, when Saddam Hussein's Iraqi army invaded Kuwait, the world immediately took notice. Politicians sprang into action, and world markets quickly reacted to an unstable situation. By virtue of the global communications and technology that make such information instantly available, westerners also became more aware of persons from around the globe in a personal, existential way. This was also fostered by the ease and frequency of air travel to other parts of the world, as well as by the immigration of citizens of other nations to the West, especially in the post-colonial era. Thus it came to pass that westerners came into more meaningful face-to-face contact with adherents of the world religions, heightening their awareness of and interest in religious visions other than their own dominant Judeo-Christian tradition.

These factors – the Columbus factor, the Reformation factor, the Enlightenment factor, the scholarship factor, the western crisis factor, the Asian renewal factor, and the globalization factor – help to explain the West's growing awareness of religious and cultural plurality. For many in the West, this picture presents a dilemma, particularly for committed believers in the Judeo-Christian tradition. To take the Christian case, it is often perplexing for believers to reconcile what seems to be the dominant Christian view of other religions ("Christianity is true and other religions aren't, which must mean that only persons who confess the name of Jesus Christ receive salvation") with what their lived experience tells them to be the case ("Non-Christian religions seem to possess at least *some* truth, and many of their adherents whom I know are devout, well intentioned, and highly moral – can their ultimate fate really be so bleak?").

Christian responses to religious plurality

Before elaborating a Christian theological response to this situation of religious plurality based on the principal sources of the Bible and tradition, we must first clarify the matter of an appropriate existential and ethical response to a world characterized by religious "manyness." How are Christians to conduct themselves as they interact with the members of other faith communities? First of all, we must ever bear in mind that all persons have been created in the image of God; all persons are therefore worthy of dignity and respect regardless of their religion. Second, Christians are obligated to love their fellow human beings just as God loves the *world* (John 3:16), in the sense that they are to treat their neighbors with fundamental concern for their well-being (i.e., the golden rule). Even if we disagree theologically with the beliefs of others, we are nonetheless required to conduct ourselves civilly and in the spirit of Christian charity. It is both an irony and a tragedy of history that so much hatred and violence have been justified in the name of religion, for which Christianity must also confess its culpability. This unfortunate history points to the need for understanding and dialogue among the religions of the world, especially when given today's precarious geo-political situation and the possibility for massive violence. With these important ethical maxims in mind, which should undergird and qualify any approach to the world's religions, we turn now to the contours of a Christian theology of religious plurality.

Biblical perspectives
It is significant that both testaments of Christian scripture unfold in a religiously pluralistic environment.[6] In the case of the OT, Israel found

---

[6] On the Bible's view of religious plurality, see Plantinga, ed., *Christianity and Plurality*, ch. 1.

itself interacting regularly with the nations of the ancient Near East. In the NT, Christianity developed in a Greco-Roman world in which there were many faiths and traditions, including the faith from which the church sprang – Judaism. In light of these contextual realities, it is not surprising to find much material in scripture relevant to the issue of religious plurality. Two themes in particular stand out here.

On the one hand, there is clear emphasis on creational *universality*: the God of Israel is the Creator of all there is, the divine King who desires fellowship with creatures (Gen. 1–2) and has revealed something of the divine life to all of creation (see Ps. 19; Rom. 1). In light of human rebellion, God chose to save a creation gone awry, all of whose nations are the object of divine concern (see e.g., Amos 1–2), by implementing a plan of redemption for the whole *kosmos* (John 3:14–15) in which God desires the salvation of all (1 Tim. 2:4).

On the other hand, there is also in scripture a strong theme of redemptive *particularity*: there is but one true God (see Deut. 6:4; 1 Kings 18), who chooses to work out a plan of salvation through a particular people with specific instructions for human living spelled out in the covenant (see Deut. 5–6). Out of this covenant history a messiah is promised. The NT subsequently makes special claims about the uniqueness and particularity of Jesus of Nazareth as the sole savior of the world. It ascribes to him the one name through which humanity is saved (Acts 4:12), the name above all names to whom every knee shall bow (Phil. 2:9–11), and proclaims that he is the one mediator between God and humanity (1 Tim. 2:5). These biblical themes of universality and particularity pose the theological question as to their proper relationship. Can they be reconciled? If so, how?

Historical perspectives

In continuity with the biblical world, the early church is one of the periods in history when Christians most keenly felt the reality of religious plurality. In patristic Christianity, two divergent approaches to the tension between the universal and particular strains of scripture begin to be seen, strategies which would be repeated time and again throughout the history of the tradition. To put it succinctly, one emphasized biblical universality and stressed Christianity's continuity with other religions; the other stressed particularity and emphasized Christianity's discontinuity with other religions.

The second-century Justin Martyr was a convert to Christianity with a pronounced background in Greek philosophy, which at that time was highly religious in nature. In becoming an apologist for the new faith, he sought to make sense of his pagan past *vis-à-vis* his Christian present. His general strategy is to argue that although Christianity is *the* truth, there is also truth in the non-Christian world.[7] Justin's key argument as to why truth can be found outside of Christianity focuses on the concept of *logos* (see p. 425). Whereas Christ is *the* Logos, the Word of God made flesh for our redemption, as the mediator of creation the seed of this *logos* – creation's logic, sense, and rational structure – has been spread throughout space and time. According to Justin, the seeds of the *logos* in the non-Christian world are thus a source of general revelation: everyone has a fragmentary knowledge of the *logos*, which ultimately points to the truth of Christ. Glimpses of the truth expressed by the philosophers, therefore, are due to their discovery and contemplation of some aspect of the *logos*. But since they did not know the full *logos*, they often ended up in half-truths and contradictions. Accordingly, Christianity is superior to paganism because only Christians truly love and worship the Logos made flesh in Jesus Christ. Philosophy possesses only partial truth, but it is nonetheless a preparation for the gospel and a gift of God.

Justin's view that philosophy is rather continuous with Christianity was emphatically rejected by Tertullian, who is the eminent representative of the discontinuous approach to the non-Christian world. Because he regarded philosophy as folly and the source of heresy, he chose a rather antagonistic strategy with respect to Greco-Roman thought, attacking non-Christian beliefs and practices wholesale in light of his understanding of Christian truth. In the process, Tertullian articulated what became a classic view of Christianity's relationship to philosophy, reason, and culture, captured in the famous rhetorical question: "What has Athens to do with Jerusalem?" Tertullian argues that God's final revelation in Christ was foretold in the OT, communicated to the apostles, passed on to the church, and expressed in the church's creeds, doctrines, and preaching.[8] There is no need to look for truth outside of Christianity, and no possibility of finding salvation outside of the church. The implication for Christianity's relationship with other religions is rather obvious.

Another noteworthy statement in patristic Christianity on the matter of non-Christian religions is that of Augustine. In *The City of God*, he responds to the charge that Christianity was to blame for the sack of Rome in the early fifth century, since it led the Roman Empire away from its traditional gods. Augustine seeks to refute those who think that pagan gods should be worshipped either to gain advantage in this life or with an eye to salvation in the life to come. In his view, worship is due to the one true God alone.

---

[7] See Justin Martyr, *First Apology*, 242–89.
[8] See Tertullian, *Prescriptions Against the Heretics*, 31–64, quotation at 36, translation amended.

Christian truth, moreover, shows other gods to be false and therefore unable to give this-worldly aid or eternal life. Augustine's critique of polytheism, however, did not prevent him from admiring and appropriating philosophical monotheism, especially that of Neoplatonism. In his own synthetic way, therefore, Augustine was heir to the strategies of *both* Justin and Tertullian.

After the patristic period, in the age of Christendom (from Constantine to early modernity), the church generally assumed and emphasized discontinuity between Christianity and the other religions – that is, to the degree that the church was even aware of other faiths at all. The Athanasian Creed reflects this attitude, maintaining that the church possesses all necessary religious truth. It emphasizes that for salvation, believers must confess certain key doctrines, especially those that concern the Trinity and Christ: "Whoever desires to be saved must above all things hold the catholic faith."[9] As such, this creed is a statement of the principle that outside of the parameters of orthodoxy, of which the church is guardian, there is no salvation (*extra ecclesiam nulla salus est*). In the lengthy history of Christendom, this doctrinal-ideological position was generally assumed and at times insisted upon with considerable regimen (e.g., the Inquisition).

A second period in Christian history in which the question of religious plurality was particularly alive was the modern period. The important and influential view suggested by liberal Protestantism (e.g., Ritschl and Harnack; see pp. 527–8) tended to regard non-Christian religions as testimony to general revelation and, in an evolutionary sense, *preparatory* to Christianity (in a way not unlike that of Justin Martyr). Within this general revelation there is the particular revelation of God in Jesus Christ that stands out as *fulfilling* and definitive, making Christianity the highest religion.

Another significant modern view of non-Christian religions was articulated by Ernst Troeltsch (1865–1923), the eminent representative of the "history of religions school."[10] Troeltsch believed that Christianity must be regarded as one religious phenomenon among many in the Greco-Roman world. Emphasizing historical individualities over abstract universality, his convictions prompted him to conclude that because history is the realm of the transitory, the contingent, and the relative, Christian attempts to establish the ultimate and enduring validity of Christian revelation and

---

[9] "Athanasian Creed," in Pelikan and Hotchkiss, eds., *Creeds and Confessions*, I: 676.
[10] See Ernst Troeltsch, "The Place of Christianity Among the World Religions," in *Christianity and Plurality: Classic and Contemporary Readings*, ed. Richard J. Plantinga (Oxford: Blackwell, 1999), 211–22.

truth in history *vis-à-vis* other religions have all failed. Christianity is not absolutely true or ultimately valid, says Troeltsch, but is relatively true – true for those of us who live in the cradle of western civilization, with which Christianity is inextricably bound. His conclusion therefore is that other religions are valid for the citizens of other civilizations, just as Christianity is valid for the West. Troeltsch asks: "Who will presume to make a really final pronouncement here? Only God himself."[11] It follows for Troeltsch that the idea of conversion – and of missions in any meaningful sense – is utterly misplaced.

The early twentieth century witnessed a return to orthodoxy in Protestant theology, a redirection principally inspired by Karl Barth. Barth famously argued that revelation shows religion to be "unbelief."[12] In religion (human striving for God), human beings "speak against" (literally, contra-dict) and resist revelation (God's searching out humanity); religion is human self-justification. While religion in itself is unbelief, religion can *become* true by grace, an act of God that is analogous to God's justification of the sinner. God has designated the Christian religion as the true religion; by grace, revelation has more powerfully contradicted religion than religion has contradicted revelation. In light of his conviction that revelation means *the* revelation of God in Jesus Christ, the early Barth judges that theological reliance on general revelation is fruitless (see pp. 65–6 above). Apart from grace, all religions (including Christianity, when it neglects Christ) fail to express God's truth.

At the same time, Catholic theologians were also seeking to respond to the challenge of religious plurality. One significant effort was suggested by Karl Rahner (1904–84), the theologian so instrumental for Vatican II. To simplify Rahner's complex thought, he argues that Christianity is the absolute religion and is necessary for salvation, but that it becomes absolute for different cultures at different times – namely, only after a significant historical encounter with Christianity.[13] Those who have not sufficiently encountered Christianity are not accountable for its message. In that case, Rahner held that when such persons participate faithfully in their own religions, they do so as "anonymous Christians" – that is, as persons who have an implicit Christian faith with access to elements of God's grace within their own religions, and therefore to the possibility of the salvation that God wills universally through Christ.

---

[11] Troeltsch, "Place of Christianity," 219.   [12] See Barth, *Church Dogmatics*, 1/2: 280–361.
[13] See Karl Rahner, "Christianity and the Non-Christian Religions," in *Theological Investigations*, trans. K.-H. Krueger (New York: Crossroad, 1983), v: 115–34.

Influenced in part by Rahner's position, the Catholic Church officially addressed religious plurality in a declaration crafted at Vatican II. After its rather staunch historic conservatism, this council sought to open the arms of the Catholic Church to other Christian churches and even to members of non-Christian religions, choosing to downplay its traditional commitment to the idea that salvation is possible only through the church.[14] Vatican II sought to emphasize what most religions have in common: a common origin and a common end (i.e., God); the recognition that God's plan of salvation extends to all; and the recognition that all religions seek to answer the problems of human existence. In turning to specifics, the council arranges Christianity's relationship and proximity to the world's religions in a series of concentric circles, with Christianity at the center and other religions radiating outward, first through the monotheistic faiths of Judaism and Islam, with non-western religions (e.g., Buddhism) at the outermost edge. While the Catholic Church understands itself to be duty bound to proclaim the truth of the Catholic faith centered upon Christ, it clearly expresses an openness to other faiths.

As open and tolerant attitudes toward non-Christian religions began to be articulated by progressive Christian theologians, some more daring thinkers sought to bring about nothing less than a Copernican revolution in thinking about Christianity's relationship to the world's religions, advocating a pluralistic position on this question. The most notable representative of this new paradigm is John Hick (b. 1922).[15] Given a changing and pluralistic world, to which theology must respond, Hick takes issue with the traditional Christian assessment of other religions, a perspective that he considers to be outmoded and largely discredited. He rejects the core belief of the older theologies that God is the God of Christians alone, the assumption that God's saving activity is confined to one narrow strand in the thick rope that constitutes the history of religion. Rather than claim that non-Christians can be saved as "anonymous Christians" (following Rahner), Hick suggests that it is preferable to recognize that human beings in *all* religious traditions are in relationship with the one transcendent divine Being. This "God" answers to different names and has taken up residence in various religious communities. Therefore there is a plurality of saving paths to God. Hick locates Christian resistance to his proposal in the

---

[14] "Declaration on the Relation of the Church to Non-Christian Religions," *Nostra aetate*, in *Vatican Council II*, 1: *The Conciliar and Postconciliar Documents*, ed. Austin Flannery, rev. edn. (Northport, NY: Costello, 1996), 738–42. John Paul II operated theologically in the same vein as Vatican II. See, e.g., his encyclicals *Redemptor Hominis, Redemptoris Missio*, and *Ut Unum Sint*.

[15] See, e.g., John Hick, "Whatever Path Men Choose is Mine," in *Christianity and Other Religions: Selected Readings*, ed. John Hick and Brian Hebblethwaite (Philadelphia: Fortress, 1980), 171–90; and Hick, "A Philosophy of Religious Pluralism," in Plantinga, ed., *Christianity and Plurality*, 335–46.

traditional doctrines of the incarnation and the Trinity, and therefore pleads for Christians to give up a *Christo*centric view of religion and adopt a broadly *theo*centric position, rejecting christological orthodoxy as exclusionary (if not also largely unintelligible and therefore nonsensical). Hick suggests that we view the incarnation as a metaphorical idea, as a myth that expresses the *Christian* experience of contact with the transcendent Being, but which does not rule out other valid experiences of God in other religions with their own saving points of contact. While Hick's revolutionary approach attempts to level the playing field for a fruitful dialogue among the religions of a shrinking, interdependent, and unstable planet, it also means that Christian missions and conversion are things of the past.

A typology of perspectives

Our review of major biblical themes and some of the Christian tradition's key verdicts about non-Christian religions provides a basis for understanding the typology of positions on Christianity and the world's religions that is commonly employed by theologians today – that of exclusivism, inclusivism, and pluralism. *Exclusivism*, sometimes also called particularism, is the view that there is one exclusive way to God – all other paths being in principle excluded. Emphasizing the biblical theme of particularity, exclusivists stress that Jesus Christ is the sole mediator between God and humanity, the "only name" by which humanity can be saved (Acts 4:12). Since this special revelation has been uniquely given to the Christian church, only its members can claim salvation. In our review of the Christian tradition, Tertullian and Barth stand out as exclusivists.[16]

Inclusivism is the view that while God has a special relationship with the Christian church, people who are adherents of other religions are included in God's salvific plan for the world and may indeed find salvation even in the context of their own religion. Striving to balance the biblical themes of universality *and* particularity, inclusivists hold that salvation is accomplished by the unique atoning death of Christ on the cross, but that this may be effective for those outside of Christianity to the degree that they live in accordance with the light they have via general revelation. In general, inclusivists can be thought of as operating with a whole–part schema: what Christianity has in full, other religions can be said to have in nucleus or in

---

[16] Later in his theology, however, Barth articulates themes that temper the characterization of his position as exclusivistic. See *Church Dogmatics*, IV/3.1: 38–165. Barth's ostensible exclusivism is also complicated by his universalistic-tending doctrine of election, which appears to "limit" salvation to all humanity through Christ. See *Church Dogmatics*, II/2: §§32–5.

fragmentary fashion, which in the absence of Christianity may be an avenue to the salvation accomplished in Christ. In our review of the Christian tradition, Justin Martyr, liberal Protestants, and Karl Rahner can be characterized as inclusivists.

Pluralism is the view that the one God – or the transcendent, or the supreme reality – is God of all the peoples of the world. Each culture or tradition has its own way of conceiving and naming the one God. In other words, there are many paths to God. Pluralists thus do not consider truth to be restricted to the sacred writings and human traditions of just one religion – notably, Christianity. Rather, they endorse the existence of many revelations which provide for the reality of salvation across the religions of the world. In our review of the Christian tradition, Ernst Troeltsch hints at pluralism, while John Hick articulates it unambiguously.

Whereas exclusivism has tended to be the dominant view of the Christian tradition, especially during the period of Christendom, inclusivism (which is actually closer to exclusivism than is often assumed) has been put forward in periods where Christians were relatively more conscious of religious plurality, as in patristic Christianity and in modern Christianity. Both exclusivism and inclusivism are christocentric: Jesus Christ is central to the history of religion and is the fount of all salvation. Pluralism, on the other hand, is theocentric: it is not the founder, say, of any one religion who can be said to be central in the history of religion; rather, it is the God (*Theos*) or transcendent reality common to them all that is central.

Although it is convenient to describe this or that theologian as an exclusivist, inclusivist, or pluralist – as we in fact have done – this typology itself has some limitations, chiefly for the reason that it is rather inflexible. Given the complex theological issues that have direct bearing on how one thinks of other religions – especially the various issues of *revelation, knowledge of God,* and *salvation* – there may be different answers to the question of whether one should be an exclusivist, inclusivist, or pluralist, depending on the variable at issue. In point of fact, we have difficulty classifying our own view in a straightforward manner. On the matter of revelation, we would incline to an inclusivist position. That is, while we hold to the primacy of the revelation of God in Jesus Christ (special revelation), we also recognize the reality of God's revelation in creation across time and space (general revelation). Consequently, *contra* a rigid exclusivism, we are also inclined to an inclusivist position on the matter of knowledge of God: if there is revelation outside of Christianity, knowledge of God cannot be an exclusively Christian possession. At this point, however, the inclusivist would claim, *contra* pluralism, that because of the uniqueness and finality of the revelation in Christ, Christian knowledge of God and relationship with God are of a different quality and type than what is found elsewhere in the history of religion. Adopting an inclusivist stance on the matter of truth allows for a gradation of truth that finds its center and fulfillment in Jesus Christ, which we find a more promising basis for Christian dialogue with members of the world's religions than that accorded by an exclusivist position. On the matter of salvation, which is the central issue and concern of the typology as ordinarily used, we would adopt a position on which both exclusivists and inclusivists agree, namely that Christ is the sole *means* of salvation. If God is the sovereign Creator of all that is, and if God has chosen to become uniquely incarnate in Jesus of Nazareth with the purpose of redeeming a creation that has gone awry, this particularist fact must be acknowledged. But as regards the *scope* of salvation, which extends to all of creation, including in principle both Christians *and* non-Christians, we lean in an inclusivist direction.[17] Such a universal scope currently remains a matter of Christian hope, since the Christian story has not yet concluded, an issue we will pick up in the next chapter. Whether a person from a non-Christian tradition who has had no meaningful encounter with the Christian faith can nonetheless through grace be saved by Jesus Christ by virtue of a faithful response to the revelation they have been given – even if such a response is expressed in terms of their own religion – we happily leave up to the triune God of love.[18]

As we have seen, Christians in the West during the last century have become especially conscious of religious plurality. Accordingly, Christian theology has been engaged in the work of crafting responses to the reality of a world in which there are many religions. But while the West was preoccupied with this challenge for the mission of the church, the global face of the church itself was changing. It is to that change, which is most profoundly taking place outside of the western world, that our discussion now turns.

[17] Instructively, in the history of Christianity, one often finds verdicts that are not straightforwardly exclusivist or inclusivist, as in the case of Augustine. Augustine obviously admired Greek philosophy, and in this way he resembles Justin Martyr and inclusivism. But he also recognized the futility of paganism and argued for the superiority of Christianity, and in this way he resembles Tertullian and exclusivism. More recently, Lesslie Newbigin expressed difficulty in identifying himself as an exclusivist or an inclusivist in a straightforward manner. See Newbigin, *Gospel in a Pluralist Society*, 171–83.

[18] This sort of inclusivist position is held by venerable representatives of both the Catholic and Protestant traditions, including John Paul II and C. S. Lewis, respectively. See John Paul II, *Crossing the Threshold of Hope*, trans. Jenny McPhee and Martha McPhee, ed. Vitorio Messori (New York: Knopf, 1994); C. S. Lewis, *The Last Battle* (New York: HarperCollins, 1994).

WORLD CHRISTIANITY

The recent growth of "non-western" Christianity

The twentieth century witnessed a revolutionary shift in Christianity's center of gravity. At the beginning of the century, the great majority (about 80 percent) of Christians in the world lived in Europe and North America. By its end, the majority of Christians (about 60 percent) were found in Africa, Latin America, and the Pacific Rim of Asia. The statistics in the case of Africa are particularly revealing: in the year 1900 – in the heyday of colonialism – there were about 10 million Christians in Africa. Around 1960 – as colonialism receded – there were approximately 60 million Christians in Africa. By the year 2000 – after the collapse of colonialism – there were some 360 million Christians in Africa. Even taking into account overall population growth, this remarkable demographic shift means that the socio-cultural character of Christianity is changing significantly.[19] As Philip Jenkins notes: "If we want to visualize a 'typical' contemporary Christian, we should think of a woman living in a village in Nigeria or in a Brazilian *favela*."[20] It seems clear that the numbers of Christians in the southern and eastern hemispheres will continue to rise dramatically. Importantly, as Christianity becomes an increasingly non-western religion, the shape of the church and the contours of its mission will inevitably be changed.

The "dean" of the study of world Christianity is the Scottish historian Andrew Walls, who has a special interest in the emergence, shape, and significance of African Christianity. Upon arriving in Sierra Leone as a young scholar with an Oxford doctorate in patristics, Walls was ready to instruct "the younger churches" about the significance of the early church. What he found, much to his surprise, was that he was living and teaching in a situation that very much resembled the patristic church of early Christianity. Just as Christians in the fledgling church wondered about the relationship of their new faith to currents in the Greco-Roman world, so have African Christians sought to make sense of the relationship between their new faith and their cultures' religious past: "Conversion is turning; and Christian conversion is turning towards Christ. This means that the process

---

[19] On the statistics presented here, see Joel A. Carpenter, preface to *The Changing Face of Christianity? Africa, the West, and the World*, ed. Lamin Sanneh and Joel A. Carpenter (New York: Oxford University Press, 2005), vii–viii; Jenkins, *Next Christendom*, 1–6; and Lamin Sanneh, *Whose Religion Is Christianity? The Gospel Beyond the West* (Grand Rapids, MI: Eerdmans, 2003), 14–15.
[20] Jenkins, *The Next Christendom*, 2.

of conversion involves turning what is already there."[21] According to Walls, as cultures become converted to Jesus Christ, they contribute to the ongoing "translation" of the gospel and the church into new cultural forms that reinvigorate Christianity. These historical and cultural translations are themselves dependent on the incarnation of Jesus Christ – the paradigm translation of God's good news into human form.[22] The point is clear: as Christianity returns from its centuries-long sojourn as a predominantly western religion to being a truly *global* faith, the very shape of the church and its beliefs will be dynamically changed (see Illustration 14.1).

While Christians in various parts of the world seek to understand their faith and live their Christian lives, they will develop expressions of faith and ways of living that differ – perhaps markedly – from the traditions of the West, challenging traditional notions of the identity and mission of the church. In what follows, we will take stock in very broad terms of the basic contours of some important emerging non-western manifestations of the one, holy, catholic, and apostolic church.[23]

Latin America

The Christian church in Latin America is already half a millennium old. The different forms and expressions of that church are all closely connected, at least historically, to the colonialist version of Christianity brought by Spanish and Portuguese *conquistadores*. Accordingly, traditional Latin American Christianity has been largely Catholic, mostly patterned on the Catholicism of the Old World. In fact, a strong majority of Latin America remains Catholic, with much traditional theology, liturgy, and church culture deeply embedded in the local churches and societies of Latin America.

But old-world Catholicism has not remained unaffected by Latin American culture. This inevitable contextualization and transformation of the faith began already in the colonial era itself, even if it accelerated at the end of the colonial period.[24] The subtle, and sometimes revolutionary, revision of aspects of Christianity into distinctively Latin American cultural forms can be seen in Mexico, for example, in the convergence of the indigenous penchant for

---

[21] See Andrew F. Walls, *The Missionary Movement in Christian History* (Maryknoll, NY: Orbis, 1996), xiii–xix, quotation at xvii.

[22] Ibid., 29.

[23] It bears pointing out that the kind of Christianity that is growing outside the West does not neatly fit the traditional categories used in the West for parsing Christian traditions and denominations – that is, Orthodox, Catholic, and Protestant.

[24] Dana Robert, "Shifting Southward: Global Christianity since 1945," *International Bulletin of Missionary Research* 24, no. 2 (April 2000), 53.

Illustration 14.1 Peter Paul Rubens's *Adoration of the Magi* (1626), depicting the biblical episode that adumbrates the global dimensions of the gospel of Christ and his multicultural church.

communion with the dead with the Catholic celebration of All Saints' Day and All Souls' Day – resulting in the well-known *día de los muertos* (Day of the Dead). An additional Mexican example is the combination of indigenous racial and cultural identity with Catholic devotion to the Virgin Mary as seen in the famous dark-skinned Virgin of Guadalupe.[25]

[25] On the broader theological and cultural considerations connected with the Virgin of Guadalupe, see Jenkins, *Next Christendom*, 108–12, 117–19.

Beginning in the 1960s, Latin American "liberation theologians," sensing a need for independence from the European and North American church, began to pay further attention to their own Latin American context. Lamenting especially the political and economic legacy of colonialism, they mobilized their theological reflections to address the pressing needs and concerns of the poor (see pp. 561–2). In meetings at Medellín in 1968 and Puebla in 1979, the bishops of the Latin American Catholic Church recognized on behalf of the continent's people a deep longing for liberation and issued a call for the church to advocate on their behalf.[26] This recognition by the church had significant ecclesiological consequences: careful account of the poor and their struggle for liberation became more central to the Latin American Catholic Church's mission, even though some of the more radical forays in this direction were met by deep suspicion on the part of the church authorities in Rome.[27] For the sake of the gospel, liberation theology contends, the church must struggle with the question of social justice, for all human persons should be able to live with dignity as they make choices about their own lives. As Gustavo Gutiérrez (b. 1928), the father of Latin American liberation theology, argued, in recognizing the wrongness of poverty, the church is required to protest against the conditions in which the poor live and suffer, as well as to live in solidarity with them. Here we see the theme of the "preferential option for the poor," a central tenet of liberation theology.[28] Just as God is especially attuned to the plight of the poor, so also should the Christian church prioritize their plight and needs. The streams of the Christian church that have become influenced by liberation theology are especially marked by their concern for justice, as well as the expression and practice of the gospel in social, economic, and political terms.

In a world of historical oppression and political repression, this kind of witness of the church has sometimes taken the form of a witness unto death – martyrdom. Among the most prominent examples of martyrdom in Latin America are the murders of Archbishop Oscar Romero in El Salvador in 1980, and six priests from the Jesuit university in San Salvador in 1989, a fate from which theologian Jon Sobrino escaped because he happened to be

---

[26] See Medellín's statements on the role of the church in working for justice and peace, in Second General Conference of Latin American Bishops, *The Church in the Present-Day Transformation of Latin America in the Light of the Council*, II: *Conclusions*, 3rd edn. (Washington DC: Secretariat for Latin America National Conference of Catholic Bishops, 1979), 32–57, henceforth referenced as *Medellín*.

[27] The disciplinary action taken by the Catholic hierarchy against Brazilian theologian Leonardo Boff can be taken as a paradigm case. See Harvey Cox, *The Silencing of Leonardo Boff: The Vatican and the Future of World Christianity* (Oak Park, IL: Meyer-Stone, 1988).

[28] Gutiérrez, *Theology of Liberation*, xxvii.

lecturing in Asia at the time of his fellow Jesuits' massacre. Sobrino contends that the Latin American church's experience of martyrdom is a participation in the dynamics of sin and salvation that were present in Jesus' own life, ministry, and cross.[29] In such a context, it makes sense that the liberationist wing of the Latin American church emphasizes the Christian God as the "God of life."[30] Christian discipleship is in turn a matter of the church actively and concretely opposing the forces of the world that harm the poor and dispossessed, unmasking them as the "idols of death."[31] History is the battleground of putative deities – the death-dealing forces of power and wealth in the world, and the life-affirming God of Jesus Christ – a struggle in which the church is called to participate. According to Ignacio Ellacuría, one of the 1989 Jesuit martyrs, the true church is called to witness to Christianity's resurrection hope by taking history's victims, or the "crucified people" (i.e., the economically, politically, and socially poor who meet with an untimely death), down from the cross, by acting on their behalf.[32] Through such activity, the church becomes the "church of the poor." Once again, we see here a vision of the church that differs from traditional ecclesiologies. In calling the church to be a church of and for the poor, liberationist Christianity in Latin America poses some serious challenges to traditional western conceptions of what it means for the church to be the true church, stressing the need for "right practice" (orthopraxis) beyond sheer confessional or doctrinal adherence to "right belief" (orthodoxy).

In large part an intra-Catholic challenge to traditional Catholicism in Latin America, liberation theology has become a well-known (and controversial) movement in Latin American Christianity. In recent years, however, Protestant Christianity, which is usually termed "evangelical" Christianity in Latin America, has been rapidly rising in prominence and significance – something that is also broadly true of "world Christianity" in general.[33] Sociologist David Martin describes the emergence of evangelical Christianity in Latin America as taking on "hurricane force" in the 1960s, as the population of evangelicals jumped from approximately 5 million to 40 million in about twenty years. This explosion of Protestantism has been especially strong in its charismatic and Pentecostal forms, which represented just over 2 percent of

[29] Jon Sobrino, *Witnesses to the Kingdom: The Martyrs of El Salvador and the Crucified Peoples*, various translators (Maryknoll, NY: Orbis, 2003), esp. chs. 4–6.
[30] See Gustavo Gutiérrez, *The God of Life*, trans. Matthew J. O'Connell (Maryknoll, NY: Orbis, 1991).
[31] Sobrino, *Jesus the Liberator*, 180–92.
[32] See Ignacio Ellacuría, "The Crucified People," trans. Phillip Berryman and Robert R. Barr, in *Mysterium Liberationis: Fundamental Concepts of Liberation Theology*, ed. Ignacio Ellacuría and Jon Sobrino (Maryknoll, NY: Orbis, 1993), 580–603.
[33] See Jenkins, *Next Christendom*, 6–8.

Latin America Protestantism in the 1930s, but over 50 percent by the 1980s.[34] Martin attributes this phenomenal growth in part to the breakdown of the social/religious synthesis of traditional Latin American Catholicism.[35] It is among the poor and less educated that evangelical Christianity has made its most rapid inroads on the Latin American continent, in contrast to liberation theology, which appealed more frequently to the intellectual classes.[36] While "Pentecostal" is an adjective whose roots lie in the western world, it is often used to describe this relatively new burst in Latin American Christianity due to the fact that healings, speaking in tongues, and direct revelations are characteristic of these expressions of Christianity.[37]

In contrast to the overt and usually left-leaning political proclivities of liberation theology, the evangelical/Pentecostal churches of Latin America have often been described as relatively apolitical. Accordingly, many liberation theologians have criticized both Protestant and Catholic versions of "Pentecostalism" as a quietism that is susceptible to manipulation by conservative political elements.[38] But many scholars caution against this judgment.[39] Some argue that much of evangelicalism's "apolitical" talk represents more of a disgust with traditional forms of politics (and the traditional church's role in such political structures) than a rejection of politics altogether.[40] Suggesting that Latin American evangelicalism is not inherently apolitical, Martin argues, for example, that the communitarian focus of many such churches has actually served in a quite liberative way to give voice to previously voiceless women in Latin America.[41] And Eldin Villafañe's *The Liberating Spirit: Toward an Hispanic-American Social Ethic* is often pointed to as a (albeit North American Latino) representation of what a new "liberation theology" from the perspective of Latin American Pentecostal evangelicalism might look like.[42]

---

[34] David Martin, *Tongues of Fire: The Explosion of Protestantism in Latin America* (Oxford: Blackwell, 1990), 49–50.

[35] Ibid., 280.   [36] Ibid., 266. Cf. Jenkins, *Next Christendom*, 65.

[37] Martin, *Tongues of Fire*, 163–84.

[38] See, e.g., Jon Sobrino's critique in *The True Church and the Poor*, trans. Matthew J. O'Connell (Maryknoll, NY: Orbis, 1984), 233.

[39] See, e.g., Hannah W. Stewart-Gambino and Everett Wilson, "Latin American Pentecostals: Old Stereotypes and New Challenges," in *Power, Politics, and Pentecostals in Latin America*, ed. Edward L. Cleary and Hannah W. Stewart-Gambino (Boulder, CO: Westview, 1997), 232–4.

[40] See Martin, *Tongues of Fire*, 233–68.

[41] Ibid., 181. And in his important study of the worldwide rise of Pentecostalism, Harvey Cox suggests more globally that such forms of Christianity flourish when traditional religious options have ceased to meet people's spiritual, personal, and social needs, and as such unleash "liberating energy" into society. See Cox, *Fire from Heaven: The Rise of Pentecostal Spirituality and the Reshaping of Religion in the Twenty-first Century* (Reading, MA: Addison-Wesley, 1995), 315.

[42] Eldin Villafañe, *The Liberating Spirit: Toward an Hispanic-American Social Ethic* (Grand Rapids, MI: Eerdmans, 1993).

In short, the rather different challenges to traditional Latin American Catholic Christianity that emerge from liberation theology and Pentecostal evangelicalism may not be entirely at odds with one another as is often thought. And it is clear that the shape taken by the future Latin American churches will provide ongoing challenges to the worldwide church – especially in the northern hemisphere – as it continues to grapple with its identity and mission as the body of Christ.

Africa

Christianity has had a presence in northern Africa since the early church, as well as in a few places in sub-Saharan Africa. But most of sub-Saharan Africa has been characterized historically by indigenous religious observances and beliefs, which are commonly called "primal religions." Similar to Latin America, the more prevalent presence of the Christian church in sub-Saharan Africa is linked to the age of colonialism, when the European powers brought their faith with them in their exploration and exploitation of foreign lands. As Africa has entered a post-colonial Christian era, the church has ironically blossomed both in terms of numbers and in the indigenizing of Christian belief and practice. In this context, a key issue for the African church has been that of its distinctive identity.

One of the prominent attempts to forge a Christian identity in the post-independence, post-missionary African church has focused on the African struggle against oppression and inequality – that is, African liberation theology, highly profiled in the South African struggle with apartheid.[43] But another way of addressing the issue, focusing on cultural identity, is exemplified by Kwame Bediako (1945–2008), a theologian from Ghana. Following Andrew Walls (his teacher), Bediako argues that the translatability of the Christian gospel (both linguistically and culturally) means that God speaks to people, including Africans, in their mother tongues.[44] This leads Bediako to reflect ecclesiologically on the relationship between Christianity and indigenous, pre-Christian African culture. Such primal religions were generally dismissed as insignificant by missionaries in the colonial era. For example, at the World Missionary Conference held in Edinburgh in 1910, missionaries rejected the notion that African primal religion and religious experience could serve as a "preparation for

---

[43] E.g., Allan A. Boesak, *Black and Reformed: Apartheid, Liberation, and the Calvinist Tradition*, ed. Leonard Sweetman (Maryknoll, NY: Orbis, 1984).
[44] See Bediako, *Jesus in Africa*, 49–62. Cf. Sanneh, *Whose Religion is Christianity?*, 69–73.

Christianity," since they assumed that Africans had little or no knowledge or sense of God. Given this western missionary attitude and practice, the resulting loss of memory by Africans of their religious past made it difficult for the African church to forge its own Christian identity. Today, however, such pre-Christian traditions are increasingly seen as integral to the health of the African Christian church.[45]

According to Bediako, the recognition of the importance of indigenous ("primal") traditions by the African church and its theologians has produced a sustained discussion of the question "as to how, and how far, the 'old' and the 'new' in African religious consciousness could become integrated into a unified vision of what it meant to be African *and* Christian."[46] Answers to this question have varied. Some have seen a deep continuity between the old and the new, not viewing Christianity as something foreign to Africa, but regarding African Christian experience more as a modification of existing primal religious experience. Others have posited a more moderate continuity between primal religion and Christianity, one that sees the Christian message as relevant for Africa, while also counseling faithfulness to African ancestral traditions. Yet others hold that there is a radical discontinuity between the old and the new, one in which the distinctiveness of the Christian gospel rules out a positive evaluation of pre-Christian religion. Between these perspectives lie several mediating positions. On one such dialectical view, while *pre*-Christian religion must be taken seriously, *Christian* experience, especially *African* Christian experience, has an integrity of its own. In other words, Christian faith can legitimately and authentically be translated into an African context. The Christian message should interact with – shape and be shaped by – the experience of being African as the church forges its identity and lives out its mission.[47]

Bediako himself has contributed in an important way to the development of a distinctive African Christian culture by exploring in particular the connection between Jesus Christ and the role of ancestors in African primal religion.[48] Ghanaian Christians, according to Bediako, see Jesus, like their ancestors, as having the function of mediating between them and the spirit world. But because the ancestors themselves as human beings require salvation, Jesus shows himself to be the only *true* mediator between God and humanity.[49] Bringing the NT book of Hebrews together with the

---

[45] Ibid., 50–3.   [46] Ibid., 53.   [47] Ibid., 54–6.
[48] See Bediako, "Jesus in African Culture: A Ghanaian Perspective," in *Emerging Voices in Global Christian Theology*, ed. William A. Dyrness (Grand Rapids, MI: Zondervan, 1994), 93–121.
[49] Ibid., 102.

African view of ancestors, Bediako argues that Jesus surpasses all other ancestors. The latter "remain essentially *human* spirits," but Jesus, being fully divine
yet having become incarnate and having suffered death for sinners, "is the only
real and true Ancestor and Source of life for all mankind, fulfilling and transcending the benefits believed to be bestowed by lineage ancestors."[50] Bediako
thus suggests that the African church must develop (and live by) a christology
that is commensurate with traditional orthodox christology, but should do this
by means of African categories and practices that flow from genuinely indigenous cultural traditions.

Despite the flourishing of Christianity in many parts of Africa, the African
church also faces a formidable set of challenges. One of the most significant of
these is the growth of rather rigorous forms of Islam on the African continent,
which produces a situation where Christian communities and Muslim communities frequently live side by side – and that not always harmoniously, but
often with much discontent and struggle for power. This is, of course, a
challenge that the Christian church also faces elsewhere in the world, especially
in Asia and the Middle East. Concerning the interface of these monotheistic
goliaths, Philip Jenkins conjectures (with no small dose of sensationalism):
"A worst-case scenario would include a wave of religious conflicts reminiscent
of the Middle Ages, a new age of Christian crusades and Muslim jihads.
Imagine the world of the thirteenth century armed with nuclear warheads
and anthrax."[51] The religious differences between Christianity and Islam that
have historically led to much violence and social struggle are intensified on the
African continent by the broader political, social, and economic problems that
beset African nations – think, for example, of Nigeria. With these conditions,
the African church finds itself in a trying crucible, one representative of the
broader challenge to the global church to honor the truth and distinctiveness of
its own confession and life, while living peaceably and charitably with the
"other."

Asia

While making generalizations about the situation of the church in Latin
America and Africa is already an endeavor fraught with countless difficulties
and requiring numerous qualifications, such a task is nearly impossible with
respect to the sprawling and diverse continent of Asia. The issues that shape
the theology, worship, and life of the church in Kerala, India, for one small
example, are quite different from those present in the church in Papua,

---

[50] Ibid., 117–18. [51] Jenkins, *Next Christendom*, 13; also see 168–71.

Indonesia.[52] To simplify an enormous task, we shall content ourselves by focusing on the tensions that confront the church in China, given that China is the most populous nation on earth and one whose global influence and power are quickly on the rise.

Christianity has long had a marginal presence in China, a presence that was challenged and reshaped in the face of the Maoist revolution leading to the establishment of communism in China in 1949. In general, the Christian church has been viewed with suspicion by the Chinese government, which is officially atheistic. One of the first institutional forms taken by Christianity after the Chinese Civil War was the Three Self Patriotic Movement – the three selves of "self-government, self-support, and self-propagation" – originally formed in the early 1950s as a Christian society tightly bound to and dedicated to the flourishing of the nation of China. In the attempt to allay governmental fears about a western-influenced Christianity, Y. T. Wu, its first bishop, established the Three Self Movement in order to forge a genuinely Chinese form of the church that could resist the western colonialism that the new China was trying to overcome.[53] Since 1958, when the traditional Protestant denominations were disbanded in China, the Three Self Patriotic Movement (in tandem with the China Christian Council, beginning in 1980) has served as the officially sanctioned institution of the Christian church in China. It is under a certain amount of control on the part of the communist government and continues to serve a cultural role in fostering the stability of society and in promoting a vision of the government as the leading institution for the good of Chinese society.[54]

While many Christians have, with varying degrees of enthusiasm, chosen to participate in the Three Self Patriotic Movement, many other Chinese Christians have considered the political and governmental restrictions placed upon this movement to represent an overly burdensome stricture on their faith. For this reason, there is a rather broad house-church movement in China that opts for an expression of Christian faith that is detached from official state control, but one that as a result engenders much more scrutiny on the part of the Chinese Communist Party and governmental

---

[52] See the essays by Philip L. Wickeri and Charles E. Farhadian in *Christian Worship Worldwide: Expanding Horizons, Deepening Practices*, ed. Charles E. Farhadian (Grand Rapids, MI: Eerdmans, 2007), 71–95, 171–95.

[53] See Gao Wangzhi, "Y. T. Wu: A Christian Leader Under Communism," in *Christianity in China: From the Eighteenth Century to the Present*, ed. Daniel H. Bays (Stanford, CA: Stanford University Press, 1997), 338–50.

[54] On the complex history and institutional connections of the Three Self Patriotic Movement with respect to the Chinese government, see Alan Hunter and Kim-Kwong Chan, *Protestantism in Contemporary China* (Cambridge: Cambridge University Press, 1993), 21–65.

agencies.[55] From afar, the tendency of western Christians in liberal democracies is to assume that there must be a major disjunction between the Three Self church and the house churches. While this is true to a degree, some scholars argue that rather than seeing the Three Self Movement as an institution that has compromised Christian faith in the face of pressure, and the house churches as those that heroically stand against government persecution, it is better to see the two as partners in a mutually fruitful relationship, even if neither side may see it quite that way. Paul Freston, for example, has suggested that the government's fear of pushing too many of its citizens toward the house churches leads it to give the Three Self Movement a fairly long leash, which then makes it possible for the Three Self church to advocate for Christianity in general, something the house churches are less able to do, given government suspicion.[56] Whatever may be the case, it is also necessary to mention that a consortium of house-church groups in China have clearly stated that their reason for not joining the Three Self Patriotic Movement is the division of loyalties that would result: "Three Self churches accept the state as their governing authority: their organization and administration are governed by the government's religious policy ... House churches take Christ as their head, and they organize and govern their churches according to the teachings of Scripture."[57] Moreover, despite their desire not to alienate themselves entirely from the Three Self Christians, the house-church groups have charged that "in many spiritual matters there is serious deviation in the Three Self Church."[58]

With these tensions, the Chinese church exemplifies the many difficult questions that arise when the church of Jesus Christ is pressured by society or government to shape its life and ministry in a certain way. While it is overt governmental pressure in the case of China, in the West it is often a covert social pressure that attempts to restrict the scope of the church's voice and ministry – as in the trend to confine "religion" to the private and individual sphere. In this crucible of faith, some Christians may regard modest compromise as acceptable for the greater good of Christian existence, while others will regard persecution as the necessary price for the church's autonomy and its fidelity to Christ as Lord. The answers to such contextual questions, of course, are not simple, and they depend upon a number of considerations.

---

[55] Hunter and Chan prefer the term "autonomous Christian communities" over the more typical "house churches" terminology. On the phenomenon more generally, see ibid., 81–8.

[56] Paul Freston, *Evangelicals and Politics in Asia, Africa, and Latin America* (Cambridge: Cambridge University Press, 2001), 104–5.

[57] Included in Appendix B of David Aikman, *Jesus in Beijing: How Christianity is Transforming China and Changing the Global Balance of Power* (Washington DC: Regnery, 2003), 304–5.

[58] Ibid., 294.

But this is the ever-present ecclesiological challenge to the worldwide church that confesses Christ as Lord, a communion that wrestles with what it means to be *in* the world but not *of* it.

THE FUTURE OF THE CHURCH

Clearly, the face of the Christian church in the world is changing. The West is becoming increasingly post-Christian and Christianity is becoming increasingly post-western. This waxing and waning of fortunes presents both challenges and opportunities for the Christian church.

While it is generally much safer to pronounce on the past than predict the future, it seems clear that, barring major catastrophes, the trends away from Christianity and involvement with the church in the West will continue for the foreseeable future.[59] Increasing recognition of the reality and claims of religious traditions other than Christianity will likely continue to occupy the attention of western churches, which seek to address not only the challenge of religious plurality (the question of the identity of God) but also the challenge of secularity (the question of the existence of God).

It also seems clear that the trends toward Christianity outside the West, especially in the global south, will continue for some time to come. As Christianity grows and develops in Africa, Asia, and Latin America, operating in a context that is different from that of "the West," and with a temperament that is less defensive and accommodating than its western sibling, Christianity in "the Rest" (of the world) is likely to become the pulsating epicenter of this 2,000-year-old religious tradition. Since different contexts are giving rise to diverse contextual theologies and ecclesial expressions, special effort will be required to foster a global theological conversation and ecclesial cooperation.

Perhaps the most recent change of leadership in the Roman Catholic Church brings many of these challenges and questions into focus. John Paul II (in office from 1978 to 2005) was the first non-Italian pope since the sixteenth century. The appointment of his successor, Benedict XVI, followed this tradition-breaking but nonetheless Eurocentric pattern. Was the appointment of Benedict XVI an indication from one of Christianity's major traditions that the fight for Christian Europe and the West is not yet over? Who might Benedict XVI's eventual successor be? Will the

---

[59] Philip Jenkins suggests that the growth in Christianity, e.g., in Europe, will come largely through the influx of immigrants from the Christian south and east. See Jenkins, *God's Continent: Christianity, Islam, and Europe's Religious Crisis* (Oxford: Oxford University Press, 2007).

Catholic Church again choose a European? Or might the next pope hail from Latin America or Africa as a symbol of the seismic shifts in the topography of the church? Whatever be the case, the shape of the identity and mission of the church will undoubtedly be affected, perhaps even surprisingly transformed, as it moves into the future, a future filled with the assurance of Christ's abiding presence in the church (Matt. 28:20) and of God's redemptive promise for all creation. To that hope-full subject our discussion now turns.

FOR FURTHER READING

Cox, Harvey, *Fire From Heaven: The Rise of Pentecostal Spirituality and the Reshaping of Religion in the Twenty-first Century* (Reading, MA: Addison-Wesley, 1995).

Heim, S. Mark, *Salvations: Truth and Difference in Religion* (Maryknoll, NY: Orbis, 1995).

Hick, John, *An Interpretation of Religion: Human Responses to the Transcendent*, 2nd ed. (New Haven, CT: Yale University Press, 2005).

Jenkins, Philip, *God's Continent: Christianity, Islam, and Europe's Religious Crisis* (Oxford: Oxford University Press, 2007).

  The Next Christendom: The Coming of Global Christianity (Oxford: Oxford University Press, 2002).

Newbigin, Lesslie, *The Gospel in a Pluralist Society* (Grand Rapids, MI: Eerdmans, 1989).

Plantinga, Richard J., ed., *Christianity and Plurality: Classic and Contemporary Readings* (Oxford: Blackwell, 1999).

Walls, Andrew F., *The Missionary Movement in Christian History* (Maryknoll, NY: Orbis, 1996).

CHAPTER 15

Hope and the future

INTRODUCTION

Eschatology is, most literally, the study or doctrine of the "last things" (*eschata*). As systematic theology's last formal topic, eschatology typically addresses those events envisioned for the end of history, such as the second coming of Christ, the resurrection of the dead, and the final judgment – events that lead to the final, eternal state of heaven or hell. But as Jürgen Moltmann has strongly argued, eschatology should not only be seen as the concluding chapter of Christian theology, preoccupied with history's culminating events. Rather, at its best, it is a vision of hope grounded in the life, death, and resurrection of Christ that ought to inform all doctrines and mobilize Christian practice in the present.[1] In this broader sense, eschatology concerns the basic dynamics of Christian hope.

HOPE SPRINGS ETERNAL

To hope is human. We all hope daily for a myriad of things both consciously (e.g., for success in the day's activities or world peace) and tacitly (e.g., that the sun will rise or that evil will not befall us). When we reflect upon our multifarious hopes, we can identify some common features about them that facilitate a general characterization of hope: hope is an expectation of some good that we long to realize, but which lies beyond our immediate or ultimate control to effect. In breaking this working definition down, we first note that hope is an expectation of *some good*. No one hopes for that which will not benefit oneself or others in some way, though the good in question can be variably, even perversely, defined. Further, hope has the texture of *expectation*, since the good to be realized is future. Such an expectation contains a degree of emotion: it is a *longing* or anticipation that excites, inspires, or enthralls us. C. S. Lewis described the most intense form of this longing as joy.[2] Moreover, the good that we long for we consider *realizable* – it is not mere fantasy, but is in the realm of possibility, though it may at times present itself as a "hope against hope" in the face of incredible odds. And finally, the good that we hope to realize *lies beyond our immediate or ultimate control to effect*. We typically do not hope, at least actively, for that which we can readily bring about. For example, most of us (unlike many across the globe) do not hope to eat dinner tonight, but take this for granted along with a host of other ordinary affairs in life. The German term *Sehnsucht* is a helpful synonym for hope that illustrates hope's fundamental dynamic. Usually translated "longing" or "yearning," *Sehnsucht* is a combination of two words, seeing (*sehen*) and seeking (*suchen*). In hope something good and realizable is *seen*, but not yet possessed; it is therefore *sought* with a longing expectation.

Since there are many gradients and degrees of hope, from the trivial (I hope my team wins the game), to the serious (I hope my mother's cancer stays in remission), to the sublime (I hope there is life after death), it is helpful to make a distinction between *hopes* (plural, small "h") and *Hope* (singular, capital "H"). Let us consider *hopes* to be our various earthly, historical aspirations that we entertain in life this side of death, what we

---

[1] Moltmann, *Theology of Hope*, 15ff.
[2] C. S. Lewis, *Surprised by Joy* (New York: Harcourt Brace Jovanovich, 1956), esp. pp. 17ff.

regard as more or less possible to realize in our (or our children's) lifetime. In distinction from these penultimate hopes, but not necessarily in separation from them, *Hope* can be regarded as humanity's more concentrated and ultimate longing for the good we desire beyond death – that brute reality which by all empirical observation does not appear to be an optimal end to life. Most people hope that death does not have the final say; we therefore long not only for continued existence but for a better life beyond death. If death were the final word, it would seem to make a mockery out of life. Most people believe that life cannot be so cruel – to have lived and loved and then be cast into oblivion. Most people therefore incline to think that life must have more design and purpose scripted into it, and therefore have Hope – Hope in a constellation of goods that transcend death.

For pedagogical purposes, we can break down this complex of death-transcending goods that constitutes most people's ultimate Hope into four basic components.[3] First, such Hope entails belief in a transcendent source of life who has the power to preserve life beyond physical death – a source of life typically called "God." Second, it entails the belief that God cares for people – especially, subjectively speaking, for "me" – and can grant us individual immortality. Third, it includes the belief that goods are acknowledged and wrongs righted, that justice prevails and the good triumphs. And finally, it holds that after this reckoning, this triumph of the good, there obtains an eternal enjoyment of the good in a place called heaven. Typically put, (1) God, (2) immortality of the soul, (3) final judgment, and (4) eternal life in heaven – these comprise the basic constellation of Hope (capital "H") that most people long for beyond death, and without which life finally makes little sense.

But is such Hope realistic or realizable? Is it humanly reasonable to hold such a constellation of ultimate beliefs? The deists thought so. These religious philosophers of the Enlightenment, who prided themselves on believing only that which was rational to hold, maintained that these transcendent beliefs were not only reasonable, but in fact necessary for the functioning of any just and moral society. Take Herbert of Cherbury, for instance, who is widely acknowledged as the architect of English Deism. He judged that such ultimate hopes are etched within us as "common notions" – as ideas that are rationally certain, universally apprehensible, and necessary for life – namely, that there is a supreme God, the designer of life, who is all good, just, and moral, and who therefore ought to be worshipped

---

[3] The following analysis is especially true of cultures influenced by monotheistic belief, which, when given the world-historical influence of Judaism, Christianity, and Islam, includes a majority of the world's population.

through right moral conduct since there is a judgment of the immortal soul for reward or punishment after this life.[4] To the deists, without these eschatological incentives, moral and civil life could not be easily guaranteed or even make sense.

Whether one thinks these major items of Hope are rationally demonstrable or not, they do seem quite reasonable to many people, or at least they are hoped for, since without them life appears dark and tragic, if not absurd. In fact, most Christians also seem to affirm these four as the central features of Christian Hope. But in truth, left as they are, these beliefs do not fully reflect the biblical portrait of salvation; rather, they tend to convey a gnostic sense of salvation – that of the escape of the soul from an evil material world. The genius of Christian Hope, properly understood, is that it is hope rooted in and for this world – both its good space and time.

In light of the full sweep of the biblical narrative, Christian Hope is not so much that the soul takes flight to God upon death, having been judged in some individual sense worthy of the pure spiritual state of heaven. Rather, true Christian Hope is much more "earthy." Instead of us simply going to God, it is God who finally comes to us. Instead of the solo flight of the soul, it is the whole embodied person who is raised from the dead. Instead of merely a private and individual judgment upon death, final judgment is also public, historical, and perhaps even collective. And instead of heaven being the final state, the final eschatological hope is for the renewal of all things, a new heaven *and earth*. Christian Hope in its fullest sense envisions Christ as God-in-the-flesh returning visibly to earth, raising the dead, administering justice, and making a home with us in a renovated cosmos. Put chronologically, Christ's second coming, the resurrection of the dead, the final judgment, and a new heaven and earth – these are the four basic pillars of what we will call an *ecumenical eschatology*, that which all Christians everywhere and across time (Catholic, Protestant, Orthodox) should be able to agree upon if they confess either the Apostles' Creed or the Nicene Creed, since these are the four basic eschatological beliefs emphasized in these ecumenical creeds. It is these four pillars of Christian Hope that will structure our systematic treatment after we first elaborate some biblical and historical perspectives on Christian eschatology.

Hope springs eternal, Alexander Pope once penned.[5] Humanity cannot live without hope; nor can a vibrant Christianity. The intimate relationship

---

[4] Herbert of Cherbury, "Common Notions," 169–81, esp. 178.
[5] Alexander Pope, *Essay on Man*, in *The Poems of Alexander Pope*, ed. John Butt (New Haven, CT: Yale University Press, 1963), Epistle 1.3.

between Christian hope, faith, and love has long been noted, taking a cue from Paul's exhortation in 1 Corinthians 13:13: "And now faith, hope, and love abide, these three." In the Roman Catholic tradition, these three are known as the *theological virtues*, and are understood as mutually reinforcing dispositions or habits of the soul that are given and nurtured by divine grace, since they are beyond sheer human ability to cultivate. In a similar vein, John Calvin highlighted the near-reciprocal relation of hope and faith: "Hope is nothing else than the expectation of those things which faith has believed to have been truly promised by God. Thus, faith believes God to be true, hope awaits the time when this truth shall be manifested."[6] Given this intimate relation between faith and hope, Moltmann suggests that Christian theology can just as appropriately be described as "hope seeking understanding" (*spes quaerens intellectum*) as it is classically "faith seeking understanding" (*fides quaerens intellectum*).[7] Hope is as essential to Christian life and thought as is faith. Only together can they engender authentic Christian love.

BIBLICAL ESCHATOLOGY

In elaborating a biblical eschatology, the notion of the kingdom of God is crucial, since it is the most central and overarching concept that unites the OT and NT. In the biblical narrative, we have stressed, the kingdom of God is not just a redemptive category, but is coterminous with creation. From the very beginning the Bible depicts God as King, one who creates a realm – the good space of creation – over which God's benevolent reign is to historically hold sway – the good time of creation. In this kingdom God has given humanity pride of place and a special responsibility to wear God's face and promote God's concerns in the world (as the image of God). This general human vocation is in fact depicted as a blessing to flourish, to be fruitful, and to tend to creation (Gen. 1:26–8; cf. 2:15). But human rebellion constructs a rival kingdom and the earth is convulsed (Gen. 3ff.). In the midst of this self-destructive history, Yahweh takes the initiative in setting things right by beginning small, by reclaiming a slice of humanity and a slice of creation, a chosen people (Israel) in a special land (Canaan), as the emissary of the divine mission to reclaim all peoples and lands. The elective promise to Abraham of a flourishing people, a fruitful and peaceable land, so as to be a blessing to the nations (foundationally, Gen. 12:1–3) must be seen as the means to reinstate God's blessing of the earth, which was

---

[6] Calvin, *Institutes*, 3.2.42.   [7] Moltmann, *Theology of Hope*, 32–6.

originally intended to take place through humanity's general vocation as inscribed in the *imago Dei*.

Old Testament hopes

According to Jewish theologian Abraham Heschel, Judaism was unique among the ancient near-eastern religions because it put a premium on *time* – consecrating, for example, the sabbath and the historical festivals – more than it did on *space* or place, as in a sacred mountain, river, or rock.[8] This makes human history – the drama of time – meaningful on the stage of the good earth, propelled principally by God's promises for the future and the expectation of their fulfillment. This hope for the future historical fulfillment of divine promise is an eschatological hope, the hope that "things at last" (cf. *eschata*) will be made right, that God's benevolent and just kingdom will finally fully come.

In the course of Israel's history, particularly during the low points of the destruction of the northern kingdom and exile of southern Judah, it was the prophets who especially articulated hopes for the ultimate triumph of Yahweh's kingdom. These eschatological hopes took the following concrete forms:

1. There was the growing expectation that Yahweh's kingdom would be ushered in by a special agent, an "anointed one" or *messiah*. We noted in Chapter 9 that there were actually a variety of messianic expectations in pre-Christian Judaism, the most popular one being that of a king in the lineage and likeness of David who would vindicate Israel and reign in righteousness (e.g., Pss. 2; 110; Isa. 9; 11; Jer. 23:5–6). But there also developed, especially during the intertestamental period, expectations of an ideal priest, an eschatological prophet, and, most noteworthy, an apocalyptic "Son of Man" – a supernatural heavenly agent who would come on the clouds to judge the nations and vindicate Yahweh's kingdom (based originally on Dan. 7:13ff.).[9]

2. This kingdom expectation included the hope of the *restoration of Israel* to its land, a return of the exiles to Canaan, a homeland that would flourish beyond any of its former glories, secure with God's presence in the temple (see Ezek. 34ff.).

3. Part and parcel of the restoration of exiled Israel was the promise of a *new covenant* (Jer. 31:31ff.), one more effectual than the Mosaic covenant by

[8] Heschel, *Sabbath*, esp. 3–10. [9] See Collins, *Scepter and the Star*, passim.

virtue of the law being written within the human heart, a covenant of forgiveness in which God would remember sin no more.

4. In parallel fashion, there was the promise of the *outpouring of the Spirit* in an unprecedented way (Joel 2:28–31), whereby all God's people – male and female, young and old, slave and free – would be variously anointed and animated by God's Spirit.

5. There developed especially during the intertestamental period the hope in the *resurrection of the dead*, as is seen in Daniel 12:2: "Many of those who sleep in the dust of the earth shall awake, some to everlasting life, and some to shame and everlasting contempt" (cf. also Isa. 26:19).

6. A *final judgment* was also envisioned for the end of days. The prophets typically referred to this as the "Day of the Lord," when Yahweh would come in judgment not only of God's own people, but of the world at large (e.g., Joel 2:30–1; Isa. 13:9–11).

7. Finally, there was the larger hope for a *new heaven and earth* (Isa. 65:17–25; 66:22–3), for a blossoming of life beyond the curse of the fall into sin, where the whole world would experience *shalom* – the fullness and completeness of well-being and of right relations – the longed-for peaceable kingdom.

The general OT hope for the ultimate triumph of God's kingdom, as concretized in these particular hopes, was a forward-looking and therefore *eschatological* hope.

New Testament realization

The astonishing claim of the NT is that these eschatological or end-time hopes have broken into history in the events surrounding Jesus of Nazareth. The NT proclamation is that in Christ's incarnation – his life and ministry, death and resurrection, ascension and sending of the Spirit – the eschaton, that anticipated final age of salvation, has arrived, albeit in a rather unexpected meek and gentle form and not yet in cataclysmic power. This sets up a basic tension in the NT literature between a salvation that has definitively arrived, but which has not been fully realized, a tension between the "already" and "not yet." This tensive historical dynamic qualifies the various dimensions of eschatological hope.

Take the messianic expectations, for example. The NT claims that these were fulfilled in Christ, but in unexpected ways. While he was acclaimed the son of David and messianic king, he did not conquer like a warrior king, but ironically as a suffering servant, riding "triumphantly" on a donkey, crowned with thorns, and ascending only an ignominious cross, not a royal throne. The expectation of apocalyptic triumph is now anticipated as a function of his second coming in power and glory (cf. Rev. 19). Similarly, as the Son of Man he did not come on the clouds to deliver salvation and judge the nations, but in lowliness inaugurated these realities through his death and resurrection. As the final apocalyptic judge, Christ is still to come.

Judgment therefore is both already and not yet. Christ's sacrifice on the cross as a once-and-for-all atonement for sin anticipates the final judgment, since it forgives sin now in the present. Those who respond in faith, through confession and repentance, are now "in Christ," in a new situation in which there is no longer any condemnation (Rom. 8:1). Nonetheless, Christ will come back to judge the living and the dead, both believer and unbeliever, for the works they have done in the flesh (John 5:28–9).

Resurrection is the inseparable corollary of Christ's death, the vindication of his life and ministry, and the essential foundation of Christian faith. It has both already happened in the person of Christ, and not yet fully come to pass in the general resurrection of the dead. In NT perspective, Christ is the "firstfruits" (1 Cor. 15:20ff.) or "firstborn" (Col. 1:15–18) of those who have died, guaranteeing the general resurrection of the dead. More than just the resurrection of a single individual, therefore, Christ's resurrection is the beginning of the new creation, of the complete renewal and renovation of God's good but frustrated creation. Believers in Christ already anticipate this salvation, since the power of Christ's resurrected life effects in them a new creation, "a new birth into a living hope" (1 Pet. 1:3). As Paul puts it: "So if anyone is in Christ, there is a new creation: everything old has passed away; see, everything has become new!" (2 Cor. 5:17). Yet believers long for that day when they will be fully clothed in a resurrected and glorified body, unburdened by sin, suffering, and death.

This salvation is currently mediated by the Holy Spirit, who is the eschatological gift. Anticipated at the end of days (Joel 2), the Holy Spirit is radically poured out at Pentecost (Acts 2) to inaugurate the new era won by Christ's death and resurrection and to make his salvific life present in the world. As the vivifying life of the new creation, the Spirit is a pledge, deposit, and guarantee (2 Cor. 1:22; 5:5; Eph. 1:14) of the fullness of salvation yet to come. The Spirit of the new creation is present in the world – primarily in the body of Christ, the church – but not yet fully in the transformation and glorification of the entire creation.

Therefore the new heaven and earth, the new creation, has begun, as Christ's church can already taste "the powers of the age to come" (Heb. 6:5); yet believers groan in the Spirit with all creation awaiting the redemptive drama to fully play itself out in hope that the whole creation will be freed from its bondage to decay (Rom. 8:18ff.).

Salvation therefore has an eschatological framework – it is already here and realized, but not yet fully. OT promises have already been fulfilled, but not in their definitive apocalyptic form. This classic eschatological tension is also seen in the most comprehensive eschatological horizon, that of the kingdom of God.

Jesus himself announces that the kingdom has come in his person and ministry, as he proclaims a new era of God's favor: "The Spirit of the Lord is upon me, because he has anointed me to bring good news to the poor. He has sent me to proclaim release to the captives and recovery of sight to the blind, to let the oppressed go free, to proclaim the year of the Lord's favor" (Luke 4:18–19). Jesus demonstrates that the kingdom has come by his mighty works, especially by casting out demons and binding Satan so as to plunder his kingdom (Matt. 12:22–9; cf. Luke 10:17–20; Rev. 12:9). For the time being, however, like unto its Lord, the kingdom is present in meek and humble form. It is like a small mustard seed which will eventually grow exceedingly large (Mark 4:31), or like leaven that works its way through the whole batch of dough (Luke 13:20–1). In short, the kingdom "has come" in the person of Christ; one merely needs to receive it: "Blessed are the poor in spirit, for theirs is the kingdom of heaven" (Matt. 5:3). God's kingdom is a present reality and possession "in Christ," which is why in Paul's writings the frequent reference to the *Lord* Jesus Christ has largely replaced talk of the "kingdom of God." Nevertheless, the full and cosmic realization of the kingdom is yet outstanding – it is still a future hope, to which both the NT and the pains of present experience poignantly testify. The kingdom of God is both *already* here in the person and work of Christ and in the renewing work of the Spirit, and *not yet* fully here in eschatological consummation.

From the NT perspective, therefore, what the OT anticipated for the end of history is now understood to occur in two phases – the first and second comings of Christ. This is why the NT begins to speak of this messianic age between Christ's two advents as "the last days" (Acts 2:17; 2 Tim. 3:1; Heb. 1:2), "the end of the ages" (1 Cor. 10:11; Heb. 9:26) or "the last hour" (1 John 2:18). Yet there still remains a definitive "last day" (John 6:39–40; 11:24; 12:48), a coming age associated with Christ's second coming that will witness the consummation of these eschatological hopes. Christ's first advent guarantees the latter, and it is their historical continuity that accounts for the NT expectation that the *parousia*, or Christ's second coming, is very near. NT scholar Oscar Cullmann offered a helpful analogy for thinking about this eschatological tension when he compared Christ's first coming to a decisive battle in a war (e.g., D-Day in WWII, which determined the course of the war), and Christ's second coming to the victory day of that war (e.g., VE-Day, when the Allies finally triumphed in Europe). Whereas the decisive battle for the kingdom of God has been won by Christ's death and resurrection, we still live in a time of struggle – the war continues, with battles that may even include setbacks (as was the Battle of the Bulge after D-Day). Nevertheless the outcome is assured and will be effectuated at the second coming.[10]

This NT sense of a salvation already inaugurated is typically called "realized eschatology," a salvation already experienced in history, which is then distinguished from "future eschatology," the consummation of these eschatological realities. This affirms a historical continuity of salvation between the already and not yet: what has already been established in history continues to work in history presently and will be consummated in the future on the same historical timeline. In this way the NT continues the OT's priority on time in the arena of space as the locus of God's creational and redemptive kingdom.

HISTORICAL PERSPECTIVES: THE WANING AND WAXING OF BIBLICAL ESCHATOLOGY

This *historical* dynamic of NT eschatology has not always been appreciated in Christian thought. Persistent gnostic tendencies have tempted the Christian tradition to focus more on an otherworldly heaven as the final locus of the kingdom of God rather than a historical and this-worldly new heaven and earth. Such a vertical orientation was reinforced, as we saw in Chapter 6, by the long-lasting Aristotelian-Ptolemaic cosmology that literally placed God's dwelling at the outer limits of the cosmos in the ethereal heaven. The Christian journey to God was largely viewed as an ascent to heaven, an orientation seen in Dante's classic *The Divine Comedy*, which narrates the travels of the Christian pilgrim from hell, through purgatory, to heaven. In the third and final installment of this journey, "Paradise," Dante the pilgrim travels through the cosmic spheres to the empyrean heaven and the final goal of salvation, that of beholding the glory of God – the beatific vision of the divine essence.

Though it is a generalization to say that this *transcendental eschatology* has dominated the Christian tradition – since that tradition contains some minority reports – the tenacity of a heaven-oriented eschatology continues

[10] Cullmann, *Christ and Time*, 84.

to be evident today: much of popular Christianity conceives the final state as the salvation of the soul in heaven, not as the resurrection and glorification of the whole person in a new heaven and earth.

Against this background, the NT dynamics of a *historical eschatology* already realized but not yet fully consummated were significantly eclipsed in doctrinal history – that is, until the category of history came fully into its own in the nineteenth century. With this heightened historical consciousness came the rise of historical criticism and a greater historical scrutiny of the biblical text. Quests were famously launched for the historical Jesus. In the midst of this historiographical flurry, NT scholars such as Johannes Weiss and Albert Schweitzer began to recover the thoroughly eschatological orientation of Christ's life, ministry, and prophetic task, arguing that the primitive Christian gospel could not be understood apart from its apocalyptic context. This recovery of biblical eschatology eventually worked its way from biblical studies into systematic theology. In his *Theology of Hope*, Jürgen Moltmann launched an entire theological agenda to recapture the dynamics of historical eschatology. Lamenting that eschatological themes had largely functioned as a mere appendix to much of Christian theology – treated only at the end of systematic theology and treating only future eschatological realities – Moltmann touted the primacy of hope:

From first to last, and not merely in epilogue, Christianity is eschatology, is hope, forward looking and forward moving, and therefore also revolutionizing and transforming the present. The eschatological is not one element *of* Christianity, but it is the medium of Christian faith as such, the key in which everything in it is set, the glow that suffuses everything here in the dawn of an expected new day.[11]

Rooting his thought in the cross and resurrection of Christ, Moltmann argued that just as the resurrection (to life) contradicts the cross (of death), so does the coming new creation inaugurated by the resurrection stand in contradiction to the powers of death of our present age as epitomized by the cross. This vision of the coming kingdom of God therefore should be revolutionary and transformative of present life, because it is the true reality to which history is moving, as already rooted in the gospel events and as present and approaching in the power of the Spirit.

One can safely say that in theology today the dynamic of realized and future eschatology is a given in biblical studies and significantly appreciated in systematic theology, even though this eschatological dynamic has not always filtered down into popular Christianity. The eschatological tension

---

[11] Moltmann, *Theology of Hope*, 11.

between a salvation (or kingdom of God) already realized, and one not yet fully so, has been assumed throughout our discussion of previous doctrines, and will also frame our treatment of the four main pillars of eschatological hope that constitute future eschatology.

A SYSTEMATIC CONSIDERATION OF ECUMENICAL ESCHATOLOGY

The second coming of Christ

Just as the first coming of Christ is key to realized eschatology (the already), the second coming of Christ is the linchpin of future eschatological hopes (the not yet). Without the second coming the other pillars of what we are calling an ecumenical eschatology are vacuous, since they depend theo*logically* on this apocalyptic event. It is for good reason that the very first Sunday of the Christian calendar (the first Sunday of Advent) celebrates the second coming, since this is the *sine qua non* of Christian Hope. The triune God's coming to the world, while definitive in the first coming of Christ, is not fully complete until the second coming, when the resurrected, ascended, and glorified Son becomes the lead agent of the general resurrection of the dead, the judgment of all people and nations, and the renewal and glorification of all things in a new heaven and earth – that is, when the kingdom has fully come and God will be all in all (1 Cor. 15:28).

Within the broader Christian church, however, the expectation of Christ's second coming has fallen on hard times for a variety of reasons. First, Christians reared and immersed in a modern scientific culture tend to have a harder time, whether actively or tacitly, embracing the supernatural, of which the second coming is a spectacular example. Second, the predominance of the belief that the final state of salvation involves the ascent of the soul to heaven directly upon death (i.e., transcendental eschatology) detracts from the necessity and finality of the second coming.

A third notable reason why many Christians find the second coming less than palatable is the particular presentation of it that has dominated the popular media. What is almost exclusively portrayed is a dispensational approach to end-time matters (see below), an approach that insists on a very detailed sequence of events of disaster and calamity leading up to the second coming, a tribulation from which true believers are spared, having been "raptured" out of the world. Given its popularity, many Christians (not to mention non-Christians) think it is the only doctrinal option concerning belief in the second coming, and because of their dismay with the implications of dispensationalism they are wary of any talk or consideration of the second coming.

A fourth major reason involves the so-called "delay of the parousia." *Parousia* is a technical term for the second coming, which, having been promised by Jesus himself, was expected by the NT church to occur at any time (see, e.g., 1 Cor. 7:25–9). Given the nearly two millennia now since Christ's promise, the delay of the parousia becomes a problem not so much because of its sheer unfulfillment, but because it parallels the problem of evil. Not until the second coming will evil be vanquished. Until that happens, the persistent problem of suffering can easily overwhelm one to the point of despair, a melancholy that can dampen and debilitate hope in history's resolution – namely, the full coming of God's kingdom. The continuing delay of the parousia tests Christian hope, which sometimes flags in the face of overwhelming evil: "How long, O Lord?" (cf. Rev. 6:9–10).

Only the second coming will resolve the problem of evil, since only an extra-historical resolution will suffice to redress history's woes. The second coming of Christ *is* that Christian hope, a hope that is realistic since it is based on a first coming of a transcendent one from outside of history, one who has lived and suffered in this world of violence and evil, but who has overcome. If Jesus Christ as the eternal Son of God is believed to have come once (a supernatural divine intervention), it is not a great stretch to believe in his coming again, a coming that is necessary for immortality (resurrection), justice (judgment), and the renewal of all things (new heaven and earth).

The question of the millennium

Historically, the expectation of Christ's second coming has usually been framed by millennial perspectives. Millennialism derives from the belief that Christ's advent is associated with a 1,000-year reign on earth, based on the apocalyptic text of Revelation 20:1–10. Various millennial views have evolved throughout Christian history. The earliest form is known as *historic premillennialism*. This position holds that Christ will return in dramatic, apocalyptic fashion *prior to* setting up a golden age on earth, a 1,000-year reign of peace, prosperity, and renewal before the general resurrection, final judgment, and inauguration of the eternal state. Held quite widely by the early church fathers, including Justin Martyr, Irenaeus, and Tertullian, this early premillennialism was significantly shaped by the "millennial day" theory. Taking quite literally the metaphor that a thousand years are like a day in God's sight (Ps. 90:4; 2 Pet. 3:8), the seven-day creation account was read as a prophecy portending an earthly history of 6,000 years followed by a millennium of God's sabbath rest into which all the OT eschatological descriptions of the new heaven and earth were placed (e.g., Isa. 11:6–9; 65:17ff.).

In the western church, historic premillennialism was superseded by what is termed *amillennialism*, especially due to the significant and lasting influence of Augustine, who forsook the former perspective in favor of the latter.[12] Convinced by the interpretation of Tyconius, who wrote the first treatise on biblical hermeneutics (*Book of Rules*) and who read the book of Revelation in more symbolic fashion, Augustine rejected the idea of a literal 1,000-year reign of Christ on earth. Rather, he took the "millennium" of Revelation 20 to symbolize the church age, that period of time between Christ's first and second coming. In other words, the millennium is *now*, the reign of Christ in church and kingdom, and the second coming will lead directly to the general resurrection, final judgment, and final state. Augustinian amillennialism was the dominant eschatological perspective in medieval Catholicism and was generally embraced by the Reformers and their traditions.

The rise of the modern world, however, witnessed yet another variation – that of *postmillennialism*. A close cousin to amillennialism, postmillennialism holds that the coming of Christ will occur *after* a golden age of Christian civilization of considerable duration (not necessarily a literal 1,000 years). Postmillennialists optimistically hold that the preaching of the gospel will convert the nations, including the Jews, bringing an unprecedented era of peace, prosperity, justice, and righteous living which will welcome Christ at his second coming. The preeminent American theologian Jonathan Edwards (1703–58) is postmillennialism's most famous proponent, whose experiences in the Great Awakening fueled his belief in the triumph of Christianity. Postmillennialism's association with modern western civilization and its scientific and technological gains has not escaped critics' notice (e.g., the modernist myth of unending progress is a secularized version of this eschatology), nor has the decline of postmillennial belief in the face of twentieth-century horrors.

Meanwhile historic premillennialism witnessed a revival in the post-Reformation era. One caught up in such speculation was James Ussher (1581–1656), Archbishop of Ireland. Presupposing the "millennial day" theory of 6,000 years of human history followed by a millennium of God's rest, Ussher attempted to reckon the time of Christ's premillennial return by calculating with painstaking research the time of creation, which he placed on October 23, 4004 BCE.

---

[12] See Augustine, *City of God*, 20.7.

The cataclysmic events of the French Revolution also ushered in a phase of Protestant premillennial speculation. It was in this nineteenth-century phase that *dispensationalism*, so prevalent in today's end-times frenzy, was born. The patriarch of dispensationalism is John Nelson Darby (1800–82), who, in light of his own reading of scripture, made a novel separation between OT ethnic Israel, for which God had an earthly plan and destiny, and the NT multicultural church, for which God had a heavenly plan and destiny. Accordingly, Darby did not view the NT church as a fulfillment or continuation of OT Israel, as was traditionally held. In his view, all the divine promises to OT Israel must be literally fulfilled in the land of Canaan. This framework begets the dispensational preoccupation with predictive prophecy (within a strict inerrantist view of scripture). Most of these biblical prophecies will be fulfilled after the so-called "rapture" of true believers, their sudden disappearance from the earth – another novel interpretation promoted by Darby. The rapture constitutes the first phase of Christ's return, and inaugurates a seven-year tribulation where the Jews are persecuted by the Antichrist, who will ultimately be defeated by Christ's glorious appearing at the end of the seven-year tribulation, after which Christ will set up his millennial reign for 1,000 years.

Dispensationalism became a core belief in twentieth-century American fundamentalism, and was especially popularized by Hal Lindsey's *The Late Great Planet Earth* (1970) and subsequent writings wherein Lindsey indicated that the generation that witnessed the rebirth of Israel as a nation (which happened in 1948) would be the world's last generation (based on the "parable of the fig tree" in Matt. 24:32–4).[13] Since then, a dispensational preoccupation with the end times has dominated the popular evangelical media. Virtually every televangelist, radio preacher, or publication that speculates on end-time affairs does so from a dispensationalist perspective. The prevalence of dispensationalism was recently demonstrated by the popularity of the *Left Behind* books, a bestselling novel series, which fictionally embellishes the classic dispensational scenario and countdown to Armageddon.[14]

But dispensationalism is highly questionable on biblical, theological, and ethical grounds. First, the biblical exegesis for virtually every idiosyncrasy of the dispensational schema is suspect – particularly when it argues for the separation between God's plan for ethnic Israel and the multicultural

---

[13] Hal Lindsey and Carole C. Carlson, *The Late Great Planet Earth* (Grand Rapids, MI: Zondervan, 1970).

[14] Tim LaHaye and Jerry B. Jenkins, *Left Behind: A Novel of the Earth's Last Days* (Wheaton, IL: Tyndale, 1995). This was the first in a series of sixteen novels.

church, the so-called "rapture" of the church, and the seven-year tribulation with its very detailed sequence of events just prior to Christ's second coming (as a literal and chronological interpretation of Revelation 6–19). Second, the dispensationalist view of prophecy is reductionistic, fixating on predictive prophecy, which is read very literally as "history written in advance." Third and more importantly, the ethical implications of dispensationalism are dire. It easily produces a fatalism concerning the future since that future is considered already etched in stone, and encourages a passivity concerning larger social issues, including the environmental crisis, which in its various forms (e.g., the prospect of nuclear, biological, or chemical holocaust) does indeed confront today's world with an apocalyptic specter – one of our own making (and unmaking?). In such fashion, the *Left Behind* perspective is one of the best contemporary examples of a gnostic Christianity that believes that Christians need not trouble about the world, for our home is a transcendent heaven (of which the "rapture" may be the quintessential gnostic symbol). In the *Left Behind* perspective, Christians are not responsible for the care of creation or for the attempt to reverse the conditions that threaten our mutual destruction, since this contemporary ecological sensitivity runs contrary to the dictates of predictive prophecy. There are other problems with the dispensationalist stance as well, including an unhealthy fascination with calamity and a geopolitical racism that stereotypes whole countries and nationalities as enemies of God (e.g., Russians, Arabs, Chinese).

That dispensationalism is such a loud voice in popular Christianity and the popular media – a voice of dogmatic certitude that seems at times to have considerable political influence in the United States, even on its foreign policy – is disturbing and warrants a critique. We do not believe it represents responsible or informed Christian thinking on end-time hopes, let alone Christian witness to human responsibility in the world. While dispensationalism is a Christian voice, it is an overly outspoken member of the family that must be challenged by those who reject its claim to best represent the Christian name in the world at large.

To locate and predict the second coming of Christ on a specific timetable of events or sequence of "signs of the times" – always a sensation and therefore a media event – is contrary to the dominant motif of scripture that Christ will come surprisingly as a "thief in the night" – at a time that no one knows, not even the angels or incarnate Son, but only God the Father (Matt. 24:36). Hope for the second coming is an expectation that the church should always foster, since Christ's promise is that the time is near (e.g., Rev. 22:7). This is why the church is encouraged to pray the "maranatha" prayer: "Amen. Come, Lord Jesus" (Rev. 22:20). But while we wait and yearn and hope and pray, we are enjoined to further Christ's concerns in the world. The three parables of Matthew 25 are particularly instructive here, since they conclude the so-called Olivet Discourse, Christ's prophetic, apocalyptic instruction concerning the end (Matt. 24–5). The parable of the ten bridesmaids counsels readiness for the bridegroom's coming (25:1–13), the parable of the talents encourages the investment of one's abilities while the master is away (25:14–30), and the parable of the sheep and goats teaches a judgment based on one's treatment of "the least of these" – the hungry, thirsty, stranger, naked, and imprisoned (25:31–46). In other words, hope and expectation of Christ's return require responsible participation in creation and society.

In the final analysis, the whole millennial issue may in fact be misplaced. Richard Bauckham, in his book *The Theology of the Book of Revelation*, argues convincingly that the function of the classic millennial text, Revelation 20:1–10, is really quite limited: it serves to vindicate the martyrs.[15] Though the martyrs, the epitome of the witnessing church, appear to be crushed by history and the power of the Beast, like unto their Lord who triumphed by humiliation (cf. Rev. 5), their sacrificial lives will be vindicated as a participation in the saving power of God. In other words, they are the true victors by means of their self-sacrifice, and therefore they reign with Christ. To read anything else into this text, such as a full-blown millennialism as traditionally conceived, is precisely that – a reading into. But in point of fact, much has been read into the 1,000-year language of Revelation 20 – most importantly, the OT passages concerning the new heavens and earth (e.g., Isa. 65:17ff.). This has had the effect of robbing the new heaven and earth – the renovation of the cosmos – of its final status as the endgame of God's salvation, which has then allowed a transcendent heaven to more easily substitute for the eternal state. This is eminently ironic, since the book of Revelation itself ends with the new heaven and earth in which heaven comes down to earth (in the symbol of the New Jerusalem), indicating that God's will is then done on earth as it is in heaven (cf. the Lord's Prayer). In the concluding chapters of the Christian canon, one cannot find a transcendent heaven as the final state. While the historical issue of the millennium may be conceptually misplaced, of all the millennialisms it is amillennialism that best approximates the biblical dynamics of the kingdom of God.

---

[15] Richard Bauckham, *The Theology of the Book of Revelation* (Cambridge: Cambridge University Press, 1993), 106–8.

The resurrection of the dead

The central NT hope for individual immortality is found in the resurrection of the dead, a hope grounded in Christ's resurrection. Strikingly, the OT does not manifest a well-developed or pronounced expectation of resurrection. Statements about Yahweh delivering the righteous from the depths of Sheol – the nondescript place of the dead – by and large have metaphorical reference to *this* life and its death-threatening snares (e.g., Pss. 30:3; 86:13; 103:3–4). Ultimately, however, the general OT concept of Sheol functions as an expression of hope that death may not have the final say (cf. Job 19:25–6). One such statement, Psalm 16:10, became the OT touchstone for Peter's NT claim of Christ's resurrection: "For you will not abandon my soul to Hades [OT Sheol], or let your Holy One experience corruption" (Acts 2:27). More explicit OT images of resurrection apply to the national hope of a revived and preserved Israel (Ezek. 37:1ff.; Isa. 26:19). There is in fact only one OT text that explicitly speaks of the resurrection hope for individuals, Daniel 12:2 (quoted above). But as this text is likely from the second century BCE, it underscores the fact that only in intertestamental apocalyptic literature did the hope for a general resurrection from the dead become explicit, as reiterated in such literature as 2 Maccabees, and especially in the book of Wisdom. That the resurrection was a common but not universal expectation in first-century Judaism is seen in the debate between the resurrection-affirming Pharisees and the resurrection-denying Sadducees (see Acts 23:6–9).

NT faith, however, lives or dies with the resurrection of Jesus Christ, as Paul confirms in his great chapter on the resurrection, 1 Corinthians 15: "If Christ has not been raised, then our proclamation has been in vain and your faith has been in vain" (v. 14). Moreover, "If the dead are not raised, 'Let us eat and drink, for tomorrow we die'" (v. 32). For Paul in particular and the NT witness in general, the resurrection of Christ is depicted as the dawn of the new creation, since Christ is raised as the "firstborn" (Col. 1:15–18) and "firstfruits" (1 Cor. 15:20) of those who have died. Christ's resurrection makes the new creation available now to the Christian community as a spiritual rebirth (realized eschatology), which is considered a kind of firstfruits of all that God created (Jas. 1:18) that anticipates the general resurrection of the dead and the renewal of all things – the new heaven and earth (Col. 1:20; Eph. 1:10; Rev. 21, esp. v. 5). In short, the NT overwhelmingly intones the future resurrection of the dead as the central Christian eschatological hope.

The Christian emphasis on the resurrection is a far cry from the Platonic and Neoplatonic view that the rational soul possesses immortality by virtue of its own intrinsic eternality or divine character. This dualistic depreciation of the body is certainly part of the reason why Paul asserts that the gospel is "foolishness" to the Greeks (1 Cor. 1:18–25), even as Paul's own preaching in Athens about the resurrection was largely scorned (Acts 17:16–34). In fact, the NT itself never speaks of the "immortality of the soul" (nor do the ecumenical creeds). Rather, it declares that God alone is immortal (1 Tim. 6:16), and teaches that human immortality is entirely dependent upon God. Instructively, the NT Greek words for "immortality" and "incorruption" are found predominantly in 1 Corinthians 15, Paul's concentrated treatise on the resurrection. There it is asserted that immortality or incorruption is to be received only at Christ's second coming as an attribute, it appears, of the whole person, both body and soul.

The centrality of the resurrection of the dead as *the* Christian hope, accordingly, takes the reality of death very seriously, a reality that is not so easily faced and which requires genuine lament and an earnest process of grief. As mere words often fail us in confronting death, our grief and hope are often better engaged by the arts, such as music. For this reason, one of the most prominent and profound themes in the history of western music is the specter of death in view of the Christian anticipation of the resurrection. As we indicated in Chapter 8, Gustav Mahler searchingly explored the dialectic of death and resurrection in his second symphony ("Resurrection") (for works by other composers on this theme see Table 15.1). Instructively, Mahler gets to the actual theme of resurrection only in the fifth and final movement, having first wrestled with human suffering, anguish, and the grief of death at great length. As reflected in Mahler's symphony, the poignancy and jubilation of the resurrection can be appropriately celebrated only if death is truly recognized as "the last enemy" (1 Cor. 15:26).

Table 15.1 *Other notable compositions about death and the hope of resurrection*

Composer	Work
Johann Sebastian Bach (1685–1750)	*St. John Passion, St. Matthew Passion*
Wolfgang Amadeus Mozart (1756–91)	*Requiem*
Giuseppe Verdi (1813–1901)	*Requiem*
Johannes Brahms (1833–97)	*A German Requiem*
Gabriel Fauré (1845–1924)	*Requiem*
Olivier Messiaen (1908–92)	*And I await the resurrection of the dead*
Henryk Górecki (1933–)	*Symphony no. 3 (Symphony of Sorrowful Songs)*
Arvo Pärt (1935–)	*St. John Passion*

The question of the intermediate state

But if the general resurrection is the central Christian hope for the individual's overcoming of death, this raises the question of what happens to persons between death and resurrection. We will briefly map out four basic positions on this question, largely pivoting on the variable of whether or not the "soul" is a constituent aspect of the human person that is separable from the "body."

What is known as the doctrine of the *intermediate state* has been the majority position of the Christian church since at least Augustine. It basically holds that upon death the soul, created immortal by God and therefore separable from the perishable body, goes to be with Christ in heaven, but is yet to be reunited with the body in the resurrection at Christ's second coming. Advocates of this position point to a number of NT passages that seem to indicate an intermediate state, such as the parable of Lazarus and the rich man (Luke 16:19–31), Christ's words to the penitent thief on the cross, "truly I tell you, today you will be with me in Paradise" (Luke 23:43), or Paul's assertion that to be absent from the body is to be present with the Lord (2 Cor. 5:8; cf. also Matt. 10:28; Phil. 1:21–3; Rev. 6:9; 20:4). With such texts in mind, this position attempts to account for the scriptural principle that nothing, not even death, can separate us from the love of God in Christ (Rom. 8:38–9).[16]

Second, the Roman Catholic conception of *purgatory* is a variation of the doctrine of the intermediate state. According to this teaching, believers who have died without attaining the necessary holiness to enjoy the beatific vision – beholding the glory of God in heaven – require an intermediate time of purgation. While the notion of purgatory has been embellished over the years with many speculative details – such as calculations of duration and the nature of the refining discipline – it is still regarded in Catholic thought today as a place between death and final judgment where believers continue to work out their salvation, a process of purification of any residual sin (cf. 1 Cor. 3:10–15).[17] This position attempts to account for the scriptural principle that without holiness no one will see God (Heb. 12:14).

A third basic position is known as *psychopannychia*, or "soul-sleep." Intimated by many of the early church fathers before Augustine's influence became dominant, psychopannychia was embraced by many Anabaptists

---

[16] For a full statement and defense of the doctrine of the intermediate state, see John W. Cooper, *Body, Soul, and Life Everlasting: Biblical Anthropology and the Monism–Dualism Debate*, 2nd edn. (Grand Rapids, MI: Eerdmans, 2000).

[17] See *Catechism of the Catholic Church*, 291.

around the time of the Reformation. (Interestingly, John Calvin's earliest theological writing was entitled *Psychopannychia* [1534], penned as a refutation of the doctrine in favor of the traditional intermediate state.) This teaching maintains that at death the soul enters into an unconscious, sleep-like state, only to be reawakened at the resurrection. This position attempts to account for the pervasive NT use of sleep as a metaphor for death, in addition to the weight it puts on the resurrection. Soul-sleep was more recently defended by Oscar Cullmann as capturing the dominant NT perspective.[18]

A fourth position can simply be termed *resurrection from the dead*. Though occasionally anticipated in church history (e.g., Petrus Pomponatius [d. 1525]), this position gained in popularity in the twentieth century among philosophers and theologians, due in no small measure to more holistic approaches in anthropology, including studies in brain physiology. Rejecting the view of the separability of the soul from the body as a questionable inheritance from Platonism, advocates of this position hold that human beings are psychosomatically unified. Whatever the "soul" is, it cannot exist apart from the body. Thus, when persons are physically dead, they are fully dead – both body and soul. The whole person, therefore, awaits re-creation at the general resurrection. This position seeks to capture a biblical holism concerning the human person, to take death more seriously as the "last enemy" (1 Cor. 15:26), and to put full weight on the resurrection as the central NT hope.

There are, to be sure, many variations of these four positions based on other considerations or theological variables, including whether judgment day is at death or the second coming, whether eternality is conceived of as timelessness (eternity) or unending time (everlastingness), and whether the final state is considered a transcendent heaven or a new heaven and earth. The question of the intermediate state is complex, and each position has its relative strengths and weaknesses. We will not attempt to adjudicate this debate, but prefer to remain agnostic as to its outcome, since we do not think scripture speaks loudly or clearly enough on this speculative area. That said, however, we do offer one pertinent observation: while the majority of the Christian tradition has held to some form of the intermediate state – the idea that the soul survives death to be with Christ in heaven – this has overwhelmingly functioned for most Christians, tacitly, as *the final state*, drawing remarkably close to the Platonic hope of the immortality of

[18] Oscar Cullmann, *Immortality of the Soul or Resurrection of the Dead? The Witness of the New Testament* (New York: Macmillan, 1964).

the soul. This is a problem, since it robs Christian hope of its unique dynamic concerning the second coming of Christ, the resurrection of the dead, and life in a new heaven and earth. Any teaching that diminishes the centrality of Christ's second coming and the eschatological chain of events it sets in motion is not faithful to the central NT affirmation that the avenue to everlasting life is the resurrection of the dead.

Final judgment

The OT assertion that God will judge *all* peoples parallels the recognition that Yahweh is the sole Creator God: "Rise up, O God, judge the earth; for all the nations belong to you!" (Ps. 82:8). This point is punctuated in the "all nations" prologue to Israel's history, Genesis 1–11, where God the Creator judges primal humanity (Gen. 3), the world in the Noahic flood (Gen. 6), and all peoples with the confusion of languages (Gen. 11). Like these universal judgments, the OT envisions a final judgment called the "day of Yahweh" (e.g., Isa. 2:12ff.). Judgment in the OT is about justice – it not only punishes evildoers, but secures equity and relief for the poor and oppressed, both bringing down and lifting up (e.g., Deut. 10:17–18; Ps. 72:1–4). God's judgment is impartial, beginning even with the Israel of God (the OT preoccupation), for whom the day of Yahweh's coming is envisioned as a dark day in the absence of social justice and righteousness (e.g., Amos 5:18–24).

During the intertestamental period, the rise of apocalypticism heightened the sense of the universality of God's judgment, not only over human beings but also over supernatural entities, and emphasized the vindication of God's persecuted but faithful remnant. This period also introduced the apocalyptic figure of the "Son of Man" (cf. Dan. 7:13–14), who comes triumphantly on the clouds in the name of Yahweh to execute universal judgment. The NT identifies Christ's second coming with the appearance of this apocalyptic figure. Accordingly, the OT "day of Yahweh" is called by Paul the "day of Christ" (e.g., 1 Cor. 1:8). The NT continues the OT emphasis on judgment *qua* justice, as seen already in the parable of the sheep and goats, which indicates a judgment based on one's treatment of "the least of these" – the hungry, thirsty, stranger, naked, and imprisoned (Matt. 25:31–46). So while judgment has already been anticipated in Christ's atoning sacrifice, whereby those who are "in Christ" are no longer under condemnation (Rom. 8:1), there nevertheless remains a universal judgment of works. For the Christian, this underscores the essential relation between justification and sanctification – the notion that saving faith will manifest itself in good works (cf. Jas. 2:14–26; 1 Cor. 3:10–15). In the final judgment, everything that is hidden will be revealed (e.g., Luke 12:2ff.). Without a final judgment, the problem of evil could never be addressed satisfactorily, for there would be no ultimate justice in the world.

The question of hell

The issue of final judgment, however, raises the question of hell. The OT does not really develop the concept of hell, since, as noted above, Sheol is simply the nondescript place of the dead, a land of darkness and shadowy existence. Only in the intertestamental period does a distinction emerge between the fortunes of the righteous and the wicked in Sheol, as is reflected in the NT parable of Luke 16:19–31, where Hades (= Sheol) is depicted as two compartments separated by an impassable chasm, one where the beggar Lazarus is comforted in "Abraham's bosom," and one where the miserly rich man is tormented. Hell, by contrast, is the English word that generally translates the Greek *Gehenna*, which refers in the NT to the eschatological place of punishment after Christ's second coming and final judgment. Gehenna refers most literally to the Valley of Hinnom just south of Jerusalem, which in the OT was a place of child sacrifice (2 Kings 16:3; 21:6), desecration (2 Kings 23:10), and anticipated judgment (Jer. 7:32; 19:6ff.), and where Jerusalem's refuse was burned. It is therefore an apt symbol of sin, woe, and the fire of judgment.

It has often been pointed out that in the NT Jesus speaks of hell more than anyone else, characterizing it, for example in Matthew 25, as a place of darkness, weeping, and gnashing of teeth (v. 30), as an eternal fire for demons and human beings (v. 41), and as an unending punishment (v. 46). Based on these meager biblical descriptions, but largely following Augustine, the majority opinion in western Christianity conceived of hell as an eternal state of retributive punishment for unrepentant sinners, and it was largely depicted in physical terms as a place in the earth where people suffered incessant bodily torment.[19] Such mappings of the infernal regions – in word or picture – could get quite graphic, resembling the vindictive punishments of a medieval torture chamber. One might think of Dante's *Inferno* in this respect, where the various levels of hell contain many a ghastly punishment.

But more spiritual depictions of hell have also been proffered, beginning already with Origen, which construe hell more as a spiritual state of separation from God, whether of unfulfilled desire, remorse, or self-incurred psychological anguish. Such a conception would better capture the sensibilities

---

[19] Augustine, *City of God*, Book 21, ch. 9.

of most contemporary theology, as reflected, for example, in C. S. Lewis's *The Great Divorce*, where hell is depicted as a "state of mind," a "shutting up of the creature within the dungeon of its own mind" – in essence, God's respecting the freedom of humans to reign in their own self-constructed and self-absorbed hells.[20]

The stark nature of hell as an eternal entity has raised some perplexing questions across the centuries. Does not an eternal damnation of many creatures (as traditionally conceived) represent a defeat of the divine program of salvation, especially if God is conceived of supremely as love? How can *temporal* sins merit *eternal* punishment? Is God's sense of justice that much different from our own? The answers to these questions, of course, are complicated by other theological factors such as the nature and strength of human free will, the nature and strength of divine grace, and the nature of election/predestination to salvation.

Given the unfathomable character of hell (and largely out of compassion for its prospective inhabitants), it is understandable that theologians have entertained alternatives to this infernal, eternal destiny. One proposal is that of *annihilationism*, which holds that instead of eternal punishment the wicked will cease to exist – whether they are actively destroyed by God on the assumption that humans are created with immortal souls, or passively annihilated on the assumption that humans are created mortal, but that those who fail to attain the gift of eternal life will simply pass into oblivion.

A more sanguine alternative is that of *universalism*, which holds that all humans (or even all creatures) will ultimately be saved. A variety of universalisms have been proposed across the centuries, the more simple denying even the existence of hell (i.e., all people are God's children who go immediately to heaven), the more complex holding that there is a hell, as a place of justice, but that hell is not of eternal duration and will eventually be emptied of its denizens. Hell on this account takes on the purpose and contours of a purgatory. Whatever the form, this universalistic hope has been a minority but persistent voice in the history of Christian theology, embraced by a litany of notable theologians. Its first major advocate was Origen, who tentatively proposed the possibility of an *apokatastasis*, a final restoration of all things (cf. Acts 3:21), including even the devil.[21] Origen was followed in this inclination by both Gregory of Nazianzus and Gregory of Nyssa, among others, as the notion of universal reconciliation found greater play in Eastern Orthodoxy. Represented by the Anabaptists and pietists in

---

[20] C. S. Lewis, *The Great Divorce* (New York: Simon & Schuster, 1974), 64ff.
[21] See Origen, *De Principiis*, 1.6.

the West, this universalistic strain was renewed by Schleiermacher, and even seems to be an implication of the theology of Karl Barth. Whether liberal, neo-orthodox, or otherwise, one can find many hopeful advocates of *apokatastasis* in contemporary theology.

In his little book *Dare We Hope "That All Men Be Saved"?*, Catholic theologian Hans Urs von Balthasar answers the title question in the affirmative.[22] He notes that the NT contains two sorts of statements – those that speak of the eternal judgment of hell (documented above), and those that speak of God's desire and ability to save all people (e.g., 1 Tim. 2:1–6; Rom. 5:12–21; 11:32; 2 Pet. 3:9). Von Balthasar observes that most of the former are pre-Easter sayings of Jesus, reflecting his prophetic office of the call to repentance and employing the apocalyptic images of judgment and hell of his first-century milieu. Such "threat discourse" emphasizes the gravity of the decision that people are called to make *for* God and against sin. The universalist passages, on the other hand, are for the most part post-Easter, written in light of the completed work of Christ that ensures salvation. Von Balthasar warns against reconciling these particularist and universalist strains either by subordinating the universalist to the particularist, in which case one presumes the final fact of a well-populated hell (as has been the tradition since Augustine), or by subordinating the particularist to the universalist, making the *apokatastasis* into a dogmatic statement (as von Balthasar accuses Barth of doing). Given that we stand in the middle of the biblical drama in the decisional "day of salvation," not knowing its final outcome, both remain possibilities. But since universal salvation remains a *possibility*, it is something we can *hope* for – indeed, argues von Balthasar, Christian love *obligates* us to hope for the salvation of all and to work toward that end. What other attitude would be warranted in light of this possibility? C. S. Lewis also entertains this hope in *The Great Divorce*, quoting Julian of Norwich that it may yet be the case that "all will be well, and all will be well, and all manner of things will be well."[23]

The new heaven and earth

The last feature of our ecumenical eschatology concerns "life everlasting," as the Apostles' Creed puts it, or "life in the age to come," as the Nicene Creed

---

[22] Hans Urs von Balthasar, *Dare We Hope "That All Men Be Saved"?*, trans. David Kipp and Lothar Krauth (San Francisco: Ignatius, 1988). The quotation in the title comes from 1 Timothy 2:4, which indicates that God "desires everyone to be saved."

[23] Lewis, *Great Divorce*, 124.

has it.[24] Given the full biblical story, this final state of redemption is best understood as a "new heaven and earth" – that is to say, a renovated and glorified cosmos.

Historically speaking, a renewed creation has not been the primary candidate for the final state of redemption. Those honors have typically gone to "heaven" alone. As we have recurrently noted, the dominant image of salvation in much of the Christian tradition – and which forcefully lingers in the popular imagination today – has been that of the flight of the disembodied soul to the heaven of God's transcendent dwelling. We have contended throughout this text that this represents a gnostic tendency, signaling a denigration of the doctrine of creation. It is important to remember that creation is first described in Genesis 1:1 as "the heavens and the earth," a literary figure of speech (i.e., merismus) defining the totality of the cosmos by its extremities (its heavenly heights and earthly depths). Heavens here obviously represent an aspect of the creation. In point of fact there are basically three different realms of reference for "heaven" in the biblical narrative: (1) the *atmospheric heaven* of the wind, clouds, rain, and the like; (2) the *astral heaven* of the planets, stars, and constellations; and (3) the *third heaven*, the place of God's dwelling, whither Paul was once caught up (2 Cor. 12:2). It is this "third heaven" that most have in mind as the final locus of salvation. Yet heaven in this sense, according to the broader NT witness, is at best an intermediate state, not the final state. If the doctrine of the intermediate state proves true, then believers do "go to heaven" to be with Christ until the resurrection of the body. But even in the doctrine of the intermediate state – by definition – the final state must be regarded as a new heaven and earth, a renovation of the current heavens and earth, since this is the final witness of scripture.

Beyond the persistent influence of gnosticism, perhaps part of the reason a renewed creation has been neglected as the final state is the paucity of explicit biblical references to a new heaven and earth, of which there are only four. The first two occur in the closing chapters of Isaiah, 65:17–25 and 66:22–3, which speak eschatologically of the "peaceable kingdom," of the wolf and the lamb feeding together, and the like (see Illustration 15.1).

Largely because of the mention of death (65:20), these visionary texts have not been appreciated as pointing to the final state. Therefore premillennialists over the years have relegated such texts to the period of the millennium (Rev. 20:1–6), the supposed 1,000-year hiatus between Christ's second coming and the final state. The two NT texts that speak of the new

---

[24] Pelikan and Hotchkiss, eds., *Creeds and Confessions*, 1: 163, 669.

Illustration 15.1 *The Peaceable Kingdom* (*c.* 1844–5), by the Quaker artist Edward Hicks, based on Isaiah 11:6–8.

heaven(s) and earth, however, underscore the need for a progressive under-standing of revelation, since they clearly refer to the final state. The reference in 2 Peter 3:13 is set in the context of the "present heavens and earth" undergoing judgment in which "the earth and everything that is done on it will be disclosed" – that is, "found" or "revealed" in the sense of "judged," rather than "burned up" or "destroyed" as most translations have misleadingly conveyed (v. 10). Beyond such judgment, states 2 Peter 3:13, "we wait for new heavens and a new earth, where righteousness is at home." And the fourth and last reference is found in John's vision of the end in Revelation 21:1, the chapter *after* the millennium text, where John sees a new heaven and earth, as symbolized also by the New Jerusalem (the city of God) descending from heaven to earth. Here God will manifestly dwell among creatures on earth, where death is no more since the old order of things has passed away:

Then I saw a new heaven and a new earth; for the first heaven and the first earth had passed away, and the sea was no more. And I saw the holy city, the new Jerusalem, coming down out of heaven from God, prepared as a bride adorned for her husband. And I heard a loud voice from the throne saying,

> "See, the home of God is among mortals.
> He will dwell with them as their God;
> they will be his peoples,
> and God himself will be with them;
> he will wipe every tear from their eyes.
> Death will be no more;
> mourning and crying and pain will be no more,
> for the first things have passed away."   (Rev. 21:1–4)

If the conclusion of any story must be read in order to appreciate the full meaning of that narrative, then the fact that the Christian Bible ends on the note of an everlasting new heaven and earth – a glorified creation, after or beyond which there is no ethereal eternity – is most significant. The heaven of God's dwelling – the so-called "third heaven," where God's will is perfectly realized, and from which God acts upon the fractured earth – descends, creating a new heaven and earth. Put most simply, this eschatological vision is the fulfillment of the Lord's prayer: "Thy kingdom come, thy will be done, on earth as it is in heaven."

Beyond these four references to a new heaven and earth, the fact that a renewed creation is the ultimate fulfillment of Christ's redemption is necessitated by the very doctrine of creation (as an inherently good creation). This is especially true if, as we have argued, creation itself is the original and proper locus of the kingdom of God. The goal of salvation is the kingdom of God – God's dynamic reign over God's realm, which is the breadth and depth and history of creation itself. But perhaps most telling for this creational goal of redemption is the centrality of the resurrection as the key salvific event. If the central eschatological hope is the resurrection of the dead, and if this means more than simply the ascension of the soul into heaven, but indicates an embodied existence, then the resurrection becomes the primary analogue for the renewal of the cosmos from the principalities and powers of death. Resurrected bodies, it would seem, need a renovated world in which to live and move and have their being. The bodily resurrection of Jesus Christ and his now glorified existence form the pattern and basis of our hope for resurrection, as well as that of a renewed creation, one that is so suffused with God's presence and Spirit that there is no longer any decay, suffering, or death – a complete state of glorification in which "God may be all in all" (1 Cor. 15:28). This would be the ultimate fulfillment of the promise contained within the name Yahweh – namely, that of the divine presence with God's people in the midst of creation (see pp. 79–80 above).

A vision of "everlasting life" in a new heaven and earth is a far cry from an immaterial heaven as the final state. The latter has reinforced an eschatological sense of discontinuity and dissimilarity with our present life in creation, often leading in spiritual practice to a gnostic contempt for the world, a concentration on an inner and individualistic spirituality, and a preoccupation with a narrow concept of evangelism that attempts to "save souls" from the sinking ship of the world. An eschatological vision of a new heaven and earth, however, accentuates a greater continuity and analogy with life in the present heaven and earth. It is important to note in this connection that the Greek word utilized for "new" in the NT is *kainos*, which connotes something along the order of "new in nature" or "new in kind," rather than *neos*, which signifies "new in time or origin."[25] The new heaven and earth therefore are not completely new, but new (and radically so) in nature or quality, bearing some real, ontological analogy to and historical continuity with this creation. Again, the primary analogy for this is Jesus Christ, whose resurrected and glorified existence bears both a similarity to and continuity with his earthly life and existence, even in its transformed incorruptibility. Applied to creation at large, the theological and ethical implications of these dynamics of analogy and continuity are considerable, since they underscore that salvation is both holistic and historical. Since it is all of creation that will be redeemed, there is no area of life that falls outside the reach or implications of the gospel – whether it be political, social, economic, environmental, or any other facet of life. And since that kingdom is coming down the road of this history, what we do in this space and time counts in heralding and anticipating its coming.

The question of hope

We do live in apocalyptic times – an apocalypse of our own making, since it is humanity that has created the conditions of our world's possible demise. For such times we need an apocalyptic vision, the vision of a new heaven and earth, which is a vision of what is possible, because of what we believe and hope will happen. In this light, the Christian church as the new humanity is called to hunker down in this place and time to herald and prepare the way of the Lord, the coming kingdom of God, which stands in judgment on fallen and fractured principalities, powers, and persons, and which promises everlasting life in the world to come.

---

[25] "Kainos," in Kittel and Friedrich, eds., *Theological Dictionary of the New Testament*, III: 447–9.

At the conclusion of one of his parables, Jesus asks: "When the Son of Man comes, will he find faith on earth?" (Luke 18:8). Given the inseparability of the theological virtues, Jesus' question is just as much about hope and love as it is about faith. While we wait for Christ's return, Christian faith must be nourished by a robust sense of hope and find expression in works of love. Christian theology is a quest for these virtues of faith, hope, and love seeking understanding and expression. All people are invited to contribute to this endeavor, a theological and practical wrestling with God and with humanity for the sake of God's creational kingdom.

FOR FURTHER READING

Balthasar, Hans Urs von, *Dare We Hope "That All Men Be Saved"?*, trans. David Kipp and Lothar Krauth (San Francisco: Ignatius, 1988).

Bauckham, Richard, *The Theology of the Book of Revelation* (Cambridge: Cambridge University Press, 1993).

Cooper, John W., *Body, Soul, and Life Everlasting: Biblical Anthropology and the Monism–Dualism Debate*, 2nd edn. (Grand Rapids, MI: Eerdmans, 2000).

Cullmann, Oscar, *Immortality of the Soul or Resurrection of the Dead? The Witness of the New Testament* (New York: Macmillan, 1964).

Grenz, Stanley J., *The Millennial Maze: Sorting out Evangelical Options* (Downers Grove, IL: InterVarsity, 1992).

Moltmann, Jürgen, *Theology of Hope: On the Ground and the Implications of a Christian Eschatology*, trans. James W. Leitch (New York: Harper & Row, 1967).

Wright N. T., *Surprised by Hope: Rethinking Heaven, the Resurrection, and the Mission of the Church* (New York: HarperOne, 2008).

PART III

Historical survey of Christian theology

The third part of this book offers a historical survey of Christian theology through its five significant theological epochs: the patristic, medieval, reformational, modern, and contemporary periods. This section can be read profitably and independently before, during, or after Parts I and II, depending on readers' interests or needs. This historical narrative of doctrinal theology reinforces, expands, and places in larger context the "historical development" sections of the individual Christian doctrines that are the subject of the chapters in Part II.

CHAPTER 16

Theology in the patristic era (c. 100–500)

THE BIRTH OF CHRISTIANITY

The life, death, resurrection, and ascension of Jesus Christ initiated a new religious movement in human history. The band of followers attracted by "the Way" of Jesus (see Acts 9:2) quickly became a "church," claiming to experience through the risen Christ and the Holy Spirit the liberating power of God. This new movement, however, did not arise in a vacuum, but sprouted from particularly Jewish roots within a Greco-Roman cultural matrix.[1]

---

[1] An important source for the following account of the historical context of the rise of Christianity is Everett Ferguson, *Backgrounds of Early Christianity*, 2nd edn. (Grand Rapids, MI: Eerdmans, 1993).

The Jewish roots of Christianity

The genesis of the Christian church is inseparably linked to the history of Israel, not only its classical period as recorded in the Hebrew Bible, but also the period known as Second Temple Judaism, which produced the inter-testamental literature. Jesus was hailed by his followers as the Davidic kingly Messiah or Christ who would restore the fortunes of Israel, a nation that for centuries had labored under foreign rule. Christians saw in Jesus the fulfill-ment of the promises made to Israel by the God who chose the Hebrew people in Abraham, brought them out of Egypt, and pledged the nation's future vindication. NT writers therefore interpreted the life of Jesus by appeal to the Jewish scriptural texts, later known in Christianity as the "Old Testament." By Jesus' time, the covenant people were known as the "Jews," named after the descendants of the remnant of the southern tribes of Israel (i.e., Judah) who had returned to the promised land of Palestine after the Babylonian exile of 586 BCE. By the end of this "Second Temple" period (from the rebuilding of the Jerusalem temple around 515 BCE to its destruc-tion in 70 CE), Judaism had been affected by the Hellenization of the ancient world (see below), had seen the restoration of political Israel through the Maccabean revolts (*c.* 167–164 BCE), and had witnessed the subsequent kingly-priestly rule of the Hasmonean dynasty and its fall to the waxing Roman Empire. By this time the Jewish "diaspora" (the dispersion of Jews after the Babylonian exile) had spread throughout the Mediterranean world, and a variety of sects had developed within Judaism. Some, like the Zealots, desired further Maccabean-style revolt against the Roman governors of Palestine. Two other very different groups, the Pharisees and Sadducees, attempted to define Judaism by means of divergent interpretations of the *torah* (law) of Moses. Still others, like the Essenes, aspired to an ideal of separation from the world, and lived in apocalyptic expectation of divine judgment of complacent Israel and vindication of the faithful and holy few. All of these groups variously left their mark on the fledgling Christian church.

The Greco-Roman world of early Christianity

This genetic connection to Israel is only part of the story of the birth of Christianity, for the shape of the Christian church and its theological ideas was also molded in the context of Greco-Roman antiquity. The Jewish world into which Jesus Christ was born had been under the cultural influence of the Greek-speaking world for over 300 years, followed by the political dominion of Rome for the better part of a century.

The pervasive presence of Greek language, culture, and learning in the eastern Mediterranean world was largely the result of the military conquests of Alexander the Great (356–323 BCE). Through Alexander's exploits, the Greek population spread abroad, disseminating Greek culture, language, philosophy, and religion, a process known as Hellenization (*Hellas* = Greece). This cultural matrix accounts for the language of the NT, which was written in Greek. Due to Hellenization, the earliest Christian theologians found it impossible to grapple with and communicate the ideas of Christian faith apart from dialogue with the Greek intellectual tradition, including reflection on its philosophical questions, such as the relationship between the One and the many – how the absolute unity of supreme being relates to the diversity of the empirical world (see pp. 85–6).

The Hellenized world was captured by the armies of Rome in 63 BCE. Under Caesar Augustus, relative peace, the so-called *pax Romana*, came to the ancient world, including the Palestine of Jesus' birth. The Romans ruled over a diversity of peoples and lands, largely adopting and endorsing Hellenistic culture, while at the same time striving to fortify Roman political rule. The overarching policy that governed all other Roman policies was commitment to the spread of the empire,[2] the foundation of which was thought to be the good favor of the traditional Roman gods. To the extent that Judaism and her stepdaughter, Christianity, refused to acknowledge those gods, persecution threatened.

This Greco-Roman milieu was the larger world into which Christianity was born, as reflected in the NT writings, such as the book of Acts. That chronicle of the early church begins with the ascension of the risen Christ and the evangelical efforts of the apostles in Jerusalem, the center of the Jewish world. It ends with the apostle Paul proclaiming the gospel in Rome, the center of the Hellenized world. Between these cultural locales lie the tensions inherent in the early Christian church and its theology. In response to the remarkable life, death, and resurrection of this *Jewish* man, Jesus of Nazareth, who in the eyes of his followers was the fulfillment of the hopes of Israel, it was in a land of *Hellenistic* culture and Roman rule that Christians began to articulate their faith. Thus it should not be surprising that, over time, the early church, heavily populated by Hellenized Jews and Gentiles, had increasing difficulty recognizing, appreciating, and preserving the distinctive Jewish elements of Jesus' person and life, even as these were manifest in the inspired NT writings that tell and interpret his story. The early theology of the Christian church, traditionally called the "patristic"

---

[2] Ibid., 21.

period (after the *pateres*, the "fathers" of the church), bears the stamp of this cultural ambiguity. Its search for Christian identity and cultural relevance was marked by both direct conflicts and strained syntheses with its Hellenistic milieu. The story of patristic theology is thus the narrative of the gradual, dynamic, and often difficult assimilation of these diverse inheritances.

THE PATH TO ORTHODOXY: THE SEARCH FOR CHRISTIAN IDENTITY

The "apostolic fathers"

Theology has never simply been a matter of reflecting upon the inspired Christian texts. Though written mostly in the first century, the NT canon was in fact not definitively "closed" until the late fourth century (pp. 435–7). The earliest stages of Christian theology therefore involved an intensive dialogue with the Hebrew scriptures and the growing set of Christian literature that would come to comprise the NT, as well as a dialogue with the larger culture. The broad historical category that designates the theology done in the late first to mid-second century is that of the "apostolic fathers," a name given to such writings because they were originally thought to have been produced "in apostolic times" by disciples of the apostles.[3] Accordingly, some of these writings, such as the *Shepherd* of Hermas and the letters of Clement of Rome, were considered "inspired" and authoritative by many early Christian communities. As it turns out, most of these authors probably did not know the apostles, but there is certainly an "apostolic" air about their writings. Altogether, these rather diverse writings represent an initial post-apostolic stage in the search for Christian theological identity.

The preoccupations of the apostolic fathers reflect, of course, the concerns of the fledgling church, especially regarding its organization and proper functioning. In a letter to the church in Corinth, Clement, probably the bishop of the church at Rome, advocates a "top-down" church polity that was common in this era (*1 Clement*, c. 95). Clement exhorts the Corinthians to follow Christ's supreme example of humility. In a Stoic vein, he encourages the Corinthians to foster a harmonious kind of church life that mirrors the harmonious order of the cosmos. This harmony is

---

[3] Williston Walker, Richard A. Norris, David W. Lotz, and Robert T. Handy, *A History of the Christian Church*, 4th edn. (New York: Scribner, 1985), 41.

achieved in obedience to the bishops, who are connected to the apostles in a line of apostolic succession.[4] Similarly, Ignatius of Antioch (*c.* 35–*c.* 107) was one of the first to speak of the church as "catholic," a term he used to stress the unity and universality of the church. For Ignatius, this implied a hierarchical model of the church, since the one who represents the unity of the church and secures the local church's place in the catholic church is the bishop.[5]

Christology was also a prominent theological concern of the apostolic fathers. For example, in many of his arguments Clement implied that Christ existed before creation, which is why he could regard Christ as the one speaking through many of the Psalms.[6] Similarly, Ignatius of Antioch opposed those who saw Jesus as a merely human Jewish teacher (the so-called Ebionites), emphasizing in contrast that Jesus also transcends history. Ignatius demonstrates the fact that very early in the history of theology, the conviction of Christ's preexistence was important to many, even if it was not until the fourth century that the logical implications of that conviction for Christ's divine status were fully appreciated and elaborated.

But other writings of the apostolic fathers came close to the very position that Ignatius rejected. For example, the treatise known as the *Shepherd* of Hermas espoused a "Spirit christology." According to this text, the Holy Spirit came to indwell the naturally born Jesus of Nazareth, resulting in the person Jesus Christ. Because this indwelled "flesh" lived rightly, he was made a partner with the Spirit and lifted up to God. Therefore, it is doubtful, in contrast to Clement and Ignatius, that the writer of this text regarded Jesus as the preexistent Son.

Ignatius also affirmed Jesus' true humanity and opposed early forms of "docetism," the view that Jesus was really a heavenly being and only seemed (Gk. *dokeo* = seem) to be human. Ignatius stressed the truth of Jesus' humanity, including the fact that he was truly born of a woman and really lived on *this* earth. So we see in this early period a diversity of theological opinion, even on major questions. The church was still in the early stages of doctrinal formation in its march toward orthodoxy. Yet in Ignatius' resistance to Ebionism and docetism we can see, for example, the seeds of what would become the "two-natures" christology officially endorsed at the Council of Chalcedon in the fifth century, even if the full implications of this teaching were as yet unclear.

---

[4] Ibid., 17.
[5] Justo L. González, *A History of Christian Thought*, 3 vols., 2nd edn. (Nashville, TN: Abingdon, 1987), 1: 77.
[6] Ibid., 1: 65.

Theology amid persecution: martyrdom and the apologists

Professing to be a Christian prior to the early fourth century was frequently fraught with danger. While the Roman Empire of the early centuries of the church often showed great religious tolerance, there were occasionally intense persecutions of Christians. These trials served as one of the crucibles in which early theological identity was refined.

The result of these persecutions for many Christians was martyrdom. Ignatius of Antioch, for example, likely wrote his letters on his way to be executed in Rome. The term "martyrdom" is derived from the Greek word *martys*, which means "witness." Martyrs were those who witnessed to Christ by accepting death rather than renounce their Christian confession. The church viewed the martyr's acceptance of such a fate as a means of witnessing to Christ's own martyrdom and thereby participating more fully in his death in the hope of sharing in his resurrection.[7]

These persecutions were the result of various charges leveled at the early Christians. The theologians who took upon themselves the task of defending the fledgling church against such accusations are known as the "apologists." One early apologist, Athenagoras (second century), in his treatise *A Plea Regarding Christians*, documents the range of these charges.[8] The most common accusation was that of atheism, due to the Christian failure to worship the civic Roman gods, including the emperor himself. Implicit in this accusation was the charge of treason for following Christ rather than Caesar. Athenagoras admits that Christians are guilty as charged, *if* the gods in question are the gods of Rome. But Christians are *not* in fact atheists, because they worship the one true God, who is Father, Son, and Holy Spirit. A second charge was cannibalism, rooted in Christians' sacramental language of eating the body and drinking the blood of Christ in the Lord's Supper. Athenagoras tries to show the absurdity of this accusation by pointing out that Christian believers are not even allowed to kill. How, then, can they eat human flesh? Christians, rather, are life-affirming – they avoid the gladiatorial spectacles and even oppose abortion (a common practice at that time). A third charge was that of sexual immorality, as read

---

[7] The account of Polycarp's execution in 155 CE is especially illustrative of the early church's theological interpretation of martyrdom. See "The Martyrdom of Saint Polycarp, Bishop of Smyrna," ed. and trans. Massey Hamilton Shepherd Jr., in *Early Christian Fathers*, ed. Cyril C. Richardson, Library of Christian Classics (Philadelphia: Westminster, 1953), 149–58.

[8] Athenagoras, *A Plea Regarding Christians*, ed. and trans. Cyril C. Richardson, in *Early Christian Fathers*, ed. Cyril C. Richardson, Library of Christian Classics (Philadelphia: Westminster, 1953), 300–40.

into the early Christians' secret meetings with those whom they called their "brothers and sisters." Athenagoras insists that since followers of Christ even oppose lust, they certainly do not practice illicit sexual intercourse. Chastity is in fact integral to the Christian life. In responding to all of these charges, Athenagoras asks the emperor to grant the same religious toleration and protection to Christianity as he accords other religions.

The apologists, however, not only defended the Christian faith against attacks but also tried to make a positive case for its reasonability, attractiveness, and continuity with the best wisdom of classical antiquity. The most famous apologist, Justin Martyr (*c.* 100–*c.* 165), exemplifies this approach. While Justin did expend much energy in defensive mode, many of his efforts were geared toward showing the compatibility of Christian truth and the philosophical wisdom of antiquity. To this end, Justin developed what has become known as his Logos doctrine.[9] *Logos* is a complex and multivalent Greek term in ancient philosophy, but it predominantly referred to the rational structure of the cosmos. According to Justin, this same Logos or "reason" that has always been present in the world, funding the quest for philosophical truth, became incarnate in Jesus Christ. Thus Christianity, in knowing and worshipping this Christ, is the highest form of truth, one that takes up and completes the partial truth of philosophy. Those who live rationally and virtuously, even before Christ or apart from the Christian church (such as the ancient Greek philosophers), are participating in the same Logos that became flesh in Jesus Christ. Thus Justin links the Christian claim that Jesus Christ is the "Truth" (John 14:6) with a positive affirmation of "truth" in Greek philosophy. This is his way of claiming Christian truth as truth for all human beings, thereby making a universal and public case for Christianity.

Clement of Alexandria (*c.* 150–*c.* 215) took a similar tack, finding continuity between the truth of Christianity and the truth of Greek philosophy, albeit with an interesting twist: the God of the Jews was in fact the source of Greek wisdom as well, with the latter serving as the means by which the pagan world was prepared for the gospel of Christ. States Clement: "Perchance, too, philosophy was given to the Greeks directly and primarily, till the Lord should call the Greeks. For this was a schoolmaster to bring the Hellenic mind to Christ, as the law was for the Hebrews. Philosophy, therefore, was a preparation, paving the way for him who is perfected in Christ."[10]

---

[9] Justin Martyr, *First Apology*, 242–89.   [10] Clement, *Stromata*, Book 1, ch. 5, translation amended.

Heresy and the checkered path to "orthodoxy"

In their defense of basic Christian beliefs *vis-à-vis* the intellectual and political challenges of the day, the apologists contributed significantly to the formation of early Christian theological identity. In the late second century and throughout the third century another factor began to assume a prominent role in this theological quest, namely, "heresy." The word "heresy" comes from the Greek *hairesis*, which originally referred to a party or minority within a larger group, but later came to refer to an "opinion" – that is, a false and misguided one that deviated from settled convention. "Heresy" and "heretic" were terms used by those who considered themselves to be defending the traditional and correct teaching of the church in order to brand those whose (rather idiosyncratic) teaching diverged from this majority opinion. However, it is more the case that Christian orthodoxy developed in large part *through* the church's wrestling with heresy. In other words, the defining of heresy was one of the central catalysts that facilitated the emergence of what came to be understood as "orthodoxy" (right opinion or doctrine).

Since Christianity initially arose as a Jewish sect, it is not surprising that one of the earliest so-called "heresies" in Christian history was an attempt to preserve the Jewish purity of the church. This heresy, usually known as "Ebionism" and also characterized as a "Judaizing" heresy, actually has its roots in the first century of the church's existence, as can be seen in Acts 10, 11, and 15. Here, the basic dilemma was that of determining how much of the Jewish law, the *torah*, was still normative for Christians, many of whom were Gentiles (i.e., non-Jews). On this question the Ebionites believed that in order to become a Christian one also had to become a Jew, since they regarded the Jewish law as normative for Christianity. This concern for the Jewish character of Christianity led the Ebionites to preserve Jewish monotheism in the strictest possible sense (Yahweh = the Father alone). In their view, therefore, there was no room for consideration of Jesus as a preexistent participant in the divine being. They held that Jesus was not the eternal Son of God, but due to his perfect adherence to the Jewish law he was adopted into that role through the Spirit's descent upon him at his baptism (i.e., a Spirit christology). Given its deprecation of the deity of Jesus, Ebionism would later lend its name to one of the two major types of christological heresy, the other being *docetism*, which, conversely, denigrated Jesus' humanity.

Docetism was embraced by Marcion (d. *c.* 150), the founder of an early second-century sect known as *Marcionism*, whose teaching was diametrically opposed to Ebionism. Marcion thought that Christianity should be purged of all Jewish elements in its belief, in its worship, and especially in its authoritative writings. He therefore developed a canon of scripture that rejected the entire OT, as well as the particularly Jewish sections of the NT, retaining only the Gospel of Luke (shorn of Jewish elements) and a truncated version of Paul's letters that emphasized Paul's criticism of the Jewish law. Moreover, Marcion found it difficult to believe that Jesus was truly human. His reasons for holding this view lie in his dualistic theology and cosmology. According to Marcion, the inferior OT God (Yahweh) reigns through justice and law in the evil realm of matter. Conversely, the true NT God revealed in Christ reigns through grace and love in the good spiritual realm. In this framework, Jesus could not be truly human, for that would involve him in the evil material realm. As such, Marcion taught a form of docetic christology in which Jesus merely *seems* to be human.

In terms of the doctrine of God more generally, two different forms of "monarchianism" were prevalent in the third century, views that would become heretical foils to the emerging doctrine of the Trinity. Both of these monarchianisms shared the Ebionite concern for the radically monotheistic unity of God as the "one source" or "one ruler" (*monarche*) of all. The first of these, *adoptionism* or dynamic monarchianism, is primarily associated with the work of Paul of Samosata (third century), who, desiring to preserve the strict monotheistic unity of God against growing trinitarian trends, claimed that only the Father is truly and essentially divine. The Son, Jesus Christ, did not exist before his human birth, but was a mere man who was specially filled by God's spirit with messianic power. According to Paul, Jesus was not personally divine, but was at some point adopted by the Father to be the Son of God.

Modalism or modalistic monarchianism was the second major attempt to preserve a radical monotheism in view of the church's waxing trinitarianism. This form of monarchianism, often associated with the name of Sabellius, protested that the increasingly popular Logos theology (which we saw in Justin Martyr) jeopardized the oneness of God, a oneness construed as a single, indivisible entity. If the Word of God, the Logos, is a person distinct from the Father, then it seems that two gods are affirmed. Consequently, the modalists claimed that God is a simple, single monad that expresses itself in three operations, which are not eternal divine identities or discrete persons. Since there are no distinctions in God, the

Son and Spirit are simply ways in which the one person of God appears to the world (see pp. 119–20).[11]

The most significant heresy of the patristic age, however, in terms of its widespread effect upon the development of orthodox doctrine, was *gnosticism* (see also pp. 153–5). Gnosticism flourished in many forms in Christianity, although it also appeared in Jewish and philosophical versions. Derived from the Greek word for "knowledge" (*gnosis*), gnosticism held that salvation comes via a secret, esoteric knowledge that is not accessible to everyone. The gnostics claimed to possess a special revelation that imparted to them the *true* meaning of life and Christian ideas.

The claim to special *gnosis*, however, is only one feature of gnosticism. As in the teaching of Marcion (who could be considered a proto-gnostic), the key to its intellectual and theological framework is a thoroughgoing dualism. There are two "gods," one an inferior evil principle associated with the physical universe, and the other a good principle associated with true deity and the spiritual realm. The sensible, material world is essentially an evil creation of the vengeful deity of evil and darkness, typically called the *Demiurge*. On the gnostic view, human beings are essentially souls who have fallen away from the goodness of their spiritual existence into the dirt of matter, with the material realm being the source of all human evil. Accordingly, salvation was primarily understood by the gnostics to be a matter of escape from the material world. Since one's present existence is that of a good spirit or soul being trapped in an evil body, salvation requires the realization that one's true essence and hope are only spiritual. What is thus called for is escape from physical entrapment. Through the secret knowledge (*gnosis*) of one's *real*, spiritual origin and destiny, one may through rigorous asceticism and contempt of the world begin to transcend the material mess of the here and now and return upon death to one's true heavenly home.

This dualistic system of theology, cosmology, and soteriology has considerable consequences for christology, since within this gnostic framework Jesus Christ as the revealer of salvation is considered divine, but it is impossible for him also to be regarded as truly human. As in Marcion's teaching, if Jesus had been truly human, it would mean that he was polluted by the evil realm of matter and would be unable to rescue people from it. It must be the case, therefore, that Jesus only *seemed* to be human. Thus gnostic christology is docetic – Jesus appeared as a human being but did not truly assume human flesh.

---

[11] See Kelly, *Early Christian Doctrines*, 120.

Gnosticism was a significant impetus for the early church's forging of theological identity. Because gnosticism implies docetism, most major theological rebuttals of gnosticism strongly affirmed the reality of the incarnation as the centerpiece of their critique. Gnosticism also compelled the church to clarify its assessment of the status of creation and the scope of redemption. As we shall see, the most important theologians of the second and third centuries were galvanized by the gnostic threat in developing these key doctrines.

Irenaeus

One major second-century theologian whose work focused on refuting heresy was Irenaeus of Lyons (*c.* 135–*c.* 200). His treatise, *Against Heresies*, contains lengthy expositions and critiques of the prominent gnostic systems of his day, especially that of Valentinus, who characterized the created order as an "abortion" that resulted from a fall among the heavenly beings. Irenaeus' theological rebuttal of gnosticism was crucial for the development of the doctrines of God, creation, and redemption.

To the gnostic contention that the true God and the god who created this physical world are different, Irenaeus developed a battery of theological responses. First, he emphasized the doctrine of creation out of nothing (*creatio ex nihilo*), the teaching that before creation there was nothing but the good God. All that exists comes from God and is therefore in itself good – including the material realm. The same triune God created not only the heavens, but also the earth. Second, Irenaeus insisted that God not only made the world but also remains intimately involved in the world. God the Father created by means of his "two hands," the Son and the Spirit, through whom the triune God remains involved with history. This means that God really interacts with the material world of time and space, something that would be either senseless or blasphemous to the gnostics.

Irenaeus' reflections on redemption are closely connected to his understanding of creation. He holds that within the good creation, God creates human beings for a process of maturation. Humanity is created in its infancy, so to speak, and must grow and mature in order to come of age. Irenaeus therefore gives an important and positive role to *history* as the sphere in which human beings are enabled to actualize their potential by *choosing* to remain faithful to their creator. Adam and Eve's sin, however, arrests this process of maturation, and as a result all humanity is imprisoned by the devil. Within this framework of creation and sin Irenaeus develops his understanding of redemption as a "recapitulation" (see pp. 267–8 above). Drawing upon a Pauline motif found in Romans 5:15–21 and 1 Corinthians 15:22, 45, Irenaeus portrays Jesus Christ as the "second Adam," who reverses the effects of the disobedience of the "first Adam." Whereas the first Adam succumbed to the temptation to be like God, Christ resists the temptation to become his own God. Whereas the first Adam quickly disobeyed, the second Adam remained steadfast in obedience and faithfulness. Whereas the first Adam and his seed are imprisoned by Satan on account of Adam's disobedience, the second Adam's obedience leads to the imprisonment of Satan and the release of sinners. This reversal happens through Christ retracing the life-path of Adam, this time living rightly through all the stages of human existence and reversing the effects of the fall.[12] While death resulted from Adam's disobedience, through Christ's perfect obedience all are saved from death. In this way Christ's death cannot be separated from his incarnation and life, in which he sums up all the stages of human existence; yet his life is incomplete apart from his death. For Irenaeus it is through this process of recapitulation that creation is brought to its completion.[13] Salvation, accordingly and *contra* gnosticism, is the fulfillment of creation, not an escape from it.

Tertullian

Marcionism, modalism, and gnosticism formed the horizon against which the North African theologian Tertullian (*c.* 160–*c.* 225) developed his theology, which was especially influential for the western church. Tertullian is perhaps best known for his antipathy to the integration of pagan philosophy and Christian faith. His famous rhetorical question, "What has Athens to do with Jerusalem?," which has resounded throughout the ages, was intended to imply that Judeo-Christian knowledge and wisdom are wholly distinct from pagan philosophy.[14] Tertullian even claims that all heresies have their roots in the philosophical tradition of Athens. Accordingly, he argues that the wisdom of the OT and the simple gospel of Christ are sufficient for theology and Christian faith; the subtleties and novelties of philosophy will only lead the church astray. In actual practice, however, Tertullian's position is much more complicated. The fact that he himself, whether wittingly or unwittingly, made theological use of philosophy

---

[12] Irenaeus, *Against Heresies*, 391.
[13] Irenaeus even suggests that this process of sin and salvation was *necessary* for the fulfillment of creation. In other words, salvation could not have happened apart from sin and the coming of Christ as the second Adam. Thus some of his statements seem to necessitate evil.
[14] Tertullian, *Prescription Against the Heretics*, 36, translation amended.

(especially Stoicism) suggests that he is best taken to mean that the wisdom of Jerusalem trumps and transforms the wisdom of Athens and Rome, since the Logos made flesh, Jesus Christ, is the fulfillment and clarification of all philosophical forms of the Logos.

Tertullian is also important for the development of the doctrines of Christ and the Trinity. With respect to christology, he emphasized against the gnostics that salvation comes through the authentic humanity of Jesus.[15] Tertullian also anticipates the "two-natures" understanding of Christ that would develop in the fourth and fifth centuries: there are two "substances" in Christ that remain united but still distinct; the divine Logos is clothed with human flesh, rather than changing into flesh.

With respect to the Trinity, one of Tertullian's most important contributions was the coining of the very term *trinitas*, along with other trinitarian terms, in the course of his debate with the modalists. In his conception of the Trinity, God (the Father) is never alone, but eternally exists with the Word and Spirit, possessing these in himself each as "another." But this intrinsic threeness of God's being is more fully manifested in the way God interacts with creation in salvation. The Son is "generated" from the Father for the purpose of creation and incarnation and only at that point becomes a distinct "person," a true second in addition to the Father.[16] Consequently, Tertullian is not as clear as later theologians about the eternal status of the Son as a person *vis-à-vis* the Father. But he certainly regards God's threeness to be integral to the divine unity, understood as a oneness of the divine "substance" (*substantia*) in three divine "persons" (*personae*), two other terms he adapts for trinitarian use. Tertullian forges his trinitarian terminology and conceptuality particularly against the modalists, who posited only one person in God.

Origen

A third major theologian who contributed to the development of orthodoxy in the debate with heresy was the Alexandrian theologian Origen (*c.* 185– *c.* 254). Origen was a brilliant and disciplined thinker who was the first theologian to take a systematic or topical approach to the doctrines of Christian faith. He is significant for a number of theological contributions. For one, he is famous for continuing the Alexandrian tradition of the

---

[15] See Basil Studer, *Trinity and Incarnation: The Faith of the Early Church*, trans. Matthias Westerhoff, ed. Andrew Louth (Edinburgh: T. & T. Clark, 1993), 67.
[16] Tertullian, *Against Praxeas*, chs. 5–7.

allegorical interpretation of scripture. According to this method, while one must take the face value of scripture seriously – that is, the literal sense – the "spiritual" person will discern a deeper moral, intellectual, and spiritual connotation of the text: the allegorical sense.

Origen's trinitarian reflections remain his most important legacy. Pressing beyond Tertullian, Origen clearly teaches that the distinctions between Father, Son, and Spirit are eternal and intrinsic to God, not merely pertaining to the relationship between God and creation. Origen taught that the Son is eternal and has his personal being from the Father ("eternal begottenness"). But some of his statements also suggest a subordinationist arrangement among the three members of the Trinity. The Father is the sole *arche* of the Godhead (*autos Theos*); the Son is a "second God" (*deuteros Theos*); and the Spirit is a "third God" (*tritos Theos*).[17] While for Origen all three persons of the Trinity are distinguished from creatures, some later thinkers (not without reason) took Origen to mean that each of the three possesses a different and unequal grade of divinity, an ambiguity in Origen himself that is reflected in the Arian controversy of the fourth century (see pp. 437–9).

Origen also proposed a radical scope for God's reconciling grace. He advocated the *apokatastasis* – the ultimate restoration of all things in creation, including Satan – a doctrine that has resurfaced periodically throughout the Christian tradition as a minority opinion.

Origen was a controversial figure. Despite his contributions to the church's developing orthodoxy, Origen himself was later branded by the church as a heretic on account of some of his theological proposals (especially his belief in the preexistence of human souls). Heavily influenced by the Middle Platonism of his day, his theology betrayed certain affinities with gnosticism, even though he himself claimed to follow the true knowledge of the church, over against gnostic pseudo-knowledge.

The development of creeds

While these major theologians were developing their theology in polemical dialogue with various forms of heresy, the institutional church was also formulating its authoritative teachings, a process that eventuated in the early creeds. Already in the second century there had emerged the notion of a "rule of faith" (*regula fidei*), which referred to a summary statement of the main teachings of Christian belief that was usually recited liturgically. The

---

[17] Kelly, *Early Christian Doctrines*, 128.

rule of faith was intended to differentiate orthodox Christianity from heterodox belief. Even though seasoned orthodoxy and clearly identifiable heresy were mostly products of the fourth and fifth centuries, the idea of orthodoxy and the branding of certain forms of teaching as heresy were present much earlier. Given the slow process of Christian self-definition, the rule of faith was rather fluid at this stage, with different communities using different versions of it without a standard form or fixed wording.

More stable and formal statements of basic Christian belief developed toward the end of the second and beginning of the third century. In the West, the so-called "Old Roman" Creed was one of the first offspring of the rule of faith. It functioned both as a catechetical tool to instruct new converts and as a means of confessing one's status as a true believer. The Apostles' Creed, widely used in western churches today, evolved from the Old Roman Creed. Many of its elements are directed against specific heretical understandings of the faith.[18] For example, the creed's emphasis on the Virgin Mary being the mother of Jesus effectively rules out both Ebionism (which denies the virgin conception) and docetism (which denies the humanity of Jesus). The affirmation of the resurrection counters the gnostic claim that salvation ultimately entails escaping the material realm. The Nicene Creed (the major creed of the East, still used today) emerged in the course of the trinitarian controversies of the fourth century, which we will discuss below. The Athanasian Creed has also been used in the western churches, though it was not written by Athanasius and is actually a fifth-century Latin document reflecting the Augustinian tradition. In each case, these normative statements emerged through confrontation with heresy.

The Constantinian shift

As we have seen, for the first two-and-a-half centuries of its existence, the Christian church lived as a minority community, often despised and rejected, within the political empire of Rome. As we saw earlier, this led to the occasional persecution of the church due to Christians' refusal to participate in aspects of Roman life or because of the perceived threat of Christian belief to the well-being of Rome. This situation changed radically in the early fourth century.

Largely in response to the growth of the Christian population in the Roman Empire, the emperors Constantine (in the West) and Licinius (in the East) recognized Christianity as a legal religion through the Edict of

---

[18] See González, *History of Christian Thought*, 1: 153–4.

Illustration 16.1 The Constantinian Cross, overlaying the first two letters of the Greek word *Christos* (*chi* = X and *rho* = P), was in Constantine's vision accompanied by the words, "In this sign, conquer." This symbol subsequently became the emblem of the Roman armies.

Milan in 313.[19] A mere decade later, Constantine's forces defeated Licinius, and Constantine assumed control of the whole empire. Whatever the authenticity of Constantine's "conversion," due to his purported vision that in the sign of the cross he would conquer, Constantine became the first Christian emperor and quickly established Christianity as the *de facto* official religion of the empire.

This change in Christian fortunes brought with it the curtailing of persecution, ushering in a new era in Christian history. Christianity was now a legal religion that had the approval of the emperor, who, in adopting the religion of the God of Jesus Christ, implicitly relinquished any of his own claims to divine status. In an ironic twist, the religion of the crucified Christ now had the endorsement of the world's most powerful empire, a political shift that brought protection and certain advantages to the previously persecuted church.[20] But this shift also meant that Christian faith and theology were often co-opted or at least appropriated for the purposes of the reigning powers. The armies of Rome, for example, now bore the Christian (Constantinian) cross, not as a symbol of power through weakness, but of power through military might (see Illustration 16.1).

This change led to new tensions, not least of which was the involvement of the political powers of the empire in the affairs of the church. This new religio-political situation, commonly referred to as Christendom, forms

[19] See Rodney Stark, *The Rise of Christianity: How the Obscure, Marginal Jesus Movement Became the Dominant Religious Force in the Western World in a Few Centuries* (Princeton: Princeton University Press, 1996), 4–10.
[20] Justo González makes the interesting point that Christian art very quickly took on a more triumphalistic character than it had before (*History of Christian Thought*, 1: 261).

the context for the theological debates of the fourth and fifth centuries, debates which are of signal importance in the gradual and dialectical path to Christian orthodoxy in the patristic age.

CONCILIAR ORTHODOXY: DEFINITIVE
CHRISTIAN IDENTITY

The New Testament canon

In the post-Constantinian era, Christian theology was preoccupied with the doctrines of the Trinity and of Christ. But an equally significant, though more gradual, fourth-century development was the closing of the NT canon. "Scripture" had always played an important role in theology, even in the work of the NT writers themselves. Those writers and the earliest Christian theologians, however, had in mind primarily the Hebrew scriptures in their Greek translation (Septuagint), which came to be known as the "Old Testament," whose basic (but not final) canonical shape was in place by the time of Jesus. The idea of a closed body of Christian inspired and authoritative writings actually emerged rather slowly. Analogous to the notion of "orthodoxy," prior to the late fourth century, there existed only what we might describe as a "canon in progress," with different Christian communities employing different writings as authoritative in their worship and catechesis.

The word "canon" originally referred to a reed which was used as a measuring stick, thereby serving as a norm or ideal standard. By the end of the fourth century, the theological sense of the term was that of a fixed series of writings that were normative for Christian faith and practice. The canon took its final shape through a long historical process. Strikingly, it is not until the mid-fourth century that we have the first complete listing of the twenty-seven books that constitute the definitive canon of today's NT. While most of the books canonized as the NT were written in the first century, it was by a painstaking and sometimes conflictual process that the church discerned its authoritative Bible.

How exactly did Christian communities decide which writings deserved special status? Scholars have suggested that four primary and interrelated criteria were at play in canonical judgment.[21] First, writings could be

---

[21] See Harry Y. Gamble, *The New Testament Canon: Its Making and Meaning,* Guides to Biblical Scholarship (Philadelphia: Fortress, 1985), 67–71. In this excellent introductory treatment, to which the following is indebted, Gamble also rightly warns us to remember that these criteria can only be discerned retrospectively and were not formally in the minds of the participants in these debates as "four criteria."

included in the canon only if they were either directly written by the apostles of Jesus or clearly reflected apostolic teaching – the criterion of *apostolicity*. A second criterion was *catholicity*: was a given writing relevant to the whole church rather than limited in application to only a specific community? Catholicity sometimes stood in tension with apostolicity, as in the case of many of Paul's letters, which though genuinely apostolic were addressed to particular communities. This criterion means that truly authoritative Christian writings had to be public and significant for all. Third, in the later stages of the canonization process, writings were considered worthy of the canon only if they agreed with the "rule of faith" – the criterion of *orthodoxy*. The final criterion was that of *traditional usage*. Writings were accepted into the canon only if they had a well-established place in the life of the ecumenical or worldwide church. As with the other criteria, however, this was a necessary but not sufficient condition for inclusion in the canon, since some of the writings of the apostolic fathers, such as *1 Clement* and the *Shepherd* of Hermas, for example, were excluded from the canon despite their widespread use in churches.

In surveying the process of canonization historically, therefore, we see that in the late first century there was no NT, but only the apostolic reflection upon the life and fate of Jesus in the light of the Hebrew scriptures. This body of apostolic proclamation and oral teaching was eventually set down in a series of writings. As oral teaching and tradition became less and less stable, early Christian communities came to rely more and more on the written texts.

By the middle of the second century there is evidence of the use of multiple gospels, as witnessed by Justin Martyr, for example, who still considered them to be less authoritative than the OT. Irenaeus in the 180s provides us with the earliest evidence of a theologian arguing for the exclusive authority of only four gospels – Matthew, Mark, Luke, and John – but his very argument shows that this practice was not yet universal.[22] A similar process took place with Paul's letters. It appears that a community consisting of his followers who continued his teaching after his martyrdom in Rome searched out the letters that Paul had written to various churches, possibly wrote other letters that faithfully embodied his teaching, and edited and circulated his writings. Some of these letters circulated quite early, such as Romans and 1 Corinthians, which were known to Clement of Rome in the late first century. Irenaeus possessed a collection of Pauline letters by the

---

[22] See Irenaeus, *Against Heresies*, 3.8.

180s. By the end of the second century, Paul's works were a highly regarded portion of the fledgling canon in progress.

Other writings had more checkered histories of acceptance. The book of Revelation, for example, was highly regarded in the West by the end of the second century but was still distrusted in the East. Hebrews, conversely, was highly regarded in the East but distrusted in the West because of its apparent claim that forgiveness was impossible after baptism (e.g., 6:4–8; 10:26–31). The "catholic epistles" (James, 1–2 Peter, 1–3 John, and Jude) were not widely used in the second century, but the book of Acts had achieved widespread usage by the end of the second century. In short, much, but not all, of the NT canon had taken form by the end of the second century.

The third century saw a further sifting of texts that helped to clarify the final shape of the canon, although many communities continued to use writings that were not ultimately included. It was the fourth century that witnessed the formalization of the canon. Early in that century, the catholic epistles, the writings of the apostolic fathers, and Revelation were still disputed books in some quarters. But by 367 in the East, a letter written by Athanasius, the champion of Nicene orthodoxy, included a canonical list that contained the twenty-seven books of the NT that are accepted today – the earliest evidence of the definitive Christian canon (see Table 16.1). This list was soon embraced also in the West, as affirmed by the councils of Carthage in 397 and 418. After a long process, the basic shape of the Christian canon, albeit largely acknowledged from the late second century onward, had taken its final form as the NT we recognize today.

The trinitarian controversy

The basic issue that drove the early development of the doctrine of the Trinity was the need to clarify the relationship between Jesus Christ and

Table 16.1 *Canonical lists in the early church*

Source	Number of NT books accepted	NT books omitted or disputed
Muratorian Canon (2nd or 4th cent.)	22, as well as Wisdom of Solomon and *Apocalypse of Peter*	Hebrews, James, 1 Peter, 2 Peter, one letter of John
Origen (3rd cent.)	24	Acts, James, Jude
Eusebius (311)	22	James, Jude, 2 Peter, 2 and 3 John
Athanasius (367)	All 27	

God the Father. As noted earlier, Origen was interpreted by some theologians as relating Christ to God the Father in a subordinationist way. One such interpreter was Arius (d. 336), a presbyter of Alexandria, who in 318 began to proclaim that the Son of God was a creature, thus setting off the Arian crisis, which is often also called the "trinitarian controversy" (also see pp. 121–3 above). Arius held to a notion of God as absolutely one, utterly transcendent, and uniquely eternal. Because of these commitments, he interpreted the NT statements about the "begetting" of Jesus from God the Father (e.g., John 1) quite literally as implying that Christ was created, since one who is begotten is created and thus cannot be eternal and fully divine. For Arius, while Christ is a mediating and saving figure, and can even be called "God" as a manner of compliment, he is still properly regarded as the highest creature.[23]

Alexander (d. 328), the bishop of Alexandria, and his presbyter, Athanasius (*c.* 296–373), argued to the contrary that if Jesus Christ were not truly God, then it would be impossible for him to accomplish redemption. Because they understood salvation primarily as a matter of being brought into participation with the divine nature (deification – see pp. 268–70 above), the only mediator who could accomplish such a work must himself be divine. To their cause, they rallied Origen's notion of "eternal begottenness" as a way of showing the distinction of Jesus from the Father, but also his co-eternity and hence co-divinity. They argued that while indeed the Son as Son has his being from the Father, he has *eternally* been the Son of the Father. As such, he is fully God. In this way they considered the Arian position to represent an improper reading of the various NT texts that spoke about the relationship between the Son and the Father.

This dispute eventually became so contentious that it even threatened the political stability of the Roman Empire, a situation that Constantine inherited when he assumed the rule of the eastern part of the empire in 324. To quell this bitter dispute, he convened an ecclesiastical council in Nicea in 325. This first of seven so-called ecumenical councils supported the position of Alexander and Athanasius, and ruled against Arius. It affirmed the eternal begottenness of the Son from the Father by stating that he was *homoousios* – "of the same essence" – with God the Father. This affirmation was undergirded by the conviction that only the Creator could possibly redeem creation from its sin.[24] Thus the original Nicene Creed (to be distinguished from the Nicene-Constantinopolitan Creed of 381, which is known in churches today as the Nicene Creed) speaks of Jesus Christ as "God from God, light from light, true God from true God, begotten not

---

[23] Kelly, *Early Christian Doctrines*, 229.   [24] Pelikan, *Christian Tradition*, 1: 203.

made, consubstantial with the Father."[25] Strikingly, however, this original form of the creed says little about the Holy Spirit.

While the Council of Nicea set a decisive theological trajectory that would eventually determine "orthodox" trinitarian theology in both the East and the West, it did not immediately settle the Arian controversy, as the Arian and Athanasian parties continued to spar. One of the central issues under debate was the propriety of the *homoousios* clause.[26] Some eastern church leaders were convinced that Nicea's language of *homoousios* was modalistic, since they reckoned that if Father and Son were "of the same essence," this could imply that they were the very same person. Because it was unclear to them how, on the *homoousios*, the trinitarian persons were really distinct from one another, they offered a counter-proposal, suggesting that the Son is of an essence "similar to" (*homoiousios*) that of the Father. Although this party is sometimes called "Semi-Arian," in actuality they agreed in most essentials with the Nicenes, as most of them did not consider the Son a creature with a beginning in time. Meanwhile the Cappadocian theologians (see pp. 443–4) had helped to clarify the basic trinitarian terminology, thus explaining how the trinitarian members could share one divine essence (*ousia*) while remaining distinct persons (*hypostaseis*).

In 381 a second ecumenical council met, in Constantinople, reaffirming the decisions of the Council of Nicea and again condemning Arian theology. After nearly sixty years, the Nicene cause had finally won the day. The Council of Constantinople produced a definitive revision of the Nicene Creed (the one we use today) that affirms the full deity of the Son and also says much more about the Holy Spirit, thus reflecting Athanasius' and the Cappadocians' intervening work of arguing for the full deity of the Spirit. By this time the classic formulation of the doctrine of the Trinity had been established, with different terms used in Greek and Latin respectively: three divine persons (*hypostaseis* or *personae*) who share one essence or substance (*ousia* or *substantia*).

The christological controversy

The debates leading up to Nicea and the controversies that transpired between Nicea and Constantinople forged the orthodox consensus and conviction that Christ the Son is equal to God the Father in deity. But the NT also clearly portrayed Jesus as a human being. How can he be *both*

---

[25] "The Creed of Nicaea," in Pelikan and Hotchkiss, eds., *Creeds and Confessions*, I: 159.
[26] On these positions see González, *History of Christian Thought*, I: 280–3.

divine *and* human? How can we make sense of this dual constitution of his person? After the resolution of Nicene orthodoxy, these were the issues involved in the *christological* controversies of the fourth and fifth centuries (see pp. 235–41).

In this post-Nicene age a rivalry between two christological "schools" developed, based on quite subtle yet important distinctions. To simplify, the *Alexandrian* school emphasized the divinity of Christ and the unity of his person, often to the detriment of his full humanity. By contrast, the *Antiochene* school emphasized the humanity of Christ and the difference between the "two natures" of Christ's being, often to the detriment of the unity of his person.

The contrasting tendencies of these schools can be seen by comparing Apollinarius and Theodore of Mopsuestia. The Alexandrian theologian Apollinarius (*c.* 310–*c.* 390) wanted to emphasize the full divinity of Christ and leave no doubt that Christ was only *one* person. He therefore interpreted the incarnation as a true "union" between human nature and the Logos (the eternal second person of the Trinity) in which the Logos overshadowed and glorified Jesus' humanity. Apollinarius explained his position in terms of the dualistic anthropology of his day: the Logos replaces the human soul (or spirit) and unites itself with a human body, with the result that Christ is one person.

While Apollinarius had shown how Jesus could be only one (divine) person, he did so at the expense of Christ's full humanity. His christological suggestion was widely criticized. Gregory of Nazianzus, one of the Cappadocians, famously retorted that this proposal put in jeopardy the very salvation that the incarnation was supposed to accomplish: "For that which He has not assumed He has not healed."[27] Whatever aspect of human nature is not taken up into union with the Logos is not made a participant in the sinlessness of divinity. Therefore the soul, on Apollinarius' position, was not cleansed from its sin. Dismayed by Apollinarius' christology, the Council of Constantinople condemned his views in 381.

But it was the Antiochenes who railed most vociferously against Apollinarius, arguing that his views endangered the true humanity of Jesus. For Theodore of Mopsuestia (*c.* 350–428) the full obedience of a truly *human* being was necessary for the redemption of humanity. Accordingly, he portrayed the incarnation as the indwelling of the second person of the Trinity in a human being. Yet Theodore differentiated so sharply between the human

---

[27] Gregory of Nazianzus, "To Cledonius the Priest Against Apollinarius" [Letter 101], trans. Charles Gordon Browne and James Edward Swallow, in *Nicene and Post-Nicene Fathers*, 2nd series, ed. Philip Schaff and Henry Wace (Grand Rapids, MI: Eerdmans, 1993), VII: 440.

Jesus, who was portrayed in the gospels as suffering, and the divine Logos, who in the theological mindset of that era was by definition incapable of suffering, that the Alexandrians suspected him of teaching that there were two persons of Jesus Christ.

By the fifth century the popular Alexandrian idea of *Theotokos*, referring to Mary as the "bearer of God," became the center of this controversy. The basic rationale behind the term is that if Christ is one person whose identity is divine, then the Christ-child to whom Mary gave birth must be called "God." To the Antiochene theologian Nestorius (*fl.* fifth century), however, the *Theotokos* idea appeared to endanger God's very deity, since God could certainly not have a beginning in a human mother. That would make God changeable and contradict the divine eternality. Closely following Theodore, Nestorius insisted that the incarnation was a "conjunction" or indwelling rather than a union between the Logos and humanity. The divine Logos and the human being Jesus are conjoined morally. Though Nestorius denied the accusation, the Alexandrians charged him with preaching two "Sons," one of them human and the other divine.

Cyril of Alexandria vehemently opposed Nestorius, considering that Nestorius' christology smacked of adoptionism. He strongly supported the *Theotokos* concept, even making it into a battle cry, since in his mind this concept showed that Jesus was the very person of the Logos (and hence the agent of salvation). So he described the incarnation as the true *union* wherein the Word assumed human nature (both body *and soul, contra* Apollinarius), rejecting the language of conjunction or mere indwelling.

Cyril was more careful to guard the full humanity of Jesus, however, than another Alexandrian, Eutyches (*c.* 380–*c.* 456), who depicted the incarnation as a metamorphosis of Christ's divine and human natures into a third sort of thing (*tertium quid*) – a hybrid God-man – that resulted from the Logos's union with human nature. Eutyches stressed such a radical transformation of the human nature that the Antiochenes once again wondered how Jesus' full and true humanity was maintained. It was at this time that Pope Leo of Rome was asked to weigh in on this important debate.

Leo responded with a treatise, known as his *Tome*, which criticized Eutyches. Leo emphasized that the distinction between Christ's two natures is irreducible.[28] They are united in one person, but the characteristics proper to each nature are retained. He even says that each of Christ's

---

[28] Leo of Rome, "The Tome of Leo," trans. William Bright, in Hardy and Richardson, *Christology of the Later Fathers*, 365.

Table 16.2 *The basic affirmations of the first four ecumenical councils*

The Council of Nicea (325)	Affirmed the full deity of Jesus Christ as Son of God, that he was *homoousios* with God the Father (*contra* Arius)
The Council of Constantinople (381)	Confirmed the full deity of Christ (*contra* Arianism), and also affirmed his full humanity (*contra* Apollinarius)
The Council of Ephesus (431)	Affirmed the unity of Christ's personhood (*contra* Nestorius), though it was a divided council
The Council of Chalcedon (451)	Affirmed the unity of Christ's personhood (*contra* Nestorianism) and the duality of his natures (*contra* Eutychianism)

"forms" carries on its own "activities" (*contra* Eutyches), but in communion with the other (*contra* Nestorius). While some Alexandrians continued to suspect Leo of a crypto-Nestorianism, he did reject a rigid separation between the divine and human natures.

In 451 the fourth ecumenical council was held at Chalcedon, which attempted to balance these positions.[29] The Chalcedonian definition states that there is *one* person of Jesus Christ which consists of *two* natures – true deity and true humanity (including both a human soul and body), natures that retain their distinctive characteristics even in the incarnational union. The *Theotokos* idea is also affirmed, thus making clear that the human person of Jesus Christ is in fact the second person of the Trinity. The Chalcedonian statement additionally makes four important negations that rule out the extremes of the Alexandrian and Antiochene schools. Against the Antiochenes, Chalcedon affirms that the divine and human natures are united without separation or division, and against the Alexandrians it states that the union takes place without confusion or change in the natures. In this way the Alexandrian insistence on the *Theotokos* is met, and the Antiochene concern for the irreducible distinction of the two natures is also met. Thus in a very real sense the Chalcedonian definition is a compromise. But we will see in the next chapter that this rather balanced compromise did not end the church's christological disputes.

EAST AND WEST AND THE IDENTITY OF TRADITIONS

The preceding narrative recounts the major theological debates of the patristic age with respect to the canon, the Trinity, and the person of Christ. Whereas the latter two debates were centered in the eastern part of the Roman Empire,

---

[29] The third "ecumenical" council, in Ephesus in 431, consisted largely of mutual condemnations and political maneuvering.

the influence of the West was not absent. While together accepting the orthodox statements, particularly the Niceno-Constantinopolitan Creed of 381, the East and West eventually developed distinctive forms of theology and piety, which we will explore further in the next chapter. Each tradition, however, rooted itself strongly in the thought of a major patristic antecedent. The eastern Byzantine tradition largely harked back to the Cappadocians, while the western Latin tradition regarded Augustine as its patriarch.

The Cappadocians

We have already mentioned the "Cappadocians" or "Cappadocian fathers" in conjunction with the trinitarian debates that occurred between the councils of Nicea (325) and Constantinople (381). These three eastern fathers, the brothers Basil of Caesarea (*c.* 330–*c.* 370) and Gregory of Nyssa (*c.* 330–*c.* 395) and their close friend Gregory of Nazianzus (*c.* 329–*c.* 389) were all influential bishops and impressive theologians. Their labors extended throughout the latter half of the fourth century and were decisive for the theological agenda of the eastern Byzantine tradition that developed in the Middle Ages, especially in their mystical orientation and endorsement of deification soteriology – participation in the divine nature (treated in the next chapter). Our focus here will be on their contributions to the doctrines of the Holy Spirit and the Trinity, which served to clarify the logic of these basic ecumenical beliefs.

As we saw earlier with Athanasius, one of the arguments against the Arians for the full deity of the Son was soteriological in nature. If Jesus brings salvation, and salvation is somehow a participation in the being of God (i.e., deification), then Jesus himself must fully share in the divine nature. The Cappadocians extended this logic to the Spirit as well: if the Holy Spirit brings sanctification, along with the Father and the Son, then it must be the case that the Holy Spirit also shares the divine essence.[30] By affirming the *divinity* of all three persons of the Trinity, the Cappadocians opposed the "Pneumatomachians" ("Spirit-fighters"), who rejected the extension of Nicea's logic to the Holy Spirit.

The Cappadocians' most significant contribution to the doctrine of the Trinity was the forging of a language and logic to clarify its basic threeness-and-oneness relation (see pp. 123–5 above). The technical terms *ousia* and *hypostasis* had often been confused in the Greek-speaking East, where they

---

[30] Gregory of Nyssa, *On the Holy Trinity*, trans. Henry Austin Wilson, in *Nicene and Post-Nicene Fathers*, 2nd series, ed. Philip Schaff and Henry Wace (Grand Rapids, MI: Eerdmans, 1993), v: 328.

typically functioned as synonyms. The Cappadocians brought clarity to this situation by giving *hypostasis* a sense that was differentiated from *ousia*. While retaining *ousia* for the single divine essence common to the three members of the Trinity, they utilized *hypostasis* for their individuated existence. Father, Son, and Spirit, therefore, were three *hypostaseis* who share one *ousia*.[31] While this distinction helped a great deal in the East, it still occasioned confusion in the West, since *hypostasis* translated most literally into Latin as *substantia*, their basic oneness term. The West therefore suspected the Cappadocians of promoting tritheism – belief in three divine substances or gods.

In his short treatise *On Not Three Gods*, Gregory of Nyssa addresses the problem of Christianity's seeming tritheism. He begins with his famous "three men" analogy of Peter, James, and John, three humans who share a single "humanity," but who nevertheless remain three particular human beings. Comparing this to the Trinity, if there are three persons who share one "Godhead" or deity, why – following the "three-men" analogy – can we not say that there are three gods? Gregory claims that in the case of the three humans, we actually witness a customary and unproblematic "misuse of language."[32] We do in fact use the generic term in a specific sense. If we were speaking correctly, he implies, we would not say three *humans*, but that there are three *persons* who share one humanity, using different words for the general and the particular. His use of this social analogy serves to underscore the distinction of the three divine persons or *hypostaseis*.

Gregory of Nazianzus and Basil also experimented with social analogies for the Trinity, contributing to the Cappadocian reputation for maintaining the threeness of the trinitarian persons better than their western counterpart, Augustine. They did, however, privilege the Father as the principle of trinitarian unity. As the "fount of divinity," the Father was considered the eternal "cause" of the Son and the Spirit. It is in fact their "procession" from the Father that differentiates the persons one from another by according each a peculiar characteristic: the Father is uniquely *unbegotten*; the Son is *begotten* of the Father; the Spirit is *breathed from* the Father. While this doctrine of processions would become standard trinitarian fare, Augustine would locate the trinitarian unity elsewhere, and the West would wonder if the East did not unduly subordinate the Son and the Spirit to the Father.

[31] See Gregory of Nyssa, "Letter 38," trans. Jackson Blomfield, in *Nicene and Post-Nicene Fathers*, second series, ed. Philip Schaff and Henry Wace (Grand Rapids, MI: Eerdmans, 1993), VIII: 137–41.
[32] Gregory of Nyssa, "On 'Not Three Gods,'" in Hardy, *Christology of the Later Fathers*, 257.

Augustine

The pivotal patristic figure in the West was unquestionably the North African theologian Augustine (354–430), whose theology set the agenda for the subsequent Catholic and Protestant traditions. After a tumultuous spiritual journey, recounted in his now classic *Confessions*, Augustine became a Christian, a priest, and eventually a bishop and a major player in the theological disputes of his day (see Illustration 16.2).[33] In pointed contrast to the Cappadocians, Augustine rejected a social analogy for the Trinity, preferring instead a psychological analogy based on his understanding of the rational soul as the point of divine likeness in humanity (as *imago Dei*). Just as the individual human soul admits of three faculties – mind, knowledge, and love – so also the one God admits of three "persons" – Father, Son (Word), and Spirit (Love). This unipersonal, psychological analogy better fits Augustine's methodological starting point for the Trinity, which privileges the one divine essence (*substantia*) as his principle of divine unity, in contrast to the Cappadocian emphasis on the Father. Augustine's trinitarian reflections had lasting influence on the course of western trinitarianism. Moreover, his emphasis on the Holy Spirit as the "bond of love" between the Father and the Son sowed the seeds of the western idea that the Spirit proceeds from both the Father *and* the Son (the so-called *filioque* addition to the Niceno-Constantinopolitan Creed), a source of further East–West division. Since we address these trinitarian issues more fully in Chapters 5, 11, and 17, our focus here will be on Augustine's role in the Donatist and Pelagian controversies, and his influential theology of history.

Augustine played a major role in two prominent North African controversies. The first of these, the Donatist controversy, was occasioned by the question concerning the status of those whose faith had faltered during the Diocletian persecutions before the legalization of Christianity – particularly those priests who under pressure of persecution surrendered their scriptures. A party known as the "Donatists" regarded those who had renounced their faith as "traitors" and believed that any ordinations performed by "traitor" bishops were invalid. This controversy was raging when Augustine became bishop of Hippo in 395.

Whereas the Donatists seemed to demand a perfect personal holiness of true Christians, Augustine argued to the contrary that the holiness of the church is found only in its head, Jesus Christ. The church certainly includes

---

[33] Augustine, *Confessions*. For an excellent biography of Augustine see Peter Brown, *Augustine of Hippo: A Biography*, 2nd edn. (Berkeley, CA: University of California Press, 2000).

Illustration 16.2 Botticelli's depiction of Augustine at his desk.

sinners, but the church is nonetheless holy because it participates in Christ's holiness. So the unworthiness of a well-meaning priest does not negate the validity or efficacy of a sacrament, such as ordination, since it is really Christ who is there at work.

Another major debate in which Augustine was involved is known as the Pelagian controversy.[34] Pelagius was the most notorious of a handful

---

[34] For a representative treatise of Augustine against Pelagius, see *On Nature and Grace.*

of figures who were teaching that even after Adam's sin, human beings possess unmitigated free will and therefore can achieve, by agency of their own works, true perfection. Sin, rather than being a *state* into which one is born, is merely an *act* committed against God. Grace, accordingly, is simply the God-given empowerment of the natural human faculties that allows people to do the right thing, as illumined by God's law and the example of Christ. Salvation is thus something earned by virtue of one's works.

In opposition, Augustine argued that no human being can remain sinless because of the infection of human nature by Adam's sin (i.e., original sin). Sin is both a disease and a state of guilt that all human beings inherit. Human freedom with respect to God and the achievement of holiness is therefore compromised, since the will is bent toward sin. In short, we exist in a sinful condition. Grace, then, must be supernatural – the infusion of Christ's resurrected life in the human being that restores the will and makes obedient action possible. Grace – the presence of Christ in the soul – is the basis of salvation. In this approach Augustine bequeathed to the western tradition the doctrine of original sin and an insistence on the primacy and necessity of grace.

Finally, Augustine developed a theology of history that captivated the theological and political imagination of the West. His remarkable work, *The City of God*, written between 412 and 426, was especially influential in the Middle Ages for its vision of church and world in the march of human history. In 410, the city of Rome had been sacked by invading "barbarian" tribes. In lamenting the empire's demise, many began to blame Christianity for Rome's weakened political stance, even suggesting that Romans should return to their pagan roots and gods. Augustine wrote *The City of God* to defend Christianity against these charges. He develops the metaphor of two cities, an earthly one and a heavenly one, whose complex interactions explain the vicissitudes and fortunes of history. The two cities represent two "societies" based on contrary loves – love of God and love of self. The City of God has the destiny of eternal life, while the City of the World is destined for eternal death.[35] Augustine proposes an interpretation of world history in terms of the relationship between these two cities.

According to Augustine, since the City of the World is based on earthly loves, it is impermanent. Thus the sack of Rome should not surprise anyone – all earthly empires are bound to fall. But he also sees the City of

---

[35] See Augustine, *City of God*, 14.28; 15.1; 19.17, 27–8.

Table 16.3 *Timeline of theology in the patristic era*

History of theology			World history
		400 BCE	
		356–323	Conquests of Alexander the Great
		300	
		218–201	Second Punic War
		200	
		c. 167–164	Jewish Maccabean Revolts
		100	
		65–63	Rome conquers eastern Mediterranean world
Birth of Jesus	*c.* 4		4	Death of Herod the Great
		I	
Death of Jesus	*c.* 30 CE		
Paul writes 1 Thessalonians (his earliest letter)	*c.* 50		64 CE	The Fire of Rome during reign of Emperor Nero
Clement of Rome sends letter to Corinth	*c.* 95		70	Destruction of Jerusalem and Jewish temple
		100 CE	
Death of Marcion	*c.* 150		132	Jewish Bar Kochba rebellion
Justin Martyr writes *First Apology*	*c.* 150		
Irenaeus writes *Against Heresies*	*c.* 180		180	Death of Emperor Marcus Aurelius
		200	
Origen writes *De Principiis*	*c.* 215		
Death of Tertullian	*c.* 225		
Paul of Samosata's heresy condemned	268		284	Diocletian becomes Roman emperor
		300	
Council of Nicea	325		313	Edict of Milan
Athanasius' *Festal Letter*	367		324	Constantine takes over eastern Roman Empire
Council of Constantinople	381		395	Eastern and western empires split permanently
		400	
Death of Augustine	430		410	Sack of Rome by Alaric and the Visigoths
Council of Ephesus	431		
Council of Chalcedon	451		476	The fall of the Roman Empire (trad.)
		500	

the World as playing a positive role. Temporal and proximate goods can certainly come from this city – for example, relative peace is possible. God in fact makes use of the City of the World in pursuit of divine ends. The heavenly city, on the other hand, is the eternal, eschatological reign of God. It has entered history provisionally in Israel, but in a more decisive way with the Christian church. All history is on a march toward this city – it alone is the true commonwealth, the city whose life is based on love of God.[36] The church looks forward to being ushered finally and fully into that city, but here and now is called to exist as a pilgrim community within the earthly city.

In actual history, however, these two cities cannot be separated. The church, the anticipatory version of the City of God, is bound up with the City of the World. The world gains from the church, but the church also benefits from the best that the world has to give, such as its quest for peace. It is in this context (as well as in his political battles with Donatism) that Augustine developed his theory of the just war.[37] The wise and Godly person must sometimes resort to worldly means, such as war, in order to achieve the relative good in an attempt to approximate the peace of the City of God that can never be fully attained in the City of the World.

As we shall see in the next chapter, Augustine's work was pivotal for the formation of western theological identity in the Middle Ages. Similarly, the theological paths blazed by the Cappadocians were crucial for the development of Byzantine theology in the East. Both traditions represent the fruit of the ground-breaking developments of patristic theology.

FOR FURTHER READING

Augustine, *The City of God*, trans. Henry Bettenson (London: Penguin, 1972).
  Confessions, trans. R. S. Pine-Coffin (Harmondsworth: Penguin, 1961).
Brown, Peter, *Augustine of Hippo: A Biography*, 2nd edn. (Berkeley, CA: University of California Press, 2000).
Ferguson, Everett, *Backgrounds of Early Christianity*, 2nd edn. (Grand Rapids, MI: Eerdmans, 1993).
Gamble, Harry Y., *The New Testament Canon: Its Making and Meaning*, Guides to Biblical Scholarship (Philadelphia: Fortress, 1985).
Hardy, Edward Rochie, and Cyril C. Richardson, eds., *Christology of the Later Fathers*, Library of Christian Classics (Louisville, KY: Westminster John Knox, 1954).

[36] Ibid., 19.23.   [37] Ibid., 19.7.

John of Damascus, *Exposition of the Orthodox Faith*, trans. S. D. F. Salmond, in *Nicene and Post-Nicene Fathers*, 2nd series, ed. Philip Schaff and Henry Wace (Grand Rapids, MI: Eerdmans, 1993), IX: 1–101.

Kelly, J. N. D., *Early Christian Doctrines*, 2nd edn. (New York: Harper & Row, 1960).

Pelikan, Jaroslav, *The Christian Tradition: A History of the Development of Doctrine*, vol. 1: *The Emergence of the Catholic Tradition (100–600)* (Chicago: University of Chicago Press, 1971).

CHAPTER 17

Theology in the Middle Ages (c. 500–1400)

INTRODUCTION: DIVERGING TRADITIONS

The previous chapter surveyed the topography of patristic theology, the cornerstone of the Christian church's subsequent doctrinal development. In that period we saw the seeds of the schism that would later develop between the eastern and western provinces of the church, with the Cappadocian theologians in the East and Augustine in the West setting the tone for their respective theological traditions. While the divide between East and West as formalized in 1054 is a complicated matter involving a variety of factors – including linguistic, cultural, and political considerations – this chapter can address only the major theological developments of these diverging traditions. Our survey of the theology of the Middle Ages will first examine some of the important features and controversies of Byzantine theology in the Greek-speaking East before proceeding to a more detailed review of Latin theology in the West.

BYZANTINE THEOLOGY

After Constantine became emperor of the eastern Roman Empire in the early fourth century, he chose the city of Byzantium as his imperial seat. Though that city was quickly renamed Constantinople, in the popular mind it was still known as Byzantium. As the imperial capital, Constantinople became such a major and influential center of theology that the tradition it produced is still known as "Byzantine." One should keep in mind, however, that the term "Byzantine theology" refers more widely to the Greek-speaking theology of the entire eastern Mediterranean region, including the work done by theologians in other major centers, most notably Alexandria and Antioch, a tradition which later became known as "Eastern Orthodoxy."

Key theological accents

The basic theological method that came to typify the Byzantine tradition was, by and large, historically retrospective in its outlook. That is to say, Byzantine theology located its primary theological warrants in the patristic past, in the tradition of the great "fathers" of the church. Accordingly, an appeal to the authority of the great councils and influential theologians was a central feature of its style of theology.[1] Theologians such as Athanasius, the Cappadocians, and Cyril of Alexandria, encountered in the previous chapter, became the authorities to which later Byzantine theologians appealed in defense of their own theological views. This argument "via tradition" was never a simple matter, however, since theologians on different sides of the same issue could often claim the same fathers as their antecedent authorities.

In addition to seeking patristic precedence, Byzantine theology tended to be rather mystical in temperament. This mystical bent was largely shaped by a profound sense of the divine ineffability (unutterability), which made

---

[1] See Pelikan, *Christian Tradition*, II: 16–30. Our account of Byzantine theology in this chapter is indebted to Pelikan's masterful work.

the very possibility of theological discourse problematic. How is it possible to speak the truth – or to have knowledge – about a God who is by definition unknowable? Jaroslav Pelikan points out that Greek theologians of this period tended to regard their theology as a "knowing ignorance," often claiming that the only way to know the unknowable God was "to speak in negatives."[2] Thus Byzantine theology was by and large a negative theology, which is more technically known as *apophaticism* (Gk. *apophasis* = denial) – a theology that proceeds by way of stating what God is *not* (the *via negativa*), since what God *is* remains incomprehensible.[3] One of the key developments in this approach came from Gregory Palamas (1296–1359), who claimed, based on patristic thinkers such as the Cappadocians, that the divine *essence* (God *in se*, God in God's self) is unknowable – only negative statements can be made about it. It is only the divine *energies* (God *pro nobis*, God's actions toward humanity) that are susceptible of positive knowledge. Palamas' essence/energies distinction has since been a fundamental tenet of Orthodox theology.

These tendencies in theological method – appeal to tradition and apophatic mysticism – converged in the East's rather remarkable consensus concerning the concept of salvation, which was generally understood to be a matter of "deification" (*theopoiesis* or *theosis*; also see pp. 268–70 above). Deification refers to the elevation of human beings through Christ to mystical participation in the triune reality of God. For this central soteriological theme, the Byzantine theologians followed the lead of Athanasius and the Cappadocians.

Coupled together, the apophatic tendencies of the Orthodox Byzantines and their appeal to the tradition of the great "fathers" led to a relative decline in theological creativity in this period. While certain developments inevitably took place, the cardinal theological virtue was not innovation, but continuity – the repetition in new situations of the foundational contributions of the Greek patristic theologians and the great ecumenical councils.

Continued controversy and the later ecumenical councils

In the previous chapter (as well as Chapters 5 and 9) we followed the formative controversies of patristic theology through the first four ecumenical councils: Nicea (325), Constantinople (381), Ephesus (431), and Chalcedon (451). These four councils all took place in the eastern region of the Roman Empire and therefore concerned controversies primarily of the

---

[2] Ibid., II: 32. [3] For more on the *via negativa*, see pp. 90–1 above.

Greek-speaking church, even though none of these councils lacked the influence of the Latin West, particularly the involvement of the Roman pope. After the fifth century three other major councils took place that are also known as "ecumenical" councils but reflect even less of the influence and input of the Latin-speaking West.

It was largely the continuation of the christological controversies that prompted the final three ecumenical councils in the East. As noted above, the fourth ecumenical council of Chalcedon struck a rather balanced compromise between the divergent christological schools of Alexandria and Antioch. But Chalcedon's christological definition did not settle all of the disputes regarding the person of Christ. Indeed, its deliberations were followed by some rather passionate and often chaotic confrontations between the supporters of Chalcedonian diophysitism (the council's claim that Christ has two [*dio*] natures [*physeis*]), and the so-called Monophysites (those who claimed that Christ possesses only one [*mone*] nature [*physis*]).[4]

During the first stage of these controversies, the Monophysites feared that Chalcedon did not sufficiently secure the unity of Christ's person and therefore had unwittingly lapsed into a Nestorian division of his person. They thought that it was better to talk about one "nature" in order to affirm the unity of Christ's person, even though the Monophysites themselves did want to respect the difference between Christ's humanity and his divinity in the incarnation.[5] The debate between the supporters of Chalcedon and the Monophysites led, through a winding political and theological maze, to the calling of the fifth ecumenical council in 553, known as Constantinople II. While this council upheld the theology of Chalcedon, it tried to emphasize more strongly the unity of Christ's person, albeit in such a way that Chalcedon's clear distinction between the human and divine natures was not undermined.

Although Constantinople II reaffirmed Chalcedonian "two-natures" christology (diophysitism), it did not resolve the Monophysite controversy, for there remained an unanswered question: What precisely is a "nature" and of what does it consist? To take the most controversial test case, does the "will" belong to a nature, such that Christ in possessing two natures also possesses two wills, or does that faculty belong to a person, such that Christ possesses only one will?[6] Some theologians who wanted to split the difference between

---

[4] There were some Nestorian communities and theologians who also participated in these debates. But the most influential debates were between the Monophysites and the pro-Chalcedonians.

[5] See the summary discussion of González, *History of Christian Thought*, II: 77–82.

[6] On this question see Pelikan, *Christian Tradition*, II: 62–75.

Monophysitism and Chalcedonian diophysitism held that there were two natures in the person of Christ but suggested that he possessed only one will – the position known as *monothelitism* (*mone* = one; *thelema* = will). Their basic argument, in emphasizing the unity of Christ's person, was that will is a feature of personhood, not nature. Since Christ is only one person, he must have only one will. But the Chalcedonian party again disagreed, associating will with nature and thus claiming that Christ has two wills (*diothelitism*).

It was this divisive debate that occasioned the sixth ecumenical council in 680–1, known as Constantinople III. This council ruled that since the will belongs to nature, Chalcedon's language of two natures implied two wills in the person of Christ. Moreover, it explained that these two wills are in harmony with each other because, due to Christ's sinlessness, his human will always obeys his divine will. In this way, the council attempted to preserve the difference between Christ's humanity and divinity but also to secure their close personal unity. The hope was that this reaffirmation of Chalcedon would speak to the concerns of the Monophysites and the Nestorians. To the extent that it did not, these heterodox communities continued to distance themselves from the mainstream church. The fifth and sixth ecumenical councils (Constantinople II and III) largely resolved the christological question from the official standpoint of the church – that is, Chalcedonian christology – although Nestorian and Monophysite churches have continued to exist independently to this day. Aside from the pope, the West was involved only tangentially in these discussions, since the Latin tradition largely accepted Chalcedon as unproblematic.

The next major crisis in the eastern church centered on the use of icons in worship. Unsurprisingly, this was at its core another christological disagreement. In 726 the eastern emperor, Leo III, out of mixed motives, prohibited the use of icons in the church (ostensibly fearing that people were confusing the icons with the reality that they represented, hence lapsing into idolatry). He accompanied his decree with the symbolic action of destroying an icon of Christ that had long stood over the entrance of the imperial palace in Constantinople. This act resulted in public riots in protest and earned a condemnation from the patriarch of Constantinople, the leader of the eastern Byzantine church. When the pope in the West found out about this event, he complained that Leo's decree implicitly contradicted the two-natures christology of Chalcedon, which points to the possibility of the finite (humanity) serving as a vehicle for the infinite (deity). If this is the case with Christ himself, why not also with symbols of Christ?

To help resolve this "iconoclastic controversy," the eastern theologian John of Damascus (655–750) proposed a distinction between *veneration*

Table 17.1 *The basic affirmations of the last three ecumenical councils*

The Second Council of Constantinople (553)	Affirmed Chalcedon's diophysitism (two natures in Jesus Christ) against the monophysites
The Third Council of Constantinople (680–81)	Affirmed diothelitism (two wills in Jesus Christ) against the monothelites
The Second Council of Nicea (787)	Warranted the veneration of icons in Christian worship

(*proskynesis*) and *worship* (*latreia*). With respect to icons, the former is proper and acceptable, while the latter is not, since God alone is worthy of worship. John claimed that an icon is simply a likeness that causes one's mind to think of the original that is represented by the likeness. Veneration of an icon therefore has the purpose of aiding worship – for example, worship of the Christ who is represented by the icon.[7] Moreover, given the unique case of Christ, if his humanity is real and is one with the divine Logos, as Chalcedon had claimed, then veneration of an image is eminently appropriate. In other words, the incarnation itself warrants the use of iconography. John suggested that use of icons in this way is really no different from the way in which Christ is worshipped through the veneration of the gospels, albeit with images instead of words. The iconoclastic controversy occasioned the seventh and last ecumenical council, known as Nicea II and held in 787, which decreed that veneration of icons was an acceptable practice.

The filioque *controversy*

The distinctive identity of the Eastern Orthodox church was forged in no small part by its controversy with the West over the question of the Holy Spirit's relationship to the Father and the Son. The original Niceno-Constantinopolitan Creed stated simply that the Spirit "proceeds from the Father." Drawing from the trinitarian theology of Augustine, however, the West eventually added the term *filioque* ("and the Son") to the creed, thus confessing that the Spirit "proceeds from the Father and the Son."[8] This revision, which had developed gradually in western liturgy and was first formalized in a regional synod held in Toledo, Spain (589), was officially

---

[7] See John of Damascus, *Exposition of the Orthodox Faith*, Book 4, ch. 16.
[8] Cf. the original version and the western revision in Pelikan and Hotchkiss, eds., *Creeds and Confessions*, 1: 163 and 672.

added to the creed by the pope in 1014. This creedal revision was the central *theological* factor that precipitated the schism between the Roman Catholic Church in the West and the Orthodox Church in the East.

The eastern church objected strenuously when it learned of this western amendment – in part because the western church had altered an *ecumenical* creed unilaterally without the consensus of the universal church. Issues of proper ecclesiastical protocol and theological governance were at stake. But even more, the particular creed and point of doctrine that had been revised by the West touched a deep nerve in the theology, piety, and liturgy of the East. As we noted above, one of the central characteristics of Byzantine theology was its reliance upon the tradition of the great church fathers and councils of the early church. The Niceno-Constantinopolitan creed was sacrosanct in the Greek-speaking East; the West's unilateral tampering with it was considered impious, if not blasphemous.

On the theological point of the procession of the Spirit, the East had traditionally focused on the person of the Father as the principle of trinitarian unity. As the fount of divinity, the one who eternally begets the Son and from whom the Spirit eternally proceeds, the Father is the person who unites the three persons of the Trinity as one God. Textually, the East pointed to the second half of John 15:26, which describes the Spirit as the one who "comes from" or "proceeds from" the Father. On this view, the Father's person is the source or fount of the divine life, which the Son and Spirit eternally share through their processions from the Father. Eastern theologians worried that the West's *filioque* clause implied two sources of divinity – Father and Son – in addition to unduly subordinating the Spirit to the first two persons of the Trinity.

For the West a variety of theological points were at stake. First, western theologians tended to appeal to the first half of John 15:26, which speaks of *Jesus* sending the Spirit from the Father, citing other texts as well, such as John 20:22, which describes Jesus breathing the Spirit on his disciples. Second, the West at this time was contending with the Arianism that was still flourishing among the Germanic tribes – a heresy that had already run its course in the East. Pointing to the Son as co-source of the Spirit served to emphasize the Son's deity, his unity of divine essence with the Father. Finally, this revision to the creed also enabled the West to more faithfully follow Augustine's view of the Spirit as the bond of love between Father and Son.

From the seventh to the eleventh centuries the East and West grew further apart on this issue, sometimes debating with each other and sometimes ignoring each other. Fueled by the customary ecclesial power struggles between these two regions of the church, in addition to the linguistic and cultural divisions that had long permeated their relationship, the *filioque* controversy led to the formal schism between East and West in 1054. Each tradition subsequently went its own way theologically and ecclesiastically. And when Constantinople (modern-day Istanbul) was conquered by Muslim armies in 1453, the center of gravity of Eastern Orthodoxy shifted to Eastern Europe and Russia, lands which were the missionary fruits of the Byzantine church's labors. Meanwhile the Latin West had been developing its own distinctive theological style.

LATIN THEOLOGY

The "Dark Ages" and Carolingian theology

Characterizations of historical periods tend to betray the values and assessments of the historians who name them. Both "Dark Ages" and "Middle Ages" are famous cases in point. "Dark Ages" was a term that traditionally referred to the period of time that spanned from the end of classical antiquity (around the time of Augustine and the decline of the Roman Empire) to the rebirth of classical learning in the Renaissance of the fourteenth century. The adjective "dark" implied that the light of learning had nearly been extinguished, with civilization left in peril. In actual fact, while some of those days were dark, at many times and in many places learning was alive and well in the West, particularly in the world of the monastery.[9] While not as pejorative a characterization, the term "Middle Ages," which is more commonly accepted and employed today, still implies that culture and learning in "medieval" times were only treading water, so to speak, between the high points of classical civilization and the Renaissance. Today the term "Dark Ages," if used at all, more commonly refers only to the half-millennium that spans from the fifth to the eleventh century (now often called the *early* Middle Ages). With respect to theology, it must be conceded that the early Middle Ages did not match the theological output and vitality of the patristic period. The later Middle Ages, however, witnessed the rise of scholasticism, which produced impressive theological developments. Given, therefore, the relative truth of the characterization "Dark Ages," our treatment of the early Middle Ages will be brief.

---

[9] For a popular account of the role of Irish monks in copying and preserving manuscripts in this period, see Thomas Cahill, *How the Irish Saved Civilization* (New York: Doubleday, 1995).

Against the idea that learning was defunct in this period, we must note that a renaissance of sorts occurred beginning with the rule of Charlemagne in the mid-eighth century and continuing in what is called the Carolingian Empire.[10] There was a significant revival of education in this period, which included, among other things, a renewed emphasis on the learning and literacy of the clergy. We have already seen how in this period the western church had been developing a distinctive understanding of the procession of the Holy Spirit (expressed in the *filioque* clause) that hastened the schism with the eastern church. Other discussions and debates from the eighth to the early eleventh centuries centered upon such themes as Christ's pre-existence, the nature of predestination, the doctrine of the virgin birth, and the nature of the human soul.[11] One topic that especially exemplifies early medieval theological concern was that of the presence of Christ in the Eucharist or Lord's Supper, since upon this issue turned the important question of the accessibility and availability of saving grace.

An early version of this debate occurred between a theologian named Radbertus (*c.* 790–*c.* 860) and his contemporary Ratramnus (fl. ninth century). Radbertus claimed that the presence of Christ in the Eucharist was both physical and spiritual. The physical presence is actually the real flesh or human body of Jesus, which God multiplies in the Supper so that it can be present in many places and times. Ratramnus disagreed, arguing that such a doctrine made little sense, for how could a physical body, which is by definition present in only one place at a time, be in numerous places at once? Christ is present, he argued, only spiritually and can be seen only through faith, not with the physical eye. It was the view of Radbertus, however, that came to be generally accepted.

A renewal of this debate took place nearly three centuries later, toward the end of the early Middle Ages. Berengar of Tours (*c.* 1010–88) began to argue against the view of Radbertus, which had become the popular view, insisting instead that the elements of the sacrament, bread and wine, remained precisely that – bread and wine. Berengar's argument was largely an appeal to reason. He did not think that Radbertus' traditional view made sufficient rational sense, even though it was well attested in the theological heritage. He claimed, much in line with Ratramnus centuries earlier, that Christ is present only spiritually in the Eucharist, especially since Christ's body had ascended to heaven.

---

[10] See Rosamond McKitterick, *The Frankish Kingdoms under the Carolingians* (London: Longman, 1983).

[11] For a rather concise summary, see González, *History of Christian Thought*, II: 107–42.

Berengar was opposed by a powerful church leader named Lanfranc (*c.* 1010–89), who was the head of a monastery school at Bec in France. Lanfranc defended the traditional view against Berengar's challenges. He claimed that the physical body of Christ is really present in the Supper by virtue of the bread and wine being transformed in their essence (what would later be characterized in Aristotelian terms as "substance"), even though their appearance (what would later be distinguished as "accidents") remained that of bread and wine. Lanfranc's position, eventually known as "transubstantiation," won the day in the medieval Catholic Church, being declared dogma in 1215 at the Fourth Lateran Council. Transubstantiation was later given its most precise formulation by Thomas Aquinas in the thirteenth century. But Berengar is particularly important because he shows the slow but growing emphasis in theology on *reason* in relation to faith. How exactly reason is related to faith became a debated question in the high Middle Ages, especially as the movement known as scholasticism developed.

Early scholasticism

Christianity's encounter with the Islamic world (most notoriously during the Crusades) was another medieval development with far-reaching theological consequences. This centuries-long interaction brought western Christians into renewed contact with Greek philosophy, especially that of Aristotle, many of whose texts were lost to the West but recovered through contact with the Arabic world, where they had been cherished and preserved. This sparked a renewed interest in philosophy and a new inquiry into the question of theology's relationship to philosophy. Around this time (latter eleventh century) an innovative approach to education began to develop, which is known as *scholasticism*. Scholastic approaches to theology utilized reason in a methodologically self-conscious way in order to systematize theological truth. As implied by its name, the development of scholasticism or "school theology" largely took place in the burgeoning universities of medieval Europe in the mid twelfth to thirteenth centuries (e.g., Paris, Oxford, and Cambridge), even though some of the earliest "scholastic" theologians were monks who taught at church schools of various kinds. The scholastics endeavored to establish theology as an ordered inquiry – in other words, as a science (Lat. *scientia* = knowledge). The science of theology would attempt to articulate the Christian faith in a clear, coherent, and comprehensive fashion. One of the first major scholastic theologians in whose theology reason and faith make a self-conscious liaison was Anselm of Canterbury.

Anselm of Canterbury

Anselm (1033–1109) was a student of Lanfranc at the monastery at Bec. When Lanfranc became the archbishop of Canterbury in 1063, Anselm became the prior of the monastery school and later the abbot of the monastery. Then, in 1093, Anselm followed Lanfranc's footsteps once again when he was appointed archbishop of Canterbury. Among the many achievements for which Anselm has become an important figure in the western tradition, three stand out as especially noteworthy: his theological method, his famous argument for God's existence, and his interpretation of Christ's saving death.

As discussed in Chapter 1 above, Anselm described theology as a matter of "faith seeking understanding" (*fides quaerens intellectum*), drawing upon and developing the Augustinian sense of theology as a restless journey toward the truth and wisdom of God. Anselm suggests that *faith* is actually a starting point for rational inquiry which can open up new doors of understanding that would otherwise be closed: "I do desire to understand a little of your truth which my heart already believes and loves. I do not seek to understand so that I may believe, but I believe so that I may understand."[12] His idea is that seeking a deeper *understanding* of the received faith enriches and confirms the truth of what is believed. We should also note the implication: only those who believe can truly understand. Anselm's "faith seeking understanding" has become a classic definition of theology. Accordingly, Anselm puts a high premium on reason, applying it to the difficult theological issues of his day.

His actual theological method, however, betrays a more rationalist bent, as much of the time he strives to answer issues, questions, and heresies not with scripture or tradition, but with the resources of reason alone, so as to *demonstrate* the truth of the faith that is believed. In Anselm's view, such an approach will enable the theologian to understand scripture and tradition better, because the understanding made possible by reason will have illuminated the believing mind. The hidden premise in Anselm's method is that the doctrines held by Christian faith are *not* irrational, but are fully consistent with reason and can therefore be proved rationally.

Anselm's "ontological" argument for God's existence exemplifies his reasoned approach (also see pp. 171–2 above). In considering the lofty being of God as "that thing than which nothing greater can be thought," Anselm begins by musing about the "fool" in Psalm 14 who says in his heart

---

[12] Anselm, *Proslogion*, 244.

that "there is no God."[13] Anselm argues that though the fool "understands" what is said when God is defined as "that thing than which nothing greater can be thought," the fool is actually claiming that such a being exists only in people's minds, but not in reality. Anselm reasons that such a claim on the part of the fool is evidence of the fool's folly, for "certainly that than which nothing greater can be thought cannot exist only in the understanding. For if it exists only in the understanding, it is possible to think of it existing also in reality, and that is greater."[14] The atheistic fool therefore holds a contradictory position: while accepting the idea of a most perfect being, he then denies that perfect being one of the qualities needed for it to be "most perfect" – namely, existence – thus contradicting the very definition of God that the fool accepts and claims to understand. Though not considered wholly compelling even in his own day, Anselm's ontological argument has provoked much discussion throughout the centuries, and even enjoys vigorous debate today.[15]

Anselm's method of using reason in a rigorous way to demonstrate the truths believed in faith is also exemplified in his interpretation of the reconciling work of Christ (also see pp. 271–3 above).[16] Drawing upon the feudal society of his day in making sense of the God–human relationship, Anselm likens sinful human beings to vassals who have offended and dishonored their lord by robbing him of something rightfully his. Thus in order to make "satisfaction" for their offense in view of God's honor, they must repay God and make restitution for their disobedience. The only other option that would preserve the divine honor is for humanity to be punished. However, if God were to punish all human beings with damnation, Anselm reasons, God's good designs for humanity would be defeated. So satisfaction is the only option befitting the divine character. However, since human beings owed God *perfect* and complete loyalty, it is impossible for them to repay God, because even a single moment of disloyalty falls short of perfection. Since satisfaction for humanity cannot be achieved by a mere human being, redemption is possible only through a "God-man," one who is fully divine (since only God *can* make satisfaction) and fully human (since only humanity *ought* to make satisfaction). The God-man Jesus Christ freely gives himself up to a death that he did not deserve. He thus merits

---

[13] Ibid.   [14] Ibid., 245.
[15] For a discussion of some of these debates, as well as his own attempt to maintain the kernel of the argument, see Alvin Plantinga, *The Ontological Argument: From St. Anselm to Contemporary Philosophers* (Garden City, NY: Anchor, 1965).
[16] Anselm of Canterbury, *Why God Became Man*, in Fairweather, ed., *Scholastic Miscellany*, 100–83.

a reward that he does not need, which is graciously applied to human beings as the satisfaction they themselves could not provide.

Anselm's reflections on the atonement set the agenda for later discussions in the West. In one way or another, almost all subsequent interpretations of Christ's death either draw upon or criticize Anselm, a tribute to the enduring nature of his contributions to atonement theology. Moreover, his work more broadly helped to shape the emerging enterprise of scholastic theology.

Peter Abelard

Another significant theologian of early scholasticism was a monk and scholar named Peter Abelard (1079–*c.* 1142). Though Abelard was an extraordinarily popular teacher at the emerging University of Paris, his life took a romantically tragic turn when the family of his secret wife, Heloise, found out about their love affair and had Abelard castrated.[17] Abelard also encountered professional difficulties due to the opposition engendered by his creative, even daring, theological ideas. His influential work *Sic et Non* (Yes and No) compiled seemingly contradictory quotations from scripture and the fathers of the church and attempted to resolve the theological tensions that lay within them.[18] This approach became known as "dialectic" because of the way in which its "dialogue" between opposing viewpoints served as the rational medium of the quest for truth.

One of the differences between Abelard and his older contemporary, Anselm, can be seen in their approach to the theological enterprise. Whereas Anselm claimed: "I believe in order that I might understand," the sense of Abelard's view appears to be: "I understand in order to believe," thereby reversing the order of Anselm's definition. It is not surprising therefore that Abelard was much more willing to rethink and revise the theological tradition than was Anselm, for whom reason was a tool for confirming the received beliefs of the church. However, Abelard was not a sheer rationalist, for he still generally accepted the truth of the ecumenical teaching of the church and considered its core confession to be basically consistent with reason. Nevertheless, he held the conviction that reason is necessary to bring out the true implications of Christian teaching – to truly believe the faith – and that reason will sometimes require a critical revision of certain doctrines of the church.

---

[17] On this remarkable affair see James Burge, *Heloise and Abelard: A New Biography* (San Francisco: HarperSanFrancisco, 2003).

[18] Peter Abelard, *Sic Et Non: A Critical Edition*, ed. Blanche B. Boyer and Richard McKeon (Chicago: University of Chicago Press, 1976).

In this vein, Abelard is important in proposing a different understanding of the atonement than traditionally received. He rejected both the patristic ransom theory and Anselm's satisfaction theory, objecting to the latter because he doubted Anselm's claim that atonement could have been achieved *only* by the satisfying work of the God-man. Logically, God could have saved humanity simply by a declaration of mercy. Therefore Abelard appears to think that Christ's death is not a sacrifice or a means of satisfaction, but that Christ provides salvation by virtue of his teaching and personal example of God's love:

Through his unique act of grace manifested to us – in that his Son has taken upon himself our nature and preserved therein in teaching us by word and example even unto death – he has more fully bound us to himself by love; with the result that our hearts should be enkindled by such a gift of divine grace, and true charity should not now shrink from enduring anything for him.[19]

This thread of Abelard's view is sometimes called a "moral-influence" or "subjective" theory of atonement, and prefigures the nineteenth-century classical liberal perspective on Christ's work. While such a label can certainly be justified by the quotation just cited, it is not entirely fair, since Abelard also thought that grace is objectively available on the basis of Christ's death as administered through the sacraments of the church.

Peter Lombard

Born shortly before Anselm's death, Peter Lombard (*c.* 1100–60) was a French theologian whose major contribution to the history of theology was a work known as the *Sentences*.[20] Similar to the dialectical approach of Abelard, this work compiled quotations from the great fathers of the church on central theological topics and commented on them, with the goal of resolving their apparent contradictions on the path toward the truth. While not widely used during his lifetime, Lombard's *Sentences* became the standard text for western theology in the high Middle Ages. Students were commonly taught from the *Sentences*, with the teacher reading Lombard's work while interjecting his own interpretive and critical comments. Given the centrality of Lombard's text, one of the rites of passage for budding theologians was the requirement to produce their own commentaries on the *Sentences*.

[19] Peter Abelard, "Exposition of the Epistle to the Romans," in Fairweather, ed., *Scholastic Miscellany*, 283.
[20] Peter Lombard, *Sententiae in IV Libris Distinctae* (Grottaferrata: Editiones Collegii S. Bonaventurae ad Claras Aquas, 1971).

The school of St. Victor

Roughly contemporaneous with Lombard, an order known as the Augustinian Canons established a house of study in Paris, named "St. Victor," which soon became an important theological center.[21] The first major theologian to emerge from this "school" was Hugh of St. Victor (d. 1142). Platonic in his inclinations, as was commonly the case at that time, Hugh took a rather mystical approach to theology, considering theology to be primarily a matter of spiritual ascent to God.

In this ascent to God, the sacraments play an important and integral role for Hugh.[22] Faithful to the Augustinian tradition, he recognized that contemplation of God cannot take place apart from grace, which is dispensed by God through the sacraments. Sacraments in Hugh's understanding, following Augustine, are material elements that represent, signify, and contain God's invisible grace. Since they *represent* grace, there must be some kind of appropriate similarity between the element and what it represents (e.g., wine aptly represents Christ's blood). Since the elements *signify* something beyond themselves, the words of institution (e.g., "This cup is the new covenant in my blood") are necessary to clarify the connection. And since the elements actually *contain* grace, they contribute to sanctification and thereby foster the Christian's ascent to contemplation of and mystical union with the triune God. In this way Hugh's mystical theology contributed to the clarification of sacramentology.

Roughly one generation after Hugh, a theologian named Richard of St. Victor developed and extended certain Victorine tendencies. With Hugh, Richard regarded theology as a discipline that fosters the soul's ascent to contemplation of God, yet he more clearly distinguished three steps in this spiritual process.[23] First, theology as *lectio* (reading) is a matter of studying the literal meaning of scripture and theological doctrines – this Richard likens to crawling. Second, when the theologian advances to the *meditatio* (meditation) stage of the discipline, he is involved in seeing behind mere literal words to the mind of God which is hidden therein – this Richard compares to walking. The highest form of theology and peak of this ascent is *contemplatio* (contemplation), a matter of truly communing with God by virtue of a mystical vision of the divine – this Richard likens to flying.

[21] See Stephen Ferruolo, *The Origins of the University: The Schools of Paris and Their Critics, 1100–1215* (Stanford, CA: Stanford University Press, 1985), 27–46.

[22] Hugh of St. Victor, *On the Sacraments of the Christian Faith*, trans. Roy J. Deferrari (Cambridge, MA: Medieval Academy of America, 1951).

[23] Richard of St. Victor, *Selected Writings on Contemplation*, trans. Clare Kirchenberger, Classics of the Contemplative Life (London: Faber & Faber, n.d.), 136–7.

Perhaps Richard's most important contribution to the heritage of theology, one that many twentieth-century theologians have drawn upon, concerns his "argument from love" for the trinitarian nature of God, an argument he proposed in order to rationally bolster the traditional dogma of the Trinity. Taking up the Johannine definition, "God is love" (1 John 4:8), Richard reasons that God must be a plurality of persons, since no one can properly love by simply loving himself or herself: "For charity [i.e., true love] to exist, then, it is necessary for love to tend to another; where plurality of persons is lacking, therefore, there simply cannot be charity."[24] But could not God simply be one person who is love by loving created persons? Richard rejects that possibility, because such love would not be the highest kind of love, which is possible only between equals. So only another divine person could be wholly deserving of the love of God. There must then be at least two persons in God for God to be love. But Richard then appeals to the shared nature of true love to argue for three persons. Two cannot share love, since their love would be locked up within themselves and could potentially be a selfish kind of love. So there must be a third person in the divine Trinity for the definition of God as love to make sense of love's highest form and noblest manifestation.

High scholasticism

The mendicant orders

As we move into the latter stages of the twelfth century and the period that follows, theological contributions become more and more tied to two religious orders that emerged around the turn of the thirteenth century. These two religious societies became known as the "mendicant" orders (Lat. *mendicans* = beggar) because their members were sworn to poverty and simplicity, and therefore were to subsist by begging for food and clothing.

The Franciscan order was founded by Francis of Assisi (*c.* 1181–1226). Although born into a wealthy family, Francis renounced his wealth and tried to imitate the simple life of Christ and his apostles. For Francis, such simplicity meant that he should try to live as austere a life as possible. Because he was suspicious of the intellect and therefore skeptical of scholastic theology, Francis developed a more practical "theology of life" based on the incarnation. He held that the incarnation had transformed the very fabric of the cosmos such that all creation was infused with the grace and

---

[24] Richard of St. Victor, *On the Trinity*, in Fairweather, ed., *Scholastic Miscellany*, 330.

glory of the triune God who could be encountered therein, even through inanimate creatures such as "brother sun" and "sister moon."[25]

The various followers attracted to Francis were eventually organized as a formal Catholic "order" in 1210. This order aspired to emulate the poverty, humility, and simplicity of Christ that were central to the piety of Francis. Though this order possessed rather anti-intellectual tendencies in its origins, through the work of Alexander of Hales and Bonaventure the Franciscan order became a powerful theological and intellectual force.

The second mendicant order, the Dominicans, was founded by a Spaniard named Dominic (*c.* 1174–1221) with the aim of aiding his missionary work among heretical communities. Similar to the Franciscans, the Dominicans were itinerant in nature, not possessing property, but were committed solely to spreading the gospel through preaching. As such, they became known as the "Preaching Friars." Unlike the Franciscans, however, this order did not begin with a bias against the intellect, and would eventually produce the towering theological figure of the Middle Ages – Thomas Aquinas. Both the Dominicans and the Franciscans eventually became well represented in the great European universities, even though there was much resistance at first from more established religious orders as to whether scholars from the mendicant orders ought to be allowed such prestigious positions.

Bonaventure

The greatest theologian produced by the Franciscan order, arguably, was Bonaventure (1221–74). Following the lead of Alexander of Hales before him, Bonaventure was instrumental in transforming his order into a movement of great learning and intellectual sophistication. Similar to most theologians in the Augustinian tradition, Bonaventure advocated a rather mystical brand of theology that was strongly indebted to Neoplatonism. He especially emphasized the ascent to God by means of the illumination of Christ, the Logos. Bonaventure held that since creation takes place through the mediating role of the Logos, it is based on the Ideas in the mind of the Trinity. Creation therefore bears the imprint of its Creator as trinitarian patterns are present throughout the world. This Logos-structured cosmos provides access to God and has implications for all human knowledge.

---

[25] See the helpful discussion by Margaret R. Miles, *The Word Made Flesh: A History of Christian Thought* (Malden, MA: Blackwell, 2005), 159–60.

In his influential *The Mind's Journey to God*, Bonaventure uses the metaphor of a ladder to describe the spiritual quest for God.[26] Similar to Richard of St. Victor, Bonaventure suggests that the first "rung" of the ladder to knowledge of God is examination of the physical, sensible world. Here the human mind is filled with delight when it sees the connectedness of the whole cosmos via the Logos. God is seen *in* the sensible world as one discerns vestiges of the Trinity in it (e.g., that the measurement of magnitude necessarily involves the three components of length, breadth, and depth).[27] The second rung of the ladder involves the examination of the image of God in the human mind itself, which Bonaventure understands in terms of Augustine's psychological analogy (see p. 127 above). Stepping to the third rung, the human mind is brought to the rapture of contemplation of God – seeing the Trinity in more mystical terms, a contemplative glimpse of the triune nature of God. Similar to the mystical Victorines, Bonaventure understands contemplation in rather ecstatic terms, as a vision of God that is beyond discursive, ordered thought, where the mind is filled with the beauty of God.

Through the illuminating light of the Logos, human creatures can ascend to knowledge of and communion with the triune God. For Bonaventure, this mystical ascent also had implications for the place of theology in the university. Since God as Supreme Being is at the summit of human knowledge, this means that theology – that realm of learning most directly concerned with God – is the "queen of the sciences." Bonaventure thought, in a very Augustinian sense, that knowledge in all disciplines was made possible by the illumination of the Logos. As such, philosophy and other forms of inquiry are subordinate to, but finally integrated by, theology.

Thomas Aquinas

Of all theologians, it is undoubtedly the shadow of Thomas Aquinas (c. 1225–74) that looms largest over the Latin theology of the Middle Ages. While Aquinas' theology was controversial in its own day, it eventually came to be recognized as the most significant theological contribution of the time. Thomism, as it came to be called, was instrumental in guiding the Catholic Reformation in the latter half of the sixteenth century, and was eventually declared to be official Catholic teaching in the late nineteenth century. Thomas's massive and influential works *Summa contra*

---

[26] Bonaventure, *The Mind's Journey to God*, trans. Lawrence S. Cunningham (Chicago: Franciscan Herald Press, 1979).
[27] Ibid., 38.

Gentiles and the *Summa Theologiae* have cemented his reputation in the history of theology.

Aquinas was born in Italy, but spent much of his career in France after deciding as a young man to join the Dominican order (much to his family's chagrin). His early studies and teaching at the University of Paris would decisively shape the nature and purpose of his theological project. One of the most controversial aspects of Aquinas' theology was his heavy (though not uncritical) use of the philosophy of Aristotle, whom Thomas esteemed as "the philosopher." Although many of the important works of Aristotle had been lost to the Christian West, they were preserved in the Islamic world, where a distinctive Aristotelianism was cultivated. In the thirteenth century this Aristotelianism made its way to Europe and took its fledgling universities, such as the University of Paris, by intellectual storm. With this discovery, some Catholic philosophers and theologians became so enamored of the descriptive power of Aristotle's thought – his sharp logic and precise categories – as to virtually posit a "two-truth theory." On the one hand there was religious truth, which was more symbolic, mythological, and non-demonstrable (e.g., *creatio ex nihilo*); on the other hand, there was philosophical truth, which, illuminated by Aristotle's thought and distinctions, was conceptually clear, demonstrable, and therefore more compelling, but which could not secure the essential truths of Christian faith. In short, this rediscovery of Aristotle occasioned a serious intellectual challenge to traditional Christianity. In the midst of this rationalist challenge, Aquinas took up his pen in apologetic response.

Thomas thought that philosophy in general and Aristotelian philosophy in particular could play an important but limited role in Christian theology. His understanding of the relationship between theology and philosophy is often called his "synthesis," because of the particular way in which he brings together faith and reason, grace and nature. Aquinas thought that all truth could be divided into two categories. First, he held that some truths about God could be known by reason's analysis of *nature* (i.e., creation via general revelation). It was at this point that philosophical resources became important to him, especially Aristotle's philosophy, as a rational tool to examine nature or the truths about God in creation. For example, Thomas held that God's existence and attributes can be known through reason and philosophy.[28] However, Thomas also recognized that the highest truths about God cannot be discerned by reason's application to nature. Truths such as the triune nature of God or creation *ex nihilo* could be known only through

---

[28] Thomas Aquinas, *Summa Theologica*, 1.2–11.

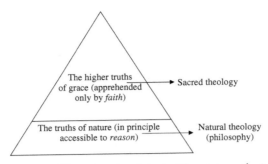

Figure 17.1 The unity of truth in the Thomistic synthesis

faith's dependence on *grace* (i.e., scripture via special revelation).[29] In other words, reason alone can demonstrate something about God by reflection on the cosmos, reasoning from its effects to God as their cause. But reason cannot penetrate the deeper truths about God. Grace and faith alone make that possible. (See Figure 17.1.)

It is important to recognize that in his synthesis Thomas did not propose a two-step theological method, as some interpreters have understood him. He does not mean that one must first use reason alone to justify belief in God's existence before relying on faith to know God as Trinity. For Thomas it is more a matter of different *kinds* of truth – truths that *can* be demonstrated through reason and truths that *cannot* be demonstrated and therefore must be *believed* through faith.[30] Thomas recognized that many people for various reasons – for want of ability or time, for example – would simply need to believe on the basis of scripture and church authority even some of the things that can *in principle* be demonstrated by reason. In fact, the things of God knowable by reason are already implied in the truths of special revelation and therefore can also simply be grasped by faith. One straightforward example: if one believes through faith that God is triune (unknowable by reason alone), then the truth that God exists (in principle knowable through reason alone) is also presupposed in that truth of faith.

Thomas thus regarded reason alone to be a limited source for theology, yet a significant tool. Reason is capable of much, but it must be complemented by faith. The synthetic nature of Thomas's approach is apparent in his famous statement that "grace does not destroy but perfects nature."[31]

[29] Ibid., 1.32.1.
[30] See Arvin Vos, *Aquinas, Calvin, and Contemporary Protestant Thought: A Critique of Protestant Views on the Thought of Thomas Aquinas* (Grand Rapids, MI: Eerdmans, 1985).
[31] Aquinas, *Summa Theologica*, 1.1.8.

In other words, what can be known theologically through grace completes the truth that can be known philosophically through nature. Thus knowledge of God through grace and faith brings a deeper, more comprehensive, and more adequate understanding of God.[32]

The character of Thomas's synthesis and the important role of Aristotelian philosophy in his theology are most evident in his doctrine of God. Since we examine this doctrine at some length in Chapter 4 above, we will not replicate that discussion here. Rather, we will focus our attention on Thomas's important doctrines of atonement and justification, since the former proposed an important revision of Anselm's influential satisfaction theory of atonement, and the latter became a key resource for the Catholic Reformation, particularly at the Council of Trent in its response to Protestant understandings of justification.

Aquinas' understanding of Christ's saving death is quite involved and multifaceted. His treatment of salvation as *redemption* provides a good entrance to his basic thought. Aquinas rejected Anselm's assumption that the salvation of humanity from sin must come through either satisfaction *or* punishment. According to Aquinas, satisfaction takes place *through* the cross *as* a substitutionary punishment that Christ bears in place of sinful humanity.[33] (The Reformers Luther and Calvin later followed Aquinas in this shift.) According to Thomas, sin brings about a twofold problem for human beings. First, they owe a debt to God that can be paid only through punishment. Second, they are enslaved to sin, which distorts their relationship with God. Christ's atoning work must therefore address both of these problems. According to Thomas, Christ's passion and death make satisfaction for sin precisely by paying the debt that human beings owe God. The cross is the presentation to God of something that God loves – Christ's perfect life – more than what God hates – the offense of sin.[34] Inasmuch as Christ's death is a temporal punishment for sin, it serves as the satisfying punishment that humanity does not have to pay. God provides this redemption in order to restore the harmony between God and humanity.

Christ's death addresses the second problem, human bondage to sin, because it merits grace. From the infinite value of his voluntary sacrifice, not only is humanity's debt deserving punishment paid, but a superabundance of merit is also produced, which is superintended by the church as dispensed through the sacramental system. By accessing this "storehouse" of merit, forgiveness for sin can be obtained, which breaks the hold of sin over humanity. Baptism, for example, applies Christ's payment of debt to humanity, and

[32] See ibid., 1.12.13.   [33] See ibid., 3.48.4.   [34] Ibid., 3.48.2.

the Lord's Supper conveys the grace of forgiveness that enables right human behavior.[35] While Christ's death and God's grace alone suffice for salvation, Thomas thought that God required human beings to experience some punishment in themselves in order to produce sorrow for sin. Thus he regarded *penance* – the sacrament of genuine contrition, confession of sin, satisfaction by works, and priestly absolution – also as a means of grace.[36]

Christ's atonement pays the debt for sin (through the substitutionary punishment of the cross) and makes saving grace available to humanity. Aquinas' doctrine of justification shows how, on his view, grace affects the human being – in other words, how forgiveness and liberation from the bondage of sin become a reality in a person's life. But to grasp the effect of justifying grace on humanity first requires an understanding of how Thomas viewed the created state of humanity.[37] According to Aquinas (who draws here upon Augustine), humanity was created in a state of justice, which means that its faculties were properly ordered: the lower powers of the body were subservient to the higher faculties of the soul, which itself answered to God. The soul's deference to God's will was possible because of a supernatural grace that was given with creation. However, the fall into sin meant that the supernatural grace was lost. Fallen humanity, accordingly, is stuck in the natural plane. And since the soul in this state no longer responds to God, it is impossible for it to rule over the lower powers of the body. Sin, in short, brings about a situation of injustice or corrupted order. Justification, then, is the restoration of right order within the human person.

Using Aristotelian categories, Aquinas says that since justification is a movement from a condition of injustice to a condition of justice, the basic components of any movement are present: a mover, the movement, and the effect of the movement. In strong anti-Pelagian fashion, Thomas regards God's grace as the Mover in the process of justification. Through the sacraments of the church (which grant access to Christ's abundance of grace) God's grace is infused into the human soul. Since free will is constitutive of humanity, the movement that results from justifying grace involves a double movement of the human will: the will freely inclines *against sin* and *toward God* in faith.[38] The effect of this double movement of the will as enabled by God is the remission of sins. In this instantaneous process, which happens through participation in the sacraments, the human will is really changed (meaning that Aquinas sees the category of sanctification as part of the process of justification), a change made possible by the operation of God's grace in Christ, with which the human will is enabled to

---

[35] See ibid., 3.69, 79.   [36] Ibid., 3.84.5.   [37] Ibid., 2a.113.1.   [38] Ibid., 2a.113.3–5.

cooperate. As we shall see, some of the important figures in later medieval theology diverged significantly from this understanding of justification, a shift that helped to precipitate the Reformation.

Late scholasticism

John Duns Scotus

While Anselm is properly considered the eminent theologian of the early scholastic period, and Aquinas the ambassador of high scholastic theology, it is more difficult to name a patron theologian for what can be called "late" scholasticism. One candidate is John Duns Scotus (c. 1265–1308). On the one hand, Scotus perpetuated the Thomistic synthesis between reason and faith – especially its confidence in the possibilities of reason via natural theology. But on the other hand, Scotus also inaugurated one of the major shifts away from Thomistic theology. While he left ample room for metaphysics (i.e., the study of "being" by means of reason), and even advocated a rational proof for God's existence from the contingency of being,[39] Scotus was less confident than Thomas regarding *how much* reason alone could demonstrate about God. He thought that most of the traditional proofs for God's existence, for example, such as Thomas's "Prime Mover" argument, failed to prove the existence of a transcendent God, but showed only the need for a first mover *within* the world. He also considered only some of the divine attributes, such as infinity, to be knowable through reason. Others, such as omnipotence and immensity, which Thomas had regarded as falling within the sphere of reason's capability, Scotus considered knowable only through faith.[40] Scotus' diminished confidence in reason in comparison to Thomas can be attributed to his relative prioritization of the divine will over the intellect.[41] Whereas Thomas thought that the divine intellect guided and controlled the divine will, so that God commands things (will) that God knows to be good (intellect), Scotus emphasized the freedom of the divine will more strongly. This shift, which downplayed the intrinsic rationality of the cosmos by seeing it more as the product of the divine will than of the divine rationality, began to erode the high medieval synthesis of reason and faith. Scotus' work paved the way for William of Ockham (see below), whose work severely undermined the Thomistic synthesis.

Scotus also contributed to Mariology, the growing theological reflections concerning the Virgin Mary that had begun during the Carolingian period

---

[39] See Richard Cross, *Duns Scotus*, Great Medieval Thinkers (New York: Oxford University Press, 1999), 15–23.

[40] Frederick Copleston, *A History of Philosophy*, II: *Medieval Philosophy* (New York: Image, 1993), 250–2.

[41] González, *History of Christian Thought*, II: 311; Copleston, *History of Philosophy*, II: 538–41.

and were continued by other medieval theologians, most notably Anselm. In particular, he supported the doctrine of the *immaculate conception* of Mary, which was later declared to be a dogma by the Catholic Church (nineteenth century). Given a high view of Mary as exalted mother of Christ, Scotus thought it made sense to think of her as being redeemed in a more perfect way than the rest of humanity – that is, by the prevention of her reception of original sin in the first place through an "immaculate" conception.[42] This idea became widespread later on as Mariology grew in popularity and as people employed this doctrine for different reasons than Scotus – namely, to explain Jesus' conception without original sin, since in Augustinian terms original sin was widely considered to be transmitted through biological reproduction.

William of Ockham

The important theological shifts beginning with Scotus – the chastening of reason, the emphasis on faith and special revelation, and the relative priority of the divine will – took more radical form in the theology of William of Ockham (*c.* 1285–1347). More than Scotus before him, Ockham emphasized the absolute priority of God's will (i.e., voluntarism). He held that in God's absolute power, God could have created a world order very different from the one we know; God could have designated other things as "good" than the moral order we in fact have, for on Ockham's view, things are good only because God wills them. In the Thomistic synthesis, by contrast, the rationality of creation, including its moral order, was rooted in the divine rationality. Human reason could grasp reality because reality itself was the product of the divine intellect. But with Ockham, the order of reality is the product of the divine will, not necessarily guided by the divine intellect. With Ockham, the foundations of Thomas's synthesis began to erode, since the theologian had to rely much more radically on faith in special revelation rather than on reason tied to general revelation. For if the natural order is not necessarily a lens into the being and intellect of God, it becomes increasingly difficult to draw conclusions about God's nature and intellect by analyzing God's effects in the world, for the cause of those effects is the free, even arbitrarily free, divine will, not the divine intellect. Given his view of the absolute contingency of the world on God's will, Ockham ruled out any use of reason to prove God's existence from the effects or order of the world. Indeed, reason became only a tool for thinking clearly about the things of faith. Ockham and his disciples fancied themselves as adherents to a "modern way" of theological thought (*via moderna*), whereas Thomas and

---

[42] Cross, *Duns Scotus*, 132–3.

even Duns Scotus, in their minds, were seen as outmoded representatives of an old way of doing theology (*via antiqua*). With the rise of the *via moderna* the Thomistic synthesis fell on hard times, as reason was significantly attenuated by the emphasis on the divine will and the corresponding need to rely on faith and special revelation via scripture.[43]

Another key feature of Ockham's critique of the Thomistic synthesis between faith and reason was his revised view of the status of "universals" – the important medieval debate concerning how general truths unify our experience of the concrete, particular things in the world (see Table 17.2). According to theologians such as Thomas, who held a position known as *realism*, universals exist in reality and are known as the mind abstracts from particular things (e.g., trees) the universal ideas (e.g., "treeness") that are the essence or inherent form of those particulars. To know "treeness," for example, is to know the real essence or form of trees. Grasping these universal essences allows the theologian/philosopher to use reason to demonstrate necessary truths in the realm of particulars.[44] Other thinkers, however, considered universals to be real, but only as intellectual concepts – the position known as *conceptualism*. While Ockham's position is perhaps best regarded as a form of conceptualism, his view came to be known as *nominalism* – the view that universals were simply symbols or names (*nomina*) that we use to group similar particulars together.[45] In claiming to know a "universal" here, such as "treeness" or "goodness," one is simply comparing particulars by noting their similarities, not coming to know through reason the very essence of trees or the good. On this view, there is in fact no real form or essence that can be known through reason.[46] For the science of theology, this meant that reason was increasingly viewed as unable to develop universally applicable concepts from sensible reality that could be applied in a more eminent way to the divine, with the result that the theologian was forced to rely more radically on faith to understand the being of God.

Ockham also furthered a shift begun by Scotus and others in the doctrine of justification. He held that God freely (or arbitrarily, depending on how one evaluates Ockham's position) chooses to reward basic good works of the human being with the gift of sanctifying grace. Accordingly, the person who

[43] Harry Klocker, *William of Ockham and the Divine Freedom* (Milwaukee, WI: Marquette University Press, 1992), 91–105.

[44] Diogenes Allen and Eric O. Springsted, *Philosophy for Understanding Theology*, 2nd edn. (Louisville, KY: Westminster John Knox, 2007), 114–15.

[45] See William of Ockham, *Philosophical Writings*, ed. and trans. Philotheus Boehner, Nelson Philosophical Texts (Edinburgh: Nelson, 1957), 35–45.

[46] Allen and Springsted, *Philosophy for Understanding Theology*, 116.

Table 17.2 *Typology of views of universals*

Universalia ante rem	Universals exist *before* particular things	Extreme realism (e.g., Plato)
Universalia in re	Universals exist *in* particular things	Moderate realism (e.g., Aristotle, Aquinas)
Universalia post rem	Universals exist *after* particular things • as concepts in the mind	Conceptualism (e.g., Ockham?, Kant)
	• as mere names (*nomina*) given to them	Nominalism (e.g., Ockham?, poststructuralism)

"does what is in him" (*facere quod in se est*) merits sanctifying grace through a lower "congruent merit." Reception of this sanctifying grace enables further good works that properly earn the reward of forgiveness through a higher "condign merit." In short, the role of good works in salvation is accentuated in Ockham's framework, although he and his followers did not consider this view to be Pelagian in character, because God's original choice to reward this initial turning of the human will toward righteousness was itself an act of grace alone. But whereas for Thomas justification takes place on the basis of God *knowing* that a real change has transpired in the believer by means of divine grace, for Ockham justification takes place simply because God *willed* (albeit graciously) to reward good works with forgiveness. The result of Ockham's emphasis on the divine will in justification was therefore an increased emphasis on the role of human works in salvation.

CONCLUSION

Raised theologically in the tradition of the *via moderna*, Martin Luther would eventually conclude that the Ockhamist view of justification was indeed Pelagian, tantamount to a works righteousness. At the same time, he imbibed the *via moderna*'s emphasis on the freedom of the divine will and its critique of natural theology. Luther's theology therefore represents both a critique and an embrace of this new brand of theology. These features of the *via moderna*, along with its subversion of the Thomistic synthesis, led to a series of instabilities that portended revolutionary changes in the theological world. Later in the fourteenth century the intellectual tide known as the Renaissance washed across Europe, a movement that disparaged scholastic theology and desired to reach back to the glories of antiquity in order to renew culture and learning, including the discipline of theology. The Renaissance also contributed to the important

Table 17.3 *Timeline of theology in the Middle Ages*

History of theology			World history
		500	
Second Council of Constantinople	553		
Synod of Toledo adds *filioque* clause to the Nicene Creed	589	565	Justinian the Great, emperor of the Byzantine Empire, dies
		600	
Lombards renounce Arianism	650	c. 610	Muhammad receives first divine revelation, founds Islam
Third Council of Constantinople	680–1	637	Jerusalem conquered by Arab forces
		700	
Beginning of Iconoclastic controversy	726	711	Islamic conquest of Spain begins
Second Council of Nicea	787	768	Charlemagne becomes king of the Franks
		800	
		800	Charlemagne crowned emperor by Pope Leo III
Cyril and Methodius evangelize Germany	860		
		900	
Conversion of Olga of Russia	950		
Norway declared to be a Christian kingdom	995	962	Otto the Great crowned Holy Roman Emperor
		1000	
Death of Anselm of Canterbury	1033		
"Great Schism" between eastern and western church	1054	1066	Battle of Hastings, Norman conquest of England
Pope Urban II calls the First Crusade	1095	1100	
Beginning of Second Crusade	1145	c. 1150	Founding of the University of Paris
Beginning of Third Crusade	1189		
		1200	c. 1209 Founding of the University of Cambridge
Transubstantiation declared dogma at Fourth Lateran Council	1215	1215	Magna Carta
Thomas Aquinas begins the *Summa Theologiae*	c. 1265	1271	Marco Polo journeys to China
		1300	
William of Ockham dies	1348	1337	Beginning of Hundred Years War
Beginning of Papal schism between Rome and Avignon	1378	c. 1350	Bubonic plague ("Black Death")
Death of John Wyclif	1384	1400	

upheavals in the late medieval/early modern European world that produced the Protestant Reformation, the theology of which is the topic of the next chapter.

FOR FURTHER READING

Bonaventure, *The Mind's Journey to God*, trans. Lawrence S. Cunningham (Chicago: Franciscan Herald Press, 1979).

Bray, Gerald, "The *Filioque* Clause in History and Theology," *Tyndale Bulletin* 34 (1983), 91–144.

Cross, Richard, *Duns Scotus*, Great Medieval Thinkers (New York: Oxford University Press, 1999).

Fairweather, Eugene R., ed., *A Scholastic Miscellany: Anselm to Ockham*, Library of Christian Classics (Philadelphia: Westminster, 1956).

Pelikan, Jaroslav, *The Christian Tradition: A History of the Development of Doctrine,* vol. II: *The Spirit of Eastern Christendom (600–1700)* (Chicago: University of Chicago Press, 1974).

    The Christian Tradition: A History of the Development of Doctrine, vol. III: *The Growth of Medieval Theology (600–1300)* (Chicago: University of Chicago Press, 1978).

Thomas Aquinas, *Summa Theologica*, 5 vols., trans. Fathers of the English Dominican Province (Westminster, MD: Christian Classics, 1948).

CHAPTER 18

Theology in the Reformation period (c. 1400–1700)

THE LATE MEDIEVAL CONTEXT OF CHURCH
AND SOCIETY

When Martin Luther famously published his Ninety-five Theses in Wittenberg, he did not intend to create a new church or denomination, but set out to spur on the reform of the Catholic Church of his day. That his attempt at reformation in fact produced the Reformation cannot, however, be comprehended by the sheer force of his theological ideas. Like all major epochs in church history, the Reformation was occasioned by a range of social, political, and cultural forces, in addition to ecclesiastical and theological concerns. Before examining the key issues in the theology of the Reformation, we will briefly survey the harrowed landscape of the church and society of Luther's day that readied his world for major ecclesiastical and theological change.

In Chapter 17, we reviewed the rise of the so-called *via moderna*, associated above all with the name of William of Ockham, which undermined the Thomistic synthesis between nature and grace, and placed a greater emphasis on human works in justification than did previous theologies. The theological flux stirred by the *via moderna* was one key factor that helped to destabilize the medieval church. While Luther's Reformation project would continue the *via moderna*'s skepticism concerning the ability of human reason to discern God through the natural world, he reacted vociferously against an Ockhamist construal of justification, in part because of how its emphasis on human works in salvation encouraged other abuses in the church.

The typical view of salvation at this time held that participation in the Mass, climaxing in the celebration of the Eucharist, brought forgiveness for sins. However, the contrite sinner still needed to perform a modest "satisfaction" (such as fasting or almsgiving), so as to acknowledge the gravity of sin in a more personal way. Ordinarily this "satisfaction" took place through the sacrament of penance. But it was increasingly believed that the act of satisfaction could also be provided by an "indulgence" – a certificate purchased from the church that replaced the prescribed act of satisfaction (for those living) or time in purgatory (for the dead). The system of indulgences came to be abused, however, when utilized to finance the church's construction of opulent new buildings. By Luther's time, this practice had degenerated to such a level that the brokers of indulgences were virtually peddlers selling their wares.

This brazen sale of indulgences was a manifestation of the growing wealth and accompanying corruption of the institutional church. Above all, the office of the papacy was in disarray in the centuries preceding the Reformation, as epitomized by the papal schism between 1378 and 1415, in which different sectors of the church and different national royalties supported different popes, one living in Rome and the other in Avignon, France. Such disunity, compounded by cases of corruption and egregious wealth in the church hierarchy, began to erode many people's confidence in and obedience to the pope. By the early fifteenth century there was a strong counter-movement to papal abuse known as conciliarism (*concilium* = council), which claimed that ecumenical councils were the highest authority in the church, an authority binding even on the pope. The important Council of Constance (1414–18) was convened in this spirit of conciliarism.

While such corruption and abuse were waxing in the church, Renaissance humanism was contributing significantly to the impetus toward reform. Scholars in this movement were rediscovering the great learning of Greek and Roman antiquity, and in this recovery came to believe that the glories of that classical period could and should be restored in their own day. Over against the medieval emphasis on the sin and misery of humanity in stark contrast to the glory and sovereignty of God, the humanist purveyors of the "rebirth" (*renaissance*) of antiquity accentuated the possibilities of human knowledge, ingenuity, and beauty that characterized the ancient world, heralding them as a standard and goal for their own culture. Scholars such as Erasmus of Rotterdam (*c.* 1466–1536) stressed the importance of studying ancient languages and of reading ancient texts – in short, of getting "back to the sources" (*ad fontes*), the battle cry of the humanists.[1] In harking back to the classical beginnings of the Christian era, the Renaissance ignited an intra-Catholic movement for reform, since it produced a greater historical consciousness that placed the medieval church in critical historical perspective.[2] As one scrutinized and privileged the Greek NT and the writings of the early fathers, it became clear that some of the beliefs or practices of the medieval church were either absent or handled quite differently in the early church. These earlier sources, which depicted a simpler and more pristine Christianity, provided a standard for reform, according to the thinking of many humanists who sought to address the problems in the church of their own day.

In addition to these ecclesiastical and cultural factors, a series of events and shifts in broader medieval society also rendered that world susceptible to major change. Two centuries before the Reformation, northern and

---

[1] Among many other things, Erasmus is famous for his edition of the Greek New Testament.

[2] See J. R. Hale, *Renaissance Europe: Individual and Society, 1480–1520* (Berkeley, CA: University of California Press, 1977), 198.

western Europe began to experience a widespread process of urbanization, as people from the countryside moved into cities in hopes of greater economic prosperity and social opportunity. The result for most, lamentably, was continued poverty, as the increased population in urban areas was not matched by a rise in food production and employment opportunities, leading to a series of famines. It was in this dire situation that the Black Death (i.e., bubonic plague, *c.* 1350) hit Europe and spread quickly through the dense and unsanitary cities of the day. Some areas were hit harder than others, but approximately 30 percent of the European population was wiped out by this epidemic. While the worst effects of the plague had passed by the time of the Reformation in the early sixteenth century, medieval Europe was keenly aware of the nearness of death and brevity of life, and lived with a collective sense of morbidity.[3] This obsession with death only fueled concern for the afterlife, thus inflating the sale of indulgences.[4]

During these same centuries European nationalism was on the rise. Rather than identifying themselves as citizens of the "Holy Roman Empire," people were coming to view themselves more as "French" or "Swiss" or "German" or "Italian" within these emerging nations. This growth in nationalism threatened the temporal power and authority of the Catholic hierarchy, and also fueled various wars that troubled this period.

Meanwhile, technology was becoming more sophisticated and efficient. The principal advance in technology that affected the Reformation was the invention of the printing press by Johann Gutenberg (*c.* 1450). This early revolution in information technology stimulated a growth in literacy, whetted an appetite for worship in the local vernacular, and made possible the proliferation of literature upon which the Reformation depended. All these factors made late medieval Europe ripe for significant change.

THE LUTHERAN REFORMATION

Martin Luther

Martin Luther (1483–1546) received his early education from teachers influenced by the *via moderna*, especially the thought of Gabriel Biel (*c.* 1420–95), whose Ockhamist theology dominated the universities of

---

[3] Carter Lindberg, *The European Reformations* (Oxford: Blackwell, 1996), 27.
[4] See Owen Chadwick, *The Early Reformation on the Continent*, Oxford History of the Christian Church (Oxford: Oxford University Press, 2001), 71–7.

Luther's day. The idea that some human effort, some initial turning of the will toward God, was necessary in order for one to merit sanctifying grace was therefore part of his early theological understanding. By his own account, Luther struggled spiritually in his younger years, including his early teaching days at Wittenberg (1513–19), wrestling with his inability to be righteous before God. He constantly felt unworthy before a holy God and feared the imminent danger of divine judgment.[5] Along with his struggles, Luther was also lecturing on the Bible (including the Psalms, Romans, and Galatians). Sometime between 1514 and 1515 he was struck by the insight that the righteousness of God spoken about in Romans 1:16–17 is not the impossibly high standard of divine righteousness by which God *judges* sinful humanity, but rather refers to the *gift* given to sinful humanity by God through Jesus Christ. This insight led Luther to a new understanding of God's justification of humanity that plunged him into controversy for the rest of his life as his new theology ignited the Protestant attempt to reform the Catholic Church. This view of justification led Luther to attack the practice of selling indulgences, which he did in 1517 in the publication of his famous Ninety-five Theses, an event generally considered to mark the beginning of the Reformation. Although it was long assumed that Luther first promulgated these theses by nailing them to the door of the castle church in Wittenberg, most historians now dispute that claim.

Justification

The doctrine of justification became the heart and soul of Luther's theology – a teaching that he regarded as the quintessence of Christian truth. In part, Luther's reinterpretation of justification must be seen as a reaction to the *via moderna* understanding of his teachers. One of his earliest writings, the *Heidelberg Disputation* (1518), clearly rejects the idea that justification must be precipitated by an initial act on the part of the sinner: "The person who believes that he can obtain grace by doing what is in him [*facere quod in se est*] adds sin to sin so that he becomes doubly guilty."[6]

While Luther employed a diversity of images and idioms to speak of justification,[7] all of them presuppose the idea that Christian righteousness is a gift from God that judicially or forensically confers a righteousness that is not the believer's own, but rather is "alien" to him. The righteousness by

---

[5] Lohse, *Martin Luther's Theology*, 33.
[6] Luther, *Heidelberg Disputation*, in *Luther's Works*, xxxi, ed. Harold J. Grimm and Helmut T. Lehmann (Philadelphia: Fortress, 1957), Thesis 16.
[7] See Althaus, *Theology of Martin Luther*, 226–7.

which God justifies the sinner is never a feature of the human soul itself, never the possession of the sinner, but something that is *attributed* to him. Drawing upon Paul's reflections on Abraham in Galatians 3 and Romans 4, Luther develops the idea that justification is God's "imputing" or "reckoning" or "attributing" to us something that in fact does *not* belong to us – namely, Christ's righteousness. Viewed from another angle, justification is God's decision in forgiveness not to impute, reckon, or attribute to us that which *does* in fact belong to us – namely, our sin. Drawing upon the metaphor of the church's marital union with Christ (Eph. 5), Luther writes:

And if they are one flesh and there is between them a true marriage ... it follows that everything they have they hold in common, the good as well as the evil. Accordingly the believing soul can boast of and glory in whatever Christ has as though it were its own, and whatever the soul had Christ claims as his own ... Christ is full of grace, life, and salvation. The soul is full of sins, death, and damnation.[8]

Because Christ's righteousness is alien to the Christian, the form it takes in the Christian can only be faith, which is always a response to the divine word of forgiveness. Faith itself is never a "work," since it is actually the disavowal of one's own works, a matter of trusting in God's grace alone.

Because justification is God's *declaration* of the sinner's innocence, even while sin in *actuality* remains part of one's life until the eschaton, Luther could describe the Christian in tensive terms as being simultaneously justified and yet a sinner (*simul iustus et peccator*).[9] While feelings of guilt and inadequacy are unnecessary because of Christ's saving work on behalf of humanity, the honest Christian ought not to have any false illusions about his own sinful character – which perdures – lest a works righteousness creep into his Christian life. Good works have a legitimate place only as a free response to justification; they are never in any way the ground or precondition of justification.[10]

Theology of the cross

Luther thought that the utter dependence on God that was required for salvation carried over into the theological enterprise itself. That is to say, Luther's theological epistemology mirrors his soteriology.[11] Just as sinful humanity tends to glorify its own works, relying on those works for its own salvation, so also a sinful approach to knowledge of God relies primarily on

---

[8] Martin Luther, *On Christian Liberty*, trans. W. A. Lambert and Harold J. Grimm (Minneapolis, MN: Fortress, 2003), 18–19.

[9] Luther, *Lectures on Romans*, 125.   [10] Luther, *Christian Liberty*, 33–74.

[11] Althaus, *Theology of Martin Luther*, 27.

the visible works of creation, as discerned by our own natural abilities to know God. Luther associated this method with the natural theology of medieval scholasticism, calling it a "theology of glory" and considering it an expression of pride tantamount to works righteousness. By contrast, Luther advocated a "theology of the cross" (*theologia crucis*): just as true salvation can be found only in Christ's suffering, so also a true and reliable knowledge of God can be found only in God's suffering in Christ. Accordingly, just as faith in God's act of salvation is an expression of appropriate humility, so also a focus on God's act of revelation – in the most unlikely place, the cross, where God is wretched and torn in Christ – is the most appropriate theological point of departure. The true theologian, the "theologian of the cross," does not attempt to pry into the "invisible things of God" (cf. Rom. 1) as though they could be directly or easily deciphered; rather, the true theologian "comprehends the visible and manifest things of God seen through suffering and the cross."[12] Faithful Christian theology, therefore, must not be founded on philosophical notions of God, but on the "foolishness of the cross" (see 1 Cor. 1:18–25) – the locus of true theological wisdom.[13] For Luther, the theology of the cross is the expression of faith (rather than works) in the form of theological method. The practical implication of Luther's theology of the cross was that God's revelation in scripture ought to be the focus of the theologian's efforts, reinforcing in no small measure one of the basic battle cries of the Reformation: *sola scriptura* (by scripture alone).

Law and gospel

Another key feature of Luther's theology that parallels his central affirmation of justification by faith is his distinctive understanding of the relationship between law and gospel. For Luther, law and gospel represent the two forms in which God addresses humanity, two forms that cannot be separated from each other, but remain in a dialectical relationship.[14] "Law" refers to God's created law; it is the expression of God's righteous demand on all human beings, those rigorous divine requirements for human behavior. Due to sin, however, the law becomes an impossible demand. Therefore its main function, according to Luther, its so-called "theological use," is to condemn and accuse humanity by reminding it of its sinfulness and need for God: "The foremost office or power of the law is that it reveals original sin and its fruits. It shows human beings how deeply they have fallen and

---

[12] Luther, *Heidelberg Disputation*, Theses 19–20.   [13] Ibid., Thesis 30.
[14] Althaus, *Theology of Martin Luther*, 251.

how their nature is completely corrupt. The law must say to them that they have no God ... Thus they are terrified, humbled, despondent, and despairing."[15] If humanity had not fallen into sin, the law would be experienced as a good and achievable demand, but because of the fall, it functions to condemn humanity for its sin.[16]

The law therefore serves to prepare the sinner for the gospel, the grace of Christ: "It is certain that man must utterly despair of his own ability before he is prepared to receive the grace of Christ."[17] The gospel of grace, in short, is Christ – his person, work, death, and resurrected life – who fulfills the righteous requirements of the law in our place; the gospel is Christ's justifying work, which alone meets the demands of the law that sinners themselves cannot fulfill.

Luther viewed law and gospel as permanent realities in the Christian life. Because justification is a judicial declaration rather than an actual change in the sinner's life, the law remains necessary for the sinner to be reminded of his sin, so that he can continue to rely on Christ in faith. While the law, on account of sin, only produces despair that the law itself cannot remedy, it points us to the gospel, which resolves that despair by providing justification in Christ. Appreciating the law and our sinfulness while at the same time relying on Christ's justifying grace in the gospel becomes for Luther a perpetual tension that characterizes the whole Christian life. Even scripture in all of its parts contains *both* law *and* gospel. When scripture serves to impress upon a person his sinfulness, it functions as law (what Luther also called the "letter"); when it reminds a person of Christ's saving work, it functions as gospel (what Luther also called the "spirit").

Sacraments

Another way in which Luther diverged significantly from Catholicism, but which also kindled disagreements within Protestantism, concerned his sacramentology. He considered only three of the traditional seven Catholic sacraments to be legitimate – baptism, the Eucharist, and penance, albeit the latter in an indirect sense inasmuch as it points back to baptism. For Luther, sacraments were indispensable as pithy, tangible, "earthy" expressions of God's word. They have the same proclamatory content as the preached gospel, but they take a more material form that is a spiritual aid

---

[15] Luther, *Schmalkald Articles*, Part 3, art. 2.

[16] Luther also allowed for a second, "civil" use of the law, namely, that it serves to restrain sin in society and allow for civil order. See Lohse, *Martin Luther's Theology*, 271.

[17] Luther, "Heidelberg Disputation," Thesis 18.

to human beings as material creatures. He identified the essence of the sacraments as the saving activity of God in Christ which they proclaim.[18] Since God's work is the object of sacramental proclamation, faith is the appropriate human response that makes the sacraments efficacious – over against the Roman Catholic view, which held that the sacraments were effective "by their very operation" (*ex opere operato*).

Baptism is the sacramental sign of God's justifying work in Jesus Christ, signifying Christ's death and resurrection, in which the believer is included.[19] Baptism is both the sign of God's promise and the act of God's prevenient grace. Even though Luther considered infant baptism to be an appropriate practice (indeed, an apt expression of humanity's utter dependence on the activity of God in Christ), he viewed it in its orientation to the future faith of the baptized as the receipt of the promise represented by the baptismal event. Infants participate in the faith of those who bring them to be baptized, until the time when they themselves come to faith.

Luther's main reflections on the Lord's Supper were developed in reaction to the reigning Catholic understanding of the mass as a re-sacrifice of Christ in which the substance of the bread and wine are actually transformed into the body and blood of Christ (i.e., transubstantiation). Luther regarded transubstantiation as a particularly unhelpful and misleading philosophical sophistry.[20] Rather than saying that a substantial transformation takes place in the Eucharist, he preferred to say, more mysteriously, that the body and blood of Christ are present "in, with, and under" the elements, which remain just bread and wine. This position has historically been termed *consubstantiation* (in contrast to transubstantiation). Just as in Christ's incarnation true deity is present *with* (Lat. *con*) authentic humanity, so also in the Lord's Supper the risen and exalted humanity of Christ – which participates in the characteristics of his divinity, such as omnipresence – is present everywhere the sacramental elements are consecrated.

Philipp Melanchthon

One of Luther's closest colleagues was Philipp Melanchthon (1497–1560). Melanchthon largely consolidated and extended the Lutheran Reformation, but also differed from Luther in important ways, thereby infuriating some other Lutherans.[21] Melanchthon was more willing than Luther to

---

[18] See Martin Luther, *The Babylonian Captivity of the Church*, ed. A. T. Steinhäuser, Frederick C. Ahrens, and Abdel Ross Wentz, in *Three Treatises* (Philadelphia: Fortress, 1970), 184–5.
[19] Ibid., 190.   [20] Ibid., 144–52.   [21] See González, *History of Christian Thought*, III: 103–10.

compromise on certain theological matters, with both the Roman Catholic Church and the Reformed/Calvinist wing of the Reformation. For example, he did not condemn the papacy as trenchantly as Luther, and he was more willing to retain penance as a sacrament in its own right. Being more of a humanist, Melanchthon also affirmed human free will to a greater degree than did Luther, who generally emphasized human inability before God.[22] Similar to Reformed thinkers such as John Calvin, Melanchthon even held to a more positive use of the law as a guide to gratitude.[23] Moreover, Melanchthon gave more credence than Luther to the doctrine of general revelation, although, like all theologians throughout the Christian era, he stressed that natural knowledge of God through creation is far from the saving knowledge of God through Christ.

Melanchthon is particularly significant in the Christian tradition as the primary author of the central Lutheran confessional writing – the Augsburg Confession, first drafted in 1530.[24] Melanchthon later revised it in an attempt to foster reconciliation between the divided branches of Protestantism, casting it in a relatively less "Lutheran" form. These later editions of the Augsburg Confession contributed in part to a series of controversies in the Lutheran churches, some of which are detailed in the next section. Melanchthon's *Loci Communes*, the first Protestant systematic theology, became a key work for the later Protestant orthodox theologians in their efforts to systematize the theological fruits of the Reformation.

Lutheran controversies and the Formula of Concord

Later in the life of Melanchthon, and continuing after his death, Lutheranism was wracked by a series of controversies that basically centered on the question of what is *authentic* Lutheranism and what compromises could rightly be made with other churches.[25] An early division in Lutheran circles developed between the so-called Gnesio-Lutherans (genuine Lutherans) and the so-called Philippists. In general, the Gnesio-Lutherans strove to hold strictly to the teachings of Luther himself, while the Philippists, in contrast, adopted Melanchthon's more conciliatory attitude toward the Catholic Church and the Reformed churches. Most of these controversies were resolved by the Formula of Concord in 1577, a statement

---

[22] Luther's rejection of free will before God is seen in his retort to Erasmus, in *The Bondage of the Will*.
[23] In his later years, Luther was less resistant to this positive use of the law than in his early theology.
[24] See "Augsburg Confession," in Pelikan and Hotchkiss, eds., *Creeds and Confessions*, II: 53–118.
[25] González, *History of Christian Thought*, III: 111–32.

Table 18.1   *The uses of the law according to the Formula of Concord*[a]

First use	*Civil* – restrainer of sin in society
Second use	*Theological* – accuser of the sinner
Third use	*Didactic* – guide to thankful living

[a] The Calvinist tradition affirmed these three uses of the law, but inverts the order of the first two, identifying the theological function of the law as its first use, and the civil function of the law as its second use.

of faith developed for the purpose of reconciling the various branches of Lutheranism that adjudicated most of these debated points.

One significant conflict among these Lutheran groups is known as the antinomian controversy. A theologian by the name of John Agricola, following Luther's original law–gospel understanding, argued that the law had no positive place in the Christian life because repentance must come from faith, which can be produced only by the gospel. His opponents followed Melanchthon in supporting a more positive "third use" of the law, in which the law functions as a guide to the Christian life, as a way of expressing one's gratitude to God for salvation in Christ. The Formula of Concord took the side of the Philippists, affirming the third use of the law, in addition to its so-called first or civil use (restrain sin in society) and its second or theological use (accuse the sinner) (see Table 18.1).

Another divisive debate was the adiaphoristic controversy. In an effort to make peace with some Catholic authorities, Melanchthon and others had allowed that some Catholic practices need not be condemned by Protestants, because they concerned "non-essential" matters known as *adiaphora* (literally, "things indifferent"). On their view, concessions such as accepting the veneration of saints were appropriate as long as Christians held to the essentials of the gospel – principally, the doctrine of justification by faith. Melanchthon and company were widely criticized by Gnesio-Lutherans for having squandered the Lutheran inheritance. In the latter party's view, in a time of doctrinal turmoil there can be no "things indifferent," for all things Catholic imply a contradiction of the doctrine of justification. Melanchthon and his supporters argued that such a position would do away with Christian freedom of conscience – one of the essential tenets of the Reformation. In addressing this controversy, the Formula of Concord accepted the distinction between *adiaphora* and essentials, but also admitted that differing contexts and extenuating circumstances could elevate certain *adiaphora* to the status of "essentials."

A further series of controversies, the most famous of which was the synergistic controversy, centered on the role of the human will in salvation.[26] Does the will "work with" (*synergo*) God's action in conversion, or is conversion simply one work (*monergon*) – the irresistible work of God upon the helpless sinner? Melanchthon and the Philippists, following their humanist inclinations, thought that there must be some role for the will – it must at least cooperate with grace by pursuing good works in order for salvation to be retained. The Gnesio-Lutherans, following Luther's early writing on *The Bondage of the Will*, thought that the will was entirely enslaved to sin until grace acts upon it.[27] The Formula of Concord ruled against the synergists that the human will of itself can do nothing – neither to effect conversion nor, after conversion, to enable us to follow the law of God; such progress can be made possible only by the Holy Spirit.

In the end, the Formula of Concord generally accepted the more traditional Lutheran interpretation on various issues, following the stricter Gnesio-Lutheran line. But it did make some key concessions to the Philippists, such as the positive third use of the law. Most importantly, it reaffirmed the Augsburg Confession, which remains the Lutheran tradition's central confession to this day.

THE CALVINIST REFORMATION

Our historical survey of the Reformation up through the Formula of Concord highlights the major theologians, themes, and events that contributed to the development of Lutheran theology from its infancy through its young adulthood. But there was another distinctive wing of Protestantism developing at the same time, at first largely in Switzerland, but then also in Germany and other areas of Europe – the "Reformed" or Calvinist wing of the Reformation.[28]

Huldrych Zwingli

While the name of John Calvin is typically associated with the Reformed tradition in the minds of most people, he was not the "father" of Reformed

---

[26] See Robert A. Kolb, *Bound Choice, Election, and Wittenberg Theological Method: From Martin Luther to the Formula of Concord*, Lutheran Quarterly Books (Grand Rapids, MI: Eerdmans, 2005).

[27] On the different theological concerns that produced this controversy, see Robert A. Kolb, "Historical Background of the Formula of Concord," in *A Contemporary Look at the Formula of Concord*, ed. Robert D. Preus and Wilbert H. Rosin (St. Louis: Concordia, 1978), 29.

[28] A useful source on the Reformation in Switzerland in general is Bruce Gordon, *The Swiss Reformation*, New Frontiers in History (Manchester: Manchester University Press, 2002).

Protestantism. That title rightly belongs to Huldrych Zwingli (1484–1531), a contemporary of Luther who served as a military chaplain and then as an influential pastor in the Swiss city of Zurich.[29] Many of Zwingli's theological differences with Lutheranism stemmed from his great appreciation for Renaissance humanism in general and thinkers such as Erasmus in particular. In this respect, his path was similar to that of Melanchthon. His reforming activities in Zurich began in 1519, a mere two years after the publication of Luther's Ninety-five Theses, when he began to attack the doctrine of purgatory and the custom of praying to the saints, among other Catholic beliefs and practices.

Similar to Luther, Zwingli considered the witness of scripture to be the sole norm of truth for the church and its theology, over against church tradition. However, he did not agree with the stark contrast that Luther placed between law and gospel, but related these in a more positive manner that became typical of the Reformed tradition and its thinkers, such as Calvin. Another key difference from Luther was Zwingli's emphasis on the irreducible distinction between the humanity and the divinity of Jesus Christ. He disagreed with Luther's idea that after the resurrection the humanity of Jesus shares in the attributes of his divinity, such as omnipresence, a position that for Luther ensured that Christ's humanity could be physically present in the Lord's Supper wherever it is celebrated. In Zwingli's view, the humanity of Jesus remains simply human, even in the incarnation.[30] This christological affirmation led Zwingli to a symbolic understanding of the Eucharist.[31] In his eyes, the humanity of Christ cannot be present in the sacramental elements, because it remains localized in his – albeit glorified – body in heaven. So the Eucharist is a symbolic remembrance of the death and resurrection of Christ, who is "present" in the Supper only by virtue of the faith of the Christian participant. Zwingli's strong attachment to this symbolic view, and Luther's firm commitment to the idea that the humanity of Christ was really and physically present "in, with, and under" the sacramental elements, was the main reason why the emerging Swiss Reformation under Zwingli and the German Reformation under Luther were unable to come to doctrinal agreement at the Marburg Colloquy of 1529. While the two sides agreed or came very close in most other doctrinal matters,

---

[29] See Ulrich Gäbler, *Huldrych Zwingli: His Life and Work*, trans. Ruth C. L. Gritsch (Philadelphia: Fortress, 1986).

[30] Huldrych Zwingli, *An Exposition of the Faith*, in Geoffrey W. Bromiley, ed., *Zwingli and Bullinger*, Library of Christian Classics (Philadelphia: Westminster, 1953), 251.

[31] Huldrych Zwingli, *On the Lord's Supper*, in Bromiley, ed., *Zwingli and Bullinger*, 185–238.

neither Zwingli nor Luther would budge on their views of the Lord's Supper, famously hindering these two Protestant traditions from officially joining forces in their reforming efforts.

John Calvin

The second-generation reformer John Calvin (1509–64) was born in France, but achieved fame as the primary progenitor of the Reformed tradition in Switzerland. Calvin worked for the majority of his career in Geneva, which he established as one of the major centers of Reformed Protestantism. To Calvin go the laurels for consolidating and systematizing the central tenets of Reformed theology. What follows are some of the prominent themes in his theological project.

Knowledge of God

The opening words of Calvin's *Institutes of the Christian Religion* are well known: "Nearly all the wisdom we possess, that is to say, true and sound wisdom, consists of two parts: the knowledge of God and of ourselves."[32] Since human beings are creatures of God, we cannot understand ourselves apart from reference to God. When we grasp something of God's glory, we better appreciate our own lowliness and sinfulness; and when we acknowledge our shortcomings, we better understand the unsurpassable majesty and glory of God. In his initial focus on divine glory and human sinfulness, we see themes central to Calvin's theology as a whole: his lofty view of God as sovereign and holy Creator, as well as humanity's creatureliness and sinfulness.

From this point of departure Calvin goes on to state more specifically how knowledge of God is possible.[33] He points first to the knowledge of God that is part of the created structures of the human mind and conscience, as well as the natural world (what we have called general revelation in pp. 53–4 above): all human beings, he asserts, possess an "awareness of divinity" (*sensus divinitatis*), an undeniable inkling of God's reality implanted as a "seed of religion" (*semen religionis*) in human life.[34] Calvin thinks that not only is some natural knowledge of God present in human consciousness, but also that God is known through the structures of

---

[32] Calvin, *Institutes*, 1.1.1.
[33] On Calvin's theological epistemology, see Edward A. Dowey Jr., *The Knowledge of God in Calvin's Theology*, 3rd edn. (Grand Rapids, MI: Eerdmans, 1994).
[34] Calvin, *Institutes*, 1.3.1.

creation, for nature is a theater that projects the glory and majesty of God to all.[35] In short, all human beings (whether they recognize it or not) possess an inchoate knowledge of God.

According to Calvin, however, this natural knowledge of God that is generally present through the structures of creation is not a reliable knowledge, and certainly not a saving knowledge of God, because it is twisted by sinful human beings into an idol of our own making.[36] Following Paul in Romans 1, Calvin argues that the main function of this general knowledge of God, given the fall into sin, is to hold humanity accountable – to prevent human beings from pleading ignorance for their failure to worship God and to live rightly. For Calvin the only reliable way to know God is through scripture. Indeed, scripture functions as a set of "spectacles" that bring general revelation back into proper focus.[37] The Bible's revelation of God as triune creator (Father), mediator of redemption (Christ), and sanctifier of the church (Spirit) is necessary to come to a reliable and saving knowledge of the true God.

Providence and predestination

For better or worse, Calvin is probably best known for his doctrine of predestination, which is integrally bound up with his rigorous doctrine of divine providence – God's superintendence of the world. As the Creator, God is the sovereign lord over all creatures. In fact, God is so sovereign that even the most evil of creatures, such as Satan, cannot help but obey God. Calvin's doctrine of providence explains why this must be the case, since providence for him means that God both actively preserves and *governs* all of creation. For Calvin, this excludes any notions of luck, chance, or fortune, because the sovereignty of divine providence means that God's will determines all things that come to pass. Calvin is unequivocal on this point – he means that God actively and specifically ordains *all* particular things that happen in the world.[38]

While Calvin appears to articulate a form of divine determinism in his view of providence, he does not want to exclude human freedom. So he asserts that even though God specifically ordains every happening – whether human or natural, good or evil – God often works through human intermediaries who are still responsible for their actions.[39] He rejects the idea

---

[35] Ibid., 1.6.2.   [36] Ibid., 1.4.2–4.   [37] Ibid., 1.6.1.

[38] Ibid., 1.16.4. Calvin even suggests that all things – both good and bad – are expressions of God's curse or blessing (1.16.5).

[39] Ibid., 1.17.

that God simply "permits" free human actions, however, stating that God is the primary cause of all actions performed by human agents. In other words, Calvin adopts a form of *compatibilism* to assert that acts determined by God are "compatible" with their being freely chosen by human agents (in this regard he appeals to Paul's talk about Pharaoh in Romans 9). In response to this view, some of Calvin's contemporaries objected that if God is the cause, then human agents should not be held responsible for their evil actions. Calvin replies that while God does not command evil, we still would not perform evil acts unless God (actively) willed them. It is at this point that Calvin appeals to the mysterious nature of the divine wisdom that enables God to *use* evil instruments for good. Exemplifying his compatibilism, Calvin states that even in the worst of human crimes, such as murder, we must "clearly contemplate God's righteousness and man's wickedness, as each clearly shows itself."[40]

Given this portrait of the divine activity in providence, it is not surprising that Calvin emphasizes God's sovereignty in the matter of salvation as well. He considers salvation to be something that God has determined or "predestined" without respect to the merits or actions of human beings themselves. Predestination is the eternal divine decree, by which "eternal life is foreordained for some, eternal damnation for others."[41] In Calvin's view, the reason for election and reprobation (i.e., damnation) is simply God's good pleasure. For those foreordained to salvation, predestination is an expression of God's mercy; for those foreordained to destruction, it is an expression of God's justice (since all are sinners through Adam who justly deserve punishment).

This doctrine has become Calvin's most notorious teaching, provoking ardent defenses on the one hand and vociferous critiques on the other hand.[42] Calvin himself recognized the thorny nature of predestinarian thought, but nevertheless regarded it as the clear teaching of scripture (especially in his interpretation of Romans 9–11). While his view of the matter may raise certain questions about the justice of God, Calvin himself on most theological occasions highlights God's love. Putting the best face on it, Carter Lindberg writes: "First and last for Calvin, God is not a celestial tyrant but a loving parent who cannot forget her nursing child, and a father who gives good things to his children."[43] It is the loving and saving character of God that is asserted most strongly in Calvin's christology and soteriology,

---

[40] Ibid., 1.17.9.   [41] Ibid., 3.21.5.
[42] For our discussion of the sensitive issue of predestination, see pp. 353–8 above.
[43] Lindberg, *European Reformations*, 267.

even though his deterministic views of providence and predestination continue to cast a shadow on his theological contributions.

Christ and salvation

Calvin accepted the Chalcedonian declaration that Jesus Christ, as mediator of salvation, was both divine and human. In agreement with Zwingli, who rejected Luther's idea that Christ's resurrected humanity shares in the divine attributes, Calvin emphasized the irreducible difference between Christ's humanity and his divinity.[44] This led him to a distinctive understanding of the presence of Christ in the Lord's Supper in comparison to the views of both Luther and Zwingli (see below).

When he turns from the person to the work of Christ, Calvin focuses his attention on Christ's threefold office (*munus triplex*) – the three anointed offices of the OT which Jesus fulfills: prophet, king, and priest.[45] As prophet, Jesus is the herald of the Father's grace, whose teaching provides the knowledge necessary for salvation. As king, he reigns over God's domain, which here and now is primarily a spiritual kingdom. As priest, Christ intercedes before God the Father for sinners, and makes reconciliation possible through his substitutionary death, in which the wrath of God is assumed by Jesus when he pays the penalty for sin on the cross (see pp. 273–4 above).

Calvin stresses, however, that Christ's salvific work would do sinful humanity no good without the action of the Holy Spirit uniting the sinner to Christ.[46] Through the Spirit's gift of faith, human beings enjoy a twofold fruit of union with Christ: justification and sanctification. Calvin largely followed Luther in his doctrine of justification, seeing it as God's judicial act of forgiveness and imputation of the righteousness of Christ. However, Calvin emphasized the doctrine of sanctification more strongly than did Luther. On the one hand, he saw the law (in its so-called third use) as a guide for the process of sanctification, since it gives us knowledge of how God wants us to live. But on the other hand, Calvin, much like Luther, was under no illusions regarding the continuing presence and debilitating effect of sin, even in the life of the Christian. So he suggests that the quintessence of sanctification is constant repentance – a deepening sense of our own inability to live righteously and of our need to depend more fully on God. Only through continued repentance is progress in holiness possible.[47]

---

[44] Calvin, *Institutes*, 2.14.1.　[45] Ibid., 2.15.　[46] Ibid., 3.1.1.
[47] Ibid., 3.3.

Table 18.2 *The presence of Christ in the Eucharist*

Catholicism	Transubstantiation	Christ is physically present in the Lord's Supper as the elements transform into the substance of the body and blood of Christ while retaining their accidental qualities.
Luther	Consubstantiation	Christ is physically present in the Lord's Supper by virtue of his omnipresent humanity, which is found "in, with, and under" the sacramental elements.
Calvin	Spiritual presence	Christ is spiritually present in the Lord's Supper by virtue of his divine omnipresence, as discerned by the faith of the believing participant.
Zwingli	Symbolic memorial	Christ is present only symbolically in the Lord's Supper as the gospel events are commemorated by the faith of the believing participant.

Sacraments

Similar to Luther, Calvin holds to a basically Augustinian definition of sacrament, namely, that it is a "testimony of divine grace toward us, confirmed by an outward sign." But Calvin's continuation of the definition strikes a note that was more muffled in Luther's sacramentology: "with mutual attestation of our piety toward him."[48] More strongly than Luther, therefore, Calvin emphasizes that faith (engendered and empowered by the Spirit) is utterly central to the sacramental event and its efficacy, even though the event itself points to the promises of God. Like Luther, he sees baptism as the sacrament of initiation into the Christian life and accepts infant baptism as an appropriate practice. But in his view of the Lord's Supper he differs significantly from Luther. Whereas Luther affirmed the physical presence of Christ in the Eucharist due to his christology, Calvin argues that Christ is not physically present, since, given his insistence on the abiding difference between the two natures of Christ, he thought that the body of Christ is locally present only in heaven. But Calvin did not go as far as Zwingli in rejecting the real presence of Christ in the Supper; rather, he held that Christ is truly present in *spiritual* form, since the divine Logos as the second person of the Trinity is present everywhere (see Table 18.2).

THE ENGLISH REFORMATION

Any account of the development of Christian theology in the era of the Reformation would be incomplete without addressing sixteenth-century

---

[48] Ibid., 4.14.1.

reform efforts in England. The English Reformation, however, did not contribute as much in the way of theological innovation as the reformational developments on the continent. Moreover, only a few words can be said about the English Reformation before the discussion leaves the terrain of historical theology and becomes more of a social history of the church in England. The story of this tradition's emergence is closely linked to King Henry VIII (who reigned over England from 1509 to 1546), his various affairs and wives, and the ecclesiastical whims of his children, in addition to central reformational convictions that made their way to the British Isles.[49] More for personal and political motives than for theological reasons, Henry led the English church in its initial break from Roman Catholicism. Even though doctrines such as justification by faith were included in the first confessional document of the Church of England, the Ten Articles of 1536, many Catholic doctrines and practices were retained, such as praying for the dead. Under the influence of Protestant advisors, Henry's young son, Edward VI (who reigned from 1547 to 1553) furthered the cause of Protestantism. It was during Edward's reign that Thomas Cranmer (1489–1556), the archbishop of Canterbury, wrote the famous *Book of Common Prayer*. In this prayer book, which embodies the emerging theology of the Anglican Church, a distinctive balance is struck between the Lutheran and Reformed wings of the Reformation, with many Catholic liturgical elements also included. However, when Edward died, his successor and half-sister Mary Tudor (who reigned from 1553 to 1558) tried to revive Catholicism, during which time many Protestant leaders such as Cranmer were either executed or exiled. But upon "Bloody Mary's" death, her half-sister Elizabeth (who reigned from 1558 to 1603) consolidated the balance of Cranmer's *Book of Common Prayer*, which typifies the theology and liturgy of the Anglican Church even to this day. As a result, while many Catholic liturgical elements were kept in the Anglican liturgy, Protestant theology features prominently (e.g., the primacy of scripture), albeit often couched in rather generic language so that Protestants of all persuasions would feel comfortable. Many of the Catholic elements were retained in the church's life because they were considered *adiaphora*, a point to which the English Puritans would later and strongly react in their desire to carve out a purer biblical form of Protestantism in England.

While the church in England developed its own distinctive ecclesial and theological identity (i.e., "Anglican"), the church in Scotland took on a

---

[49] For a comprehensive examination of the English Reformation, see G. W. Bernard, *The King's Reformation: Henry VIII and the Remaking of the English Church* (New Haven, CT: Yale University Press, 2005).

strongly Calvinist character, largely through the labors of John Knox (*c*. 1513–72). In one of his exiles from Scotland during the bloody reign of Mary Tudor, Knox took refuge in Calvin's Geneva. Here he adopted much of Calvin's theology, such as a strong predestinarian orientation and "presbyterian" church polity, although he was also significantly influenced by the writings of Zwingli. Knox was thus the chief architect of Scottish Presbyterianism, one of the major streams of the Reformed tradition.

THE RADICAL REFORMATION

The reformation efforts of theologians such as Luther, Zwingli, and Calvin were seen by some European Christians as an insufficient protest against the status quo, particularly since a number of Catholic beliefs, practices, and customs (e.g., penance, infant baptism, a close relationship with the civil state) were retained by various reformers. Those who made this critique and desired further reform of the church – to make it faithful to the word of scripture in every detail – became known as the "radical" reformers. In their view, the *adiaphora* should be radically pared down, and the church should attempt to practice *only* that which is expressly commanded in scripture. Although the term "Radical Reformation" is commonly used, it is potentially misleading as a general rubric because the different groups that wanted to take the Reformation further often worked for this advance along quite different paths and by quite different means. The term, therefore, is a generalization that rather tenuously holds together a diversity of impulses.[50]

The wing of the Radical Reformation that became known as "Anabaptism" (i.e., rebaptism) had its public beginnings in Zurich in 1525. Some church members and pastors in Zurich who thought that infant baptism was biblically unjustified defied Zwingli and the Zurich city council by publically rebaptizing one another, holding that baptism was valid only following a personal confession of faith. Their practice was regarded by mainstream Protestants and Catholics alike to be theologically inappropriate. It was also considered politically insubordinate, given the close alliance that then existed between church and state, such that the Anabaptists were quickly persecuted for their beliefs and practices. Sometimes they were even drowned as a brutally ironic recompense for their beliefs regarding (re)baptism.

---

[50] See Lindberg, *European Reformations*, 199–227.

Most Anabaptists, as well as other participants in the Radical Reformation, were skeptical of the early Reformation's close relationship with the various governments and princes in middle Europe. They judged that most Christians were too closely allied with, and therefore insufficiently set apart (i.e., holy) from, the sinful powers of the world, as the Anabaptists customarily affirmed a strong dichotomy between the church and state. Since the church is called *out* of the world, followers of Jesus Christ should not participate in sinful worldly ways of doing things, such as depending on the sword of state to settle ecclesial-theological debates. That these separatist traditions did not want to depend on the civil magistrates distinguishes them from the so-called "Magisterial Reformation" – namely, those branches of the Reformation (i.e., the Lutheran, Reformed, and Anglican) that were closely allied with various civil authorities to further their cause of reform. The Anabaptist traditions were therefore usually pacifist, regarding "spiritual" weapons as the only ones appropriate for the church of Christ. Such a sentiment is well expressed by Menno Simons (1496–1561), one of the premiere Anabaptist theologians: "Christ is our fortress; patience our weapon of defense; the Word of God our sword; and our victory a courageous, firm, unfeigned faith in Jesus Christ. And iron and metal spears and sword we leave to those who, alas, regard human blood and swine's blood about alike."[51]

THE CATHOLIC REFORMATION

We already noted that Martin Luther did not intend to form a new church or a new denomination, but simply wanted to "reform" the Catholic Church. As such, he was following the efforts of previous Catholic reformers such as John Wyclif and Jan Hus roughly a century before him. Similarly, Renaissance humanism had already played an important role in "reforming" the medieval Catholic Church by reminding it of the original sources of divine revelation and stressing the contemporary degradation of the church against the backdrop of its earlier glories. There were also other reform efforts in the Catholic Church of the late fifteenth and early sixteenth centuries, such as the conciliarist movement to reform the papacy. Thus any assessment of the Catholic Church in the Reformation age must bear in mind this variety of Catholic reform movements that either pre-dated or emerged independently of the Protestant Reformation. But it is also the case that many of the reforms of the Catholic Church took place in response to

[51] Menno Simons, *The Complete Writings of Menno Simons*, trans. Leonard Verduin (Scottdale, PA: Herald, 1956), 198.

the challenge of Protestantism. This response is commonly called the Counter-Reformation.[52]

The Counter-Reformation

Pope Paul III (pope 1534–49) was more aware than his predecessors of the problems of corruption and declining morality in the church, conditions that facilitated an exodus of Catholic faithful to the emerging Protestant churches. He therefore led an effort to curb many of the abuses of ecclesiastical power. But at the same time he also restored the Inquisition in the attempt to purify the Catholic ranks of any infiltration by Protestant doctrine.

One of the central vehicles of the Counter-Reformation was the Society of Jesus (or Jesuit order), founded by Ignatius of Loyola (1491–1556). Formerly an ambitious knight who was wounded on the field of battle, Ignatius was converted to a rather ascetic Christian lifestyle. He attracted a band of followers that came to follow a set of *Spiritual Exercises* that he authored. These exercises involved a month-long cycle of guided prayer, often practiced in the context of a retreat from ordinary life, and were intended to help the reader purify his will in order to obey God more purely and willingly.[53] The *Exercises* employed military imagery as one of their central metaphors, stressing that the Christian life is a matter of becoming an increasingly faithful soldier of the cross, something attained only by profound reflection on one's own sin in contrast to the sinless life of Christ.

The group clustered around Ignatius eventually swore an oath of poverty and of obedience to the pope, and was approved as a religious order in 1540. Henceforth, the Jesuits would be a major tool of the papacy in its resistance to the spread of Protestantism, although theologians of other orders were also instrumental in this effort. Many of this era's greatest Catholic theologians belonged to the Jesuit order.[54] Robert Bellarmine (1542–1621), a Jesuit theologian and eventual archbishop, spent a significant portion of his career arguing for the spiritual primacy and authority of the pope against Protestant critiques of the papacy. One of his contemporaries, Francisco Suárez (1548–1617), was instrumental in reestablishing the significance of the theology of Thomas Aquinas in this period through his composition of a

---

[52] On this period of Catholic Reformation in general, see Michael A. Mullett, *The Catholic Reformation* (London: Routledge, 1999).

[53] See Ignatius of Loyola, *Spiritual Exercises and Selected Works*, ed. George E. Ganss, The Classics of Western Spirituality (Mahwah, NJ: Paulist, 1991).

[54] See González, *History of Christian Thought*, III: 199–236.

commentary on key doctrines in Thomistic theology. In his efforts, Suárez followed the lead of another Spanish Jesuit, Luis de Molina (1535–1600), in approaching the thorny questions of divine grace, human freedom, and the foreknowledge of God, with the suggestion that God predestines people to salvation or damnation based on a non-causative "middle knowledge" of how people will respond to the offer of grace. Their goal was to reconcile divine action in grace with a robust sense of human freedom, although their proposal was severely criticized by many of their own Catholic contemporaries.

Most of these theologians were professors at Catholic universities in Europe. As time went on, it was especially the Jesuit order that secured a dominant place in Catholic educational institutions. But in addition to their reputation for education and scholarship, the Jesuits were also significant representatives of the papacy in Catholic missions. Jesuits such as Francis Xavier (1506–52), one of Ignatius' original cohort, and Matteo Ricci (1552–1610) attempted to evangelize the Far East. Ricci is an often cited example of the controversial tendency of some Jesuit missionaries to significantly accommodate Catholic doctrine to the cultural world of the East – as, for example, in his staking out common ground between ancestor worship in Confucian society and the Catholic practice of praying to the saints.

The Council of Trent

As a significant part of his attempt to reform the church, Paul III called a council that met off and on in the Italian city of Trent during the years 1545 to 1563. While this council tried to revitalize the practical life of the church in a variety of ways, it also reacted in a rather defensive way to Protestantism. For example, it rejected the Protestant ideas that scripture was more normative than tradition and that the Mass could be celebrated in languages other than Latin. It also reaffirmed the *seven* Catholic sacraments, endorsing transubstantiation as the Eucharistic mystery. Over against the Anabaptists in particular, it reiterated the claim that infant baptism removes original sin: "If anyone denies that infants, newly born from their mothers' wombs, are to be baptized, even though they be born of baptized parents ... let him be anathema."[55] As a general assessment, therefore, this council's part in the Catholic Counter-Reformation

[55] *Canons and Decrees of the Council of Trent*, trans. H. J. Schroeder (St. Louis: Herder, 1950), fifth session, no. 4 (p. 22).

included little by way of theological reformation. It did, however, clarify accept-able Catholic teaching on the doctrine of justification by harking back to the views of Thomas Aquinas over against the views of the later medieval theolo-gians that strongly emphasized the role of works. But Trent did not go so far as to say that justification takes place by faith *alone*: "If anyone says that the sinner is justified by faith alone, meaning that nothing else is required to cooperate in order to obtain the grace of justification, and that it is not in any way necessary that he be prepared and disposed by the action of his own will, let him be anathema."[56] In a rather Thomistic vein, however, Trent did affirm that justification happens only through the prevenience of God's grace (see p. 326 above).[57]

POST-REFORMATION THEOLOGICAL CURRENTS

This chapter has concentrated on the epochal theological developments that took place during the fifteenth and sixteenth centuries. The next chapter will largely pick up around the dawn of the eighteenth century. What, then, of the seventeenth century? Fewer key theological developments took place in this century, as the Catholic world generally remained satisfied with the decisions of Trent, and as the Protestant world spent its efforts consolida-ting and systematizing the earlier insights of the Reformers.

Protestant orthodoxy

The consolidation of Reformation theology took place in large part through a group of movements commonly summarized as "Protestant orthodoxy." In both Lutheran and Reformed circles theologians attempted to clarify and codify the body of truths expressed and implied by the theological develop-ments of the Reformation. Given this basic project, theological innovation was not a key feature during this period. In this Protestant endeavor, much use was made of the philosophy of Aristotle as an aid in systematizing the theology of the Reformation (somewhat ironic, given this philosopher's pilloried reputation during the initial phase of the Reformation itself). Both Lutheran and Reformed orthodoxy generally used a more "scholastic" method, similar to that of medieval scholasticism, where each topic was broken down into a series of questions and examined from a variety of angles.

---

[56] Ibid., sixth session, canon 9 (p. 43).   [57] Ibid., sixth session, canons 1–3 (p. 42).

In the developing Lutheran tradition, much thought was given to bringing together the seminal insights of Luther and the more systematic approach of Melanchthon.[58] Lutheran orthodox theologians, for example, devoted themselves to clarifying and categorizing the emphasis on the primacy, inspiration, and authority of scripture (following the *sola scriptura* principle). One result of their efforts was the development of verbal theories of inspiration, where the words of scripture themselves were considered the very words of God, simply dictated to human scribes. This movement also focused heavily on developing the systematic implications of the doctrine of justification, which was viewed by these Lutheran theologians as the principal teaching of scripture.

The Reformed orthodox devoted much more attention to Calvin's doctrine of predestination, often concentrating on the logical ordering of the eternal divine decrees (i.e., decretal theology).[59] Debates raged regarding whether the negative pole of predestination, that is, reprobation, was logically decreed *prior* to the fall into sin (supralapsarianism) or *posterior* to the fall into sin (infralapsarianism). This period of Reformed theology also witnessed the controversy with the Arminians (followers of Jakob Arminius [1560–1609]), who held that predestination takes place not solely on the basis of God's sovereign freedom, but on the basis of God's foreknowledge of the response of the elect to the offer of grace. Due to this controversy, strict Calvinist theology emphasized even more firmly that Christ's atonement is "limited," that is, efficacious only for the elect, and that election is unconditional, stemming only from God's "good pleasure."

Puritanism

As noted above, some Christians in England thought that the Anglican Reformation preserved too much Catholicism, especially under the guise of *adiaphora*, and believed that the ongoing task of the church was to continue to reform itself in a manner more faithful to scripture. One result of their ongoing protests was the translation and publication of the King James Bible (or Authorized Version) in 1611. This movement of "Puritanism" became known for its austere morality and, for many Puritans, a strong adherence to traditional Calvinist theology. For example, the Westminster

[58] For the standard theological compendium of Lutheran orthodox dogmatics, see Heinrich Schmid, *The Doctrinal Theology of the Evangelical Lutheran Church*, 3rd edn. (Minneapolis, MN: Augsburg, 1961).
[59] For the standard theological compendium of Reformed orthodox theology, see Heinrich Heppe, *Reformed Dogmatics*, trans. G. T. Thomson, ed. Ernst Bizer (London: Allen & Unwin, 1950).

Confession of Faith, the result of the labors of Presbyterian Puritans, emphasizes scripture as the sole authority for faith, the centrality of predestination, and the importance of God's covenant of grace through Christ. Many Puritans emigrated to North America, eventually making a significant imprint on the laws and institutions of the United States.

Pietism

Protestant Orthodoxy left the impression on many that Christian faith was largely a matter of having right beliefs (for the Lutherans, above all on justification; for the Reformed, above all on predestination). As a reaction to this overly cognitive approach to Christian faith, pietism emphasized the experiential dimension of Christianity. This movement focused its attention on the affective experience of rebirth in Christ – personal conversion to a new way of living. Given their experiential focus, the pietists were quite rigorous in their devotion to personal holiness. As seen in the work of its key representative, Philipp Jakob Spener (1635–1705), the pietist movement was broadly Protestant in its devotion to scripture and its emphasis on the priesthood of all believers, but rather novel in its particular emphasis on the experience of love in the community and its relative lack of interest in doctrinal matters.[60]

CONCLUSION

In the post-Reformation period we see anticipations of the later Enlightenment challenge to Christianity in Europe. Pietism, for example, stepped in the direction of an anthropologically centered form of Christian faith. A stance of doctrinal skepticism gradually became more common, for example, in marginal movements such as Socinianism (late sixteenth to early seventeenth centuries), which rejected the doctrines of the Trinity and incarnation on the ground of their irrationality. While Protestant Orthodoxy strongly emphasized reason as central to the theological enterprise, theirs was a reason tightly tethered to the traditional faith of the church. But as reason came to be regarded as autonomous and authoritative in its own right, we see the emergence of the rationalism that would decisively influence theological discussions within early modernity.

---

[60] Philipp Jakob Spener, *Pia Desideria*, trans. Theodore G. Tappert, Seminar Editions (Philadelphia: Fortress, 1964).

Table 18.3 *Timeline of theology in the Reformation period*

History of theology			World history
		1400	
Execution of Jan Hus at the Council of Constance	1415	1431	Burning of Joan of Arc
		c. 1450	Invention of printing press by Johannes Gutenberg
Birth of Erasmus of Rotterdam	c. 1466	1453	Muslim conquest of Constantinople
Birth of Luther	1483	1492	Columbus "discovers" the New World
		c. 1498	Leonardo da Vinci completes *The Last Supper*
		1500	
Luther's Ninety-five Theses	1517	1508	Michelangelo begins to paint the Sistine Chapel
Augsburg Confession	1530		
Henry VIII declared head of Church of England	1534	1547	Ivan the Terrible becomes Czar of Russia
Final edition of Calvin's *Institutes of the Christian Religion*	1559		
End of the Council of Trent	1563	1564	Birth of William Shakespeare
Formula of Concord	1577	1572	St. Bartholomew's Day Massacre
		1600	
King James Bible published	1611	1607	Founding of Jamestown, Virginia
Synod of Dort	1618–19	1618	Thirty Years War begins
		1636	Founding of Harvard College
Westminster Confession	1646	1642	English Civil War begins
Birth of Johann Sebastian Bach	1685	1687	Newton's *Principia Mathematica*
		1700	

FOR FURTHER READING

Bromiley, Geoffrey W., ed., *Zwingli and Bullinger*, Library of Christian Classics (Philadelphia: Westminster, 1953).

Calvin, John, *Institutes of the Christian Religion*, trans. Ford Lewis Battles, ed. John T. McNeill, Library of Christian Classics (Philadelphia: Westminster, 1960).

Heppe, Heinrich, *Reformed Dogmatics*, trans. G. T. Thomson, ed. Ernst Bizer (London: Allen & Unwin, 1950).

Lindberg, Carter, *The European Reformations* (Oxford: Blackwell, 1996).

Lohse, Bernhard, *Martin Luther's Theology: Its Historical and Systematic Development*, trans. Roy A. Harrisville (Minneapolis, MN: Fortress, 1999).

Luther, Martin, *On Christian Liberty*, trans. W. A. Lambert and Harold J. Grimm (Minneapolis, MN: Fortress, 2003).

Pelikan, Jaroslav, *The Christian Tradition: A History of the Development of Doctrine,* IV: *Reformation of Church and Dogma* (1300–1700) (Chicago: University of Chicago Press, 1984).

Schmid, Heinrich, *The Doctrinal Theology of the Evangelical Lutheran Church*, 3rd edn. (Minneapolis, MN: Augsburg, 1961).

CHAPTER 19

Theology in modernity (c. 1700–1960)

INTRODUCTION: PRELUDE TO THE MODERN WORLD

The dawn of the modern world is typically located in the so-called "Age of Reason" (seventeenth–eighteenth centuries), and more particularly in what has been termed the eighteenth-century "Enlightenment project" (Jürgen Habermas). The novel intellectual mood and cultural ethos of modernity brought many new and unprecedented challenges to Christianity – most acutely, challenges to the credibility of its basic beliefs and doctrines. Protestant theology in particular would take on a variety of new forms as it sought to make its way in a "world come of age."

The history of the modern world is in large part a story of *secularization*. Secularization (Lat. *saeculum* = "world" or "age") is, most simply, "the world coming of age," the world discovering itself in its own autonomy, freedom, and relative independence. Secularization more particularly is the process of understanding the world increasingly in its own natural terms without direct recourse to supernatural explanation – that is, understanding the world and its activities (e.g., science, politics, economics) in terms of their own structural integrity. The historical factors contributing to this growing secular outlook are, of course, many and varied, and include economic (e.g., the rise of the middle class), technological (e.g., the invention of the printing press), and geo-political (e.g., the European discovery of the "new" world) developments. But there are two intellectual and two religious developments that especially facilitated the rise of the modern world.

Intellectually, the *Renaissance* (c. 1350–1600), that "rebirth" of classical, Greco-Roman culture via the return to classical texts (*ad fontes* – "to the sources"), initiated a new humanism against the backdrop of medieval Christianity. In the medieval world, humanity was overshadowed, if not overwhelmed, by divine transcendence. But Renaissance humanism put humanity back into the picture of life in a prominent way (literally, as a third dimension emerged in painting, that of depth perspective, which portrayed human beings interacting historically in their own dignified space-through-time; see Illustration 19.1).

This changed historical perspective energized a new quest of learning and inquiry across the field of human endeavor, both in the arts and in the sciences, a quest less encumbered by the authority of church tradition. In this respect, the Renaissance serves as the midwife of the modern period. The *scientific revolution* of the seventeenth century is its direct result; its keynote was the shift from a geocentric to a heliocentric view of the cosmos, as first proposed by Copernicus, bolstered by Kepler, and promoted by Galileo, who famously clashed with the Roman Inquisition. More than just the scientific discovery that the Earth revolves around the Sun, heliocentrism initiated a whole cultural revolution, since it overthrew the long-standing Aristotelian-Ptolemaic cosmology that grounded medieval society. The medieval cosmology had scorned the physical earth in view of spiritual heaven, and had ascribed a fixed and proper place to everything under the aegis of divine providence, including social roles (i.e., ascriptivism). As a new understanding of physical motion emerged,

Illustration 19.1 Masaccio's *Holy Trinity* was one of the first Renaissance paintings to employ depth perspective. By means of this technique Masaccio brings humanity into the depiction of God as Trinity at the event of the cross, in various levels of participation: most immediately Mary and John the Baptist, and then Masaccio's patrons, who serve as a bridge to our contemporary response. Compare Masaccio's realism to Rublev's two-dimensional Trinity icon (Illustration 5.2), both painted, strikingly, within a decade of each other.

and as the natural laws that govern the universe were plotted from astronomy to zoology with mathematical precision and experimental rigor, a new cosmological paradigm emerged – that of the Newtonian world, so named after its most brilliant light, Isaac Newton, whose *Principia Mathematica* (1687) provided the mathematical proof for the Copernican revolution (see pp. 157–8 above).

Religiously, the *Protestant Reformation* aided the rise of the modern world, since it hastened the dissolution of the central authority of the medieval Catholic Church. Luther's dramatic protest at the Diet of Worms (1521) that he could not recant his dissenting position because it was "neither safe nor right to go against conscience" came to stand as a paradigm of the individual discerning his own truth before God.[1] This "freedom of conscience" or "priesthood of all believers" weakened the dependence upon ecclesiastical authority and spawned a whole variety of new religious traditions: Lutheran, Reformed, and Anabaptist. The reformers' advocacy of the "two kingdoms" as an attempt to quell the long-standing conflict between pope (church) and emperor (state) created greater public space for the state: God has a spiritual kingdom of the left hand – the church, ruled by the gospel and word – but also a temporal kingdom of the right hand – the state, ruled by law and human reason. Each of these realms has its own integrity and sphere of responsibility and should not interfere with one other. Similarly, the reformers' teaching on "secular calling" (vocation) also carved out more dignified space in the world, since in order to fulfill one's Christian vocation one need not enter the priesthood or holy orders, but could fulfill that calling in ordinary professions – be it doctor, lawyer, butcher, or candlestick-maker. Though relatively bloodless for half a century, the Reformation's religious fragmentation of medieval Christendom eventually combined with national ambitions and civil strife to unleash a century of wars of religion, whose brutality is epitomized in the St. Bartholomew's Day Massacre (1572) and whose devastation was unprecedented in the Thirty Years War (1618–48). European civilization appeared to be on the verge of collapse.

THE ENLIGHTENMENT

These intellectual and even religious forces of secularization contributed to the rise of the Enlightenment, that intellectual mood and cultural ethos that stamped its imprint on the modern world. Roughly synonymous with the "Age of Reason," historians have seen the Enlightenment as an attempt to establish western society on a new, more stable, and agreeable basis. Given the breakdown of medieval Christendom, in which religion was the common civil bond – indeed, given the religious wars that seemed to contradict the very ideal of Christianity and of civil society – a new foundation for European society was proposed: that of enlightened reason.

[1] Cited in Lohse, *Martin Luther's Theology*, 200.

Basic features of the Enlightenment

To simplify, there are four central ideas of the Enlightenment. First, there was an *appeal to harmonious nature*. Given that the world was being scientifically discovered in its natural integrity, as a place of natural law, order, and regularity – a veritable well-oiled machine – this seemed to offer a dependable and universal basis for truth. Truth, most simply, was to be found in the natural order of things. One merely had to discover the natural laws that govern something and let them work, just as in nature, whether this be in politics (hence republicanism: that government is best that governs less) or in *laissez-faire* economics (hence capitalism: Adam Smith's *The Wealth of Nations* [1776]).

Closely related to this objective basis of truth in nature is its subjective appropriation in human understanding. The human mind is also subject to natural laws, laws of logic and understanding. Once these are clarified in appropriate rationalist or empiricist ways (see below), they assert on the basis of harmonious nature the *authority of human reason*. For the Enlightenment philosopher, reason supplants faith in navigating the world.

The primacy of reason entails a *rejection of tradition*. Any received authority, be it the Bible, creed, or pope, need not be accepted *per se*, and should not be accepted unless its assertions can pass the bar of reasoned examination. Traditional authorities, it was held, impaired the freedom and independence of the self-legislating rational conscience. Human autonomy was in; heteronomy was out.

Finally, these emphases also produce a *belief in progress*, a heady optimism of what human beings can do in the world by means of their own rational powers in order to create a just and humane civilization, one that flourishes politically, socially, economically, and above all ethically, since right moral conduct was a major concern of Enlightenment philosophers. In short, the Enlightenment was highly idealistic about human potential.

Philosophical developments

While the revolutionary developments in science and technology became the principal engine of modernity, they were accompanied by important developments in philosophy. Just as Christian theology in the patristic, medieval, and reformational periods cannot be understood apart from various philosophical influences – whether for good or ill, whether consciously employed or tacitly assumed – so also theology in the modern period cannot be grasped apart from that era's philosophical developments. These philosophical trends are also essential for understanding the Enlightenment view of the authority of reason.

Such developments have a rather clear point of departure in René Descartes (1596–1650), who is considered the father of modern philosophy. Trained as a Jesuit in the spiritual exercises of Ignatius Loyola, and deeply distressed by the religious conflict of the Thirty Years War, Descartes set out to establish a more certain basis for human agreement by way of scientific inquiry. In a thought experiment, Descartes attempted to doubt away everything he had ever learned until he came to something he could no longer doubt – namely, that *he was doubting*, which was a form of thinking, hence the famous "I think, therefore I am" (*cogito ergo sum*). From this indubitable foundation in human consciousness, Descartes went on to deduce what he considered to be a body of sure and certain truths, most strategically by securing the existence of God as an innate idea through a version of the ontological argument.[2] He thus provides the keynote for modern thought: it begins with doubt (of tradition) and is founded upon the certainty of human subjectivity. Descartes clarifies the *rationalist criterion of truth*: one should believe only that which is indubitable or self-evident and what can be *deduced* from its premises. Such knowledge should approximate mathematical clarity and certainty, since for Descartes geometry was the ideal model of sure and certain truth.[3]

In contrast to mathematical models, Francis Bacon (1561–1626), Descartes' near contemporary, promoted experimentation as the key to emerging modern science. Bacon was convinced that modern empirical science could "put nature to the rack" – subdue the natural world and harness her secrets for the technological benefit and happiness of humanity. For Bacon, such scientific "knowledge is power," and will enable humanity to build the ideal society, as sketched out in his *The New Atlantis*. John Locke (1632–1704), however, is typically considered the father of modern empiricism. Locke believed that the human mind was a "blank slate" (*tabula rasa*) containing no innate ideas (such as the idea of God).[4] All knowledge therefore begins in sense experience. Locke clarifies the *empiricist criterion of truth*: one should believe only that for which there is sufficient evidence and which can be verified or falsified *inductively* through experimentation. Whereas Descartes was interested only in clarifying a method of scientific inquiry, and still assented to traditional church authority in matters of religion and ethics, Locke drew his circle of truth around the whole body of human knowledge, including religion and ethics. While Locke actually

---

[2] Descartes, *Meditations on First Philosophy*, meditation 3.   [3] See Descartes, *Discourse on Method*, pt. 2.
[4] John Locke, *An Essay Concerning Human Understanding*, ed. Kenneth P. Winkler (Indianapolis: Hackett, 1996), 2.1.2.

thought that there was much in traditional Christianity that was reasonable, for which we have sufficient evidence, he is largely classified as a deist in religious persuasion.

Immanuel Kant (1724–1804) is another major figure in modern philosophy, and in many respects epitomizes Enlightenment thought, as sounded in his famous essay "What is Enlightenment?":

Enlightenment is man's release from his self-incurred tutelage. Tutelage is man's inability to make use of his understanding without direction from another. Self-incurred is this tutelage when its cause lies not in lack of reason, but in lack of resolution and courage to use it without direction from another. *Sapere Aude* [dare to know]! "Have courage to use your own reason!" – that is the motto of enlightenment.[5]

In his complex philosophical system, Kant attempted to synthesize the rationalist and empiricist trends. With Locke and the empiricists he believed that all knowledge begins in sense perception; yet Kant was also concerned to stake down absolute and universal truth, which cannot be derived by way of empirical induction (one can only arrive at high probability). He therefore also agreed with Descartes and the rationalists that there were innate ideas, which he took to be universal categories of logic and thought in the human mind that organize our sense data. In this way, Kant believed that he had completed a "Copernican revolution" in epistemology: rather than thinking, as naively before, that our minds conform to objects as they really are in the world (which our minds re-present as ideas, as, for example, in Aquinas' "adequation of the mind to the thing"), it is actually human subjectivity that organizes sense perception and structures our world.[6] This means that we cannot really know the things of the world as they are "in themselves" (*Ding an sich*, which Kant also called *noumena*), but only as they put in their appearance to us (*phenomena*).[7] The effect of Kantian epistemology was to put in jeopardy knowledge of the objects of classical metaphysics, such as God, immortality, and freedom. Kant solidified the modern turn to human subjectivity. It is within human subjectivity and by human reason, not by external authority, that the affairs of life are adjudicated.

Enlightenment challenges to Christian belief

While many Enlightenment thinkers were not antagonistic toward Christianity *per se* as much as they were desirous of bolstering its credibility in light of developing scientific and philosophical thought, in their pursuit

---

[5] Kant, "What is Enlightenment?," 3.　　[6] Kant, *Critique of Pure Reason*, 22.　　[7] Ibid., 265–75.

of a more rational approach to religion it was the revelational particulars of Christian belief that eventually lost out. This rationalist challenge affected both belief in God in general and the particular doctrines of traditional orthodoxy.

Belief in God in general

The rather diffuse movement known as *Deism* emerged as the rational religious philosophy of the Enlightenment. Generally speaking, the deists held that God created the world so well in its natural integrity that it runs superbly on its own and does not need any divine supervision, much as a master clockmaker makes an autonomous clock (i.e., the Newtonian world). Deists emphasized God as the *creator*, for which they found the teleological argument, or argument from design, most compelling. But they had no need for God as the *intervener*, such as providential sustainer or incarnational redeemer. They did, however, still retain God as the final judge, as the necessary enforcer of the human moral project for which Deism was deeply concerned, since human beings have, by rational belief and moral necessity, immortal souls. Deism therefore embraces the transcendence of God but has little if any place for the immanence of God in the world.

But the rational bases for belief in the deistic God were soon challenged, especially by the likes of David Hume (1711–76). As a thoroughgoing empiricist, Hume was skeptical that human beings could plumb the essence of things, let alone achieve high probability in epistemic endeavors, since human knowledge can only make associations based on sense experience. In his *Dialogues Concerning Natural Religion*, Hume provided a critique of classic teleological (design) and cosmological (causal) arguments for God's existence, arguing, among other things, that given the imperfection, chaos, and suffering in the world we cannot thereby infer a God (first cause or highest intelligence) who is all-benevolent. Indeed, Hume revived Epicurus' ancient argument for atheism based on the world's evil (see pp. 207–8 above).[8] The problem of evil in general was heightened in Enlightenment thought, whose rational sensibilities no longer accepted the facile reconciliation of evil with a beneficent divine providence. In light of tragic events such as the devastating Lisbon earthquake of 1755, Voltaire's *Candide* famously parodied the "theodicy" argument of the rationalist philosopher Leibniz, that this was "the best of all possible worlds."[9]

[8] Hume, *Dialogues*, pt. 10.
[9] Voltaire, *Candide*, trans. Richard Aldington, in *The Portable Voltaire*, ed. Ben Ray Redman (New York: Penguin, 1977), ch. 4.

As modern science would continue to develop, plotting the workings of the world in its natural integrity as a well-oiled machine run by natural laws, less and less was God needed as an explanatory principle of the world's workings. The cosmos, in turn, was significantly demystified and God was increasingly pushed to the periphery of human knowledge, a tendency that would eventually facilitate the rise of modern atheism (see p. 93). The distant God of Enlightenment Deism is a first step in this direction, a trend compounded by an intensifying problem of evil.

Christian belief in particular

In addition to this secularizing trend toward atheism, the Enlightenment also launched a series of challenges to the specifics of Christian theology. As human reason achieved heightened status, the essential Christian belief in divine revelation was diminished, if not eliminated. While John Locke still found much in traditional, revealed Christianity reasonable (*The Reasonableness of Christianity*, 1695), deists like John Toland (*Christianity Not Mysterious*, 1696) and Matthew Tindal (*Christianity as Old as Creation*, 1730) found the category of revelation superfluous to the essentials of religion that could be derived by human reason through nature. This Enlightenment trend toward a rational religion is epitomized by Immanuel Kant's *Religion within the Limits of Reason Alone* (1793).

This depreciation of revelation in view of human reason was part and parcel of a growing anti-supernaturalism that found acute expression in the critique and rejection of miracles. Given a mechanistic cosmos of recurring natural law, French rationalist Denis Diderot famously proclaimed that he would not believe in a resurrection of a dead man were the entire Parisian population to testify to it. And David Hume, while not ruling out the possibility of miracles, strictly speaking, held that such reports could not be accorded historical credibility on balance with our experience of regularity today, anticipating the criterion of "analogy to today" of modern historical criticism.[10]

Scripture accordingly was dislodged from its place of authority and came under increasing scrutiny. While the Enlightenment proper (eighteenth century) was generally dominated by rationalism and the rationalist critique of the contents of scripture, it was the empiricist approach that eventually won the day. The increasing success of empirical science ultimately placed

---

[10] David Hume, *An Enquiry Concerning Human Understanding and Selections from A Treatise of Human Nature* (LaSalle, IL: Open Court, 1945), section 10.

greater emphasis on experience and historical particularity. Out of this trend historiography emerged as a self-conscious critical science in pursuit of "what actually happened" (Leopold von Ranke).[11] Approached as any other historical human document, scripture was put to the historical-critical test and was in many respects found wanting.

Other traditional Christian doctrines were also put to the rational and historical test and summarily dismissed. The doctrine of the Trinity, for example, was considered to be more influenced by Greek philosophical modes of thought than by the NT itself, and was chided by unitarian and atheist alike for being incoherent. The doctrine of original sin, for another example, was seen to be a novel historical development in Augustine's thought, one that was certainly incompatible with an enlightened assessment of human potential.

All of these critical, skeptical trends came especially to bear on christology. As Christ's miraculous resurrection was discounted, so also were his deity and incarnation, as well as the creedal tradition's teaching of his "two natures." The focus became exclusively the historical human Jesus. Hermann Samuel Reimarus (1694–1768), for example, saw in Jesus an aspiring messiah who taught the natural truth of religion (Deism), but who died a tragic death. His disciples then stole his body and fabricated the resurrection story and therewith the Christian gospel. Reimarus' posthumously published Wolfenbüttel Fragments (1778) are considered to have launched the "quest of the historical Jesus," which over different phases has attempted to ferret the real "Jesus of history" out of the church-embossed "Christ of faith."[12] The christological result has been to view Jesus as a moral example, a significant personality, or a teacher of important religious truths, but not as the incarnate Son of the eternal God.

THEOLOGICAL RESPONSES TO THE ENLIGHTENMENT

The rationalist-historicist challenge of the Enlightenment elicited a variety of Christian responses. Since the Enlightenment was mostly a western European phenomenon, Eastern Orthodoxy did not engage it until much later (see pp. 525–7). But neither did Roman Catholicism officially until around the time of Vatican I in the nineteenth century (see pp. 524–5). While certain

---

[11] See Leopold von Ranke, *The Theory and Practice of History*, ed. Georg G. Iggers and Konrad von Moltke, trans. Wilma A. Iggers and Konrad von Moltke (Indianapolis, IN: Bobbs-Merrill, 1973), 137.
[12] See Schweitzer, *Quest of the Historical Jesus*.

strains of Protestantism also dismissed this modernist challenge (e.g., Protestant orthodoxy, pietism), many Protestant theologians approached the rise of modernity as a serious and unavoidable issue that threatened the credibility of Christian belief and of Christian witness in the world. While the rest of this chapter examines theologians and theologies that in one way or another address this modernist challenge, the first two responses to the Enlightenment that we consider come from philosophers with influential theological proposals.

Immanuel Kant

While Immanuel Kant is in many respects the quintessential Enlightenment philosopher, endorsing those tenets central to that intellectual movement, he also signals the end of Enlightenment *rationalism*. (The "reasoned" methods of the empirical and historical sciences, however, would continue to assert the Enlightenment hegemony in modernity in opposition to traditioned perspectives.) Crediting Hume for having awakened him from his "dogmatic slumber," in his *Critique of Pure Reason* Kant attempted to demonstrate the limitations of human reason *qua* reason to discern the world as it really is. As we saw above, in the process, Kantian epistemology put in jeopardy a knowledge of the supersensible realities of classical metaphysics, such as God, the immortality of the soul, and human freedom. But Kant thought that these essential religious realities, which his own critique barred as objects of theoretical knowledge or speculative reason, could be established on a firmer basis, as the necessary or "transcendental" conditions of *practical reason* – that is, as the rational structure and precondition of moral experience. It is for their sake that Kant makes the famous claim that "I have therefore found it necessary to deny *knowledge*, in order to make room for *faith*."[13]

In his analysis of human morality, Kant arrives at a "supreme principle of morality," a universal law of moral experience which he calls the "categorical imperative": "Act only on that maxim through which you can at the same time will that it should become a universal law."[14] In other words, it is the rational duty of persons to always do what is universally right regardless of circumstances. Kant then reasons that the condition

[13] Kant, *Critique of Pure Reason*, 29.
[14] Immanuel Kant, *Groundwork of the Metaphysic of Morals*, trans. and ed. H. J. Paton (New York: Harper & Row, 1964), 88.

that makes the human moral project possible is *freedom*, which empowers the moral project toward the supreme good of happiness; but since such virtue and happiness are not fully achievable in this lifetime, this requires the *immortality* of the soul for its final perfection. There must then be a *God* whose judgment and power can effect the ultimate synthesis between morality and happiness – humanity's *summum bonum*. So in Kant's view, that which theoretical reason could not positively identify – freedom, immortality, God – practical reason can.[15]

Kant therefore establishes religion on morality; morality in turn comprises for Kant the one, true, universal religion. It is this ethical concern that colors Kant's conception of Christianity, which he considers to be the highest exemplification of rational moral religion – that is, once shorn of its mythological elements. This ethical reduction of Christian theology is seen quite clearly in his *Religion within the Limits of Reason Alone*. There the locus of revelation is found not in scripture but in each person's practical reason (i.e., the categorical imperative); morality thus becomes the exegetical principle of biblical interpretation. Accordingly, Jesus Christ is viewed as the human archetype – the ideal of humanity – one that is already ever present in the human moral consciousness (and thus technically not requiring a particular empirical person in order to exemplify it).[16] Jesus is the personified good idea, whose purported heavenly descent and virgin birth merely symbolize the divine origin and purity of the good principle resident within us all. Moreover, Jesus' death on the cross is not an atonement for the "radical evil" which we ourselves freely choose, since such personal debt "can never be discharged by another person, so far as we can judge according to the justice of our human reason."[17] Rather, we judge ourselves and expiate our own guilt as we turn continually to the "new man" in death and resurrection – our rational self – as symbolized by the gospel events. In short, Christ is merely an example of the messiah that resides within us all. Kant's religion noticeably reduces to a "works righteousness." Since individuals make themselves either morally good or evil, "there exists absolutely no salvation for man apart from the sincerest adoption of genuinely moral principles into his disposition."[18] While Kant may have thought that he was rescuing Christianity from Hume's skepticism and his own critique of rational metaphysics, the room he left for faith was significantly vacated of orthodox theological content.

---

[15] Immanuel Kant, *Critique of Practical Reason*, ed. and trans. Mary Gregor, Cambridge Texts in the History of Philosophy (Cambridge: Cambridge University Press, 1997), 102–111.
[16] Kant, *Religion Within the Limits*, 54–60.   [17] Ibid., 66.   [18] Ibid., 78.

Georg W. F. Hegel

The profound philosophical thought of Georg W. F. Hegel (1770–1831) is difficult to summarize in short order. Hegel attempted to meet the Enlightenment challenge to belief in God along with the Kantian critique of pure reason by developing an all-encompassing idealistic ontology (theory of being) wherein the rational and historical are the truly real. Hegel's philosophy strove to overcome traditionally conceived opposites, such as subject–object, freedom–necessity, particular–universal, abstract–concrete, and being–becoming, by viewing reality as a dynamic, evolving process in which "identity-in-difference" is "taken up" (*aufgehoben* = sublated) into a greater whole. For example, in Hegel's philosophical logic or "dialectic," *Being* interrelates with its opposite *non-Being* in a dynamic process of *Becoming*, a dialectic often explained through the triad thesis–antithesis–synthesis, though that language was mostly utilized by the German idealist Fichte.

Given Enlightenment developments, Hegel was deeply concerned that we cannot know the great truths of religion – principally, God – "in themselves" by means of theoretical reason (given Kant's phenomena/noumena distinction and his argument that these can be established only by way of practical reason). Accordingly, Hegel's philosophy offers a speculative *tour de force* to secure direct knowledge of God: God as *Geist* ("Spirit" or rational "Mind" – like Aristotle's view of God as self-thinking thought) is in a "trinitarian process" of coming to consciousness in and through world history. God as abstract Spirit or ideal Being (symbolically the Father, much like a thesis) confronts and is poured out in its opposite, the concrete, material World (symbolically the incarnation *and* death of the Son – i.e., non-Being – like an antithesis), so as to be "taken up" (*aufgehoben*) in the Becoming or history of the world as Absolute Spirit (symbolically the Holy Spirit, the synthesis). In this God–world relationship and march of world history, God comes to consciousness in and through human rational consciousness and its various forms of expression – culture, art, religion. Human awareness of God therefore is direct awareness and apprehension of God's own self-consciousness. In this way, Hegel purported to rescue the great orthodox doctrines of Christianity by means of speculative reason.

Hegel's philosophy, as opaque as it is, has been subjected to radically different interpretations. The so-called "right-wing Hegelians" – for example, P. K. Marheineke and F. C. Baur – interpreted Hegel's thought as compatible with Christian belief. But the "left-wing Hegelians" have taken Hegel in the direction of atheism. The most famous of these,

Ludwig Feuerbach (1804–72), thought that Hegel had the God–world relationship backwards: it wasn't God who was coming to self-consciousness through human subjectivity; rather, it was human subjectivity that was coming to self-consciousness through the concept of God. Accordingly, Feuerbach thought that the notion of God was a projection of the human imagination, a human fancy that actually served a deleterious function – to alienate human beings from their own good nature and potential. For Feuerbach, all theology was really anthropology, and to face up to this truth would liberate humanity for positive social and political action in the world. Given his elaboration of the projectionist theory of theistic belief, Feuerbach is considered the father of modern atheism (see pp. 93–7 above).

Karl Marx (1818–83) draws on both Hegel and Feuerbach in his historically influential communist ideology. Taking Hegel's dialectic in a strictly materialist fashion as a history of class conflict, Marx argued that it is these economic relations that give rise to social structures and the ideas that justify existing relations. Drawing on Feuerbach, Marx regarded "God" as nothing more than a human projection, and interpreted religion as an ideology that economically and politically justifies the opulence of the rich and the squalor of the poor. Although religion expresses the "sigh of the oppressed," it also serves as the "opium of the people," doping the pain of their present existence by promising otherworldly recompense.[19] Therefore religion, in Marx's view, served no liberating function for present inequities, and must give way to atheism if the just society is to emerge.

Friedrich Schleiermacher

Friedrich Schleiermacher (1768–1834) was the first significant Protestant theologian to grapple with the intellectual challenges of the Enlightenment ethos. By virtue of his novel theological method, he established himself as the "father of modern theology," and generated a legacy that endures to the present. While Schleiermacher was raised in the Reformed tradition, he was also significantly influenced in his youth by pietism. In seminary he began to have doubts about his Protestant orthodoxy and became curious about the larger intellectual world around him. Enrolling in the University of Halle, Schleiermacher imbibed its philosophical currents, especially Kantianism, on his way to becoming a Reformed pastor, and eventually a

---

[19] Marx, *Selected Writings*, 72.

hospital chaplain in Berlin (1796). Berlin at this time had fallen under the cultural spell of romanticism.

While romanticism shared the Enlightenment rejection of tradition (especially authoritarian, dogmatic belief systems), it was also a reaction to the cold rationalism of the Enlightenment itself. Typically regarded as a period of literature and arts of the late eighteenth to mid-nineteenth centuries (e.g., Goethe, Wordsworth, Coleridge), romanticism emphasized inward feeling and emotion, imagination and vision, novelty and adventure, and the (nonconformist) growth of individuality, even to the point of eccentricity. Religiously, the romantic mood tended toward otherworldliness, stimulating a longing (*Sehnsucht*) for the whole, a mystical desire to envision the infinite in all finite things. Goethe's Faustian cry, *Gefühl ist Alles* ("feeling is everything"), became a motto for many romantics.

In Berlin, Schleiermacher embraced the romantic spirit with its emphasis on feeling. Coupled with his pietistic bent toward inwardness, this helped to catalyze for Schleiermacher a middle way between traditional Protestant orthodoxy (supernaturalism), which he considered crippled by Kant's critique of reason, and the rigid Enlightenment rationalism of Deism (naturalism). Schleiermacher first proposed his "mediating theology" in his early *On Religion: Speeches to its Cultured Despisers* (1799), a work of apologetics addressed to Berlin's cultural elite who largely considered religion to be *passé*. In these speeches Schleiermacher attempts to rescue religion, and therewith the Christian faith, through the category of *feeling*. Religion, he suggests to his skeptical audience, is neither primarily a way of *thinking*, as in the science of physics or metaphysics, nor primarily a way of *acting*, as in ethics. Rather, religion is most fundamentally *Gefühl* or feeling:

> The contemplation of the pious is the immediate consciousness of the universal existence of all finite things, in and through the Infinite, and of all temporal things in and through the Eternal. Religion is to seek this and find it in all that lives and moves, in all growth and change, in all doing and suffering. It is to have life and to know life in immediate feeling, only as such an existence in the Infinite and Eternal. Where this is found religion is satisfied ... Wherefore it is a life in the infinite nature of the Whole, in the One and in the All, in God, having and possessing all things in God and God in all.[20]

True religion, states Schleiermacher, is a "sense and taste for the Infinite."[21] Thus, rather than following the way of theoretical reason (Deism, and even Hegel), or the way of practical reason (Kant), Schleiermacher grounds

[20] Schleiermacher, *On Religion*, 36.   [21] Ibid., 39.

religion in feeling, a pre-reflective intuition and consciousness of the eternal, infinite whole in God.

This point of departure frames Schleiermacher's theological enterprise. He contends, however, that such a universal religious intuition comes to expression only in concrete historical religions, most supremely within Christianity. Like his contemporary Hegel, Schleiermacher is committed to the importance of history as the mediator of truth (a post-rationalist Enlightenment emphasis). Historic Christianity is one expression of fundamental human religious experience, and its theological doctrines are secondary reflections on that experience.

Schleiermacher's theological proposal is most thoroughly expressed in his magisterial *The Christian Faith* (two editions, 1821–2 and 1830), which is generally acclaimed the most significant Protestant dogmatics since Calvin's *Institutes*. It is here that Schleiermacher articulates his classic formula of religion as "the feeling of absolute dependence" on God, and explicates Christian doctrine neither on the basis of scriptural propositions (as in Protestant scholasticism), nor through Enlightenment rationalism (as in Deism), but on the basis of a systematic and historical analysis of contemporary Christian consciousness, or what he termed the "Christian affections": "Christian doctrines are accounts of the Christian religious affections set forth in speech."[22] In this unique endeavor, Schleiermacher was concerned to delineate a Christian theology that did not conflict with the advances in modern science and philosophy – particularly the deliverances of natural and historical science. As a result of his theological method, Schleiermacher proposed many revisions of classic Christian doctrines.

Take the doctrine of God, for example. God is the reality that corresponds to our feeling of absolute dependence. Following Kant, Schleiermacher holds that we cannot know God "in God's self" (*Ding an sich*), but only in our dependent experience: "All attributes which we ascribe to God are to be taken as denoting not something special in God, but only something special in the manner in which the feeling of absolute dependence is to be related to Him."[23] Schleiermacher's heavy emphasis on dependence, however, led him to conceive of God's omnipotence as the causal and determining ground of everything, so as to leave little room for a reciprocal relation of creatures to God (such as in petitionary prayer). It also, more starkly, led him to attribute sin and evil to divine causality. Moreover, Schleiermacher had little concern for the doctrine of the Trinity (which, as traditionally

[22] Schleiermacher, *Christian Faith*, §15 (p. 76).   [23] Ibid., §50 (p. 194).

formulated, he found fraught with logical problems), since it was not an immediate experience or utterance of the religious consciousness. He treated this doctrine only briefly at the conclusion of *The Christian Faith*, but elsewhere stated his preference for a modalistic conception of the Trinity. In a similar vein, he considered sin to be that which impugns God-consciousness. It is primarily "God-forgetfulness" or self-conscious "alienation from God."[24] Given this emphasis, Schleiermacher revisits the classic Augustinian doctrine of original sin and reinterprets it in more historical and social categories (see pp. 198–200 above).

Redemption through Christ, accordingly, involves a restoration of our sense of absolute dependence or God-consciousness. Finding the classic doctrine of Christ's "two natures" problematic, since he thought it was illogical that one person could possess two natures, Schleiermacher proposes a functional christology: Jesus Christ is not a preexistent divine being, but rather is a human person who possessed an "absolutely potent God-consciousness" manifest in a life of perfect dependence on God.[25] His perfect God-consciousness reflected God's redemptive activity in and through him, an activity which itself constitutes his divinity: "The Redeemer, then, is like all men in virtue of the identity of human nature, but distinguished from them all by the constant potency of his God-consciousness, which was a veritable existence of God in Him."[26] This redemptive life of Christ, however, is not immediately available to the individual in spiritual or mystical experience, but is only mediated historically through the society of the church. It is through the church that "the Redeemer assumes the believers into the fellowship of his unclouded blessedness, and this is his reconciling activity."[27]

Schleiermacher attempted to mediate Christianity to his modern intellectual times. By rooting theology in human consciousness and feeling, he sought to overcome opposition to Christianity as a rigid propositional orthodoxy (Protestant scholasticism) or a moral authoritarianism (Kantianism). But many have questioned the price he paid in toning down the supernaturalism of traditional Christianity, since Schleiermacher's theological agenda ruled out the miraculous. It is primarily for this reason that many regard Schleiermacher as the father not only of modern theology, but also of Protestant liberal theology. Whatever one's estimate of his theological program, Schleiermacher's shadow looms large over theology in the modern era and even persists in the present.

---

[24] Ibid., §11.2 (p. 54) and §§62–3 (pp. 259–64).
[25] Ibid., §96 (pp. 391–8).   [26] Ibid., §94 (p. 385).   [27] Ibid., §101 (p. 431).

Roman Catholicism and the First Vatican Council

Given the pervasive character of Enlightenment thought, especially in the developing empirical and social sciences, many individual Catholic thinkers were exploring their own syntheses of modern ideas and Catholic belief. The official teaching office of the church as rooted in the papacy, however, adopted a defensive posture, since it was committed to maintaining the classical faith believed "everywhere, always, and by all" (Vincent of Lérins, d. *c.* 445). Accordingly, the Vatican's "Index of Prohibited Books" swelled. In view of the political and cultural turmoil of the French Revolution (the political symbol of Enlightenment), the Napoleonic wars, the breakup of the Holy Roman Empire, the revolutions of 1848, and the loss of the Papal States – movements all quite antagonistic to the Catholic Church and its traditional role in society – the hierarchy of the church as concentrated in the papacy reacted strongly against the modern forces of liberalism.

This reaction is seen most clearly in the papacy of Pius IX (1846–78). Though he was initially a reforming pope, a forced exile from the Vatican embittered him to liberal reform and the modern ideas that inspired it. He therefore set on a course to consolidate papal authority for all aspects of the church (Ultramontanism) over and against national and local trends to invest regional bishops with greater authority (Gallicanism or episcopalianism). Pius subsequently published the "Syllabus of Errors" (1864), which claimed for the Church all control of science, culture, and education, and concluded by denying that "the Roman Pontiff can and should reconcile and adapt himself to progress, liberalism, and the modern civilization."[28] Besides his proclamation of the dogma of the Immaculate Conception of the Virgin Mary (1854), Pius IX is best known for convening the First Vatican Council (1869–70), the first church council since Trent (1545–63) in the Reformation era.

Vatican I's dogmatic constitution on the Catholic faith, *Dei Filius*, clarified traditional Catholic belief. While affirming the Thomistic position that God "can be known with certitude by the natural light of human reason from created things," it warned of the current rationalist and anti-supernaturalist trends sweeping across Europe and forbade conclusions of science that were contrary to the Catholic doctrine of faith.[29] The dogmatic constitution on the church of Christ, *Pastor aeternus*, declared the world-wide primacy of the pope by asserting his infallible teaching authority:

We teach and explain that the dogma has been divinely revealed: that the Roman Pontiff, when he speaks *ex cathedra*, that is, when carrying out the duty of the

---

[28] Denzinger, *Sources of Catholic Dogma*, 442.　　[29] Ibid., 443, 451.

pastor and teacher of all Christians in accord with his supreme apostolic authority
he explains a doctrine of faith or morals to be held by the universal Church,
through the divine assistance promised him in blessed Peter, operates with that
infallibility with which the divine Redeemer wished that His church be instructed
in defining doctrine on faith and morals; and so such definitions of the Roman
Pontiff from himself, but not from the consensus of the church, are unalterable.[30]

Vatican I thus spelled the triumph of Ultramontanism, which centralizes
all ecclesiastical power in the papacy, and confirmed Pius IX's antagonistic
positions on the growing rationalism and liberalism of modern times.
While many Catholic faithful responded positively to this shoring up of
the church's authority, Pius IX's bulwark against modernity would not last
long. For example, John Henry Newman (1801–90), who converted to
Catholicism in 1845, and who did not consider the promulgation of papal
infallibility a prudent move, continued with his influential historical studies
of the formation of Christian doctrine in critique of conceptualist scholastic
categories. And already in the late nineteenth century a so-called "modernist" school of Catholic theologians emerged; they entertained scientific,
historical, and critical methodologies in their theological work, as, for
example, Alfred Loisy in his important biblical studies. Such scholarship
would swell in the twentieth century, providing new syntheses of Catholic
confession and contemporary culture. But the official sanctioning of "modern" Catholic thought would not take place until Vatican II (1962–5).

Eastern Orthodoxy

While the Byzantine Orthodox tradition reached its zenith in Gregory
Palamas (c. 1296–1359), after the fall of Constantinople in 1453 that intellectual tradition faded for nearly three and a half centuries. A revival stirred
only in the nineteenth century with the establishment of various theological academies of the Russian Orthodox Church and translations of Greek
patristic texts into Russian. These academies, however, were quite conservative, if not scholastic, in their Orthodox "appeal to tradition" (see
pp. 452–3 above).[31]

---

[30] Ibid., 457.
[31] For a helpful summary of these modern developments in Eastern Orthodox theology, see Aristotle
Papanikolaou, "Orthodox Theology" section of "Theology in the Nineteenth and Twentieth
Centuries," in *The Encyclopedia of Christianity*, ed. Erwin Fahlbusch (Grand Rapids, MI: Eerdmans,
1999), v: 414–18; and Rowan Williams, "Eastern Orthodox Theology," in *The Modern Theologians*, ed.
David F. Ford (Oxford: Blackwell, 1989), II: 152–69.

The so-called "Russian school" of Vladimir Solovyov (1853–1900) and Sergei Bulgakov (1871–1944), however, did engage western philosophical currents, especially those of German idealism. Solovyov developed a philosophical theology that came to be called *sophiology*. According to Solovyov, since God is *Sophia* (Gk. = Wisdom) and has created the world in wisdom, all of creation reflects God and bears an intrinsic relation to God's life. By analogy with deification (the central Orthodox soteriological emphasis), which manifests the reconcilability of Creator (deity) and creature (humanity), all of creation as created wisdom is caught up in the process of reconciliation with God the divine *Sophia* – a union of opposites in a unique synthesis of transcendence and immanence (a version of what is called *panentheism* = all things in God). Bulgakov furthered Solovyov's sophiology along more orthodox trinitarian lines, emphasizing the *kenosis* – the self-emptying, self-giving – of the trinitarian persons, not only in the incarnation and crucifixion of Christ, but also in the act of creation itself and its reconciliation at large.[32] By means of their sophiology, Solovyov and Bulgakov provided a link (the relationship between God's divine *Sophia* and created wisdom) and warrant for theological engagement with all disciplines of human inquiry.

Solovyov and Bulgakov's sophiology was opposed by the "neo-patristic school," whose major representatives Georges Florovsky (1893–1979) and Vladimir Lossky (1903–58) both played a role in the "Sophia Affair" (1935) that judged sophiology heretical. The neo-patristic school insisted that Orthodox theology could not be extricated from the language and conceptuality of its foundational eastern patristic texts, that is, that it could not be "de-Hellenized" or westernized without distorting its orthodoxy. Lossky in particular considered sophiology's rather panentheistic synthesis of theology and philosophy to impugn the distinction between God's transcendence and immanence, since, harking back to Palamas's basic distinction, he thought that the transcendent divine *essence* was beyond being and unknowable, while the immanent divine *energies* – God's communication and communion with us – were knowable. Lossky considered *Sophia* to be a divine attribute that belonged solely to the latter.[33] Accordingly, Lossky emphasizes an apophatic approach to theology, one in which human reason must remain silent in the face of God's reconciliation of opposites, such as

---

[32] See Sergei Bulgakov, *Sophia: The Wisdom of God: An Outline of Sophiology*, Library of Russian Philosophy (Hudson, NY: Lindisfarne, 1993).
[33] Vladimir Lossky, *The Mystical Theology of the Eastern Church* (Crestwood, NY: St. Vladimir's Seminary Press, 1976), 80–81.

in the incarnation, where God (the divine Logos) and that which is not God (Jesus' humanity) become one. Similarly deification, the salvific union of Creator and creature, can be appropriated only in mystical experience that transcends human comprehension.

Liberal Protestantism

While there have been many different forms of "liberal" Christianity, a category as broad as one's definition of liberalism, one Protestant version of theological liberalism has become classic – that associated with Albrecht Ritschl (1822–89), whose school of thought flourished in the generation leading up to WWI. At first a Hegelian in his studies of the NT, Ritschl enthusiastically embraced Kant and Schleiermacher *en route* to becoming a leading systematic theologian. Reflecting the Kantian critique of speculative reason, Ritschl locates religious knowledge in the practical realm of "value judgments."[34] Ritschl's theology, accordingly, is decidedly anti-metaphysical, since the Christian religion can have only a practical-moral foundation and content. Traditional dogmatic affirmations such as the Trinity and the deity of Christ are ruled out of epistemic bounds, since we cannot know God *in se* but only *pro nobis* – God in God's effects on us. This one true God (unitarianism) is known in "trinitarian" effect through the life of Christ (who only ideally preexisted in the mind and intention of God the Father) and the history of the church.[35] Here Ritschl attempts to give a more rigorous biblical and historical foundation for Christian belief than that laid down by Schleiermacher. It is nonetheless the religious experience of the Christian community that determines the value and content of Christian theology. That content, judges Ritschl, centers on the "kingdom of God," which Ritschl defines in his magnum opus, *The Christian Doctrine of Justification and Reconciliation*, as the moral "organisation of humanity through action inspired by love."[36] In this kingdom, God the Father is revealed as love in Jesus' personality, life, teaching, and vocation; Jesus' ministry offers us justification and reconciliation from our selfish and ignorant "kingdom of sin" for ethical action in this world. Ritschl's program of the "moralizing of dogma" would continue as a broad school through major thinkers such as Wilhelm Hermann, Ernst Troeltsch, and Adolf von Harnack.

---

[34] Ritschl, *Justification and Reconciliation*, III: 203–11.
[35] Ibid., III: 272–4.   [36] Ibid., III: 12; cf. III: 280, 334–5, 610.

Harnack (1851–1930), eminent church historian at the University of Berlin (1888–1921), was the last great continental Ritschlian. His series of lectures entitled *What is Christianity?* became a popular and influential statement of Protestant liberalism. According to Harnack, Jesus taught a simple gospel, not about himself, but about the one God and Father, which distills to these three great truths: "Firstly, the kingdom of God and its coming. Secondly, God the Father and the infinite value of the human soul. Thirdly, the higher righteousness and the commandment of love."[37] This is the enduring truth of the gospel, the essential kernel that can do without the time-conditioned husk of the biblical worldview with its apocalyptic landscape of angels, demons, and reports of miracles, as well as the dogmatic formulations of Christian tradition – especially Trinity and incarnation – since these are the result of the weedy intrusion of Greek philosophy on the pure soil of the gospel.[38] For Harnack, in true Kantian fashion, morality is the soul of Christian religion.

Harnack's liberalism concentrated on the individual, beating the Augustinian refrain of "God and the soul" (Harnack was a staunchly conservative supporter of Kaiser Wilhelm II's administration and its imperialistic war aims). Walter Rauschenbusch (1861–1918), however, the most prominent Ritschlian in America and leading spokesperson for the "social gospel" movement, was concerned to apply this "ethical kingdom" to the project of "Christianizing the social order," for which he laid out an ambitious agenda for social, political, and economic reform.[39]

NEO-ORTHODOXY

Neo-orthodoxy is the generic name given (originally by its critics) to the twentieth-century movement launched by Karl Barth in reaction to the prevailing nineteenth-century Protestant liberalism. The "neo-orthodox" theologians were generally united in their opposition to liberalism by stressing humanity's *inability* to rightly know God and conduct its life – in short, sin – and therefore the need for God's external word of revelation, justification, and empowerment – in short, grace. Given this dialectic of sin and grace, neo-orthodoxy is also known as "dialectical theology." It has also been termed a "theology of crisis" (Gk. *krisis* = judgment), since it emphasized

---

[37] Harnack, *What is Christianity?*, 46.
[38] Adolf von Harnack, *Outlines of the History of Dogma*, trans. Edwin Knox Mitchell (Boston: Beacon, 1957), 5.
[39] See, e.g., Walter Rauschenbusch, *Christianizing the Social Order* (New York: Macmillan, 1912); and Rauschenbusch, *A Theology for the Social Gospel*, Library of Theological Ethics (Louisville, KY: Westminster John Knox, 1997).

the divine word of judgment on human pretense (e.g., liberalism) in a time of crisis (WWI and WWII). By and large, neo-orthodox theologians returned to the orthodox themes of the Protestant Reformation, but in a way they considered tailored to their twentieth-century context. "Neo-orthodoxy," however, is no cookie-cutter theology, since its "representatives" exhibit a wide spectrum of theological orientation and content. This will especially be seen in the distance between Barth's and Tillich's theologies.

Karl Barth

Karl Barth (1886–1968) was undoubtedly the most significant Protestant theologian of the twentieth century, with some even hailing him as a modern-day church father. Raised within the Reformed tradition, Barth pursued theological studies at various universities, imbibing the Ritschlianism of the day, especially through his teachers Harnack at Berlin and Hermann at Marburg. Ordained in the Reformed Church, Barth was pastor of a small church in the Swiss border town of Safenwil from 1911 to 1921. In this humble setting, Barth found that his liberal sermons did not meet the needs of his blue-collar parishioners. He was also significantly dismayed when his former teachers, especially Harnack, unabashedly signed a manifesto in support of Kaiser Wilhelm II's imperialist war aims (1914). All this drove Barth back to the text of scripture, wherein he discovered "the strange new world of the Bible,"[40] a world quite different from the "culture Christianity" and theological bankruptcy of liberal Protestantism.

The initial fruits of Barth's study of scripture came in the form of a commentary on *The Epistle to the Romans* (1919), the second edition of which (1922) was significantly reworked and constituted Barth's bold theological manifesto against liberalism. In it Barth taps the then underappreciated thought of Søren Kierkegaard (1813–55), who had opposed the Hegelian-influenced theology of his Danish Lutheran Church by arguing for the antithesis of the God–humanity relationship (and thus the decisive need for grace in view of human sin) rather than their rational synthesis as in Hegel's thought. States Barth:

If I have a system, it is limited to a recognition of what Kierkegaard called the "infinite qualitative distinction" between time and eternity, and to my regarding

---

[40] Karl Barth, "The Strange New World within the Bible," in *The Word of God and the Word of Man* (New York: Harper & Row, 1957), 28–50.

this as possessing negative as well as positive significance: "God is in heaven, and thou art on earth." The relation between such a God and such a man, and the relation between such a man and such a God, is for me the theme of the Bible and the essence of philosophy.[41]

From this juncture on, Barth would emphasize God as the "Wholly Other," who is not captive to human subjectivity (as he considered to be the case in any form of natural theology), but is always the sovereign subject of divine revelation, a revelation that comes in judgment of human ability and culture, yet with the offer of justifying grace in Jesus Christ.

Barth held a series of professorships in theology at Göttingen (1921), Münster (1925), and Bonn (1930). With the rise of Hitler and the Nazis, Barth opposed the "German Christians" in their attempt to meld Christianity with the policies of National Socialism, and almost single-handedly drafted the Barmen Declaration (1934), which became a founding document of the resisting Confessing Church in Germany. The Barmen Declaration clearly sounds the Barthian notes of God's self-revelation in Christ over and against other sources or norms of revelation:

Jesus Christ, as he is attested for us in Holy Scripture, is the one Word of God which we have to hear and which we have to trust and obey in life and in death. We reject the false doctrine, as though the church could and would have to acknowledge as a source of its proclamation, apart from and besides this one Word of God, still other events and powers, figures and truths, as God's revelation.[42]

On account of his refusal to swear an oath of allegiance to Hitler, Barth was dismissed from his teaching post in Bonn. He then took a position at Basel (1935), the city of his birth, where he taught and wrote for the rest of his life.

Barth's systematic theology is elaborated in his massive *Church Dogmatics*, a thirteen-volume work begun in 1932 and still unfinished by the time of his death in 1968. In this daunting opus with its many exegetical, historical, and constructive forays, Barth works through the various theological topics in view of his emphasis on God's sovereign freedom in revelation – a theology "from above" over against any form of natural theology "from below," whether it be classical liberalism as rooted in Schleiermacher or classical Roman Catholic theology as rooted in Aquinas (Barth's two principal foils). Barth's resulting theology contains a number of unique slants on classical doctrines, giving some warrant to the term "*neo*-orthodoxy," a label which Barth himself resisted.

[41] Karl Barth, *Epistle to the Romans*, trans. Edwyn C. Hoskyns, 6th edn. (London: Oxford University Press, 1933), 10.
[42] "Barmen Declaration," in Pelikan and Hotchkiss, eds., *Creeds and Confessions*, III: 507.

In his emphasis on revelation as the Word of God encountering us, the single source of Christian theology, Barth distinguishes three forms of the word of God.[43] At the heart and center of this framework stands Jesus Christ, the Word of God *revealed/incarnate*. The event of the incarnation or "Christ event" is the definitive form of God's self-revelation, which, we will see, Barth understands in a unique trinitarian way. The Bible is a second form – it is the word of God *written*. For Barth, the Bible is not authoritative in and of itself, but only as a faithful witness to the Christ event, revelation proper, through the activity of the Holy Spirit. Barth did not regard scripture as a repository of propositional truth, and he was not opposed to biblical and historical criticism in exegetical matters. Scripture's authority is authenticated by mediating the self-revelation of God in Christ. In short, scripture becomes the word of God in witness to Christ. The word of God *proclaimed* in the church's ministry is a third form of God's word to us. Again, the church actually proclaims the word of God when, through the Spirit, it provides a faithful witness to scripture's testimony to Christ.

Barth develops his understanding of revelation in conjunction with the doctrine of the Trinity. Unlike the theological trend following Thomas Aquinas, who treated the Trinity only subsequent to a consideration of the One God (a natural theology), and unlike the theological trend following Schleiermacher, who broached the doctrine only minimally and at the conclusion of *The Christian Faith*, Barth takes up the Trinity at the very beginning of his *Church Dogmatics*. This is because, for Barth, the Christian understanding of revelation and the doctrine of the Trinity imply each other.[44]

According to Barth, in any act or event of revelation we can distinguish three formal aspects: the *revealer*, the *revelation* itself, and the effect of that revelation, its *revealedness*. Moreover, when we inquire into the biblical witness we can distill its material concept of revelation down to this: "God reveals Himself as Lord," which Barth calls the root of the doctrine of the Trinity.[45] Putting these formal and material elements together, we get this: God the Father is the Revealer, whose self-revelation is found in Jesus Christ, the Son of God, whom Barth calls the "objective reality" of revelation,[46] and which revelatory result is the actualizing of the divine lordship in the life of the believer by means of God the Spirit, whom Barth calls the "subjective reality" of revelation.[47] Since Barth conceives of Christian revelation exclusively as the *self*-revelation of God, revelation is always a

---

[43] Barth, *Church Dogmatics*, I/1: 88–124.   [44] Ibid., I/1: 310–12.
[45] Ibid., I/1: 306.   [46] Ibid., I/2: §13.   [47] Ibid., I/2: §16.

personal encounter with the trinitarian God. As self-revelation, the trinitarian event of revelation guarantees the singular subjectivity of God in revelation (including the miracle of reception in the believer by means of the Spirit). God's own lordship over revelation thereby precludes any distortion of divine revelation and knowledge of God by means of human subjectivity – the very distortion which Barth considers to have taken place in the legacy of natural theology (Catholicism or liberalism), and which, absent special revelation, falls prone to Feuerbach's critique that theology is mere anthropology. We will take up Barth's polemic against natural theology in the next section in connection with his famous debate with Emil Brunner.

Barth's emphasis on the *self*-revelation of God leads him to ascribe personhood in the typical sense of personality, subjectivity, or consciousness only singularly to God, preferring "modes of being" (*Seinsweisen*) to describe the trinitarian members severally. While some have thus charged Barth with surreptitious modalism, there is little debate that Barth's efforts helped to revive the doctrine of the Trinity in the twentieth century against the backdrop of its modern neglect.

On the basis of his trinitarianism, Barth offered a reformulation of the divine attributes (which, since Thomas, had largely been treated prior to trinity doctrine). Conceiving of God the Trinity principally as "the One who loves in freedom,"[48] Barth grouped the divine perfections under the two rubrics of love and freedom, replacing the more traditional categories of incommunicable or transcendent attributes and communicable or immanent attributes, respectively. Barth elaborates this with such artistry and equipoise as not to play off the divine freedom against the divine loving, but to show how they condition each other.[49] Accordingly, he elaborates the perfections in complementary pairs, first under the category of divine loving, where the first term represents love while the second term clarifies the freedom of that love. He then reverses their order under the category of divine freedom, where the second term of each pair integrally qualifies the loving character of that freedom (see Table 19.1). For Barth, God as Trinity transcends the world (*contra* Hegel), but in his sovereign freedom he has lovingly determined to be God for us.

Barth's revelational Trinity and reconfiguration of divine attributes come to bear on his conception of election, resulting in another unique reformulation of an orthodox (especially Reformed) doctrine. Unlike the traditional Calvinist eternal decree of double predestination, whereby God from eternity decides which individuals will be saved and which will be damned,

---

[48] Ibid., II/1: 322.   [49] Ibid., II/1: §30–31.

Table 19.1 *The perfections of God, according to Karl Barth*

The perfections of the divine loving	The perfections of the divine freedom
Grace and holiness	Unity and omnipresence
Mercy and righteousness	Constancy and omnipotence
Patience and wisdom	Eternity and glory

Barth understands God's free eternal determination to concern God's own self – as the one who loves in freedom.[50] Election accordingly takes place in Jesus Christ, in whom God determines covenantally to be for another – for us. Uniquely, Jesus Christ is both the one elect and the one reprobate person, suffering God's wrath on the cross, so that all may be accepted by God.[51] Election takes place *in Christ*, who, though truly divine as the electing God, is also the representative of all humanity (see also pp. 355–8 above). The implications of Barth's doctrine of election lean decidedly toward universal salvation, a point on which Barth himself was coy.

Barth's recovery of God's transcendental freedom as Trinity, but gracious revelation to us in the incarnation, death, and resurrection of Jesus Christ, launched a revolution in theology against the backdrop of traditional Protestant orthodoxy and the "culture Protestantism" of liberalism. Again, while the label "neo-orthodoxy" has its limitations, it remains a convenient way to group those who followed Barth's train in the attempt to negotiate the contours of an orthodox faith in the face of liberalism and an ongoing modernity. While Barth's theology remains controversial at many points, his theological achievement is such that all subsequent theologians have had to engage him as a serious dialogue partner.

Emil Brunner

One of Barth's neo-orthodox allies was Emil Brunner (1889–1966), professor of theology at nearby Zurich from 1922 to 1955, though an early clash over general revelation unfortunately strained their personal relationship until late in life. Brunner's neo-orthodoxy independently complemented Barth's, and was actually more influential in the formative stages of dialectical theology in Britain and America, given Brunner's travels there, the early English translations of his works, and his more accessible theological presentation and style of writing. While he published widely, Brunner's

[50] See, e.g., ibid., II/2: 49, 76.   [51] Ibid., II/2: 346–54.

mature thought is found in his three-volume *Dogmatics*, published from 1946 to 1960.

Beyond the core themes of dialectical theology over against liberalism and Protestant orthodoxy, Brunner is especially known for developing a theological personalism. Drawing from the existentialism of Kierkegaard, but especially the I–Thou personalism of Ferdinand Ebner and Martin Buber, Brunner emphasized revelation as a *personal* encounter with God in Christ. Following Buber in particular, Brunner stressed that Christian truth is not a matter of impersonal, objective, I–it relationships, such as propositions in the Bible, creedal formulations, or having the right theological beliefs – all impersonal, objective statements; rather, Christian truth is a matter of personal, subjective, I–Thou encounter with God in Christ:

> To know [God] in trustful obedience is not only to *know* the truth, but through God's self-communication to *be* in it, in the truth that as love is at the same time fellowship. The truth about man is founded in the divine humanity of Christ, which we apprehend in faith in Christ, the Word of God. This is truth as encounter ... which makes us free by restoring to us our true being, our being in the Thou, and our being for the Thou.[52]

Unfortunately, Brunner is best known today for his controversy with Barth over the question of the efficacy of general revelation.[53] In a 1934 essay entitled "Nature and Grace," Brunner argued that there must be some "point of contact" within sinful humanity for the call of the gospel by virtue of humanity's creation as *imago Dei* and by way of God's revelation in nature (i.e., general revelation). By this "point of contact," he meant a basic consciousness of sin and of one's need for God that serves as a presupposition for encountering the good news of the gospel and the call to repentance. Barth's quick and forceful reply was "*Nein!*" – there is *no* point of contact in sinful humanity for responding to the gospel; any human capacity and response are the miraculous work of the Holy Spirit. Barth chastised Brunner for advocating an un-Calvinistic synergism of grace and human effort, and for opening the door to a natural theology reminiscent of Catholicism and liberalism. Although Barth's position on general revelation and natural theology was consistent with the logic of his theology, his vehemence toward Brunner can be accounted for only by the principal crisis of his time – his opposition to the "German Christians," who by means of a natural theology were compromising the gospel with the Nazi agenda. Barth's theological prominence would continue to overshadow

---

[52] Emil Brunner, *Truth as Encounter*, trans. Amandus W. Loos *et al.*, rev. edn. (London: SCM, 1964), 21.
[53] See Brunner and Barth, *Natural Theology*.

Brunner's career, even though Brunner was a major neo-orthodox theologian in his own right.

Dietrich Bonhoeffer

Of all the major neo-orthodox theologians, the life and thought of Dietrich Bonhoeffer (1906–45) are especially fraught with enduring mystique. This is particularly due to the circumstances surrounding his early death – he was executed by the Nazis for his participation in a conspiracy to assassinate Hitler. For his courageous resistance, Bonhoeffer has been hailed as a modern-day Christian martyr.

Bonhoeffer grew up in an aristocratic, nominally Lutheran family, but showed a proclivity for theology at an early age. Having received his doctorate in theology at the University of Berlin at the age of twenty-one (his teacher Harnack wanted him to become a church historian), Bonhoeffer gravitated early, but not uncritically, to Barth's theology. After some pastoral work in the Lutheran Church and a lectureship at Berlin, the course of Bonhoeffer's life and theology would be indelibly shaped by the rise of National Socialism (1933).

Bonhoeffer became a founding member of the Confessing Church and directed a number of its clandestine seminaries, most famously at Finkenwalde (1935–7). Out of these experiences came Bonhoeffer's most popular work, *The Cost of Discipleship* (1937), which, as an exposition of the Sermon on the Mount, denounced various forms of "cheap grace," and called for the "costly grace" of following Christ in the world:

Costly grace is the gospel which must be sought again and again, the gift which has to be asked for, the door at which one has to knock.

It is costly because it calls to discipleship; it is grace, because it calls us to follow *Jesus Christ*. It is costly, because it costs people their lives; it is grace, because it thereby makes them live. It is costly, because it condemns sin; it is grace, because it justifies the sinner. Above all, grace is costly, because it was costly to God, because it cost God the life of God's Son.[54]

Bonhoeffer himself thought that his most important contribution was the crafting of a well-integrated theological ethics, one that overcame the *deontological* Kantian ethic (deducing ethics on the basis of an impersonal principle, such as the imperious categorical imperative) in favor of an ethic more *teleological* (oriented to ends/consequences) and *contextual* (oriented

---

[54] Bonhoeffer, *Discipleship*, 45.

to circumstances) in nature. Published only posthumously as *Ethics*, Bonhoeffer's approach in general attempts to discern the "form of Christ" in every situation.[55] Written during the conspiracy years, as can be read between its lines, Bonhoeffer's *Ethics* wrestles with the question of responsible Christian action in the face of egregious evil.

For scholars, Bonhoeffer's fragmentary *Letters and Papers from Prison* (mostly smuggled out during his two-year incarceration) holds a special place in his theological legacy. Half-way through his imprisonment, Bonhoeffer wrote to his former student and friend (and future biographer) Eberhard Bethge: "You would be surprised, and perhaps even worried, by my theological thoughts and the conclusions that they lead to."[56] He goes on in this letter and subsequent others to speak, somewhat ominously, about a "religionless time" that is coming in a "world come of age." For Bonhoeffer this means that the Christian church will have to learn to live and speak about God in a "secular way," as though belief in God were no longer a safe assumption or a given presupposition.[57] In order to capture the "profound this-worldliness of Christianity," Bonhoeffer begins to sketch out a non-religious interpretation of Christianity.[58]

What Bonhoeffer was reflecting on in these provocative letters, papers, and poems was the debilitating effects of secularization on the Christianity of his time. While his own rudimentary thoughts in response are best interpreted in the context of his whole theology and as a continuation of its christological and creational vectors (and therefore not a radical breach in his ethical theology), some theologians of the 1960s would latch on to certain of these rhetorically charged snippets and interpret Bonhoeffer in a much more radical way (see pp. 544–5 below). Bonhoeffer is recognized today as a rich source of theological and ethical reflection, a tribute to one who followed Christ into the crucible of Gethsemane.

Rudolf Bultmann

Rudolf Bultmann (1884–1976) was the prominent biblical theologian of the neo-orthodox era, serving as professor of NT at the University of Marburg

[55] See, e.g., Dietrich Bonhoeffer, *Ethics*, ed. Ilse Tödt, Heinz Eduard Tödt, Ernst Feil, and Clifford Green, trans. Reinhard Krauss, Charles C. West, and Douglas W. Scott, Dietrich Bonhoeffer Works 6 (Minneapolis, MN: Fortress, 2005), 76–102.
[56] Dietrich Bonhoeffer, *Letters and Papers from Prison*, ed. Eberhard Bethge, tr. R. H. Fuller *et al.*, enlarged edn. (New York: Macmillan, 1972), 279.
[57] See, e.g., ibid., 279–82, 325–9.
[58] Ibid., quotation at 369, sketch of non-religious interpretation at 380–3.

from 1921 to 1951. His theology was similar to that of Barth and company in its reaction to classical liberalism and in stressing that God is "Wholly Other," who graciously comes to us in the event of revelation, the gospel of Christ. But Bultmann's "theology of the word" was quite unlike Barth's in adopting a particular philosophical lens through which to view biblical theology – that of existential philosophy, primarily as articulated by Martin Heidegger, who was Bultmann's colleague at Marburg from 1923 to 1928.

Bultmann is best known for his program of "demythologization" – his attempt to reinterpret the mythological imagery of the NT so as to capture the true meaning of the gospel. Presupposing a Newtonian world (a closed mechanistic system of cause and effect) and a Kantian epistemology (a division between the phenomenal world of sense/science and the noumenal world of transcendent faith), Bultmann was convinced that "modern man" could no longer accept the mythological worldview of the biblical text with its three-tiered universe (heaven, earth, hell) and commonplace miraculous interventions.[59] But unlike his classical liberal teachers, Bultmann did not slough off these mythical elements in pursuit of the universal ethical truths manifested in Christianity; rather, he attempted to reinterpret them for the truth of the kerygma – the proclamation of the gospel wherein sinful humanity encounters God's saving grace.

That revealed truth, Bultmann argued, correlated with Heidegger's existentialist analysis of the human situation – particularly Heidegger's emphasis on the historicity of human being and the quest for authentic existence by resolute and responsible life decisions (versus inauthentic existence in which the self is lost out of anxiety, care, and despair among a world of objects). Bultmann thought that existentialism provided the analogical hinge between modern humanity and the essential content of the NT, and was therefore the necessary "pre-understanding" (*Vorverständnis*) for interpreting the truth of the gospel.

So, for example, the NT depiction of the second coming of Christ and the end of this world ought not to be taken literally, but should impress upon us the truth that "today is the day of salvation," that our lives have an end which requires of us now a decision of ultimate significance – a resolve for authentic human existence. Such authenticity is found in the gospel of Christ, which mediates God's liberating judgment. A response in faith to the truth of Christ's death and resurrection (the latter of which is not to be taken literally, but represents the rise of faith in the disciples) enables us

---

[59] Bultmann, "New Testament and Mythology," in *Kerygma and Myth: A Theological Debate*, ed. Hans Werner Bartsch (New York: Harper & Brothers, 1961), 1–8.

to die to our inauthentic selves and to live a life of authentic obedience to God.[60]

In his theology, Bultmann did not want to root the gospel in the facticity of history, since he thought that the modern acids of criticism had eroded that historical foundation, as manifest in the failure of "the quest of the historical Jesus" documented by Schweitzer. Since, in Bultmann's view, faith cannot be rooted in objective historical truth (which would thereby serve as its own justification), it can only be received as a miracle of God through the proclamation of the "Christ of faith."

Bultmann's theology was quite controversial for its reduction of Christian theology to the anthropological categories of existentialism, and for its begging the issue of the historical Jesus. While his insights into the existential dimension of Christianity have largely been appreciated, his "no quest" of the historical Jesus eventually stimulated a "new quest" among his students, such as Ernst Käsemann, which would also bear fruit in the eschatological theologies of Wolfhart Pannenberg and Jürgen Moltmann (see pp. 555–60 below).

Reinhold Niebuhr

Reinhold Niebuhr (1892–1971) is the earliest significant representative of "neo-orthodoxy" in America, though he had his own criticisms of the Barthian and Bultmannian versions. Niebuhr was principally a social ethicist whose overall thought has been characterized as "Christian realism." As an American theologian, Niebuhr's concentration on social ethics reflects the pragmatism that is the unique stamp of the American intellectual tradition.

Raised in a pietistic yet socially liberal German-Reformed tradition, Niebuhr first served as pastor of a German Evangelical church in Detroit from 1915 to 1928. There Niebuhr actively engaged the political, social, economic, and racial conflicts and injustices that beset his working-class congregation within a booming car industry. This practical pastoral context led him to a critical stance toward industrial capitalism in favor of socialism and to a rejection of the naive optimism of his theological education in liberalism, even though he would retain distinct affinities with the social gospel movement. Niebuhr became professor of "applied Christianity" at New York's Union Theological Seminary in 1928, where he remained until his retirement in 1960.

---

[60] See, e.g., ibid., 38–43.

At the heart of Niebuhr's "Christian realism" is a recovery of the Augustinian-Reformed doctrine of sin. In contrast to liberalism's view of the basic goodness of humanity and human potential to achieve moral progress, even perfection, Niebuhr believed that the classic Christian conception of sin had proven itself over and over again to be an empirical reality in history. Only a frank acknowledgment of human sin, argues Niebuhr, makes for a realistic social ethic.

Niebuhr's mature thought is summed up in his magnum opus, *The Nature and Destiny of Man*, based on his Gifford Lectures of 1940. There he elaborates a theological anthropology that emphasizes human beings as created and finite, whose core identity is found in relation to God as *imago Dei* and not by virtue of their rational faculties. Principally through anxiety and insecurity, human beings fall into sin, either by way of sensuality (underestimating our stature as image-bearers of God) or pride (overestimating our stature as creatures of God).[61] Ethically speaking, while the individual person may aspire to the selfless *agape*-love of Jesus in relation to one's neighbor, this is not realistic for social groups in which human selfishness and will-to-power are compounded. The proper *social* ethic therefore is one of *justice*, which can only be proximate and imperfect in balancing out the freedoms and equality of persons, a justice that may even require on occasion the use of physical coercion. Accordingly, the kingdom of God in history, like Jesus' ethic of love of neighbor, remains an "impossible possibility."[62] These concerns led Niebuhr to emphasize the cross of Christ as the centerpiece of Christian revelation, which paradoxically reveals the divine judgment for sin *and* (in due recognition of the former) the divine love and forgiveness of sin.

As Niebuhr experienced the rise of totalitarianism, Nazism, WWII, and the ensuing Cold War, he came to argue strongly for democracy, and became an important ethical voice in post-WWII America and American policy. His political realism is well captured in his aphorism: "Man's capacity for justice makes democracy possible; but man's inclination to injustice makes democracy necessary."[63] While Niebuhr was "neo-orthodox" in his rejection of liberalism, he did not posit a radical analogical disjunction between God and humanity as did Barth, and he was critical of Bultmann's program of demythologization, since he held that central

---

[61] Niebuhr, *Nature and Destiny of Man*, I: 178–240.
[62] Reinhold Niebuhr, *An Interpretation of Christian Ethics* (New York: Seabury, 1979), 62–83.
[63] Reinhold Niebuhr, *The Children of Light and the Children of Darkness: A Vindication of Democracy and a Critique of its Traditional Defense* (New York: Charles Scribner's Sons, 1960), xiii.

Christian "myths," while not to be taken literally or scientifically, were
essential to Christian meaning even in a modern world.

Paul Tillich

Paul Tillich (1886–1965) was a very popular, highly acclaimed, and influential theologian at the height of his career in America. Born and raised in
Germany, Tillich emigrated to the United States in 1933 when, mostly on
account of his socialist writings, he was declared an enemy of the state by
the Nazis. Niebuhr helped Tillich secure a position at Union Theological
Seminary, where he spent most of his career. On the spectrum of neo-
orthodox theologians, Tillich is at the opposite end from Barth, while
showing clear affinities with Bultmann's approach.

Tillich is best known for his "method of correlation," which correlates
questions that arise in philosophy with answers that derive from theology.
In Tillich's own words: "Philosophy formulates the questions implied
in human existence and theology formulates the answers implied in divine
self-manifestation under the guidance of the questions implied in human
existence. This is a circle which drives man to a point where question and
answer are not separated."[64] What especially colors Tillich's theology is the
particular branch and type of philosophy he privileges for asking the
questions of theology – namely, ontology, understood as an analysis of
the structures of human being and existence. This "existentialist ontology,"
significantly influenced by twentieth-century existential philosophers such
as Heidegger and Sartre, asks the relevant contemporary questions – What
is being versus non-being? What is authentic human existence? – to which
Christian revelation supplies the answers. Tillich insisted that theology
must be "answering theology."[65] For Tillich, however, in order for those
answers to be relevant in their *material* content, they must be expressed
in the *form* of the philosophical question. So, for example, an analysis of
human existence unveils its finitude and the constant threat of non-being,
which raises the question of being itself as ever-enduring and beyond non-
being, which is the question of God. Theology then answers this philosophical inquiry. States Tillich: "God is the answer to the question implied
in human finitude. However, if the notion of God appears in systematic
theology in correlation with the threat of non-being which is implied in
existence, God must be called the infinite power of being which resists the

---

[64] Paul Tillich, *Systematic Theology*, 3 vols. (Chicago: University of Chicago, 1976), 1: 61.
[65] Ibid., 1: 59–66.

Table 19.2 *Timeline of theology in modernity*

History of theology		World history	
	1700		
		1715	Death of King Louis XIV of France
Beginnings of First Great Awakening	1730		
	1750		
Death of Jonathan Edwards	1758	1755	Lisbon Earthquake
		1763	Seven Years War ends
Schleiermacher's speeches *On Religion*	1799	1776	American Declaration of Independence
	1800		
Beginnings of Second Great Awakening	1830	1789	French Revolution begins
		1814	Congress of Vienna
		1821	Death of Napoleon
John Henry Newman converts to Catholicism	1845	1837	Victoria becomes Queen of Britain
	1850		
Promulgation of the Immaculate Conception of Mary	1854	1859	Darwin publishes *The Origin of Species*
Kierkegaard's *Attack on Christendom*	1854	1861	Beginning of American Civil War
First Vatican Council begins	1869	1889	Birth of Adolf Hitler
	1900		
World Missionary Conference in Edinburgh	1910	1914	Beginning of WWI
Barmen Declaration	1934	1933	Nazis come to power in Germany
Execution of Dietrich Bonhoeffer	1945	1945	End of WWII
		1947	Gandhi leads India to independence
	1950		
		1953	Death of Josef Stalin

threat of non-being. In classical theology this is being itself."[66] Hence Tillich's preference for "being-itself," "ground of being," or "power of being" as names for God instead of the personal biblical names, which Tillich regards as symbols that can be reinterpreted. Similarly, Jesus Christ is the "new being" sought for in answer to all the anxieties, guilt, and evil that are laid bare by existential analysis of the human condition. Such correlations logically and rigorously structure Tillich's systematic theology.

Of the so-called neo-orthodox theologians reviewed here, Tillich's theology is the most controversial, since it subordinated biblical and confessional

[66] Ibid., 1: 64.

terminology and conceptuality to the categories of his ontological analysis. Many critics have seen in Tillich's project a wholesale accommodation of confessional Christianity to a novel philosophical theology. Tillich himself was quite conscious that he was offering an alternative to classical (e.g., Thomistic), liberal (e.g., Ritschlian), and "neo-orthodox" (Barthian) approaches to theology. He offered his synthesis of philosophy and theology as an apologetic project, directed primarily to intellectuals in a modern secular culture "come of age." Tillich's basic apologetic concern nonetheless continues to predominate in contemporary theology.

FOR FURTHER READING

Allen, Diogenes and Eric O. Springsted, *Philosophy for Understanding Theology*, 2nd edn. (Louisville, KY: Westminster John Knox, 2007).

Barth, Karl, *Dogmatics in Outline*, trans. G. T. Thomson (New York: Harper & Row, 1959).

Bonhoeffer, Dietrich, *Discipleship*, trans. Martin Liske, Ilse Tödt, Barbara Green, and Reinhard Krauss, ed. Geffrey B. Kelly and John D. Godsey, Dietrich Bonhoeffer Works 4 (Minneapolis, MN: Fortress, 2003).

Grenz, Stanley J., and Roger E. Olson, *20th-Century Theology: God and the World in a Transitional Age* (Downers Grove, IL: InterVarsity, 1992).

Tillich, Paul, *The Courage to Be* (New Haven, CT: Yale University Press, 1952).

CHAPTER 20

Theology in the contemporary period
(c. 1960–present)

THEOLOGY IN THE TURBULENT 1960S

We begin our review of contemporary theology in the 1960s, the decade that witnessed the waning influence of neo-orthodoxy – due in large measure to the retirement or death of its leading theologians – and the rise of new theologies and theological emphases. Just as western society was in ferment, so also was theology. Still reeling from WWII, in which both Auschwitz and Hiroshima revealed the technological horrors of which modern industrial states were capable, the contemporary world would continue to live under the Damocles' sword of nuclear holocaust in the frigid tensions of the Cold War.

The 1960s were a decade of turbulence, manifesting aspirations for a new society (in the United States: John F. Kennedy's social Camelot, Lyndon B. Johnson's "great society"), the civil rights and peace movements, racial riots and student rebellions in protest of social injustice and an intensifying Vietnam war, and a growing consciousness of ecological degradation – conditions, among others, that would stimulate new and even more radical initiatives in Christian theology.

It is tempting to entitle this chapter "Theology in the postmodern period," since the sixties are as good a candidate as any for marking the dawn of postmodernity. As a time referent – the emergent period *after* modernity – we have little objection to equating this contemporary era with postmodernity. But since the postmodern label was consciously applied to this period only later, and since "postmodern" can carry weighty philosophical baggage that does not, more narrowly, characterize all the theological movements of the contemporary era, we will reserve our description of postmodernity until later in this chapter. What we can say in anticipation and in general at this juncture about the various theologies of the contemporary world is that they are more sensitive to historical, relational, contextual, linguistic, and global concerns than those of their modern counterparts – concerns, we will see, that generally reflect the postmodern mood.

Death-of-God and secular theologies

The radical nature of the 1960s is especially reflected in the "death-of-God" theology. Harking back to Nietzsche's parable of the madman, whose proclamation of the death of God was a prescient description of the course of western secularization that appeared to make God obsolete (see pp. 95–6 above), the death-of-God theologians attempted to address the radical secularization of modern life. In this venture they (quite unjustly) rallied to their cause Dietrich Bonhoeffer, whose prison letters had somewhat cryptically called for a "religionless Christianity," affirmed the "profound this-worldliness" of Christianity, and reflected on living "without God" in a "world come of age" (see p. 536 above).[1] William Hamilton and Thomas J. J. Altizer were the principal proponents of the death-of-God theology, whose jointly authored book, *Radical Theology and the Death of God* (1966), represents the high-water mark of the movement.[2]

---

[1] Bonhoeffer, *Letters and Papers*, 278–82, 369–70, 325–9.
[2] Thomas J. J. Altizer and William Hamilton, *Radical Theology and The Death of God* (Indianapolis, IN: Bobbs-Merrill, 1966).

Convinced by the critique of Nietzsche and other nineteenth-century atheists that classical Christian theism was not only obsolete, but also incompatible with human freedom and dignity, they attempted to relieve Christian belief of its outmoded supernaturalism. In this seemingly short-lived movement, largely sensationalized by the media (e.g., *Time* magazine), Altizer's proposal in *The Gospel of Christian Atheism* (1966)[3] proved to be the most radical and full of theological ingenuity. Drawing deeply from Hegel, Tillich, and William Blake, Altizer proposed an extreme kenotic *theology* – that in the incarnation and death of Christ, God (conceived of unitarianly) had not only vacated a position of divine transcendence but had actually died to the divine identity, "emptying" the divine self completely into history and humanity. This was the ultimate sacrifice on God's part so that human beings, now liberated from an inhibiting divine patriarchy, could live free lives of moral responsibility, for which Jesus Christ (shorn of the resurrection) becomes the model of love of neighbor.

While not as radical or atheistic, a wave of "secular theologies" accompanied the death-of-God movement in an attempt to mediate Christian faith to a "world come of age." Such a theological venture can be seen in Paul Van Buren's *The Secular Meaning of the Gospel* (1963)[4] or in John A. T. Robinson's *Honest to God* (1963).[5] The latter was a most popular book that purported to satisfy Bonhoeffer's "non-religious" prison agenda. Drawing heavily from Bultmann's program of demythologization and Tillich's non-supernatural philosophical theology, Robinson proposed that God is found in the depth experiences of human love and freedom. To be a Christian therefore is (borrowing Bonhoeffer's words) to be a "man for others" – caught up in the basic human responsibilities of life in this world – a perspective, proposes Robinson, that overcomes any stultifying preoccupation with otherworldly transcendence or fracturing dichotomy of sacred (eternal) and secular (temporal).

Another popular book at this time promoting secular theology was Harvey Cox's *The Secular City* (1965).[6] In a similar vein, Cox viewed the process of secularization not as antithetical to Christian faith, but as actually generated by the dynamics of biblical faith in history and therefore a liberating development toward human maturity, a liberation that is analogous to the exodus. Since God is the Lord of history, Cox argued, the

[3] Thomas J. J. Altizer, *The Gospel of Christian Atheism* (Philadelphia: Westminster, 1966).
[4] Paul M. Van Buren, *The Secular Meaning of the Gospel* (New York: Macmillan, 1963).
[5] John A. T. Robinson, *Honest to God* (Philadelphia: Westminster, 1963).
[6] Harvey Cox, *The Secular City* (New York: Macmillan, 1965).

church must step outside of its sacred confines in order to discern and participate in the ways that God is working in the world at large, such as in movements of equality and social change (e.g., civil rights). For this new perspective Cox proposed the image of the "secular city" as embodying the goals of the kingdom of God, which include human maturation and social responsibility. While Cox was severely critical of the death-of-God theologians, he nonetheless concluded his book by wondering whether a new name for "God" might not be needed to capture the new reality of Christian life in the secular city.

While the death-of-God and secular theologies of the 1960s were rather short-lived "pop" theologies, they aptly reflect the radical and revolutionary spirit of that decade. Their basic concerns, however, would linger and gestate in subsequent theology.

Process theology

Process theology also came into its own in the 1960s, though, unlike the previous two theologies, it became an enduring school of thought, chiefly in academic circles. Bearing a formal resemblance to the thought of Pierre Teilhard de Chardin (1881–1955), the Jesuit priest who proposed a unique synthesis of Christian theology and evolutionary thought (see p. 549), process theology is directly rooted in the metaphysics of the British mathematician-philosopher Alfred North Whitehead (1861–1947). In order to keep in step with scientific discovery, especially that of evolutionary thought and Einstein's physics of relativity, Whitehead proposed a new metaphysics – a general description of the universal principles required to explain the particulars of experience in a dynamic world as scientifically understood.[7] Unlike the older metaphysical systems that attempted to stake down the true reality of *Being*, relegating *becoming* to a non-essential and inferior status, Whitehead's metaphysic attempts to account for reality as a dynamic and ever-changing process. As a novel proposal (although reminiscent of the ancient Greek philosopher Heraclitus), Whitehead's philosophy has its own distinctive language and conceptuality.

Since Whitehead understood that every cosmology implies a theology, he sketched out the basic contours of the God–world relation within his system.[8] With some modifications to Whitehead's thought, Charles Hartshorne (1897–2000) was one of the first to elaborate its implications

---

[7] Alfred North Whitehead, *Process and Reality: An Essay in Cosmology* (New York: Macmillan, 1929).
[8] See Whitehead, "God and the world," in ibid., 512ff.

for Christian theology, which crystallized into a movement in the 1960s, winning a number of notable disciples, including John Cobb Jr. and David Ray Griffin.[9]

Process theology is unabashedly a philosophical or natural theology, since its conception of God functions as the chief exemplification of the basic process metaphysic. Process theologians are severely critical of the classical theistic conception of God as adorned with attributes that logically render God statically transcendent and impassively aloof from the world, as well as directly determinative of all the world's operations with nary a reciprocal relation with creatures. Rather than this omnipotent, all-controlling, and efficient cause (and therefore coercive power) of the world, process theologians emphasize God as the universal source of order and value in the world, who by persuasive power lovingly lures all things toward the realization of their potential.

God therefore is radically immanent in the world in process theology, intrinsically related to every "actual occasion," changing and suffering with the world while luring it on to greater creativity and value. In this panentheistic (i.e., everything-in-God) conception of the God–world relation, God does not *really* transcend the world, but does so only logically or abstractly by embodying the principles and possibilities of the world process. Process panentheism openly rejects the doctrine of creation "out of nothing" in favor of "creation out of chaos."[10] This means that in process thought, God cannot be conceived of apart from the world, as in an immanent Trinity, since God is in actuality the intrinsic principle of the world's workings.

Similarly, Jesus Christ exemplifies the process metaphysic. Rejecting the classical doctrine of the "two natures" and therefore the personal preexistence of Christ, process theology tends to view Jesus as the thoroughly human one who manifests in an exemplary way the "creative transformation" that can take place in faithful response to the call of God. Accordingly, process theology in general has little use for the confession of the Trinity, except perhaps in regarding the persons as symbolic labels for different principles or moments of the process metaphysic. But process theology as a whole is constrained not by traditional theological formulations but by issues of contemporary relevance, for which Whitehead's philosophy is a key and controlling factor.

[9] See John B. Cobb and David Ray Griffin, *Process Theology: An Introductory Exposition* (Philadelphia: Westminster, 1976), for a helpful introduction to process theology.
[10] Ibid., 65.

Process theology bears a kinship with the radical theologies in the attempt to make the Christian faith relevant to a scientific "world come of age," and in disdaining any separation between the sacred and the secular. It is also a rather radical theology from an orthodox point of view, dismissing many traditional confessional constants in the name of a public – philosophical or natural – theology.

CATHOLIC THEOLOGY AND VATICAN II

During the transitional 1960s, the ferment and clamor for change that were spreading throughout the western world were also felt in Catholic theology. The pioneering event that brought ground-breaking change into the Catholic Church was the Second Vatican Council, held from 1962 to 1965, which officially reversed the church's antithetical stance toward modernity. As discussed in the previous chapter, the official mindset of the nineteenth-century Catholic Church, as codified by the First Vatican Council, was strongly opposed to the winds of change that were sweeping across Europe in the wake of the Enlightenment. The changed mentality that found its zenith at Vatican II was the result of a long period of theological renewal that stretches back to the first half of the twentieth century, when many Catholic theologians began to develop visions of church doctrine that addressed the challenges of modernity.

Twentieth-century Catholic theological reform

The most significant changes in the trends in Catholic theology orbit around a movement known to many of its proponents as *ressourcement*, a "return to the sources" of Christian doctrine in scripture and the foundational theology of the early church. To its opponents, however, this movement was pejoratively regarded as an intrepid *nouvelle théologie*, a "new theology" that diverged dangerously from the well-trodden paths of the church's tradition. The theologians of this movement worked against what they perceived as the overly traditionalist forms of Catholic theology that were ossified in the Thomistic scholasticism that had been declared official Catholic teaching in the nineteenth century. Some *ressourcement* theologians, such as Jacques Maritain and Étienne Gilson, returned to the theological corpus of Thomas Aquinas with fresh eyes, often emphasizing the congruence of his work with scripture and patristic theology, or by focusing on the intersections between Thomism and the offerings of modern philosophical movements, such as existentialism.[11] Others, such as Henri de Lubac and Hans Urs von Balthasar, focused on reappropriating the theological resources of the early church and the broader medieval era in a creative way.

Still other theologians focused their attention on the intersection between traditional Catholic dogmas, modern philosophical insights, and the advances of modern science. One of the most controversial examples of a Catholic dialogue with modern science was the attempt of Pierre Teilhard de Chardin (1881–1955) to synthesize Catholic doctrine with evolutionary theory. Teilhard viewed God as radically immanent in (if not the veritable deep structure of) the complexity and immensity of nature. He portrayed the incarnation of Christ and the continuing work of Christ's body, the church, as a decisive impulse in the evolution of humanity (as the apex of all nature) toward what he called the "Omega point,"[12] resulting in the interpenetration of Creator and created in each other.[13] As noted above, Teilhard's theories bore much affinity with the Whitehead-inspired efforts of process theology.

The pioneering efforts of Karl Rahner (1904–84) represent one of the most prominent instances of progressive Catholic theology's attempt to construct a dialogue between traditional dogma and modern sensibilities. Rahner's work was an especially important impulse in paving the way for Vatican II, at which he served as an influential theological advisor. Rahner attempted to use modern philosophies (such as idealism and existentialism) and scientific perspectives as frames for his accounts of Christian dogma. In general, Rahner adopted what he called (employing Kantian conceptuality) a "transcendental" approach to theology, where he tried to show the anthropological conditions by which it was possible for Christian doctrine to find a home in the modern ethos. That is, he draws upon the basic elements that appear constitutive of being human as profound points of contact for Christian claims, claims which in turn can be shown to fulfill humanity's deepest longings. Thus one of the very first questions he takes up in his *Foundations of Christian Faith* is: "What kind of hearer does Christianity anticipate so that its real and ultimate message can even be heard?"[14] For Rahner, humanity is

---

[11] E.g., Étienne Gilson, *Thomism: The Philosophy of Thomas Aquinas*, trans. Armand A. Maurer and Laurence K. Shook (Toronto: Pontifical Institute of Mediaeval Studies, 2002). This book was first published in 1919 and went through five subsequent editions.

[12] Pierre Teilhard de Chardin, *The Phenomenon of Man*, trans. Bernard Wall, rev. edn. (New York: Harper & Row, 1965), 254–72.

[13] E.g., Pierre Teilhard de Chardin, *The Divine Milieu* (New York: Harper & Row, 1960), 46–7, 122.

[14] Karl Rahner, *Foundations of Christian Faith: An Introduction to the Idea of Christianity*, trans. William V. Dych (New York: Crossroad, 1978), 24. This work is Rahner's major summary of the themes of his theological project.

oriented toward spiritual self-transcendence and is therefore by nature capable of hearing and receiving divine revelation, which in turn fulfills the very being of humanity.[15] Accordingly, Rahner roots his account of Christian teaching in an existentialist anthropology, seeing Christianity's offer of "salvation" as something that human beings can intelligently grasp because the theological question of salvation is in fact implied by the existential questions and aspirations present in human life.[16]

Rahner utilizes this transcendental approach in other areas of theology, such as christology. Humanity's intrinsic longing for an "Absolute Savior" is the precondition for the intelligibility of orthodox christology, which Christianity presents as a description of the true historical Savior who fulfills humanity's basic hope.[17] Rahner also employs this transcendental christology in a way that is similar to the efforts of Teilhard de Chardin, to show the "intrinsic affinity and the possibility of a reciprocal correlation" between the Christian dogma of the incarnation and a contemporary evolutionary understanding of the world.[18] Rahner argues that in view of the evolutionary progression in the world from mere matter to the self-transcendence of spirit, as seen especially in human knowledge of God, it is possible to interpret the incarnational union between God and humanity – the preeminent act of divine grace – as bringing with it the fulfillment of the natural evolutionary process.[19] While the particulars of Rahner's theology did not always meet with widespread agreement, his broader goal of relating the theology of the church to the modern ethos in a dynamic way became one of the defining features of the Second Vatican Council.

This goal of theological renewal served as the intellectual counterpart to another theme that was commonly stressed by progressive Catholic theologians of this era – namely, the practical need for renewal in the life and structures of the church. In his ecclesiological work, for example, Yves Congar attempted to mitigate the hierarchical flavor of Catholicism by emphasizing the communitarian character of the church and the evangelical significance of the laity.[20] This goal of ecclesial renewal became a predominant theme for the council.

[15] Rahner, *Hearer of the Word: Laying the Foundation for a Philosophy of Religion*, trans. Joseph Donceel (New York: Continuum, 1994), 45–54.
[16] Rahner, *Foundations*, 39–41.   [17] Ibid., 228–9.   [18] Ibid., 179.   [19] Ibid., 199–201.
[20] E.g., Yves Congar, *Lay People in the Church: A Study for a Theology of the Laity* (Westminster, MD: Newman, 1957). After the council, this was also emphasized by Küng, *The Church*, 370–87.

The Second Vatican Council

With these theological developments as backdrop and stimulus, Pope John XXIII announced a Second Vatican Council in 1959, although its meetings did not begin until the fall of 1962. John himself died during one of the council's early adjournments, so leadership of the proceedings was taken over by his successor, Paul VI, in 1963. While there were some efforts on the part of the Roman hierarchy to ensure a relatively conservative tone of the council and its resulting documents, a more progressive theological and ecclesiological spirit eventually dominated.

In many ways, the final document produced by the council, *Gaudium et spes* ("Pastoral Constitution on the Church in the Modern World"), best exemplifies the theological spirit of the council. It begins by emphasizing the common struggles and hopes that Christians share with all human beings: "Nothing that is genuinely human fails to find an echo in their hearts."[21] The document then examines the changing cultures, problems, and aspirations of the modern world in relation to the church's claim that Christ bears the meaning of and salvific hope for all history. For example, in taking up the issue of modern atheism, *Gaudium et spes* criticizes such disbelief as an attempt to show that "man is an end to himself."[22] But it also allows room for the church and its members to dialogue and cooperate with atheists in the broader human quest for order and justice.[23] The document takes this critically appreciative approach in its examination of a variety of issues confronting the modern human race, including cultural trends, market economics, politics, war, and nuclear weapons.

This transformed understanding of the relationship between the Catholic Church and the modern world also prompted the council's endorsement of the use by Catholic biblical and theological scholars of the "modern methods" of historical and theological study that had been viewed with such distrust by Vatican I.[24] In response to the traditional concentration on the church's hierarchy and ordained "religious," the council gave a pronounced emphasis to the missional role of the laity, both within the structure of the church and in the transformation of the broader society: "It is the Lord himself, by this Council, who is once more inviting all the laity to unite themselves to him ever more intimately, to consider his interests as their own, and to join in his mission as Saviour. It is the Lord who is again sending

---

[21] Vatican II, *Gaudium et spes*, in Austin Flannery, ed., *Vatican Council II, 1: The Conciliar and Post-Conciliar Documents*, rev. edn. (Northport, NY: Costello, 1996), 1. All references to Vatican II documents will be taken from this volume, with citations given by paragraph number in the document.
[22] Ibid., 19.   [23] Ibid., 21.   [24] *Gravissimum educationis*, 11.

them into every town and every place where he himself is to come."[25] While the council did not deny the hierarchical nature of the church, it sought to soften the intensity of its top-down structure by emphasizing the religious significance of the secular work of the laity.[26] In an attempt to make the theology and mission of the church more accessible and meaningful to its rank-and-file members, the council also sanctioned a simplification of the rites of the Mass, as well as the use of vernacular languages in the Mass.[27]

By any measure, Vatican II was a watershed event in the life and theology of the Catholic Church, one that also exerted significant influence in the realm of Protestant theology and church life. While the council certainly achieved much in the way of bringing the church "up to date" (*aggiornamento* – one of the key phrases of its proceedings), the longer-term implications of its decisions were a matter of considerable debate among Catholic theologians afterwards. One group, exemplified by von Balthasar and Joseph Ratzinger, attempted to stay carefully within the spirit and intent of the council, emphasizing its continuity with more traditional Catholic teaching; other theologians, such as Rahner and Hans Küng, wanted to pursue what they regarded as the progressive vectors of the council, advocating further theological and ecclesial reform. These two groups eventually founded rival theological journals – in the case of the more progressive wing, the journal *Concilium*, and in the case of the more conservative group, the journal *Communio*. These journals became important vehicles for the development of these diverging visions of the future after Vatican II. The emergence of Latin American liberation theology in the early 1970s (see pp. 561–2) is a key example of the more progressive reading of Vatican II. The lengthy papacy of John Paul II (1978–2005) was an especially influential instance of the more conservative interpretation of the council, as visible in the Vatican's skeptical reception of liberation theology during the 1980s and '90s. Since Cardinal Joseph Ratzinger was one of the primary agents of the conservatism of John Paul's papacy, it is not surprising that his own papacy as Benedict XVI (beginning in 2005) is continuing in a rather traditional direction.

EASTERN ORTHODOX THEOLOGY

Eastern Orthodoxy theology, though traditionally resistant to change, has more recently entertained modifications of its centuries-old traditions. In view of the recent trinitarian renaissance in western theology, which has gravitated to more Cappadocian-inspired models of the Trinity, Orthodox

---

[25] *Apostolicam actuositatem*, 33. [26] *Lumen Gentium*, 18–38. [27] *Sacrosanctum concilium*, 34–6.

churches have been open to initiatives directed toward the healing of the East–West split in Christendom that was formalized in 1054, due in large measure to the controversial *filioque* clause (see pp. 295–6, 302–3, 456–8 above). For example, in 1965 Pope Paul VI of the Roman Catholic Church and Patriarch Athenagoras I of the Orthodox Church mutually retracted their churches' nearly millennium-old condemnations of each other.

The neo-patristic school of Florovsky and Lossky (see pp. 526–7 above) has given birth to a second generation of Orthodox theologians. Of these, John Zizioulas (1931–) is perhaps the most significant. Now titular metropolitan bishop of Pergamon, Zizioulas has developed a more personalist understanding of deification and ecclesial being, toning down Lossky's more apophatic mystical approach.[28] Given the revelation of the trinitarian God, Zizioulas argues, the Cappadocians effected a revolution in ontology, redefining "Being" from meaning an impersonal and abstract "nature" to meaning *communion* – as ultimately grounded in the communion of the trinitarian persons.[29] Deification, therefore, the key event of salvation as mediated by the Eucharist, the liturgical center of Orthodox theology, is a participation in the divine nature (2 Pet. 1:4) in an eminently *personal* way – as our union with the person of Christ brings us into the interpersonal trinitarian life. Moreover, human beings truly become persons only in union with Christ, which means in the church. Personhood therefore is "ecclesial being," and is supremely characterized, like the trinitarian members themselves, by *ecstasis* – living outside oneself for others.[30] Zizioulas's formulation calls into question the central Palamite essence/energies distinction in Orthodoxy, since the persons of the Trinity belong to the divine *essence*, that which was previously considered in principle unknowable, whose being *is* the communion in which the church knowingly participates. Zizioulas's project is controversial within Orthodoxy, however, since it draws from insights of twentieth-century personalist philosophy, which construes personhood in a way that some regard as inconsistent with the patristic understanding of divine personhood as *hypostasis*.

Currently, Orthodox theology is becoming more socially conscious than has traditionally been the case.[31] A reconsideration of Bulgakov's trinitarian sophiology is also leading some Orthodox theologians to broader points of

---

[28] For a detailed comparison of Lossky and Zizioulas, see Aristotle Papanikolaou, *Being with God: Trinity, Apophaticism, and Divine–Human Communion* (Notre Dame, IN: University of Notre Dame Press, 2006).

[29] John Zizioulas, *Being as Communion: Studies in Personhood and the Church* (Crestwood, NY: St. Vladimir's Seminary Press, 1985), 15–49.

[30] Ibid., 49–65.   [31] See Papanikolaou, "Orthodox Theology," 418.

contact with culture and other disciplines of inquiry. Such trends promise even greater ecumenical dialogue and cooperation with western churches in further reconciliation and healing of the East–West schism in witness to the catholicity of the one church of Christ.

HISTORY AND ESCHATOLOGY IN PROTESTANT THEOLOGY

While the 1960s were a time of renewal and change in Catholic theology, above all through the significance of Vatican II, it was also a time of creative theological development in Protestant circles. We have already seen some of the Protestant theological efforts of the period in the death-of-God, secular, and process theologies in the United States and England. But many other Protestant theologians – in parallel to the efforts of their Catholic counterparts – also strove to keep theological rhythm with a changing world, albeit in a more orthodox key. In general, these efforts were decisively informed by the theological revolution wrought by the work of Karl Barth (see pp. 529–33). Barth challenged the Christian world to let God's voice of revelation speak through scripture, rather than relying primarily on the voice of human religious experience. His consistent christocentrism, thoroughgoing use of a trinitarian grammar, and the subtle contextuality of his theology *vis-à-vis* his era's political realities all influenced a new post-Barthian generation of European Protestant theologians who attempted to take Barth's revolution forward while remedying what they took to be its shortcomings.

One theologian who stayed rather close to the Barthian line is Eberhard Jüngel (1933–), one of Barth's most acclaimed students. In addition to his own Lutheran emphasis on justification, Jüngel's work draws heavily upon Barth's account of how speech about God can take place through the revelatory act of the triune God, in addressing the intersection between the metaphysics of Christian doctrine and the hermeneutical challenges of interpreting that doctrine for today's world.[32] Jüngel develops a trinitarian view of God over against classical theism and modern atheism in order to argue that, through the revelatory story of God's identification with humanity in the incarnation and the justification of sinners through Christ's cross,

---

[32] Eberhard Jüngel, *Justification: The Heart of the Christian Faith: A Theological Study with an Ecumenical Purpose*, trans. Jeffrey F. Cayzer (Edinburgh: T. & T. Clark, 2001); and Jüngel, *God's Being is in Becoming: The Trinitarian Being of God in the Theology of Karl Barth; A Paraphrase*, trans. John Webster (Grand Rapids, MI: Eerdmans, 2001).

the "unspeakable" God has been rendered knowable.[33] While Jüngel's theology has exerted much influence in the German-speaking world, his significance is rising among English-speaking theologians, due in large part to the translation and expository efforts of John Webster.[34]

Other theologians took the insights and impulses of Barth's theology in quite innovative directions, avenues of which Barth did not entirely approve. These proposals were, of course, varied and diverse, but a significant number of them focused on the related issues of the *historical* character of God's revelatory and saving action, and the *eschatological* nature of salvation history. Along these lines, we shall focus our attention on two theologians of Jüngel's stature whose influence has been more international and wide-ranging – Wolfhart Pannenberg (1928–) and Jürgen Moltmann (1926–).

Wolfhart Pannenberg

As one whose conversion to Christianity was largely intellectual in impulse, Pannenberg's theological project has concentrated on the question of *truth*. In his view, the only sufficient reason for being a Christian is that the gospel is indeed true and the God of that gospel is the true God.[35] Christian theology therefore has the responsibility to *demonstrate* the truth of the beliefs of Christian faith.[36] While this approach may seem straightforward at first glance, it becomes a subtle and complex matter when one recognizes that Pannenberg regards "truth" as a matter of the coherence of all reality. Therefore theology, in an interdisciplinary way, must take account of the "nontheological knowledge of humanity, the world, and history, and especially of what the statements of philosophy that deal with the question of reality have to say about these themes." Pannenberg desires to bring all these into dialogue with Christian claims that flow from God's revelation in Christ, in order to show "the universal coherence and therefore the truth of Christian doctrine."[37] Accordingly, Pannenberg's theological works include significant dialogues with the disciplines of natural science, cultural anthropology, and

---

[33] Eberhard Jüngel, *God as the Mystery of the World: On the Foundation of the Crucified in the Dispute between Theism and Atheism*, trans. Darrell L. Guder (Grand Rapids, MI: Eerdmans, 1983), *passim*, e.g., 231; on the narrative dynamics of theological hermeneutics, see 299–314.

[34] John B. Webster, *Eberhard Jüngel: An Introduction to His Theology* (Cambridge: Cambridge University Press, 1986).

[35] Wolfhart Pannenberg, *An Introduction to Systematic Theology* (Grand Rapids, MI: Eerdmans, 1991), 4–5.

[36] Wolfhart Pannenberg, *Systematic Theology*, trans. Geoffrey W. Bromiley, 3 vols. (Grand Rapids, MI: Eerdmans, 1991–1998), 1: 48–61.

[37] Ibid., 1: 49.

critical history. He devotes much attention to the philosophical portrayal of God (i.e., natural theology), which functions as a critical norm for the truth of Christian theology, but which also requires theological correction in light of God's decisive revelation in Christ.[38] Thus Pannenberg follows the general intent of Barth (under whom he studied for a time) to let revelation guide theology, but refuses to divorce divine revelation from "natural" knowledge of God. He strives instead to plot the relationship between the two, integrating both natural and scriptural sources of knowledge of God.

Most prominently, it is the issue of *history* that penetrates the whole of Pannenberg's theological corpus. Pannenberg takes great pains to show that divine revelation, as presented by scripture, comes through the medium of history, given that Christianity claims to root itself in specific historical events – above all, the cross and resurrection.[39] For this reason, the theological task of demonstrating the truth of Christian faith must take seriously the issue of historicity: "The statement that Jesus was crucified under Pontius Pilate is a historical statement the truth of which we have to judge by ordinary historical standards."[40] But more broadly, the scope of universal history is the arena in which the question of God must ultimately be decided, and it is therefore the arena in which Christian theology must do its work of arguing for the truth of Christian faith: "As the revelation of God in his historical action moves towards the still outstanding future of the consummation of history, its claim to reveal the one God who is the world's Creator, Reconciler, and Redeemer is open to future verification in history, which is as yet incomplete, and which is still exposed, therefore, to the question of its truth."[41] In other words, the verification of Christian truth is eschatologically pending.

Pannenberg's concern for history gives shape to his particular approach to christology. He refuses to adopt a christology "from above" – that is, a traditional approach that presupposes the preexistence of Christ and then proceeds to examine how it could be the case that a member of the Trinity could descend into our reality so as to become human. Rather, Pannenberg advocates a christology "from below" – that is, one that looks through accepted historical methods at the man Jesus and "inquire[s] about how Jesus' appearance in history led to the recognition of his divinity."[42] To start "from above," Pannenberg claims, "is to leap past the justifiable demand that all christological statements about Jesus Christ must be vindicated in

[38] Ibid., 1: 73–118. Cf. Pannenberg, *Metaphysics and the Idea of God*, trans. Philip Clayton (Grand Rapids, MI: Eerdmans, 1990).

[39] Pannenberg, *Systematic Theology*, 1: 230–57.   [40] Ibid., 1: 56.   [41] Ibid., 1: 257.

[42] Wolfhart Pannenberg, *Jesus – God and Man*, trans. Lewis L. Wilkins and Duane A. Priebe (Philadelphia: Westminster, 1968), 34.

terms of his historical reality and an exposition of it."[43] That is to say, the traditional approach begs the question of truth. By contrast, Pannenberg's approach "from below" strives to look first at the historical particularity of Jesus in order to see how God's reality intersects with the world in Jesus himself. This means giving significant attention to the resurrection as the key historical event in the NT's portrayal of Jesus' divinity. In doing so, Pannenberg devotes much attention to the question of the historicity of the resurrection, appealing to historiographical grounds for its facticity.[44] Pannenberg then argues theologically that the historical event of the resurrection itself must be seen as *constitutive* for the very deity and preexistence of Jesus. In his novel view, the validation and confirmation of Jesus' radically human life by God's eschatological act of resurrection has "retroactive force," such that the *historical* event of the resurrection itself makes it the case that Jesus has *eternally* been the Son of God.[45] It is through this sense of retro-activity, taken ontologically, that Pannenberg thinks his christology from below preserves the incarnational truth of the traditional christology from above – that Jesus is eternally existent as the second person of the Trinity. Pannenberg's "retroactive ontology" has engendered much debate among critics, who generally find it a perplexing and inscrutable claim.

The fabric of Pannenberg's christology – as both historically and eschatologically oriented – is essentially the fabric of his broader theological enterprise. Revelation in its irreducibly historical nature is also irreducibly eschatological, for it looks forward to the conclusion of history. Because God's revelation is rooted in history, it must of necessity be confirmed in history – that is, eschatologically. In short, the truth of Christianity is at stake in history, and only the future eschatological action of God will definitively decide whether Christian belief is true.[46] Since Christian theology's claims have as their eschatological "premise" the actual coming of God's kingdom, that event, more than the efforts of theologians, will demonstrate the truth of Christian theology.[47]

Jürgen Moltmann

While Pannenberg is often classified as a "theologian of hope" due to his eschatological orientation, it was Jürgen Moltmann's *Theology of Hope*

---

[43] Pannenberg, *Systematic Theology*, II: 281.   [44] Ibid., II: 346–63.
[45] Pannenberg, *Jesus – God and Man*, 135–41. Pannenberg has softened this point in his later work. See, e.g., *Systematic Theology*, I: 331, II: 345–6, 364–6.
[46] Pannenberg, *Systematic Theology*, I: 330–2.   [47] Ibid., III: 531.

(1964) that catapulted him to theological prominence and won him that title early in his career. Moltmann's theology bears the stamp of his experience in WWII and in a British prisoner-of-war camp, when, in despair over the destruction and death perpetrated by his German nation, Moltmann discovered in the Bible the God who in Christ suffered with him and who rose from the dead to new life. It is this basic gospel dialectic of cross and resurrection that forms the dynamic of Moltmann's theology of hope.

Moltmann was one of the first systematic theologians to take up the rediscovery by twentieth-century biblical scholars of the thoroughly eschatological nature of the NT and to think through its implications for the range of Christian doctrines. *Theology of Hope* revitalizes biblical eschatology as a doctrine of Christian hope for this world and as a way of orienting all theology. In Moltmann's words, rather than eschatology being merely an appendix of Christian theology concerned only with "last things,"

from first to last, and not merely in the epilogue, Christianity is eschatology, is hope, forward looking and forward moving, and therefore also revolutionizing and transforming the present. The eschatological is not one element of Christianity, but it is the medium of Christian faith as such, the key in which everything in it is set, the glow that suffuses everything here in the dawn of an expected new day.[48]

In Moltmann's eschatology the cross and resurrection are key: just as Christ's resurrection to life contradicts the powers that led to his death on the cross, so also the new creation inaugurated by his resurrection stands in contradiction to the present powers of sin and death in the world, promising hope for the renewal of all things in the coming kingdom of God and pressing for renewal in the present. In this eschatological orientation Moltmann found a new direction for theology "after Barth," whom he once thought had "said everything and said it so well."[49]

In his second major work, the influential *The Crucified God* (1973), Moltmann deepened his reflections on the cross in the tradition of Luther's *theologia crucis*. The cross, he asserts, must become the critical criterion of all Christian theology, standing in judgment of triumphalistic versions of Christianity and conceptions of God that justify authoritarian relations of power and unjust societies – a political dimension of theology to which Moltmann is ever sensitive, given his experience of Nazi Germany. In opposing as unbiblical the traditional conception that God is immutable and cannot suffer (the apathy axiom), Moltmann understands the cross as a

---

[48] Moltmann, *Theology of Hope*, 16.
[49] Jürgen Moltmann, *A Broad Place: An Autobiography*, trans. Margaret Kohl (Minneapolis, MN: Fortress, 2007), 47.

trinitarian event between Father, Son, and Spirit that reveals the God who is passionate love, who is vulnerably affected by and voluntarily suffers for creatures. By advocating the trinitarian God of pathos, Moltmann addresses the objections of modern atheists who protest that belief in God, classically conceived, is incompatible with both human freedom and the rampant evil in the world. It is the theodicy issue that especially weighs on Moltmann here, who sees in the crucified Christ God's identification with both the godforsaken (victims) and the godless (perpetrators), a perspective that makes Christian theology possible "after Auschwitz." In this vein, Moltmann has been keen to engage in Jewish–Christian dialogue and to tap neglected Jewish sources for Christian theology.

The Church in the Power of the Spirit (1975) completes what has been called Moltmann's early trilogy, wherein he surveys the whole of theology through a particular lens – first the resurrection of Easter Sunday, second the cross of Good Friday, and, in this third major work, the outpouring of the Spirit on Pentecost. Moltmann here elaborates the church's active involvement in the world, broadly and secularly conceived, as a participation in the Spirit's mission to transform the world in anticipation of God's promised future – a "messianic ecclesiology." The particular political accents of this trilogy have led Moltmann to be regarded as a key proponent of political theology.

After this trilogy, Moltmann embarked on more systematic "contributions" to theology. In the first of these, *The Trinity and the Kingdom* (1980), he argues against "mere monotheism" in favor of a social conception of the Trinity – three distinct divine persons who are united in perichoretic purpose, fellowship, and love. The interactive relationships between Father, Son, and Spirit depict the "trinitarian history" of God that is at the same time the history of the kingdom of God in the world, since it is God's goal to take up all of creation into the trinitarian life "so that God may be all in all" (1 Cor. 15:28). Moltmann's subsequent theology has been rigorously trinitarian, though many critics see in his model the specter of tritheism.

In his second systematic installment, *God in Creation* (1985), Moltmann develops a trinitarian understanding of creation, especially in view of the ecological crisis. Fearing that traditional theistic models of creation emphasize divine transcendence to the loss of divine immanence, Moltmann keys on the Spirit's immanent presence in creation through which God is in all things and all things are in God. Moltmann thus advocates a panentheistic view of God and creation, but unlike process theology does not deny creation out of nothing or the Trinity's transcendent existence apart from the world. Given his view of the dynamic trinitarian history with the world, Moltmann advocates a compatibility between creation and evolution, whereby creation in the beginning (*creatio ex nihilo*) continues via evolutionary processes (*creatio continua*) but will not be complete until the divine fulfillment of the new creation (*creatio nova*).

In *The Way of Jesus Christ* (1990) Moltmann develops a "Spirit christology," but not in the adoptionistic vein that is usually associated with the term.[50] Without denying the deity and preexistence of Christ (as affirmed by his trinitarianism), Moltmann concentrates on a largely neglected feature of christology – the messianic character of the human life of Jesus, who, as the Messiah, is the one who lives by the power and energies of the Spirit. The way of Christ's life in dependence upon the Father in the power of the Spirit then becomes the way of Christian discipleship in the world.

Moltmann continued his systematic series with a holistic pneumatology, a formal eschatology, and reflections on theological method. He once characterized his theology as emphasizing "a biblical foundation, an eschatological orientation, [and] a political responsibility."[51] It is especially the political themes of Moltmann's trinitarian theology of hope that have influenced contemporary theology, particularly in the sphere of liberation theology.

THE RISE OF LIBERATION THEOLOGIES

During the post-Vatican II era, and contemporary with Moltmann's early political theology, Christian theology became increasingly sensitive to the variety of moral and structural evils that plague the human race, whether it be global poverty, cultural and institutional racism, or patriarchal sexism. Many theologians criticized the church and its doctrine as often complicit in propping up such injustices, but also claimed to find a liberating message in scripture and in the nobler elements of the Christian tradition, spawning what became known as "liberation theology." The most prominent of these liberation theologies, which cross-fertilized with and drew upon Moltmann's attempt to construct a liberating political theology for Cold War Europe, is the form that emerged on the Latin American continent.

---

[50] Jürgen Moltmann, *The Way of Jesus Christ: Christology in Messianic Dimensions*, trans. Margaret Kohl (Minneapolis, MN: Fortress, 1993).
[51] Jürgen Moltmann, *History and the Triune God: Contributions to Trinitarian Theology* (New York: Crossroad, 1992), 182.

Latin American liberation theology

Latin American liberation theology began as a largely Catholic movement, rooted broadly in the vitality and renewal that flowed through the Catholic world after Vatican II. That council had called into question the inequity of the widening gap between the rich and the poor, and had enjoined the church (and the world's governments) to use its wealth charitably in "a world today where so many people are suffering from want."[52] Such conciliar statements were taken up and augmented by councils of Latin American bishops in Medellín, Colombia (1968), and later in Puebla, Mexico (1979). Medellín described the Christian God as the "God who, in the fullness of time, sends his Son in the flesh, so that He might come to liberate all men from the slavery to which sin has subjected them: hunger, misery, oppression, and ignorance, in a word, that injustice and hatred which have their origin in human selfishness."[53] Latin American liberation theology sprang from these conciliar statements as a radicalization of the Christian approach to the problem of poverty, a problem felt acutely among the nations and peoples of Latin America.

Generally considered to be the "father" of Latin American liberation theology, Peruvian theologian Gustavo Gutiérrez (1928–) in his ground-breaking 1971 book *A Theology of Liberation*, argued that Latin American dependence on the first world thwarted the necessary "development" that was typically considered to be the way out of poverty for the third world. A more revolutionary approach was needed, one of *liberation*, which includes not only economic and political transformation, but also an "emancipation" through which impoverished humanity is enabled to become "the artisan of its own destiny" in history.[54] While Gutiérrez noted that the clamor for liberation is a social and cultural reality affecting the whole Latin American continent, he insisted that the Christian church is also called to engage in the struggle against poverty.[55] For this reason, Gutiérrez stressed that Christian theology must be a "critical reflection on Christian praxis in the light of the Word" – by which he means that theology is not merely an intellectual reflection on the *doctrines* of Christian belief, but must serve the church's concrete *practice* and mission as mandated by scripture.[56] Christian theology has the task of clarifying and deepening the church's active presence in the world, which in Latin America means contributing to the

---

[52] Vatican II, *Gaudium et spes*, 60–9, quotation at 69.
[53] Second General Conference of Latin American Bishops, *Medellín*, 33.
[54] Gutiérrez, *Theology of Liberation*, 56.   [55] Ibid., 58–71.   [56] Ibid., 11.

church's participation in the process of social liberation in witness to Jesus Christ, who offers liberation from both personal *and* social sin.[57] Salvadoran theologian Jon Sobrino explains this stance as a matter of theology concerning itself not primarily with the original Enlightenment challenge of liberation from myth through right reason (which he associates with Kant), but with the later Enlightenment's quest for concrete historical liberation from oppression through right social ordering (which he associates with Marx).[58]

A key theme that runs through the diverse theologies of the Latin American liberationists is that of a "preferential option for the poor," an idea advocated generally by Medellín in 1968 and more explicitly by Puebla in 1979.[59] Because scripture demonstrates God's concern for the "least of these" – the world's poor and oppressed – especially through the exodus story and Christ's ministry of the kingdom of God, the church is called to enter into solidarity with the poor in order to contribute to their liberation.[60] Theology has the responsibility of discerning the contours of the triune God's own preferential option for the poor so that the church can live in fidelity to its Lord by consciously serving the world's victims in a liberative way. While God's love (and therefore the church's concern) is universal – for all people – it comes to urgent expression through a particular concern for the poor and disadvantaged, who have the greatest need of God's loving power and the church's evangelical resources.

A related theme of Latin American liberation theology is its multi-dimensional notion of salvation. While recognizing the truth in the Christian tradition's emphasis on salvation as a remedy for personal sin, in the gaunt face of Latin American poverty the liberation theologians have affirmed that salvation – as the kingdom of God that transforms all reality – also includes social and economic justice as a remedy for structural and political sin.[61] This all-encompassing notion of salvation, which focuses on the historical dimensions of salvation, is often termed "integral liberation."[62]

---

[57] Ibid., 103.   [58] Sobrino, *True Church and the Poor*, 10–15.

[59] Second General Conference of Latin American Bishops, *Medellín*, 175–6. Third General Conference of the Latin American Episcopate, *Evangelization in Latin America's Present and Future*, trans. John Drury, in *Puebla and Beyond: Documentation and Commentary*, ed. John Eagleson and Philip Scharper (Maryknoll, NY: Orbis, 1979), 264–7.

[60] Leonardo Boff and Clodovis Boff, *Introducing Liberation Theology*, trans. Paul Burns (Maryknoll, NY: Orbis, 1987), 43–9.

[61] Gutiérrez, *Theology of Liberation*, 24–5, 103–5.

[62] E.g., Boff and Boff, *Introducing Liberation Theology*, 52, 60.

Black theology

Many of the same themes are present in another liberationist movement that developed about the same time as its Latin American counterpart – that of black theology, associated above all with the work of James Cone (1938–), whose first book, *Black Theology and Black Power*, was published in 1969.[63] Black theology, however, was informed specifically by the North American experience of slavery and the ongoing legacy of racism that is felt by black Americans in both personal and structural ways. As an attempt to articulate the Christian gospel and its ethical ramifications in a way that was in rhythm with the African American experience, black theology has drawn on the spiritual songs, poems, and prayers of American slaves and their descendants.[64] It has also appealed to the rather different responses of Martin Luther King Jr. and Malcolm X to the plight of blacks in American society.[65]

In order to stress the connection between black oppression and Christian faith in an unmistakable way, Cone has provocatively made the claim that "God is black." Given that "blackness" is central to the identity and self-understanding of African American people, the corresponding "blackness of God" is central to the way in which blacks know and relate to God. This idea, obviously, does not refer to divine skin pigmentation, but to the fact that God identifies with the oppressed, entering in solidarity into their situation so as to transform it: "The blackness of God means that God has made the oppressed condition God's own condition," something that Cone, in similar fashion to the Latin American theologians, claims on the basis of the election of the nation of Israel and the incarnation of Jesus Christ.[66] And similar to Latin American liberation theology's attempt to counterbalance the tradition's rather abstract emphasis on the universality of God by portraying God as the God of the poor, Cone rejects a "colorless" portrayal of God.[67] Accepting the "blackness" of God means departing from a notion of the "colorlessness" of God that is in fact a "white" view of God – an abstracted depiction of God that serves only to reinforce the social status quo. Cone's claim about God implies the call for the white church to become "black" by rejecting its whiteness, namely, its continued participation in cultural and structural sin that oppresses African Americans, and

[63] James H. Cone, *Black Theology and Black Power* (New York: Seabury, 1969).

[64] See James H. Cone, *God of the Oppressed* (New York: Seabury, 1975), 17–30.

[65] James H. Cone, *Martin and Malcolm and America: A Dream or a Nightmare?* (Maryknoll, NY: Orbis, 1991).

[66] Cone, *Black Theology of Liberation*, 63–4, quotation at 63.   [67] Ibid., 63.

instead to "become black with God by joining God in the work of liberation." It also implies the call for the black church to accept that God has
entered into their struggle for liberation and therefore to "[accept] themselves as they are in all their physical blackness."[68]

Feminist theology

A third variety of liberation theology, stressing themes common to its Latin
American and black versions, but proceeding from the reality of women's
experience, is feminist theology. If our first two varieties are protests against
the evils of poverty and racism, their feminist cousin opposes the sexist and
patriarchal character of western society and the Christian tradition. As
feminist theologian Letty Russell writes: "Domination of women by men
is an ancient and persistent form of the subjection of one human being to a
permanent status of inferiority because of sex," something that she argues is
"the most universal form of exploitation which supports and perpetuates the
other forms of exploitation in both church and society."[69] Feminist theologians point not only to the stereotyped relegation of women to the role of
mother and housekeeper, but also to the fact that in the church women have
historically been barred from serving as leaders and ministers, restrictions
that have been justified by a reading of certain NT texts that are considered
to support male "headship."

Many feminist theologians contend that these restrictive understandings
of the role of women have been reinforced by the traditional habit in
western (Christian) society of referring to God solely in masculine terms –
God as divine King, or "Heavenly Father," or the Trinity of Father, Son,
and Spirit, but in any respect referred to pronominally as "He." This has left
the impression that men, rather than women, are the ones who are truly
created in the divine image as the creaturely heirs of the divine lordship.
God's absolute power over the cosmos, according to this line of thinking, is
rightly reflected in "man's" absolute power over the whole creaturely realm,
including women. Mary Daly puts the matter most bluntly: "Since 'God' is
male, the male is God."[70]

In order to shake the church from its patriarchal language for God, some
feminist theologians have suggested gender-neutral ways of referring to

---

[68] Ibid., 66.
[69] Letty M. Russell, *Human Liberation in a Feminist Perspective: A Theology* (Philadelphia: Westminster,
1975), 29.
[70] Daly, "Qualitative Leap," 20.

God, such as "Creator" or "Parent." Others, such as Elizabeth Johnson, have proposed more radical ways of renaming God, such as the use of "Sophia" (the feminine Greek word for wisdom) and "She who is" (an interpretation of the OT divine name YHWH).[71] Sallie McFague advances the trinitarian proposal of "Mother, Lover, and Friend" as an alternative to the "Father, Son, Spirit" language of the tradition. She argues that these metaphors for God as Trinity, by being rooted in the most basic of personal relationships, are more transformative in a world where (male) misuse of power threatens the very life of creation.[72]

Feminist theologians have also focused their attention on christology and ecclesiology. For example, against the claim that Jesus' male gender was somehow intrinsically necessary to the saving purpose of the incarnation, theologians such as Rosemary Radford Ruether have argued that such a view would exclude women from participation in Jesus' renewal of humanity; it is therefore necessary to focus not on his maleness, but on his *ministry*, which he lived out in a liberative and stereotype-shattering way for the oppressed, including women.[73] If it is Jesus' liberating humanity and ministry, rather than his maleness, that makes his incarnation significant, then a key traditional argument against the ordination of women to church leadership is defused. Ruether argues that if "women are equally theomorphic," then God can be imaged equally as male and female, and women should feel empowered to preach the gospel and live it out in their lives.[74]

We could note other variants of liberation theology. For example, the confluence of black theology and feminist theology – flowing from the particular experience of black women – has produced what is known as "womanist theology."[75] All of these variations of liberation theology have influenced one another considerably since they hit the theological stage in the 1960s and '70s. Indeed, many of their key and common features, such as the recognition of structural sin, the Bible's this-worldly depiction of salvation, and the idea of a "preferential option" for the oppressed, have even found their way into much "mainstream" theology, as well as into postmodern theology in its particular concern for the ideal of justice.

---

[71] Elizabeth A. Johnson, *She Who Is: The Mystery of God in Feminist Theological Discourse* (New York: Crossroad, 1992).

[72] McFague, *Models of God*, 84–7.

[73] Rosemary Radford Ruether, "The Liberation of Christology from Patriarchy," in *Feminist Theology: A Reader*, ed. Ann Loades (Louisville, KY: Westminster John Knox, 1990), 140, 147.

[74] Ibid., 146–7.

[75] See, e.g., Delores S. Williams, *Sisters in the Wilderness: The Challenge of Womanist God-Talk* (Maryknoll, NY: Orbis, 1993).

POSTMODERNITY AND THEOLOGY

Around the 1980s theology became more self-consciously "postmodern." Although the postmodern label was already being used in other disciplines (e.g., architecture, literary criticism), as a description of a general cultural and intellectual trend in western society it became ensconced in popular parlance by Jean-François Lyotard's *The Postmodern Condition* (1984), which famously defined "postmodern" as "incredulity toward metanarratives."[76] By "metanarrative" Lyotard had primarily in mind the master story of Enlightenment science that claimed universal authority.

The postmodern condition is funded by numerous sources, including factors ideological (Nietzschean philosophy), linguistic (developments in hermeneutics and structuralism-poststructuralism), scientific (the rise of quantum physics and relativity theories), economic (the ramping up of post-WWII consumer culture), and social (the radical 1960s), among others. Though emergent postmodernity is still in a state of flux and eludes simple description, as a reaction to modernity we can briefly and generally characterize the postmodern condition as follows.

1. Whereas modernity made an *appeal to harmonious nature* (the mechanistic Newtonian world) as the basis of *universal truth* that is objective, timeless, and supracultural – a unified worldview (Lyotard's "metanarrative") – postmodernity is resigned to a plurality of perspectives (cf. the relativistic Einsteinian world), holding "truth" to be more participatory in nature and relative to a particular community – a diversity of narratives or worldviews.

2. Whereas modernity held to the *authority of reason*, construing the individual as an autonomous rational substance and self-determining subject who could attain knowledge that is objective, certain, and dispassionate, postmodernity touts a more communally based understanding of normativity, recognizing that the human knower is historically, culturally, and linguistically embedded and conditioned, and that human knowledge is value-laden, subjective, relational, and indeterminate. The postmodern condition also places greater value on the emotions, intuitions, and the aesthetic as modes of human knowing.

3. Whereas modernity entailed a *rejection of tradition* as an inferior, heteronomous, if not superstitious form of authority that impeded individual freedom and moral responsibility, postmodernity has greater place for

---

[76] Lyotard, *Postmodern Condition*, iv.

traditioned perspectives as essential narratives of community, the formative web of corporate truth and social responsibility.

4. Whereas modernity indulged in an optimistic *belief in progress* based on its sanguine assessment of human potential to achieve scientific and technological mastery over nature and society – the myth of unending progress (fueled by the western industrial age as symbolized by the factory) – postmodernity is pessimistic about modern progress, recognizing that life is fragile and that the modern project has not only bumped up against its limits, but has actually created the conditions of apocalypse for all (nuclear holocaust, ecological disaster). Postmodernity therefore sends out a clarion call for a new paradigm of life (communicated through the global information age as symbolized by the computer).

If this is the general postmodern condition as a reaction to modernity, then many of the theologies we have reviewed in this contemporary period qualify as "postmodern," with some of them – especially process, liberation, and feminist theologies – over time becoming more self-consciously "postmodern." But there is a more extreme version of postmodernity that seems to undermine the very enterprise of theology itself.

Radical postmodernism in theology

This radical strain of postmodernism is largely rooted in the thought of Friedrich Nietzsche, who not only famously pronounced the death of God and therefore the loss of a transcendent ground for anchoring life, knowledge, and ethics, but also attacked the Enlightenment conviction that knowledge, truth, and value could be grounded in abstract, objective, universal reason. To Nietzsche those so-called "truths" distorted the particulars of human experience. With a keen eye to the metaphorical nature of language, Nietzsche viewed "truth" perspectivally – as a function of language employed in specific cultural contexts which served the purpose of human "will-to-power," sometimes positively as a creative function of human potential (e.g., Nietzsche's prescription of "Overman"), but more often negatively as a cloak for selfish interests and power relations (e.g., Christian "slave morality"). As a nihilist, Nietzsche held that human interest as expressed in language creates its own reality.

Nietzsche's ideas dovetail with poststructuralist views of language and culture that maintain that all linguistic systems are socially constructed. Here words (signifiers) bear no necessary or structural relation to human thought or the external world (the signified), but are rather an arbitrary play of language. Michel Foucault (1926–84) is one prominent poststructuralist who has developed this strain of thought into a critique of grand narratives and social systems that mask knowledge as power and underwrite structures that unjustly exclude "the other."

Jacques Derrida (1930–2004), however, is probably the most famous post-modern philosopher, best known as an exponent of *deconstruction*. By understanding philosophy (and theology) as a form of literature, thereby denying its (historically self-assumed) privileged position to adjudicate truth, Derrida attacks the "logocentrism" of the western tradition, which posited an ultimate "word" or "presence" – whether God or the subjective self – as a "transcendental signifier" to serve as a foundation and demarcation of truth. Given these poststructuralist suppositions, Derrida's deconstruction involves the critical analysis of language and texts (= "writing") to show that they cannot bear the weight of reference to the objective truth they claim, and that we are left finally with the endless self-referential interplay of signs and interpretation.

While Derridean postmodernism would appear uncongenial to the theological enterprise, Mark C. Taylor's *Erring: A Postmodern A/Theology* attempts to show the contours of such a theology given the deconstructive critique.[77] Acknowledging up front his sympathy for Nietzsche, "one of the greatest prophets of postmodernism," Taylor suggests that "deconstruction is the 'hermeneutic' of the death of God."[78] Given this atheistic assumption, Taylor sketches in Part I ("Deconstructing Theology") how the death of *God* leads to the disappearance of the *self* created in God's image and to the loss of a meaningful or redemptive *history*, impugning the notion of an authoritative *book* of scripture. Given the "erasure" of these traditional key themes of theology, Taylor in his second part ("Deconstructive A/Theology") offers his deconstructive reformulation of these key themes. God is replaced by *writing* as the divine milieu, the linguistic environment in which the decentered self, now only an insubstantial *trace*, meanders in purposeless *mazing grace* in companionship with an unfinished *erring scripture*. It is interesting to note that Taylor elaborates the death of God in terms of a radical kenosis, drawing from Altizer's work, whose own ongoing atheology also took on explicit deconstructionist overtones. Taylor is quite cognizant that his playful theological proposal is "heretical" by orthodox standards, confirming Derrida's own early contention that deconstruction "blocks every relationship to theology."[79]

---

[77] Mark C. Taylor, *Erring: A Postmodern A/Theology* (Chicago: University of Chicago Press, 1984).
[78] Ibid., 3, 6.
[79] Quoted in ibid., 6. Cf. John D. Caputo, *Philosophy and Theology*, Horizons in Theology (Nashville, TN: Abingdon, 2006), for an alternative interpretation of Derrida's relation to theology.

Narrative and post-liberal theology

An alternative to radical postmodernism, yet very much concerned with the linguistic turn in contemporary philosophy, can be found in the rise of narrative theology, particularly as this comes to expression in George Lindbeck's proposal for a post-liberal (i.e., a postmodern) theology. Lindbeck is part of the "Yale school" of theology, known for its sensitivity to narrative as rooted in Hans Frei's *The Eclipse of Biblical Narrative* (1974).[80] In this seminal work Frei argued that in the face of Enlightenment and historical criticism, most western theology had been duped into divorcing Christian truth from the meaning inherent in the biblical story, elevating some other historical truth or ideal as the external criterion of the biblical narrative – as, for example, in the quest of the (real) historical Jesus. This emerging divide between biblical theology and historical criticism affected both liberals, who reduced the meaning and use of the Bible to the eternal truths it symbolized about God and humanity, and conservatives, who defensively fixated on scripture's historical facticity. Against this modernist trend, Frei argued that scripture was a "realistic narrative" in which form and meaning are inseparable. The authoritative truth of scripture is the meaning conveyed by the biblical story, not some other foundational truth; and it is within this story that the Christian is to live and interpret reality.

Following Frei's lead, George Lindbeck in his *The Nature of Doctrine* (1984) advocates a "cultural-linguistic" theory of religion in contrast to "cognitive-propositional" (conservative, premodern) and "experiential-expressive" (liberal, modern) models. Drawing from more recent insights in cultural anthropology (especially Clifford Geertz) and linguistic theory (especially Ludwig Wittgenstein), Lindbeck's cultural-linguistic model views religions as "comprehensive interpretive schemes, usually embodied in myths or narratives and heavily ritualized, which structure human experience and understanding of self and world."[81] Thus unlike the experiential-expressivist model (Lindbeck's primary foil), which posits some foundational or universal religious experience as prior to its expression in various religious patterns, myths, and stories, Lindbeck's model views the narrative structure of religion as the matrix that gives birth to and nurtures religious experience. Religious experience, he argues, is analogous to a language that one learns – for the Christian, within the

---

[80] Hans Frei, *The Eclipse of Biblical Narrative: A Study in Eighteenth and Nineteenth Century Hermeneutics* (New Haven, CT: Yale University Press, 1974).

[81] George Lindbeck, *The Nature of Doctrine: Religion and Theology in a Postliberal Age* (Philadelphia: Westminster, 1984), 32.

cultural-linguistic matrix as articulated in its foundational narrative texts, the Bible. Doctrines, accordingly, function like grammatical rules of the Christian "language-game." Rather than as universal "propositions" or merely "expressive symbols" of universal religious experience, doctrines are best conceived as particular "rules" that regulate the life of faith, nourishing Christian identity, belief, character, and action in the world. Lindbeck sketches a post-liberal vision of Christian theology that is intra-textual, in which the Christian narrative is the lens that "absorbs the world, rather than the world the text."[82]

Narrative theology, though quite a diverse movement, has attracted many thinkers who see it as an approach that facilitates a distinctive and unapologetic Christian theology that goes beyond the modernist crisis in theological method – particularly over the nature and function of scripture – an approach that takes seriously the storied nature of human experience and therefore the historical-linguistic sensitivities of postmodernity. Many have also seen in narrative a promising avenue to connect theology and ethics. Of these Stanley Hauerwas stands out, whose narrative approach to ethics emphasizes the Christian community as formative of Christian character. This "virtue ethics," Hauerwas maintains, is inextricable from – and indeed should be prioritized in – theology in witness to the truth of the Christian story.[83]

GLOBAL CHRISTIANITY AND THE SHAPE OF THEOLOGY

While postmodernity has been integrated into theology in both radical and more moderate ways, the recognition of cultural context has become paramount in contemporary theology, even by theologians who do not self-consciously adopt the label of "postmodern." This is especially true in the present global situation, in which Christianity is experiencing a boom in the so-called third world or global south, a pattern that is the mirror image of the church's relative decline in the first world of the north. As we explained in greater detail in Chapter 14, the demographic shift in Christianity is remarkable: Around the year 1900, about 80 percent of the world's Christians lived in the global north (Europe and North America), but a century later about 60 percent of Christianity was situated in the global south (Africa, Latin America, and parts of Asia), with church growth rates

---

[82] Ibid., 118.
[83] See, e.g., Stanley Hauerwas, *The Peaceable Kingdom* (Notre Dame, IN: University of Notre Dame Press, 1983); and Hauerwas, *A Community of Character: Toward a Constructive Christian Social Ethic* (Notre Dame, IN: University of Notre Dame Press, 1981).

soaring in the region of sub-Saharan Africa in particular. If Christian theology is by its very nature contextual – in reflection of its key event and doctrine, the incarnation – then the flourishing of Christian faith in the global south portends increasing changes in the shape and contours of theology. The challenges faced in new contexts will provoke new theological questions and formulations. Such ground-breaking reflection, for example, is certain to flow from Christianity's sometimes fractious interaction with Islam, another monotheistic religion with which it coexists at close quarters in parts of Africa and Asia.

While Latin American liberation theology is one example of the theological innovation and transformed biblical interpretation that have emerged from Christianity in the global south, it is the result of the much longer gestation of Christianity in Latin America, dating back to the conquests of the fifteenth and sixteenth centuries. In other parts of the south, where the presence of Christianity is relatively more recent yet still fraught with the ambiguous legacies of colonialism, further varieties of liberation theology have appeared. For example, in the struggle against apartheid in South Africa, a form of liberation theology emerged that consciously drew upon North American black theology and Latin American liberation theology. While he is more of a churchman than an academic theologian, the thinking of Anglican archbishop Desmond Tutu is a good example of this liberationist impulse in South Africa.[84] Such globalized liberation theology also appeared in South Korea under the rubric of "minjung theology," with the Korean term *minjung* used to denote the class of people who suffer as the result of the systems of the broader society. From this perspective, God's saving work in Jesus Christ converges, through the power of the Holy Spirit, with the *minjung*'s protesting and populist movement for the democratizing and humanizing of Korean society.[85]

While the liberationist versions of global Christianity have been prominent in their influence on the broader theological enterprise, Christian theology has also been indigenized in specifically cultural ways, some of which have proven to be controversial in the accommodations they make to non-western culture. For example, Jung Young Lee, a North Korean who spent much of his career teaching in the United States, argued that the Christian doctrine of the Trinity could be inculturated for Asians in connection to the yin/yang

---

[84] E.g., Desmond Mpilo Tutu, *Hope and Suffering: Sermons and Speeches*, ed. Mothobe Mutloatse and John Webster (Grand Rapids, MI: Eerdmans, 1984).

[85] See Suh Nam-dong, "Historical References for a Theology of Minjung," in *Minjung Theology: People as the Subjects of History*, ed. Commission on Theological Concerns of the Christian Conference of Asia, rev. edn. (Maryknoll, NY: Orbis, 1983), 177.

duality of Asian culture and philosophy.[86] Just as the symbols yin and yang represent polar moments that cannot be separated from each other, so also Father, Son, and Spirit are distinctive persons who cannot be understood apart from their connection to one another. The three persons of the Trinity are "in" one another in a way that bears affinity to the way in which the principles of yin and yang, while distinct, remain "in" each another. In addition to what he perceived as the formal congruence of the Taoist world-view with trinitarian thinking, Lee also connected other principles of Asian culture to the particular persons of the Trinity, such as the idea of *ch'i* – the force that animates the human body – which he regards as an Asian point of contact for the Christian view of the Holy Spirit.

In the realm of African theology, John Mbiti has argued that the traditional western emaciation of soteriology, where salvation is reduced to a matter of the individual soul, is significantly corrected by the fusion of traditional African culture and a fresh *African* reading of the Bible. In traditional African culture, there is no rigid split between the spiritual and the physical, but "physical threats have spiritual consequences and spiritual threats have physical consequences."[87] Thus, in order to be at home in African culture, Christian salvation has to be understood in an all-encompassing or cosmic sense – one that is also more compatible with the Bible than the individualized salvation of the tradition.[88] Additionally, Mbiti argues that since there is only one God, the God known in traditional African religion must be the same as the triune God of Christianity, even if the Trinity's full identity is only partially grasped. Since Jesus Christ as revealed in the NT is a person of the Trinity – the true God – it is necessary to recognize his presence in partial and cloaked form in traditional African religion: "He is the unnamed Christ, working in the insights that people have developed concerning God."[89] Because the salvation that Jesus brings fits with the problems and hopes of African culture, Jesus is therefore the fulfillment of the African religion in which he is present in a concealed way.

Lamin Sanneh predicts that the linguistic and cultural translation of the Bible and Christian theology into an African matrix will lead to a creative and innovative transformation of Christian faith. Rejecting the fear that this transformation entails syncretism (and subtly implying that this is more a

---

[86] Jung Young Lee, *The Trinity in Asian Perspective* (Nashville, TN: Abingdon, 1996).

[87] John S. Mbiti, *Bible and Theology in African Christianity* (Nairobi: Oxford University Press, 1986), 156.

[88] Ibid., 165.

[89] Mbiti, "Is Jesus Christ in African Religion?," in *Exploring Afro-Christology*, ed. John S. Pobee (Frankfurt: Peter Lang, 1992), 21–9, quotation at 28.

Table 20.1 *Timeline of theology in the contemporary period*

History of theology			World history
		1960	
Death of C. S. Lewis	1963	1961	Construction of Berlin Wall
Second Vatican Council ends	1965	1965	Vietnam War escalates
Death of Karl Barth	1968	1967	Six Day War between Israel and Arab nations
Second Conference of Latin American Bishops	1968	1969	*Apollo 11* lands on the moon
		1970	
Moltmann publishes *The Crucified God*	1972	1972	Terrorist attack at Munich Olympics
		1973	OPEC oil embargo
John Paul II becomes pope	1978	1974	President Nixon resigns due to Watergate scandal
Third Conference of Latin American Bishops	1979	1979	Iranian seizure of US embassy in Tehran
		1980	
		1980	Lech Walesa organizes Solidarity trade union in Poland
Death of Karl Rahner	1984	1985	Mikhail Gorbachev becomes General Secretary of USSR
Founding of Jesus Seminar	1985	1988	End of Iran–Iraq War
New Revised Standard Version of the Bible published	1989	1989	Fall of the Berlin Wall
		1990	
Publication of the *Catechism of the Catholic Church*	1992	1992	Conflict begins in former Yugoslavia
Wolfhart Pannenberg completes *Systematic Theology*	1993	1993	First attack on World Trade Center
Catholic–Lutheran *Joint Declaration on Justification*	1999	1997	Hong Kong returned to Chinese control
		2000	
Rowan Williams becomes archbishop of Canterbury	2003	2001	Terrorist attacks on USA
		2004	Tsunami in Indian Ocean
Benedict XVI becomes pope	2005	2008	Global economic crisis
		2010	

matter of a new cultural expression of right Christian belief – i.e., ortho-doxy), Sanneh nevertheless maintains that the form of such theology will be significantly different.[90] Taking the East African Maasai ethnic group as an example, Sanneh writes that they

---

[90] On syncretism, see Sanneh, *Whose Religion is Christianity?*, 44.

speak in their so-named African Creed of believing as a community rather than as individuals, and instead of casting their creed in cognitive abstract terms of the seen and unseen, of Christ as eternally begotten of the Father, God from God, light from light, begotten not made, etc. [i.e., the language of the Nicene Creed], they speak of a journey of faith in a God who out of love created the world and us, of how they once knew the High God in darkness but now know this God in the light.[91]

Sanneh suggests that this indigenized Christian theology will be of benefit to the whole church, in no small part because, unlike the Nicene Creed, it does not bear the "scars of bitter theological battle."[92]

Presently in the West and north the theological reverberations of Vatican II continue to resonate in the Catholic world, the eschatological-political insights of post-Barthian theology continue to exert their influence in the Protestant world, and the various expressions of liberation theology continue to challenge the church and its theology. But it is likely that some of the most significant contributions to Christian theology in our contemporary postmodern era will come from the places in the world where the church is flourishing most dynamically – the global south. The question remains, however, whether theologians of the first world will care to listen to other brothers and sisters in the collective enterprise of theology – a wrestling with God and humanity for the sake of the world at large.

FOR FURTHER READING

Caputo, John D., *Philosophy and Theology*, Horizons in Theology (Nashville, TN: Abingdon, 2006).

Cobb, John B., and David Ray Griffin, *Process Theology: An Introductory Exposition* (Philadelphia: Westminster, 1976).

Cone, James H., *God of the Oppressed* (New York: Seabury, 1975).

Moltmann, Jürgen, *Experiences in Theology: Ways and Forms of Christian Theology*, trans. Margaret Kohl (Minneapolis, MN: Fortress, 2000).

Pannenberg, Wolfhart, *An Introduction to Systematic Theology* (Grand Rapids, MI: Eerdmans, 1991).

Papanikolaou, Aristotle, *Being with God: Trinity, Apophaticism, and Divine–Human Communion* (Notre Dame, IN: University of Notre Dame Press, 2006).

Parsons, Susan Frank, ed., *The Cambridge Companion to Feminist Theology* (Cambridge: Cambridge University Press, 2002).

Rahner, Karl, *Foundations of Christian Faith: An Introduction to the Idea of Christianity*, trans. William V. Dych (New York: Crossroad, 1978).

Sanneh, Lamin, *Whose Religion is Christianity? The Gospel Beyond the West* (Grand Rapids, MI: Eerdmans, 2003).

[91] Ibid., 59.   [92] Ibid., 60.

Theological glossary

The chapter or chapters cited at the end of the glossary entries indicate where one can find the most extensive discussion of the term. Terms with no chapter reference are generally used throughout the book, with no extensive discussion at any single point.

accommodation. The theological idea that God adjusts or adapts revelation so that it is suitable or fitting to human understanding, given the conditions of human finitude and sinfulness (Chapter 3).

adoptionism. The christological position, most famously represented by Paul of Samosata, that Jesus of Nazareth was not personally divine as a preexistent being, but was at some point in his life, typically at his baptism, specially adopted by the Father to be the messianic Son of God (Chapters 9 and 16).

Alexandrian school. One of two famous ancient "schools" of theology (the other being the Antiochene school), which was largely oriented to Platonic thought, resulting in an allegorical approach to scriptural exegesis, and an emphasis in christology on the transcendent deity of Christ and the unity of his person, at times leaving in question the authenticity of Christ's humanity (Chapters 9 and 16).

amillennialism. A millennial perspective which holds that the millennium of Rev. 20 is a symbol of Christ's reign in the church and the kingdom of God in the present messianic age between Christ's first and second comings. Championed by Augustine, amillennialism became the dominant eschatological view of the Roman Catholic and mainstream Protestant churches (Chapter 15).

analogia entis. Literally, "analogy of being." The supposition that God's creation bears an analogy to God's own character, such that the truth, goodness, and beauty of creation are a reflection of God's perfect being as Truth, Goodness, and Beauty. This supposition is important for a realist understanding of theological language and knowledge of God (Chapters 3 and 6).

analogy. In theological language, a way of speaking about God that draws a comparison between God and creation that involves both likeness and unlikeness (e.g., God as the perfect Father is both like and unlike human fathers). Analogy is a middle way between *univocity* (speaking about God and creatures in the identical sense of a term) and *equivocity* (speaking about God and creatures in a completely different sense of a term) (Chapter 3).

annihilationism. Offered as an alternative to the traditional view of an eternal punitive hell, the proposal that at death unbelievers are annihilated and cease to exist (Chapter 15).

anthropodicy. Literally, "the justice of humanity." The corollary question to theodicy: How can a free (semi-potent) and good (semi-benevolent) humanity be justified in the face of the massive evil and suffering it perpetrates and for which it is responsible (Chapter 8)? (*See also* theodicy.)

anthropology, theological. From Gk. *anthropos* = humanity. The doctrine of humanity in relation to God, which typically includes discussion of human identity as the *imago Dei* and the distortion of human nature, behavior, and calling that results from sin (Chapter 7).

anthropomorphism. In theological speech, attributing "human form" or characteristics to God (Chapter 3).

anthropopathism. In theological speech, attributing "human pathos" – human feelings, passions, or sufferings – to God (Chapter 3).

Antiochene school. One of two famous ancient "schools" of theology (the other being the Alexandrian school), which was largely oriented to Aristotelian thought, resulting in a literal-historical approach to scriptural exegesis, and an emphasis in christology on the genuine humanity of Christ and the distinction of his natures, at times leaving in question the unity of his person (Chapters 9 and 16).

apatheia. Synonymous with "impassibility," the classical theistic idea derived *via negativa* that God cannot suffer, be affected, or experience emotion (Chapter 4).

apocalyptic. From Gk. *apokalypsis* = revelation. A genre of literature that arose in the intertestamental period, best illustrated in the biblical corpus by Daniel and Revelation, the latter also known as the Apocalypse from its very first word. Apocalyptic literature typically contains a visionary disclosure of God's will concerning the end of days, drawing in sharp relief the promise of God's final resolution to the problem of evil, including the coming divine judgment upon unrighteousness, and the vindication of the righteous. Accordingly, "apocalyptic" can also refer to the earth-shattering, cataclysmic events of the end of this world (Chapter 15).

Apocrypha. A term coined by Jerome in his work on the Vulgate (the Lat. translation of the Bible) to identify those intertestamental books, from Tobit to 2 Maccabees, which were included in the Septuagint (the Gk. translation of the OT), but were not present in the Hebrew Bible. While such books were rejected by the Reformers as canonical, they were largely retained in Roman Catholicism and Orthodoxy as "deuterocanonical."

apokatastasis. Offered as an alternative to the traditional view of an eternal punitive hell, the proposal that God will ultimately restore all things in creation (see Acts 3:21). This hope for universal salvation was famously entertained by Origen, and has since been a minority report throughout the course of doctrinal history (Chapter 15).

Apollinarianism. The christological view, rooted in Apollinarius' theology, that in the incarnation the preexistent person of Christ, the divine Logos, took the place of the human rational soul of Jesus of Nazareth, rendering him less than fully human. This position was rejected at the Council of Constantinople (381), which affirmed that Christ was fully human, in both body and soul (Chapters 9 and 16).

apologists. The name given to a group of early church fathers, including Justin Martyr and Athenagoras, who took up the pen in intellectual defense (Gk. *apologia*) of Christian belief and practice against critics' various charges (Chapters 1 and 16).

apostolic fathers. The name given to a group of late first- to mid second-century writings that were originally thought to have been produced by the disciples of Jesus' apostles, such as the *Shepherd* of Hermas and the letters of Clement of Rome (Chapter 16).

appropriations. The teaching that certain works of the Trinity toward the world are "appropriated" in theological speech to one or another of the trinitarian persons because they seem "most appropriate" to that person – principally, creation to the Father, redemption to the Son, and sanctification-glorification to the Spirit. The theory of appropriations was necessitated by the teaching that the operations of the Trinity toward the world are singular or "indivisible" (*opera trinitatis ad extra sunt indivisa*) on account of the supposition of divine simplicity (Chapter 11).

Arianism. In tandem with modalism, Arianism represents a second major foil in the development of trinitarian doctrine. Based on the teaching of Arius, this position held that Jesus Christ was the preeminent creature begotten in time by God the Father to mediate the relationship between an infinite, eternal, and unknowable God and a finite, temporal, and searching world. Arianism was rejected by the councils of Nicea (325) and Constantinople (381), which both ruled that Jesus Christ was *homoousios* – of the same eternal divine essence – with God the Father, thus affirming the full deity of Christ (Chapters 5, 9, and 16).

atheism. Most basically, a denial of the existence of God. Atheism admits of various nuances and temperaments, including practical varieties (practical denial of the relevance of God [cf. Ps. 14:1]) and philosophical versions (intellectual denial of the reality of God) (Chapter 4).

atonement. A synonym for "reconciliation," the term "atonement" has come to be particularly central in English-language theological terminology, such that a wide variety of explanations of *how* Christ brings salvation or reconciliation have come to be known as "atonement theories." Used as a general rubric, atonement theories are conceptual elaborations that draw out the logic and implications of central biblical metaphors concerning Christ's saving work. Most literally, the concept of atonement focuses on the fact that Christ's work brings a new situation of unity between estranged parties – God and humanity – such that they are once again right or "at one" with each other, hence *at-one-ment* (Chapter 10).

biblical theology. The branch of theology that focuses on theology's basic biblical source. Biblical theology is the study and interpretation of the Bible, with an eye to ascertaining what the text means theologically – most broadly, about the triune God, creation, and their relation, or any particular topic therein. Along with historical theology and philosophical theology, biblical theology is one essential component of systematic theology (Chapter 1).

canon. Originally referring to a reed used as a measuring stick, and therefore by extension a norm or ideal standard, the theological sense of "canon" is that of a fixed series of writings that were normative for Christian faith and practice – the authoritative Christian Bible, including the thirty-nine OT and twenty-seven NT books, and, in the Catholic and Orthodox traditions, the books of the Apocrypha (Chapter 16).

canonization. The lengthy process through which the books of the Bible were acknowledged by the catholic church as authoritative, as weighed by the issues of apostolicity, catholicity, orthodoxy, and traditional usage. The earliest extant canonical list of the twenty-seven books that comprise the NT today is found in Athanasius' *Festal Letter* of 367 (Chapters 3 and 16).

charismata. Literally, the "things given." The gifts of the Spirit, such as serving, teaching, encouraging, prophecy, healing, and speaking in other tongues, among other gifts (see Rom. 12:4–8; 1 Cor. 12–14) (Chapter 11).

Christ. Gk. equivalent to the Hebr. "messiah." See Messiah.

Christendom. Most particularly, the state of affairs from Constantine up through the modern period in which Christianity was the official or assumed religion of the empire or state (e.g., the Holy Roman Empire). During this span of many centuries, especially in the Christian West, the church became a formidable political and social institution, influencing the state's affairs and functioning as a civil religion (Chapters 14, 16, and 17).

christology. From Gk. *christos* = messiah. The doctrine of Christ, which typically includes discussion of his personal identity as both divine and human, and his work of atonement that brings salvation (Chapters 9 and 10).

Christus victor. Literally, "Christ the victor." A dominant view of Christ's work in the early church, emphasizing the military metaphor of Christ's kingly triumph over the enemies of Satan, sin, and death. This broad "atonement" motif is often coupled with the ransom theory of atonement (Chapter 10).

church fathers. The leading thinkers and writers of the foundational patristic era of Christian theology, usually differentiated between Latin fathers, such as Tertullian and Augustine, and Greek fathers, such as Athanasius and the Cappadocians (Chapter 16).

communicatio idiomatum. Literally "communication of attributes." In classical christological thought, the ascription of the attributes of both the divine nature and the human nature to the one person of Jesus Christ in order to account for his dual identity in the scriptures and the various characteristics that (presumably) manifest his divine and human capabilities, from powerful miracles to human weaknesses (Chapter 9).

compatibilism. Most basically, the position held by thinkers who wish to maintain both a determinist/predestinarian view of the God–world relationship and the moral responsibility of humanity. Compatibilists hold that acts determined by God are "compatible" with their being freely chosen by human agents (Chapters 8 and 18). (*See also* incompatibilism *and* determinism.)

conceptualism. In the medieval debate over the status of "universals," conceptualism was often conflated with nominalism, but actually occupies a position between nominalism and realism. Best represented by William of Ockham, conceptualism holds that universals exist in the mind as universal concepts without any external substantial reality. To know "treeness," for example, is to know only the formal mental concept of trees (Chapter 17). (*See also* nominalism *and* realism.)

contextualization. Theological sensitivity to the contexts in which Christian theology must be articulated, translated, and embodied, as well as those contextual forces that personally impinge upon and shape the theologian – including historical, cultural, economic, social, political, racial, and other factors, forms, and institutions. Contextualization involves the recognition that theology does not happen in a vacuum, but that both practitioner and audience are embedded in complex contexts that must be taken into account (Chapter 2).

cosmological argument. An argument for the existence of God on the basis of cause and effect, reasoning from the effects of the world (*kosmos*) to God as First Cause. The first four of Thomas Aquinas' famous "Five Ways" are variations of the cosmological argument (Chapters 3 and 4).

creatio continua. Literally, "continuing creation." The idea that creation is not complete "in the beginning," but is an ongoing process over time. Preferred by some theologians as more accurate to the biblical portrayal, the notion of *creatio continua* does not necessitate as distinct a doctrine of providence as traditionally embraced and is more open to evolutionary perspectives on creation (Chapter 6).

creatio ex nihilo. Literally, "creation out of nothing." The foundational tenet and linchpin of Christian creation doctrine. With meager biblical reference (see Rom. 4:17; Heb. 11:3), this theological affirmation became an important defense against gnosticism, ruling out the dualistic idea that God created out of preexistent matter (as the inferior Demiurge was held to have done) and thereby affirming both the sovereign freedom of the Creator God and the goodness of God's creation (Chapter 6).

creed, ecumenical. From Lat. *credo* = I believe. Creeds are formal summary statements of the main elements of Christian faith. The early church formulated three enduring ecumenical creeds – pertaining to the worldwide or catholic church – that are confessed by the Roman Catholic and Protestant churches today: the Apostles' Creed, the Nicene Creed, and the Athanasian Creed. Of these three, however, Eastern Orthodox churches confess only the Nicene Creed (Chapters 1 and 16).

deification/divinization. From Gk. *theosis* or *theopoiesis*. A central soteriological motif in the early church and especially in Eastern Orthodoxy whereby salvation is conceived of as a participation in the divine nature (see 2 Pet. 1:4). This motif was given classic expression by Athanasius as the central purpose of the incarnation – "For [Christ] was made man that we might be made God" – signifying that the saving life of Christ brings the incorruptible and immortal divine life to the very *being* of humanity that is beset by sin, death, and non-being (Chapters 10, 16, and 17).

Deism. From Lat. *Deus* = God. The rational religion of the Enlightenment period proposed as a unifying alternative to traditional (revealed) Christian theism with its conflicting, warring factions. Adherents to this movement, such as Herbert of Cherbury and John Toland, believed in a Supreme Being who fashioned the world so well that it runs by its own inherent laws, much as a skilled watchmaker crafts a reliable watch. Accordingly, the Creator's nature and will for humanity could be deciphered by rational observation of the natural laws of the created order. Deists laid emphasis on the moral (rational) duties of humanity while excluding the supernatural, interventionist, and immanental elements of traditional theism (Chapters 3 and 19).

deontological. From Gk. *deon* = duty. One dominant perspective in ethical theory that emphasizes obligation or duty to right moral principle. Classically represented by Immanuel Kant's categorical imperative – "Act only on that maxim through which you can at the same time will that it should become a universal law" – deontological ethics is typically distinguished from teleological or consequentialist ethics, which emphasizes ends or consequences, and from virtue ethics, which focuses on the character development of the moral agent (Chapter 19).

determinism. Most generally in theological thought, an understanding of the God–world relation or divine providence that makes God the efficient causal agent of everything that occurs, casting doubt upon the actuality of human free will (Chapters 4, 8, and 18). (*See also* compatibilism *and* incompatibilism.)

diaspora. A "scattering" or "dispersion" of an ethnic people from their homeland. Diaspora was first applied to the dispersion of the Jews after the Babylonian exile (*c.* 597–586 BCE) (see Acts 2:5–11) and then later to those expelled from Judea by the Romans (70 CE). Together, these Jewish exiles made up the "Jewish diaspora" – those living outside the land of Israel.

diophysitism. Following the Council of Chalcedon (451), the position that affirms that Christ has two (*dio*) natures (*physeis*), one divine and one human. Diophysitism was re-confirmed by the fifth ecumenical council of Constantinople II (553) against the monophysites, who, in the fashion of Eutyches, held that Christ had only one nature, a fusion of deity and humanity (Chapters 9 and 17).

diothelitism. The position that affirms that Christ has two (*dio*) wills (*thelema*), a divine will and a human will. Diothelitism was affirmed by the sixth ecumenical council of Constantinople III (668) against the monothelites, since it was seen as a necessary corollary to Chalcedonian diophysitism (Chapters 9 and 17).

dispensationalism. Rooted in the thought of John Nelson Darby (1800–82), dispensationalism is a variation of premillennialism that presupposes a sharp distinction between OT ethnic Israel and the NT multicultural church, champions a literalist interpretation of predictive prophecy, and posits a detailed sequence of end-time events including the "rapture" of the church and a seven-year tribulation before the millennium, which will be inaugurated by Christ's second coming. Dispensationalism is the predominant eschatological view of fundamentalist and some evangelical churches (Chapter 15).

docetism. From Gk. *dokein* = to seem or appear. The early christological heresy that affirms Christ's deity to the depreciation of his humanity. Docetism is rooted in the gnostic supposition that matter is evil and beneath the dignity of the true spiritual God, casting doubt upon the integrity of Jesus' incarnate life, including the veracity of his bodily suffering and resurrection. In this perspective, Christ only *seems* or *appears* to be human (Chapters 6, 9, and 16).

dogmatics. The systematic study of Christian beliefs (doctrines and dogmas). In tandem with ethics, dogmatics is one important component of systematic theology (Chapter 1).

dualism. Most generally, a metaphysical system or worldview that posits two (*duo*) ultimate realities or first principles, as in the classic gnostic dualism of spirit (God) and matter (world). A metaphysical dualism typically defaults to an ethical dualism, involving other binary oppositions such as soul (good) and body (bad) (Chapter 6).

Ebionism. The early christological heresy that denied Jesus' divinity. The Ebionites, an early Jewish-Christian sect, believed that Jesus was the Messiah, but, due to their strict interpretation of monotheism (Yahweh = the Father alone), denied his preexistent deity. Ebionism eventually became the name for one of the two major types of early christological heresy (Chapters 9 and 16). (*See also* docetism.)

ecclesiology. From Gk. *ekklesia* = church. The doctrine of the church, which typically includes discussion of the notes, sacraments, and mission of the church (Chapter 13).

ecumenical. From Gk. *oikoumene* = world. "Ecumenical" refers to the universal, worldwide, or catholic church. For example, "ecumenical creeds" are those statements of belief that are accepted by the worldwide church; similarly, the "ecumenical movement" strives to recapture the unity of the church throughout the whole world.

election. God's choosing of a particular person or group – in the Bible, for example, the nation of Israel or the community of Christ. In systematic theology, the doctrine of election centered more on the issue of God's electing grace in the salvation of the individual. Election became especially tethered to issues of divine foreordination or predestination, functioning as the positive counterpart to reprobation (Chapter 13).

Elohim. The most common generic name for "God" in the Hebrew scriptures, Elohim connotes strength and authority and is accompanied in the OT by many descriptive terms – for example, "God of gods" (Deut. 10:17) or "everlasting God" (Isa. 40:28) (Chapter 4).

epistemology. From Gk. *episteme* = knowledge. The science of knowing. Epistemology inquires into the nature of human knowing and understanding.

eschatology. From Gk. *eschata* = last things. The doctrine of Christian hope for the fulfillment of history, which typically includes discussion of the second coming of Christ, the resurrection of the dead, the final judgment, and the eternal state of salvation (Chapter 15).

eschatology, historical. A horizontal orientation to eschatology that sees the fulfillment of eschatological realities in the historical future, and conceives of final salvation as the resurrection of the dead in the everlasting new heavens and earth. Contrasted to transcendental eschatology (Chapter 15).

eschatology, transcendental. A vertical orientation to eschatology that sees the fulfillment of eschatological realities in a timeless transcendent eternity, and conceives of final salvation as the escape of the soul to a pure spiritual heaven. Contrasted to historical eschatology (Chapter 15).

eternality. As used in this text, eternality is a neutral term that admits of two alternative connotations, correlating with the English synonyms "eternity" and "everlastingness." (1) Classically speaking, divine eternality was understood within a Greek metaphysic to entail God's *timelessness* – the idea that God is wholly outside of time, and therefore experiences all temporal events as an "eternal present" and simultaneous whole (eternity). (2) In revisionist thought divine eternality is understood to entail God's *timefullness* – the idea that God is from everlasting to everlasting, has always been and will always be, but that the trinitarian life manifests a temporal sequence or history with events past, present, and future to the divine persons (everlastingness) (Chapter 4).

ethics. The field of inquiry concerned with right, good, and virtuous character, behavior, and action. A Christian theological ethics roots itself in the revelation of God's character and will, and as such is a constituent part of systematic theology as a complement to dogmatics, ever leading theology from more theoretical to more practical considerations (Chapter 1).

Eutychianism. The christological view rooted in the theology of Eutyches, who, assuming a strict correlation between personhood and nature, proposed that since Christ was only one person he must also have but one nature. Eutyches conceived of this nature as a third sort of entity, a fusion of deity and humanity, wherein the latter is basically absorbed by the former. His view was rejected at the Council of Chalcedon (451), which affirmed that Christ is one person with two distinct natures. Eutyches' thought persisted in the form of monophysitism (Chapter 9).

evil. The disruption of *shalom* in creation, usually as the result and consequence of creaturely rebellion against God's will. Evil is a power that causes misery, suffering, and destruction in the world. It is variously categorized, including moral, natural, and structural evil (Chapter 8).

evil, moral. Most basically sin, which itself is both an instance of evil and a cause of evil. Moral evil occurs when acts perpetrated by accountable moral agents result in adverse consequences, suffering, and destruction (Chapter 8).

evil, natural. Suffering or destruction due to natural processes or forces, such as the adverse consequences of tornadoes, earthquakes, diseases, and the like (Chapter 8).

evil, structural/systemic. Moral evil that is inscribed in the very structures of human life; the adverse consequences of unjust social, economic, and political structures, such as racism, poverty, and exploitation (Chapter 8).

exclusivism. Along with inclusivism and pluralism, exclusivism (also called particularism) is one of the three main positions on the question of whether salvation is possible outside of the church. Emphasizing the biblical theme of particularity, this view holds that salvation is possible only through Jesus Christ and is granted only to those who have a conscious knowledge of the gospel, since there is "no other name" through which humanity can be saved (Acts 4:12) (Chapter 14).

exemplarism. In christology, concerning the *person* of Christ, the position that views Jesus not as essentially divine, but only as an exemplary human teacher or moral leader (as do the deists); concerning the *work* of Christ, the position that views Christ's saving life and death in terms of exemplary love, with the cross as the supreme example of self-sacrificial love (as in Abelard) (Chapters 9 and 10).

filioque. Literally "and the Son." The western addition to the Nicene Creed stating that the Holy Spirit proceeds from the Father "and the Son," an implication of Augustinian trinitarianism. This unilateral addition to the creed became the focus of the theological debate that eventually led to the formal split between the culturally differing western Roman Catholic Church and the eastern Byzantine Orthodox Church in 1054 (Chapters 11 and 17).

functionalism. In christology, the position that locates Jesus' "divinity" in the particular work or activity that God performs through him. Functionalism is famously exemplified by the christology of Friedrich Schleiermacher (Chapter 9).

geocentrism. The dominant cosmology or scientific worldview in ancient and medieval times up to the sixteenth-century Copernican revolution (heliocentrism). Largely influenced by Aristotle's physics and Ptolemy's astronomy, this view of the cosmos considered the heavens (from the moon on up) to be a realm of unchanging perfection, while the material earth at the center, by contrast, was considered the dregs of the universe. In theology this reinforced a transcendental eschatology, positing a far distant heaven as the final locus of salvation while depreciating the material earth and human body (Chapters 4 and 6).

gnosticism. From Gk. *gnosis* = knowledge. A diverse heretical movement that broadly challenged the early church, gnosticism held that salvation comes via a secret, esoteric knowledge that is not accessible to everyone. Gnostic thought is based on a radical dualism of spirit and matter, positing two gods, the true God of the transcendent realm of pure spirit (of whom Christ is the revelatory emissary), and the inferior god who fashioned the physical world, the Demiurge or creator god. Since gnostics regard matter as intrinsically evil, they depreciated the body, held that Christ's incarnation was only apparent (*see* docetism), and viewed salvation as an escape from the material world. Gnosticism helped to stimulate the development of creation doctrine and its orthodox implications (Chapter 6).

heliocentrism. The new cosmology that parallels the rise of modern science and displaced Aristotelian-Ptolemaic geocentrism. By viewing the Sun rather than the Earth as the center of the solar system, the sixteenth-century Copernican revolution was not only a scientific advance, accurately plotting the course of the heavens, but also a social revolution in challenging many cultural – including theological – ideas that were reinforced and inscribed in Aristotelian geocentrism (Chapters 4 and 6).

Hellenization/Hellenism. From Gk. *Hellas* = Greece. Due significantly to the military campaigns of Alexander the Great, the gradual dissemination of Greek culture, language, philosophy, and religion in the larger Mediterranean world, which the Romans largely adopted. It is this Hellenistic ethos that provides the larger context for the text of the NT (written in Greek) and patristic theology. Hellenism refers to the culture of the Greco-Roman world (Chapters 4 and 16).

heresy. From Gk. *hairesis*, which refers to a false and misguided "opinion." "Heresy" and "heretic" were terms used by those who considered themselves to be defending the correct teaching of the church to brand those whose teaching diverged from its majority opinion (Chapter 16).

hermeneutics. From Gk. *hermeneuein* = to interpret. Hermeneutics is the science of interpretation that elaborates "principles" that should guide the interpretation of the biblical text, including matters of original audience, literary genre, and intra-canonicity, among other principles (Chapter 3).

heterodoxy. Literally, "different opinion" or "other opinion." Heterodoxy refers to views that differ from the orthodoxy or "right opinion" of the church in its established doctrines. The divergences of heterodoxy are sometimes referred to more pejoratively as "heresy."

historical theology. The branch of theology that focuses on the historical sources of Christian doctrine. Historical theology examines the content and development of theological ideas in their context through the course of the Christian tradition. Along with biblical theology and philosophical theology, historical theology is one essential component of systematic theology (Chapter 1).

homoiousios. Literally, "of similar (*homoi*) essence (*ousia*)." The preferred term of many in the eastern church to secure both the Son's deity and his personal distinction from God the Father, given their initial suspicion that the Nicene *homoousios* implied a modalist interpretation of the divine persons. Through Athanasius and the Cappadocians, most eastern homoiousians were won over to the *homoousios* as appropriately delineating the trinitarian relations (Chapters 5 and 16).

homoousios. Literally, "of the same (*homo*) essence (*ousia*)." The key term at the Council of Nicea (325) that affirmed in pointed condemnation of Arius' position that Jesus Christ possessed a divine nature, status, and dignity equal to that of God the Father. Although debated fiercely after Nicea, *homoousios* was eventually confirmed at the Council of Constantinople in 381 (Chapters 5, 9, and 16).

hypostasis. Literally, that which "stands beneath." *Hypostasis* was originally synonymous with *ousia* as a word for "essence" (as in the original Nicene Creed), but came to be differentiated and used in trinitarian thought as the classic threeness term for the Father, Son, and Spirit in their distinct, discrete personhood, making this term synonymous with *prosopon* (Gk.) and *persona* (Lat.) (Chapter 5).

hypostatic union. A technical term in christology to capture the Chalcedonian affirmation that both the divine and the human nature are united in the one person (*hypostasis*) of Jesus Christ, making the second person of the Trinity or Logos identical with the person of Jesus of Nazareth (Chapter 9).

immanence. In Christian theology, the idea that God is *within* creation, a complement to the affirmation that God transcends creation. Divine immanence takes many different forms, given the variety of involvement of Father, Son, and Spirit with the world in creation and redemption (Chapter 6).

immutability. The classical theistic idea derived *via negativa* that there is no change in God. This divine attribute was primarily directed against the view that God could be acted upon from without, since that would make God the passive object of creaturely action. But it was also thought that if God is perfect, *any* change in God would involve either a diminishment of divine perfection or an admission of its lack (Chapter 4).

impassibility. Synonymous with *apatheia*, the classical theistic idea derived *via negativa* that God cannot suffer or experience emotion (Chapter 4).

inclusivism. Along with exclusivism and pluralism, inclusivism is one of the three main positions on the question of whether salvation is possible outside of the church. Striving to balance the biblical themes of God's universal love *and* particular provision of salvation, this view holds that salvation is accomplished by the unique atoning death of Christ on the cross, but that God may extend this salvation to those outside of Christianity to the degree that they live in accordance with God's will as made known in general revelation – even through the forms of their own religion. What Christianity possesses in its full recognition of Christ, other religions have in fragmentary fashion, which in the absence of Christianity in a culture may be an avenue to the salvation accomplished in Christ (Chapter 14).

incompatibilism. Most basically, the position held by thinkers who consider a determinist/predestinarian view of the God–world relationship to be "incompatible" with the moral responsibility of humanity. Incompatibilists typically reject a hard determinism in the name of accountable (libertarian) human freedom (Chapters 8 and 18). (*See* compatibilism *and* determinism.)

indivisibility. *See* simplicity.

intermediate state. On the question of the state of the Christian between death and resurrection, this is the majority position of the Christian church since at least Augustine. It holds that upon death, the soul, created immortal by God and therefore separable from the perishable body, goes to be with Christ in heaven. This intermediate state will give way to the person's final state when the soul is reunited with the body in the general resurrection of the dead at Christ's second coming (Chapter 15).

justification. In its most literal sense, "justification" refers to the "becoming just" or "becoming righteous" of the sinful human being. It is generally associated with God's gracious forgiveness of sin through faith in Christ, although a variety of interpretations of the precise dynamics of justification have developed over the Christian centuries (Chapters 12, 17, and 18).

kenosis. Literally, "emptying." A word used in verbal form in Philippians 2:7 to refer to the self-humbling of Christ in the incarnation. The term is of special significance in an interpretation of the person of Christ known as "kenotic christology," a doctrinal position which proposes that upon the event of the incarnation and through the period of his humiliation the preexistent Son of God voluntarily relinquished or "emptied" himself of all maximal divine attributes, powers, prerogatives, and/or glory that were incompatible with his becoming truly and fully human (Chapter 9).

liberalism, Protestant. The Protestant intellectual tradition that dominated nineteenth- to early twentieth-century theology, associated with Ritschl, Harnack, and Troeltsch. This tradition attempted to interpret Christian theology in terms amenable to modern European intellectual culture. The result was a form of Christian theology that emphasized questions of historicity, religious experience, and natural science, often producing doctrinal claims that diverged significantly from traditional orthodoxy (Chapter 19).

Logos. Literally "word" or "reason," *logos* is a multivalent term in Greek culture and philosophy. In the Middle Platonism that was popular in the Hellenistic world, *logos* referred philosophically to the (divine) rational structure of the cosmos, which the human rational soul, as microcosm, could discern. Since the Gospel of John had identified Christ as the Logos (1:1), this concept seemed to offer a natural intellectual bridge for the Christian gospel into Hellenistic culture. In christological thought, Logos became a technical term for the preexistent person of Christ as the eternal Son of God. Most generally, however, the term refers to the reasoned account or study of a certain subject area, such that *logos* about *Theos* (God) is the discipline of *theology* (Chapters 1, 5, 9, and 16).

Logos-anthropos. The model typical of the Antiochene school in fifth-century christological debates. Given the Antiochene emphasis on the integrity of Christ's humanity, this model conceived of the incarnation as the eternal Logos or second person of the Trinity conjoining himself to the whole human person (*anthropos*) of Jesus of Nazareth (Chapter 9).

Logos-sarx. The model typical of the Alexandrian school of fifth-century christological debates. Given the Alexandrian emphasis on the unity of Christ's person, this model conceived of the incarnation as the eternal

Logos or second person of the Trinity assuming human flesh (*sarx*). While early versions of this model (such as that of Apollinarius) posited that the Logos unites himself only with a human body, later versions emphasized that the Logos unites himself with human nature, both body *and* soul, in the incarnation (Chapter 9).

Marcionism. An early second-century sect founded by Marcion (d. *c.* 150), who viewed Christianity and Judaism as polar opposites. In promoting a dualism close to gnosticism, Marcion set up an antagonistic relationship between the inferior OT God (Yahweh), who reigns through justice and law over the evil realm of matter, and the true NT God revealed in Christ, who reigns through grace and love over the good spiritual realm. Accordingly, Marcion thought that Christianity should be purged of all Jewish elements in its belief, worship, and authoritative writings. He therefore developed a canon of scripture that rejected the entire OT as well as the particularly Jewish sections of the NT (Chapter 16).

Messiah. Literally, "anointed one." A term whose linguistic root in the OT is frequently used to denote the anointing and special role of the Israelite king. The expectation of a Davidic king became the covenant people's primary messianic hope, though there were also priestly and prophetic conceptions of the messiah. These messianic hopes catalyzed during the latter stages of the OT and especially waxed during the intertestamental period. In the NT, Jesus is portrayed as the fulfillment of these messianic hopes, as translated into his Greek title of "Christ," which since Paul has for all practical purposes become a proper name. Jesus the Christ or Messiah indicates that the primary biblical identity of Jesus is that of a special agent anointed to do God's salvific bidding (Chapter 9).

metanarrative. A "master story" or "totalizing account" that claims to capture the basic and singular truth of reality. Postmodernism has been defined as "incredulity toward metanarratives" (Lyotard), since this movement regards such master stories as oppressive ideologies, benefiting insiders (as powerbrokers of the truth) to the exclusion of others (Chapters 2 and 20).

metaphor. A figure of speech in which a meaning is "carried across" or "transferred" from one thing to another; an implied comparison – e.g., "God is my rock." In recent years, theology has become increasingly aware of the metaphorical character of all language – especially theological language, since it must invoke the creaturely realm to describe the Creator. This recognition has produced much discussion about theological method and what grounds and governs the metaphors privileged in theological description (Chapter 3).

metaphysics. Most basically, the inquiry into the nature of ultimate reality or first principles; closely related to ontology. Metaphysical issues are unavoidable in theological study, which offers to this inquiry the resources and suppositions of revelation. At its broadest, the Christian metaphysic is a duality of Creator and creature (Chapter 6).

Middle Platonism. A combination of Platonic, Aristotelian, and Stoic thought that was influential from the first century BCE to the second century CE as part of the Hellenistic milieu of early Christianity. In reflecting on the fundamental philosophical question of "the One and the many," Middle Platonism tended to view God as an impersonal principle of Supreme Being which accounts for finite being – "God" as the immaterial, transcendent, and utterly singular ground, unity, and structure of being, the veritable fullness of life. This philosophical conception of God was influential in patristic discussions of the doctrine of God (Chapters 4 and 16).

millennialism. The belief that associates a thousand-year (millennium) reign of Christ on earth with his second coming, based on the apocalyptic text of Rev. 20:1–10. Four major varieties of millennialism have developed over the course of church history: historic premillennialism, amillennialism, postmillennialism, and dispensational premillennialism (Chapter 15).

modalism. Along with Arianism, one of the two major trinitarian heresies of the church. According to modalism, God is a simple, single monad that manifests itself in three operations, which are not eternal divine identities or discrete persons. Since there are no distinctions in God, the Son and the Spirit are simply ways or "modes" in which the one person of God appears in the world (Chapters 5 and 16). (*See also* Sabellianism.)

monism. Most generally, a metaphysical system or worldview that posits one ultimate reality or first principle, typically God. While monism is usually synonymous with pantheism, there are also other varieties, such as idealism or naturalism (Chapter 6). (*See also* naturalism.)

monolatry. The worship (*latreia*) of only one god. In Israel's polytheistic context, the command to worship her covenant God (as seen in the *Shema* of Deut. 6:4) was merely an injunction to worship Yahweh alone to the exclusion of the other deities of the day (see Exod. 20:23). Israel's monolatry eventually developed into full-fledged monotheism – the deeper claim that there *is* only one true God (Chapters 4 and 5).

monophysitism. The view that Jesus Christ possesses only one nature (*mone* = one; *physis* = nature). The basic logic of this position is that since Christ is only one person, he must possess only one nature, since nature and person on this view are considered roughly equivalent. This position was declared heterodox at the councils of Chalcedon (451) and Constantinople II (553) (Chapters 9, 16, and 17).

monotheism. The claim that there is only one true God. In the Judeo-Christian tradition monotheism has primarily to do with the Creator/creature distinction: more than just Israel's national god, Yahweh is the only true God because Yahweh is the Creator of heaven and earth, and therefore the God of all nations. In this light, all other purported "deities" are creaturely idols (Chapters 4, 5, and 6).

monothelitism. The view that Jesus Christ, despite his two natures, possesses only one will (*mone* = one; *thelema* = will). The basic logic of this position is that will is a feature of personhood rather than "nature." Since Christ is only one person, as decreed by the Council of Chalcedon (451), he must have only one will. This view was declared heterodox by the Council of Constantinople III (680–1) (Chapters 9 and 17).

Montanism. A late second-century heretical movement, named after one of its founders, Montanus, that laid claim to a special baptism and charismatic empowerment of the Spirit that privileged this particular community with God's final revelation, including prophecies of the imminent end of the world. Montanist enthusiasm for immediate experience of the Spirit spread throughout the Mediterranean basin, disrupting many area churches (Chapter 11).

mortification. Along with vivification, one of the essential components of repentance and sanctification. Mortification signifies a "dying to self," as the sinner turns away from sin toward reliance on God, something that can take place only through Christ's grace (Chapter 12).

mystery. In theology, mystery typically functions as an acknowledgment of the transcendence of God and the finitude of human understanding. Mystery is a term subject to various connotations. *Mysterium salutis* ("mystery of salvation") refers to something that was previously hidden, but is now revealed for our salvation (e.g., Eph. 3:4–5), approximating the Pauline understanding of mystery. *Mysterium stricte dictum* ("mystery strictly speaking") refers to something that is undiscoverable by human reason alone and therefore requires revelation (such as the doctrine of the Trinity). *Mysterium logicum* ("logical mystery") refers to the justification of paradoxical or even contradictory claims in theology due to the incomprehensibility of its subject-matter, God. *Mysterium communionis* ("mystery of communion") refers to the fact that loving relationships between persons, whether human or divine, constitute an inviting horizon of mystery that can never be fully comprehended (Chapter 5).

naturalism. A form of monism, naturalism is the metaphysical system or worldview that posits matter as the singular first principle or ultimate reality. According to this view, there is nothing to the world or humanity beyond their physicality. Naturalism therefore champions atheistic evolutionary thought (Chapter 6).

natural theology. The project of making theological claims on the basis of human reason and its reflection on the natural world. Natural theology refers to theology done on the basis of general revelation, apart from special revelation, as for example in the traditional – cosmological, teleological, and ontological – "proofs" of God's existence (Chapter 3).

neo-orthodoxy. The twentieth-century movement launched by Karl Barth in reaction to Protestant liberalism. Neo-orthodox theologians returned to the orthodox themes of the Protestant Reformation, but in a way they considered appropriate to their twentieth-century context – hence "neo-orthodox." With many differences among them, neo-orthodox theologians were generally united in their opposition to liberalism by stressing humanity's *sinful* inability to rightly know God and conduct its life, and therefore the need for God's *gracious* external Word of revelation, justification, and empowerment (Chapter 19).

Nestorianism. The christological view, rooted in the theology of Nestorius, which, assuming a strict correlation between nature and personhood, proposed that since Christ has both a divine and a human nature, he must also be two persons. This view was most definitively rejected at the Council of Chalcedon (451), which affirmed that Christ was only one person, albeit in two natures (Chapters 9 and 16).

nominalism. In the medieval debate over the status of "universals," nominalism was the extreme view that universals are simply symbols or names (*nomina*) that we use to group similar particulars together. In claiming to know a "universal," such as "treeness" or "goodness," one is simply comparing particulars by noting their similarities, not coming to know through reason the very essence or objective substance of trees or the good. On this view, there is in fact no real form or essence that can be known through reason (Chapter 17).

omni-attributes. From Lat. *omnia* = all. Attributes of God that result from the *via positiva* method of classical theism. Since God is the supreme cause of the good of the world, desirable features of finite existence (such as power, knowledge, presence, or goodness) are maximized when ascribed to God, yielding the divine attributes of omnipotence, omniscience, omnipresence, and omnibenevolence (Chapter 4).

ontological argument. An argument for the existence of God that, presupposing that existence is an attribute of perfect being (*on*), reasons that God as the maximally perfect being must, by definition, necessarily exist. The ontological argument was first famously proposed by Anselm of Canterbury and has been vigorously debated since (Chapters 6 and 17).

ontology. From Gk. *on* = being, the science of being. Ontology inquires into the nature of what is, whether divine Being or creaturely being, an inquiry that is closely related to metaphysics (Chapters 4, 5, and 6).

ordo salutis. Literally, "order of salvation." The theological question that took on importance in the Reformation and post-Reformation era of specifying the logical (or chronological) ordering of the key components of individual salvation. The question of the *ordo salutis* centered on how facets of salvation such as justification, sanctification, regeneration, and conversion are related to one another (Chapter 12).

orthodoxy. Literally, right (*orthos*) Christian opinion or belief (*doxa*). In the Catholic tradition, orthodoxy refers to adherence to the doctrines that have been believed "everywhere, always, and by everyone" in the catholic church (Vincent of Lerins). In Eastern Orthodoxy, the term has come to be the official label for the Christian communion that orients itself to the beliefs of the church fathers, who are seen as the successors of Christ's apostles. In Protestantism, "orthodoxy" is generally taken to mean fidelity to the biblical text and the tradition's best interpretations of it (Chapters 1 and 17).

orthopraxy. Right (*orthos*) Christian practice (*praxis*). Orthopraxy is a concrete way of living that tangibly befits orthodoxy – right Christian doctrines and principles (Chapter 1).

ousia. Most literally, "essence." One of the key terms that emerged in the patristic church to describe the oneness or unity of the three persons of the Trinity. Theologians such as the Cappadocians argued that *ousia* properly refers to the one divine essence or nature that Father, Son, and Spirit share, despite their clear distinction as three persons (Chapter 5).

panentheism. In the question of the God–world relationship, the family of views which argues that all things (*pan*) are in (*en*) God (*Theos*). Most prominently associated today with process theology, panentheism is typically criticized for insufficiently maintaining the qualitative difference between God and the world, although more orthodox construals that embrace the Creator/creature distinction as secured by *creatio ex nihilo* doctrine have also been proposed (Chapter 19).

pantheism. The most prominent form of monism, pantheism literally means that "all things (*pan*) are God (*Theos*)." Pantheism is a metaphysical system or worldview that posits one ultimate reality, God. Since God or the divine alone possesses reality, all creatures must be divine in some real and realizable sense (Chapter 6).

parousia. Literally, "presence." "Parousia" became a technical term for the second coming of Jesus Christ, implying that at his return, the world will enjoy his enduring presence as Lord of creation (Chapter 15).

patripassianism. Literally, the suffering (*passio*) of the Father (*pater*). This term was used as a pejorative code word for modalism in patristic theology. If Father, Son, and Holy Spirit are simply modes of the single person of God, then it follows that the Christ suffering on the cross is also actually the Father. This view was considered problematic in doctrinal history mostly because of its association with the modalistic heresy, but also because it violated the assumed axiom of divine apathy or impassibility (Chapter 5).

patristic. The period of the "fathers" (Gk. *pateres*) of the church, spanning roughly 100 CE to 500 CE, in which the foundations of Christian theology were laid (Chapter 16).

penal substitution. A theory of the atonement that interprets Christ's saving death as a substitutionary bearing of the punishment that human beings owe for sin. In freely giving himself up to a sacrificial death, Christ bears God's wrath and pays the penalty for sin in humanity's place (Chapter 10).

perichoresis. In reference to the Trinity, a term first found in John of Damascus' *The Orthodox Faith* (eighth century), which connotes the "mutual indwelling," "interpenetration," and "fellowship" of the trinitarian persons. Based on the oneness or "in-ness" of Father and Son as portrayed in John's gospel (e.g., 10:30), the term *perichoresis* emphasizes the unity of the Trinity in view of the distinction of persons (Chapters 5 and 9).

philosophical theology. In its narrower sense, philosophical theology discerns what may be known about God through human reason and has historically focused on the project of rationally demonstrating God's existence and attributes. However, if the term "philosophy" can also refer more broadly to human learning in its wide array of forms, then a broader sense of philosophical theology refers to the engagement of theology with all disciplines of human inquiry – the interaction of the current state of human wisdom with the themes of Christian faith (Chapter 1).

philosophy. Literally, the "love of wisdom." In its classical and broadest sense, philosophy refers to the truths resulting from human inquiry in a wide range of domains. Philosophy involves the truths of reason and experience as they are discovered through the breadth of the arts and sciences. In this broad sense of human learning, philosophy serves as one of the three sources and norms of theology (Chapter 1).

pluralism. Along with exclusivism and inclusivism, pluralism is one of the three positions on the question whether salvation is possible outside of the church. This view holds that the one God – or the one transcendent reality – is present to all the peoples of the world, regardless of their particular religion. Each culture or religious tradition therefore has its own way of approaching, conceiving, and naming that single transcendent reality. Since there are many paths to God, truth can never be restricted to the sacred writings or human traditions of just one religion. Rather, the pluralistic perspective supposes the existence of many different revelations of God, which provide salvation through the many religions of the world (Chapter 14).

pneumatology. From Gk. *pneuma* = spirit. The doctrine of the Holy Spirit, which typically includes discussion of the person and work of the Spirit as the third person of the Trinity (Chapter 11).

pneumatomachianism. Literally, "Spirit-fighters." A pejorative label given to those in the mid-to late fourth century who denied that the Holy Spirit was equal in divinity to Father and Son. The pneumatomachians were also called *Tropici* (Chapters 11 and 16).

postmillennialism. A millennial perspective which holds that the second coming of Christ will occur *after* a golden age of Christian civilization of considerable duration – the "millennium" of Revelation 20, although not necessarily a literal 1,000 years. Flourishing in the modern period, postmillennialists optimistically believed that the preaching of the gospel would convert the nations, bringing an unprecedented era of peace, prosperity, justice, and righteous living to the world, which would welcome Christ at his second coming (Chapter 15).

postmodernism. Beginning roughly in the 1960s, postmodernism is regarded as the dawning intellectual mood and cultural ethos that must of necessity come *after* modernity, given the latter's destructive and exclusionary legacy. In contrast to the modernist belief in the powers of human rationality and inevitable progress, postmodernism reckons with the destructive underside of technological progress, the inevitable subjectivity of truth, and the marginalizing function of "metanarratives," among a collage of other postmodernist themes (Chapters 2 and 20).

practical theology. In its most technical sense, practical theology deals with how theology is applied in the life of the church, and includes the fields of homiletics (preaching), liturgy (worship), pastoral care, Christian education, and church government. In a broader sense, however, all Christian theology should be seen as practical theology, since theology at its best is concerned with how doctrines intersect with life in the world (Chapter 1).

praxis. As rooted in Aristotle's understanding, and as utilized in theology today, praxis is the ongoing dialogue (dialectic) between theory and practice. The dialectics of praxis underscore that thinking and action are never done in isolation from each other, but always condition each other. Attention to praxis is part of the theological sensitivity to issues of contextualization and is a central concern of liberation theology (Chapter 20).

predestination. The view, typically associated with Augustine and Calvin, that God eternally chooses which human beings will be saved through grace (the "elect") and which human beings will be condemned for their sin (the "reprobate") (Chapters 13 and 18). (*See also* election *and* reprobation.)

premillennialism, historic. A millennial perspective that holds that the second coming of Christ will happen in dramatic, apocalyptic fashion *prior to* the establishment of a golden age on earth, a 1,000-year reign of peace, prosperity, and renewal that will occur before the general resurrection, final judgment, and inauguration of the eternal state of salvation. Largely embraced by the early church before the influence of Augustine's amillennialism (Chapter 15).

prosopon. Most literally, "face." As a synecdoche, *prosopon* took on the sense of "person" and became one of the differentiating terms that emerged in the Greek-speaking patristic church to denote the three persons of the Trinity in their distinction from one another. *Prosopon* is a threeness term that parallels the Gk. *hypostasis* and the Lat. *persona* (Chapter 5).

providence. When understanding creation primarily as "creation in the beginning," providence is the complementary systematic category that refers to God's active and ongoing work of "providing" for creation by way of preservation and governance. Preservation concerns the way that God continues to sustain creation in its natural integrity; governance concerns the way that God intervenes in the affairs of the world so as to direct history to God's desired goal. Together, creation and providence traditionally sum up the basic God–world relationship (Chapter 6). (*See also creatio continua.*)

psychopannychia. Literally, "soul-sleep." On the question of the state of the person between death and resurrection, this position maintains that the soul enters into an unconscious, sleep-like state, to be awakened only at the resurrection. *Psychopannychia* attempts to account for the NT's pervasive use of sleep as a metaphor for death, as well as the weight it puts on the resurrection as the central eschatological hope (Chapter 15).

ransom. A popular view of Christ's work in the early church, emphasizing the financial metaphor of Christ's death as an exchange that liberates humanity from its enslavement. Christ offers himself as a ransom for humanity, which sold itself to the devil by means of its sin. This broad "atonement" motif is often coupled with the *Christus victor* theory of atonement (Chapter 10).

realism. In the medieval debate over the status of "universals," realism was the view that the mind can abstract from particular things (e.g., trees) the universal ideas (e.g., "treeness") that are the essence or inherent form of those particulars. To know "treeness," for example, is to know the real objective essence or form of trees. This means that universals exist in reality. Grasping these universal essences allows the theologian/philosopher to use reason to demonstrate necessary truths in the realm of particulars (Chapter 17).

recapitulation. Irenaeus' chief account of the saving work of Christ based on Paul's Adam typology (see, e.g., Rom. 5:12–21). As the second Adam, Christ "re-lives" the life of the first Adam, retracing his steps and experiencing all of the stages of human life. Unlike the first Adam, however, who faltered in obedience to God, Christ does not succumb to temptation, but remains faithful and obedient to God. In this work of "summing up" or recapitulating the trial of human life, Jesus Christ sanctifies humanity and provides salvation (Chapters 10 and 16).

regula fidei. Literally, "rule of faith." In the early church, the "rule of faith" referred to a summary statement of the main teachings of Christian belief. Such statements were used liturgically and catechetically with the intention of serving as a "rule" for the Christian life of faith. While the rule of faith had a rather flexible form, with different communities using different versions of it, such statements served as predecessors of later creeds (Chapter 16).

reprobation. God's condemnation of some human beings to eternal damnation, usually conceived of as part of an eternal predestining decree of God. Reprobation is the counterpart to election in theories of double predestination (Chapters 13 and 18).

revelation, general. The disclosure of a natural knowledge of God via the structures of creation. This universally accessible revelation is thought to be apprehended by human reason, intuition, or conscience, resulting in what is typically called natural theology (Chapter 3).

revelation, special. The disclosure of a special knowledge of God via divine redemptive acts and words. This particular revelation is apprehended by faith (through the work of the Holy Spirit), resulting in what is typically called sacred theology (Chapter 3).

Sabellianism. Rooted in the thought of Sabellius, Sabellianism is the classic form of modalism and as such functions as a synonym for this early trinitarian heresy (Chapter 5). (*See also* modalism.)

sacraments. Fixed rites of the church which symbolically communicate the gospel as "means of grace." In the western-Augustinian tradition, a sacrament is traditionally defined as a visible sign of an invisible grace. Nearly all Christian traditions accept baptism and the Lord's Supper as sacraments, since they symbolize quite forthrightly the chief events of the gospel – Christ's death and resurrection – and were specifically commanded by Jesus himself. Some traditions, such as Roman Catholicism, however, argue for additional rites (such as penance and marriage) as sacraments (Chapter 13).

sanctification. The process in the Christian life of becoming holy (Lat. *sanctus* = holy); the gradual and life-long progression of being conformed in disposition and behavior to the image of Christ through God's grace. Along with justification, sanctification is a key component of soteriology (Chapter 12).

satisfaction. The key concept of Anselm's theory of atonement. Through their sin, human beings have stolen from God the perfect fidelity that they owe. Since they are unable to make "satisfaction" or restitution for their robbery, God sends Jesus Christ to make satisfaction on their behalf through his perfect life and gracious death (Chapters 10 and 17).

scholasticism. The movement of theology practiced by medieval "school-men" or scholastics, which attempted to establish theology as an ordered inquiry – in other words, as a science. Scholasticism strove to articulate the whole of Christian doctrine in a clear, orderly, and sophisticated fashion, with special attention to the proper use of rationality in a methodologically self-conscious way. As implied by its name, the development of scholasticism or "school theology" primarily took place in the burgeoning universities of medieval Europe (e.g., Paris, Oxford, Cambridge), although some of the earliest scholastic theologians were monks who taught at church schools (Chapters 4 and 17).

scripture. From Lat. *scriptura* = writing. Synonymous with the biblical text, which tells the story of God's relation with creation, scripture is generally considered to be an "inspired" and authoritative text, and is therefore typically regarded as the primary source and norm of Christian theology (Chapters 1 and 3).

secularization. From Lat. *saeculum* = "world" or "age." Secularization refers to the world "coming of age," the world discovering itself in its own autonomy, freedom, and relative independence, especially during the Enlightenment period. More particularly, secularization is the process of understanding the world and its various activities (e.g., science, politics, economics) increasingly in their own natural terms and structural integrity without direct recourse to supernatural explanation or divine governance (Chapters 4 and 19).

Septuagint. The Greek version of the Hebrew Bible translated over the course of the third to first centuries BCE in Alexandria, Egypt. The term *septuaginta* denotes "seventy" on account of the legend that seventy Jewish scholars independently arrived at the same translation – hence its abbreviation, LXX. The Septuagint contains the books of the Apocrypha and is the textual tradition overwhelmingly used in NT references to the OT.

shalom. Literally translated as "peace." *Shalom* in the Hebrew Bible connotes fullness and wholeness of well-being, the vital flourishing of all things in right relationships – with God, humanity, and nature at large. *Shalom* describes God's intention for creation and God's promise for the new creation (Chapters 7, 12, and 15).

Shema. The central theological confession of ancient Israel in the OT. From Deuteronomy 6:4, this confession is called the *Shema* from its first Hebrew word, "Hear." It is traditionally translated: "Hear, O Israel, the LORD (*YHWH*) our God (*Elohim*) is One." In its original setting, the *Shema* was an injunction to monolatry – the worship of only one god, YHWH, the God of the Israelites, as opposed to other gods – and is best translated along the lines of "Hear, O Israel, Yahweh is our God, Yahweh alone" (Chapters 4 and 5).

Sheol. In the OT, *Sheol* can refer simply to the grave, but also to the nondescript place of the dead, a land of darkness and shadowy existence. Rather than a clear conception of an afterlife, *Sheol* largely functions as a metaphorical contrast to the fortunate life of the living. In the intertestamental and NT periods, *Sheol* translates into the Greek *Hades*, becoming a place of conscious existence, expressing the hope that death will not have the final say (Chapter 15).

simplicity, divine. The classical theistic idea derived *via negativa* that God is one singular, utterly indivisible entity. This divine attribute, also known as indivisibility, was part and parcel of a Greek philosophical conception of the divine that influenced Christian views of God beginning in the patristic period, creating a tension with trinitarian affirmations (Chapters 4 and 5).

sin. Anything in thought, word, or deed that opposes the will of God and distorts the harmony of creation. Sin is often interpreted as rebellion against God by free moral agents who resist God's will, resulting in corruption and evil in the world (Chapter 7).

sin, actual. The acts of sin that human beings commit and for which they are individually guilty. Actual sin is typically understood as something that is fostered by the tendencies inculcated in people by original sin and is also manifested as structural or systemic sin (Chapter 7).

sin, original. The idea that because all of humanity is united as an organic whole, all instances of sin in the world must be traced to a common origin, such as the "original" sin of Adam and Eve. The traditional Augustinian view of original sin claims that Adam and Eve's sin infected human nature, such that all people who are subsequently born into that nature inherit the guilt and sinful inclinations that resulted from their first sin, since sin is part and parcel of the human nature that is passed on in the reproduction of the human race (Chapter 7).

sin, structural/systemic. Sin that transcends individual persons and becomes a force or dynamic that permeates the institutions, attitudes, structures, and systems of society. The notion of structural and systemic sin involves the recognition that the sins of persons in the world also combine to form larger corporate realities – such as poverty, sexism, and species extinction – that result from patterns and structures of human society rather than from particular individuals (Chapter 7).

Son of Man. A phrase sometimes used in the OT to describe a human being (e.g., Ezek. 2:1), but which takes on greater significance as a "messianic" conception as it appears in the book of Daniel (7:13–14) and in the intertestamental period. This title refers to an agent of Yahweh who will descend with power from the heavenly realm to establish the kingdom of God and vindicate the nation of Israel through judgment, a motif that sometimes melded with the hope for a powerful Davidic kingly messiah. In the gospels, "Son of Man" is Jesus' favorite self-designation and likely encapsulates his basic understanding of his messianic mission (e.g., Mark 14:62) (Chapter 9).

soteriology. From Gk. *soteria* = salvation. The doctrine of salvation, typically including discussion of justification, sanctification, and the Christian life (Chapter 12).

subsistent relation. The construct in western trinitarianism (with roots in Augustine and as systematized by Aquinas) that conceives of the trinitarian "persons" or *hypostases* not as discrete personal entities, but as sheer "relations" within the one divine substance. This interpretation of the persons is due to the assumption of divine simplicity, which allows only one substantial thing in God – the singular divine essence with which each of the three persons is identical. As subsistent relations, the Father *just is* the individuating characteristic of fatherhood (*paternitas*) in the divine essence, the Son *is* the relation of sonship (*filiatio*), and the Spirit *is* merely the characteristic of being breathed out (*spiratio*) (Chapter 5).

systematic theology. The synthetic branch of theology that endeavors to integrate biblical data, historical insights, and the fruits of human learning into a systematically ordered, coherent, and constructive statement about the triune God, creation, and their relation. As such, systematic theology draws upon the best of biblical theology, historical theology, and philosophical theology in order to render an account of the big picture of Christian faith (what Christians believe and how they should live) by examining the content and interaction of component Christian doctrines and their practical implications (Chapter 1).

teleological. Oriented to purpose or ends (Gk. *telos*). Among other uses, this term refers to approaches in ethics that tether the ethical act to the results it intends to bring about. Teleological ethics are closely related to consequentialist ethics and typically contrasted with deontological ethics (Chapter 19).

teleological argument. An argument for the existence of God that reasons from the purpose (*telos*), order, or design of the world to the Intelligent Mind or Designer behind it. Also known as the "argument from design," the teleological argument is the fifth of Thomas Aquinas' famous "Five Ways" (Chapters 3 and 4).

tertium quid. Literally, "third thing." It was the view of Eutyches that in the incarnation the Logos so unites himself to human nature that the result is a "third thing," a divine-human hybrid or fusion in which the deity of Christ overtakes and divinizes his humanity. Ruled out by the Council of Chalcedon (451), Eutyches' position anticipated the later view known as monophysitism (Chapters 9 and 16).

theodicy. From Gk. *Theos* (God) and *dike* (justice). A term coined by the philosopher Leibniz to denote the attempt to "justify God" as being both all-powerful (omnipotent) and all-good (omnibenevolent) in the face of evil. In its most specific sense, the term "theodicy" refers to arguments that attempt to specify why God and evil are compatible realities; in its broadest sense, theodicy refers to the general problem of evil (Chapter 8).

theology. From *Theos* (God) and *logos* (word, speech, account). The discipline of speaking carefully and responsibly about God. In its broadest sense, theology refers to the elaboration of a reasoned account of God, creation, and their relation (Chapter 1).

theology proper. The doctrine of God. Since the term "theology" is often used in a general sense, the term "proper" is sometimes appended to denote "talk about God" in the most particular sense – the specific doctrine of God (Chapter 4).

Theotokos. Literally, "bearer of God." In the patristic Greek-speaking church, a popular liturgical custom developed of referring to the Virgin Mary as *Theotokos*, a belief and practice held especially dear by the Alexandrian school. For the Alexandrians, the *Theotokos* was a necessary confession because it affirmed the "communication of attributes" (*communicatio idiomatum*) and therefore strongly underscored the personal unity of Christ's deity and humanity by implying that the eternal Logos *is* the person Jesus who was born of Mary. The orthodoxy of this affirmation was secured by its inclusion in the definition of the Council of Chalcedon in 451 (Chapters 9 and 16).

tradition. The deposit of theological and practical wisdom offered by the Christian church throughout the breadth of its history as transmitted in its creeds and confessions, liturgies, practices, biblical commentaries, and theological writings. Along with scripture and philosophy (human learning), tradition is one of the three main sources and norms of Christian theology (Chapter 1).

transcendence. In Christian theology, the idea that God is *beyond* creation, a complement to the affirmation that God is immanent in creation. Divine transcendence affirms that God surpasses and cannot be reduced to the creaturely level, since God is the Creator and Lord of the cosmos (Chapter 6).

transubstantiation. The Catholic view, declared dogma at the Fourth Lateran Council in 1215, that in the Lord's Supper, the body and blood of Christ are physically present by virtue of the bread and wine being transformed in their essence ("substance"), even though their external appearance ("accidents") remains that of bread and wine (Chapters 13, 17, and 18).

Trinity, economic. The Trinity viewed from the perspective of salvation history. "Economic Trinity" refers to the three persons of the Trinity in their dynamic work of creation and redemption (Chapter 5).

Trinity, immanent. The Trinity viewed from the perspective of eternity. "Immanent Trinity" refers to the three persons of the Trinity in their essential relationships with one another, even apart from creation (Chapter 5).

universalism. Offered as an alternative to the traditional view of an eternal punitive hell, the eschatological perspective that holds that all human beings (or even all creatures) will ultimately be saved. This belief has taken a variety of forms, the more simple denying even the existence of hell, and the more complex holding that there is a hell as a place of justice, but that hell is not of eternal duration and will eventually be emptied (Chapter 15). (See also *apokatastasis*.)

via negativa. Literally, the "negative way." The method of ascertaining the divine attributes in classical theism by saying what God *is not*. Since God is different from the world, and not subject to the un-desirable attributes of finite existence, God must possess the opposite of those creaturely qualities. Hence reflection on the (ostensibly) prob-lematic characteristics of composition, change, passibility/suffering, and temporality in the world yields the negative divine attributes of indivisibility, immutability, impassibility/apathy, and eternality (Chapter 4).

via positiva / eminentiae. Literally, the "positive way" or "way of eminence." The method of ascertaining the divine attributes in classical theism by saying what God *is*. Since God is the eminent ground and cause of all the good and desirable things in the world, God must possess those attributes in maximal measure. Hence reflection on the characteristics of goodness, power, knowledge, and presence in the world yields the positive divine attributes of omnibenevolence, omnipotence, omniscience, and omni-presence (Chapter 4).

vivification. Along with mortification, one of the essential components of repentance and sanctification. Vivification signifies new life in the Holy Spirit, the sinner's coming alive to faithfulness and obedience as a new creation through the grace of Christ (Chapter 12).

vocation. From Lat. *vocatio* = calling. Most generally, the calling of the corporate church and individual Christians to participate in God's saving renewal of the created order. More narrowly, the term referred in tradi-tional Catholic theology to someone's calling to a religious order or the priesthood. In Protestant theology, vocation was broadened to refer to a person's calling to any kind of profession or occupation, "sacred" or "secular," through which one serves God and lives out his or her Christianity (Chapter 12).

Vulgate. The definitive Latin translation of the Bible, commissioned by Pope Damasus in 382 and attributed largely to the labors of Jerome. The

Vulgate includes the books of the Apocrypha and became the official Latin Bible of the Roman Catholic Church.

Yahweh. The personal and covenantal name of God given to Israel (see Exod. 3:14). Called the Tetragrammaton or "four consonants," since ancient Hebrew did not possess letters for vowels, the name YHWH remains unspoken by most Jews (often referred to simply as "The Name") but is otherwise written and pronounced as "Yahweh" and rendered in most English Bibles as Lord. As the particular covenantal name of God, Yahweh expresses the promise of God's faithful presence to sojourning Israel (Chapters 4 and 5).

Bibliography

Abelard, Peter, "Exposition of the Epistle to the Romans," in *A Scholastic Miscellany: Anselm to Ockham*, ed. Eugene R. Fairweather, Library of Christian Classics, Philadelphia: Westminster, 1956.

    Sic et Non: A Critical Edition, ed. Blanche B. Boyer and Richard McKeon, Chicago: University of Chicago Press, 1976.

Abraham, William J., *The Divine Inspiration of Holy Scripture*, Oxford: Oxford University Press, 1981.

Aikman, David, *Jesus in Beijing: How Christianity is Transforming China and Changing the Global Balance of Power*, Washington DC: Regnery, 2003.

Allen, Diogenes, *Christian Belief in a Postmodern World*, Louisville, KY: Westminster John Knox, 1989.

Allen, Diogenes, and Eric O. Springsted, *Philosophy for Understanding Theology*, 2nd edn., Louisville, KY: Westminster John Knox, 2007.

Althaus, Paul, *The Theology of Martin Luther*, trans. Robert C. Schultz, Philadelphia: Fortress, 1966.

Altizer, Thomas J. J., *The Gospel of Christian Atheism*, Philadelphia: Westminster, 1966.

Altizer, Thomas J. J., and William Hamilton, *Radical Theology and the Death of God*, Indianapolis, IN: Bobbs-Merrill, 1966.

Anselm of Canterbury, *Proslogion*, in *The Prayers and Meditations of Saint Anselm*, trans. Sister B. Ward, Harmondsworth: Penguin, 1973.

    Why God Became Man, in *A Scholastic Miscellany: Anselm to Ockham*, ed. Eugene R. Fairweather, Library of Christian Classics, Philadelphia: Westminster, 1956, 100–83.

Aristotle, *Categories*, in *The Basic Works of Aristotle*, ed. Richard McKeon, New York: Random House, 1941.

Athanasius, *On the Incarnation of the Word*, in *Christology of the Later Fathers*, ed. Edward Rochie Hardy and Cyril C. Richardson, Library of Christian Classics, Louisville, KY: Westminster John Knox, 1954, 55–110.

Athenagoras, *A Plea Regarding Christians*, ed. and trans. Cyril C. Richardson, in *Early Christian Fathers*, ed. Cyril C. Richardson, Library of Christian Classics, Philadelphia: Westminster, 1953, 300–40.

Augustine, *The City of God*, trans. Henry Bettenson, London: Penguin, 1972.

    Confessions, trans. R. S. Pine-Coffin, Harmondsworth: Penguin, 1961.

On Baptism, Against the Donatists, trans. J. R. King, in *Nicene and Post-Nicene Fathers*, 1st series, ed. Philip Schaff, Grand Rapids, MI: Eerdmans, 1993, IV: 411–514.

On Nature and Grace, in *Four Anti-Pelagian Writings*, trans. John A. Mourant and William J. Collinge, The Fathers of the Church 86, Washington DC: Catholic University of America Press, 1992, 22–90.

The Nature and Origin of the Soul, trans. Roland J. Teske, in *Answer to the Pelagians*, The Works of Saint Augustine 1/23, New York: New City, 1997, 473–561.

The Perfection of Human Righteousness, trans. Roland J. Teske, in *Answer to the Pelagians*, The Works of Saint Augustine 1/23, New York: New City, 1997, 289–316.

On the Profit of Believing, trans. C. L. Cornish, in *Nicene and Post-Nicene Fathers*, 1st series, ed. Philip Schaff, Grand Rapids, MI: Eerdmans, 1993, III: 347–66.

The Punishment and Forgiveness of Sins and the Baptism of Little Ones, trans. Roland J. Teske, in *Answer to the Pelagians*, The Works of Saint Augustine 1/23, New York: New City, 1997, 34–137.

On Rebuke and Grace, trans. Peter Holmes, Robert Ernest Wallis, and Benjamin B. Warfield, in *Nicene and Post-Nicene Fathers*, 1st series, ed. Philip Schaff, Grand Rapids, MI: Eerdmans, 1993, V: 471–91.

The Trinity, trans. Edmund Hill, The Works of Saint Augustine 1/5, New York: New City, 1991.

Aulén, Gustaf, *Christus Victor: An Historical Study of the Three Main Types of the Idea of Atonement*, trans. A. G. Hebert, New York: Macmillan, 1951.

Balthasar, Hans Urs von, *Dare We Hope "That All Men Be Saved"?*, trans. David Kipp and Lothar Krauth, San Francisco: Ignatius, 1988.

Barth, Karl, *Church Dogmatics*, ed. Geoffrey W. Bromiley and Thomas F. Torrance, 4 vols, various translators, Edinburgh: T. & T. Clark, 1956–75.

Dogmatics in Outline, trans. G. T. Thomson, New York: Harper & Row, 1959.

The Epistle to the Romans, trans. Edwyn C. Hoskyns, 6th edn. London: Oxford University Press, 1933.

"The Strange New World within the Bible," in *The Word of God and the Word of Man*, New York: Harper & Row, 1957.

Basil of Caesarea, "Letter 236," trans. Blomfield Jackson, in *Nicene and Post-Nicene Fathers*, 2nd series, ed. Philip Schaff and Henry Wace, Grand Rapids, MI: Eerdmans, 1993, VIII: 276–9.

Bauckham, Richard, *The Theology of the Book of Revelation*, Cambridge: Cambridge University Press, 1993.

Bauman, Zygmunt, *Modernity and the Holocaust*, Ithaca, NY: Cornell University Press, 1989.

Bediako, Kwame, *Jesus in Africa: The Christian Gospel in African History and Experience*, Yaoundé, Cameroon: Éditions Clé, 2000.

"Jesus in African Culture: A Ghanaian Perspective," in *Emerging Voices in Global Christian Theology*, ed. William A. Dyrness, Grand Rapids, MI: Zondervan, 1994, 93–121.

Berger, Peter L., *The Sacred Canopy: Elements of a Sociological Theory of Religion*, Garden City, NY: Doubleday, 1969.

Berkouwer, G. C., *Man: The Image of God*, trans. Dirk W. Jellema, Grand Rapids, MI: Eerdmans, 1962.

Sin, trans. Philip C. Holtrop, Grand Rapids, MI: Eerdmans, 1971.

Bernard, G. W., *The King's Reformation: Henry VIII and the Remaking of the English Church*, New Haven, CT: Yale University Press, 2005.

Bevans, Stephen B., *Models of Contextual Theology*, Faith and Cultures, Maryknoll, NY: Orbis, 2003.

Boersma, Hans, *Violence, Hospitality, and the Cross: Reappropriating the Atonement Tradition*, Grand Rapids, MI: Baker Academic, 2004.

Boesak, Allan A., *Black and Reformed: Apartheid, Liberation and the Calvinist Tradition*, ed. Leonard Sweetman, Maryknoll, NY: Orbis, 1984.

Boethius, "A Treatise Against Eutyches and Nestorius," in *The Theological Tractates*, trans. H. F. Stewart and E. K. Rand, Loeb Classical Library 74, Cambridge, MA: Harvard University Press, 1936, 73–127.

Boff, Leonardo, and Clodovis Boff, *Introducing Liberation Theology*, trans. Paul Burns, Maryknoll, NY: Orbis, 1987.

Bonaventure, *The Mind's Journey to God*, trans. Lawrence S. Cunningham, Chicago: Franciscan Herald Press, 1979.

Bonhoeffer, Dietrich, *Discipleship*, trans. Martin Liske, Ilse Tödt, Barbara Green, and Reinhard Krauss, ed. Geffrey B. Kelly and John D. Godsey, Dietrich Bonhoeffer Works 4, Minneapolis, MN: Fortress, 2003.

Ethics, ed. Ilse Tödt, Heinz Eduard Tödt, Ernst Feil, and Clifford Green, trans. Reinhard Krauss, Charles C. West, and Douglas W. Stott, Dietrich Bonhoeffer Works 6, Minneapolis, MN: Fortress, 2005.

"Geheimnis," in Dietrich Bonhoeffer, *Gesammelte Schriften*, ed. Eberhard Bethge, Munich: Chr. Kaiser Verlag, 1972, v: 515–20.

Letters and Papers from Prison, ed. Eberhard Bethge, trans. R. H. Fuller *et al.*, enlarged edn., New York: Macmillan, 1972.

Botterweck, G. Johannes, and Helmer Ringgren, eds., *Theological Dictionary of the Old Testament*, various translators, 15 vols., Grand Rapids, MI: Eerdmans, 1974–2006.

Bray, Gerald, "The *Filioque* Clause in History and Theology," *Tyndale Bulletin* 34 (1983), 91–144.

Bridges, Robert Seymour, and H. Ellis Wooldridge, eds., *Hymns: The Yattendon Hymnal*, Oxford: Oxford University Press, 1899.

Brock, Rita Nakashima, "And a Little Child Will Lead Us: Christology and Child Abuse," in *Christianity, Patriarchy, and Abuse: A Feminist Critique*, ed. Joanne Carlson Brown and Carole R. Bohn, New York: Pilgrim, 1989, 42–61.

Bromiley, Geoffrey W., ed., *Zwingli and Bullinger*, Library of Christian Classics, Philadelphia: Westminster, 1953.

Brown, David, *Invitation to Theology*, Oxford: Blackwell, 1989.

Brown, Peter, *Augustine of Hippo: A Biography*, 2nd edn., Berkeley, CA: University of California Press, 2000.

Brown, Raymond E., *An Introduction to New Testament Christology*, Mahwah, NJ: Paulist, 1994.

Brueggemann, Walter, *The Land: Place as Gift, Promise, and Challenge in Biblical Faith*, 2nd edn., Minneapolis, MN: Fortress, 2002.

Brunner, Emil, *Dogmatics*, II: *The Christian Doctrine of Creation and Redemption*, trans. Olive Wyon, Philadelphia: Westminster, 1952.

Man in Revolt: A Christian Anthropology, trans. Olive Wyon, London: Lutterworth, 1939.

Truth as Encounter, trans. Amandus W. Loos *et al.*, rev. edn., London: SCM, 1964.

Brunner, Emil, and Karl Barth, *Natural Theology: Comprising "Nature and Grace" by Professor Dr. Emil Brunner and the Reply "No!" by Dr. Karl Barth*, trans. Peter Fraenkel, London: Centenary, 1946.

Bulgakov, Sergei, *Sophia: The Wisdom of God: An Outline of Sophiology*, Library of Russian Theology, Hudson, NY: Lindisfarne, 1993.

Bultmann, Rudolf, "New Testament and Mythology," in *Kerygma and Myth: A Theological Debate*, ed. Hans Werner Bartsch, New York: Harper & Brothers, 1961.

Theology of the New Testament, trans. Kendrick Grobel, 2 vols., New York: Scribner, 1951–5.

Burge, James, *Heloise and Abelard: A New Biography*, San Francisco: HarperSan Francisco, 2003.

Cahill, Thomas, *How the Irish Saved Civilization*, Hinges of History, New York: Doubleday, 1995.

Calvin, John, *Institutes of the Christian Religion*, trans. Ford Lewis Battles, ed. John T. McNeill, Library of Christian Classics, Philadelphia: Westminster, 1960.

Camus, Albert, *The Myth of Sisyphus and Other Essays*, trans. Justin O'Brien, New York: Vintage, 1991.

Canons and Decrees of the Council of Trent, trans. H. J. Schroeder, St. Louis: Herder, 1950.

Caputo, John D., *Philosophy and Theology*, Horizons in Theology, Nashville, TN: Abingdon, 2006.

Carpenter, Joel A., Preface to *The Changing Face of Christianity? Africa, the West, and the World*, ed. Lamin Sanneh and Joel A. Carpenter, New York: Oxford University Press, 2005.

Carroll, Lewis, *Alice's Adventures in Wonderland and Through the Looking-Glass*, New York: New American Library, 1960.

Catechism of the Catholic Church, New York: Doubleday, 1994.

Chadwick, Owen, *The Early Reformation on the Continent*, Oxford History of the Christian Church, Oxford: Oxford University Press, 2001.

Chopp, Rebecca S., "Feminist and Womanist Theologies," in *The Modern Theologians: An Introduction to Christian Theology in the Twentieth Century*, ed. David Ford, 2nd edn., Oxford: Blackwell, 1997.

Clement of Alexandria, *The Stromata*, ed. A. Cleveland Coxe, in *Ante-Nicene Fathers*, ed. Alexander Roberts and James Donaldson, Grand Rapids, MI: Eerdmans, 1993, II: 299–520.

Clowney, Edmund P., *The Church*, Contours of Christian Theology, Downers Grove, IL: InterVarsity, 1995.

Cobb, John B., and David Ray Griffin, *Process Theology: An Introductory Exposition*, Philadelphia: Westminster, 1976.

Collins, John J., *The Scepter and the Star: The Messiahs of the Dead Sea Scrolls and Other Ancient Literature*, New York: Doubleday, 1995.

Cone, James H., *Black Theology and Black Power*, New York: Seabury, 1969.

A Black Theology of Liberation, rev. edn., Maryknoll, NY: Orbis, 1990.

God of the Oppressed, New York: Seabury, 1975.

Martin and Malcolm and America: A Dream or a Nightmare?, Maryknoll, NY: Orbis, 1991.

Congar, Yves M. J., *I Believe in the Holy Spirit*, trans. David Smith, 3 vols., New York: Seabury, 1983.

Lay People in the Church: A Study for a Theology of the Laity, Westminster, MD: Newman, 1957.

Cooper, John W., *Body, Soul, and Life Everlasting: Biblical Anthropology and the Monism–Dualism Debate*, 2nd edn., Grand Rapids, MI: Eerdmans, 2000.

Copleston, Frederick, *A History of Philosophy*, I: *Greece and Rome*, New York: Image Books, 1993.

A History of Philosophy, II: *Medieval Philosophy*, New York: Image Books, 1993.

Cox, Harvey, *Fire From Heaven: The Rise of Pentecostal Spirituality and the Reshaping of Religion in the Twenty-first Century*, Reading, MA: Addison-Wesley, 1995.

The Secular City, New York: Macmillan, 1965.

The Silencing of Leonardo Boff: The Vatican and the Future of World Christianity, Oak Park, IL: Meyer-Stone, 1988.

Cross, Richard, *Duns Scotus*, Great Medieval Thinkers, New York: Oxford University Press, 1999.

Cullmann, Oscar, *Christ and Time: The Primitive Christian Conception of Time and History*, trans. Floyd V. Filson, rev. edn., Philadelphia: Westminster, 1964.

The Christology of the New Testament, trans. Shirley C. Guthrie and Charles A. M. Hall, rev. edn., Philadelphia: Westminster, 1963.

Immortality of the Soul or Resurrection of the Dead? The Witness of the New Testament, New York: Macmillan, 1964.

Daly, Mary, "The Qualitative Leap beyond Patriarchal Religion," *Quest* 1, no. 4 (1975), 20–40.

Dawkins, Richard, *The Blind Watchmaker: Why the Evidence of Evolution Reveals a Universe Without Design*, New York: Norton, 1987.

Denzinger, Henry, ed., *The Sources of Catholic Dogma*, trans. Roy J. Deferrari, St. Louis: Herder, 1957.

Descartes, René, *Discourse on Method and Meditations on First Philosophy*, trans. Donald A. Cress, 4th edn., Indianapolis, IN: Hackett, 1998.

Dickinson, Emily, *The Complete Poems of Emily Dickinson*, ed. Thomas H. Johnson, Boston: Little, Brown & Co., 1960.

Dostoevsky, Fyodor, *The Brothers Karamazov*, trans. Constance Garnett, New York: New American Library, 1980.

Dowey, Edward A., Jr., *The Knowledge of God in Calvin's Theology*, 3rd edn., Grand Rapids, MI: Eerdmans, 1994.

Dulles, Avery, *Models of the Church*, rev. edn., New York: Doubleday, 2002.

Models of Revelation, Garden City, NY: Image Books, 1985.

Ehrman, Bart D., *Lost Scriptures: Books that Did Not Make it into the New Testament*, Oxford: Oxford University Press, 2003.

Ellacuría, Ignacio, "The Crucified People," trans. Phillip Berryman and Robert R. Barr, in *Mysterium Liberationis: Fundamental Concepts of Liberation Theology*, ed. Ignacio Ellacuría and Jon Sobrino, Maryknoll, NY: Orbis, 1993, 580–603.

Evans, C. Stephen, ed., *Exploring Kenotic Christology: The Self-Emptying of God*, Oxford: Oxford University Press, 2006.

Fairweather, Eugene R., ed., *A Scholastic Miscellany: Anselm to Ockham*, Library of Christian Classics, Philadelphia: Westminster, 1956.

Farhadian, Charles E., ed., *Christian Worship Worldwide: Expanding Horizons, Deepening Practices*, Grand Rapids, MI: Eerdmans, 2007.

Fee, Gordon D., and Douglas Stewart, *How to Read the Bible For All its Worth*, 3rd edn., Grand Rapids, MI: Zondervan, 2003.

Ferguson, Everett, *Backgrounds of Early Christianity*, 2nd edn., Grand Rapids, MI: Eerdmans, 1993.

Ferruolo, Stephen, *The Origins of the University: The Schools of Paris and Their Critics, 1100–1215*, Stanford, CA: Stanford University Press, 1985.

Feuerbach, Ludwig, *The Essence of Christianity*, trans. George Eliot, Great Books in Philosophy, New York: Prometheus, 1989.

Lectures on the Essence of Religion, trans. Ralph Mannheim, New York: Harper & Row, 1967.

Flannery, Austin, ed., *Vatican Council II*, 1: *The Conciliar and Postconciliar Documents*, rev. edn., Northport, NY: Costello, 1996.

Floros, Constantin, *Gustav Mahler: The Symphonies*, trans. Vernon Wicker and Jutta Wicker, ed. Reinhard G. Pauly, Portland, OR: Amadeus Press, 1993.

Foster, Michael B., "The Christian Doctrine of Creation and the Rise of Modern Science," *Mind* 43 (1934), 446–68.

Freeman, Kathleen, ed., *Ancilla to the Pre-Socratic Philosophers: A Complete Translation of the Fragments in Diels*, Fragmente der Vorsokratiker, Cambridge, MA: Harvard University Press, 1948.

Frei, Hans, *The Eclipse of Biblical Narrative: A Study in Eighteenth and Nineteenth Century Hermeneutics*, New Haven, CT: Yale University Press, 1974.

Freston, Paul, *Evangelicals and Politics in Asia, Africa, and Latin America*, Cambridge: Cambridge University Press, 2001.

Fretheim, Terence, *The Suffering of God: An Old Testament Perspective*, Overtures to Biblical Theology, Minneapolis, MN: Fortress, 1984.

Freud, Sigmund, *The Future of an Illusion*, ed. James Strachey, New York: Norton, 1989.

Frost, Robert, "To a Young Wretch," in *Robert Frost's Poems*, New Enlarged Pocket Anthology, New York: Washington Square, 1971.

Gäbler, Ulrich, *Huldrych Zwingli: His Life and Work*, trans. Ruth C. L. Gritsch, Philadelphia: Fortress, 1986.

Gallup, Alec M., and Frank Newport, eds., *The Gallup Poll: Public Opinion 2007*, Lanham, MD: Rowman & Littlefield, 2008.

Gamble, Harry Y., *The New Testament Canon: Its Making and Meaning*, Guides to Biblical Scholarship, Philadelphia: Fortress, 1985.

Ganssle, Gregory E., ed., *God and Time: Four Views*, Downers Grove, IL: InterVarsity, 2001.

Giddens, Anthony, *The Consequences of Modernity*, Stanford, CA: Stanford University Press, 1990.

Gilkey, Langdon, *Maker of Heaven and Earth: The Christian Doctrine of Creation in the Light of Modern Knowledge*, Garden City, NY: Doubleday, 1959.

Gilson, Étienne, *Thomism: The Philosophy of Thomas Aquinas*, trans. Armand A. Maurer and Laurence K. Shook, Toronto: Pontifical Institute of Mediaeval Studies, 2002.

Goldstein, Valerie Saiving, "The Human Situation: A Feminine View," *Journal of Religion* 40, no. 2 (1960), 100–12.

González, Justo L., *A History of Christian Thought*, 3 vols., 2nd edn., Nashville, TN: Abingdon, 1987.

Gordon, Bruce, *The Swiss Reformation*, New Frontiers in History, Manchester: Manchester University Press, 2002.

Green, Garrett, *Imagining God: Theology and the Religious Imagination*, Grand Rapids, MI: Eerdmans, 1989.

Gregory of Nazianzus, "Oration 38," trans. Charles Gordon Browne and James Edward Swallow, in *Nicene and Post-Nicene Fathers*, 2nd series, ed. Philip Schaff and Henry Wace, Grand Rapids, MI: Eerdmans, 1993, VII: 345–51.

  The Theological Orations, trans. Charles Gordon Browne and James Edward Swallow, in *The Christology of the Later Fathers*, ed. Edward Rochie Hardy, Library of Christian Classics, Philadelphia: Westminster, 1954, 128–214.

  "To Cledonius the Priest Against Apollinarius" [Letter 101], trans. Charles Gordon Browne and James Edward Swallow, in *Nicene and Post-Nicene Fathers*, 2nd series, ed. Philip Schaff and Henry Wace, Grand Rapids, MI: Eerdmans, 1993, VII: 439–43.

Gregory of Nyssa, "An Answer to Ablabius: That We Should Not Think of Saying There Are Three Gods," trans. Cyril C. Richardson, in *Christology of the Later Fathers*, ed. Edward Rochie Hardy, Library of Christian Classics, Louisville, KY: Westminster John Knox, 1954, 256–67.

  The Great Catechism, trans. William Moore and Henry Austin Wilson, in *Nicene and Post-Nicene Fathers*, 2nd series, ed. Philip Schaff and Henry Wace, Grand Rapids, MI: Eerdmans, 1993, V: 473–509.

  "Letter 38," trans. Jackson Blomfield, in *Nicene and Post-Nicene Fathers*, 2nd series, ed. Philip Schaff and Henry Wace, Grand Rapids, MI: Eerdmans, 1993, VIII: 137–41.

On the Holy Trinity, trans. Henry Austin Wilson, in *Nicene and Post-Nicene Fathers*, 2nd series, ed. Philip Schaff and Henry Wace, Grand Rapids, MI: Eerdmans, 1993, v: 326–30.

Grenz, Stanley J., *The Millennial Maze: Sorting Out Evangelical Options*, Downers Grove, IL: InterVarsity, 1992.

Grenz, Stanley J., and Roger E. Olsen, *20th-Century Theology: God and the World in a Transitional Age*, Downers Grove, IL: InterVarsity, 1992.

Who Needs Theology? An Invitation to the Study of God, Downers Grove, IL: InterVarsity, 1996.

Guder, Darrell L., and Lois Barrett, eds., *Missional Church: A Vision for the Sending of the Church in North America*, Grand Rapids, MI: Eerdmans, 1998.

Gunton, Colin E., *Act and Being: Towards a Theology of the Divine Attributes*, Grand Rapids, MI: Eerdmans, 2003.

The Promise of Trinitarian Theology, Edinburgh: T. & T. Clark, 1991.

The Triune Creator: A Historical and Systematic Study, Edinburgh Studies in Constructive Theology, Grand Rapids, MI: Eerdmans, 1998.

Gutiérrez, Gustavo, *The God of Life*, trans. Matthew J. O'Connell, Maryknoll, NY: Orbis, 1991.

"Option for the Poor," trans. Robert R. Barr, in *Mysterium Liberationis: Fundamental Concepts of Liberation Theology*, ed. Ignacio Ellacuría and Jon Sobrino, Maryknoll, NY: Orbis, 1993, 235–50.

A Theology of Liberation: History, Politics, and Salvation, trans. Caridad Inda and John Eagleston, rev. edn., Maryknoll, NY: Orbis, 1988.

Hale, J. R., *Renaissance Europe: Individual and Society, 1480–1520*, Berkeley, CA: University of California Press, 1977.

Hall, Douglas John, *God and Human Suffering: An Exercise in the Theology of the Cross*, Minneapolis, MN: Augsburg, 1986.

Imaging God: Dominion as Stewardship, Grand Rapids, MI: Eerdmans, 1986.

Thinking the Faith: Christian Theology in a North American Context, Minneapolis, MN: Augsburg, 1989.

Hall, Thomas Cuming, *The Religious Background of American Culture*, Boston: Little, Brown & Co., 1930.

Hardy, Edward Rochie, and Cyril C. Richardson, eds., *Christology of the Later Fathers*, Library of Christian Classics, Louisville, KY: Westminster John Knox, 1954.

Harlow, Daniel C., "Creation According to Genesis: Literary Genre, Cultural Context, Theological Truth," *Christian Scholars Review* 37, no. 2 (2008), 163–98.

Harnack, Adolf von, *History of Dogma*, trans. E. B. Speirs and James Millar, 7 vols., London: Williams & Norgate, 1898.

Outlines of the History of Dogma, trans. Edwin Knox Mitchell, Boston: Beacon Press, 1957.

What is Christianity?, trans. Thomas Bailey Saunders, New York: Harper & Row, 1957.

Hauerwas, Stanley, *A Community of Character: Toward a Constructive Christian Social Ethic*, Notre Dame, IN: University of Notre Dame Press, 1981.

The Peaceable Kingdom, Notre Dame, IN: University of Notre Dame Press, 1983.

Hays, Richard B., *The Faith of Jesus Christ: The Narrative Substructure of Galatians 3:1–4:11*, Grand Rapids, MI: Eerdmans, 2002.

Heim, S. Mark, *Salvations: Truth and Difference in Religion*, Maryknoll, NY: Orbis, 1995.

Heppe, Heinrich, *Reformed Dogmatics*, trans. G. T. Thomson, ed. Ernst Bizer, London: Allen & Unwin, 1950.

Herbert of Cherbury, "Common Notions Concerning Religion," in *Christianity and Plurality: Classic and Contemporary Readings*, ed. Richard J. Plantinga, Oxford: Blackwell, 1999, 169–81.

Heron, Alasdair I. C., *The Holy Spirit*, Philadelphia: Westminster, 1983.

Heschel, Abraham Joshua, *The Prophets*, Peabody, MA: Prince, 2003.

The Sabbath: Its Meaning for Modern Man, rev. edn., New York: Farrah, Straus, & Co., 1951.

Hick, John, *Evil and the God of Love*, rev. edn., New York: HarperSanFrancisco, 1977.

An Interpretation of Religion: Human Responses to the Transcendent, 2nd edn., New Haven, CT: Yale University Press, 2005.

"A Philosophy of Religious Pluralism," in *Christianity and Plurality: Classic and Contemporary Readings*, ed. Richard J. Plantinga, Oxford: Blackwell, 1999, 335–46.

"Whatever Path Men Choose is Mine," in *Christianity and Other Religions: Selected Readings*, ed. John Hick and Brian Hebblethwaite, Philadelphia: Fortress, 1980, 171–90.

Hill, William J., *The Three-Personed God: The Trinity as a Mystery of Salvation*, Washington DC: Catholic University Press, 1982.

Hoekema, Anthony A., *Created in God's Image*, Grand Rapids, MI: Eerdmans, 1986.

Saved by Grace, Grand Rapids, MI: Eerdmans, 1989.

Hugh of St. Victor, *On the Sacraments of the Christian Faith*, trans. Roy J. Deferrari, Cambridge, MA: Medieval Academy of America, 1951.

Hume, David, *Dialogues Concerning Natural Religion*, Indianapolis, IN: Hackett, 1990.

An Enquiry Concerning Human Understanding and Selections from A Treatise of Human Nature, La Salle, IL: Open Court, 1945.

Hunter, Alan, and Kim-Kwong Chan, *Protestantism in Contemporary China*, Cambridge: Cambridge University Press, 1993.

Ignatius of Antioch, "Letter to the Trallians," in *Early Christian Fathers*, ed. Cyril C. Richardson, Library of Christian Classics, Philadelphia: Westminster, 1953, 98–101.

Ignatius of Loyola, *Spiritual Exercises and Selected Works*, ed. George E. Ganss, The Classics of Western Spirituality, Mahwah, NJ: Paulist, 1991.

Irenaeus, *Against Heresies*, ed. A. Cleveland Coxe, in *Ante-Nicene Fathers*, ed. Alexander Roberts and James Donaldson, Grand Rapids, MI: Eerdmans, 1993, 1: 315–567.

Proof of the Apostolic Preaching, trans. Joseph P. Smith, Westminster, MD: Newman Press, 1952.

Jaeger, Werner, *Early Christianity and Greek Paideia*, Cambridge, MA: Belknap, 1961.

Jaki, Stanley, *Science and Creation: From Eternal Cycles to an Oscilla Universe*, Edinburgh: Scottish University Press, 1974.

Jenkins, Philip, *God's Continent: Christianity, Islam, and Europe's Religious Crisis*, Oxford: Oxford University Press, 2007.

The Next Christendom: The Coming of Global Christianity, Oxford: Oxford University Press, 2002.

Jeremias, Joachim, *New Testament Theology: The Proclamation of Jesus*, trans. John Bowden, New York: Charles Scribner's Sons, 1971.

John of Damascus, *Exposition of the Orthodox Faith*, trans. S. D. F. Salmond, in *Nicene and Post-Nicene Fathers*, 2nd series, ed. Philip Schaff and Henry Wace, Grand Rapids, MI: Eerdmans, 1993, IX: 1–101.

John Paul II, *Crossing the Threshold of Hope*, trans. Jenny McPhee and Martha McPhee, ed. Vitorio Messori, New York: Knopf, 1994.

Johnson, Elizabeth A., *She Who Is: The Mystery of God in Feminist Theological Discourse*, New York: Crossroad, 1992.

Jüngel, Eberhard, *God as the Mystery of the World: On the Foundation of the Crucified in the Dispute between Theism and Atheism*, trans. Darrell L. Guder, Grand Rapids, MI: Eerdmans, 1983.

God's Being is in Becoming: The Trinitarian Being of God in the Theology of Karl Barth: A Paraphrase, trans. John Webster, Grand Rapids, MI: Eerdmans, 2001.

Justification: The Heart of the Christian Faith; A Theological Study with an Ecumenical Purpose, trans. Jeffrey F. Cayzer, Edinburgh: T. & T. Clark, 2001.

Justin Martyr, *The First Apology*, trans. and ed. Cyril C. Richardson, in *Early Christian Fathers*, Library of Christian Classics, Philadelphia: Westminster, 1953, 242–89.

Kant, Immanuel, *The Conflict of the Faculties*, trans. Mary J. Gregor, New York: Abaris, 1979.

Critique of Practical Reason, ed. and trans. Mary Gregor, Cambridge Texts in the History of Philosophy, Cambridge: Cambridge University Press, 1997.

Critique of Pure Reason, trans. Norman Kemp Smith, New York: St. Martin's, 1965.

Groundwork of the Metaphysic of Morals, trans. and ed. H. J. Paton, New York: Harper & Row, 1964.

Religion Within the Limits of Reason Alone, trans. Theodore M. Greene and Hoyt H. Hudson, New York: Harper & Row, 1960.

"What is Enlightenment?," in Immanuel Kant, *On History*, ed. Lewis White Beck, trans. Lewis White Beck et al., Library of Liberal Arts, Indianapolis, IN: Bobbs-Merrill, 1963.

Kärkkäinen, Veli-Matti, *Pneumatology: The Holy Spirit in Ecumenical, International, and Contextual Perspective*, Grand Rapids, MI: Baker Academic, 2002.

Trinity and Religious Pluralism: The Doctrine of the Trinity in Christian Theology of Religions, Burlington, VT: Ashgate, 2004.

Kasper, Walter, *The God of Jesus Christ*, trans. Matthew J. O'Connell, New York: Crossroad, 1984.

Kelly, J. N. D., *Early Christian Doctrines*, 2nd edn., New York: Harper & Row, 1960.

Kittel, Gerhard, and Gerhard Friedrich, eds., *Theological Dictionary of the New Testament*, trans. Geoffrey W. Bromiley, 10 vols., Grand Rapids, MI: Eerdmans, 1969–76.

Klocker, Harry, *William of Ockham and the Divine Freedom*, Milwaukee, WI: Marquette University Press, 1992.

Kolb, Robert A., *Bound Choice, Election and Wittenberg Theological Method: From Martin Luther to the Formula of Concord*, Lutheran Quarterly Books, Grand Rapids, MI: Eerdmans, 2005.

"Historical Background of the Formula of Concord," in *A Contemporary Look at the Formula of Concord*, ed. Robert D. Preus and Wilbert H. Rosin, St. Louis: Concordia, 1978, 12–87.

Küng, Hans, *The Church*, trans. Ray Ockenden and Rosaleen Ockenden, London: Burns & Oates, 1967.

LaHaye, Tim, and Jerry B. Jenkins, *Left Behind: A Novel of the Earth's Last Days*, Wheaton, IL: Tyndale, 1995.

Lasch, Christopher, *The Culture of Narcissism*, New York: Norton, 1978.

Lee, Jung Young, *The Trinity in Asian Perspective*, Nashville, TN: Abingdon, 1996.

Lehman, Paul L., *Ethics in a Christian Context*, New York: Harper & Row, 1963.

Leibniz, Gottfried Wilhelm von, *Theodicy: Essays on the Goodness of God, the Freedom of Man, and the Origin of Evil*, ed. Austin Farrer, trans. E. M. Huggard, LaSalle, IL: Open Court, 1985.

Leo of Rome, "The Tome of Leo," trans. William Bright, in *Christology of the Later Fathers*, ed. Edward Rochie Hardy and Cyril C. Richardson, Library of Christian Classics, Philadelphia: Westminster, 1954.

Lewis, C. S., *The Four Loves*, New York: Harcourt & Brace, 1960.

The Great Divorce, New York: Simon & Schuster, 1974.

The Last Battle, New York: HarperCollins, 1994.

Mere Christianity, New York: Simon & Schuster, 1996.

Surprised by Joy, New York: Harcourt Brace Jovanovich, 1956.

Lindbeck, George, *The Nature of Doctrine: Religion and Theology in a Postliberal Age*, Philadelphia: Westminster, 1984.

Lindberg, Carter, *The European Reformations*, Oxford: Blackwell, 1996.

Lindsey, Hal, and Carole C. Carlson, *The Late Great Planet Earth*, Grand Rapids, MI: Zondervan, 1970.

Livingston, James C., *Anatomy of the Sacred*, 5th edn., New York: Prentice Hall, 2004.

Livingstone, David N., *Darwin's Forgotten Defenders: The Encounter Between Evangelical Theology and Evolutionary Thought*, Grand Rapids, MI: Eerdmans, 1987.

Loades, Ann, "Sacrament," in *The Oxford Companion to Christian Thought*, ed. Adrian Hastings, Alistair Mason, Hugh Pyper, Ingrid Lawrie, and Cecily Bennett, Oxford: Oxford University Press, 2000, 634–7.

Locke, John, *An Essay Concerning Human Understanding*, ed. Kenneth P. Winkler, Indianapolis, IN: Hackett, 1996.

Lohse, Bernhard, *Martin Luther's Theology: Its Historical and Systematic Development*, trans. Roy A. Harrisville, Minneapolis, MN: Fortress, 1999.

Lombard, Peter, *Sententiae in IV Libris Distinctae*, Grottaferrata: Editiones Collegii S. Bonaventurae ad Claras Aquas, 1971.

Lossky, Vladimir, *The Mystical Theology of the Eastern Church*, Crestwood, NY: St. Vladimir's Seminary Press, 1976.

Louth, Andrew, ed., *Genesis 1–11*, Ancient Christian Commentary on Scripture, Downers Grove, IL: InterVarsity, 2001.

Lundberg, Matthew D., "The Problem of Suffering and the Theology of the Cross," *Covenant Quarterly* 66, no. 1 (2008), 3–23.

Luther, Martin, *The Babylonian Captivity of the Church*, ed. A. T. Steinhäuser, Frederick C. Ahrens, and Abdel Ross Wentz, in *Three Treatises*, Philadelphia: Fortress, 1970.

The Bondage of the Will, trans. J. I. Packer and O. R. Johnston, Old Tappan, NJ: Revell, 1957.

Commentary on Galatians, ed. John Prince Fallowes, trans. Erasmus Middleton, Grand Rapids, MI: Kregel, 1979.

"The Disputation held at Heidelberg," in *Luther: Early Theological Works*, ed. J. Atkinson, Library of Christian Classics, Philadelphia: Westminster, 1962.

Heidelberg Disputation, in *Luther's Works*, XXXI, ed. Harold J. Grimm and Helmut T. Lehmann, Philadelphia: Fortress, 1957.

Lectures on Romans, ed. and trans. Wilhelm Pauck, Library of Christian Classics, Philadelphia: Westminster, 1959.

On Christian Liberty, trans. W. A. Lambert and Harold J. Grimm, Minneapolis, MN: Fortress, 2003.

The Schmalkald Articles, trans. William R. Russell, Minneapolis, MN: Fortress, 1995.

The Lutheran World Federation and the Roman Catholic Church, *Joint Declaration on the Doctrine of Justification*, Grand Rapids, MI: Eerdmans, 2000.

Lyotard, Jean-François, *The Postmodern Condition: A Report on Knowledge*, trans. Geoff Bennington and Brian Massumi, Minneapolis, MN: University of Minnesota Press, 1984.

Mackintosh, H. R., *The Doctrine of the Person of Jesus Christ*, 2nd edn., Edinburgh: T. & T. Clark, 1913.

Macquarrie, John, *A Guide to the Sacraments*, London: SCM, 1997.

McCormack, Bruce L., *For Us and Our Salvation: Incarnation and Atonement in the Reformed Tradition*, Studies in Reformed Theology and History, Princeton, NJ: Princeton Theological Seminary, 1993.

McFague, Sallie, *Metaphorical Theology: Models of God in Religious Language*, Minneapolis, MN: Augsburg Fortress, 1997.

Models of God: Theology for an Ecological, Nuclear Age, Philadelphia: Fortress, 1987.

McGill, Arthur C., *Suffering: A Test of Theological Method*, Philadelphia: Westminster, 1982.

McGrath, Alister E., *Iustitia Dei: A History of the Christian Doctrine of Justification*, 3rd edn., Cambridge: Cambridge University Press, 2005.

McKitterick, Rosamond, *The Frankish Kingdoms under the Carolingians*, London: Longman, 1983.

Macrobius, *Commentary on the Dream of Scipio by Macrobius*, trans. William Harris Stahl, New York: Columbia University Press, 1952.

Marsh, Thomas, *The Triune God: A Biblical, Historical, and Theological Study*, Mystic, CT: Twenty-Third Publications, 1994.

Martin, David, *Tongues of Fire: The Explosion of Protestantism in Latin America*, Oxford: Blackwell, 1990.

"The Martyrdom of Saint Polycarp, Bishop of Smyrna," ed. and trans. Massey Hamilton Shepherd Jr., in *Early Christian Fathers*, ed. Cyril C. Richardson, Library of Christian Classics, Philadelphia: Westminster, 1953, 149–58.

Marx, Karl, *Selected Writings*, ed. David McLellan, 2nd edn., Oxford: Oxford University Press, 2000.

Mbiti, John S., *Bible and Theology in African Christianity*, Nairobi: Oxford University Press, 1986.

"Is Jesus Christ in African Religion?," in *Exploring Afro-Christology*, ed. John S. Pobee, Frankfurt: Peter Lang, 1992, 21–9.

Meadows, Donella, Jorgen Randers, and Dennis Meadows, *Limits to Growth: The 30-Year Update*, White River Junction, VT: Chelsea Green Publishing, 2004.

Middleton, J. Richard, *The Liberating Image: The* Imago Dei *in Genesis 1*, Grand Rapids, MI: Brazos, 2005.

Migliore, Daniel L., *Faith Seeking Understanding: An Introduction to Christian Theology*, 2nd edn., Grand Rapids, MI: Eerdmans, 2004.

The Power of God and the gods of Power, Louisville, KY: Westminster John Knox, 2008.

Miles, Margaret R., *The Word Made Flesh: A History of Christian Thought*, Malden, MA: Blackwell, 2005.

Miller, Patrick D., *Deuteronomy*, Interpretation, Louisville, KY: John Knox, 1990.

Minear, Paul S., *Images of the Church in the New Testament*, New Testament Library, Louisville, KY: Westminster John Knox, 2004.

Moltmann, Jürgen, *A Broad Place: An Autobiography*, trans. Margaret Kohl, Minneapolis, MN: Fortress, 2007.

The Crucified God: The Cross of Christ as the Foundation and Criticism of Christian Theology, trans. R. A. Wilson and John Bowden, New York: Harper & Row, 1974.

Experiences in Theology: Ways and Forms of Christian Theology, trans. Margaret Kohl, Minneapolis, MN: Fortress, 2000.

God in Creation: A New Theology of Creation and the Spirit of God, trans. Margaret Kohl, San Francisco: Harper & Row, 1985.

History and the Triune God: Contributions to Trinitarian Theology, trans. John Bowden, New York: Crossroad, 1992.

The Source of Life: The Holy Spirit and the Theology of Life, trans. Margaret Kohl, Minneapolis, MN: Fortress, 1997.

The Spirit of Life: A Universal Affirmation, trans. Margaret Kohl, Minneapolis, MN: Fortress, 1992.

Theology of Hope: On the Ground and the Implications of a Christian Eschatology, trans. James W. Leitch, New York: Harper & Row, 1967.

The Trinity and the Kingdom: The Doctrine of God, trans. Margaret Kohl, Minneapolis, MN: Fortress, 1993.

The Way of Jesus Christ: Christology in Messianic Dimensions, trans. Margaret Kohl, Minneapolis, MN: Fortress, 1993.

Morris, Thomas V., *The Logic of God Incarnate*, Ithaca, NY: Cornell University Press, 1986.

"The Metaphysics of God Incarnate," in *Trinity, Incarnation, and Atonement*, ed. Ronald J. Feenstra and Cornelius Plantinga Jr., Notre Dame, IN: University of Notre Dame Press, 1989, 110–27.

Our Idea of God: An Introduction to Philosophical Theology, Downers Grove, IL: InterVarsity, 1991.

Mullett, Michael A., *The Catholic Reformation*, London: Routledge, 1999.

Murray, John Courtney, *The Problem of God: Yesterday and Today*, New Haven, CT: Yale University Press, 1964.

Newbigin, Lesslie, *The Gospel in a Pluralist Society*, Grand Rapids, MI: Eerdmans, 1989.

The Household of God: Lectures on the Nature of the Church, London: SCM Press, 1957.

Niebuhr, H. Richard, *Christ and Culture*, New York: Harper & Row, 1951.

Niebuhr, Reinhold, *The Children of Light and the Children of Darkness: A Vindication of Democracy and a Critique of its Traditional Defense*, New York: Charles Scribner's Sons, 1960.

An Interpretation of Christian Ethics, New York: Seabury, 1979.

The Nature and Destiny of Man: A Christian Interpretation, New York: Charles Scribner's Sons, 1943.

Nietzsche, Friedrich, *Beyond Good and Evil: Prelude to a Philosophy of the Future*, trans. Walter Kaufmann, New York: Vintage, 1989.

The Gay Science: With a Prelude in Rhymes and an Appendix of Songs, trans. Walter Kaufmann, New York: Vintage, 1974.

Thus Spoke Zarathustra, in *The Portable Nietzsche*, ed. and trans. Walter Kaufmann, New York: Penguin, 1982.

Norris, Richard A., Jr., ed., *The Christological Controversy*, Sources of Early Christian Thought, Philadelphia: Fortress, 1980.

Numbers, Ronald L., *The Creationists*, New York: Knopf, 1992.

O'Collins, Gerald, *The Tripersonal God: Understanding and Interpreting the Trinity*, New York: Paulist, 1999.

Origen, *De Principiis*, trans. Frederick Crombie, ed. A. Cleveland Coxe, in *Ante-Nicene Fathers*, ed. Alexander Roberts and James Donaldson, Grand Rapids, MI: Eerdmans, 1993, IV: 239–382.

Pannenberg, Wolfhart, *An Introduction to Systematic Theology*, Grand Rapids, MI: Eerdmans, 1991.

Jesus – God and Man, trans. Lewis L. Wilkins and Duane A. Priebe, Philadelphia: Westminster, 1968.

Metaphysics and the Idea of God, trans. Philip Clayton, Grand Rapids, MI: Eerdmans, 1990.

Systematic Theology, trans. Geoffrey W. Bromiley, 3 vols., Grand Rapids, MI: Eerdmans, 1991–8.

Theology and the Philosophy of Science, trans. Francis McDonagh, London: Darton, Longman, & Todd, 1976.

Papanikolaou, Aristotle, *Being with God: Trinity, Apophaticism, and Divine–Human Communion*, Notre Dame, IN: University of Notre Dame Press, 2006.

"Orthodox Theology," section of "Theology in the Nineteenth and Twentieth Centuries," in *The Encyclopedia of Christianity*, ed. Erwin Fahlbusch, Grand Rapids, MI: Eerdmans, 1999, v: 414–18.

Parsons, Susan Frank, ed., *The Cambridge Campanion to Feminist Theology*, Cambridge: Cambridge University Press, 2002.

Pelikan, Jaroslav, *The Christian Tradition: A History of the Development of Doctrine*, 5 vols., Chicago: University of Chicago Press, 1971–89.

Pelikan, Jaroslav, and Valerie Hotchkiss, eds., *Creeds and Confessions of Faith in the Christian Tradition*, 3 vols., New Haven, CT: Yale University Press, 2003.

Pinnock, Clark H., *Flame of Love: A Theology of the Holy Spirit*, Downers Grove, IL: InterVarsity, 1996.

Plantinga, Alvin, *God, Freedom, and Evil*, Grand Rapids, MI: Eerdmans, 1974.

The Ontological Argument: From St. Anselm to Contemporary Philosophers, Garden City, NY: Anchor, 1965.

Plantinga, Cornelius, Jr., *Not the Way It's Supposed to Be: A Breviary of Sin*, Grand Rapids, MI: Eerdmans, 1995.

"Social Trinity and Tritheism," in *Trinity, Incarnation and Atonement: Philosophical and Theological Essays*, ed. Ronald J. Feenstra and Cornelius Plantinga Jr., Notre Dame, IN: University of Notre Dame Press, 1989, 21–47.

"The Threeness/Oneness Problem of the Trinity," *Calvin Theological Journal* 23 (1988), 37–53.

Plantinga, Richard J., "God So Loved the World: Theological Reflections on Religious Plurality in the History of Christianity," in *Biblical Faith and Other Religions: An Evangelical Assessment*, ed. David W. Baker, Grand Rapids, MI: Kregel, 2004, 106–37.

ed., *Christianity and Plurality: Classic and Contemporary Readings*, Oxford: Blackwell, 1999.

Plato, *Republic*, in *The Collected Dialogues of Plato*, ed. E. Hamilton and H. Cairns, Bollingen Series 71, New York: Pantheon, 1961.

Plotinus, *The Enneads*, trans. Stephan Mackenna, New York: Larson Publications, 1992.

Pope, Alexander, *Essay on Man*, in *The Poems of Alexander Pope*, ed. John Butt, New Haven, CT: Yale University Press, 1963.

Rad, Gerhard von, *Genesis: A Commentary*, trans. John H. Marks *et al.*, rev. edn., Philadelphia: Westminster, 1972.

    Old Testament Theology, 1: *The Theology of Israel's Historical Traditions*, trans. D. M. G. Stalker, New York: Harper & Row, 1962.

    Wisdom in Israel, trans. James D. Marton, Nashville, TN: Abingdon, 1972.

Rahner, Karl, "Christianity and the Non-Christian Religions," trans. K.-H. Krueger, in *Theological Investigations*, New York: Crossroad, 1983, v: 115–34.

    Foundations of Christian Faith: An Introduction to the Idea of Christianity, trans. William V. Dych, New York: Crossroad, 1978.

    Hearer of the Word: Laying the Foundation for a Philosophy of Religion, trans. Joseph Donceel, New York: Continuum, 1994.

    The Trinity, trans. Joseph Donceel, New York: Crossroad, 1997.

Ranke, Leopold von, *The Theory and Practice of History*, ed. Georg G. Iggers and Konrad von Moltke, trans. Wilma A. Iggers and Konrad von Moltke, Indianapolis, IN: Bobbs-Merrill, 1973.

Rauschenbusch, Walter, *Christianizing the Social Order*, New York: Macmillan, 1912.

    A Theology for the Social Gospel, Library of Theological Ethics, Louisville, KY: Westminster John Knox, 1997.

Reid, W. S., and Geoffrey W. Bromiley, "Atone, Atonement," in *The International Standard Bible Encyclopedia*, rev. edn., 4 vols., ed. Geoffrey W. Bromiley, Grand Rapids, MI: Eerdmans, 1979, 1: 352–60.

Reimarus, Hermann Samuel, *Fragments*, ed. Charles H. Talbert, trans. Ralph S. Fraser, Philadelphia: Fortress, 1970.

Richard of St. Victor, *On the Trinity*, in *A Scholastic Miscellany: Anselm to Ockham*, ed. Eugene R. Fairweather, Library of Christian Classics, Philadelphia: Westminster, 1956.

    Selected Writings on Contemplation, trans. Clare Kirchenberger, Classics of the Contemplative Life, London: Faber & Faber, n.d.

Ricoeur, Paul, *The Symbolism of Evil*, trans. E. Buchanan, Boston: Beacon, 1967.

Ridderbos, Herman, *Paul: An Outline of His Theology*, trans. John Richard De Witt, Grand Rapids, MI: Eerdmans, 1975.

Ritschl, Albrecht, *The Christian Doctrine of Justification and Reconciliation*, III: *The Positive Development of the Doctrine*, ed. and trans. H. R. Mackintosh and A. B. Macaulay, Edinburgh: T. & T. Clark, 1900.

Robert, Dana, "Shifting Southward: Global Christianity Since 1945," *International Bulletin of Missionary Research* 24, no. 2 (April 2000), 50–8.

Robinson, John A. T., *Honest to God*, Philadelphia: Westminster, 1963.

Rogers, Eugene F., Jr., *After the Spirit: A Constructive Pneumatology from Resources Outside the Modern West*, Grand Rapids, MI: Eerdmans, 2005.

Rosenzweig, Franz, *The Star of Redemption*, trans. Barbara E. Galli, Madison, WI: University of Wisconsin Press, 2005.

Roukema, Riemer, *Gnosis and Faith in Early Christianity: An Introduction to Gnosticism*, trans. John Bowden, Harrisburg, PA: Trinity Press, 1999.

Rudolph, Kurt, *Gnosis: The Nature and History of Gnosticism*, trans. Robert McLachlan Wilson, New York: HarperCollins, 1984.

Ruether, Rosemary Radford, "The Liberation of Christology from Patriarchy," in *Feminist Theology: A Reader*, ed. Ann Loades, Louisville, KY: Westminster John Knox, 1990, 138–48.

Rusch, William G., ed. and trans., *The Trinitarian Controversy*, Sources of Early Christian Thought, Philadelphia: Fortress, 1980.

Russell, Letty M., *Human Liberation in a Feminist Perspective: A Theology*, Philadelphia: Westminster, 1975.

Russell, Norman, *The Doctrine of Deification in the Greek Patristic Tradition*, Oxford Early Christian Studies, Oxford: Oxford University Press, 2004.

Sanders, E. P., *Paul and Palestinian Judaism*, Philadelphia: Fortress, 1977.

Paul, the Law, and the Jewish People, Philadelphia: Fortress, 1983.

Sanneh, Lamin, *Whose Religion is Christianity? The Gospel Beyond the West*, Grand Rapids, MI: Eerdmans, 2003.

Schleiermacher, Friedrich, *The Christian Faith*, ed. H. R. Mackintosh and J. S. Stewart, Edinburgh: T. & T. Clark, 1928.

On Religion: Speeches to its Cultured Despisers, trans. John Oman, New York: Harper & Row, 1958.

Schmid, Heinrich, *The Doctrinal Theology of the Evangelical Lutheran Church*, 3rd edn., Minneapolis, MN: Augsburg, 1961.

Schreiter, Robert J., *Constructing Local Theologies*, Maryknoll, NY: Orbis, 1985.

Schwarz, Hans, *Christology*, Grand Rapids, MI: Eerdmans, 1998.

Schweitzer, Albert, *The Quest of the Historical Jesus: A Critical Study of its Progress from Reimarus to Wrede*, trans. William Montgomery, New York: Macmillan, 1961.

Second General Conference of Latin American Bishops, *The Church in the Present-Day Transformation of Latin America in the Light of the Council* [Proceedings of Medellín Conference of Latin American Bishops], II: *Conclusions*, 3rd edn., Washington DC: Secretariat for Latin America National Conference of Catholic Bishops, 1979.

Sharpe, Eric J., *Comparative Religion: A History*, 2nd edn., LaSalle, IL: Open Court, 1986.

The Universal Gītā: Western Images of the Bhagavadgītā, London: Gerald Duckworth & Co., 1985.

Sherman, Robert, *King, Priest, and Prophet: A Trinitarian Theology of Atonement*, Theology for the Twenty-first Century, New York: T. & T. Clark, 2004.

Simons, Menno, *The Complete Writings of Menno Simons*, trans. Leonard Verduin, Scottdale, PA: Herald, 1956.

Singer, Charles, ed., *Studies in the History and Method of Science*, I, Oxford: Clarendon, 1917.

Smith, Wilfred Cantwell, *The Meaning and End of Religion*, New York: Harper & Row, 1978.

"The So-Called Letter to Diognetus," ed. and trans. Eugene R. Fairweather, in *Early Christian Fathers*, ed. Cyril C. Richardson, Library of Christian Classics, Philadelphia: Westminster, 1953, 213–24.

Sobrino, Jon, *Christ the Liberator: A View from the Victims*, trans. Paul Burns, Maryknoll, NY: Orbis, 2001.

Christology at the Crossroads: A Latin American Approach, trans. John Drury,
    Maryknoll, NY: Orbis, 1978.
Jesus the Liberator: A Historical-Theological Reading of Jesus of Nazareth, trans.
    Paul Burns and Francis McDonagh, Maryknoll, NY: Orbis, 1993.
The True Church and the Poor, trans. Matthew J. O'Connell, Maryknoll, NY:
    Orbis, 1984.
Witnesses to the Kingdom: The Martyrs of El Salvador and the Crucified Peoples,
    various translators, Maryknoll, NY: Orbis, 2003.
Sokolowski, Robert, *The God of Faith and Reason: Foundations of Christian
    Theology*, Notre Dame, IN: University of Notre Dame Press, 1982.
Spener, Philipp Jakob, *Pia Desideria*, trans. Theodore G. Tappert, Seminar
    Editions, Philadelphia: Fortress, 1964.
Stark, Rodney, *The Rise of Christianity: How the Obscure, Marginal Jesus Movement
    Became the Dominant Religious Force in the Western World in a Few Centuries*,
    Princeton, NJ: Princeton University Press, 1996.
Stauffer, George B., *Bach: The Mass in B Minor: The Great Catholic Mass*, New
    Haven, CT: Yale University Press, 2003.
Stead, Christopher, *Divine Substance*, Oxford: Clarendon, 1977.
Philosophy in Christian Antiquity, Cambridge: Cambridge University Press,
    1994.
Stewart-Gambino, Hannah W., and Everett Wilson, "Latin American
    Pentecostals: Old Stereotypes and New Challenges," in *Power, Politics, and
    Pentecostals in Latin America*, ed. Edward L. Cleary and Hannah W. Stewart-
    Gambino, Boulder, CO: Westview, 1997.
Studer, Basil, *Trinity and Incarnation: The Faith of the Early Church*, trans.
    Matthias Westerhoff, ed. Andrew Louth, Edinburgh: T. & T. Clark, 1993.
Suh Nam-dong, "Historical References for a Theology of Minjung," in *Minjung
    Theology: People as the Subjects of History*, ed. Commission on Theological
    Concerns of the Christian Conference of Asia, rev. edn., Maryknoll, NY:
    Orbis, 1983, 155–82.
Tappeiner, D. A., "Holy Spirit," in *International Standard Bible Encyclopedia*, rev.
    edn., 4 vols., ed. Geoffrey W. Bromiley, Grand Rapids, MI: Eerdmans, 1995, II:
    730–42.
Taylor, Mark C., *Erring: A Postmodern A/Theology*, Chicago: University of Chicago
    Press, 1984.
Teilhard de Chardin, Pierre, *The Divine Milieu*, New York: Harper & Row, 1960.
The Phenomenon of Man, trans. Bernard Wall, rev. edn., New York: Harper &
    Row, 1965.
Tertullian, *Against Praxeas*, trans. Peter Holmes, ed. A. Cleveland Coxe, in *Ante-
    Nicene Fathers*, ed. Alexander Roberts and James Donaldson, Grand Rapids,
    MI: Eerdmans, 1993, III: 597–627.
The Prescriptions Against the Heretics, in *Early Latin Theology*, ed. and trans.
    S. L. Greenslade, Library of Christian Classics, Philadelphia: Westminster,
    1953, 31–64.
Treatise Against Praxeas, ed. and trans. Ernest Evans, London: SPCK, 1948.

Thielicke, Helmut, *A Little Exercise for Young Theologians*, trans. Charles L. Taylor, Grand Rapids, MI: Eerdmans, 1962.

Third General Conference of the Latin American Episcopate, *Evangelization in Latin America's Present and Future*, trans. John Drury, in *Puebla and Beyond: Documentation and Commentary*, ed. John Eagleson and Philip Scharper, Maryknoll, NY: Orbis, 1979, 123–285.

Thiselton, Anthony C., *The Two Horizons: New Testament Hermeneutics and Philosophical Description with Special Reference to Heidegger, Bultmann, Gadamer, and Wittgenstein*, Grand Rapids, MI: Eerdmans, 1980.

Thomas Aquinas, *Summa Theologica*, 5 vols., trans. the Fathers of the English Dominican Province, Westminster, MD: Christian Classics, 1948.

Thompson, Thomas R., "Deity of Christ," in *The New Dictionary of Christian Apologetics*, ed. W. C. Campbell-Jack, Gavin J. McGrath, and C. Stephen Evans, Downers Grove, IL: InterVarsity, 2006.

"*Imitatio Trinitatis*: The Trinity as Social Model in the Theologies of Jürgen Moltmann and Leonardo Boff," PhD dissertation: Princeton Theological Seminary, 1996.

"Nineteenth-Century Kenotic Christology: The Waxing, Waning, and Weighing of a Quest for a Coherent Orthodoxy," in *Exploring Kenotic Christology: The Self-Emptying of God*, ed. C. Stephen Evans, Oxford: Oxford University Press, 2006, 74–111.

"Trinitarianism Today: Doctrinal Renaissance, Ethical Relevance, Social Redolence," *Calvin Theological Journal* 32, no. 1 (1997), 9–42.

Thompson, Thomas R., and Cornelius Plantinga Jr., "Trinity and Kenosis," in *Exploring Kenotic Christology: The Self-Emptying of God*, ed. C. Stephen Evans, Oxford: Oxford University Press, 2006, 165–89.

Thornhill, John, *Modernity: Christianity's Estranged Child Reconstructed*, Grand Rapids, MI: Eerdmans, 2000.

Tillich, Paul, *Systematic Theology*, 3 vols., Chicago: University of Chicago, 1976.

The Courage to Be, New Haven, CT: Yale University Press, 1952.

Torrance, Thomas F., "The Goodness and Dignity of Man in the Christian Tradition," *Modern Theology* 4, no. 4 (1988), 309–22.

Tracy, David, *The Analogical Imagination: Christian Theology and the Culture of Pluralism*, New York: Crossroad, 1981.

Troeltsch, Ernst, "The Place of Christianity among the World Religions," in *Christianity and Plurality: Classic and Contemporary Readings*, ed. Richard J. Plantinga, Oxford: Blackwell, 1999, 211–22.

Tutu, Desmond Mpilo, *Hope and Suffering: Sermons and Speeches*, ed. Mothobe Mutloatse and John Webster, Grand Rapids, MI: Eerdmans, 1984.

Van Buren, Paul M., *The Secular Meaning of the Gospel*, New York: Macmillan, 1963.

Van Till, Howard J., *et al.*, *Portraits of Creation: Biblical and Scientific Perspectives on the World's Formation*, Grand Rapids, MI: Eerdmans, 1990.

Van Till, Howard J., Davis A. Young, and Clarence Menninga, *Science Held Hostage: What's Wrong with Creation Science and Evolutionism*, Downer's Grove, IL: InterVarsity, 1988.

Vanhoozer, Kevin J., ed., *The Cambridge Companion to Postmodern Theology*, Cambridge: Cambridge University Press, 2003.

Villafañe, Eldin, *The Liberating Spirit: Toward an Hispanic-American Social Ethic*, Grand Rapids, MI: Eerdmans, 1993.

Vischer, Lukas, ed., *Spirit of God, Spirit of Christ: Ecumenical Reflections on the Filioque Controversy*, London: SPCK, 1981.

Voltaire, *Candide*, trans. Richard Aldington, in *The Portable Voltaire*, ed. Ben Ray Redman, New York: Penguin, 1977.

Vos, Arvin, *Aquinas, Calvin, and Contemporary Protestant Thought: A Critique of Protestant Views on the Thought of Thomas Aquinas*, Grand Rapids, MI: Eerdmans, 1985.

Wainwright, Arthur W., *The Trinity in the New Testament*, London: SPCK, 1962.

Walker, Williston, Richard A. Norris, David W. Lotz, and Robert T. Handy, *A History of the Christian Church*, 4th edn., New York: Scribner, 1985.

Wallace, Mark I., *Finding God in the Singing River*, Minneapolis, MN: Fortress, 2005.

Walls, Andrew F., *The Missionary Movement in Christian History*, Maryknoll, NY: Orbis, 1996.

Wangzhi, Gao, "Y. T. Wu: A Christian Leader Under Communism," in *Christianity in China: From the Eighteenth Century to the Present*, ed. Daniel H. Bays, Stanford, CA: Stanford University Press, 1997.

Webster, John B., *Eberhard Jüngel: An Introduction to His Theology*, Cambridge: Cambridge University Press, 1986.

Weil, Simone, *Waiting for God*, trans. Emma Gruafund, New York: Putnam, 1951.

Welch, Claude, ed., *God and Incarnation in Mid-Nineteenth Century German Theology*, New York: Oxford University Press, 1965.

Westphal, Merold, *Suspicion and Faith: The Religious Uses of Modern Atheism*, Grand Rapids, MI: Eerdmans, 1993.

Whitcomb, John C., Jr., and Henry M. Morris, *The Genesis Flood: The Biblical Record and its Scientific Implications*, Philadelphia: Presbyterian & Reformed, 1961.

White, Lynn, Jr., "On the Historical Roots of our Ecologic Crisis," *Science* 155 (March 10, 1967), 1203–7.

Whitehead, Alfred North, *Process and Reality: An Essay in Cosmology*, New York: Macmillan, 1929.

Wiesel, Elie, *A Jew Today*, New York: Vintage, 1978.

Night, New York: Bantam, 1960.

The Trial of God, New York: Schocken, 1995.

William of Ockham, *Philosophical Writings*, ed. and trans. Philotheus Boehner, Nelson Philosophical Texts, Edinburgh: Nelson, 1957.

Williams, Delores S., *Sisters in the Wilderness: The Challenge of Womanist God-Talk*, Maryknoll, NY: Orbis Books, 1993.

Williams, Rowan, "Eastern Orthodox Theology," in *The Modern Theologians*, ed. David F. Ford, Oxford: Blackwell, 1989, II: 152–70.

Willis, W. Waite, Jr., *Theism, Atheism, and the Doctrine of the Trinity: The Trinitarian Theologies of Karl Barth and Jürgen Moltmann in Response to Protest Atheism*, Atlanta: Scholars Press, 1987.

Wink, Walter, *The Powers*, 1: *Naming the Powers: The Language of Power in the New Testament*, Philadelphia: Fortress, 1984.

Wolterstorff, Nicholas, "God Everlasting," in *God and the Good: Essays in Honor of Henry Stob*, ed. Clifton Orlebeke and Lewis B. Smedes, Grand Rapids, MI: Eerdmans, 1975, 181–203.

Lament for a Son, Grand Rapids, MI: Eerdmans, 1987.

World Council of Churches, *Constitution and Rules of the World Council of Churches*, available at www.oikoumene.org/index.php?id=2297, accessed November 18, 2008.

Wright, N. T., *Paul in Fresh Perspective*, Minneapolis, MN: Fortress, 2005.

Simply Christian: Why Christianity Makes Sense, New York: HarperCollins, 2006.

Surprised by Hope: Rethinking Heaven, the Resurrection, and the Mission of the Church, New York: HarperOne, 2008.

Zizioulas, John, *Being as Communion: Studies in Personhood and the Church*, Crestwood, NY: St. Vladimir's Seminary Press, 1985.

Zwingli, Huldrych, *An Exposition of the Faith*, in *Zwingli and Bullinger*, ed. Geoffrey W. Bromiley, Library of Christian Classics, Philadelphia: Westminster, 1953, 245–79.

On the Lord's Supper, in *Zwingli and Bullinger*, ed. Geoffrey W. Bromiley, Library of Christian Classics, Philadelphia: Westminster, 1953, 185–238.

Index

Made in the USA
Lexington, KY
19 April 2017